Equipment for Living

# Equipment for Living

The Literary Reviews of Kenneth Burke

Edited by
Nathaniel A. Rivers and Ryan P. Weber

Parlor Press
*West Lafayette, Indiana*
www.parlorpress.com

Parlor Press LLC, West Lafayette, Indiana 47906

© 2010 by Parlor Press
All rights reserved.
Printed in the United States of America

SAN: 254-8879

Library of Congress Cataloging-in-Publication Data

Burke, Kenneth, 1897-1993.
 Equipment for living : the literary reviews of Kenneth Burke / edited by Nathaniel A. Rivers and Ryan P. Weber.
    p. cm.
 Includes bibliographical references and index.
 ISBN 978-1-60235-144-8 (pbk. : alk. paper) -- ISBN 978-1-60235-145-5 (hardcover : alk. paper) -- ISBN 978-1-60235-146-2 (adobe ebook)
  1.  Literature, Modern--20th century--History and criticism. 2.  Literature, Modern--20th century--Reviews. 3. Literature and society. I. Rivers, Nathaniel A. II. Weber, Ryan P. III. Title.
 PN770.5B87 2010
 809'.03--dc22
                              2009052004

Cover illustration by Joseph Sellers. Used by permission.
Cover design by David Blakesley.
Printed on acid-free paper.

Parlor Press, LLC is an independent publisher of scholarly and trade titles in print and multimedia formats. This book is available in paper, hardcover, and Adobe eBook formats from Parlor Press on the World Wide Web at http://www.parlorpress.com or through online and brick-and-mortar bookstores. For submission information or to find out about Parlor Press publications, write to Parlor Press, 816 Robinson St., West Lafayette, Indiana, 47906, or e-mail editor@parlorpress.com.

# Contents

Preface   *xi*

Introduction   *xiii*

**Poetry**   *3*

  Untitled Review of *Pens for Wings* by Emanuel Morgan   *5*
  Heaven's First Law   *6*
  Deposing the Love of the Lord   *10*
  Two Kinds of Against   *12*
  Recent Poetry   *16*
  Return After Flight   *28*
  The Hope in Tragedy   *30*
  Deft Plaintiveness   *32*
  Leave the Leaf Its Springtime   *35*
  Tentative Proposal   *37*
  Fearing's New Poems   *40*

**Literature**   *43*

  Alcohol in the Eighties   *45*
  A Transitional Novel   *48*
  Felix Kills His Author   *52*
  Axiomatics   *55*
  The Modern English Novel Plus   *59*
  The Editing of Oneself   *63*
  Modifying the Eighteenth Century   *67*
  The Critic of Dostoevsky   *71*
  The Consequences of Idealism   *75*

Enlarging the Narrow House   *79*

Immersion   *82*

Ethics of the Artist   *84*

Delight and Tears   *87*

The Bon Dieu of M. Jammes   *90*

A Decade of American Fiction   *93*

Permanence and Change   *103*

While Waiting   *106*

Change of Identity   *108*

Thurber Perfects Mind Cure   *111*

The Book of Proverbs   *114*

Symbolic War   *115*

Imaginary Lines   *127*

**Drama**   *131*

Rugged Portraiture   *133*

Field Work in Bohemia   *135*

By Ice, Fire or Decay?   *138*

**Criticism of Poetry**   *141*

Van Wyck Brooks in Transition?   *143*

Belief and Art   *147*

Gastronomy of Letters   *150*

Coleridge Rephrased   *153*

Cautious Enlightenment   *155*

Exceptional Improvisation   *157*

Responses to Pressure   *159*

On Poetry and Poetics   *162*

Towards Objective Criticism   *165*

Untitled Review of *La Poesie et le Principe de transcendance* by Maurice Duval   *169*

The Sources of "Christabel"   *171*

Toward the Perfectly Poisonous   *172*

Father and Son     *176*
Untitled Review of *Wallace Stevens* by Harold Bloom     *180*
Untitled Review of *The Sovereign Ghost* by Denis Donoghue     *184*
Prelude to Poetry: Scales and Fugue     *188*

**Criticism of Literature**     *191*
On Re and Dis     *193*
A New Poetics     *197*
The Technique of Listening     *200*
The Encyclopaedic, Two Kinds of     *202*
Henry Miller and Harry Levin on James Joyce, New Directions     *210*
Untitled Review of *On Native Grounds* by Alfred Kazin     *212*
Criticism for the Next Phase     *216*
On Covery, Re- and Dis-     *219*
The Criticism of Criticism     *228*
The Dialectics of Imagery     *246*
A Sour Note on Literary Criticism     *254*
A Trail Trails Off     *257*
Exceptional Book     *260*
The Serious Business of Comedy     *263*
Kermode Revisited     *268*
Swift Now? Swift Then     *275*
Irony Sans Rust     *279*

**General Criticism**     *283*
Engineering With Words     *285*
Key Words for Critics     *289*
Action, Passion, and Analogy     *296*
Likings of an Observationist     *302*
The 'Independent Radical'     *311*

**Sociology**     *319*
Realism and Idealism     *321*

Idols of the Future  324

Hypergelasticism Exposed  328

The Age of Enterprise  332

Renaming Old Directions  337

Without Benefit of Politics  340

The Constants of Social Relativity  343

Untitled Review of *The Ethics of Competition* by Frank H. Knight  346

Homo Faber, Homo Magus  349

More Dithyrambic than Athletic  351

The Second Study of Middletown—Albert Rhys Williams on the U.S.S.R. and Ortega in Spain  356

In Quest of the Way  360

Protective Coloration  366

Storm Omens  369

A Radical, But—  370

Anatomy of the Mask  371

Property as an Absolute  374

Methodology of the Scramble  378

Synthetic Freedom  381

Spender's Left Hand  383

More Probes in the Same Spot  385

Quantity and Quality  389

The 'Science' of Race Thinking  391

Corrosive Without Corrective  394

The Work of Regeneration  398

The Carrot and the Stick, or  402

Democracy of the Sick  410

**Religion**  415

Fides Quaerens Intellectum  417

Weighted History  421

Invective Against the Father    *423*

**Philosophy**    *429*

    Righting an Ethnologic Wrong    *431*

    William James: Superlative Master of the Comparative    *433*

    Untitled Review of *Reason and Emotion* by John MacMurray    *438*

    Intelligence as a Good    *439*

    The Poet and the Passwords    *445*

    Fraught with Freight    *451*

    The Universe Alive    *454*

    Liberalism's Family Tree    *455*

    George Herbert Mead    *459*

    Monads—on the Make    *463*

    Action as Test    *466*

**History**    *469*

    Puritans Defended    *471*

    A 'Logic' of History    *473*

    In Vague Praise of Liberty    *479*

    Untitled Review of *Stalin: A New World Seen Through One Man* by Henri Barbusse    *483*

    Revival of the Fittest    *486*

**Myth**    *491*

    Untitled review of *An Introduction to Mythology* by Lewis Spence    *493*

    A Recipe for Worship    *494*

    Careers Without Careerism    *497*

    Folktale and Myth    *502*

    Myth, Method and Tragedy    *505*

**Language**    *509*

    After-Dinner Philosophy    *511*

    Idiom and Uniformity    *515*

    Poets All    *518*

Concern About English *521*
The Impartial Essence *523*
Semantics in Demotic *526*
Basic and After *530*
Words as Deeds *534*

**Art** *553*
Untitled Review of *Greek Vase-Painting* by Ernst Buschor *555*
Note on *Der Sturm* *557*
A Pleasant View of Decay *558*
Many Moods *561*
The Esthetic Strain *563*
The Esthetic Instinct *567*

**Biography** *571*
Chekhov and Three Others *573*
Art and the Hope Chest *577*
Heroism and Books *583*
Codifying Milton *585*
The Art of Yielding *587*
A Gist of Gists of Gists *591*
Goethe and the Jews *593*
Mainsprings of Character *595*
One Who Wrestled *599*
Why Coleridge? *602*
Cult of the Breakthrough *606*
The 'Christ-Dionysus Link' *610*

Appendix A: *New York Herald Tribune Books* Reviews, 1923 to 1929 *615*
Appendix B: Reviews by Journal *623*
Appendix C: Reviews in Chronological Order *635*
Acknowledgments *643*
Index *649*

# Preface

In editing Kenneth Burke's literary reviews, we tried to make very few changes to the source texts. For archival purposes, these reviews are best presented with as little alteration as possible to preserve most completely Burke's original work. The toughest decision to make was deciding what counted as a literary review. Since Burke routinely centers discussions around the analysis of texts, it is often difficult to distinguish literary criticism from metacriticism. Relying on the criteria and catalogs created by William Rueckert and extended by Richard Thames, David Blakesley, and Clark Rountree for the bibliographies now available online at *KB Journal*, reviews were determined to be those pieces that evaluated a specific text or texts and were identified by the publication itself as literary reviews.

Once collected, these reviews presented only minor editing complications. Because Burke is notorious for playing with usage for effect, his style is often unconventional. It would sacrifice some of his meaning and intent to alter clever italicizations or punctuation that does not conform to style guides; however, these reviews were also subject to the specific conventions of journals and history, such as spelling and citation style. Those anomalies that seemed to be the result of editorial decisions or contemporary conventions were normalized, but those deemed Burkeian were left intact. As a result, only minor changes were necessary, such as spelling "colour" as "color" or changing the notation of Waldo Frank's novel "Dark Mother" to *Dark Mother*.

Issues of organization were more complex. While there are several ways to present these reviews, we have decided to group them thematically to maximize their accessibility. Thematic organization will allow readers to notice trends and connections between reviews on similar topics. The categories for organization are fairly basic (e.g., fiction, poetry, sociology), and the scope of these categories is narrow enough to provide insight but broad enough to avoid specialization. Because Burke can easily turn a review of a novel into an essay on economics, the reviews are placed in categories based on the subject of the book under review. We readily admit, however, that this categorization does not reflect, to borrow again from Burke, how God himself divided-up the world. For instance, "Puritans Defended" here falls under "History"; it could just as easily have been placed under "Religion." We have self-consciously opted for, out of necessity, the Philosophy of the Bin. We recognize, as well, that the bins we have created do not necessarily contain all of Burke's collected literary reviews, and that some would count what we have discounted. Additionally, because of financial issues surrounding the permissions for Burke's reviews published in the *New York Herald Tribune Books*, those reviews do not appear in this collection. See Appendix A for an extended, critical discussion of those now excised reviews. We aimed to produce as complete and accessible a collection as various recalcitrants allowed. Within categories, reviews are grouped chronologically by journal. For example, all reviews from the journal with the earliest review are listed first, followed by those from the journal with the second earliest review. Additionally, alternative tables of content have been provided—one organized by journal, another by strict chronology—to allow readers to approach the reviews from different angles.

In compiling these literary reviews we have been aided mightily by the time and talents of others. David Blakesley has shepherded this project with the patience of a saint and guidance of a consummate educator. The Burke Literary Trust has likewise aided the project both by granting us permission to reprint Burke's work and by expressing genuine interest in the project. Many others have likewise provided support and guidance along the way. Thomas M. Rivers reviewed several versions of the introduction, as did Irwin Weiser. Jack Selzer and Robert Wess pointed the way to previously "lost" reviews. Debra Hawhee provided encouragement early on, as did the Kenneth Burke Society, which graciously awarded us the title of Emerging Burke Scholars for our work on this collection. We also want to thank these professional writing majors at Purdue University for their copyediting work on the manuscript: Kate Bouwens, Summer Carder, Alexandra Cash, Jessica Clements, Shawn Dildine, Daniel Elliott, Ryan Gardner, MacKenzie Greenwell, Kate Jackett, Mikel Livingston, Kaye Maloney, Suzie Mason, Caroline Mochel, Jennifer Norman, Holly Pierson, Patrick Qi, Francesca San Pedro, Samantha Schneider, Kristen Short, and Margaret Zahm.

We would like to thank many times over Joseph Sellers, the talented artist who produced the most excellent cover of this book. With very little direction, Joseph produced a design perfectly suited to the themes and historical contexts of many of Burke's literary reviews.

Finally, we wish to thank Jodi Rasche Rivers and Anna Lowe Weber for their love, support, and patience during the project.

# Introduction

*Nathaniel A. Rivers and Ryan P. Weber*

Kenneth Burke's critical approach resists containment. Reading through this collection, this elusiveness seems intentional. Perhaps a metaphor, or several, would be helpful. In his essay "Literature as Equipment for Living," Burke characteristically piles metaphor on top of metaphor, each helpful in describing attributes of literature while suggesting incongruent directions. Literature is medicine. Literature is strategy. Literature is attitude. Literature is vehicle. Literature is sociology. But these metaphors are not as incongruent as they seem; they are active categories. Burke writes: "Art forms like 'tragedy' or 'comedy' or 'satire' would be treated as *equipments for living*, that size up situations in various ways" (*Philosophy of Literary Form* 304). For Burke, literature is not to be passively absorbed, but actively applied. Books are strategies, written with specific attitudes, drawn from specific situations to address recurrent situations. Burke opens *The Philosophy of Literary Form*, a book about criticism that collects some of his criticism, with this very idea. "Critical and imaginative works are answers to questions posed by the situations in which they arose. They are not merely answers, they are strategic answers, stylized answers" (1).[1]

One of the many nuances of the "equipment for living" metaphor is that it applies as equally to the creation of literature as to its criticism. We seek strategies for life in literature, whether we are writing it or reading it. Burke says this about the strategizing of the author: "One seeks to 'direct the larger movements and operations' in one's campaign of living. One 'maneuvers,' and the maneuvering is an 'art'" (298). Readers, using these maneuverings, can discern different strategies in different books, so they would be wise to have available as many approaches as possible. Each book, in this way, is medicine, "designed for consolation or vengeance, for admonition or exhortation, for foretelling" (293). Reading Coleridge, reading Eliot, reading Woolf, reveals different cures for what ails us. In these cures, Burke finds "strategies for selecting enemies and allies, for socializing losses, for warding off the evil eye, for purification, propitiation, and desanctification, consolation and vengeance, admonition and exhortation, implicit commands or instructions of one sort or another" (304).

How do you easily define a critic who deploys so many metaphors for what literature is and does? How do you sum up a critic who writes in his critical treatise *Counter-Statement,* "We advocate nothing, then, but a return to inconclusiveness" (91)? Simply put, you can't. Despite being variously categorized as a New Critic, a Marxist critic, a psychoanalytic critic, Burke works beyond these tidy labels. And he means to. "The greater the range and depth of considerations about which a critic can be explicit," Burke writes in "Kinds of Criticism," "the more he is fulfilling his task as a critic" (272). His critical program is so extensive that its surface can barely be scratched here. As Paul Jay writes, "The scope and complexity of Burke's work as a literary critic makes generalizations difficult" (Jay, "Kenneth Burke"). Many critics finally solved this problem by simply referring to Burke's system as "Burkeology."

Within Burkeology, it is difficult to see Burke as a literary critic when he is more famous for his social and cultural criticism at large. Books such as *Permanence and Change, Attitudes Toward History, A Grammar of Motives,* and *A Rhetoric of Motives* use literature primarily to explore the drama of human interaction played out in language. This exploration, however, evidences the crossing of traditional genres present throughout Burke. William H. Rueckert testifies to this approach in charting the labeling of Burke's work:

> At first we thought of him as a literary critic (a role that is continuous throughout his career); then we thought of him as a social/cultural critic (another role that is continuous); then we thought of him as a language critic (not a linguist, but a critic who approached the study of human relations through the study of language). (100)

Rueckert here captures the dynamic relationship between the social, the cultural, the linguistic, and the literary as Burke envisioned them. Dennis J. Ciesielski argues that Burke's criticism "reveals and investigates the social textuality" in a way that juxtaposes the "cultural, historical, and linguistic" forces at work in everyday life. It is the "multiplicity of these discourse situations which validates Burke's investigative forays" into what Ciesielski calls "world-text" (243). If literature is equipment for living, then literary criticism is always already social, cultural, and linguistic criticism. As Rueckert parenthetically argues above, these roles are continuous; we would argue that, more importantly, they are all coterminous.

As Rueckert's statement implies, Burke began his career as a literary critic, publishing reviews in the "little magazines" and scholarly publications of the 1920s and 1930s. But with these literary reviews, Burke began to chart his career as a social and cultural critic as well. Many of these reviews were short, only a page or a column in the review section, but they were remarkable grapplings with the diverse fields of the day, including: literature, poetry, criticism, sociology, philosophy and language. As Burke tackles a work, he masterfully engages its ideas in ways that elaborate dynamic dimensions of the other's thoughts and his own. His reviews contributed to the valuable discourse in magazines such as *The New Masses, Poetry, The Nation, The New Republic*, and especially *The Dial*. Many of these magazines had a huge impact on the artistic and critical circles of their day, drawing in literary giants like William Carlos Williams, W.B. Yeats, Hart Crane, Ezra Pound, Marianne Moore, Carl Sandburg, and e.e. cummings.

Though most of Burke's book reviews are not as available as his widely printed works, thinkers across the humanities have lauded Burke's abilities as a reader and critic. W. H. Auden praised Burke's magnitude in 1941: "No isolated quotation can do justice to Mr. Burke's subtlety and good sense, and no doubts that one may entertain about the soundness of his critical position can obscure the fact that he is unquestionably the most brilliant and suggestive critic now writing in America" (59). Rueckert, who calls Burke the "omnivorous critic at large" (46), echoes Auden by asserting that "Burke is unquestionably one of our great modern critics" (100). Recent critics also cite Burke as an influence; most famously, Harold Bloom called Burke "the strongest living representative of the American critical tradition, and perhaps the largest single source of that tradition since its founder, Ralph Waldo Emerson" (qtd. in Kostelanetz 11)

These critics praise Burke for analyzing the symbolic action of language within literature to reveal how it is not just a reflection but an interpretation of reality. As Burke writes in the review "The Quest for Certainty," (1930), "a shift in the vocabulary of approach will entail new classifications for the same events." Burke calls these shifts terministic screens, because, like color filters on a camera, vocabularies work as a selection and deflection of reality and are thus an active interpretation that prescribes further action. Literature then becomes the naming of recurrent situations as a means of coping with them. The critic's job is to identify the use and usefulness of these namings, to interpret the interpretation. This leads to Jay's conclusion that literature and literary criticism are both equipment for living. Jay writes, "I think it is important to recognize, too, that criticism—and the criticism of criticism—is also treated by Burke as a broadly *social act* by which we equip and re-equip ourselves to live" ("Criticism" 29). If this critical program is performed well, it can transform literature into salvation. Rhetorician Wayne Booth writes, "[Burke] would use criticism to save the world, including the world of criticism, and he would also see literature itself as one mode that can save or damn us" (9). By posting warning signs and helpful instructions, critics help readers maximize the strategic value of a text. As Rueckert writes, critical texts are themselves equipment for living:

> Criticism also functions as part of our equipment for living—it's something that it most certainly did for Burke during his long and varied critical life. Critics are mediators between the symbolic structures and us readers; they share their knowledge with us, not because they think we are stupid, but because they see things in these texts that we don't and they are convinced that their knowledge will be useful to us. (114)

If critics look for things that the rest of us don't see, they better look in all the places we never imagined. Burke's reviews, as well as his wildly annotated personal library, evidence an uncanny reading ability, reflecting his view in the essay "Kinds of Criticism" that "At [criticism's] best, it sustains the intense contemplation of an object to the point where one begins to see not only more deeply into the subject but beyond it" (276). Richard Kostelanetz describes Burke's copy of Harold Bloom's *Wallace Stevens*, which demonstrates Burke's vigilant notetaking and marginalia in anticipation of a review in *The New Republic* in 1977 ("Untitled Review of Harold Bloom"):

> On every page are perhaps 20 inked annotations. Key words are underlined, vertical lines trace connections. In the blank pages of the back of the book and even on the flyleaves are more extensive notes, some of them referring to the book in general and others to particular passages. This is the kind of critical artifact that should be on permanent display in every university library. (25)

Because of his complexity as a reader, Burke's criticism transcends any specific school or structure. Limiting reading to formalized critical conventions risks deflecting alternate avenues of salvation and tumbling headlong into damnation. To this end, Burke is, as Charles Glicksberg writes, "A subtle and adventurous critic . . . willing to follow the trail of an idea wherever it may lead, without regard to the established sanctities of meaning" (74).

This tendency for intense contemplation, while beneficial and productive, can frustrate even the most generous of readers. Burke's dogged, even playful, explorations of specific textual elements may appear tangential. Wendell Harris comments:

> Burke creates difficulties for his readers. Much of what seems unnecessarily eccentric in his writing results from a tendency to elaborate as far as possible a limited number of ideas that strongly appeal to him . . . until they swallow everything in sight. Moreover Burke frequently seems to be writing only to himself. (453)

A first glance through these reviews could produce sympathy for Harris's critique; Burke may seem at times to write largely for his own amusement. Indeed, he almost apologizes in the review "Engineering With Words" (1923) for pursuing Gertrude Stein's *Geography and Plays* by means of a circuitous discussion of Milton.

Ultimately, though, the charge of digression is too extreme even for a man who adheres to no strict critical approach. These supposed digressions are better understood as Burke's desire to incorporate everything available to the critic, things both intrinsic and extrinsic to the text. Burke writes, "The main ideal of criticism, as I conceive it, is to use all that is there to use" (*Philosophy* 23). The biography of the writer, the social situations surrounding the work, the terms used by the writer and reader, politics, history, economics, ecology, physiology, and psychoanalysis—all provide fruitful insight into a text.[2] This broad scope caused Andrew King to look back with pleasure on the rise of Burkean criticism, with its adherents across disciplines like English, communications, sociology, philosophy, and even economics and political science. King writes, "While Burkean critics concentrated on a single finite text, they placed it in a rich historical and political context" (Enos et al. 367). Recent scholarship continues this tradition by using Burke's "equipment for living" concept as a fruitful metaphor in investigating a wide variety of texts: the poetry of William Carlos Williams (Clark), the aesthetics and social impact of jazz and punk music (Veneciano; Matula), the ethics of Renaissance literature (Grossman), the rhetoric of religious discourse (Smith; Lewis), the work of Ralph Ellison (Pease), and parodic texts like *Spaceballs* and *Mad Magazine* (Ott and Bonnstetter; Carabas).

The ability of the equipment for living metaphor to reveal resonance within so many disciplines and texts reveals Burke's inclusive approach, which employs several critical methods to search a text for strategies. Because of his desire to treat literature as equipment for living, Burke always looks for the best parts of even the worst books. He calls this strategy *discounting*. Discounting is a generosity in reading that selects the criteria most likely to produce usable insights from a text, guided by the understanding that no text can do or say everything at once. Burke writes, "By proper discounting *everything* becomes usable" (*Attitudes* 244). If literature is equipment for living, then no one book, no one piece of equipment, is going to be useful in every situation.

Though Burke demands usefulness in literature, this does not imply that he favors the practical over the aesthetic. In fact, *Counter-Statement* erodes that binary. Literature is useful because it is beautiful. Burke argues that the opposition between practical and aesthetic "vanishes when a machine is beautiful. Accordingly, to ask that the aesthetic set itself in opposition to the practical is to ask that the aesthetic be one specific brand of the aesthetic" (111). Literature functions as equipment, but the metaphor enhances, not maligns, the role of eloquence in art. Authors who wish to be simply and blatantly didactic are better off using "the pamphlet, the political tract, the soap-box oration" (189) as the equipment to spread their message. Literature must arouse and satisfy the desires of readers with a form that parallels experiences outside of art. It must craft evocative, moving symbols that provide "a terminology of thoughts, actions, emotions, attitudes, for codifying a pattern of experience" (154). These symbols encapsulate with great power and resonance the complexities of society, providing readers with new perspectives and strategies for their situations. For further discussion of aesthetics and usefulness as components of equipment for living see Appendix A.

Given how Burke unites usefulness with aesthetics, it is not surprising that his reviews often highlight the power of symbol, literary form, beauty, and eloquence to generate attitudes in readers. Discussing this in the review "A New Poetics" (1925), Burke writes that "art, by its subtle insinuations of what aspects of life are to be desired and what to be avoided, contributes moral standards in that manner which seems most penetrative: by unaware absorption." A critic's work involves uncovering the prescribed action inherent in literary symbols. As Burke argues in the review "Symbolic War" (1936), the attitudes offered by poets function as incipient action:

> . . . the nonpartisan, imaginative poet writes, "Beware, a storm approacheth." As propagandist he adds, "Go thou, and buy rubbers." The critics of the "proletarian" school . . . have done us a service in recalling how often the poet, in this imperfect world, is in effect writing, "Go thou, and buy rubbers" when he is only *aware* of writing,[3] "A storm approacheth." In the mere act of warning us what to beware of, he suggests the kind of measures to be taken.

This search for "measures to be taken" is the driving force behind the reviews in this collection. Satisfaction in reviewing never came to Burke through the writing of a plot summary and the awarding of stars. He is far more interested in charting the aesthetics of a work and navigating through its most fruitful branches, whether literary or critical. To this end, he may even violate the more standard conventions of reviewing, giving unannounced spoilers or ignoring a plot entirely as it suits his purposes.

Indulgent, perhaps, but Burke was always ultimately interested in the way a book could reflect, inform, reshape, or contain situations. A perusal of this volume reveals instance after instance when Burke evaluates literature in terms of its strategy and style. In the review "Fraught with Freight," Burke argues that Thomas Mann's writing provides symbolic strategies for the situations outside of art. "At times his work suggests to me, not a personality, but a battlefield, an expanse of suffering soil across which the fluctuant and indeterminate conflicts of our day are waged momentously." When reviewing *One Season Shattered* in the review "Deft Plaintiveness" (1936), Burke notices in James Daly a childlike quality that, while appealing, is ultimately insufficient. "I am a little afraid of it, since it does not equip us explicitly for battle." Given art's relevance to life, then, it seems natural that Burke favorably evaluates Joseph Krutch's *Experience and Art* (1932):

> Mr. Krutch, rightly, I think, questions those schools of literary criticism which would relegate the enjoyment of poetry to a mere "make-believe" corner of the mind. He holds that art bears upon the coordinates of living in general, giving us those emphases in the imaginative sphere which are relevant to "other human interests," to man's "other activities" outside of art.

It is from this basis that he reviews Horace Gregory's *Chorus for Survival*, emphasizing in "The Hope in Tragedy" (1935) the ability of tragic stories to transform human sorrow into strength: "Within the frame of the tragic attitude, we do not seek to sterilize our aberrations, but to *harness* them, to make them *serve*, and with the help of criticism to build assets out of liabilities." A failure to symbolically encapsulate experience is also seen as a major failing of Glenway Wescott's *Apple of the Eye*, as Burke reviews it in "Delight and Tears" (1924). It is not enough that readers can enjoy the book as if it "actually occurred in one's own life," because the work does not invent "symbols which adequately summarize for us the emotional and ideological complexities in which we are involved." This distinction is an important corrective to those who would reduce the "stylized answers" approach to what Burke calls in the essay "Equipment for Living" "easy consolation" (298), evidenced in books that provide readers clichéd relatability or an unearned sense of success without offering sustainable symbols for future experience.

Often, Burke's quest for applicability is so irresistible that he will highlight through discounting aspects of the same work which are and are not useful to reader's situations. When writing "William James: Superlative Master of the Comparative" (1936), Burke praises James for the pragmatic application of his thought process: "It promoted a kind of any-port-in-a-storm attitude, annoying perhaps to lovers of the symmetrical when it takes the metaphysical guise of pluralism, but extremely helpful for the moral jugglings we must manage in this imperfect world." At the same time, he wonders if James alone is all the equipment modern readers need: "Yet, as we finish the account of his work, we are led to wonder whether, for all his inclusiveness, he could give us a full equipment for today. One is struck, for instance, by an almost total absence of historical and economic considerations. The mention of politics is rare, and naïve." Similar critical tactics enacted in "Coleridge Rephrased" (1935) analyze I. A. Richards, whom Burke lauds for investigating the current relevance of Coleridge's work:

> Expertly translating passages from Coleridge into terms that more easily reveal their relevance to the present, [Richards] enables us to glimpse the ways in which a poet's myths may be of the utmost importance to mankind in the most pragmatic sense conceivable: by providing the framework through which our minds may be organized and ordered.

Simultaneously, Burke wonders if the usability of Richard's own work is tarnished because it ignores the role of economics and propaganda (a term, incidentally, which is not wholly pejorative for Burke): "Such thoughts would suggest the possibility that, to be completely serviceable for our needs, [Richards's] book should not so cursorily dismiss the 'propagandist' element in poetry today."

Even when not completely allied with the author, Burke gleans something from his reading. In "Corrosive Without Corrective" (1938), he finds value in Thurman Arnold's *The Folklore of Capitalism:* "The book is certainly not to be considered an alternative to Marxism, as many reviewers have proposed; but if read by readers who discount it from the angle of a Marxist critique, it is very serviceable indeed." Burke employs a similar strategy in "Words as Deeds" (1975), discounting behaviorist scientists by prioritizing the terminology he believes they neglect:

> But by a dramatistic reinterpretation, much of their work can be of great use, in helping to suggest the proper admonitions when we are attempting to sum up just what is involved in our being the kind of symbol-using, speech-acting

animal we are, as viewed in terms of MOTION, ACTION, and ATTITUDE.

In the end, Burke is always interested in ways that literature allows readers to better understand the complex situations of their own lives. Occasionally, this act involves including details from his own, as he does in "Imaginary Lines" (1962) when he relates Shirley Jackson's *We Have Always Lived in the Castle* with his own experience "of truly apocalyptic terror" at the planetarium or when he compares reading James Daly's *One Season Shattered* (1936) to seeing the framed aphorism "Laugh and the world laughs with you—weep and you weep alone" on a wall from his childhood. At one point, Burke admits to imbibing as a way of approaching more appropriately the poetry of Hart Crane. Experience can clarify art, and art can clarify experience, as it does in Thomas Mann's *Joseph and His Brothers*. Burke writes in the review "Permanence and Change" (1934) about readers recognizing recurrent situations in art:

> They were the "key" situations of the tribe that had evolved them, after all that could be forgotten had been forgotten and all that could not be forgotten had been made salient. They were not "facts," as legalistic precedents are, but communal works of art. And when the individual understood his own role by reference to them (saying, "I am like Jacob," or "This situation is like Leah's") he was being himself and a member of his group simultaneously.

Some readers will notice that this review shares its title with one of Burke's earlier books, but the similarities do not end there. Many of these reviews are quite revelatory of Burke's later writings, referencing and anticipating them both directly and indirectly. Before it appears in *Permanence and Change,* Burke's wily old trout, the famed example of overcoming trained incapacity, makes a cameo in the review "Poets All" (1933). Elsewhere, Burke gives a unique definition of perspective by incongruity in his review "Corrosive Without Corrective" (1938). Other characteristic Burkean concerns are more subtle but just as pervasive. His obsession with form is everywhere, but those interested in finding specific manifestations might do well to examine "Engineering with Words" (1923) and "Delight and Tears" (1924). Burke is also quite fond of revealing the influence of terministic screens wherever he can, and he makes fascinating explorations into their operation in "Heaven's First Law" (1922) and "Intelligence as a Good" (1930). If parts of Burke are everywhere in these reviews, some reviews find much of Burke encapsulated, with "Words as Deeds" and "Kermode Revisited" perhaps, being the most thorough discussions of his larger works. Burkeology abounds in this collection, and Burke's fingerprints are all over these reviews. Even titles reflect his concern with terminology, situation, and applicability: "The Criticism of Criticism" (1955), "On Covery, Re- and Dis-" (1953), "Renaming Old Directions" (1935), "Cautious Enlightenment" (1936), "The Editing of Oneself" (1921), "A Gist of Gists of Gists" (1937).

These concerns create a complexity and nuance which make Burke hard to pin down. Burke chases many leads in these reviews, but the constant approach is active reading that values literature as equipment for living. Burke writes, "You will note, I think, that there is no 'pure' literature here. Everything is 'medicine'" (*Philosophy* 293). Literature can act not only as medicine, but as strategy, as attitude, as vehicle, as sociology. If Burke conceives of literature as medicine, then think of these reviews as prescriptions. If he conceives of literature as strategy, then think of this book as the war room. If Burke conceives of literature as equipment for living, then consider this book the blueprint.

## Notes

1. Burke quotes this passage in his review of J.L. Austin, "Words as Deeds."

2. Though Burke clearly breaks from the mold of any specific literary critical tradition, it is likewise inaccurate to classify him under every critical approach. No one critic can cover all ground or use all terms, as Burke himself would acknowledge, especially since many current critical vocabularies were unavailable. However, many scholars have found Burke's critical vocabulary compatible with current terminology. See, for instance, Phyllis M. Japp's "'Can This Marriage Be Saved?': Reclaiming Burke for Feminist Scholarship" or Dustin Bradley Goltz's "Perspective by Incongruity: Kenneth Burke and Queer Theory."

3. This does not imply that Burke believes writers are always unaware of the broader implications of their symbols, though Burke would argue that certain critical vocabularies are better suited to drawing out these implications, what Burke would call their use.

## Works Cited

Auden, W. H. "A Grammar of Assent." *The New Republic* 105 (14 July 1941): 59. Print.

Booth, Wayne C. "Kenneth Burke's Way of Knowing." *Critical Inquiry* 1 (Fall 1974): 1–22. Print.

Goltz, Dustin Bradley. "Perspective by Incongruity: Kenneth Burke and Queer Theory." *Genders* 45. June 2007. Web. 30 Oct. 2009.

Burke, Kenneth. *Attitudes Toward History*. 1937. 3rd rev. ed. Berkeley: U of California P, 1984. Print.

—. *Counter-Statement.* 1931. Berkeley: U of California P, 1968. Print.
—. "Kinds of Criticism." *Poetry* 68 (Aug. 1946): 272–82. Print.
—. *The Philosophy of Literary Form.* 1941. Berkeley: U of California P, 1973. Print.
Carabas, Teodora. "Tales Calculated to Drive you MAD: The Debunking of Spies, Superheroes, and Cold War Rhetoric in Mad Magazine's 'SPY vs SPY.'" *The Journal of Popular Culture* 40.1 (2007): 4–24. Print.
Ciesielski, Dennis J. "Secular Pragmatism: Kenneth Burke and the [Re]socialization of Literature and Theory." *Kenneth Burke and the 21$^{st}$ Century.* Ed. Bernard L. Brock. New York: SUNY P, 1999. 243–67. Print.
Clark, Miriam Marty. "Art and Suffering in Two Late Poems by William Carlos Williams." *Literature and Medicine* 23.2 (2004): 226–40. Print.
Enos, Richard Leo, et al. "Interdisciplinary Perspectives on Rhetorical Criticism." *Rhetoric Review.* 25.4 (2006): 357–87. Print.
Glicksberg, Charles I. "Kenneth Burke: The Critic's Critic." *The South Atlantic Quarterly* 36 (1937): 74–84. Print.
Grossman, Marshall, ed. *Reading Renaissance Ethics.* New York: Routledge, 2007. Print.
Harris, Wendell. "The Critics Who Made Us: Kenneth Burke." *The Sewanee Review* 96.3 (Summer 1988): 452–63. Print.
Japp, Phyllis M. "'Can This Marriage Be Saved?': Reclaiming Burke for Feminist Scholarship." *Kenneth Burke and the 21st-Century.* Ed. Bernard L. Brock. Albany: SUNY P, 200: 113–30.
Jay, Paul. "Criticism as Equipment for Living." *Horns of Plenty, Malcolm Cowley and His Generation.* 2.1 (Spring 1989): 27-39. Print.
—. "Kenneth Burke." *The John Hopkins Guide to Literary Theory and Criticism.* Baltimore: John Hopkins UP, 2005. Web. 25 Oct. 2009.
Kostelanetz, Richard. "A Mind That Cannot Stop Exploding." *New York Times Book Review* (15 Mar. 1981): 11, ff. Print.
Lewis, Camille Kaminski. *Romancing the Difference: Kenneth Burke, Bob Jones University, and the Rhetoric of Religious Fundamentalism.* Waco: Baylor UP, 2007. Print.
Matula, Theodore. "Pow! To the People: The Make-Up's Reorganization of Punk Rhetoric." *Popular Music and Society* 30.1 (Feb. 2007): 19–38. Print.
Ott, Brian L., and Beth Bonnstetter. "We're at Now, Now: *Spaceballs* as Parodic Tourism." *Southern Communication Journal* 72.4 (2007): 309-27. Print.
Pease, Donald. "Ralph Ellison and Kenneth Burke: The Nonsymbolizable (Trans)action." *boundary 2* 30.2 (2003): 65–96. Print.
Rueckert, William H. *Encounters with Kenneth Burke.* Urbana: U of Illinois P, 1994. Print.
Smith, Erin A. "'Jesus My Pal': Reading and Religion in Middlebrow America." *Canadian Review of American Studies* 37.2 (2007): 147–81. Print.
Veneciano, Jorge Daniel. "Louis Armstrong, Bricolage, and the Aesthetics of Swing." *Uptown Conversation: The New Jazz Studies.* Ed. Robert O'Meally, Brent Hayes Edwards, and Farah Jasmine Green. New York: Columbia UP, 2004. 256–77. Print.

# Equipment for Living

# Poetry

*One man attains self expression by becoming a sailor, another by becoming a poet.*

*—Counter-Statement* (53)

# Untitled Review of *Pens for Wings* by Emanuel Morgan

*Pens for Wings* by Emanuel Morgan
*The Freeman*, 3 June 1921, 286

It has been said that by the law of permutations if you juggle the Greek alphabet long enough you will get the *Iliad*. By juggling with the most incompatible images Emanuel Morgan in his *Pens for Wings* at least succeeds in reconstructing with surprising aptness three score or more modern poets. Whether it is Mr. T.S. Eliot, "The wedding cake of two tired cultures," or Mr. William Carlos Williams, "Carbolic acid in love," this skillful prestidigitation is applied with singularly accurate results. Mr. Chesterton, for instance, is revealed as "a Cardinal on a merry-go-round," while poor Mr. Arthur Symons is nearly destroyed when the toss comes to "enchanted Roquefort." Mr. Walter de la Mar is reproduced as dreamily as one of his own lines by "a door-knob in the mist." What with *Spectra* and *Pens for Wings,* Emanuel Morgan threatens completely to outdistance his intimate and associate, Mr. Witter Bynner. The book is illustrated with caricatures by Messrs. Ivan Opffer and William Saphier, a happy combination, since Mr. Opffer's predilection for the generous thumb-smear method complements Mr. Saphier's trim hair-lines and silk-stockinged silhouettes.

# Heaven's First Law

*Sour Grapes* by William Carlos Williams. The Four Seas Company
*The Dial*, February 1922, 197–200

It had once been my privilege to see a page written by William Carlos Williams on which he undertook to reproduce nine times the lovely sunshine thought, "Order is Heaven's first law." Now, by the fifth time, the poet became noticeably impatient, and from the seventh on the copy was completely unreadable. The ninth version was a mere wavy line, broken in four places. At first I took this to be quite damning; but on second thought, what use could Williams make of order? He thinks in an entirely different set of terms. To add organization to his poetry would have no more meaning than to insist that his lines begin in alphabetical rotation.

What Williams sees, he sees in a flash. And if there is any correlation whatsoever, it is a certain determined joyousness in a poet who would find it awkward to weep. For as his arch-enemy has noted, Williams is a bad Freudian case whose poetry is certainly not allowed to come out the way it came in. But beyond this very reasonable prudency, which he shares with no less an artist than Flaubert, consistency falls away.

No, Williams is the master of the glimpse. A line of his, suddenly leaping up out of the text, will throw the reader into an unexpected intimacy with his subject, like pushing open a door and advancing one's nose into some foreign face. Given a subject, he will attack it with verve, striking where he can break through its defense, and expecting applause whenever a solid, unmistakable jolt has been landed. It would be mere idleness to give his *ars poetica* in more presumptuous terms. The process is simply this: There is the eye, and there is the thing upon which that eye alights; while the relationship existing between the two is a poem.

The difficulty here lies in conveying the virtues of such a method. For the method itself is as common as mud. The minute fixating of a mood, an horizon, a contrast; if one finds there any unusual commendation for Williams it is not in the excellence of his poetics, but in the excellence of his results. His first virtue, therefore, lies in the superiority of *his* minute fixations over those of his ten million competitors. He is a distinguished member of a miserable crew.

Honest people who really think highly enough of words to feel unhappy when they are vague will rejoice that Williams's new volume, *Sour Grapes,* is more sober in this respect than the *Improvisations.* For the *Improvisations* were not finally satisfactory. Clear notes were there in abundance, but they were usually preceded and followed by the usual modern data for mental tests. (How beautiful the association of ideas would have been in art if used in one work, by one man, for one page, and for some end other than that of a beautiful association of ideas.) True, by the mere dissatisfaction of their context, such momentary beatitudes of expression received their full share of enthusiasm, but having twenty sentences of chaos to heighten one sentence of cosmos is too much like thanking God for headaches since they enable us to be happy without them.

*Sour Grapes,* however, skips a generation and takes after the volume, *Al Que Quiere.* And in these two works, it seems to me, Williams is at his best, since here he is not handicapping his remarkable powers of definition, of lucidity. You may wonder, perhaps, just why the poet is going off in some particular direction; but you are always aware just what this direction is. Here also his inveterate lustiness is up to par; for Williams knows Walt Whitman's smile down to the last wrinkle. If there are logs in the grate, he puts a match to them; if it is a warm Easter morning, he throws off his coat. And if, behind it all, there is evidence of a strong tendency towards transgression, towards, let us say, the mountains of Tibet or a negro harem in Madagascar, such things are there as an irritant rather than as a subject. The face value of the poems will always remain the definition of the poet's own gatepost. His peculiar gifts of expression, if nothing else, dictate this simplification. Williams evidently realizes that his emotions are one thing and his art another, and that those who wish to go beyond his minute fixations can find a great deal more implicated in them; but in the meantime, let the minute fixations suffice.

I should say, therefore, that Williams was engaged in discovering the shortest route between object and subject. And whether it is a flamingo befouling its own tail, or the tired ogling at little girls, or trees stark naked in a wind, one must always recognize the unusual propriety of his poetry, the sureness and directness with which he goes at such things. A fact with him finds its justification in the trimness of the wording.

If a man is walking, it is the first principle of philosophy to say that he *is not* walking, the first principle of science to say that he is placing one foot before the other and bringing the hinder one in turn to the fore, the first principle of art to say that the man is *more than* walking, he is *yearning;* then there are times when scientist, philosopher, and poet all discover of a sudden that by heavens! The man is walking and none other. Now, a good deal of this discovery is in Williams' poetry, and, if I understand the word correctly, is contained in his manifesto praising Contact in art. For I take Contact to mean: man without the syllogism, without the parade, without Spinoza's Ethics, man with nothing but the thing and the feeling of that thing. Sitting down in the warmth to write, for instance, Kant might finally figure it out that man simply must have standards of virtue in spite of the bleakness of the phenomenon/noumenon distinction, and that this virtue could be constructed on the foundations of a categorical imperative. But Williams, sitting down in the warmth to write, would never get over his delight that the wind outside was raging ineffectually; and, in his pronounced sense of comfort, he would write:

JANUARY

Again I reply to the triple winds
running chromatic fifths of derision
outside my window:
                      Play louder.
You will not succeed. I am
bound more to my sentences
the more you batter at me
to follow you.
                      And the wind,
as before, fingers perfectly
its derisive music.

Seen from this angle, Contact might be said to resolve into the counterpart of Culture, and Williams becomes thereby one of our most distinguished Neanderthal men. His poetry deals with the coercions of nature—and by nature I mean iron rails as well as iron ore—rather than with the laborious structure of ideas man has erected above nature. His hatred of the idea in art is consequently pronounced, and very rightly brings in its train a complete disinterest in form. (Note: Form in literature must always have its beginnings in idea. In fact, our word for idea comes from a Greek word whose first meaning is "form.") The Contact writer deals with his desires; the Culture writer must erect his desires into principles and deal with those principles rather than with the desires; the *Urphenomen,* in other words, becomes with the man of Culture of less importance than the delicate and subtle instruments with which he studies it.

Williams, however, must go back to the source. And the process undeniably has its beauties. What, for instance, could be more lost, more uncorrelated, a closer Contact, a greater triumph of anti-Culture, than this poem:

### THE GREAT FIGURE

Among the rain
and lights
I saw the figure 5
in gold
on a red
firetruck
moving
with weight and urgency tense
unheeded
to gong clangs
siren howls
and wheels rumbling
through the dark city.

# Deposing the Love of the Lord

*Selected Religious Poems of Solomon Ibn Gabirol.* Translated into English Verse by Israel Zangwill. Edited by Israel Davidson. The Jewish Publication Society of America.
*The Dial*, August 1924, 161–162

On reading through this collection of devotional poetry, the reader must first of all be impressed by the constancy of the subject-matter. Here the poet keeps his eye focused long and lovingly on one thing, which is God and His Creation. But there is also a certain deadly disproportion here: it seems that in spite of his prolonged focus, Gabirol had not succeeded in finding an eloquence equal to his engrossment. The first inclination is to lay this discrepancy to the translator; it is appalling to sit down and translate an entire book of verse, and it would be readily pardonable if that imaginative inventiveness which is the best communicant of conviction—if not the proof of it—were found missing in the result. For too often Gabirol assures us rather than persuades; loving the Lord, he deposes accordingly. It is a record without pungency; at least if one is allowed to examine churchly texts for their sheer cunning of diction, boldness of image, for the *picturesqueness* of their passion, in short, rather than for its *honesty*.

But in Mr. Davidson's introduction to this volume there is material which justifies us in laying this skepticism against the original rather than the translation. For Gabirol wrote his religious poems at a time when it was the accepted thing to write religious poems, or, as the Rev. Matthew Henry says of Nehemiah, wrote "where religion was in fashion, and an air of it appeared on men's common conversation." Gabirol wrote "according to the genius of the place," and the genius happened to be one of piety—and while this does not in any way invalidate the sincerity of his poems, it does justify us in laying less importance upon his religious engrossment than we might have done otherwise. Especially since we are told the additional fact that if the devotional lyric was in vogue, it was Gabirol who contributed most to breaking down this vogue, as he was perhaps the first writer of *secular* Hebrew verse.

"Where religion was in fashion," then, Gabirol inaugurated a profane tradition, which indicates that his engrossment in the Lord was by no means a complete thing with him, and may explain our feeling that Gabirol, in his proper business of recalling that Vast Gulf between Self and Maker, conveys less to us of God's greatness than of his own smallness.

On the whole, the poems in unrhymed translation are much the better, and this is especially true of the long closing rhapsody where the original, we learn from Mr. Zangwill, was rhymed, but very freely and irregularly; perhaps poet and translator both have profited by this greater liberty. This, for instance, has something of the true Biblical ellipsis:

> Calling unto the void and it was cleft,
> And unto existence and it was urged,
> And unto the universe and it was spread out.

In this poem Gabirol could become eloquent over the astronomy of his day. And perhaps one explanation of the paleness in most of his poems is that too often he was accepting the fashion of praising the anthropomorphic Creator, whereas in reality he already had the modern touch of being more interested in the Creation. In any case, it is only when he starts moving among the astral bodies that we get any sense of splendor in his faith. For the documents of his religious fervor seldom flower. The great bulk of his lines are at best neutral; they are the mere labels of religious experience, the signs without the persuasion, the typical rather than the excellent.

One might draw a moral: The poet must possess the whole sincerity of his subject if he is to produce art, and the poet must have something *beyond* sincerity to produce art. The art-emotion transcends the emotion of his subject-matter. Beginning with engrossment in his material, the artist hunts the means to his expression, and these means in turn become hypertrophied into an aim of themselves. But both steps are equally necessary, for the invention of means is the result of engrossment in the material. With Gabirol there was no invention to become hypertrophied; the result is documentary truth without persuasion.

# Two Kinds of Against

*No thanks* by e. e. cummings. The Golden Eagle Press
*Poems* by Kenneth Fearing. Introduction by Edward Dahlberg. Dynamo
*The New Republic*, June 1935, 198–199

Despite superficial differences, e. e. cummings' *No thanks* and Kenneth Fearing's *Poems* have important ingredients in common. Both poets have an exceptional gift for the satirically picturesque. Both specialize in rhetorical devices that keep their pages vivacious almost to the extent of the feverish. Both are practiced at suggesting the subjective through the objective. And both seem driven by attitudes for which there is no completely adequate remedy in the realm of the practical (with Cummings, a sense of isolation—with Fearing, an obsession with death).

Cummings has more range, which is not always a virtue in his case, as much of his wider scope is devoted to cryptic naughtiness of an immature sort, a somewhat infantile delight in the sexual parts, alembicated confessions that seem unnecessarily shy and coy (material which, I suspect, Cummings would have abandoned long before now, had he not discovered a few processes of stylistic chemistry for extracting the last bit of ore). And like the chronic invalid who comes to identify his doctor with his disease, hating them interchangeably, he is dissatisfied not only with the current political and economic texture, but also with the "famous fatheads" and "folks with missians" (vindictively misspelled) who would attempt its radical cure. Fearing can be buoyed up with the thought of a situation wherein "millions of voices become one voice" and "millions of hands . . . move as one." But Cummings sees the process from the other side, as he strikes at those "worshipping Same," says they "got athlete's mouth jumping on & off bandwagons," and in not very loving verse lambastes the "kumrads" for being deficient in love.

But even a lone wolf cannot feel wholly content without allies. Hence, as with belligerent capitalist states, his occasional nondescript alliance with anyone who will serve (witness his scattering of somewhat shamefacedly anti-Semitic aphorisms, usually consigned to cryptogram, but still "nonsufficiently inunderstood"). As we read *No thanks* carefully, the following picture emerges: For delights, there is sexual dalliance, into which the poet sometimes reads cosmic implications (though a communicative emphasis is lacking). For politics, an abrupt willingness to let the whole thing go smash. For character building, the rigors of the proud and lonely, eventually crystallizing in rapt adulation of the single star, which is big, bright, deep, near, soft, calm, alone and holy—"Who (holy alone) holy (alone holy) alone."

Cummings' resistance to man-made institutions of any kind serves to stimulate a romantic sense of communion with nature (even the mercurial must have *some* locus of constancy); and the best work in the volume is unquestionably his natural description: the hush of snow falling or fallen; the solemn times when "emptied. Hills. Listen."; a bird in flight; the "mOOn Over tOwns mOOn"; rain that can "move deeply," with life and sex burgeoning in response; the bursting forth of a "white with madness wind" that tears "mountains from their sockets" and makes "writhing alive skies"; Poe's version of the jangling and tintinnabulation of the bells, bells, bells, brought up to date; the spread of "twilight's vastness"; and an elegiac piece, an account of the poet ascending a hill by the sea

> at dusk
> just when
> the Light is filled with birds—

a poem so intense, and so well sustained, that we greatly resent the few spots where his mannerisms threaten to undo the mood.

We might say that Cummings' biology is good, but his history is too bad. As historian, at the best he must niggle:

> little
> mr Big
> notbusy
> Busi
> ness notman.

And at the worst, he must attack in the lump:

> news alimony blackmail whathavewe
> and propaganda

—an attitude too non-negotiable for a society to run a growing concern on.

Fearing's clearly formed philosophy of history gives his work much better coordination and direction as satire. Cummings the antinomian symbolizes refusal as the little boy that won't play. Fearing, the poet as politician, can offer a take-it-or-leave-it basis of collaboration, a platform, a communist set of values that makes for an unambiguous alignment of forces and a definite indication of purpose. He has a frame of reference by which to locate his satire. Whereas Cummings as satirist is driven by his historical amorphousness into *personal moods* as the last court of appeal, Fearing can attack with the big guns of a *social framework*. He can pronounce moral judgments; and remembering Juvenal or Swift we realize what an advantage this is, for any invective, implicit or explicit, is strongest when the inveigher is appealing to a rigorous code of likes and dislikes. Whereas both poets are alive to the discordant clutter about us, Cummings tends to be jumpy, shifty, look-for-me-here-and-you'll-find-me-there. (After reading him for an hour or so, I show the tetanic symptoms of a cocaine addict.) Fearing is better able to take on something of the heavy oratorical swell, which he manages by an exceptional fusion of ecclesiastic intonations (the lamentation) and contemporary cant (slang, business English, the imagery of pulp fiction, syndicated editorials and advertising).

An inverted Whitman, Fearing scans the country with a statistical eye; but where Whitman sought to pile up a dithyrambic catalogue of *glories,* Fearing gives us a satirically seasoned catalogue of *burdens.* Whitman, the humanitarian, could look upon a national real-estate boom and see there a mystical reaching out of hands. Fearing conversely would remark upon the "profitable smile," the "purpose that lay beneath the merchant's warmth." This method leads at times to the mechanical device of indictments held together by a slightly varied refrain, but for the most part the poet is as ingenious as he is sincere. I know of no better patent, for instance, than this way of saying (in "1933") that the official pronouncements are crooked and that the organization to reinforce the crookedness is terrifyingly efficient:

> You heard the gentleman, with automatic precision,
>     speak the truth.
>   Cheers. Triumph.
> And then mechanically it followed the gentleman lied.
> Deafening applause. Flashlights, cameras, microphones.
>   Floral tribute. Cheers.

His "Dirge" to the average man winds up superbly by the use of slang interjections:

And wow he died as wow he lived,
> going whop to the office and blooie home to sleep and
>> biff got married and bam had children and oof got fired,
zowie did he live and zowie did he die . . .

It is harder in limited space to illustrate Fearing than cummings, as Fearing does not get his effects so succinctly. But I might give one more instance of his skill. Readers will recall the often cited remark of Eliot's wherein he characterizes his "general point of view" as "classicist in literature, royalist in politics and anglo-catholic in religion." One may greatly respect Eliot for his important attainments, and still enjoy the deftness of Fearing's reference to

> That genius, that litterateur, Theodore True,
>> St. Louis boy who made good as an Englishman in
>>> theory, a deacon in vaudeville, a cipher in politics,
>> undesirable in large numbers in any community.

Through the volume, Fearing's discerning hatred of all that the "fetishism of commodities" has done for us, as regards the somewhat prospering as well as the destitute, is brilliantly conveyed, along with a quality of reverie, of fears and yearnings that delve far deeper than the contemporary.

# Recent Poetry

*An Omnibus Review*

*Selected Poems* by Marianne Moore (Introduction by T. S. Eliot). Macmillan
*Six Sides to a Man* by Merrill Moore, with an epilogue by Louis Untermeyer. Harcourt, Brace
*Man with a Bull-Tongue Plow* by Jesse Stuart. Dutton
*Strange Holiness* by Robert P. Tristram Coffin. Macmillan
*Panic, A Play in Verse* by Archibald MacLeish. Houghton Mifflin
*Vienna* and *Poems* by Stephen Spender. Random House
*Collected Poems, 1929–1933,* & *A Hope for Poetry* by C. Day Lewis. Random House
*Dance of Fire* by Lola Ridge. Smith and Haas
*A Winter Diary and Other Poems* by Mark Van Doren. Macmillan
*Permit Me Voyage* by James Agee with a foreword by Archibald MacLeish. Yale UP
*Poems, et cetera* by David Greenhood. Helen and Bruce Gentry
*Chorus for Survival* by Horace Gregory. Covici-Friede
*No Thanks* by e. e. cummings. Golden Eagle Press
*Poems* by Kenneth Fearing (Introduction by Edward Dahlberg). Dynamo

*The Southern Review,* July 1935, 164–177

A survey of recent poetry should begin with the *Selected Poems of Marianne Moore,* as Miss Moore would merit special honors by the members of her own Guild. It is customary to think of her as adept at expressing a tiny corner of experience—but inasmuch as this corner is close to the very core of poetry, a reader who is willing to meet her work halfway, bringing something in exchange for what he would take, may discover in her observations a quality or method that can be applied to many matters beyond her particular subjects. "These people liked small things," she writes—and she is one of them—yet behind her miniatures there seem to lie larger equivalents, as a sprawling city is the equivalent of its neat contours on a map, or as one may learn something radical about the history of centuries by watching a few children at play in the backyard. She shows sympathy with little animals, not for their lowliness, but because of their exceptional precision, the "great amount of poetry in unconscious fastidiousness." She describes vessels at sea that "progress white and rigid as if in a groove," or the mountain goat, "its eye fixed on the waterfall which never seems to fall," thereby exemplifying her kind of remoteness; and if she were discussing the newest model of an automobile, I think that she could somehow contrive to suggest an antiquarian's interest. There is nothing more unlike her work than a steamroller, a difference which probably explains why she has included in her collection a withering attack upon one, beginning

> The illustration
> is nothing to you without the application.
> > You lack half wit. You crush all the particles down
> > into close conformity, and then walk back and forth on
> > them.

The great steamroller of political and economic necessities which has been flattening us out may prevent the general public, and even many poets, from feeling the full value of Miss Moore's work. Her linguistic subtlety may often be lost on those who were not listening attentively enough to be surprised. Her deft invention of something that might be called the "poetic editorial" may not communicate its savor to us after we have been too violently assailed by the "big bow wow stuff" all about us. And if we read hastily, her conversational understatement may conceal from us the range and boldness of her responsiveness, as in her astounding poem, "An Octopus of Ice." In his introduction to the volume, T. S. Eliot selects the word *genuineness* as the mark of her work. *Greatness,* he says, is a quality for the future to decide upon—but the *genuineness* of a work can be discerned by an author's contemporaries. At a time when people are everywhere climbing upon bandwagons, let me hasten on this issue at least, to climb upon a bandwagon with Mr. Eliot. He writes: "The *genuineness* of poetry is something which we have warrant for believing that a small number, but only a small number, of contemporary readers can recognize." I wish hereby to enlist formally in this distinguished company—and to state my conviction that all those of Miss Moore's Guild, all poets of all persuasions, should vote with me and Eliot for Miss Moore's *genuineness.*

It is not merely a correspondence of name that takes me next to *Six Sides to a Man,* a collection of sonnets by Merrill Moore, with an "Epilogue, by way of advertisement," by Louis Untermeyer. I should not dare to call Merrill Moore a steamroller, after the mean things that have been said about one—and I will admit that nearly every writer must seem somewhat blunt if we pick up his work just after laying down Miss Moore's—but his gusto and dash are wholly the opposite of Miss Moore's meticulousness. Mr. Untermeyer, writing less as editor and critic than as accountant, calculates that Dr. Moore, who is now thirty-one, has written "approximately twenty-five thousand idiomatic, hybrid, or 'American' sonnets." These sonnets suffer considerably from lack of revision—but if you read them as hastily as they were written, hurrying rapidly from one to the next, you will gradually come to see a "way of life" emerging, as the poet details the incidents of his day with an almost gluttonous curiosity. It is modesty on his part to call himself but six-sided. He seems to have as many sides as there are subjects—and what we get is a sequence of quick, haphazard matchings, for he has learned to be engrossed in experience as a clutter. That is: by finding things very *noteworthy,* he can avoid the discouragement of those who find things very *disordered.* This mode of "acceptance" may go far to explain his great vitality.

Dr. Moore is a kind of urban Jesse Stuart. Like the author of *Man With a Bull-Tongue Plow,* he mars the sonnet (the most statuesque of forms) by adapting it to the conveniences of completely impromptu statements, getting something that has fourteen lines, with approximately ten syllables to the line, but is otherwise wholly free to follow the dictates of accident. And he writes with the same rough spontaneity as Jesse Stuart ("blurt out your dreams"), though the world of the Kentucky mountaineer is a much simpler one—and whereas Stuart does not revise because of naïvete, Moore probably forgoes revision because of restlessness. Moore speculates easily on much that Stuart would tend to lump together as a vague forbidding Shape, to be hated as it encroached upon the simplicities of his people, who resent the abstractions of politics, finance, and the law, and who in maturity ask the same protectiveness of the soil as a mother provided them in childhood. "Love in the flesh is greater than the mind," writes Stuart, all of whose poems spring from the most concrete of facts. And it should be noted that this rustic poet, unlike most urbanized poets of the soil, writes poems as full of characters as a novel. Nature for him does not point towards privacy and remoteness, but towards the barn dance. This mind that yields to reverie as it follows the turning sod is well stocked with gossip and local lore, in which the inhabitants of the graveyard still figure because their stories remain a vital part of the community.

The other aspect of Nature (as a place of symbolic communion for a man essentially lonely) is to be found in Robert P. Tristram Coffin's *Strange Holiness.* Mr. Coffin has something of Miss Moore's engrossment in the fastidious ways of animals—but whereas she can consider them primarily as connoisseur, Mr. Coffin for all his admiration remembers that on occasion he must destroy them, when they threaten to crowd him from his farm. His poem, "The Haters," recounting the forms of life (the "dispossessed") that struggle to assert themselves in opposition to his plans and purposes ("It is by the cellar they come first") perhaps gives most clearly the quality of his mind, the way in which comfort and discomfort, kindness and cruelty, are intermingled for him. The poet is made devout by the look of terror in a shot or frightened animal's eye. He can convey to us, quite solemnly, the uneasy expectancy of a summer night, as a storm slowly approaches. The pleasures he celebrates have a touch of melancholy, even when he notes the

> Gentle purrs that came and went
> In the cat stretched out content.

Almost persecutionally encircling him, there is the burning animation of non-human life. Hence he can write a brilliant lyric on bees, "shooting hot from flower to flower"; and his contemplative tributes to a cow being milked are very moving. In "First Flight" he characteristically employs the narrative of an airplane ride purely as a means of reaffirming in a new way his attachment to the soil. Only occasionally does his somber mythology get too much for us: we may accept it that the spider is not unkind, but simply industrious and scrupulous in her fashion—yet he does perhaps strain at our limits of endurance when suggesting, in his poem "The Bull Inside," that this turbulent animal has accepted a check upon himself, somewhat in line with neo-Humanist doctrines of decorum, "for the sake of small calves to come." And there are times when his sense of natural awesomeness makes us realize why men have been driven to machines, business, finance, and the state, whereby they may, with distinct relief, contemplate not mystery, but either craft or quackery, not sacrosanct wisdom the thought of which makes us breathe wrong, but the foibles of comedy—not man in nature, but man in society.

Indeed, one might roughly distinguish the tragic from the comic by saying that the tragic deals with man in nature, while the picture of man in society is comic. But one should have to modify this statement forthwith, by admitting that the materials of comedy themselves become tragic when some aspect of society is treated as a *force*. The distinction applies to Archibald MacLeish's new play in verse, *Panic,* which has for its subject a phenomenon so essentially social as a collapse in our financial institutions, yet contrives to give the theme a fully tragic quality. One could only guess why an author as well acquainted with business phenomena as MacLeish, an editor of *Fortune,* should choose to picture a Wall Street crash in so magical a fashion.

It is possible that the almost religious accents of fatality present here stem from some desire for symbolic self-immolation on the part of the author. This poem is not written to herald the rise of the masses, but as a dirge for the fall of a banker. The Marxian "scientific" prophecies of capitalist decay are transformed into the tonalities of a Shakespearean soothsayer, or a mystic foreboding of death such as permeates the opening of a play by Maeterlinck. The only fully developed characters are the banker McGafferty and his mistress Ione—and as a matter of fact, one of the most effective scenes in the play profits by the contrast between the super-personal or non-personal quality of the plot in general and the intimate conversation of this couple (the interweaving of private relationships and broad historic trends such as distinguishes Malraux's novel of the Chinese revolution, *Man's Fate*).

No one seems to have noted how greatly the role of the messenger in Greek drama has been magnified in *Panic*. The course of the action is maintained by a steady bombardment of news: as read aloud by a throng "in a street before an electric news bulletin of the Times Square type—moving words in lighted letters," as read from the tape of the ticker in McGafferty's office, and as received by telephone. While all the world collapses, the organized distribution of public intelligence remains in perfect order. Indeed, we have scarcely witnessed the grim intrusion of The Blind Man and his radical companions in McGafferty's office, before we hear the voices of the people in the street reading the same information from the flicker of the news bulletin. Reports continue to pour in, until the banker finally wilts before the suggestiveness of their climactic arrangement. The logic of life and effort as he knew it is gone—and he is made ready to destroy himself.

The success with which MacLeish has met the problem of writing poetic drama makes me very enthusiastic about *Panic*. I consider it no slight triumph for a man to take a current issue, surrounded with the most realistic connotations, and treat it in a style neither pompous nor lame. Here again, I think, MacLeish has solved much of his problem by recourse to news. For many of the speeches that would have been least amenable to poetic formalization (such as lists of bank failures) are given the necessary amount of distinction, while still seeming "natural," by reason of the fact that they are phrased in the tone of headlines or telegrams. When the people from the street are reading from the bulletin, or Immelman is reading from the ticker, the correspondence is of course complete. But again and again we find the plot upheld by information or judgments whose expression gravitates about the conventions of news-writing. For this reason lines can seem "natural" even when beginning bluntly with nouns (the appropriate definite or indefinite article being omitted), and when marked by forms of ellipsis totally alien to conversational syntax (as when a character says: "He helping is hope").

MacLeish asserts in his introduction: "The classical rhythm equivalent to American speech would be more nearly the trochee or the dactyl than the iamb of blank verse." But I hold that this remark really applies most aptly to written forms, the headline and telegraphic styles. Indeed, it is where the plot is carried by monologue (as the plot of history is conveyed in the daily press by monologue) that MacLeish's style truly observes his injunction to "*descend* from stressed syllables" rather than (as in blank verse) "*rise toward* stressed syllables." The further his play departs from recitation and the closer it comes to true dramatic dialogue, the stronger is the tendency of the ear to hear the lines as iambic, regardless of his typographical divisions. But as evidence of how subtly MacLeish elaborates the headline conventions, and as corroboration for my belief that in his reliance upon news (both as the core of his dramatic causation and as the key for his style) he has solved the poet's problem of acquiring both *conventionalization* and "naturalness" at once, I might quote this fragment from a speech by The Blind Man:

> Knowing
> Never for what fault or
> Failing of ours is altered the
> World's future suddenly—Spilling of what blood:
> Thing done or not done:
> Holy duty forgotten—Knowing neither the fault nor the
> Finder—nevertheless
> We know well His messenger!
> Death we have always known!

MacLeish writes that "the rhythms of contemporary American speech ... are nervous, not muscular; excited, not deliberate; vivid, not proud." Which may or may not be true—but as I read the above verses, I felt that their peculiar quality of "nervousness," "excitement," and "vividness" was not that of *speech* at all, but the strange mixture of jerkiness and fluency that impresses one when following the galvanic convulsions of a news ticker.

A poet's symbols probably aim at "condensation" in this way: If he had had a certain attitude towards his parents at one period in his life, and if at other periods he had had an attitude of the same quality towards his companions, his studies, his art, and finally his politics, he might attempt to "integrate" himself by inventing symbolic devices that telescoped all these segments into one. Thus, were we discerning enough, MacLeish's imaginative identification of himself with the banker who wills to die could probably be traced to the point where his present political emphasis is found to merge with his earlier esthetic one. The symbolism of self-immolation has always been present in his work—and in MacLeish there is a parricidal ingredient. During his days as an esthete, he revealed something of the emotional elements in his *ars poetica* when he likened a good line of verse to the firm resounding of the ax as it sinks into the tree. We may not be extravagant if we remember, in this connection, that the tree is a "patriarch," that it stands as the symbol of shelter and authority (oh woodman, spare it)—hence we may suspect what devious condensations are taking place when this poet, on turning from estheticism to politics, pictures a capitalist leader (a "father"?) made ready to die.

The suggestion becomes more plausible when we note, in the young English Communist poets, a clear attempt at the coordinating of their politics with their earlier family relationships. They talk explicitly of their old quarrels with the father (quarrels which, they hint on occasion, even led to sexual gnarling)—and they explicitly merge this old relationship with their new political emphasis by a somewhat magical doctrine of ancestor-worship. In the surprising reversals of this doctrine, a man intellectually reborn can *choose* his forbears. Thus Stephen Spender, in his recent poem, "Vienna," concerns himself deeply with such symbolic reorganization. "I think often of a woman," he says—and ends the stanza of his tribute to her,

> It surely was my father
> His dry love his dry falling
> Through dust and death to stamp my feature
> That made me ever fear that fortunate posture.

In the men who died fighting at the Karl Marx Hof in Vienna, however, he finds a "father principle" for his new self—and his poem ends

> These are
> Our ancestors.

The same symbolic pattern lies at the base of C. Day Lewis's work. His long essay, "A Hope for Poetry," printed in his volume of *Collected Poems,* begins with a figure of speech quite relevant to my thesis: "In English poetry there have been several occasions on which the younger son, fretting against parental authority, weary of routine work on the home farm, suspecting too that the soil needs a rest, has packed his bag and set out for a far country." He proceeds to claim "Hopkins, Owen and Eliot as our immediate ancestors." He cites Stephen Spender's poem, "I think continually of those who were truly great," as indication of what "real ancestors" are. And he quotes from Auden's *The Orators:*

> It wasn't till I was sixteen and a half that he (an uncle) invited me to his flat. We had champagne for dinner. When I left I knew who and what he was—my real ancestor.

I most prize in our poets, as distinct from the simple rationalistic pamphleteer, publicist, or economist, the fact that they are alive to the full complexities of human readjustment. Implicit in their work is the knowledge that, with an honest and earnest man, any notable shift of cultural emphasis requires a great deal of "consolidation." A change in political affiliations, for instance, may not be merely a choice of expedients, as the more superficial pragmatists would suggest; it may involve all sorts of other factors grounded in one's past. One may not feel that, for him, the particular concern of the three English poets with their "ancestry" is important. The important thing to me is their clear awareness of the fact that a man's need of "integration" or "fusion" involves factors more complex, and closer to "magic," than rationalistic oversimplifications of political necessities can reveal.

Lola Ridge is similarly concerned with symbolic mergers in her *Dance of Fire,* issued in a cover and jacket of deeply glowing bronze that arrestingly announces the tenor of her work. As for "condensation": in the twenty-eight sonnets of her "Via Ignis" she evolves a kind of dithyrambic metaphysics about the symbol of fire. With Heracleitan thoroughness she finds us "living in a dynasty of fire," "still in the midst of the fire dance," for "the flame that breaks down, fuses and forms is still burning nakedly in humanity." Hence our agitation—to which she holds out the hope that "we may come forth, for a period, into the time of light." Thus we have a universal burning, existence as trial by fire—and we have a transcendent burning, light. Her sonnets are a highly ritualized statement of her key metaphor. By the unifications of her myth, all that is most significant in experience is drawn together: the "infuriate spark" in us, and in our "blood singing to the ancient horn"; the "tind'rous structure of the heart"; the

> lambent menace in the brain,
> Too fraught with tensions, which the blood inspires
> In radiant passage;

the upheavals of storm, the sea, and nebulae; the "music over heaven"; the sun; the "silver truce," "effulgence on the waters glistering"; "the lion and the burning dove"; the jungle, history arising from the jungle, the Chosen sacrificed for history, and finally, since such rigorous pursuit will usually call forth in some form its own negation, we come to poems on the "Ice Heart," the "vise of glaciers closing," and her apostrophe:

> Draw near, O near, to the ice-heart! abase
> This blood before the white contagious death
> Till it congeal in harmony.

There is no better proof of her deep attachment to her symbolism than the lovely sonnet "Is not this April of our brief desire" (where she Platonically interprets spring as the frail manifestation of some vaster awakening), or in her devout saluting of the dawn. But the full reward of her earnestness is to be seen in "Three Men Die," a tribute which one can justly call exalted, to the secular martyrs, Sacco and Vanzetti, themselves pictured in light, their nerves burnt in the raw electric fire. Many a poet will be found to have made devotional services of his own, semi-private compensations for the lacunae or irrelevance in the symbols of institutional religion. But no one could be more definitely focused upon such effort than Lola Ridge in her recent volume.

If I were required to characterize Mark Van Doren's *A Winter Diary and Other Poems* in but one word, I should use the word "humble." I do not mean that this poet makes a thriving business of humbleness (as the Frenchman Francis Jammes has done quite effectively). I refer to the fact that, when gripped by emotions, the author of these candid poems makes his reports, not with Byronic assertiveness, not with the air of one who would suggest that generous portions are his birthright, but apologetically—with timidity, regret, sorrow, and (at times of encouragement) gratitude. As a consequence, though his verse is lacking in brilliance, it does possess a subdued kind of poignancy. The long opening poem, a modernized extension of Whittier's "Snowbound" (plus something of the moralistic schedule we get in Milton's "L'Allegro" and "Il Penseroso"), the record of a city family's sojourn in the country from fall to spring, will not satisfy those who demand that the line of poetry be packed—yet in its unassuming way it suggests the appropriate seasonal moods with penetration, and sets the memory to vibrating. Though mainly a record of mild delights, the poem made me quite melancholy, having as it does so many lines that seemed to me wholly gray ("Slap, slap, the sound of car chains going by"). There is also a sonnet sequence, a troubled account of love, the quality of the whole well pointed in these opening lines:

> I said: It will not blow this way again;
> The branches of my life too soon are old;
> The wind is kind to early-withered men
> Lest they remember and confess the cold.

> I said, and scarcely knew that it was I,
> Hanging my leaves there in the springless year.
> I said; and did not listen to a high,
> Loud sound of March that filled the woods with fear.
> Then it was all around me, till at last
> Love like a hurricane of hate was blowing
> Bruising me everywhere. Yet I was fast,
> And stood among the ruins of his going.
> > Only the after stillness came and showed
> > These blossoms on me everywhere, like blood.

And perhaps not unrelated in essence, we have another long poem, "The Eyes," suggesting an obsession of guilt prior to offense. The many short lyrics reinforce the note of sad decline that seems to motivate the poet's output, one of the best formed being "This Amber Sunstream," which ends

> No living man in any western room
> But sits at amber sunset round a tomb.

James Agee's *Permit Me Voyage*, which bears the endorsement of a foreword by Archibald MacLeish, I find somewhat difficult to characterize. One must respect it for its firm workmanship throughout, but at the same time one must feel that the poet is still somewhat ambiguous as regards the coordinates he lives by (no great disgrace, as he is still in his twenties). His "Epithalamium" is an extremely able record of the marriage night, with tactful interspersing of attendant meditations. And a symbolic narrative, "Ann Garner," gives an impressive sense of rigor by picturing the stone-like kernel of silence that fell upon a woman whose child was still-born. "Life was in death," he writes, as he symbolizes purgatorial moods, symbolic curses. The book also contains a long "Dedication" in prose that in Amy Lowell's day would doubtless have been called "polyphonic." A rhetoric of pity and anger, it reveals the great complexity of the issues to which the author is alive, is succinct, and shows considerable canniness of appraisal.

Another volume in the "promising" category is David Greenhood's *Poems, et cetera*. Like most poets of the Southwest, he is much given to visual imagery, to the evocation of vague moods by sharp perceptions. In "The Life of a Hunter," a succession of prose paragraphs, the analogy between girl and deer is drawn out deftly, and with freshness. And one is shaken by the ominous speed of his "Aphorism":

> Westward of the road the white cloud rose,

> Eastward hove the vulture,
> Earthward bowed the high-hung Jew
> Introducing culture.

Much of his verse was obviously written at a time when his energies were not yet fully engaged or directed. They have the melancholy of potentialities unemployed, with the result that poetry has for him too many of the associations that go with incompletion. Hence the harsh decision of his envoy:

> Singers with sacred nerves,
> Mourners for the fallen leaf,
> We are writing tonight too many poems
> Awake with watchman and thief.

Poets should always be ready to vow such treachery—but as they mature, they should find ever maturer reasons for failing to abide by their vow. In Greenhood's case, I should imagine that his aphoristic gift, coupled with the adolescent association that poetry has for him, will most likely lead him into a period of analytic prose.

I must end somewhat "unscientifically" by the mere mention of three other books, which are treated summarily not because they are unimportant (I consider all three of importance) but because I have written about them for publication elsewhere, and I should not feel justified in repeating myself here. I refer to Horace Gregory's *Chorus for Survival* (which I am reviewing for *Poetry*) and e. e. cummings' *No Thanks* and Kenneth Fearing's *Poems* (which I am reviewing for *The New Republic*). Though sharper in his circumstantial references to the details of his times than Lola Ridge, Gregory resembles her in his turn for metaphysical unification—and I prefer the greater proportion of the critical which Gregory mixes with his sustained musicality. He is wholly at home in the current mode of seeing people *statistically*, noting about the individual his traits as member of a group. The attitude may show in the depiction of long historic movements—or we may find it in tribal migrations so brief as one evening's traffic jam, as in the poem beginning

> Under the stone I saw them flow,
> express Times Square at five o'clock
> eyes set in darkness, trampling down
> all under, limbs and bodies driven
> in crowds, crowds over crowds, the street
> exit in starlight and dark air
> to empty rooms, to empty arms,

> wall paper gardens flowering there,
> error and loss upon the walls.

One will find little current verse of greater scope and pliancy than that of *Chorus for Survival*.

Cummings seems to have got himself into a surprising tangle which keeps him fluctuating between the cryptic and the moony, the comic and the mystically ecstatic—and he frequently grows vindictive in ways that show more fancy and invention than maturity. His satiric gift is crippled by his exaggerated individualism, which a jumble of integrity and pig-headedness has prompted him to intensify in opposition to the current collectivist emphases (he had learned so well the ways of the antinomian that his very aptitudes tend to hold him at this stage). So we find him carrying on a kind of guerilla warfare against all camps, with catch-as-catch-can tactics finally involving him in anti-Semitic elucubrations that do him no credit. But his tendency to snipe at authority in every form helps his output in one notable respect: by stimulating a sense of isolation, it indirectly prods him to stress a compensatory "oneness" with the dramatic events of landscape and season—and some of his purely descriptive poems are excellent of their kind.

Kenneth Fearing, whose book is very accurately located by Edward Dahlberg's introduction, is almost the exact fit for our needs of the moment. For this reason, like a cartoonist he is limited in the range of his devices—but within this range he attains great suavity (the tonality of plaint and brooding that underlies his slang making for ceremoniousness). And there is no contemporary poet who is neater at noting with ironic corrosion the grotesque injustices of our ailing economic structure, in the "flophouse, workhouse, warehouse, whorehouse, bughouse life of man."

# Return After Flight

*Theory of Flight* by Muriel Rukeyser. Foreword by Stephen Vincent Benet. Yale UP
*The New Masses*, February 1936, 26

If one would find corroboration for the thesis that even the most practical of acts may have symbolic features, one should certainly examine this interesting volume of poems by Murial Rukeyser. The formal poet might make a poem of airplane flight, in which by his choice of imagery he conveyed the emotional overtones the act of airplane flight had for him. Or the practical mechanic might write of flying, purely by way of contributing to the data of aeronautics. But in Murial Rukeyser we find a clear convergence of the two. She made a practical study of the subject; and at the same time she felt the symbolic aspects of her interest.

The result is a work that can awaken, in the sympathetic reader, a profound responsiveness.

And the record of her experience, though told in a concatenation of isolated poems, is very close to the heart of drama. We get first a kind of long preamble, a collection under the general head, "Poem Out of Childhood." It shows, as it were, her "preparation," the quality of experience that made the thought of flying be the appropriate answer to her moods. It is only in the dramatic sense that we could call them poems of "childhood" as regards the section following, the "Theory of Flight" proper.

As we read through this second section, we begin to see emerging the modes of this strange initiation rite she has imposed upon herself. From a distance, she surveys the cruelty and arduousness of the contemporary world. At once aloof and observant, she comes upon an attitude that duplicates, in her own immediate terms, the educative passing of Dante through hell. And quite in keeping with the materials of thought uppermost today, it is the airplane motor that takes over the protective role of Virgil as her guide.

Thus, as we begin to feel stirred when we observe the import of the verses that close the purgatorial journey. "Flight is intolerable contradiction," she says—the very choice of the word "contradiction" giving us some clue as to the remade nature of her mind. "We bear the bursting seeds of our return." And she concludes, in lines that, while good in themselves, become magnificent in their context:

> Now we can look at our subtle jointures, study
> our hands, the tools are assembled, the maps unrolled,
> propellers spun, do we say *all is in readiness:*
> *the times approach, here is the signal shock:*?
>
> Master in the plane shouts "Contact":
> master on the ground: "Contact!"
>     he looks up: "Now?" whispering "Now."
>     "Yes," she says.    "Do."
>     Say yes, people.
>     Say yes.
>     YES.

For what has she thus symbolically prepared herself? We learn in the last poem of the book, "The Blood is Justified."

The range of relevant material she handles, in making this work an experience involving the entire personality and not merely a schematically "before and after" object lesson for schoolboys, is imposing in its richness. She remains competent and composed, even in the dangerous regions of magic: blood, fire, the pit, the father, the owning of names, ritual, the abyss-motif of perspective, the "going round and around" in the swing-music of the gyroscope, the upper and nether spheres, the mounting of stairs—all these secret ingredients are called upon, along with an affectionateness that evokes our confidence.

In having such a writer on their side, Communists have a worthy ally.

# The Hope in Tragedy

*Chorus for Survival* by Horace Gregory. Covici, Friede
*Poetry*, July 1935, 227–230

When we consider the great proportion of urban material embodied in Gregory's work, it may seem perverse of a critic to call the basic patterns of this poet's mind *agrarian*. Yet there is a sense in which the adjective applies almost as well to him as to the writer whose work seems to have had most effect in shaping him, D. H. Lawrence (a master whose significant vices Gregory has avoided with phenomenal tact). By an agrarian pattern of mind I mean a marked sense of periodic recurrence, of seasonal repetitions—observation largely shaped by the feeling that what has been still is and will be. In the typical urban attitude, history is a straight line, moving ever onward, leaving old things behind it, and coming into regions wholly new. It is "progressive," whereas the agrarian attitude is cyclical.

Motivated by the mystery of the seed, with its confluence of past, present, and future (life as born of death), the agrarian pattern is in essence tragic. Its concern with problems of rebirth makes for many variants of the Phoenix symbol. And we may expect to find here, in one guise or another, the vision of a marmorean Atlantis that lies, still perfect, its palaces intact, its marbles posturing in heavy twilight, at the bottom of the sea.

The agrarian pattern is that of the "Eternal Now." It brings the past to us, not as of antiquarian interest, as a collection of curios in a museum, but as another version of the present. The events of today, however concretely noted (and Gregory can note them as concretely as does any barrister's indictment before a Grand Jury) are at the same time fused with a sense of long perspective, whereby the poet is *close-to* and *remote-from* simultaneously. In his case, a specific intimate event, existing in its particularities but once, is reported with an overtone of migrations and historic sweeps. The poet observes through a screen of myth, so that what he sees bears the markings of this screen upon it. (The result is not "illusion," since the sense of relationship embodied in the myth is as "real" as anything else in the universe.)

Thus, Gregory is realistic and visionary at once, noting accurately, almost photographically, while his "metaphysical head" remembers that the ocean's roll and the expanse of continents lie significantly about the fringes of his details. Historic telescoping comes natural to him:

> New York closed into Rome, Rome into Egypt, Cosmopolis, and only darkness there.

Having called him tragic, we might define our meaning further by distinguishing between the tragic and the hygienic. The hygienic would solve all problems by sterilization. Is one beset? Locate the germ, and kill it. The tragic attitude, based upon the mysteries of the seed, of life-from-death, cannot accept the methods of hygiene as a solution for our fundamental ills. Within the frame of the tragic attitude, we do not seek to sterilize our aberrations, but to *harness* them, to make them *serve,* and with the help of criticism to build assets out of liabilities. It would sluice the demonic lightning into wires; it would control by reins.

For such reasons, Gregory's poetry is not always accepted by his political allies as assisting their immediate purposes. At first glance, the tragic attitude can appear to make for an acceptance of institutional maladjustments whereby the investor should "resign himself" in the most approved classic manner, to the burden of clipping coupons, and the impoverished, who cannot share the prosperity, are advised at least to attempt sharing the good taste (the Humanists' irritating philosophy of decorum). But only the most superficial reading of Gregory can lead one to assume that his basically non-hygienic attitude is reactionary in implication. There are many forms of "resignation"; we may also "resign ourselves" to protest—and appeal to the tragic attitude would be woefully misused if it were taken to justify acceptance of a toothache where there is a dental surgeon handy.

To read Gregory's three books of verse in succession is to note a gradual enlargement of his rhythms, which began with a sharpness sometimes almost hectic, and have slowly expanded to attain something like the gravity of rivers. Such progress in maturing, such grip upon the sustaining of his musicality, would indicate that he is at peace with his methods. The long invocation, *Tell us that love returns,* establishes a mood which he proves himself well equipped to maintain. And the ballad-like *Through streets where crooked Wicklow flows* is a terrifying picture of poverty done with the fullest poetic skill. I shall be surprised if it does not earn recognition as a poem exemplifying in the noblest manner the issues now upon us.

# Deft Plaintiveness

*One Season Shattered* by James Daly. Centaur Press.
*Poetry*, August 1936, 282–285

There were several aphorisms, printed and framed, in a room I remember from childhood. One said: "If whiskey interferes with your business, give up your business" (it was evidently an ironic plea for temperance, but I was bewildered because, taking it seriously, I couldn't make sense of it). There was another about talkative mothers-in-law. A third, the one that bears particularly upon our present purposes, ran as follows: "Laugh and the world laughs with you—weep and you weep alone."

When reading Daly's lovely poems, in his recent volume *One Season Shattered,* I was made to remember this room and my moods as I used to shop about in it, examining its lore. For all their technical maturity, the poems made me recall almost fearfully the sense of uneasiness I experienced there. In some vague way, when in that room, I wept, and wept alone. So do these verses. Religiosity is many things, but one of its important ingredients is what I might call the "socialization of loneliness." The religious man, said Nietzsche, thinks only of himself. But to think of oneself, in this real world, is to think of ways that will assemble those like oneself, to seek one's band. Thus, the utterance is at once monologue and universal summons.

In Daly, the two terms of our formula are present. Emphasize the first term, *socialization,* and you get to his profoundly plaintive plea for Communism, "Storm Warning." "Economics" means "housekeeping." And the poet, always close to origins, spontaneously feels again the correctness of the metaphor, and calls for a house fit to live in, a house that will withstand the inclement weathers of history. Yet emphasize the second term, *loneliness,* and you come upon a severe sense of personal property, imaginings of a realm "Outside the Earth":

> a portaled world
> To inhabit vastly and possess alone.

Poetry being a selection, it is not always certain how much or how little of one's practical self one ropes off to form the personality of the poetic self. The happiest men, doubtless, are those in whom the practical self and the poetic self can be identical. But there is restlessness in those who, as poets, build an *imperium in imperio*. Daly seems to be of this latter sort. He maintains in his art a plaintiveness that does not wholly encompass the adult world. It is basically childlike. But this childlike quality, when rienforced by adult knowledge as with him, can exert a most penetrating appeal. I am a little afraid of it, since it does not equip us explicitly for battle.

Mann somewhere mentions "that sense of strangeness, which in an earlier age would have been called saintliness." Since "saintliness" has been dropped from our working vocabulary, the "sense of strangeness" must bear its burden without the encouragement of the earlier euphemism. Daly is clearly one of Mann's "outsiders"—and perhaps my love for Mann inevitably foretells my susceptibility to the modes of appeal in Daly. The subtlety of his rightness is like the subtlety in a right tone of voice: the critical, quantitative, conceptual words for defining it are not yet at hand.

But there are some points where the matter emerges for discussion. We can note, for instance, how the "outsider" attitude in his earlier poems attains its obvious symbolic equivalent in the nature of his titles: "He walks alone by a lake-shore; He asks an old question, new to him; He reads the Book of Job—and he pretends her death." He looks upon the poetic *I* as *he*, with the outsider attitude, as though this articulate self were a mere *tenant* in the house of the inarticulate body. He goes to woman as across a bridge. He even spontaneously denies himself the solace of friendly personalizations: for when he turns to the thoughts of a father, he thinks in terms of *defeated* courage, and says with almost Greek severity:

> See your heart's proud city razed; and know
> The destroyer was in some fierce way yourself,
> An inward flaw, destruction in your soul.

And when he turns to thoughts of a mother (He *mourns* for his mother), we quickly get to the "moaning of the tide"—whereat we recall the first poem in his book, "He thinks of Life, the protean Eternal She," and learn that life is an ocean in which the poet would drown himself. Thus are mother, life, infinity, and death inexorably brought together in the magical fusions of the "unconscious," so that the cards are stacked in advance: there seems little likelihood of pulling a good time out of that setup.

In sum, what do we have? So far as this reviewer is concerned, we have a collection of poems that reawaken vividly the deepest of old responses. Their success within this frame comes from the tactfulness of complete sincerity. Their accent is as correct in the carrying-out of its purpose as are the gestures of a skilled actor. One feels arrested, one feels startled—an event which, in critical shorthand, we could signalize by saying simply that one feels a kind of beauty.

# Leave the Leaf Its Springtime

*New Poems* by Frederick Mortimer Clapp. Harper & Bros.
*Poetry*, July 1937, 226–229

If you are one of those readers who feel that there can be far more poetry in a compact definition than in the over-expansion of an image, I believe you will continually find eventfulness in Clapp's *New Poems*. Clapp can demarcate situations with scholastic compression. "Luxor lies ruins," he writes, in his poem "Peering at Pharaohs"—and I don't see how you could do more with that. The two initial *l*'s, the two final hard *s*'s, with the middle monosyllabic word, as bridge, combining both—that seems to me gratifying, workmanlike language. It is the kind of accomplishment Clapp has often.

With such stylistic equipment he goes forth to encounter danger; at which point we must introduce our "however." (If one wanted a 'scutcheon for the family tree of modern thought, I propose as heraldic legend that strange device, *N'eanmoins*.) Clapp's economy of production has its attendant rigor ("rigor" as in "rigor mortis"). One is led to speculate on the difference between an Egyptian, looking at an Egyptian mummy when Egyptian culture was alive, and ourselves looking at the mummy in a museum now, when its culture is dead. The poet, viewing the archaeological object under glass, hears outside an aeroplane; he imagines "the steep spiral climb / Of that mechanic hawk." By varying incantatory entrances, each firmly constructed, he returns us to the same uneasy mood, such feeling perhaps as one might get on leaving the traffic-laden streets on a hot summer day and entering a cool, dark church (someone else's church).

There are fears that one dare not confront, lest he be turned to stone. They are a Gorgon's head. But if he makes for himself a stylistic mirror, he can observe the monster thus reflected—and he is not rigidified. The unexpected bottleneck in the economy of such production is this: It is when the poet is *not* viewing Gorgon's heads in the protective mirror of his style, it is *then* that he is turned to stone. Or, translated: Our present poet can contemplate death with mastery; it does not freeze him; but when he holds his ingenious mirror up to *life,* he becomes petrified. He has an obol for crossing Acheron (even our great assertive steamships become her "Acherontic liners")—but he passes out this obol constantly, which is a punishment.

Within these contextual limits, Clapp's naming is expert. Here are, cautiously appraising,

>     clear cold eyes
> That make of me an alien.

The strict inventory discloses that days were spent "in a grass-fire of activity." The sexual act serves for "defying the Macrocosm." He observes how

> new astronomic ice ages set in
> and new conventions of original sin.

As I became formed to the pattern, towards the end of his book I noted a poem entitled "Birth." On the basis of past evidence, I ventured: "Somehow this birth will be a dying." Partially, the poet outwitted me. He treats, with delicacy, of an opening leaf. He gets us to opening with it. But, he rounds out the matter thus:

> Why does it tremble so on its stem?
> Is it, its fulness found,
> Tugging in an ecstasy of vitality still unconsumed
> Towards disembodiment?

I felt that one should try hard to leave the leaf its springtime. However, the taking-away can be done in slovenly fashion or well. And Clapp often does it very well—positively, assertively, by scrupulous stylistic building.

# Tentative Proposal

*The Mediterranean, and Other Poems* by Allen Tate. Alcestis Press
*Reactionary Essays on Poetry and Ideas* by Allen Tate. Chas. Scribner's Sons
*Poetry*, May 1937, 96–100

It has never been hard for me to understand why, in the face of too much talk about "progress," one should say: "In that case, call me a reactionary." Or why overzealous faith in scientific panaceas might make one even prefer to see a world go hang rather than see it happy by such dismal tests (observing, first, that the excess of zeal is fantastic in its credulousness; and second, not wanting comfort on such a plane even if it were obtainable). If, furthermore, one is a poet, and deeply so, as Mr. Tate is—and if one, with the scrupulosity of poets, has formed his expression around the coordinates of death, seeing everything, as it were, as a projection, or attentuation, of the mood one might feel when delivering, or hearing, a funeral oration—one will presumably have invested too thoroughly in an art that is *at home* with death for him to feel our current hygienic cant as other than a threat to his very character. That, too, I can understand. Or, on seeing what has been done with *ambition* in recent centuries, I can understand why one might want to speculate again on the sounder insight of *humility*.

But I can less well understand why such an earnest and discerning man would permit himself to "freeze" on these issues, to freeze too soon, thereby being forced to uphold tendencies that he need not uphold. I should cite Thomas Mann, who is as thorough as any contemporary writer, who sees how much more complex the problems of human relationship are than the coordinates of naïve materialistic science make them out to be, and who can pay tribute to the powers of darkness while warning against the powers of darkness.

Mr. Tate disturbs me. For he is exceptionally penetrating, both as critic and poet. To read his book of poems and his book of essays together, as I have just done, is to be stirred.

In my disturbance, I began looking for a quick solution. I began looking for some rule of thumb, as writers of reviews must, something handy, that might serve here as a point of departure. There is, of course, the ready availability of matters to do with "class." There is the "cue" derivable from the statement: "The Negro, who has long been described as a responsibility, got everything from the white man." One may stickle at the vandalism of that. But I am going to risk an even blunter formula, that could be associated with it, but might apply as well to men of much different views.

What I feel the lack of, throughout both essays and poems, is *physicality*. How much of a poet's "soul," I have often dared ask myself, stems from the simple fact that he doesn't *do* enough, in the purely muscular sense of doing? While voicing great resentment of abstractions, Mr. Tate suggests something of the abstract and managerial in his notions of social and poetic purpose. There are those who lift and carry; there are those who oversee those who lift and carry; and there are those who, insofar as the processes of overseeing and being overseen are in order, may stand somewhat aside from both. Mr. Tate, as we clerics have ever been, seems sometimes the super-overseer and sometimes the forgetter, but too little of the physical mover.

Ethically, the cleavage tends toward a breach of this sort: Concepts of humility do not attain their counterpart in menial acts. They become truncated, somewhat of a soul without a body (as colonies or monastic orders were not). They become insignia. And the abstract is inevitable, since it is not grounded; it yearns for immediacy, without paying enough attention to the entrance into immediacy, which is through the body (i.e., "mimetic"). Do we not all tend to become too "efficient" in our function as "clerics" (a tendency permitted to some in every age, but often even drastically required of us today)? No purely contemplated South, I believe, no sanctioned and cherished ancestry, no refurbished feudalism however humane, even no "progressive" solution, can be the antidote to such abstraction. Our social drama must be reconstructed on the basis of the body as an actor. It is because of such beliefs that I call his statement about the Negro "vandalism" (vandalism is that which robs everyone).

From this rough-and-ready formulation, many attendant reservations might be deduced. Does not its violation account in great part for the forbidding rigor of his verse, its preference for granite rather than for litheness? The results are sometimes deeply impressive. His metaphysical "Shadow and Shade" is a poem that I shall return to often, both for what it says, and for what it gives inklings of, beyond the saying. And repeatedly, I find his remarks on other writers astounding in their incisiveness and imaginativeness. Yet, in both his critical perception and his poetic expression, I feel no preparatory cult and practice of doing. In politics, we get at most the vestiges of the managerial genius in such statesmen as Calhoun. In poetry with religious hankerings, we get austere purgatorial moods (forgetful that, whatever this world is, it is not wholly the disembodied state of purgatory).

His poetry, I should say, marks the reward of such selectivity. His technical criticism is its conceptual parallel in worth. And his social exhortations are its corresponding deficiency. They make him say "Faugh!" where he might have said "I'm sorry." They make him say "Turn back" where he might have said, "Let's try to go on, and come out on the other side."

# Fearing's New Poems

*Dead Reckoning* by Kenneth Fearing. Random House
*The New Masses.* February 1939, 27–28. Also in *Philosophy of Literary Form*

"The alarm that shatters sleep, at least, is real" . . . Before you have finished one stanza in a poem by Kenneth Fearing, you have felt the trend of it stimulus, and have set yourself to the proper mode of expectation and response. I know of no poet who can swing you into his stride with greater promptness. Taking as his characters the stock situation of modern history's problem play, he offers us a slogan-laden "science of last things," in imagery found among the piles of the metropolis. Confronted by all the alloys, substitutes, and canned goods that are offered us by the priesthood of business, the catch phrases of salesmanship and commercialized solace, Fearing has put the utilitarian slogans to a use beyond utility, as he rhythmically sorrows, with their help, assigning them to an interpretative function in his poems that they lack in their "state of nature."

By his method, you may peer beyond some trivial advertisement to discern despair, migration, even "Amalgamated Death" (since the poet, after a secular fashion, is given to carrying out the churchman's injunction: "Thou shalt live a dying life"). The handwriting in a letter becomes the handwriting on the wall; and I feel sure that, with his expressive resources, he could readily transmogrify a pat salutation like "Dear Sir" into a prognosis of the vast collapse of Western culture.

Perhaps the quickest way to characterize his book is by a paragraph of cullings, one from each poem, that convey the quality of the poet's burden: "shadows that stop for a moment and then hurry past the windows" . . . "the phone put down upon the day's last call" . . . "until then I travel by dead reckoning and you will take your bearings from the stars" . . . "it is late, it is cold, it is still, it is dark" . . . "fill in the coupon" . . . "how the moon still weaves upon the ground, through the leaves, so much silence and so much peace" . . . "Lunch With the Sole Survivor" . . . "is it the very same face seen so often in the mirror" . . . "not until we've counted the squares on the wallpaper"

... "on the bedroom floor with a stranger's bullet through the middle of his heart, clutching at a railroad table of trains to the South" ... "It is posted in the clubrooms" ... "a privileged ghost returned, as usual, to haunt yourself?" ... "CAST IN THE ORDER OF DISAPPEARANCE" ... "tomorrow, yes, tomorrow" ... "soothed by Walter Lippmann and sustained by Haig & Haig" ... "if now there is nothing" ... "the empty bottle again, and the shattered glass" ... "as armies march and cities burn" ... "ask the stones, so often walked" ... "the natives can take to caves in the hills, said the British MP" ... "wages: DEATH" ... "Take a Letter" ... "with the wind still rattling the windows" ... "why do you lay aside the book in the middle of the chapter to rise and walk to the window and stare into the street" ... "Dance of Mirrors" ... "this house where the suicide lived" ... "something that we can use, like a telephone number" ... "Wait, listen."

There is a risk here, in the "statistical" quality of the perspective by which the poet sizes up the "thousand noble answers to a thousand empty questions, by a patriot who needs the dough." There is such limitation of subject matter as may come of taking the whole world as one's theme. All people look like ants, when seen from the top of the a skyscraper—and the poet's generalized approach often seems like the temptation of a high place. Connected with this is an over-reliance upon accumulation and repetition, traits that derive also from his disposition to establish a very marked pattern, which he expands as a theme with variations. Hence, for my part, the items I liked best were "Pantomime" ("She sleeps, lips round, see how at rest" ... ), a poem of tenderness and meditation that is very moving, and the opening "Memo" ("Is there still any shadow there, on the rainwet window of the coffeepot" ... )—where the generalized plaint is introduced in less head-on fashion. "Devil's Dream" (a kind of "There but for the grace of God goes our author" theme) is another poignant accomplishment, by reason of a more personal note. The author's rhetoric of attack ranges from the slap to a tearing of the hair (with perhaps his "En Route" among the most successful of the generalized statement); and all his lines bear convincing testimony—in speech swift and clear—of estrangement in a world awry, where many are asked to face the emptiness of failure in order that a few may face the emptiness of success.

# Literature

*We ask only to leave the entire matter vague—to say that a work may be popular and good, popular and bad, unpopular and good, unpopular and bad. It may be widely read and ineffectual, widely read and influential, little read and ineffectual, little read and influential.*

—*Counter-Statement* (91)

# Alcohol in the Eighties

*Painted Veils* by James Huneker. Boni and Liveright
*The Literary Review (New York Evening Post)* October 30, 1920

Mr. Huneker has just bridged a large lacuna in American letters. In *Painted Veils* he has given us our own little version of that panting period at the end of the last century which went racing though all the big cities of the Occident. We can now sit back proud in the knowledge that America was as ferocious as the rest of them. If France had its absinthe and its curacao, and England and Germany ditto, we now know on the authority of *Painted Veils* that vigorous young Americans went about with an occasional Dora whose "body was like a white satin stove," and conquered frequent violent "hookers." In *Painted Veils,* the Eighteenth Amendment is flaunted egregiously. The book should have three stars on the label. It is 110 proof.

The novel opens with Esther's coming to New York back in the '80s with only a hundred dollars in her pocketbook. But Esther is a difficult problem for the reader. Here is a young girl, coming to New York, poor and an orphan, yet she is neither duped, nor beset by plotting scoundrels, nor overwhelmed by the splendor of the city. In fact, as soon as Esther arrives she begins a business-like exploitation of every one who tries to befriend her. She has a voice, she has come to have a career, and she sets out on this career the first day. Within a short time she has used New York for all that it seems to be worth to her at that time, and goes off to Europe. With her temporarily out of the way Mr. Huneker turns attention to Ulick, who is a dramatic critic well up on the arts, with a Parisian training, but living in New York at the advice of his friend, Remy de Gourmont.

Ulick had had one brief mix-up, *incognito* with Esther before meeting her in New York, and the memory of it still itches him. However, there is nothing to do but find consultation in other fidelities, a predicament which Ulick manages quite well. But Esther has been going steadily ahead with her conquests, and returns to New York toward the close of the book a famous Wagnerian singer. Along with her fame she has considerably increased the range of her vices. The outcome of it all is a discovery which is as disgusting as the author intended it to be; then various characters are buried, and the book is over.

*Painted Veils* is a remarkable essay in assimilation, as I suppose a novel by a critic should be. With marked Baudelairean morals, it also has bits after the St. James version, a generous application of the psychoanalytic nomenclature, passages in the manner of our newest fragmentary writers, a few sentences of the thriller type, and, most of all, frequent borrowings from James Huneker, the critic. Mona at times has the flavor of Schnitzler's Anna in "Der Weg ins Freie." There is Huysmans, both in the intermingling of dogma and plot, and in the predilection for riot. The characters often mediate in a series of quotations from the most select authors. The *purpureus pannus* of Esther nude before the mirror is a newly imagined re-rendering of the classic theme of painting. For pages on end the author will transfer his authority to some other author he has read and admired.

The outcome of it all, then, is a "literary" novel. The characters are alternately ideological and mulierose, they are intelligent, and above all, talky. A continuous attempt at valuations—by no means new, but still vital—runs through the volume, although they are usually stuck in the mouth or head of some character. The book is allowed to fluctuate as it wills—action, criticism, analysis, generality; surely, Mr. Huneker was trying to do what Ulick contemplated: "To write a story, not all empty incident, nor yet all barren analysis. Neither Henry James, nor Dumas."

I do not know how long it takes to make a bomb. But Mr. Huneker testifies that *Painted Veils* was written in barely more than a month and a half. It was written, then, as speedily as it seems. It was hardly more than a racy conversation. The rough spots were never corrected, but, in compensation, the good spots are all the swifter. Mr. Huneker took his little fling, and a fling is never quite beyond reproach. Again, a fling is more likely to be an hilarious affair, where the smile crystallizes on your face every now and then, turns sickly, but soon regains its spontaneity.

This spontaneity is the most striking quality of the book. The index cards in the public libraries have a record like this after Mr. Huneker's name: (1859- ); yet here comes Mr. Huneker with a volume that is nothing if not young. It is hard to believe when you read *Painted Veils* that Mr. Huneker was once a contemporary of waxed flowers and antimacassars, family albums, and the sheaf of wheat, "over the fence is out," and fathers that asked young men who called three times in succession whether their intentions were honorable.

Uplifts having gone out of fashion, James Huneker is one of our leading down-lifters. For a time, at least, Gallicism seems to be climbing toward ascendancy over Victorianism. And with a sympathy for Gallicism comes a parallel questioning of America. We are coming to accept it not only docilely, but almost with gratitude, when we learn that "Ulick, despite his fondness for minced pie and Philadelphia scrapple, could not endure the national cuisine.' 'We are barbarians compared with the French,' he openly asserted, 'who know how to eat, drink, and think.'" In all probability, one nation is as stupid as another, however. But for better or worse, we are on our way; Victorianism never dreamed of such a neat cacophony as "They sang, and their voices were heavy with wine, passion, and incipient catarrh."

There is no break between the Huneker of the ethic-less criticisms and Huneker of *Painted Veils*. His treatment is completely unhampered, and will prove decidedly too unhampered for those who prefer calling a spade a teaspoon. And what with *The Genius* and *Jurgen* and *Painted Veils,* it seems that that super-Adam-and-Eva, that pre-Hebronian couple, Lingam and Yoni, have been gaining great vogue of late.

# A Transitional Novel

*The Dark Mother* by Waldo Frank
*The Literary Review* (*New York Evening Post*), November 1920, 6

A number of years ago, Professor Münsterberg defined the three successive stages of a nation's existence as provincial, cosmopolitan, and national. At that time he judged America to be emerging from the cosmopolitan stage into the national. In other words, we were reaching the culmination of our development in approaching the ante-bellum chauvinism of Germany and France. Although the war may have had the effect of disintegrating this attitude in Europe, war and our increased foreign trade are just marking the true beginnings of the national spirit in America.

Concomitant with an interest in the political and economic sides of our national development comes the interest in our development as an intellectual and social unit. Beginning a few decades back with the epic novels of Frank Norris, we have since then refined upon the study of ourselves, with such results as Van Wyck Brooks's subtle posing of Mark Twain against the background of our dying puritanism, and Waldo Frank's sublimated press-agenting, *Our America*.

There is one type of contemporary intellectual American who thinks he must flee from America. There is another group of artists concerned mainly with themselves and the manifestation of themselves in their medium; their environment is of merely accidental importance, employed or discarded for some purely subjective reason. A third kind is trying to distil some essence which they can call America, to give us some national integrity which can begin a tradition for us, form the sproutings of a purely indigenous culture. Such a man is Waldo Frank.

I don't know just why it is, but these alchemists in search of the gold of American unity have nearly always been rhapsodists; perhaps it is because Whitman was a rhapsodist. In any case, they usually interpret America in terms of breathlessness. They record a fever chart. We must be written about in a *tempo agitato,* in restlessly vacillating curves of rhythm. Speed, then, and syncopated noise are the first principles of American unity? I question it.

In illustration of this, I recall reading the opening chapter to *Our America,* that masterful frenzy of American corruption and chaos, *The Land of the Pioneer.* I was buried in the history room of the library, where a man was frowned on for whispering. The air was stuffy and artificially still. But as I read I no longer received the impression of my surroundings. I got into the feel of 200 years of American herculeanism. I saw our origins as white dashes, monstrous errors, gigantic diseases. As I left the library America seemed to me something terrifying, something beautifully wrong, something moon-mad and money-mad and joy-mad and hate-mad.

I stepped out on Forty-second Street. The day was mild and confident. One chap stopped to light a cigarette. A young woman was trotting a little lap dog. I went into Bryant Park and observed people dozing in the sun. Two girls were giggling and eating peanuts. I sat in the park a while, and then went home on the elevated. It was crowded, but there was no confusion. That evening I went to visit a friend, and found him playing pinochle with his parents. After a number of equally harmless and placid observations I wondered just where this feverish America was. I felt that I had been tricked. . . . No wonder Waldo Frank disapproves of the pragmatists!

In his present novel, *The Dark Mother,* Mr. Frank applies the same general mentality. His characters struggle through a world of superlatives. This, for instance, is a good sample of his method of approach:

> Her sleep was a strange thing. No real dreams—streakings of thought and dream ran through her night like falling flames. So that her night was neither sleep nor waking. It was an endless trembling between two worlds, it was a part of Chaos. She lay there and her body was a restless weight holding her down. She was like a little boat tossed at anchor by a broken sea. Her body and her consciousness: these were the anchor. They kept her from running wild with the waves. And the waves kept her from being quiet at her anchor. She was torn. She was a continuous play of hindered movement.

It is done well, frequently with beauty. The only question is that of its initial validity. The characters suffer too often; or rather, we are *told* that they do this excessive suffering. For it is only rarely that these characters are seen in actual operation; but these rare places are remarkable. The Judas-psychology of Tom guying his dear friend in the presence of two ninnies, for instance, is unforgettable. And Cornelia's suicide is handled with a certain business-like directness.

Broadly stated, the story is about a dreamy young man from the country whose whole body and soul are bent upon remaining exalted. He is the country cousin endangered in a Big City. In it Mr. Frank intends to hint at those unexpressible nuances of relationship which arise among people of affection. But his book operates on latent motives. He gives too much to the emotions and not enough to the intellect. As a consequence, we suddenly stop moving with the author, and see quite coldly that hearts are broken and souls endangered. The turmoil of diction continues, but it has lost significance. Surely, Mr. Frank is a more convincing narrator in his essays.

*The Dark Mother* is decidedly a transitional novel. Although it was written in 1917–1918, Mr. Frank is already doing something different with his methods of writing prose. For I think it is safe to suppose that "Under the Dome," a short story which was published this September, was written after *The Dark Mother*. Free verse is well enough established now, but free prose is only beginning. Writers of English prose who got beyond the standard dribble of the modern English novel are floundering temporarily in the chaos of a more sensitive medium, a more pliant form. Mr. Frank is one of the foremost of these martyrs in America. *The Dark Mother* is a lost cause, so far as the medium goes. For it is transitional; it is neither the novel, nor something distinct from the novel. Judged as a novel, it does not satisfy; and there is nothing else to judge it by.

Experimentation with the novel will be done at a dreadful sacrifice. For a novel normally takes at least a year to produce. Now, if at the end of a year the experiment is not satisfactory, that means a good portion of a man's life gone. In verse the experiment was less fatal. The comparatively short time it takes to produce a unit of poetry is not significant. This is perhaps the reason why prose is only now beginning to break, after the poetic revolt is nearly established.

In any case, Waldo Frank is *en route* for something or other. At present his mind is still cluttered up with innumerable *clichés*, which may be true or may be false, but are *clichés* all the same. It is a *cliché*, for instance, to think that every time your hero looks at a New York street you have to lyricize on the great brute city. It is a *cliché* to write in terms of great elations and great miseries when human beings think in terms of mild comforts and irritating discomforts. It is a *cliché* to assume that one is made cynical and broken by familiarity with the ways of the world, while idealism is a sort of divine stupidity.

Of course, any one can see beyond the *cliché*. The difficulty is to *produce* beyond the *cliché*. The man who can write "She trudged through the bright pink snow" has the proper equipment. Or this about a song sung by foreigners in a travelling railway car:

> The melody throbbed higher. Sharp flashings of desire were now in the women's voices; the men's were weary and disconsolate, dying down. The song was over.
> A new silence lay in the car. The car ran on, subdued in it and sweetened.

# Felix Kills His Author

*Moon-Calf* by Floyd Dell. Alfred A. Knopf
*The Literary Review* (*New York Evening Post*), 1 December 1920

The Endymion motif, I imagine, is a very difficult one to handle. Just how, for instance, is one to treat his hero? Certainly, as a youth he must not be like the other boys, which is a rather well-worn path. Further, he would write a good deal of poetry. Again, he would "come home at dusk, his head with its cluster of yellow curls bent over a book which he read as he walked, another volume held tightly under his arm."

As the hero-poet is brought up in Middle Western towns, he must begin to worry as to whether he likes certain girls or really loves them. At times when he is silent, as is the way with poets, people will suggest that it is because a cat has his tongue. There are further girls to be kissed on the rollercoaster, and there must be a love affair beginning with moonlight on the river. Occasionally a sentence will occur about "being true to one's soul."

Floyd Dell has solved this problem by making his book a frank study of mediocrity. Brought up in mediocre surroundings, with a mediocre sentimental equipment, the hero writes verse which is mediocre and meets all sorts of mediocre people. Later on, as the hero grows older, he goes through a few denim love affairs, works at indifferent jobs, and plans a crude novel. As the book nears its close, a series of love scenes occur which nearly destroy us with their mediocrity, love scenes evolving along the following lines:

> She came and put her arms around him. "Felix, dear, I'm so sorry. I—I didn't know you cared—like that."
> 
> He looked up, his face grotesquely twisted with sobs. "You didn't know I cared?"
> 
> "No," she whispered. "Not in that way. Did you really love me so much?"
> 
> He looked at her tragically. "What happened?" he asked. "What really came between us? I can't quite believe it."

She smoothed his hair. "I don't know," she said slowly. "It does seem strange, doesn't it? We loved each other so much. And then—"

The sum and substance is that she marries another man, and the hero goes down the road with a sudden illumination; he will escape to Chicago. Trifling as it is, it is his one emergence above the dead level of existence.

The danger of such a subject, of course, is that the mediocrity of the hero may penetrate the author's presentation. This nearly happened in the case of Flaubert; but Flaubert was saved by his hatred for his Frederic Moreau. In Floyd Dell's case the hate seems to be lacking. Indeed, the author seems almost complacent with his hero's avid grasp of atheism, socialism, and other patently high-brow theses which throbbed among the high-school intellectuals of a decade or so back.

And as a consequence, Mr. Dell finally succumbs. His first chapter, a chapter dealing with the hero's antecedents, and therefore written before Felix could get a grip on him, is a piece of gratifyingly terse writing; a kind of apotheosized business English. But when Felix enters, the good writing is over. Only once or twice after that is the author able to rise above his cretin. He gets down a couple of Middle Western interiors with accuracy, for instance, and writes two positively magnificent pages about a crippled boy. This cripple is introduced out of the void; he is placed before us in a few lines; we accept the entire significance of his mania for playing at God; and then his is dismissed, gone out of the book entirely.

After that Mr. Dell resigns himself to his task. His words develop a dull and unpenetrative edge, while his form is not at all illuminative. One is lost in a meandering of incident which has been given no significance by any concerted impulse, any synthetic grasp of the subject, any consistent overtone or generality. The book, which is the story of a life, takes on no more composition than life itself would have. To make a distinction between two possible kinds of fiction, it would be a diary rather than an essence, which is to say, the facts without an implication. We learn such things, for instance, as that the hero does not know French or German, things which point to no basic conception. Even the chapter ending becomes slovenly, resorting to such unhappy closes as "Good," said Felix. "Let's!" or "One *can't* get everything the island has to offer and still have a carefree home."

Judging from this first novel of his, it is safe to prophesy that Floyd Dell is to belong to no school, to ride no literary hobby horse. Glancing over the world of modern writers to define just what Mr. Dell is not, I should say first of all that he does not fall among the verbalists. Roughly, the verbalists are those who are trying to restore the ecstasy of the proscenium speech. In

France another phase of verbalism is the *reduction ad absurdum* of the Dadaistes: here the word is dignified to a height beyond mere meaning, a murmur of the prophet under an anæsthetic. And if what I have seen of Walter Hasenclever's work is representative, I should say that the post-war verbalist movement in Germany is an attempt to supplant the sentence by the word, to find the shortest possible synthesis for an idea, and to gain a peculiar effect on human lostness by this method.

There are also the fragmentarists, which Floyd Dell is not. The fragmentarists are working on the value of the disjointed, carrying out a theory which William Carlos Williams has captured very precisely: "The speed of the emotions is sometimes such that thrashing about in a thin exaltation of despair many matters are touched but not held, more often broken by the contact."

Furthermore, there are all the neo-Catholics and their non-believing disciples; one side of the movement makes for an ingenuous mysticism, the other for the rabies of a defenestrated Christian. There are still other movements, ranging from the attempt to reconstruct the sentimental side of Hellenism, through the attempt to destroy the novel, to the attempt at developing the expressiveness of mere typographical arrangement. Another group is trying to follow up the technique bequeathed it by the world's last genius, Jules Laforgue. Their attempt is to be sad by means of a scientific nomenclature.

But in the meantime, placed quite immune above the battle, undisturbed by all this blind theorizing and futile tentative, Floyd Dell purls happily, "And Felix was immersed again in the day dreams which books unfolded for him . . . her sweet and friendly presence . . . the poignant wonder of night . . . Felix breathed freely once more . . . he walked away, framing the words in rhythmic sequence."

# Axiomatics

*The Mask* by John Cournos. George H. Doran Company
*The Dial* 68, April 1920, 496–499

There are dreadful people I have met who think that to be of any value, a work of art must have magnitude. They appraise art by its bulk and its momentum if hurled, while a symphony for eighty pieces would, in their scheme of judgment s, be eighty times as important as a sonata. To have concocted Big Moments, to have dealt in everybody's heart-throbs, to have approached some sort of exaltation, is to have merited their ultimate benediction. They have waded through Dreiser, wallowed in English trilogies, and gulped great waves of 1850 Russian epilepticism. But it never occurs to them that a horn tooting away for dear life might be ridiculous. . . . Over against their almost universal trombonism, if one is to plead that the world still has taste, can be mentioned a scraggly number of tinkerers with the harpsichord. The harpsichord was a frail instrument, somewhat glib, although not more so than the Moralités Légendaires of Laforgue, or some of de Gourmont's excursions. We are in sad need of a trombone here in America to toot the value of the harpsichordists.

But the harpsichordists do not belong in a discussion of *The Mask*. I mention them simply because Up induces the thought of Down, and systole is accompanied by diastole; because I couldn't read *Cannan* without remembering *Les Chevaux de Diomede*. Mr. Cournos, that is to say, plays the trombone; and for a comparative beginner, he plays it well.

Mr. Cournos is very seriously immersed in the floods of life. In a novel that is evidently the redoing of a vivid personal experience—d'Aurevilly said that we all had two or three of such plots in our sack—he writes with all the fervour of a Dostoevsky. For like Dostoevsky, he is manipulating the throbbing realities. Life is a struggle for adjustment, a painful attempt to resolve things. These efforts begin when the newborn sees blurred movings with unfocused eyes, and end, I suppose, with death. All of which is a banal outlook on life, and has produced masterpieces.

The objection to misery and struggle as an impetus to art is that it takes the caution out of a man. The violent surge of things to be said pushes one recklessly on, so that he has no time for questioning his aesthetics. Standards have to be taken for granted; if the house is to be erected hastily, we must grab the hammer and nails nearest at hand. By this I do not necessarily mean that the book is dashed off at top speed. Samuel Butler spent years with his *Way of All Flesh,* and yet whenever he came to it, he came not as an artist but as one of the immersed-in-lifers. He *may* have talked technique from night till morning, but his book was always bigger than he was, like life itself. There is not a single trial of skill in the whole volume. Earnest things were to be expressed adequately, and he expressed them as adequately as his earnestness could enable him. The same might be said of the author of *The Mask.*

The fault with this earnest adequateness shows most noticeably in the disturbing breaks of the narrative, frequent in both books. The reader is lugged ten or twenty years ahead of the story for a few pages, and then just as suddenly dumped back again. Autobiographical associations have proved stronger than the demands of the medium, so that for the sake of a full truth the author will snatch at anything. This makes it impossible to develop concomitantly with the hero of the novel. A reader's receptivity is a very frailly built mechanism which is always disrupted by such rough handling. If the opening sentence of a book prognosticates one kind of story, the reader unconsciously adapts himself to whatever kind it promises to be. But if the story does not abide by the laws of its kind, it cannot be entirely satisfactory, even though we theoretically approve of its transgressions. There are many sorts of writing in which any kind of a break is possible—I can think of no happier example of this than Gide's *Nourritures Terrestres*—but if one is setting out at this late date to do something *compelling,* something drastically *true to life,* something *vibrant with human interest,* he must recognize that the medium is already pretty thoroughly established for that sort of thing; and that if he is after verisimilitude with heart and soul, he must have a better reason than mere convenience for breaking the steady march of his narrative.

The embarrassing predicament of *The Mask* is that it is a reasonably good book. Now a reasonably good book is peculiarly elusive. One cannot tumble all over himself with praise of it, nor can he object to it without a futile qualification of every statement. Mr. Cournos, like so many of our present-day writers, goes about his work with intelligence, an impeccable keenness of vision, and some thoroughly arrived attitudes. It is safe to suppose that he has read Freud, a couple of essays on zoology, and a weekly with some shade of radical politics. Consequently, one cannot get at him. He is impregnably *aware.* Such people are skilled in the art of giving just as much as can be endured, and no more. John Gombarov's stepfather Suffers in Silence for so many pages, but is always discretely muddied with some domestic detail as he is on the verge of becoming a hero. Occasionally a pompous train of oratory is organized, only to be rained on at the last moment. Whereas in the old code comedy was introduced to keep us from suffering too strongly, it is wisely inserted here to forestall our protests. And as I say, the enraging thing is that such subterfuges are successful. Writers of reasonably good books are preeminently slippery; they are not to be walked on with comfort. When their book is completed, they can lie back and observe us moving nervously along on ice-creepers.

Heaven alone knows what is to become of the novel. As early as 1884 Huysmans was sick of it, and began his series of compilations with *A Rebours*. But on the whole, although it is so short-lived, it has become astonishingly autocratic. Keen minds have accepted it as naïvely as the infallibility of a pope. In spite of the hemorrhage of verse that is splattering about the earth, I suppose there is still one novel published for every poem. Huysmans, Gide, de Gourmont, Joyce, Lewis—I can think of no others who have showed any interest in even *stretching* the novel, unless Romains be added for safety's sake. The French Academy goes on with its sterile coronations, and across the Channel ten (10) established reputations still heave their annual mountain. Yet if perfection can kill a thing, the novel should have died at the end of the century, since Mann had already written his Buddenbrooks. However, most people have easily avoided this dilemma by not knowing Mann.

The novel is too rigid a form to express an age like the present. We need something that admits easily of interruption, digression, and the mounting of hippogriffs. Perhaps we shall develop a form, or a formlessness, after the fashion of Petronius' escapades. Indeed, our kinship with late Latin is continually becoming more evident. We are squarely in one of the Dark Ages, a period of transition and uncertainty, or perhaps better, a period of *marked* transition, since Goethe says we are always in transition: *der Uebergang, der Uebergang zum Uebergang, des Uebergangs Uebergang zum Uebergang, and des Uebergangs Uebergang zu des Uebergangs Uebergang.* We, like them, are essentially Orphic rather than Olympic. Without their Christianity, we have their Christian retreatism. We have their love of the catalogue, their joy in vituperation, their interest in broad, ugly words. Some of the most notable writers of the last decades have drawn from late Latin. Of all these, perhaps the most representative is Léon Bloy, with his polysyllabic spew, his tetanic disgust, and his crushing in of the heads of the bourgeois.

Practically all of these men, of course, are French. This is to be expected, for although we northern barbarians have been assuming for three hundred years that we are quite in the flow of things, the fact is that Rome has only now reached as far as Paris. In all probability this Romanization will continue; let us trust that Latin is still more permanent than correspondence courses. And in the meantime, if a Russian temperament chooses to write under English influences, we can expect interesting books, intelligently and honestly written, with perhaps such pearls of style as this:

> And, having caught with all this a sense of inevitable fatality which attends upon those born to incur the steady displeasure of the gods, he felt that now he could go on with the tragi-comic play with keen interest, even amusement, that indeed, to some degree he could assist, if need be supplant, the demoniac prompter.

# The Modern English Novel Plus

*Night and Day* by Virginia Woolf. George H. Doran Company
*The Voyage Out* by Virginia Woolf. George H. Doran Company
*The Dial*, May 1921. 572–575

If symbolism was carried off by a collection of Greeks, Jews, Spaniards, Germans, Americans, and Belgians writing French, France is no worse off than England, where letters since the Nineties seem to have been maintained by one Pole, two Americans, and a horde of Irishmen. Germany at least had the vitality left to produce a philosophical historian as late as 1917, but Spengler according to his own testimony is the dying gasp, while all of occidental Europe enters upon the winter of its civilization.

In any case, the Spenglerian doctrine is not endangered any by Virginia Woolf's *Night and Day,* where we learn in five hundred pages, against a background of afternoon teas and the names of philosophers, that Katharine loves Ralph but is engaged to William who is also chafing under the bondage since he has come to care more for Cassandra, while Ralph has concealed his love from Katharine, and Mary loves Ralph in vain so that in the end she must strive to forget, but Katharine and Ralph are united by her mother—concealing a tear of happiness—and Cassandra and William ditto.

The appearance of *Night and Day* is all the more astonishing in that it was preceded by *The Voyage Out,* a first novel in which Mrs. Woolf had made a distinct advance upon the representative modern English novel. The book was marked at times by a peculiar loneliness of vision. Or perhaps better, a readjustment of the angle of approach. This quality is to be found, for instance, in the passage where the ship on which the action of the novel is taking place is suddenly treated as it is seen by the passengers of other vessels, so that it becomes simply "a ship passing in the night." It is present when the heroine's first serious moonings are shattered by the rousing appearance of an English battleship, or when the illness which is to cause her death is introduced in this wise:

> Owing to the heat and the dancing air the garden too looked strange—the trees were either too near or too far, and her head almost certainly ached. She was not quite certain, and therefore she did not know, whether to tell Terence now, or to let him go on reading. She decided that she would wait until he came to the end of a stanza, and if by that time she had turned her head this way and that, and it ached in every position undoubtedly, she would say very calmly that her head ached.

It is to be found in the self-serious conversation of two friends while one of them is cutting his toe nails. Or the description of a hotel attained by giving a two-or-three-line glimpse at each separate and unrelated entity. Or the sudden memory of a drizzly day in London when the book has us baking in the steady heat of the Amazon.

In its weakest exemplification, the tendency shows up in the following kind of attack, a method which has been squeezed and sucked dry by our neo-Whitmanites, and which the earnest editors of *Contact* would probably dispose of very rightly as "modern traditionalism":

> It was as though the room were instantly flooded with water. After a moment's hesitation, first one couple, then another, leapt into mid-stream, and went round and round in the eddies. The rhythmic swish of the dancers sounded like a swirling pool. By degrees the room grew perceptibly hotter. The smell of kid gloves mingled with the strong scent of flowers. The eddies seemed to circle faster and faster, until the music wrought itself into a crash, ceased, and the circles were smashed into little separate bits.

Without this shift of attitude, her material is composed of the characteristic English-novel accessories. Mr. Pepper is a vegetarian pedant who complains of his ailments; St John is the eunuch second-lead friend who worships the heroine awkwardly and always says the wrong thing, for which you love him; Mrs. Somebody is partially deaf, so that tragic news gains a hysterical relief by being shouted at her four times. Indeed, a great many of her characters are stock types which could be patched together from one season on Broadway.

Too often, the general mentality behind the books displays a hankering after the secrets of life, the sacred experience, the beautiful truths which are *sensed*—not *realized in crude clarity*—one more bow, in short, to the inarticulate *muqueuses*. The more important—and therefore sensitive characters—

spend a large portion of their time living as in a dream, frequently floating in so disturbingly indefinite a thing as a cloud of thought. Indeed, Mrs. Woolf's vocabulary for fixing brain states does not depart radically from that of Oliver Optic; we learn, for instance, that her hero's "mind was scaling the highest pinnacles of its alps, where there was only starlight and the untrodden snow." She also accepts with unquestioning seriousness what Benda would call the "aesthetic of love": which is to say that the Bronte throb is restored with neither additions nor subtractions. (And while on this subject it might be well to add that Mrs. Woolf's romantic men are more than a vengeance for our male authors' romantic women.)

These tendencies, however, show to much less disadvantage in *The Voyage Out,* since in this book the technical manipulation has been so thorough. It is a splendid stroke, for instance, when the heroine is dead, to dismiss her and her lover entirely, return to the hotel and summon a raging storm. For a few pages this little colony of Britishers, who have come all the way to South America and transplanted every single feature of their life in England, chat nervously while the tropical storm rips by and Rachel is known to he dead. It passes; we see it lighting far out on the ocean; the Britishers go to their rooms. One gets the smell of fresh damp vegetation . . . and the death of the heroine has been magnificently orchestrated. In fact, *The Voyage Out* is full of such careful juxtaposition of elements; Mrs. Woolf reaches the highest points in her book by just this method.

If *Night and Day* had been followed by *The Voyage Out,* one could explain very glibly that the first book was a mere blind tentative. But as the books were written in the reverse order, it seems that Mrs. Woolf did not realize her own distinctions. The same calamity happened to Louis Wilkinson, who wrote *The Buffoon,* and then went scurrying back to the usual society novel of his countrymen. As a matter of fact, the ideal development of a writer would probably be in exactly the opposite direction. Before he had attained a complete consciousness of his intentions and a mediumistic equipment with which to embody those intentions, he would be much nearer the general level of writing than after he had gotten himself really in hand. To take the example of music, it is only in their earlier compositions that Scriabine and Debussy approach the Grade 3 A splendour of the *Minute Waltz.*

But for some reason or other, literature seems to fight shy of this *Zug nach Innen.* There is the case of Sherwood Anderson in America, for instance, who is evolving on the principle that the stages of a literary artist should be, first to express one's self, then to express an Illinois butcher, and finally to express all the readwhile-runners in seven continents. (Those, that is, for whom a book is the moral equivalent of a newspaper or a box of chocolates. The work of art is received as a vague lump; the acme of critical acumen is attained in the characteristic "Have you read the latest book by—?" To become "great," a book must naturally be composed of elements which do not go beyond this preponderant public.) In America, this process of vulgarization is caused by our neo-Whitmanite hoax, which strives to make art explode like a blunderbuss. In England, perhaps, it all derives from the deadly combination of literature and the drawing room.

# The Editing of Oneself

*The Mystic Warrior* by James Oppenheim. Alfred A. Knopf
*The Dial*, August 1921, 232–235

With the advent of psychoanalysis the literature of confessions enters upon a new phase. Heretofore the confessor has been subject to emotion in such a way that his need to express himself was greater than his discretion; he maintained a wavering battlefront between pride and humility, although above and beyond it all the confessions continued. But now the confession has become an invention, made possible only by the discoveries of modern science and research. If the older confessions were written almost in spite of oneself, the newer confessions burble along like brooks. And when one has been properly "psyched," he does not even suffer a pudency before his secretly suspected virtues.

As a consequence, it is becoming the custom, when one has reached a certain age, to lay out the stades and parasangs of one's journey; and, having decided just where one is going, to tell exactly how one got there. Further, it seems there is no longer any essential difference between making a work of literary art and writing an essay on the causes of the Great War. Beginning with the result, one works back into a set of teleological connections, and then starting with the teleological connections, one works up to the result . . . a method which has produced a remarkably interesting volume in Mr. Oppenheim's *The Mystic Warrior*.

*The Mystic Warrior*, working along these lines, is born to find that "the world was a dream of beauty, an ache of loveliness." But, on the other hand, "everything spoke of death, everything whispered in my ears, 'James, you will die.'" In the beginning, therefore, Mr. Oppenheim recalls the love of life and the fear of death. "Then, after breakfast, grammar." He could not concentrate on his studies, however. "Phantasy possessed me . . . And everything was too beautiful . . . Too beautiful the blue of the sky, green of the earth, Too poignant the gleam of wonder in butterfly wings, Too aching lovely the summer fields, the glaze of the morning . . . My throat was clutched with tears . . ." Little James watches the sun go down with terror, since then he will think of death. By way of summing up here, the author passes two judgment s: "O, only one who has felt this terror knows what it is to live!" and later on: "And nobody bothered his head about it!"

With the death of his father—told with an honest homeliness of emotion which makes it one of the finest passages in the book—the boy is thrown into less general preoccupations. "But now I must take his place: I must hurry and be a man . . . Strange task for the dreamy little singer and artist!" Along with this, a period of yearning sets in:

> . . . I wanted, not to be my father,
> But to be the child encircled by my father's love . . .
> I wanted to go from the hard weary world, the torture of existence,
> The clash and dust of my brain,
> Into that cell of abnegation and quiet
> Where the invisible Beloved hovers,
> And I should give birth to the divine child,
> My inspired song, my poem, born in love.

But instead:

> Sold my love for power, converted religion into livelihood,
> And gave the artist in me to be a semi-harlot of the press.

For the next years, life is a hodge-podge of Napoleon, Lincoln, Shakespeare, Wagner, Jesus, and jobs. Above it all was a mixed ambition to conquer or redeem the world, to throw off contemplation for action. However:

> I essayed, and failed . . . song lured me again . . .
> Again the storm-cloud, again the agony,
> Again the triumph of music and vision.

"Not that there was no counter-current." He tried "To be interested in others, to join good causes, to work among the poor, And last, and greatest, to learn how to love." This love, although containing much of the metaphysical for "What did I love but the God with whom I became one . . ."—also extended to a marriage, which was not successful and forced him into hackwriting. But finally "New knowledge came . . . My marriage broke open and showed itself for what it was . . ."

> . . . I went off to a life of lonely poverty . . .

> And in that life, in anguish, listening, brooding,
> I heard from far-off the murmur of the divine music coming like a turning tide back to me . . .

The story ends here, after the author has attained the haven of his first book, *Songs for the New Age*.

In an appendix, Mr. Oppenheim discusses the problem of form as it applies to his present work. He finds that the tendency of the realistic novel has gradually been leading closer to the material of the author's life; in other words, gradually becoming a mere "thinly disguised autobiography." Mr. Oppenheim claims that the natural consequence is that we give over the thin disguise and write frankly of ourselves. It is certainly gratifying to see an author who can examine the basis of his work, although in the present instance one might dispute the cogency of his conclusion on the grounds that the increasing necessity which realism finds in thinly disguising the life of the artist points simply to the imminent bankruptcy of realism. In fact, looking beyond the novel to the realistic movement as a whole, we find that even at the opening of the century intense realism led not to autobiography, but to symbolism. The reason for this is that realism, by putting man face to face with facts *per se,* awakens over again his primitive need for animism, or *correspondences;* since man is constitutionally averse to the sterility of mere facts, and when they are placed before him in all their barrenness he must immediately make something else of them. (On the other hand, if realism has gone off into symbolism, it could be claimed for Mr. Oppenheim that he is leading it into teleology, at least giving it the added significance of getting us somewhere.)

The real objection to the frankly autobiographical "fiction" is that the mere editing of one's accidental experiences offers so little opportunity for an imaginative aggressiveness, a sense of line, mass, organization, and the like. At the very start the emphasis is placed on information rather than presentation, and as such belongs either to journalism or Wednesday prayer meetings, but not to art. Auto-biographical, certainly . . . since the artist employs only that which derives from his experiences; but the gods of Lord Dunsany are as immediately connected with experience as any photograph of an Eleventh Avenue beanery.

Since *The Mystic Warrior* is dedicated to Whitman, one finds oneself almost automatically ranging the two poets alongside of each other and comparing their methods of attack. Whitman began with a more spontaneous gluttony, a will to devour which was active even before meeting the object to be devoured. Thus, as soon as he came upon it, he could cast it into his belly without so much as a questioning glance. With Mr. Oppenheim these processes have been reversed. He begins by seeing things, examining them very carefully, and all but throwing them away entirely. Then at the last moment he remembers the obligation of gluttony which is part of his *ars poetica,* and gobbles them down almost as ravenously as the master.

For the fact is that Whitman, the genial voice of an aggressive, an expanding America—the earlier and less tarnished phase of our imperialism, that is—slashed into his material so recklessly that he has left his disciples with nothing but protest for a subject. The elation of the broad axe is gone, although a group of epigons remains which is bent on recovering this elation. While retaining an unmistakably Whitman technique, they have gone over almost as a body to Freud for material, since he seemed to offer some possibilities of new territory, less physical than Whitman's, of course, though satisfying the same yearning. But I doubt whether we have as yet discovered the formula for making synthetic artists' insight. The psychoanalytic teachings, centering as they do about a set of systematized inhibitions, chain the artist's attention almost exclusively to the shedding of these inhibitions. In a great measure, therefore, he begins with his interpretations of life prescribed for him, and with a strict education as to what he must look for; it is no wonder that his methods also are frequently adopted. Just how much farther the intrusion of psychology into art will go it is hard to say. There is at least one promising young poet and critic I know of, however, who will no longer allow psychoanalysis to be mentioned in his home.

# Modifying the Eighteenth Century

*Casanova's Homecoming* by Arthur Schnitzler. Translated by Eden and Cedar Paul. Privately printed for subscribers only
*The Dial*, December 1921, 707–710

There is one species of poet who, if he quarrels with his mistress in the morning—supposing that poets still possess such lovely baggage—writes a poem that day on quarrelling with his mistress; whereas, if he had been awakened by a piano playing next door, he would have composed some Variations on Being Awakened by a Piano. In a much broader way, Schnitzler's procedure has about it something analogous to this. Since as a much younger man, that is, Schnitzler wrote *Anatol and Reigen,* as an older man he writes *Casanova's Homecoming.* If this method succeeds, which it seems to have done in Schnitzler's case, the artist must have one highly consoling thought as he looks back over the range of his productions: he has made the world observe with interest the milestones of his own personal journey.

Casanova himself, belonging to a rather more glorious century, and one which could not go sour on the scientific dethronement of man, found the meditation of his earlier *fougues* an occupation of such a delightful nature that he simply could not help retailing them for everyone. For, as he explains in his capacity as a somewhat facile philosopher, the joys of his past are still with him because he can live them again in his memory, whereas the pains are no longer operative since he is so conscious of their being gone. But then, Casanova was not particularly interested in the Orphic, that peculiar pudency which was to capture the following century and which manifested itself in the tendency to qualify to the point of disintegration, to behold with a divided attitude, thus feeling ashamed. He was content with his facile philosophy.

The comparison is inevitable, since in *Casanova's Homecoming* Schnitzler sees so markedly nineteenth century an ending for so eighteenth century a celebrity. Where Casanova himself—if we take him at his word—found a perfect satisfaction in recalling an adventurous past which he could no longer duplicate—Schnitzler sees the chevalier broken and hideous, stripped of human dignity, and at fifty-three manoeuvring to prolong those pleasures which he had accepted with confidence fifteen years earlier. He reduces the adventurer by a series of final qualifications, when he has lost the very essence of his glory; he imagines Casanova as an old man trying to carry off an existence which sits well with a much, younger man.

Casanova is decidedly moth-eaten. What money he gets comes for the most part from petty gambling. He has two suits, one for everyday and one "for occasions." At this point he meets an old school friend, Olivo, who insists that Casanova come stay with him for a few days on his estate. There is a young woman here, Marcolina; Casanova forthwith becomes pre-occupied with this Marcolina exclusively. She, however, is completely neglectful of his prestige; she treats him with a mixture of politeness and indifference which turns to something like revulsion when he makes a few tentative moves. Also, there is Lorenzi, a young lieutenant whom Casanova suspects of being in love with her, perhaps successfully.

Sneaking out at dawn, to see if he can catch sight of Marcolina in her room, he finds the shutters closed and barred. But after a time there is a noise; dropping behind a bench, Casanova spies Lorenzi taking leave of her. His desire for Marcolina becomes intense, almost a necessity. . . . Schnitzler next centres his attention on getting Lorenzi into a gambling debt, which in a moment of *beau geste,* of the old feudal honour, Lorenzi claims he will redeem the following morning. But he has no money, and is leaving for war the next day. Casanova, who has won the thousand ducats that Lorenzi needs, in what is perhaps the most skilfully executed portion of the story, makes Lorenzi a strictly business proposition: he will give Lorenzi the money if Lorenzi pledges his word that he will arrange to have Casanova enter Marcolina's room that night, posing as her lover. Lorenzi agrees; the plan succeeds; Casanova is accepted in the darkness as the lieutenant.

It is from this point that Schnitzler begins pursuing the wretch in earnest. After describing in a highly romantic vocabulary what happened in that pitch-black room, Schnitzler begins tracing a set of wild images in Casanova's brain—a mixture of day-dreams and nightmare—Casanova awakes, stifling . . . dawn is penetrating the thick curtain, and Marcolina is looking at him in horror, at his yellow, wrinkled face. He sees, by her mute agony, the monstrosity of his age. Then Marcolina turns her face to the wall, while this lean, worn frame pulls itself out of the bed, clasps on its sword, throws on Lorenzi's robe, and leaps through the window.

Lorenzi is waiting, with his sword. Casanova, a bit cynically, pulls back his robe and shows that he is naked; whereupon, Lorenzi undresses as well. Scene: the two men facing each other, stark naked, the one young, fresh, full-muscled, the other slightly spavined with age and usage; the cool, moist lawn; the dawn still pale in the east; fencing. Lorenzi is stabbed through the heart; Casanova kisses his dead face; after which the flight to Venice begins. We end with him established as a spy, in mean quarters, preparing to give information against people who trust him implicitly.

In *Casanova's Homecoming* Schnitzler has produced both the triumph and the reduction to absurdity of his method. The story has been so simplified, so thoroughly focussed on the one subject of Casanova's decay, that every element of it shows up as an accessory. Certain parts plainly exist, for instance, to establish in the reader's mind just how splendid a figure Casanova used to be, so that we get the full force of his going to seed. As the most aggressive instance of this might be cited the staging of a sight-seeing trip to a convent, so that, as Casanova is leaving, one of the nuns can break her vow of silence by whispering his name, the name which belongs not to him as he is now, but to his former reputation. Other parts exist for the machinery of the plot, as for instance the first evening of gambling, which leads imperceptibly into the second evening of gambling, which leads to a gambling debt, by which Schnitzler can get Casanova into Marcolina's room; Schnitzler gives us one evening of gambling so that we accept the second. Or again, we have Casanova see himself in the mirror, and for no other reason than that the next morning, when he awakes with Marcolina looking at him in horror, Schnitzler can give us a cut-back to the face in the mirror, thus making the point more forceful than if he had tried to get the full significance of Casanova's wrinkles across at the last moment. So thoroughly has Schnitzler been permeated by stage technique—the painless method of insinuation, that is—that we find it again in such things as this: the story begins with our being told twice that Casanova has not seen Amalia—whom he had seduced just before her marriage—for over fifteen years, while her eldest child is only thirteen; at which point, gentlemen, we have a perfect right to await the seduction of this eldest daughter, which comes in time.

I do not recall ever having seen before a structure so elaborately propped and counter-propped. Nor a piece of prose fiction which was so much like a play with the he-saids and the she-saids written in. Schnitzler has become so thoroughly accustomed to objectivization that even when Casanova thinks, he thinks visually. Still, it should be pointed out that the plot is thoroughly in keeping with the theme, for this is the sequence to eight volumes of more or less elaborate intrigue; a plea which Schnitzler himself makes as skilfully as anything in the story, by bringing up here and there various high points out of the Memoires.

Significantly enough, a somewhat analogous theme has been handled by Schnitzler's one superior as a craftsman of German prose; I refer to Thomas

Mann's *Der Tod in Venedig*. Here, however, the *raisonneur* has been complicated and diseased by years of devotion to literature; and quite in keeping with the intricacy of von Aschenbach's brain—over against the flat "dramatic conflict" of Casanova with an eyetooth missing—the plot centres on, not a beautiful young woman, but a beautiful young Polish boy, the entire story working among half-stifled and purely cerebral transgressions.

Mann's treatment is that of a musician, rather than a playwright, which, I think, will always be the case of a subjective writer who has gone to the bottom of his methods. Whereas Schnitzler has produced something as objective as a movie scenario, Mann turns rather to orchestration, to harmonization, putting out elements not as "plants," but as themes to be picked up and developed later, and assembling his material until he has brought the very air and water of Venice to bear upon his story. Mann goes for an almost austere dignity; Schnitzler gets a clarity of evidence which might be found in the reviewer's *vade mecum,* I believe, under "Depiction, relentless." But if Mallarme's claim is just and the artist should accept first of all those properties which are fundamental to his medium, Mann is more in his province than Schnitzler, for prose fiction is as *inherently* subjective as the stage is *inherently* objective.

# The Critic of Dostoevsky

*Still Life* by J. Middleton Murry. E. P. Dutton and Company
*The Things We Are* by J. Middleton Murry. E. P. Dutton and Company
*The Dial*, December 1922, 671–674

In *Still Life* Mr. Murry gives us: an English critic's version in novel form of England's own particularly highly sophisticated type of post-war, out-of-nowhere-into-nothingness, the book ending with one lost hysterical soul weeping in perfect iambs. In *The Things We Are* Mr. Murry seems to have undergone an idyllic reaction against his own previous effort, and in expiation steers a mysteriously awakened Mr. Boston into a wife, and the company of wholesome, big-bosomed Mrs. Williams. And to our astonishment and shamefaced confusion, just when the lovers have been united, this very Mrs. Williams comes into the room and places a steaming pudding on the table. Which makes one feel that if we are to preserve Mr. Murry as a Platonist we must maintain the balance between dualities by throwing one of his novels on each side of the scale, and letting the bitterness of the one counterbalance the sweetness of the other.

As a portrait of English society, I am willing to take Mr. Murry as gospel. The sterile self-analysis in *Still Life,* the futile conversations, the almost vulgar self-consciousness: it has always been my fond belief that contemporary drawing-room England is precisely that. Yet, building upon this fundament, Mr. Murry has contrived to wind up a story with a positively astonishing skill. For the first seven or eight chapters we follow him as he takes on one responsibility after another; but unfortunately, once Mr. Murry has finished winding up his story, there is nothing to do but let it run down. Before the story is finished every last one of the characters has told us far too much about himself; and for the last hundred pages they are nothing but voices. Still, these statements are unfair; as they make no allowance for the really keen strokes which Mr. Murry keeps turning up continually, and for the discretion and freshness with which the old triangle theme is handled.

*71*

But *The Things We Are,* as I have said, starts out very plainly to supply the antidote to *Still Life.* Mr. Boston, far from deluging us with self-analyses, is an unusually rigid and silenced man, a man in whom all impressions lie buried and unuttered. Then suddenly, about half-way through the book, Mr. Boston begins to unbend; he acquires a virulent attack of normality, goes out among good wholesome people, picks up a couple of buns, falls in love with a girl, and analyzes himself as expertly as though he had been at it all his life, or as though he had been carried over bodily from Mr. Murry's earlier novel. Thus, there are simply two Mr. Bostons: one is made to feel the potentialities of this first Boston, and to see the second Boston kinetically, but one does not feel that the potential energy of the first Boston is the kinetic energy of the second. The accepted methods of effecting a character's rejuvenation are (a) to have him meet a Salvation Army lass, or (b) to have him awakened by the war. Mr. Murry's invention of simply having the character rejuvenated is more cautious, perhaps, but no more contenting.

On taking up these books of Mr. Murry's one automatically returns to the question of Dostoevsky. Mr. Murry, to be sure, has done a remarkably thorough job at making the Russian less uncouth and reducing his frenzy to the proportions proper to an English drawing-room; but the principle underlying both authors is the same. It calls, I think, for a distinction between the psychology of form and the psychology of subject-matter. Or between the psychologism of Dostoevsky and the psychologism of, say, a Greek vase. By the psychology of subject-matter I mean, I believe, what Mrs. Padraic Colum has defined as information, or science. She might as well have called it journalism. Journalism, science, biographical gossip . . . this movement of almost pure information has had a tremendous effect on modern aesthetics. Thanks to it, far too much emphasis is laid upon the documentary value of the work of art, upon art as a revelational function. We find both Mr. Matthew Josephson and Mr. Burton Rascoe, for instance, objecting to Joyce because there are more psychoanalytic facts to be obtained from the reading of Kraft-Ebbing or Freud than from *Ulysses.* And I trust soon to hear these Messrs objecting to Cezanne because his paintings do not contain nearly so much data on trees as can be found in a bulletin of the Forestry Department.

The point is that the problem of the artist lies elsewhere, and that the novel after Dostoevsky has given too much attention to the document. The document *per se,* being neither beautiful nor unbeautiful, falls into quite another plane of considerations from purely aesthetic ones. And if Dostoevsky must stand for his revelations of the human soul, then he stands as nothing other than a scientist who was improperly trained in scientific methods of presentation, and who gave us consequently a hodgepodge rather than a schematization. One might have thought that the peculiarly vigorous flourishing of science would have served rather to purge literature of any documentary obligations, just as the perfection of photography has brought about a similar release in painting. But instead, literature was swept into a sympathetic movement, and science became a burden rather than an instrument of liberation.

Perhaps, to define unescapably just how I should distinguish between the psychology of form and the psychology of subject-matter, I should pin myself to a specific illustration. We read, then, in *The Things We Are:*

> ... Bettington felt sad. It seemed to him that at the moment when he knew his friend, his friend was embarking on a great journey with him, a journey more dangerous perhaps, but far more wonderful than his own. It was too much. To have to say two farewells at the same moment was more than he could bear, more than he ought to bear; and besides, there was a strange envy in his heart. He must confess it.
> 
> "I envy you . . . old man. I can't help it; I try not to."
> 
> "I wonder you don't hate me as well."
> 
> "No, I don't hate you . . . I don't think I do. Why should I? I don't feeling you're taking Felicia away from me. The more I think about her, the more I know she wasn't mine. But envy, yes. I'm afraid it goes pretty deep, too." After a minute he added, et cetera.

Perhaps the author has established whether it is hate or envy. But I take liberty to assure the reader that he will not care. The information is there, but the issue hardly seems a contribution to beauty. Of course, I do not deny that even this sort of information could have been made beautiful, especially if—in the truest sense—it had been made more intense. But it would have been the intensity, and not the fact, which was beautiful. The accurate definition of an idea is beautiful—as in Spinoza. The accurate solution of a problem is beautiful—which doubtless explains why Euclid was included among the humanities. And which obviously suggests defining beauty as the shortest distance between two points. But there is also the functional side to beauty, and fortunately Mr. Murry has given a very fine instance of it, which I quote from *Still Life* to illustrate the psychology of form:

> Above them Anne began to sing, low enough to be singing to herself. She could hear that they were not talking, and she crooned. But the house was so still, beneath the regular beat of the rain between the gusts, that they could hear her

when her voice rose above a low humming. Neither knew what she was singing.

"Does Anne often sing like that?" said Dennis, almost whispering.

"How do you mean, 'like that'?" Maurice [Anne's lover] hardly understood the question. Then something familiar in the sound came vaguely into his memory. "I don't know. Yes, she does sometimes. But not often. . . . At least, I don't think so. . . . I don't know."

It is, quite plainly, the functional value which counts here. Mr. Murry has given us a mechanism of beauty. A program is officially announced; a blare of trumpets has been sounded. Similarly in *Macbeth* when the porter scene follows the murder scene this is no documentary *coup,* but a purely functional one. Writing in the Dostoevsky tradition, however, one underrates this really primary quality of art, and—in Mr. Murry's case, at least—attains it too seldom.

The making of this lengthy distinction, I feel, is justified in that it attempts to get at the exact quality of diffuseness which makes Mr. Murry's books a bit dissatisfying.

# The Consequences of Idealism

*Rahab* by Waldo Frank. Boni and Liveright
*City Block* by Waldo Frank. Privately printed for subscribers only
*The Dial*, October 1922, 449–452

Let us imagine a room painted in this wise: there are the walls, a window, chairs, table, food on table, and two humans. These walls are aligned as inexorably as armies; one feels their seclusion and their leaden mass. Light, however, pours through the flood-gates of the window, tumbles and seethes into the room, rolling with sheer commensurable bulk. The chairs fulfill their functions as chairs earnestly, even avidly; in a sense one might say that they are crying out to be chairs; they are more than chairs, by God, they are staunch havens of palliation, they are strong, tender arms to which our failing corporeal fibers may surrender with confidence. As to the table, note how it offers up its contents as profusely, as unstintingly, one might say, as the calyx of a lily. And that man and that woman, leaning, gravitating towards each other . . . they are waterspouts growing up out of the floor. Their arms hang limp, but countless phantom arms interlock in the air. While these two humans stand "silent upon each other, heavily."

The closing quote is from Waldo Frank, as is fitting. For our painted room is in the truest manner of *Rahab,* or *City Block.* I wish mainly to bring out the element of volition behind the author's eye. He has written elsewhere that when "feet clamber up and over a hill" the hill is already there; "the feet do not create the hill, although they have a tendency to think so." Yet his own writings are a testimony of feet which, if they do not create the hill, at least recreate it, transforming it from a mere hill, *qua* hill, to a spiritual problem, an obstacle proclaiming its identity over against the yearnings and necessities of human atoms.

In 1893 Stephane Mallarmé gave the first definite formulation of the poetics which encompasses this attitude in writing. Building on Hegel, he found in idealism the artist's right to his own universe, a right which extended even to the development of a personal idiom. Mallarmé's expert mal-writing reached a rare flowering—in such a hothouse product, for instance, as "*heureuses deux tétines.*" And the peculiar glory of these pursuits is that the artist attains thereby "*au-dessus d'autre bien, l'élément de félicités, une doctrine en memo temps qu'une contrée.*"

Waldo Frank's idiom is no less personal. But instead of Mallarmé's special-case fauns and nymphs with their icy emotions, Mr. Frank gives us the eager, pulsing universe noted above. Still, it cannot be denied that Waldo Frank's idealism emphasizes a somewhat different aspect. If Mallarmé was striving simply for beautiful possibilities, for intriguing enormities, for likely distortions which would appeal to the connoisseur acquainted with all the rules, Mr. Frank falls in rather with the German expressionists who strive to give us a version of life which shall be alas! only too true. For the last fifty years the world has been pressionistic (read, volitional) first im and then ex. If Mallarmé, looking at a man, goes beyond that man with the direct purpose of distortion, the expressionists take their man, rip off his clothing, observe the sorry nipples of his breasts, look into his viscera, and maintain that here is the real man, the *essential* man. The subtle difference is that Mallarmé has said, "Here is a distortion," and has given us one, while the expressionists have said, "Here is the very pulse of truth," and their distortion has been no less marked.

One goes into a park and sits down, and immediately, if one is an artist, the park becomes a problem. It lies there. The individual feels his edges knocking improperly against it. He is sitting in somebody else's park. Then, if he is Waldo Frank, he starts remaking that park. Exorbitant characters appear, the skyline begins to churn, mad speeches are ground out. And we have "John the Baptist," one of the most interesting stories of *City Block*. But such a park is a personal creation, and is statistically false; it is true as a reflection of Waldo Frank's temperament, true in a sense that Mallarmé's fauns are true, but completely erroneous as a gauge of our environment.

My reason for pointing this out is a somewhat complicated one. But first of all, I feel that it provides us with a criterion for approaching Mr. Frank. Thus, we have the two possibilities: a book *must* be statistically true, a whole and proper valuation of life; or it must be true in the sense that Mallarmé's fauns are true, must be a beautiful possibility created in the mind of the artist. I have consistently objected that Mr. Frank does not qualify on condition one; life as he presents it is assiduously culled, the volitional clement of the artist is over-emphasized. Or, to borrow from a colleague, M. Cowley, I should say that he has stacked the cards. However, if we admit this cheating, take it as a basis of our calculations, we must next inquire as to whether Mr. Frank cheats dextrously; we shall not ask if he is false, but if he is *superbly* false. On the whole, I think he is not, for the two books under consideration are not *finally* beautiful. They lack just that element of cold carving, that bloodless autopsy of the emotions, which allows Mallarmé so near an approach to perfection.

True, these books have many passages of thick beauty such as Mallarmé probably never dreamed of. When Mr. Frank, for instance, undresses one of his women, and opens his throat and sings thereat, the song is full and lovely. Or when, as in *Rahab* . . . but the situation must be explained more fully: Mrs. Luve is a procuress, but a procuress with her Bible and her refinements, a procuress who needs a great deal of explanation. Mr. Frank takes us through a book to explain her, and at the end we do accept his attitude—we believe that she is a delicate woman whose denigration has an almost Christlike significance. We see her, then, in the midst of her set, politicians, gamblers, crooks, whores. We hear their vulgarly minute conversation, note their unenlightened envelopment in the immediate moment; whereupon, of a sudden, the author gives a projection of each character, or, technically speaking, draws out the *song* of each character, the lyric surrender to a grand communion of passions. That is, they sit in the room, each aware of *his* apartness from the others; but each has a purer attitude within him somewhere, a naïve burst of confidence which is suppressed: it is this naïve burst which Mr. Frank gives in his lyrical projections of the characters present. *Here passion has justified itself by the discovery of an excellent subterfuge;* it is Waldo Frank at his best.

On the whole, however, I must confess that the author's intensity is too direct, lies too far beyond the subterfuge. Mr. Frank is as serious as Buddha, which is a dangerous thing to be in an age which could produce *Ulysses*. If we have to choose between an artist who is passionless and clever, and an artist who is tumultuous and non-clever, it is a sad pair to choose from, but the former would be nearer to art. Mr. Frank, as I have noted above, can be clever, but as a rule he is too precipitant. As a result, his works lack edges; one catches an abundance of rich overtones, but they obscure the note itself. What, for instance, is the structural significance of the *City Block* cycle? What is the *inevitable* centre about which it revolves? It should force itself upon us from the complexion of the work. Structure is not so priestly a thing that only the elect can glimpse it. Structure is the first principle of a work, not the last.

As to *Rahab*, the case is simpler. One does, on finishing it, get a definite retrospect. The author starts with Mrs. Luve, a procuress; then he goes back to the beginning, and gives us Mrs. Luve's career; ending upon Mrs. Luve, exactly where the book began, we now have this procuress with all the qualifications and subtilizations of 250 pages. She emerges, somehow, stationary, like a fireplug on a busy street, like a boat anchored in a fog. There is nothing priestly about this; it is, in fact, startlingly simple. The book is undoubtedly

Mr. Frank's best piece of work up to date. It is the logical culmination of *The Dark Mother,* representing directly that type of writing which the former book was feeling for. That is, Mr. Frank has found the manner which best carries his burden.... The same is true of certain stories in City Block taken as isolated units. In stories like "Under the Dome" and "John the Baptist" Mr. Frank has made just as accurate a junction between the burden and the expression thereof. That is, so far as the untrammeled, direct giving of himself is concerned, the author has attained it. These works go the whole extent of Croceanism: the expression is immediate and full.

But expression is not all of art; the rest is elegance. Mr. Frank has done a valiant task in his fight against the inhibitory baggage which American art has had to lug. His work on this score is as significant as that of Van Wyck Brooks. But both men, under the urge of their evangelism, tend to make the emphasis on expression too exclusive. It is an excellent corrective, which becomes in turn a defect if carried too far.

# Enlarging the Narrow House

*Narcissus* by Evelyn Scott. Harcourt, Brace and Company
*The Dial*, September 1922, 346–348

Having read only those portions of Rupert Hughes which are pasted on the sides of newsstands, I can hardly venture to discuss him with authority. Yet, if I were to form a tentative judgment on those summaries and blurbs, I should say that Mr. Hughes is an author who gives us something like a society drama, with characters, plot, and setting all more or less typical of some actual stratum, or condition, in society. In this I may be entirely unjust to Mr. Hughes. But in revenge I am positive that it applies to Mrs. Scott, who wrote *The Narrow House,* and who has now made that house gratifyingly less narrow in her new novel *Narcissus.*

But as Mrs. Scott is quite plainly a much more complex writer than Mr. Hughes, one feels at the start that the juxtaposition of the two names is false. To begin with, Mr. Hughes would not write like this, which I take from *The Narrow House:*

> The room closed them like a coffin. Their life was their own. It did not flow in from the street.

No, that is not like Mr. Hughes; it is like Mr. Waldo Frank. There are other passages scattered through Mrs. Scott's books which show the influence of *Ulysses,* a strain which it is safe to suppose has never defiled our great cinema novelist. However, Mrs. Scott writes:

> I'm suffering deeply, Julia. You are suffering. I see it. It is only the little person who doesn't suffer. Why do you resent me? Life is always making patterns. It has thrown us three—you and me, and your husband—into a design—a relationship to each other.

And although Mr. Hughes would probably never have stepped so circumspectly around the word "triangle," it is safe to assume that the situation has occurred to him: Lawrence immersed in his chemical work; Dudley, a young artist, lover of Julia; Julia, the wife of Lawrence, beautiful and idle. But I have spoken of Mrs. Scott's greater complexity; let us examine just how it affects her treatment of this vexing problem. First going back to *The Narrow House*.

*The Narrow House* was part of that astonishing post-war movement of anti-chauvinism among the intellectuals, a movement which attained its greatest expression in the sales of Main Street and the departure of Mr. Harold Stearns for Europe. *The Narrow House,* then, was what might be termed "professionally depressing." Like most of 1921's record, it dipped back into Zola, being somewhat more circumspect and infinitely less powerful. It showed dull, broken lives, American lives which were so weary, so hateful, that even the American sun was discovered to shine with fatigue upon them.

In her second work Mrs. Scott has cut away a great deal of this misery *praetor necessitatem*. The house is distinctly less narrow. The professional depression is for the most part lightened. Despite her public's approval of the patent gesture in *The Narrow House,* Mrs. Scott seems to have developed a distrust of it. But unfortunately, the resultant virtue is only a negative one; the author has gone through the excesses of *The Narrow House* to attain the neutralization of *Narcissus*.

At the same time she has attempted to graft upon her style elements of James Joyce and Waldo Frank. There is no objection to them as influences. There is no particular reason why writers should begin over again, when philosophers hand their apparatus from one to the other throughout the ages. Thus, my objection is neither to influences in general nor to these particular influences; but I do question the propriety of the influences as they appear in *Narcissus*.

For they produce a work which is peculiarly lacking in correlation. One feels this especially in the case of Waldo Frank, since his method is so specifically adapted to his own kind of writing. *Narcissus* is, as we have said, more or less of a society drama, wherein characters are presented for their objective reality, for their identity as people you see or shake hands with. But Waldo Frank's characters are meant to be like pebbles dropped into a pool: he tries to draw ever-widening circles around them. His plots are conceived in the same non-temporal, non-spatial tone. It is not to the point to attempt any judgment s on this method at present. But it is to the point to insist that the method is as peculiarly adapted to one set of conditions as were dinosaurs or mastodons. Transferred, it is simply bones in a glass case.

Thus, the novel fluctuates between its strict localization and this lyrical drawing of the ever-widening circles. As a result the book has no consistent drive. Even the blurb is at a loss, for it heralds "A story of a group of people who are hindered by the relaxation of old standards of conduct and don't know what to do with their new freedom." There is, to be sure, one adolescent who enters and exits at intervals throughout the book, and who is undecided concerning his future. But even here the element of social transitions is only indirectly touched upon. (For which, by the way, let us be grateful.) I spoke of the opening triangle: Dudley, the artist; Julia, the wife; Lawrence, the husband. Actuated by a set of nuances which is not completely cogent—and the vagueness arises precisely because Mrs. Scott always switches at such times from strict analysis of motives to Waldo Frank's type of lyrism—she tells Lawrence of their affair. He moves his bed into another room, and starts carrying his life from her bit by bit. She breaks off with Dudley—again by a set of elusive nuances—in the direction of a business man, and has an affair with him. After which she finally pierces Lawrence's steel on the last two pages, there is a reconciliation, and the book closes with:

> Unacknowledged, each kept for himself a pain which the other could not heal. Each pitied the other's illusion, and was steadied by it into gentleness.

Perhaps, in this fluctuation between the strict localizing of her characters and the drawing of lyrical circles, I have objected to the very thing which Mrs. Scott was aiming for. But, if we are to have two poles of treatment, we must also have their polarity. It is not sufficient to juxtapose them without reconciliation. In the truest sense, significance is lost: the significance of some modus consistently and exclusively pursued.

# Immersion

*A Book* by Djuna Barnes. Boni and Liveright
*The Dial*, May 1924, 460–461

Some considerable time past, when reviewing a book in *The Dial*, I had occasion to speak of immersion-in-life with a somewhat categorical disapproval. Since then, this has lain on the conscience. For though I still feel that the book belittled was an inferior one, and inferior precisely because of its patient and dutiful immersion in life, it has seemed that the category itself should be revised. For in art a category can be degraded or justified by the individual instance exemplifying it.

The reading of Miss Barnes' book makes the revision imperative. The author of these stories, plays, poems, and drawings is undoubtedly immersed—and to such an extent that if you have the modern interest in the mechanics of writing you must wonder how eager her preoccupations must have been to have made her miss so much. Yet her pages have a force, an ingenuity, which rises purely from the intensity of her message.

Miss Barnes seems to have seized upon the form nearest to hand, the one-acter, and to have shaped all her subjects to this simple mold. To wit: there is a situation, this situation is followed by a general jog-trot of plot for so long, and then, with only two or three hundred words to go, the author seizes a knife or a pistol, or stages an incestuous kiss, or something similar—in short, unwinds the rest of her plot with a snap, and the story is over.

If one is looking for an astute and concentrated method of writing, then, one will not find it in any of Miss Barnes' paragraphs. There are no interior designs, no "functioning" sentences. The occasional shame-faced attempts at an epigram are nearly always painful. So that we must situate the appeal of this book precisely in the vigour of her attitudes, in her immersion. Nor are these attitudes themselves unimpeachable. A great deal is weak Russian, a great deal is old stuff; Miss Barnes' vamps, for instance, are almost as pat as movie vamps.

I spoke of a force or ingenuity rising purely from the intensity of her message. The opening of her story "Oscar" is a good example of what I mean. It begins with four descriptions: a place, a woman, a man, another man. *A priori* it should be safe to say that a story should not begin with such a Walter Scott sameness. Yet these very pages have a swift stride. Of one of the men:

> He smelled very strongly of horses, and was proud of it. He pretended a fondness for all that goes under hide or hair, but a collie bitch, known for her gentleness, snapped at him and bit him. He invariably carried a leather thong, braided at the base for a handle, and would stand for hours talking, with his legs apart, whirling this contrived whip, and, looking out of the corner of his eyes would pull his moustache, waiting to see which of the ladies would draw in her feet.

The other descriptions are equally firm. The effect is probably gained by the fact that the descriptions themselves are plots. Another instance of how Miss Barnes can produce results by the sheer earnestness of her conception is in the dialogue, "To the Dogs." Gheid Storm, a direct and unsubtle young man, comes to Helena Hucksteppe "in the mountains of Cornwall-on-Hudson" to offer her himself. She proves, to the satisfaction of him and the reader, that he could not make things very interesting for this advanced and rather vampish lady. Time and again he puts out a statement, and her answer is designed to kill it; thus, a topic is exhausted by his sentence and her reply—yet Miss Barnes manages, along with this effect, to keep up the illusion of continuity in the dialogue.

In *A Book* the will to tragedy is maintained with a sureness which is very rarely met with in contemporary writing. And if the author does not convince us that her stories carry very far beyond themselves, she does make us feel that this little corner of experience she is dealing with is handled with the adequate reactions. By which I mean that we can accept the fatalities of her stories, and perhaps even feel that the last bit of plot unwinding with its snap really belonged to the texture of her subject. In her drawings this will to tragedy is equally convincing. Her portraits seem to possess that strained attitude in living which goldfish have when sucking air at the surface of a bowl. Her poetry, again, carries the same vein. At best it is hot, tight, and sullen. The whole, put into one book, produces a very satisfactory program.

# Ethics of the Artist

*Buddenbrooks* by Thomas Mann. Translated by H. T. Lowe-Porter. Alfred A. Knopf
*The Dial*, November 1924, 420–422

Although *Buddenbrooks* was written by Mann in his twenties, it is the work of a writer who, if not mature, quite obviously placed a high value upon maturity as a literary acquisition. While thanks to the solidity of the North German civilization which Mann was depicting, at this early age he had already seen people "placed," had already seen so many points in the progress of their lives from ambition to success or frustration, that he could plot the entire curve of their careers. This, I take it, is a major aspect of experience. And meditation upon this experience is one aspect of philosophy. *Buddenbrooks* is rich in both.

*Buddenbrooks* is the story of a North German merchant family through four generations, developing from a genial, normal stock which enjoyed life and took the good things of life without question, through two generations of growing introversion, where the openness to externals became less of an appetite and more of a moral obligation, finally culminating in the artist whose sensitiveness to outside impressions has "o'erleapt itself and fallen on t'other," so that he is unable to accept normal everyday life even as a duty, but takes to music and poetry like a drug. This is called the Decay of a Family. Over against this, almost as an artistic necessity, we have the rise of bolder and more unscrupulous merchants, vigorous, good-natured, destroying the older family through necessity rather than malice, as fit for living as Nietzsche's blond beast, and above all, thick-skinned. The story is pursued patiently, stroke upon stroke, often with a delicate sense of chapter development and transition; and when it is over we have this major form of a march through four generations, a curve as natural as the cycle of a storm, or the incubation of a malady.

There are certain books which are the result of a *genre,* and these books are understood and appreciated best after we know the aesthetic conditions under which they arose. There are other books (much rarer) which serve to justify a *genre,* so that the aesthetic conditions are understood and appreciated best after we know the books. *Buddenbrooks* and *Death in Venice* fall within the latter category. They are the profound justification of a typical nineteenth-century attitude, where the instability of moral dogma was compensated for by the stress of moralism, specific religion gave way to religiosity, and the physiognomy of God retreated behind the idea of divinity.

In the sharp piece of self-analysis with which Thomas Mann introduces his Betrachtungen Eines Unpolitischen, he speaks of his "conscientiousness—a quality which comprises such an essential element of my writings that one might almost say they consist of nothing else: conscientiousness, an ethical-artistic quality, to which I am indebted for whatever effects I may have gotten." This conscientiousness has a double manifestation. It is first a "morality of production" which ranks the author among the great technicians of literature. This aspect of his writing culminates in his short novel, *Death in Venice,* where almost every paragraph contains some particular reward of vigilance, some formal invention, the solution of some literary problem.

The other aspect of his "conscientiousness" is the development of an attitude towards life which is, before everything else, patient, or even cautious. The total body of Mann's work is the formulation of an ethics: not an ethical system, but an ethical proclivity, a highly complex reception of life through the modes of *"Romantik, Nationalismus, Burgerlichkeit, Musik, Pessimismus, Humor."* If I understand Paul Elmer More correctly, I should say that Thomas Mann is a skeptic in Mr. More's sense of the word. Which is, it seems to me, almost the equivalent to saying that he is fully the artist. For it is in the artist that we find formulations of life (symbolizations) which are as complex, as poised, as life itself. And perhaps what More means by skepticism, Mann means by anti-radicalism: a state of suspense before too easy a simplification. (I say easy, aware that a man may expend a whole life, and an heroic energy of discipline, in the pursuit of a doctrine, and yet have taken the "easier" channel of escape. Prior to this plunge into one direction, there is room for an initial skepticism or anti-radicalism which might deprive said man of precisely this life interest on which he will practice his energy of discipline. Over against the discipline of the soldier or the athlete—the early martyr or the modern business man—there is a discipline of evaluations, a discipline of *poise* rather than a discipline of *projection.* This is what I understand by skepticism, or anti-radicalism.)

So Mann is above all "conscientious." And it was precisely this conscientiousness which kept him from being either a *bourgeois* or a Bohemian, kept him vacillating between his sympathy for the mediocre, the blunt, the unthinking and his deep understanding of hyperaesthesia. From Goethe, through Nietzsche, he accepts "life" as the basis of values; and yet he also associates the development of the aesthetic sense with the hypertrophy of channels which are useless, even positively inimical, to the purposes of this "life."

With all this we are now familiar. This type of preoccupation is precisely what the nineteenth century left us as one of its most complex and irritating inheritances. While it is in Mann's works that the mood is recovered in all its vitality and significance; since his are the sort of books that justify the *genre*.

However, I have been seeing *Buddenbrooks* too much in retrospect, too much the way Mann himself looks back upon it in his Betrachtungen Eines Unpolitischen (Mann's craftsmanship has been rewarded in that he does not have to "renounce" his earlier work—as is the fashion—but deepens it as he proceeds). Before all else, *Buddenbrooks* is an epic novel (a large canvas with many details and people and single events, all drawn together into one organism).

It includes people who are characters, and others who are characteristic, and others who are types. At times, that is, it focuses upon strict psychological analysis, while at other times it develops caricature with the vivacity of Dickens, although without Dickens' excesses of sentiment and vulgarities of style. Or again, Mann will centre his faculties on the charting of an event, as for instance the clinical record of a death, which he can carry off with a subtle mixture of emotionalism and technicality. *Buddenbrooks* (and the English version is an admirably smooth piece of work) is one of the few "epic" novels in which the handling of major proportions has not misled the author into a neglect of line-for-line texture.

# Delight and Tears

*The Apple of the Eye* by Glenway Wescott. Lincoln Mac Veagh. The Dial Press
*The Dial*, December 1924, 513–515

I shall not forget the feeling of astonishment and—shall I say?—well-being with which, some months past, I read the opening of Glenway Wescott's *Bad Han* when it appeared in *The Dial*.* Within three sentences Mr. Wescott had established his mood, a mixture of ruggedness and lyrism. The abrupt change from these four lines to the name of his heroine served to clinch his effect. Here, in the purest sense, was action. For such movements, it seems to me, are the essence of action in art.

Mr. Wescott's novel, *The Apple of the Eye,* is a continuation of the story *Bad Han* as it appeared in *The Dial.* The novel has a kind of tripartite arrangement, in each part the focus being placed upon a different character, while the parts are held together by certain parallelings and interactions of plot and emotion. The first part is the story of Bad Han; the second centers about the love-affair between a delicate young girl and a farm-hand whose wanderlust is temporarily quieted by his attachment to this girl. In this second part a young boy, Dan, has been brought into the story; the third part now settles upon this boy, but treats him in the light of the parts preceding. One feels the reward of Mr. Wescott's method: the story does have a cumulative effect, and the ending is made richer by its strong reliance upon what has preceded.

All of which is very vague, and in no wise conveys the quality of Mr. Wescott's story. It is a book almost exclusively of emotional propulsion. Indeed, it even becomes a drenching in emotions, those softer, readier emotions which we designate usually as "feminine," an experience purely of "delight and tears" (to borrow one of his chapter heads) and is thus a kind of revival in letters, an atavism, albeit a revival which is done with such force, such conviction, that one is caught unawares, and before he knows it is deeply involved in these partings (by death or locomotion), this girl like wilted flower

---
* January and February, 1924.

left to perish, these stutterings of love, the sleep-walking in the moonlight, the call, or lure, of the city over the hills and plains. The machinery of pathos is well utilized—which, once again, fails to convey the quality of the story, for it is so obvious that the author did not think in terms of the "machinery" of pathos. His book, if it makes few demands upon the intellectual equipment of the reader, is a profoundly appealing piece of emotional writing, or one might better call it an emotional *experience,* for the reader's participation in the author's plot is intense enough to leave him in possession of the story's overtones much as one is left with the overtones of some dream or some actual event which has occurred in one's own life.

The principal objection I find to Mr. Westcott's book is its failure to widen the field of our aesthetic perceptions. And I use the word "aesthetic" very broadly here, to signify simply all perceptions which engage what Goethe calls the *organs* of art. Such perceptions are of two categories: method, technique, discoveries of procedure within the medium itself; and the far more important discovery of symbols which adequately summarize for us the emotional and ideological complexities in which we are involved. In method, Mr. Wescott's chief contribution is the bringing of a greater and more sensitive vitality to a type of book in which the typical novelist could feel very much at home. In subject-matter, the author has re-seen for us certain stock figures and situations of the contemporary story, re-seen with a keener eye, but no new angle of vision.

Yet this in itself becomes a kind of virtue. Our latent familiarity with the mold sets us for it so perfectly, that when Mr. Wescott does his act with such vigour we are able to follow him without a wrench. There is a point whereat the average suddenly transcends into the natural, and at times Mr. Wescott seems rewarded by precisely this illumination, so that his book becomes something of a racial experience, adjusting itself with sensitiveness to our desires for both satisfaction and frustration. The greatest book ever written will probably be so for the same reason. And it is here that Mr. Wescott is rewarded for having kept the commandments, and the law as the apple of his eye.

There are certain writers who, in addition to the absolute values of their work, have for me a sort of barometric interest. Such writers, for instance, as Joyce, Eliot, or Cummings, always strike me as facing an issue, as being on the verge of some new decision. I speculate on what they will do next. I feel this way also with reference to Wescott. Will his next book be a continuation of his present one (*The Apple of the Eye* ends as the somewhat autobiographic hero leaves the farm for college, and thus it could be projected into further volumes of the same sort); or will it, in some form or other, suffer that strange critical deflection (an equivalent to epistemology in philosophy?) which has started so many modern artists through some personal migration parallel to Joyce's curve from *Dubliners* to *Ulysses*?

It might be said that if Mr. Wescott chooses to repeat his present formula, we may expect him to repeat it with that creative vitality which he has already displayed. Yet the issue is much deeper; perhaps it is just as hard today to retain one's fire in the fidelity to artistic orthodoxy as is the case with religious or political orthodoxy. This is no mere accident; it is the result (both the flowering and the absurdity) of that modern specialized manner of living whereby art itself tends to become the predominant experience of the artist (his keenest hours being devoted to the perceptions of technical procedure and his weaker hours being left for the perceptions of life in general) so that he makes extensions and discoveries within his field of experience which are simply unseen by specialists in other fields who have not paralleled his experience.

But to return—Mr. Wescott is of a much more highly critical temper than his first book would seem to indicate. He is, therefore, by no means immune from the *Dubliners*-to-*Ulysses* temptation. While on the other hand the brilliancy of his first book would certainly justify him in trying to develop in the avoidance of more specialized channels.

In any case, we may for the time being content ourselves with this opportunity to welcome a work of such keen emotional appeal and stylistic vigour as are displayed in *The Apple of the Eye*.

# The Bon Dieu of M. Jammes

*Romance of the Rabbit* by Francis Jammes. Nicholas L. Brown
*The Freeman* May 1921, 211–212

Priapus at eighty-five, except for an occasional rheumatic complaint and the necessity of watching what he ate, might be expected to lead a very mellow life, sweetened by the reminiscence of his own follies. He could be visited, by those who were interested, in his pleasant little cabin on a hillside, a cabin situated in the midst of a soft, orderly lawn. Although by now quite complacent in his senescence, he would probably maintain a lingering interest in delicate young women, so that it would give him great contentment to pat them reassuringly on the shoulder. This Priapus at eighty-five, with perhaps a little amber stain on his white beard near his lips, is the Bon Dieu of Francis Jammes.

But indeed M. Jammes's Bon Dieu is distressingly careless of his dignity, as witness this description of him in the story "Paradise" which has been translated into English in the collection entitled *The Romance of the Rabbit:*

> The Bon Dieu had his hat and stick on the ground. He was garbed like the poor on the great highways; those who have only a morsel of bread in their wallets, and whom the magistrates arrest at the town gates, and throw into prison, since they know not how to write their name.

With all suspicions Manichæism safely hidden away in the records of the universities, the Bon Dieu potters about in a creation of mild conveniences, always has a few moments to spare to listen to this complaint or that, and draws his pleasure from a reservoir of cosmic devotion. The cats, recognizing his leniency, do not even bother to obey him, but, on the other hand, what greater tribute is possible than that of the sage-plant: "And full of trust and serenity, without pride or humility, a sage-plany let its insignificant odour rise toward God."

The peculiar satisfaction which comes of a tour through M. Jammes's heaven is that it has been so carefully laid out. In "The Romance of the Rabbit," for instance, the scissors-grinder's dog will be found performing his task with vigour into eternity an interesting readjustment of the Tantalus-Ixion-Sisyphus idea of the Greeks. Even though there is no knife for him to sharpen, he goes on turning the wheel, his eyes shining with "the unquestioning faith in a duty fulfilled." The wolves, too, have been carefully provided for:

> At the summit of a treeless mountain, in the desolation of the wind, beneath a penetrating fog, they felt the voluptuous joy of martyrdom. They sustained themselves with their hunger. They experienced a bitter joy in feeling that they were abandoned, that never for more than an instant—and then only under the greatest suffering—had they been able to renounce their lust for blood.

Another great instance of the Bon Dieu's delicacy of feeling in such matters is the fact that, although the general rule is that humans must not enter the animals' heavens, young girls are permitted to play in the heaven of the birds.

Such a well-ordered heaven is also reflected in a well-ordered earth. M. Jammes understands the friendly attitude of his favourite arm-chair, he listens to the symbolic croaking of the frogs, he registers the humble smell of cow-dung, and when the mother of a dead boy offers him the dead boy's wagon, a flood of tenderness fills his heart: "I felt that this *thing* had lost its friend, its master, and that it was suffering." He is content with the almost primitive reaction of animating his inanimate surroundings, or of giving speech to the little animals so that they may speak exactly as men. His expression has an exceedingly limited diapason, but it is always accurate. He sees at once the clay road shaking with heat, the panorama of fields and farmhouses broken by the churchspire, and a little bunch of half-rotten leaves pulsing above a mouse. Through it all, his point of view is so astonishingly biased, so completely safe in its Ptolemaicism, so unquestioningly rooted in his almost cosmic assurance that the world is man's, that he can write like this to a truck-garden:

> *Légumes du jardin*
> *Dites-vous*
> *Qu'il est doux*
> *attachéches á vos rames*
> *De mûrir doucement pour une sainte femme.*

It was Paul Clandel who restored M. Jammes to the faith—he has called himself a converted fawn: but even while maintaining a complete disdain for *le catholícisme des vicilles femmes,* he nevertheless expressed his theories in Catholic terms, as we may see in this paragraph from the *Mercure de France* of 1897, eight years before his conversion:

> I think that the truth lies in the praise of God: that we must celebrate this in our poems, if they are to be pure: that there is only one school, a school where, like children who imitate as exactly as possible some model of beautiful handwriting, the poets copy a lovely bird, a flower, or a young girl with charming ankles and graceful breasts.

In this peculiar mixture of Christianity and paganism there is manifest one of the richest and most productive tendencies of modern French literature.

# A Decade of American Fiction

*An Omnibus Review.*

*The Bridge of San Luis Rey* by Thorton Wilder. Longmans, Green and Co.
*The Cabala* by Thorton Wilder. Washington Square Press
*The Sun Also Rises* by Ernest Hemingway. Simon & Schuster
*Blue Voyage* by Conrad Aiken. Charles Scribner's Sons
*The Dark Mother* by Waldo Frank. Boni & Liveright
*The Enormous Room* by e. e. cummings. Random House
*Good-bye Wisconsin* by Glenway Wescott. Harper & Brothers
*The Apple of the Eye* by Glenway Wescott. Harper & Brothers
*The Grandmothers* by Glenway Wescott. Harper & Brothers
*The Time of Man* by Elizabeth Madox Roberts. The Viking Press
*Cane* by Jean Toomer. Liveright
*The Boy in the Sun* by Paul Rosenfeld. The Macaulay Company
*Manhattan Transfer* by John Dos Passos. Harper & Brothers

*The Bookman*, August 1929, 561–567

Though we still hear of dissatisfaction with the status of art in America, art is a major industry. Hundreds of thousands of skilled workmen are dependent for their sustenance upon the output of a comparatively negligible band of artists. When we consider how much union labor goes into the reproduction and distribution of some erratic gentleman's paragraphs, we may conclude that the frailest of esthetic temperaments is providing, thus indirectly, a livelihood for at least ten stalwart heads of families. And though our countrymen are told constantly that they despise art, they go on constantly showing that they love it. Between the hours of five and twelve p.m., the United States of America is devoted exclusively to transit and art, the transit being patronized by the art-goers. In the midst of much talk about working under pressure, we go on augmenting the specified hours of leisure—and for leisure, art is the only alternative to overeating, immorality and suicide.

With good art, the situation is less encouraging. But perhaps good art is merely a by-product of bad art, a notable deviation from the sounder average stock, a sport. I have never understood what would be gained by having the populace prefer Shakespeare to the Broadway school of drama. Good art is for people who cannot be satisfied with bad art. And profusion offers the best likelihood of important deviations, as the many purchasers of cheap records have enabled the perfecting of a mechanism whereby we may, at our pleasure, turn on Stokowsky playing Brahms.

That set of trivial magazines on the counter of the country drug store—do not abhor it, for it is culture. Culture is a state of society wherein one can save for eighteen volumes of Thomas Aquinas, if he will, while his neighbors are studying Hearst. As the world sleeps, with such at its pillow, you may enjoy the extreme prerogative of being left alone. The natural-born marauders are reading bad books, the lions are being milk-fed, while you are at peace to consider "a preserving and amassing of genius such as the world has never known before." Documents upon any aspect of speculation or sensibility are readily obtainable.

And we rejoice that there have been many bad books in the last ten years, for they constitute our guaranty that there have been some good ones. Yet in singling out the superior, we should not be gentle. A book which merits encouragement for a season may require vilification for a decade, and praise is best sharpened with slander.

Perhaps we should consider first, to dismiss the sooner, Thornton Wilder. *The Bridge of San Luis Rey* can be sacrificed without loss. In its own way it says, "The scroll, my lord." Its fatalism seems specious, trivial and even dishonest, as though consistency in the Maker's ways were trumped up to serve the ends of plot. *The Cabala* is much better, though questionable in that general air of selectness which it has in common with the society novels of writers like Marcel Prévost, Marcelle Tinayre, Henri Bordeaux, Henri de Régnier and Paul Bourget. We find the phrase of music or the line of a painting mentioned with easy familiarity which takes for granted the reader's deep acquaintance with the fashionable in art. And the work is vitiated at the close by that superficial coquetting with the mystic which mars *The Bridge* as a whole.

For one gift, Wilder is to be cherished. I refer, in *The Cabala,* to his succession of essays upon the various characters of his book. A queer, cracked lot, assembled in their oddity with considerable tact, they are described as in the lively letters of some traveller or visitor whose leisure among fountains and avenues leaves many energies unclaimed. "The Princess," he says, "was astonished to find such quiet mastery in a woman without a *de* and the Signora was amazed to find the same quality in a noblewoman." This is parlor talk of distinction, and *The Cabala* has much of it. Good examples of his characterizations could be chosen almost at random:

> So I led her up to Dame Edith Steuert, Mrs. Edith Foster Prichard Steuert, author of Far From Thy Ways, I Strayed, the greatest hymn since Newman's. Daughter, wife, sister, what not, of clergymen, she lived in the most exciting currents of Anglicanism. Her conversation ran on vacant livings and promising young men from Shropshire, and on the editorials in the latest *St. George's Banner* and *The Anglican Cry*. She sat on platforms and raised subscriptions and got names. She seemed to be forever surrounded by a ballet of curates and widows who at her word, rose and swayed and passed the scones. For she was the author of the greatest hymn of modern times and gazing at her one wondered when the mood could have struck this loud conceited woman, the mood that had prompted those eight verses of despair and humility. The hymn could have been written by Cowper, that gentle soul exposed to the flame of an evangelism too hot even for negroes. For one minute in her troubled girlhood all the intermittent sincerity of generations of clergymen must have combined in her, and late at night, full of dejections she could not understand, she must have committed to her diary that heartbroken confession. Then the fit was over, and over forever.

This is vivacious epitome, and it is a trick which enlivens the whole of *The Cabala*. Still, the book dies with its plot, after giving us a kind of hypothetical reality which has not gone far enough into fancy to entertain us speculatively (as does a work like Hudson's *A Crystal Age*), yet is too inventive for service as a formulation of life. The artist pronounces some number. Giving uniformity to many complex factors, he produces the typifying of an attitude. In the novel this is most often, but not invariably, done with the medium of a character. A posture like that of Childe Harold or a character like Julien Sorel contains a code of conduct beyond the limits of the fiction. Wilder, from this standpoint, does not qualify.

To take apart Hemingway's *The Sun Also Rises,* after having read it with enjoyment, is to be aghast. We find that we have read about people taking baths and getting haircuts, having another drink and giving tips to the coatman. Three people converse negligibly with one another, whereupon we learn without protest that two of them were "in fine form" that day. We watch Americans doing pleasantly in Europe all sorts of low-powered things which chroniclers of the same events in America would detail with venom and despair. We see people, vaguely cultured, whom we know to be cultured by their rigorous avoidance of all cultural topics. Hemingway provides appeal for a kind of idealized, international philandering, the trivialities of selfish and complacent people, a somewhat cut-throat crowd, whose familiarity with one another is founded upon too flimsy a basis. In this Hollywood conception of glory, no difficult thing is advocated, if we except the discipline and refinement required to behold and appraise the bullfight. Here is the "lost generation," contentedly lost. The book is particularly to be recommended to eager young girls with occasional yearnings, who associate brilliance with a rather sunny and literate form of idleness, who would like to imagine a world in which enjoyment comes easy and who, above all, have not yet been to Europe. For such reasons, I enjoyed it.

Hemingway's power of continuity in *The Sun Also Rises* is exceptional. Things follow one another with no suggestion of abruptness, a result rare in a writer whose observations are so keenly stated, since emphasis upon one fact makes for its division from the next. His short, easily riding sentences form a sure succession of narrative statements, a minimum of psychology, a maximum of behavior. Yet the hero can be a thinker. Hear him, on Page 153:

> I thought I had paid for everything. Not like the woman pays and pays and pays. No idea of retribution or punishment. Just exchange of values. You gave up something and got something else. Or you worked for something. You paid some way for everything that was any good. I paid my way into enough things that I liked, so that I had a good time. Either you paid by learning about them, or by experience, or by taking chances, or by money. Enjoying living was learning to get your money's worth and knowing when you had it. You could get your money's worth. The world was a good place to buy it. It seemed like a fine philosophy. In five years, I thought, it will seem just as silly as all the other fine philosophies I've had.

Hemingway weeds out much that is pious, or pompous; he is a good corrective, as good a corrective as listening in the street. His enthusiasm is naturally reserved for the bulls. His bullfights are scrupulous in their bloodiness—indeed, his most eager writing is expended upon the display of subtleties in the physical, where subtlety has been least exploited. At such times he is most observant and lyrical. He proves that if rock-crushing had its genius, it could be subdivided into as many gradations of experience as late love.

Of his short stories, we advocate particularly "The Undefeated," in *Men Without Women,* the spectacle of a moth-eaten toreador, expending a fiercety of determination, fighting for the recovery of past greatness and being dragged, step by step, to defeat, while the crowd looks on without sympathy. As though under glass, we watch this brutal discrepancy between efforts and results. It is Hemingway's "starkness" at his best, the employment of strong-arm methods heretofore reserved for a lower order of fiction.

There are some writers who, while the tenor of their work is admirable, manage to produce no one thing in which their best qualities converge. Despite their excellence as artists, they can claim no outstanding book. There are others whose average of attainment is lower, yet who have hit happily upon one anthology number. *The Time of Man,* by Elizabeth Madox Roberts, is far enough beyond *My Heart and My Flesh* and *Jingling in the Wind* to have been written by a different person. *The Jingling* suggests something of Chaucer, *Candide* and *Alice in Wonderland,* but remains a book of no great moment despite its distinguished antecedents. It is appealing in its literary sophistication, its incidental sallies into the picturesque. In *My Heart and My Flesh,* we remain unmoved by the heroine's aberrations, which are conveyed less by psychological disclosure than by tricks of presentation, particularly the peopling of the brain with altercating voices, conversing as in the dialogue of a play and destroying the illusion of reality by means of a form to which the illusion of reality is essential. But Miss Roberts's *The Time of Man* marks a flowering of the local-color novel. Her rustic heroine, necessarily sensitive beyond her station, is followed through a homely tragedy which recovers for us the feel of courage and our rage against injustice. One distinctly participates. Glenway Wescott has commented upon the beauty she distills out of the Kentucky dialect. This diction, though serving the ends of realism, arouses pleasures which are almost those of fantasy. Miss Roberts handles colloquial conversation with a tact undreamed of by Eugene O'Neill. The talk is as some distortion of speech might be if it were undertaken by an inventor with much linguistic subtlety, distortion made in the interests of a future form of beauty. And the heroine's monologues, as they rise out of a narrative episode to end a chapter in zealous philosophizing, seem to be a personal discovery of the author.

Conrad Aiken is of that class whose level of production is high, while the single outstanding product is still lacking. There is about Aiken some of that interest in death and desiccation which distinguishes Eliot, and which usually coexists with selectness and sparsity of output. Yet Aiken is unloosed—his work, wide in its intellectual range but narrow emotionally, attains profuse embodiment. He can extract a common quality out of varied experiences. Thus, in reading his *Blue Voyage,* one has the satisfaction of a formula intricately repeated. The formula represents a man who has derived strong moral predispositions from his upbringing, but who has intellectually superimposed upon himself a dismissal of all such emotional investments. The result is a kind of hilarious morbidity; and the hero Demarest, despite his able equipment, is without dignity, unless we can find dignity in vacillation and the willingness to admit anything. Aiken might even be somewhat of a martyr—for I believe that he is striving for a set of post-Freudian moral judgments, trying to uncover what *the good* might be if we begin with the premise that all our mental processes are trivial. Thus, *Blue Voyage* sets soberly to work focusing much sensitivity and education upon amatory engrossment's which could, by another artist, easily be made farcical. Demarest is a Puritan unhorsed. He is quick to confuse the female ankle with meditations upon abstruse metaphysical destinies. The flirtatious wenches on this boat are considered and observed by a protagonist who believes himself an erotomaniac simply because he happens to ponder upon sex for twenty-four hours a day. Yet the content of his thinking might argue a denial of his claim, proving him an observer, an outsider, who has been caught by the sexual symbol owing to its present somewhat arbitrary association with communion. His meditations are in constant deviation from their sexual starting-point, though Demarest chooses to interpret them in terms of their beginnings rather than in terms of their tangential escapes.

Regardless of wide differences, we might note one striking similarity between *Blue Voyage* and Waldo Frank's *The Dark Mother.* Aiken, like Frank, uses the technical subterfuge of projecting his characters beyond themselves. By which I mean that, after each author has shown us his characters in their realistic, more or less unexpressive guise, he transports them hypothetically to a plane of intelligence and eloquence, allows them to discuss the mainsprings of their nature with one another, converts their realism into allegory and gives us an orgiastic fraternization such as the composer of the *Choral Symphony* might have taken delight in.

In *Blue Voyage,* Aiken has dispensed with protective dignity. His claim to respect seems to lie, not in reticence, not in such "uncontemporaneous" methods as Racinean elimination, but in the brightness of his disclosures. Here, it is not the form, but the law, that excludes. And the burden of his skepticism, in this book which is built about a transatlantic voyage, is lifted by that feeling of expectancy which is a large element in the psychology of travel. By way of happy ending, the book closes characteristically with Demarest entering for the first time the illicit cabin. It is a dingy homecoming.

Can we, in this review of fiction, include *The Enormous Room* of e. e. cummings? For, though founded upon the recording of actual events, the author's incarceration in a French detention camp, it bears the marks of arrant fictionizing, might in fact even be described as the art of fabrication, the romanticizing of the realistic, the documentary lie. This is not reporting, this charitable eye for excrement, this ability to see everything startlingly, these distortions of one who, instructed to hold a mirror up to nature, obediently procured his mirror from a laughing gallery. The one thing we can know of the people in that enormous room is that they are not as Cummings asserts them to be. They have been converted into their super-selves by a freakish imagination necessarily compelled to expatiate upon its environment, pleased to read an event into happenings which, without such interpretive enterprise, would have been uneventful. Even in suffering, this quality of mind forces its owner upon a lark.

Cummings, to depict his object, assails it with a whole broadside of data; he overwhelms it; like a cartoonist, he industriously seeks the distortion of its every particular. He will look at a stomach, and find a belly; at a face and find a mug; at a chin and find three chins. It is the method of Gross. And unlike Frank, he uses the connotations of humor, to which distorting is proper.

His descriptions are often more vigorous than revealing. There is saliency for its own sake. The vigor of description may transcend its object and, even as the picture grows dim, leave us with a tingle of vigorous description. But the haze of the individual characters, which arises despite an exhaustive dwelling upon their details, assists in conveying a mass impression of the enormous room itself. Its occupants are indefinite but, as an aggregate, their swarming identity is established.

Cummings can hate irresponsibly, as in his ferocious attacks upon a nonexistent *gouvernement français*. And he can praise irresponsibly. He can dote upon Jean Le Nègre, the royal beast in this enormous room, without submitting his judgments to the final consistency of permanent companionship. He is, after all, leaving. He can rhetorically pray for their meeting in death (another enormous room, be it observed) without worrying about the fact that they would have little in common for the years intervening. He possesses fortunate irresponsibility—somewhat as adolescents can be absolute in the criticism of their elders, can be uncompromising, through not yet having had to face compromise. We follow him through this freshness, through much joyous misery, ending in a return to prosperity, comfort, assured well-being:

> My God, what an ugly island. Hope we don't stay here long. All the redbloods first-class much excited about land. Damned ugly, I think.
> Hullo.
> The tall, impossibly tall, incomparably tall, city shoulderingly upward into hard sunlight leaned a little through

> octaves of its parallel edges, leaningly strode upward into firm hard snowy sunlight; the noises of America nearingly throbbed with smokes and hurrying dots which are men and which are women and which are things new and curious and hard and strange and vibrant and immense, lifting with a great ondulous stride into immortal sunlight . . .

At times I have wished that all literature were like the music of Bach, never descending below the level of inventiveness. When nothing else is happening, the manipulation of the medium should reward our attention, providing the inarticulate reader with inarticulate delight and the analytic one with material for swift analysis. Cummings in *The Enormous Room* does meet this requirement. Though, sometimes, he relies upon slang paraphrase—and when he speaks of going through a door haughtily, "using all the perpendicular inches God has given me," we know that he has *drawn himself up to his full height.* But there is always ebullience. The author strives that the reader may relax. Should one open the book at random, wherever the eye falls the page comes to life. Granted that the life is not invariably beyond our protest—that it might often be a better quality of life—the buoyancy is to be found throughout and promptly declares itself.

Wescott is a writer of short stories. *Good-bye Wisconsin* is avowedly a collection of short stories; and his two novels, *The Apple of the Eye* and *The Grandmothers,* are sequences of short stories in disguise. Perhaps one of the best examples of his suggestive method is "The Whistling Swan," the piece which ends *Good-bye Wisconsin.* We see a young musician, who is in Wisconsin after having been subsidized abroad. There is a young girl, who loves him with a certain disturbing awe. He is trying to decide whether to remain, or to make new plans for a return to Paris. While walking in the woods, with a gun and his indecision, he comes upon a swan, which startles him and which he shoots almost before thinking. Indecision vanishes. He will remain. In the shooting of the bird, felled in a flutter of expert prose, he slays a portion of himself, that portion which was drawing him to Paris. Wescott suggests—we are at liberty to complete the psychology. An aspect of the hero's self is externalized, and he slays it. The event may be taken, not as the cause of his reversal, but as the paralleling of it. That which occurs within, by the dark and devious channels of decision, he duplicates without as the destruction of a swan. Following this symbolic elimination, he is prepared to remain, to marry, and let our gentle girl become indispensable to him.

There is a sweetly morbid effect in Wescott, as when, in *The Grandmothers,* he discusses past romance in the presence of old age. "The October afternoon on which she was buried, among her relations and his own, mingled in his memory with the afternoons of her girlhood." As we read of his pioneers, we feel that this vast continent was peopled in gloom; where there is enthusiasm, it is seen through the despair and envy of another, or in the melancholy of retrospect. He writes of Grandfather Tower: "His beard was parted in the middle, and fell on each side of a large bone button in his shirt collar; his rheumatic hands were clenched; and wherever he went, he seemed to be elbowing aside invisible people on his way." Similarly, in *The Apple of the Eye*, he takes a charming character from us, showing her body carrion after we had learned much of her difficult ways of feeling. And his short stories hint vaguely of corruption, corruption which even gains moment by being vaguely hinted.

Wescott gives the impression of one whose written frankness is kept suavely in arrears of his understanding; he diverges from his readers with discretion; determined neither to give offense nor to leave the offensive unsaid, he is necessarily unctuous. Westcott tells old stories. It is part of his success. To the circumambient he adds suavity. His pages, being liquid, flow. They flow through the mind, merging into one another, making perfect conformity. Plot and the statement of an attitude are, by his ways, skillfully interchangeable; neither is a digression from the other; both are aspects of a method essentially lyrical.

Waldo Frank we dare omit. Yet we recognize his great seriousness, recognize him even as a prophetic writer who could view with bitterness the spectacle of his work being incorporated elsewhere, piece by piece, not by plagiarists, but by artists who have in their own manner arrived at his results. Such men as Anderson we dare omit for other reasons: they have been amply appraised.

We regret the silence of Jean Toomer, after his early volume, *Cane*, a work showing the influence of Frank and Anderson jointly. Toomer takes the business of fiction very earnestly and is, perhaps, hindered temporarily by the desire to incorporate greater complexity into his work. There are many aspects of experience which must undergo a discipline of esthetic trickery before they can serve the purposes of lyric prose. And Toomer, essentially Negro in his inspiration, would surely never be content to let the singing quality depart from his work.

Paul Rosenfeld's *The Boy in the Sun* shows to advantage the impressionistic treatment which the author applies with less fitness in his criticism. Perhaps it reflects the influence of Frank in that the metaphor, the image, tends to supplant psychological analysis. Since his adolescent is left at the end, still living, and even walking "through the cold spring evening," we dare entertain the possibility of a sequel, treating of a treacherous passage from wonder to acceptance.

In *Manhattan Transfer,* John Dos Passos abandons his earlier, descriptive style for the methods of a playwright. Out of blunt materials—beaneries, seduction in the slums, low-visioned ambitions, thefts, brawls, dirty tricks—the author accumulates a grimy, but easily recognizable metropolis. Dos Passos contributes a new quickness to narrative, by a succession of pointed episodes, lives glimpsed preferably at moments of change or decision. Each event is thus a kind of miniature peripety, a plot at some culminating stage. His book affords us no new enlightenment, but it rises to the category of excellence through the sheer efficiency by which it represents its genre. The dishes-in-the-sink tradition is here carried to fulfillment.

We should also mention the appearance of Jonathan Leonard's novel, *Back to Stay.* Leonard first attracted attention when a long story of his was published in *The Second American Caravan.* With his love of oddity, his peculiar preciosity in the linking of statement and answer, his pleasant glibness, readers who seek too exclusively in novels the sense of reality might find him disappointing. Dramatic situations are allowed to trickle away, sapped by the author's and his characters' perverse gift of loquacity. But by this loss, the flavor of his repartee is more emphasized.

We shall not venture upon the future. There seems little indication of any pronounced change. We might wish for the decease of the gossip novel, as having been written frequently enough. We might plead the obligations of history, maintaining that the accumulations in this medium are sufficient. We might hope to see local color become a less important aspect of fiction, on the grounds that it can hardly be done better than it has been done by many men long since dead. We might prefer to find the greater stressing of fiction as a literary experience, a speculative activity, a method of inquiry, rather than as a form of vicarious living. Meanwhile, there are advantages in the possession of these technicians who can entertain thee, at mealtimes, on the boulevards and by thy pillow, with able and compliant prose.

# Permanence and Change

*Joseph and His Brother* by Thomas Mann. Translated by H. T. Lowe-Porter. Alfred A. Knopf
*The New Republic,* June 1934, 186–187. Also in *The Philosophy of Literary Form*

This first volume of Thomas Mann's trilogy carries us, as down a deep shaft, to old Biblical regions across which lie peaceful and pastorally melancholy landscapes. Down into the big black hole of the past we drift, until we come upon a world that lived three thousand years ago and is now, by Orphic conjuring, made to live again. The book has about it a quality that has almost vanished from contemporary fiction. It is contemplative, or ruminant—so perhaps one could speak more intelligently of its effects after a long interim of silence during which one returned to it only in memory. One must judge Mann, not as an adept in quickly caught and quickly forgotten impressions (not as the equivalent in pure art of the methods of advertising in applied art)—his value resides rather in a subtle, patient and skillfully sustained evangelism which produces changes in us capable of developing through decades.

Mann is a very thorough writer—and surely this melancholy volume, with its astonishingly complex morality, is the end-product of his thoroughness. As one reads it, one understands the solemn note that has gained prominence in his later critical writings. It seems clear that, in a pre-scientific era, Mann would have become a priest—or still farther back, in more primitive groups, he would have taken his place in the college of elders who carefully scan the tribal archives that all new acts may be judged and shaped by precedent. Indeed, as we read this reworking of the Biblical legends clustered about Isaac, Jacob, Esau, Leah, Rachel and Joseph, we get a new understanding of the part played by precedent in the matter of human motives. In earlier days, we feel, precedent was not the purely legalistic device it has since become, a way of preventing new decisions by reference to past decisions made under different conditions and for different purposes. The reference to precedent was *re-*

*vealing* rather than *obstructive,* precisely because the conditions and purposes had remained constant. Again, these precedents were not the individualized events we meet when we go back to the records of 1929 to find out what the Supreme Court ruled in the case of Johns vs. Johns. They were *mythical* precedents: they were group products—they were "right" because they took their form as a collective enterprise. They were selective and interpretative, the results of long revision at the hands of many people through many years. They were the "key" situations of the tribe that had evolved them, after all that could be forgotten had been forgotten and all that could not be forgotten had been made salient. They were not "facts," as legalistic precedents are, but communal works of art. And when the individual understood his own role by reference to them (saying, "I am like Jacob," or "This situation is like Leah's") he was being himself and a member of his group simultaneously. It is in this sense that Mann sets about to write of "people who do not know precisely who they are," and "the phenomenon of open identity which accompanies that of imitation and succession."

At least, whether one agrees with the suggestion or not, it is the feeling that one takes away with him from the reading of Mann's latest piously ironic novel. What one can do with it, I do not know. The author has simplified and idealized his point of view by eliminating attempts at modern parallels. He is not concerned with strict modern-ancient correspondences like Joyce, who would chart the new equivalents to the old wanderings of Odysseus. In the altered ways of life which technology has brought, perhaps the situations are so radically changed from those earlier pecuniary or stock-breeding days that we must abandon the attempt to understand ourselves by reference to the precedents of myth. Again, the myths are bewilderingly intermingled: they are not living art, but art in a museum. Yet even for this state of affairs, perhaps, there is a mythical parallel—for is there not everywhere the legend of the Tower of Babel that arose to confound primitive men when they were elated by such ambitions as have in recent centuries elated us, and the vast projects of building were confused by a multitude of tongues quite as our specialized vocabularies continually threaten to confuse us?

"Without passion and guilt nothing could proceed." If I chose the word "thorough" as the label that might most briefly characterize this book, it is because *Joseph and His Brothers* profoundly pursues the ramifications of this thought. The strange intermingling of kindness and cruelty which animates it could all, I believe, be shown to flow from this statement. The pervasive imagery of the pit, the phenomena of indentured service which he considers with insistence, his constant concern with the psychology of waiting, his almost fierce emphasis upon the cult of fertility, his remarks on the "upper and lower half of the sphere," his deliberate affronts to the mechanistic concepts of causality, his ironic sympathy with opportunism, his somewhat awestruck pondering on the subject of recurrence—all this, I believe, could be shown to follow, directly or indirectly, from his care as to the part which the "problem of evil" plays in the civic, or historic process. An author in search of metaphor, he makes us feel that life itself is metaphorical.

I have probably said enough to suggest that another word might replace my adjective "thorough." Mann's new book is "mystical." It brings us to the edge of things, to that fearful dropping-off place which, before the feat of Columbus, could be geographically imagined but has since usually been relegated solely to a disposition of the mind under duress, though it is brought back once more in the physical sense perhaps by the contemporary physicist's suggestion that electronic activity is like a radiation from a non-existent core (as were it to well up from some other region like water quietly moving the sand at the bottom of a spring). It is an eschatological book, dealing with the "science of last things." As such, it is disturbing, and will perhaps be rightly repudiated by happier fellows who prefer to shape their acts by contingencies alone. To live by contingencies alone is unquestionably the most comforting way to live—and contented ages have probably been those in which the concepts of duty were wholly of this specific sort, harvesting when the crops were ripe, shearing when the sheep were heavy, and coupling when the body felt the need of its counter-body. But the world of contingencies is now wholly in disarray. In our despicable economic structure, to do the things thus immediately required of us is too often to do despicable things. It is at such times, I imagine, that the question of duty naturally becomes more generalized, and attempts at defining the "ultimate vocation" seem most apropos. Mann's new book is written in this spirit.

# While Waiting

*Those Who Perish.* by Edward Dahlberg. The John Day Company
*The New Republic*, November 1934, 53

In *Those Who Perish,* Edward Dahlberg has written a novel that is forceful and poignant. A writer who approaches the contemporary disorders with a sensitiveness bordering on hyperesthesia, he is especially well equipped to picture the disintegration of individuals that is implicit in the disintegration of our economic structure. Dahlberg is adept at taking grotesque, harried and abysmal characters, and prodding them to become more and more themselves. The persons of his books whom he has selected for particular dislike, he pursues with a corrosive brand of comment which constantly crashes through their own concepts of their lives, like a heckler who breaks a debater's sequence at every point by shouting out unwieldly questions. Dahlberg's style is highly mannered, with a distinctiveness that can readily alienate whenever it ceases to attract. It builds an elaborate "superstructure" about his figures, somewhat as Cummings does in *The Enormous Room,* where he quickly gets from the object to a gigantesque projection—but in Dahlberg's case this device seldom shows Cummings' tendency toward pure playfulness; rather, it is pained and even vengeful. Dahlberg has obviously been under great strain in this ailing society, and in his writing he is settling a score.

In fluent and natural dialogue, Dahlberg gives us an important aspect of the grim interregnum that is now upon us, when the collapsing capitalist order can provide neither moral nor material security, and no alternative has been established. We see the grave unsettlement of the Jews in America, as the Nazi movement gains power and threatens to extend its doctrines to this country. We see them, when they would turn to communism as a solution, frightened by the thought that a frank allegiance to Marxism would make them members of two minorities instead of one, and this at our present stage could but multiply their risks. Dahlberg is not a sympathetic man: he tends to excoriation rather than to pity—and even while building up this dilemma he rigorously pursues the business men and Zionists who would tend toward a fascist compromise of their own instead of electing the communistic solution and welcoming a present danger in the interests of ultimate betterment. In this respect it is questionable whether his machinery of propaganda extends so far and includes so much as the needs of strategy may demand.

Stanley Burnshaw, writing on Dahlberg's book in *The New Masses*, has noted that the earlier negativistic attitude exemplified in *From Flushing to Calvary* has here found its positive counterpart: *Those Who Perish*, he says, does not contain merely the rejection of capitalism, it contains also the positive election of communism. I can only say that, so far as I was concerned, this turn from the negation of capitalism to the affirmation of communism seemed but sketchily embodied. Dahlberg's heroine, Regina Gordon, dies in a state of complete loneliness. A suicide, she swept out her arms toward "those who have the heart for tomorrow," whereupon she "smoldered into yesterday." The affirmation thus remains in the stage of the ideal, the prophetic, a vague and bewildered reaching out of hands toward the future as one sinks into oblivion. She salutes communism as a doctrine, but no character in this book has been pictured in connection with communism as an organization. As an isolated individual, Dahlberg's heroine has "seen the light," in much the old religious fashion of conversion. But to my mind the negation has not been imaginatively embodied as an affirmation until the artist gives us a positive picture of group cooperation and adjustment, shows us on the positive side what actual concrete solace and encouragement the Comrades can provide for one another. Meanwhile, we can proclaim Dahlberg as the possessor of a strong stylistic death-ray—and those characters upon whom his partisanship prompts him to train this ray wither before our very eyes.

# Change of Identity

*Judgment Day* by James T. Farrell. The Vanguard Press
*The New Republic*, June 1935, 171–172

Could one possibly read James T. Farrell's impressive Lonigan trilogy without feeling an irresistible desire to sermonize? Farrell always gives us the feeling that what he says is authentic. Hence his story of a young Chicago Irishman, bred in a typically modern-Catholic orientation, forms a ghastly attack upon the educational influences, both formal and informal, to which his representative hero is subjected. When reading his three vigorous volumes, the last of which has been published recently, one can well understand why conscientious persons raised in a thoroughgoing religion may as adults be able to tolerate nothing short of absolute atheism, manifesting an almost ferocious hatred of the God-concept, and categorically shutting off all visions of damnation by violently insisting upon the mortality of the soul.

    I admit that I have considerable sympathy with religious lore (as preserved in the formulations of the Church's philosophers, psychologists and mystics, and as manifested in a vast structure of myth and symbolism that seemed miraculous in its ability to take care of basic human difficulties). I believe the visions that give purpose and unity to historic movements are in essence religious. And I am convinced that, however secular the terminology guiding our subsequent social directions may set out to be, it will not succeed in handling the essential problems of human relationship unless it finds ways of paralleling, in its own terms, the mental patterns formed in the past by religious imagery. In this work of secular transformation, I think, the "illumination" will come primarily from our poets.

    To read Farrell's startling trilogy, however, is to feel how complete the transformation must be. At least as regards the class that provides all the important characters of his trilogy (the "low Irish" of a metropolis), Farrell repeatedly shows us, with a feverish insistence that makes the heart sink, how completely unfit the precepts of the Church are for coping with the principal morbidities of today. Primitive Catholicism may have been strongly collectivistic; and medieval Catholicism, for all its tolerance of serfdom, may have been pitted against the cults of nationalism, individualism and business; but what Farrell pictures today is a slovenly manipulation of superstition and prejudices that directly or indirectly stimulates jingoism, race hatred, sexual orgy, alcoholism, cruelty and uncritical acceptance of a drastically ailing economic structure. In this respect, the picture he draws is not new. Farrell's claim to distinction is the purely esthetic one of having given form to his own particular range of experience. But in the course of thus putting things together, he shows most poignantly, at times even terrifyingly, how the religious emphases, at least as manipulated by average priests under capitalist conditions, make spontaneously for moral disorganization through their very vocabulary of virtue. As we read we see the full irony of the situation he portrays: the fact that those who are *pushed down* by a defective economic system are *held down* by the very structure of meanings to which they turn for guidance and solace.

A morality is an equipment for living. At its best, it is a felicitously adjusted set of values which, by inducing people to despise real social dangers and to desire real social goods, promotes the maximum of cooperative conduct in the group as a whole. Yet Farrell shows us a dangerous misalliance of religious and late-capitalist values that—by combining the informal instruction of the pool room and the "can house" with dismal political thinking of the ward-heeler variety and a moral training that mainly lays the basis for pruriency—contrives in the end to promote an incongruous moral clutter (a clutter that contributes most to "cooperation" by stifling and misdirecting criticism of the current commercial framework).

Other writers may appear and give us other versions. (For, as conditions continue to tighten, we may well discern the same "class lines" forming *within* a religious orientation as outside it.) I am simply discussing now the convincing version provided us by Farrell. In his tough, fluent lingo, he gives us three novels that bear devastating evidence, on every page, of the drastically anti-social amalgam we get when run-down capitalism and religious conformism are put together—the first creating the need of accurate economic appraisals, and the second obscuring the need by a continual thundering against symptoms while causes go unquestioned.

The most interesting paradox in Farrell's trilogy to me is the extreme *moralism* that figures in his characters' decay. Their brutality and carousing are done with the most exacting sense of propriety; one can feel their scrupulous straining to "belong," in accordance with a woefully muddled system of values that (a) does not properly name the evils of their economic structure, (b) does not properly name their own individual quandaries with respect to the situation in general, and (c) attempts to make up for its inaccuracy by an elaborate tissue of promises, indulgences, and condemnations thoroughly irrelevant. In this sense, we may feel his characters' decay, not as weakness, but as a sensitive recording of the colossal moral burdens being placed upon them. Their corruption, their loss of social purpose, their confused devotion to a gang morality—all this may be considered as the crude first draft of a judgment which, if properly revised, can become correct and wholesome.

Reading the three volumes of Farrell's trilogy in succession, I noted certain shifts in treatment that I considered significant. In the first, *Young Lonigan,* which begins with Studs's graduation from St. Patrick's grammar school at the age of fifteen, we have by far the closest interweaving of Studs's character with the events about him. He is almost wholly a part of his environment—with but a slight sense of separation, best observable in the occasional feeling on the boy's part that there is a door in his mind, and the vision of his deliberately closing this door at times when he wishes to shut away untoward thoughts. In *The Young Manhood of Studs Lonigan* there enters a stronger sense of dissociation; inserted between the main chapters of the plot, there are brief interludes in italics, totally different in style (ceremonious, novelistic interpretations that suggest the "layer" method of Dos Passos).

In *Judgment Day* the element of dissociation is advanced far beyond a dualism in treatment. The mark of it is strongly upon Studs Lonigan himself. Though Studs does not die until the end of volume three, an integral part of him died after his besotted collapse at the end of volume two. *Judgment Day* opens by stressing his fear of death (a theme that had been present in the two preceding books, but now becomes major). Though still a young man, he is obsessed with the thought of his physical deterioration, and given to morose comparisons with what he *had been* or *might have been.* And for all his paucity of vocabulary, he has become somewhat the observer (much of the plot being a succession of typical city scenes, with Studs simply transferred from one to the next). Studs walks beneath a shadow (a state which has, for its one good side, a much more humane attitude towards his parents).

Returning now to my opening remarks: I believe that, however radically we transform the *dogmas* of religion, its essence must remain. And that even in a man like Farrell, whose ferocity against the Church has been turned into these energetic books, we may expect to see the religious processes perpetuated. Thus, his Lonigan trilogy might be called an initiation service—the dropping of one personality and the assuming of another in its place. And as Studs dies, leaving an unmarried woman pregnant with his child, while the radicals demonstrate in the streets, we can discern the tenor of this magic rite whereby a change of role is heralded in the symbolism of a novelist's plot.

# Thurber Perfects Mind Cure

*Let Your Mind Alone! and Other More or Less Inspirational Pieces* by James Thurber. Harper and Brothers
*The New Republic*, September 1937, 220–221

That skillful literary man, St. Augustine, has warned that one should never smite an opponent in bad grammar. Applying a loose interpretation, we could translate his wise teaching thus: If a man would carry a discussion through points A, B, C and D, don't let him think he has got anywhere, in the way of cogency, simply by lining up a good argument. For should he have a lisp, or should someone in his audience periodically sneeze in a notable way, or should there be an irrelevant voice echoing from the corridors, our hero is all Achilles' heel. Especially when there is a Thurber about.

In fact, if he should make a statement that requires as many as three sentences, and there is a Thurber about, he is as vulnerable. For Thurber may choose to hear only the first sentence, proceeding joyously and outrageously to build upon it. We generally think of funny men as irrational. But they are as rational as the constructor of a Mother Goose rhyme (who gets to his crooked house via a crooked man, crooked smile, crooked sixpence, crooked stile, crooked cat and crooked mouse). And one thing they learn early is that, if a thought requires three sentences for self-protective presentation, they would be disloyal to their method in hearing out the three. Where three parts are needed, the professional funny man just *knows* that he should stop at part one. His one Marquis of Queensberry rule is: Belts are to hit below.

A Thurber, having singled out part one, will next proceed, with perverse rational efficiency, to ponder this broken part. He will invent "case histories" with which to try it out—and of course, they won't fit.

But a mere bad fit is not enough. The funny man will also seek a situation such that his readers *want* a bad fit. If they are good Catholics, for instance, he knows it will be hard to make them meet him halfway should he decide to play havoc with an encyclical. He will lay off such dynamite, leaving it for the news itself to provide the outrageous incongruities, as when, reporting a Papal blast on communism at the time of Mussolini's triumph in Africa, the dispatch proceeded: "On the subject of Ethiopia, His Holiness was less explicit." On the other hand, readers of *The New Yorker,* in which all but two of the articles in *Let Your Mind Alone!* appeared, are likely to be less problematical when leftward-looking politics is the subject—so we get "What Are the Leftists Saying?" I thought it tearfully lame; but for all I know it may be judged by typical New Yorker readers the most devastating bit of fun since the discovery of the banana peel.

The first ten pieces, which give this volume its title, are a very amusing burlesque of psychoanalysis. The field offers a good opportunity for Thurber's phenomenal gifts. The study of the mind has brought to the fore many paradoxes. A man may *think* he is doing one thing when he is *actually* doing another. This state of affairs outrages common sense—the thought of it makes one uneasy—hence we are glad to meet that man halfway who will expend his jocular enterprise to vindicate the judgments of common sense.

There are pages that make one laugh very hard. One is glad that Thurber does his part to keep the leftward-lookers on their toes. I am even willing to concede him his constitutional right, as funny man, to start too soon, to remain dumb on purpose, dying that others may live—though he tends somewhat to flatter stupidity, making it a kind of accomplishment within reach of all, like getting drunk, as in his soothing challenges of this sort: "I know very little about electricity and I don't want to have it explained to me" (the medicinal effect of such trivializing bravado being necessary, since there are so many things now to know very little about, and we might feel like worms if we didn't have people of Thurber's authority to help mend our humiliation).

His skill at turning little domestic rows into transmogrifications of themselves is picturesque. In such scenes, I believe, the perception of his draughtsmanship is carried over. You see the people in watching the drama. Tight shoes, he says, make one walk "with the gait of a man who is stalking a bird across wet cement." And he hates women "because they throw baseballs . . . with the wrong foot advanced." There's something I had been working on since the eighth grade, and never understood until Thurber brought it clearly into consciousness by his combined skill as draughtsman and verbalizer. (Incidentally, I here select examples that I think are good—but I might illustrate his own method by adding that, were I to employ it here, I should pick out some of the weakest quips in the book and hold them up for rapt admiration.)

His drawings are good *always* for the perception his writing has *sometimes.* But I do wish he'd go after bigger game. He shoots too many cockroaches. To get such heightened value, I'd even be willing to hand him over to the reactionaries. Let him hound the "socially conscious" more consistently, in case he finds their attitude of "uplift" too much for his antinomian perversity. He need not join the author of *Redder Than the Rose*. But let him at least make an indirect contribution, in serving to keep the statements of the Left alert (though they could never be alert enough to forestall all possibility of Thurberization). I have just been reading Jacques Barzun's book on theories of racial superiority. I think fondly of what a Thurber might do by examining these documents on crooked thinking and translating them into the idiom of hilarity. But that would be asking too much (at least until his waggish remarks on cocktail parties run out—and he is so ingenious and fertile with them that I doubt whether they ever will run out). So I am willing to have him become our Lord Macaulay of fun-making, a reactionary keeper-thin of the Left. Unction must be made difficult—so let him be the deunctifyer. But as things now stand, he too is purveying a patent medicine. The trivial has its medicinal aspect—but too often he expends his talents to load the trivial with all the traffic can bear.

# The Book of Proverbs

*Racial Proverbs: A Selection of the World's Proverbs, Arranged Linguistically* by
   Selwyn Gurney Champion. The Macmillan Company
*The New Republic*, June 1939, 230

If there is any truth in the notion that the thorough cataloguing of a cultural manifestation marks its demise, this imposing exhibit suggests that the Era of Proverbs is about finished (with wisecracks, perhaps, taking their place). Here, in any case, is assembled a set of tools and weapons as handsomely formed as any that ever broke ground or skull. And what an admonishment lies there, for the writers of this copy-making age, if they could but *afford* to seek the succinct rather than the space-filling. Or, since he who says it fumblingly gets paid more for his fumble than for a clean catch (the fumble lasting longer), might it be possible, like the Elizabethans who wrote poetry after the proverb model, to find ways of filling space with the succinct?

The balances, antitheses, ratios (a: b :: c: d), alliterations, internal rhymes, triads and periodicities that characterize the form (some of these qualities, of course, being lost in translation) make statement an *event*. And the pronounced overlap of proverbs across both temporal and geographical distance, the repetition of the same paradigms in different individuations, provides correction to those who would put too much stress upon doctrines of cultural subjectivism.

Proverbs never speculate at random. The folk realism, religion and symbolism of their play grow out of work; they are shaped to a purpose. The general tenor of this purpose is best revealed in the Subject-Matter Index, where we note that entries under "Caution (anticipation, foresight, forethought, precaution, prudence)" comprise nearly three columns, "Philosophy (complaisance, contentment)" over four, "Diplomacy (cunning, subtlety, tact)" five, and "Consequence" more than six and a half. Prompted to mimicry by the style, we made up a homely proverb of our own: "A good fire burns the toast." Which, applied to the present volume, would mean: The very excellence of proverbs spoils them for straightaway reading. Rather, as here so amply assembled, they should be but *sampled*. Otherwise, one finds that his stream of consciousness is lulled to a drowsy murmur by flowing over pebbles.

# Symbolic War

*Proletarian Literature in the United States, An Anthology* edited by Granville Hicks, Michael Gold, Isider Schneider, Joseph North, Paul Peters, and Alan Calmer. With a critical introduction by Joseph Freeman. International Publishers
*The Southern Review*, Summer 1926, 134–147

Poetry, I take it, is a matter of welfare—as religion and politics are matters of welfare. And welfare, in this imperfect world, is grounded in material necessities. Even if we chose to deny these material necessities, starving or being slain in behalf of some cause, our self-abnegatory act would still be grounded in material necessities. The "material basis of reference" is as strong in the acts of those who would flout it as in the behavior of any businessman who treats financial profit and spiritual profit as interchangeable terms. It is in this sense that believe in the priority of economic factors. Some have said challengingly, and some bitterly, what Aristotle said as a matter of course: that people live together for their greater advantage. The problems of congregation center about the problems of wealth, derived from the means of production and defense. Where the available means of production and defense are ample, poverty or loss can only arise from some disorder in the modes of congregation. The dispossessed man is in a different "environment" from the man who enjoys the fruits of the society's wealth. He has a different "relation to the productive forces." And insofar as this situation sharpens his fears, hopes, and conflicts, it helps to condition his "morality."

Thus do such matters as wealth, morality, poetry, environment, production, and congregation tend to become intertwined, shaping a point of view, making for "partisans" insofar as different relationships become simplified as consciousness of "class."

However, to have pursued our speculations as far as the matter of "class-consciousness" is to realize that the relation between the "economic substructure" and the "moral superstructure" is lacking in the symmetry of one-to-one correspondences. We can belong in as many classifications as scientists or philosophers care to invent. Though a radical paper is written for a different "class" than a conservative one, we may have heard complaints from the

*115*

*contributors* to radical papers which would suggest that, to them, the *editors* of the radical paper often seem to be in the same "class" as the editors of the conservative paper. Their most intimate connection with a "class war" may be in the war between the *editor* class and the *contributor* class—and it can be a very bitter one, waged behind the lines at a moment when battles on a wider front are being fought.

Again, our "economic environment" is not wholly historical. At any given time in history, we have specific relationships to the forces of production (tools and weapons) accumulated by our society. But there is another "economic plant," the resources of the body itself, the *biologic* tools and weapons, with *their* "superstructural" counterparts (intelligence, love, hate, desire for mobility, etc.). We might call this a "human" environment or situation, wider than any given historic environment. Here enters the possibility of cultural overlap, whereby a "proletarian" may find much in common with the "late feudal" or "early bourgeois" Shakespeare.

The presence of this "human" environment, the "natural" frame of reference that is wider than the "historical," may be discussed as the tendency of the poet to "transcend" the peculiar economic necessities of his times. Not even a fish could be said to live in a totally different environment from man. The "moralities" of man and fish must tend to overlap, destroying the symmetry of complete differentiation, insofar as both "classes" live by respiration and locomotion. A happy translator might do a fairly reputable job at turning a fish's delight in gills and fins into a glorification of lungs and legs.

Many of the recent literary battles hinge about this issue. The over-simplifying advocate of "proletarian" art would stress the historic environment to the exclusion of all else (and would then invent all sorts of subterfuges and epicycles to explain a liking he might have for Dante or Aeschylus, perhaps finally deciding that they were "workers" in their field). And the oversimplifying advocate of the universally human would lay all emphasis upon the continuity of "man's burden" throughout the ages, as he incessantly confronts the critical events of birth, growth, love, union, separation, initiation, sorrow, fear, death, and the like.

In sum: we live by the goring of the ox (or some equivalent victim, be it only a vegetable). Call this relationship the biological, the universal-human, that attains its replica in the syntheses of ideology and morals ("imagination"). But it also makes a difference *whose* ox is gored. Call this relationship the historical, the partisan, making for "consciousness" insofar as the partisans tend to think of themselves as a "class" ("propaganda," "rhetoric," the "producing of effects"). As so stated, might not some of the issues dissolve? Might we not suspect that, unless men were brutes or gods (and Aristotle reminds us that they are not either) they must inevitably exemplify imagination and propaganda both? Or, to employ another trope: the nonpartisan, imaginative poet writes, "Beware, a storm approacheth." As propagandist he adds, "Go thou, and buy rubbers." The critics of the "proletarian" school (in tune with the *Zweck im Recht* analysis of law) have done us a service in recalling how often the poet, in this imperfect world, is in effect writing, "Go thou, and buy rubbers" when he is only *aware* of writing, "A storm approacheth." In the mere act of warning us what to beware of, he suggests the kind of measures to be taken.

There is also the problem of "leads." Philosophies are thinking machines—and like machines, they are frightfully "efficient." Their efficiency makes particularly for extremes in the placing of emphasis. And the proletarians, even the least intellectual of them, are philosophers. Their philosophy (the philosophy of the "class struggle") gives them "leads." And it is obvious that "leads" can on occasion *mislead*. By giving us so quickly and persuasively certain important clues as to the nature of "experience," they can incidentally prevent us from noticing other clues. In particular, those of their readers who follow other leads may sometimes find their work impoverished and "unreal," by reason of misplaced emphases. Indeed, insofar as the privileged can hire men to gore the ox for their benefit, the privileged may even afford to be above this despicable matter entirely. And they can resent the low-mindedness of those who would go back over a territory that they have happily left behind. I would answer them by quoting Goethe's admonition, that "no one walks unpunished beneath palms." Even were there no acute social issues, even if we had, here and now, an ideal "classless society," with communal property upon which to build a communality of morals (as in the monastic orders of the early Church) I should suspect that a people could forget the goring of the ox only at their peril. The neglect would be an act of pride; and pride is the basic sin not only of the Church, but of the universe. Pride: "that state of mind that goes before a fall"—the "assumption that one can walk unpunished beneath palms"—the "failure to remind oneself that all blessings are mixed blessings." The monastic orders were framed to guard against it; hence their great emphasis upon the *moral* effect of lowly occupations. A monastic order would deteriorate in proportion as the admonitions of its founder came to be forgotten, "alienation" arising as some men were "released" from too immediate concerns with the goring of the ox, which somehow got gored, while they could turn to nobler matters, and of a sudden you find the order corrupt.

As Mr. John Crowe Ransom has wisely admonished us, there is a disturbing contemporary tendency to imagine God after the analogy of central heating and dental anesthetics. He resents this cult of a deity that is merely a celestial version of "all modern conveniences." He has asked for a Jehovah, a God of wrath, a God *with thunder*. And I have paradoxically asked myself whether the "proletarian" school, for all its atheistic trappings, might come very close to meeting his requirements. Merely put "history" in place of "Jehovah"—and anger, vengeance, lamentation once again come to the fore. History, in the proletarian code, a just God, a jealous God, a wrathful God. Only at their peril can men violate its commandments. It rewards, with the rewards of a good conscience, those that give it strict obedience and glorify its prowess. But as for those that sin against it, attempting to maintain human laws in opposition to its laws, it wreaks its vengeance upon them, even unto the children of the third and fourth generation.

Thus, I should not advise one to take the atheistic trappings at their face value. Why be sidetracked if, by a mere shifting of vocabulary, a new word causes to live again a pattern of thought that had been obscured by an old word? The morality of toil was ingrained in Hebraicism. It renewed its vigor in Catholicism after the collapse of pagan Rome, an elegant world that pined away in proportion as its cultured elements became psychologically unemployed ("leisured"). But Catholicism in turn eventually ran into difficulties. Surely it is not an accident that the last monastic order before the collapse (the Franciscans), an order that just missed being anathematized as a heresy, attempted to counteract the new difficulties of work by making a vocation of the *mendicant* (somewhat as we today some-times attempt so to manipulate our fictions that unemployment itself can be turned into a profession). In keeping with the nostalgia and mystic vision of *Piers Plowman,* new vents for human effort were found through Protestantism (particularly in the new vein that could be tapped by the Calvinistic sanctions upon credit and investment). And when this solution in turn has floundered of its "inner contradictions," we find the morality of toil reborn in the emphases of socialism. It holds that there can be no leisure without decay. Were every material want to be satisfied, people could live as moral beings (without pride) only by developing *subtler* concepts of necessity. In a civilization of mechanical slaves, for instance, they might revert to Grecian concepts of effort. They might focus their attention upon the ultimate task, the development of the "perfect citizen" (shaped for the playing of his role as member of a collectivity). But that too would be toil—and, if the toil were avoided, the God of wrath, speaking through history, would once more pronounce his curse, and the proud architecture of the State would crumble.

It is for such good reasons, I think, that this new literary movement devotes particular attention to the poignancy of unemployment, and of employment under conditions of intolerable conflict. Turning to the works themselves, you will unquestionably find such subjects painfully overstressed. The strike, the lock-out, bad working conditions, the witting or unwitting agents of "exploitation," the physical and mental rigors of joblessness, the *organizing* of protest (whereby the forces of anger and anguish may not be allowed to follow their natural chaotic bent, but may be directed into rational, socially useful channels of expression)—a continual harping upon such grim themes is bothersome to us, insofar as we have been taught that we have a *right* to anesthesia. And this reviewer admits that, but for the nature of his task, he would not have read the book continuously, but would have turned to it now and then, wisely interspersing it with material more in the "glorification of the American girl" tradition. I know of one critic who, though avowedly "proletarian" in his sympathies, read the anthology while convalescing in a hospital, and developed such a "blockage" that he has not been able to review it at all. Lamentations may be more gratifying to write than to read.

Our resistance, particularly to the work of the less imaginative contributors, is justified for another reason. They are not able to "transcend" the partisan "leads" supplied by their philosophy. Their philosophy makes them quick to recognize a *propaganda situation,* and they proceed with great efficiency to build a work that emphasizes it. In fact, they become so intent upon the emphasizing of the *situation,* that they overlook the *humane* development of character. Their characters are formed in haphazard fashion, for the specific partisan purpose at hand, like the distortions of a political cartoonist. Hence, if the situation itself is burdensome to the reader, there may be nothing else in the work by which the writer can cajole him. One may hypothetically picture the two opposite procedures: that of the "partisan" writer, who begins by discovering a "propaganda situation," and proceeds to exploit it by inventing characters to fit; and in contrast, there is the "imaginative" writer, who might begin with an attachment to some very appealing character, and in the course of depicting him, might show him at work in some propaganda situation, such as the harboring of a labor leader hunted by vigilantes. Ultimately, there need be nothing at odds between the two approaches: an expression that is not truncated will encompass both. But if the partisan factor is emphasized with too much greed, it may lead to schematization of character, with nothing of appeal insofar as the situation itself lacks appeal.

An extreme instance of this is Philip Stevenson's story, "Death of a Century." Some of Stevenson's stories in the old *American Caravan,* prior to his "efficient" development of the partisan approach, were very appealing in the subtlety of their humaneness. But here he attempts to project, through an entire piece, a feeling people sometimes experience when seeing pictures and hearing stories of Rockefeller in extreme old age. He imagines a fabulously wealthy capitalist, now in his dotage, a living mummy surviving for a time after a successful revolution in the United States. Venomously, literal in his settling of scores, the author attempts to wreak symbolic vengeance upon his villain by picturing him as a victim of both revolution and old age. Not only is the result childishly repellent in the simplicity of its wish-fulfillments. It is so naïvely partisan that it defeats its purpose as partisanship. One grows indignant at the author's treatment of senility. In trying to discredit capitalism by identifying it with a decrepit old man, he quite unintentionally reminds us that no social change can remove the pathetic feebleness of age—and the more vengeful he becomes, the sorrier we feel for the scapegoat of his vengeance. Thus, the character is thin at best, and insofar as it takes on fullness, it does so at the expense of the propagandistic purpose.

There is a compensatory feature of the "propaganda situation" that should be noted, however. Whereas, in its overemphasis, it can serve as imaginative restriction, it does contribute one virtue to even the least pretentious contributions in the book. For I think that the strong sense of the propaganda situation is linked with the strong sense of an *audience* one gets when reading this anthology. This literature is written *to* people, or *for* people. It is *addressed*.

So much by way of introduction. The volume is compendious, and uneven. Yet perhaps we should single out for comment some of the more representative texts.

Robert Cantwell's story, "Hills Around Centralia," is a good example of a crucial propaganda situation embodied imaginatively. It is based upon the poignancy of the Crucifixion theme (the "benefactor" persecuted as "malefactor"). Irony of clashing moralities. The author "weights" his material propagandistically by showing us, first, the morality of the vigilantes in action, and then slowly widening our conception of the total scene by a sympathetic portrait of the strikers. Tactfully, he permits us to see how the interests of the vigilantes have led them to misinterpret the nature of a riot, while their grip upon the channels of education and publicity serves to shape "neutral" opinion in their favor. The two opposing worlds (of vigilantes and strikers) are eventually "synthesized" by a bridge device, being brought together when some impressionable boys, who had been bewilderedly subjected to the vigilante views, come upon two strikers hiding in the woods (overtones of the "little child shall lead them" theme). The author's choice of sides is made atop the ironic, the relativistic—hence, "propaganda" in the fullest sense, because profoundly humane. Strict "proletarian" morality could not be so "shifty." It would be pitted squarely against the enemy. But the farthest-reaching *propaganda* (as a device for appealing to the enemy, and not merely organizing his opposition by the goads of absolute antithesis) requires the more ambiguous talents of the diplomat (who talks to an alien camp in behalf of his own camp).

The excerpt from Jack Conroy's novel, *The Disinherited,* reveals upon analysis that the author, for all his superficial roughness, can be very sensitive in the delicacy of his formal progressions. For his tendentious situation, he draws upon our sympathies for a courageous, hard-working, but victimized mother. The "argument" falls into three parts: (1) we see the mother rejecting the thin-lipped charity that would separate her from her children; (2) we get an effectively ironic association when the son, resolving to be a "man," hears the other children playing "hide and seek," and yearns to join them; (3) the mother rigorously at toil. The chapter is rhetorically rounded off with something that might be called a coda. Apparently at a tangent, Conroy falls to telling of an incident unrelated to the matters at hand—and when he has finished, he suddenly reveals its application to his theme. It becomes a bitter device for rejecting "those canned Western Union greetings" for Mother's Day. If the reader is not moved by this turn, at once surprising and prepared, he is blessed with a tougher skin than is your present correspondent. Conroy evidently likes to think of himself as a "diamond in the rough" sort of writer; but the correctness of his form reveals a sense of propriety in the best sense of the word.

Ben Field's "Cow" is interesting as a problem in propaganda because of its vigorous attempt to combat anti-Semitism by destroying the stereotype image of the Jew and assembling a different cluster of traits in its stead. Perhaps he approaches his task a little too head on. Hence, those who respond strongly to the stereotype will tend to feel his portrait as "false," since his zeal for reconstruction gets him into the "statuesque" rather than the "humane." But its attainments may be felt despite its defects—and one must recognize the justice of its inclusion in a book of this kind, representing the attitudes of a group which, like the many religious bodies of the Hellenistic period, recruits its members by cutting on the bias across traditional distinctions of nationality and race.

Albert Halper's "Scab!" suffers from an O. Henry patness in the "well-made" conversion of the last two lines. But it makes one notable contribution in the search for propaganda situations. Halper adds this particular twist: he establishes his own point of view by showing a man who sins against it in spite of himself. He "weights" his material by giving a sympathetic plea for the strikebreaker while at the same time causing the strikebreaker to revolt against his own role. Obviously, such internal conflicts, that match external conflicts, provide a good opportunity for the dramatic—and Halper develops the possibilities with complexity, complexity enough in fact to have spared us the bluntness of the ending.

Albert Maltz's "Man on the Road" is a remarkable mixture of dream-magic and realistic shrewdness. The man with the glazed eyes, standing at the approach to the tunnel, conveys to us the overtones of the "pit," and of "living death." Yet the fact that the author built his ominous dreaming about a worker dying of silicosis (his politics prompting him to see the "news" in the West Virginia disaster without waiting for the story to "break" in our headlines) indicates how deep an author's enlistment in a practical cause may go. We observe how a writer may on occasion tie even his dreams to a party line.

I might close my reference to the story section by a mention of an excerpt, complete in itself, from Edwin Seaver's novel of white-collar workers, *The Company*. Seaver has evidently learned much from Sherwood Anderson, whose lyric mode of story-telling he applies to his idylls and laments of metropolitan life. He is particularly good at finding simple themes that suggest complex connotations. In some ways, the tendentious situation embodied in his portrait of Aarons places us strategically at the very "narrows" of the propaganda issue. Aarons works for a public relations counsel—and the public relations counsel is the proletarian propagandist in reverse. He is purely and simply the historic devil. For whereas (the proletarian propagandist would enter the region of overlap between) his group and the people for the purpose of enlisting the people *in behalf* of social change, the public relations counsel would work in this same marginal territory *to obstruct* social change. Hence the subtlety of the situation which Seaver economically depicts for us, as we see Aarons, with a revolutionary interest in this region of overlap, employed by a man whose business it is to manipulate this same region for reactionary purposes. We watch Aarons making himself at home in this schizoid state. We see him undermining the simple loyalty of the others in the office, until their self-cynicism impairs the convincingness of their copy, while Aarons has learned to harness his detestation. From the very violation of his own beliefs, he derives a perverse strength, and is finally commended by his boss in the presence of those whose confidence in themselves he has destroyed. The bowing of the head, the theme on which this brief story ends, is mutely eloquent.

I have considered the stories at some length, since they lend themselves particularly well to an analysis of the tactics underlying propagandist art. Turning to the poetry section, we note that the lyrics necessarily possess, in their *epistolary, polemic* ingredient, a level of relevance beneath which they cannot sink. There are such incidents as May Day, the burning of the books, the execution of Sacco and Vanzetti to be commemorated; there is a definite need of encouragement to equip one for the intricacies of "class struggle"—hence the strongly recitative, oratorical note that pervades this form, a form rapidly becoming almost bereft of gravitational pull. To borrow a word from capitalism, we may note that there is a "market" for occasional verse, devotional verse, and the ritualization of dogma. These poets are at the stage where Commodianus was in the upbuilding of Catholic poetry. One feels behind them the pressure and sincerity of hunger (sometimes hunger literally, more often hunger in its wider, metaphorical aspects). Much of this verse is not written merely for the eye, or even for the ear, but for the mouth. Thus, though most of these atheistic poets would be scandalized at the thought, I should say that their verse is primarily concerned, in secular guise, with the mimetics of prayer. For prayer, we are told by the shrewdest of our naturalistic explainers-away derives the force of its appeal from the first experiences of childhood when the child learns "word magic," the influencing of reality by speech (as when it summons its nurse by calling for her). Its obverse is the anathema. So we get here the building of character by the "magical" devices of petition, plaint, and curse.

Let me mention, "among those present," such pieces as: Kenneth Fearing's three declamatory poems, an amalgam of politics and sentiment. Robert Gessner's "Cross of Flame," vigorously realizing for us the incidents before the Reichstag fire. Michael Gold's "A Strange Funeral in Braddock" ("listen to the story of a strange American funeral"); and his "Examples of Worker Correspondence" suggest good possibilities, if the poet can resist the temptation to convert his wise lameness into a mannerism. Horace Gregory's "Dempsey, Dempsey," employing for polemic purposes the psychoanalytic account of the "identification" process. Alfred Hayes' "In a Coffee Pot," interesting for its transformation from the theme of *one man's unemployment* to the theme of *organized group resistance*, an "extension device" also well utilized in Langston Hughes' "Ballad of Lenin." James Neugass' "Thalassa, Thalassa" (a serviceable "idea," as he incongruously draws upon our connotations of ancient Greece when celebrating a strike of Greek freighters at Buenos Aires, though it is far better as an invention than in its working out). Kenneth Patchen's "Joe Hill Listens to the Praying," a work conducted on three levels: the sermon, Joe Hill, the poet's comments. Edwin Rolfe's "Unit Assignment," a homely but accurate account of an incident in the spreading of the doctrine. Muriel Rukeyser's "City of Monuments," the imaginative opposing of tomb and sprout. Isidor Schneider's "Portrait of a False Revolutionist" ("He'll chant red song/like a cricket all day long")—also one should note his use of the Brecht-Eisler "you must be ready to take over" theme in "To the Museums." The middle class writer's concern with scruples, in Genevieve Taggard's "Life of the Mind, 1933" and "Interior." Don West's "Southern Lullaby" (which Mr. Brooks had condemned for its sentimentality, an unfavorable diagnosis one could rephrase favorably, or part-favorably, by saying that the author undertakes the strategic feat of incongruously introducing politics into the least political of themes). And two anonymous

Negro pieces, which well illustrate how the moods of the spiritual can be drawn upon for "modern" purposes.

The "reportage" section is excellent. Perhaps it maintains the highest average of quality in the whole anthology. Nor is this an accident. I sometimes wonder whether, when Communists speak of "reality," they mean purely and simply "news." And there is a notable accuracy here. The early bards were hardly more than news peddlers. Later, when the bourgeois order became established, the resistance to the democratization of news was stubborn and powerful (since private access to news gave one a distinct commercial advantage). And Communists feel, of course, that "the news" is still being tampered with, to an extent that prevents people from seeing, in the proper proportions, the "realities" of the historic process now under way. Each of these eight items has much to recommend it. I should mention in particular the strange circumstantiality of Meridel Le Sueur's "I Was Marching." It has an almost mystical cast, that may result from the hysterical suppression of terror. Nor can one read Agnes Smedley's "The Fall of Shangpo" without being fascinated. She carefully depicts the dreadful upheavals of the human mind as archaic ways of thought are jammed brutally into new situations. John Mullen's "Mushrooms in the Factory" is brief, with a surprising touch of fancy in its ingenious way of revealing the workers' attachment to their place of work despite the many good reasons for alienation. Perhaps John L. Spivak's "A Letter to the President" is the most vulnerable article in this section. Spivak learned his trade doing "sob sister" work for MacFadden. He has brilliance, and the events he is describing make an authentic claim upon our sympathies—but it would take no princess to be disturbed by the pea of his early training beneath the twenty mattresses of his politics.

The inclusion of Clifford Odets' "Waiting for Lefty" among the plays would be enough to make the drama section valuable. I spoke earlier of the tendency to *begin* with propaganda situations and work towards character. This method of construction is more natural to the dramatist—and in "Waiting for Lefty" it flowers. Odets builds characters with strict reference to their functional necessity; his efficiency is sometimes astounding. This functional or formal emphasis prompts him to make unexpected discoveries. When the crooked labor leader says, for instance, that it is "only an hour's ride on the train" to Philadelphia, a voice pipes up: "Two hours"—and these simple words carry an enormous load. They are *eloquent* in their place, because they are rich with promise. In their trivial stubbornness, they show you which way the arrows are pointing. You are amused—and there is a strong promise that your attitude of vengefulness towards the crooks will subsequently be permitted fuller expression.

Marxism is above all an inducement to drama. It is a dramatic theory of history, for it clearly and unmistakably names the vessels of good and evil (you can't make good drama without the assistance of a villain in goading forward the plot). It is loquacious, litigious, rhetorical. In our theatres at least, the revolution has already taken place, as the old hack producers of the "give the public what it wants" school had already brought on the fatal crisis in culture, darkening one house after another by their inability to have the least notion as to what the public wants. In addition to full-sized plays, requiring considerable commercial organization, there are many short skits being produced without scenery, in political gatherings of one sort or another. At their poorest, they merely confirm the audience's prejudices, as a war play in war times. But often they "transcend" these simpler requirements, attaining a wider comic or tragic scope—and there is no reason why, as audiences develop, the talent they enlist should not develop also.

As for the specific works in this collection: Odets' "Waiting for Lefty" and Alfred Kreymborg's "America, America!" (somewhat in the manner of a morality play) will probably appeal best when read, though all the pieces can disclose virtues to those who also watch for *theatric* possibilities.

I agree with Newton Arvin that the section on criticism seems least developed. The dramatic invitation to "make a choice" may lead the critic to make his choice too soon. Here enters the problem of "suspended judgment," as against the invitation to the dramatics of invective. In fact, if one reads Michael Gold's "Wilder: Prophet of the Genteel Christ" purely as a fiction, he is likely to enjoy it much better. I could even imagine Wilder enjoying it, if he were able to think of it as a Cicero thundering against a Catiline. And in "Eagle Orator," Malcolm Cowley administers very deft punishment to Paul Engle's earlier work, "American Song." For criticism of a non-pyrotechnic nature, we should signalize Edwin Berry Burgum's appreciation of Spender, Auden, and Lewis, written from the standpoint of their serviceability in shaping revolutionary attitudes. And the essay by the younger critics, William Phillips and Philip Rahv, bears testimony that they understand the complexity and indirectness involved in the "imaginative assimilation of political content." Indeed, I believe that their reservations would require them, editors of the Communist *Partisan Review,* to be less friendly towards some of the political matter in this anthology than I have been. We should also include here a reference to Joseph Freeman's introduction which, though prolix and unnecessarily defensive, contains many acute formulations.

In conclusion: As one particularly interested in the *processes* of literary appeal, I have generally tended to consider the volume from this standpoint. I have been vague about "absolute" tests of excellence, for I frankly do not know what such tests might be. Particularly in works of a controversial nature, the imponderabilia of emotional bias strongly influence our aesthetic judgments. Hence, in dealing with a book of this sort, I thought it better to place the emphasis upon the matter of functions, which are neutral, available to anyone, like a theory of ballistics. But in the course of discussing processes, I have also found it necessary to touch somewhat upon the "way of life" that gives them meaning.

For the anthology does represent a way of life—and in this congregational feature lies the power and the promise of the "proletarian" movement as a contribution to our culture. In this movement, there is the customary high percentage of unexalted moments, as regards the field of literary representation, and even more so as regards the field of practical relationships. But taking what we have, I think we may see how the "proletarian" sort of emphases and admonitions can provide a lasting and essential stimulus to the formation of the national "consciousness."

# Imaginary Lines

*We Have Always Lived in the Castle* by Shirley Jackson. Viking
*The New Leader*, December 1962, 20–22

Once at the planetarium, while the show was on, I fell into a doze, or a daze, leaning back comfortably, peering into the artificial starry cloudlessness. Words were issuing from some indeterminate place in the man-made night. And as I listened half-asleep, my eyes glazed but not closed, of a sudden there flashed across the sky great white arcs, with numbers. The apparition caused a brief interval of confusion in my mind: between the perceiving of these startlingly sharp lines and the recognition that they were not a prodigious happening in the real sky, but a mere human invention to illustrate the meridians which can be theoretically drawn as a means of specifying longitude. In that unbalanced interval, I experienced a moment of truly apocalyptic terror.

And, without the fright, there is a somewhat related painting by Charles Demuth. It represents a calm bunching of angled roofs and a belfry. But for present purposes, the main point is: The sky is filled with arbitrary lines that repeat the forms of the architecture.

Both of these examples might help define the particular quality of Shirley Jackson's imagination, most notably her ways of shifting between the real and the fancied. It is a trick on which she has worked out many variants. And it is managed with especially appealing success in her piece of fanciful realism, *We Have Always Lived in the Castle,* a story told in a style as limpid as brooks used to be, before the days of progress.

This novel is exceptionally well built as regards the ways in which the characters serve to bring out the poetic functions of one another. The younger sister (Mary Katherine, "Merricat") bristles with odd judgments and intolerant discriminations (in keeping with Miss Jackson's likings for the lore of demonology). By contrast, the elder sister, Constance, becomes wholly believable in her patient simplicity. She is so prompt in helpfulness she never gets to the stage of recrimination, except when she blames herself.

The contrast is heightened ironically by the character of Uncle Julian, who is invalid to the extent of childishness, and who takes the maternal Constance's constant attention as a matter of course, even while also taking it for granted that she was guilty of the crime for which she had been tried and acquitted. (It is a judgment in which many of the neighbors concur, so that Constance's virtue is even somewhat like that of a savior crucified between thieves, though you can depend upon it that, in a Shirley Jackson character, any traits on the "saintly" side will have their special twists.)

In the midst of all the turmoil, something like high comedy arises from the ingenious notion of having Uncle Julian at work collecting data on the crime, while at the same time his mind wanders, so that, at particularly tense moments in the unfolding of the plot, he forgets which character is which, and falls into outbursts of righteous indignation that are quite irrelevant.

Against all three of these inmates in the "Castle" there is Cousin Charles, a fairly ordinary fellow whose average nature in this ingeniously tangled setting makes him almost heinous. We also tend to see the story largely through the eyes of Merricat, who is outstanding in Shirley Jackson's catalogue of little demons, and who rounds out the pattern by her intuitive notions about Cousin Charles as "'demon" and "ghost." The villagers perform dynamic roles in the development, too—nor should we forget Jonas, Merricat's cat, whose role as a person serves well, again and again, to keep the pot of the narrative aboiling.

One could not here discuss in detail the handling of the plot itself without somewhat spoiling the story for those readers who prefer to find out such things for themselves. But some observations can be noted. Except for a bit of padding, the story is told with perfect mastery, particularly in the way the interrelationships among the cluster of characters is handled.

The best kinds of "surprise" and "suspense" are those that one experiences when *re*-reading a book. The appeal of a story is soundest if it does not depend for its effect upon the reader's sheer ignorance of the outcome. In the case of the narrative of these odd inmates in what becomes a very run-down "Castle," we could strike this compromise:

For those who want the one-time kind of surprise and suspense (the book that is to be used once and thrown away), this story has the twist that can fully meet their demands. It is a story built around the reminiscing on a crime, the arsenic poisoning of several people (plus, we should note in the interests of imagery, much incidental concern with poison mushrooms). But the essential attitudes toward this crime are built up so integrally, the reader's ultimate interest is not confined to "who dun it" curiosity: rather, the book's best appeal is grounded in the fact that, when the disclosure comes, it is made to mesh perfectly with the salient traits of the characters. This is a more permanent advantage.

The novel's virtues, then, in sum: An exceptionally well-assorted bouquet of characters; a fanciful ending built out of quite *real* beginnings; a disclosure that, because of its relation to the kind of essence we find in characters, can go on being a disclosure after you know of it. (Ibsen is, to my mind, the greatest master of this economic test of form.) As for possible nays: The book, though not long, is a bit expanded beyond necessity; and the expansions tend to involve sheerly internal modes of repetition rather than references to life in general. But decidedly, the ayes have it.

The quality of Shirley Jackson's imagination can be most readily illustrated by comparing and contrasting this newest work with her well-known story, "The Lottery." Lurking in ordinary human sociality there is always a kind of embarrassment, insofar as the "villagers'" ways are not the ways of the writer's dreaming, storytelling self. Accordingly, when the writer "extrapolates" from this situation and its modes of estrangement, thoroughly tracking down the implications of it by drawing imaginary lines that go in the same direction but much farther, conditions are set to conceive of someone victimized by an unresolvable malaise. Thus, through the "freedom of the imagination," the embarrassments that are but lurking in ordinary social situations can be translated into terms of an excess (as when, in "The Lottery," the "villagers" meet in everyday cordiality to choose by lot from among their numbers a scapegoat whom they stone to death).

In the present, longer story, the theme of such implicit estrangement is worked out much more fully, and with much greater psychological depth (for the remarkable thing about this book is that beneath its apparent simplicity there is an exceptional range of subtlety and complexity). Merricat's superstitious magic is a kind of improvised protocol, to make up for the fact that savages so often institutionalize the symbolic treatment of awkward personal relationships which the "civilized" do not even know exist.

Indeed, the contemporary "esthetic" cult of primitive ritual may center largely in the need of poets and storytellers to improvise protocols for the handling of troublesome situations that are not otherwise recognized, situations that we "don't have a word for," but that go on recurring and plaguing us nonetheless. Shirley Jackson's playful recourse to the imagery of estrangement, the primitive and the infantile should best be thought of thus; it is the fanciful expansion of problems as realistically local to the age as bridge clubs and Westchester County.

If you keep "The Lottery" in mind, in reading the book you will see what an interesting step this new plot takes. It works out a system of moral accountancy whereby the menacing principle of the "villagers" becomes transformed into a friendly principle, and in such ways that the "resolution" builds up a kind of imaginary womb-heaven, where one's needs are taken care of by the friendly principle, without effort on one's own part.

The name of the problematical family in the book is the "Blackwoods." So while you read you might on the side note each time the words "black" or "wood" appear, reminiscent of the fatal role of the black wooden box in "The Lottery." When you put all these references together, I think you will see how that very name ambiguously epitomizes the nature of the plot. And, incidentally, in tracking down just those two words, in watching how they tie things up, you will discover for yourself the astounding kind of complexity implicit in the imaginary lines of this charming book's apparent simplicity.

# Drama

*Well, a dramatist is a professional gambler. He prefers playing with loaded dice.*

*—The Philosophy of Literary Form* (336)

# Rugged Portraiture

*Rubicon* or *The Strikebreaker* [film], dir. by Vladimir Vainshtok
*The New Masses*, April 1934

The story of a marine worker's conversion to sympathy with the Soviet way of life. The Rubicon to be crossed is the distinction between Bill Parker as a strikebreaker and Bill Parker as a solid member of his class. The parallelisms, contrasting "before" and "after," suggest somewhat the balance-sheet pattern of Thomas Mann's early story, *Tonio Kröger*, though the material is of course profoundly different. In Mann's story the two contrasted attitudes are Bohemian and bourgeois; in *Rubicon* they draw the contrast between the worker "on his own" and the worker in his group.

Bill Parker is a stoker who hates his job and finds satisfaction only in the periods of compensatory dissipation which are open to him when his ship is in port. We have here, in outline, the Customary Puritanic swing between drudgery and distraction characteristic of a man whose work lacks group motivation. In any event; Bill has nothing but the freedom of the port town to look forward to. Hence, when he arrives at Havana during a coalheavers' strike, and is told by the captain that he cannot go ashore "until the boat is coaled, he promptly sets to work with some of the other men heaving the coal into the bunkers. Later we see him ashore, as the reward of his labors. He meets the captain, drunk in a dive—and when the captain taunts him, they get into a fight, with the result that the stoker loses his job and is blacklisted. However, there is a Soviet boat in the harbor—a new hand is needed, and Bill is accepted for the job, the Soviet captain having no objection to a blacklisted man.

In the course of his brawls, Bill had defended himself with a horseshoe. He keeps this horseshoe as a trophy. It becomes the fulcrum of the plot in this wise: On reaching Leningrad, Bill goes to live in an international home for sailors, where he fraternizes with Communist workers and becomes imbued with their attitudes. He has also come into contact with a capitalist lumberman who employs him as an assistant. This lumberman attempts to sabotage a Soviet mill, since he will profit by a time-clause in his contract if delivery is delayed—but Bill recognizes his horseshoe as the implement that did the wrecking, and he exposes his employer.

For contrasted parallels, we have such events as the gluttonous eating of the men on the first ship vs. the gusty eating of those On the Soviet boat; the dissipations under the one way of life vs. the activities in education and sport under the other; dismal living quarters vs. homelike living quarters—and, over all, the horseshoe.

The play has many of those shots of machinery in motion, viewed from peculiar angles and in abrupt sequences, at which the Soviet photographers are particular apt. Again, there are several closeups of individual workers, a tradition of rugged portraiture to which Soviet films have brought a new understanding. There are some quiet skies that are noteworthy, brief studies of turbulent water, and a few very appealing Sheeler-like stills that look up into the well distributed lines of a ship's rigging.

# Field Work in Bohemia

*This Room and This Gin and These Sandwiches* by Edmund Wilson. The New Republic
*The Nation*, July 1937, 133–134

There are the people who work with materials: farmers, men in factories and on construction. There are the people who carry on the services that coordinate these acts: trainmen, telegraph operators, shipping hands. There are the people who keep the books involved in the productive and distributive pattern: the accountants, stenographers, filing clerks. There are the people who trade in the symbols by which the books are kept: bankers, financiers, speculators, promoters, business men. There are the people who coach the responses to these symbols: educators, publicists, journalists, editors, politicians. There are the "contradictions": people out of jobs, business men crippled by other business men, monopolists fighting monopolists, racketeers, gangsters, radical propagandists.

And there is a special, somewhat abstract, highly mobile group of people who may, with varying degrees of success, live off the total muddle. These are in part the people with income, and the entertainers, the artists. Materially they are rewarded, or hope to be. Occasionally they may "go away" to some earthy spot in search of, and sometimes in temporary discovery of, an idyll. When congregating they can build up a somewhat isolated world, with its own values, its own scandals, its own concepts of obligation, trial, heroism, and defeat. They are *on the fringes*—the fringes of political radicalism, of philosophy, of wisdom, of service, of the soil, of ecstasy and drought, of religion, of moralization and demoralization. They make up the stratum of life depicted in Wilson's three clever, engrossing, and moralistic plays.

The steam locomotive is said to be a very inefficient machine; but it is the essence of sound performance as compared with the operations of contemporary society—yet the social plant jerks along somehow, and while it continues it can manage to support a certain percentage of people in this mobile, abstract way of life, with their peculiar kind of secular "other-worldliness."

In particular it did so during the war and post-war periods of inflation. And Wilson here gives us a vigorous and imaginative version of this way.

The three plays are points that plot a curve. In the first, "The Crime in the Whistler Room," we get a mixture of realism and fantasy serving as the rites of initiation. It is a ritual of rebirth, a shift in perspective exemplifying in imaginative terms the following proposition: If one abandons one mode of living for another, and the two seem sufficiently at odds, one can call the second mode "life" only by feeling that the earlier mode was "death." Hence we watch a preparation for bohemian "life" in contrast with a respectable family who act like corpses. The heroine is the Beatrice who guides the hero on his journey—and she helps a lot through being got by him with child, though he appears in some of the fantastic scenes as a werewolf.

In the second play, "A Winter in Beech Street," we are wholly within this special world. I doubt whether any one else will catch as well as Wilson does here the norms of sociality that developed about the theater projects of the Provincetown Players as the American center of bohemian protest. The inventiveness of the dialogue is very appealing; one is sometimes startled out of his engrossment at the sudden realization that it is even depicting *delirium tremens* joyously.

In the third, "Beppo and Beth," we come closest to attempts at finding a way out. And after a scene of violently alcoholic protest against the void lurking beneath alcohol, with one suicide stopped only by another attempted suicide, we end:

> BEPPO: We'll get married again tomorrow and we'll take the first boat to Mexico!
>
> BETH: Why Mexico!
>
> BEPPO: Because Mexico's the place where they make those little pottery animals!
>
> BETH: You broke the little bank just now when you pulled the tapestry down.
>
> BEPPO: I know; I want to get a new one! The train to Mexico City will be our P. L. M. Express! We'll revive the old rebellion!
>
> BETH: You'd better pick up those pennies: we'll need them!

Not forgetting Chang and Chung, the Chinese servants, who had patiently, at intervals, explained to Beppo the Marxist theories of capitalist decay, and did it very well, with what looks like a good stage effect, in the midst of all the hubbub and the antics.

The talent and the incongruities of bohemianism are conveyed in lines that are bright and limpid. The void is made tremendously real, all the more so since the patter that conceals the void is given with verve. "Well, we may not have got the whole of everything," says Sally of the Beech Street Players in a moment of inventory, "but we've got something very precious at this moment—we've got this room and this gin and these sandwiches, and we've got each other's very agreeable company!" Or, as another character who has invented a new religion puts it: "All the religions of the past have either mortified the flesh in the interests of the spirit or have stinted the spirit in the interests of the flesh: and this is the first religion in history that has promoted the highest development of the spirit and at the same time facilitated the ecstasies of the flesh!"

If one would see Murger's world again, shown with an accuracy and taste for comedy that Murger's sentimentalizing made him incapable of, one should read these plays. And if one feels moralistic, he can discern on every page the pressure of the money economy behind the antics.

# By Ice, Fire or Decay?

*Paradise Lost: A Play in Three Acts* by Clifford Odets. Random House
*The New Republic* 86. April 1936. Also in *The Philosophy of Literary Form*

After having been led, by the explicitly formulated objections of some dissenters, to expect that I would dislike Odets' "Paradise Lost," I finally went to see it, and liked it enormously. I even found that the scandalous number of entrances and exits did not bother me, except in a few instances where the action was not paralleled by a similar movement in the lines themselves. And though I had in the past complained against propagandists who compromised their cause by the depiction of people not worth saving, and had been led to believe that Odets transgressed on this score, I found on the contrary that the characters, for all their ills, possessed the ingredients of humanity necessary for making us sympathetic to their disasters. To me there was nothing arbitrary about the prophetic rebirth in Leo's final speech. And as I had witnessed, not pedestrian realism, but the idealizations of an expert stylist, I carried away something of the *exhilaration* that good art gives us when, by the ingratiations of style, it enables us to contemplate even abhorrent things with calmness.

The opportunity to examine the play in print has even heightened my admiration, by revealing the subtlety, complexity and depths of the internal adjustments. For all his conscious symbolism, the author has not merely pieced together a modern allegory. His work seems to embody ritualistic processes that he himself was not specifically concerned with—and I want to discuss them briefly.

At the close of Act I, as the characters listen to Pearl playing the piano upstairs, Gus says: "And when the last day comes—by ice or fire—she'll be up there playin' away." I consider this the "informing" line of the play. "By ice or fire." It is interesting that, in *The Partisan Review,* James T. Farrell, who wrote a book called *Judgment Day,* should have objected to a work having this eschatological theme as its point of departure. But Farrell is in the stage of pure antithesis, turning his old Catholicism upside down—and hence preferring, for the time at least, the simple, hard-boiled reversal of his religious past. Odets may be more complex, admitting elements that Farrell could not admit without a corresponding expansion of his esthetic frame. Farrell's resistance is justified on the grounds of self-preservation, rather than as a mature act of critical appraisal.

Along with the "ice or fire" epigram, I should note the significant credo of Pike who, within the conditions of the play, comes nearest to the "proletarian" philosophy: "I'm sayin' the smell of decay may sometimes be a sweet smell." And taking these two passages as seminal, I should say that the play deals with three modes of "redemption"—redemption by ice, fire or decay—and finally chooses the third. Like certain ancient heresies, it pictures the "good" arising from the complete excess of the "bad," as the new growth sprouts from the rotting of the seed.

The first act rejects "redemption by ice." In its simplest objectivization, we find the situation placed before our eyes in the form of Ben's statue on the stage. The friends, Ben and Kewpie, had been under ice together; they had been skating with a third boy, when the ice broke and their friend had drowned. The spell of this "life-in-death" is still upon them. As Ben formulates it later: "We're still under ice, you and me—we never escaped!" And again: "'Did we die there?' I keep asking myself, 'or are we living?' " The first act establishes this situation—and Acts II and III show us the author's attempts to shape a magic incantation whereby the spell is broken.

Act II, by my analysis, considers and rejects "redemption by fire." It is in this way that I would locate the symbolic element underlying the remarkable realism of Mr. May, the professional firebug. Leo refuses to accept his impotent partner Sam's proposal that they solve their financial troubles by employing this man. But Pike, the proletarian furnace tender (who would thaw the ice), had proclaimed his belief in "redemption by decay." He is thus the bridge between Sam's fire solution and Leo's rebirth from decay. And we complete the pattern in the third act where, as the process of decay is finished, Leo's prophecy of rebirth sprouts from the rotted grain, and the curtain descends.

I might note other features of the internal organization. Thus, Pike's mere entrance at times foreshadows the "fatality" of the plot. For he knocks at the door (1) just as Julie has said, "When the time comes—" (2) when Gus has said he would like to "go far away to the South Sea islands and eat coconuts," and (3) when, Clara having asked "Is it the end?" Leo has answered, "Not yet." At these crucial moments, Pike's message is in the offing. But whereas the message remains the same throughout the play, Leo (the "father") must assimilate it in his own way, as he does by conscientiously completing the symbolism of the rotting grain. (The same basic pattern of thought may be seen in the "conscientious corruption" of Andre Gide, who has significantly entitled his autobiography "*Si le grain ne meurt.*")

Approached from this angle, Krutch's doubts as to the play's statistical value (its actuarial truth as a survey of the bourgeoisie) may seem less relevant. If a poet happens to have the sort of imagination that revivifies an old heresy in modern details, how would he go about it to put this imaginative pattern into objective, dramatic form? At other times, he might have externalized the pattern as a struggle between angels and demons, or between Indians and settlers, or between patriot and foe, or in the "war of the sexes," etc. At present, in keeping with current emphasis, he may symbolize it with relation to an interpretation of historic trends, where its "prophetic" truth is enough. Incidentally, the *subjective* origin of the pattern need not impair the *objective* validity of the symbols used. If the bourgeoisie is oppressed by loss of certainty, one may have many good objective reasons for externalizing the pattern of his imagination in this form, particularly as the pattern itself may have been established in the individual poet precisely by the effects of the same frustrating process.

Our approach also may have bearing upon the comments of Stanley Burnshaw, who observed in *The New Masses* that the play erred as political strategy. Inasmuch as the proletariat must expect the petty bourgeoisie to become its allies, he asks, how could people so decayed have the vitality to assist in the tremendous work of establishing a new order? This objection is justified only if one does not believe in the Odets formula for redemption, remembering only the ash and not the Phoenix that arises from the ash. But if one follows the Odets ritual to the end, the objection is weakened. By the Marxist formula, the complete "proletarian" would require no process of rebirth. He would grow up with his morality. He and it would be one. But the bourgeois would have to "come over," dropping the morality that made him and taking another in its place. Converting the situation into drama, we should require rebirth, the ritualistic changing of identity, rather than merely a superficial matter of climbing off one band-wagon and climbing on another. And we should require the dramatist to deepen and broaden the process as greatly as possible.

Thus, I question whether we can appreciate the play by a simple "scientific" test of its truth, as in Farrell's naturalistic bias, Krutch's census-taking requirements or Burnshaw's question of united-front tactics. A more integral test is to be found, I submit, in a consideration of the play as ritual. And those who respond to its ritual will be enabled to entertain drastic developments, without drawing simply upon a masochistic desire to be punished.

# Criticism of Poetry

*Once when I was analyzing the symbolism of sun and moon in Coleridge's poem, 'The Ancient Mariner,' a student raised this objection: 'I'm tired of hearing about the symbolic sun in poems, I want a poem that has the real sun in it.'*

*Answer: If anybody ever turns up with a poem that has the real sun in it, you'd better be about ninety-three million miles away. We were having a hot summer as it was, and I certainly didn't want anyone bringing the real sun into the classroom.*

—The Rhetoric of Religion (9)

# Van Wyck Brooks in Transition?

*Emerson and Others* by Van Wyck Brooks. E. P. Dutton and Company
*The Dial,* January 1928, 56–59

Mr. Brooks's recent volume comprises eight essays, six monographs on Emerson, John Butler Yeats, Randolph Bourne, Bierce, Melville, and Upton Sinclair, and two general essays on the "soil" of art. All of them bear more or less directly on a matter which has always been a primary concern with this author: the causal relationship between artist and environment. The issue, when one attempts to schematize Mr. Brooks's exhortations and conclusions, appears to have been variously met. At times he would seem to be asking that artists be accorded greater categorical respect than they now receive; but again, as in his *Amor Fati,* he suggests that too much opportunity to improve one's standard of living may be disastrous to art, that the artist should in his devotion to art become somewhat of a pariah, "that the ancient tag about 'the world forgetting, by the world forgot' really states the first principle of the conservation of energy in the literary life." Or again, he seems on some occasions to be employing the psychoanalytic technique to account for failure and at others to disclose failure where we had assumed success.

On the whole, I doubt whether Mr. Brooks ever found for his key problem any consistent solution, though in the course of his preoccupation with it he has put forth many very suggestive alternatives. The core of this attitude seems to have centered in the concept of the artist's "muse." If the inspirational aspect of art is stressed in an irreligious era—as it was in the "Seven Arts tradition"—the afflatus which was once infused into the artist from on high must now be derived from a secular source, in this case the environment. Whereupon, a good line redounds to the credit of the nation and a bad line is the fault of one's neighbors—and since the lines are preponderantly bad, the critic has much cause to accuse his countrymen. But strangely enough, in stressing the intimate connection between the artist and the race, the tendency to brand the race as unworthy coexists with the *vox populi vox dei* attitude, so that the artist seems at times to be judged a victim through expressing his environment, and at others through failing to do so. The whole antinomy being investigated along psychoanalytic lines.

In the "Emerson: Six Episodes" which opens the present work, and which was obviously the last written of all the essays published here, Mr. Brooks has advanced into a less doctrinaire territory. Indeed, the author has, to my knowledge, here given us the first "stream-of-consciousness" biography. By skilfully culling and arranging the entries in Emerson's journals, he has produced a subjective record corresponding to those workings of the busy tentative brain which we find exemplified in such writers as Joyce, Dorothy Richardson, Virginia Woolf, and Gertrude Stein, where the intelligence is brought to bear upon the processes of perception rather than upon those of ratiocination. Here we see not the transcendentalist (an aspect of Emerson which concerns us little at the present time) but the experimental mind, reasoning on a basis of bodily sensation, and respectful of its excursions. Emerson certainly does not gain in dignity by such treatment, but he is made familiar, and thus contemporary. To the "sensitive plant," which is at once the symbol and reduction to absurdity of nineteenth-century romanticism, there is here added a prompt matching of sensation with ideation. With each veering of mood, another code struggles to develop. It is a mode of thinking implicit in the change from the Cartesian *cogito, ergo sum* to the post-Kantian *volo, ergo sum* as a proof of existence.

In the "Notes on Herman Melville," though they deal with a case which Mr. Brooks defines as "the suffocation of a mighty genius in a social vacuum," we frequently and gratifyingly lose track of this theme through the obtrusion of another: the spirited admiration which the author feels for *Moby Dick*. In this essay Mr. Brooks is at his best in depicting the "trials" of the artist. And we feel for once, though perhaps the author may not have expressly wished it, that the artist's work can claim a certain priority over his environmental difficulties, that his art is the reflection of the temper by which his practical problems will be determined and met. One feels, that is, not that *Moby Dick* was written by Melville's contemporaries, but that the man who could (a) write *Moby Dick* would (b) conduct his life as he did. Such an attitude would be "non-psychoanalytic." At least, it would cancel psychoanalytic causality by stressing the consistency between character, art, and practical activities, so that both art and "life" are seen as parallel modes (each within its own terms) of the same mentality. In any case, *Moby Dick* is certainly not explained here as a "social result," but seems rather to be admired as the adequate and uncompromising expression of Melville's faculties.

In a brief prefatory note, Mr. Brooks says of *The Literary Life in America* that it contains "many statements that are certainly less true now than they were when they were written." But on the whole, the contention of the chapter (that American society is more bent upon the development of practical utility than of aesthetic receptivity) seems to be as "true" now as it ever was. At least, we fervently hope so.

The only reason I could imagine for failing to choose utility at the expense of aesthetic receptivity would be the belief that they need not be opposed to each other. When even our most responsible and capable artists chose to consider aesthetic refinement in terms of sickliness, one could hardly resent the rather Spartan distrust of art which the *bourgeois* adopted as a consequence. The aesthetic attitude, it seems to me, is defensible only if it can be advocated as a more complex form of utility. (Religion, for instance, insofar as it assists in the forming of a set of moral imperatives, is useful. "Religiosity," an attitude without theological dogma, is "aesthetic." It would be as useful a social force as religion, but religion in the past has proved simpler and more practical as a method of procuring the required minimum of order. But the value of the practical religion is limited, and the whole conditioning is so unpliant that, when established on this plane, it can like patriotism be easily converted to anti-social ends. The aesthetic "religiosity" at such times proves more practical, because more complex and thus more pliant. The "aesthetic" might thus be defined as an attempt—in terms of play, as in the "preparations" of childhood—to extend the biological adequacy of both the individual and the group.)

We suspect that the almost mechanical antinomy between "business" and "art," so pronounced a few years ago, was at bottom an economic matter, involving a political opposition which has been allowed temporarily to languish under the comparative quiescence of labor disturbances and jingoism. The "intellectual," perhaps as a Tolstoyan importation, had assumed a fraternity with the American "worker and peasant" which existed only insofar as they might have certain enmities in common. Once this negative bond had weakened, the many divergencies between the two groups were quick to assert themselves. Meanwhile the *bourgeois,* being rich, and generally virtuous, finds it impossible to occupy his time between the hours of five and twelve with anything but art, so that "expression" becomes a major industry. (Which it always was; but now, in the general prosperity, there are crumbs even for the most "select" artists—the whole scale being raised—and the *élite* are content to let Harold Bell Wright banquet if only the same conditions permit them to lunch. And thus, in Europe, we find art distrusted on the grounds that art and *bourgeoisie* are synonymous!) Further, the class which voiced such strong objections against the *bourgeoisie* were pledged by the very framing of these objections to avoid all standardized motions, and would thus have to deny themselves the right of repeating over a protracted period any slogan, even if it embodied their profoundest convictions, so that the attitude of "protest" could subside without necessarily indicating that the situation had altered correspondingly. And "less true" may only mean "less in demand."

Nor does the other aspect of his "indictment" ("the blighted career, the arrested career, the diverted career are, with us, the rule") seem any less "true." Did not the editors of this very magazine, but a few months back, editorially look in vain not for the important writers which Mr. Brooks had hoped for, but merely for "interesting" writers? Yet somehow the morale behind it all has changed—and hope and hopelessness as to the future seem to have vanished together. Artists are now well documented in their predicaments which, like prolonged plagues, though they may continue to destroy, finally cease to dismay. Whereas an editor, through a sense of justice, may deplore the circumambient mediocrity, a writer, through a sense of embarrassment, must refrain from doing so. In such plaints, for him, there is no longer catharsis. The problem has been reduced to doggedly simple terms: to write as best he may, not as the result of an ancestral hunger after izzat, nor as the expression of any driving need for vicarious existences, but because, under a continued failure to be coherent, he becomes uneasy.

# Belief and Art

*Experience and Art* by Joseph Wood Krutch. Harrison Smith & Robert Haas
*The Nation,* November 1932, 536–537

One who has read Mr. Krutch's *The Modern Temper* before reading his newest volume, *Experience and Art,* must be struck by an interesting change in the critic's point of view. The earlier book was built around the thesis that poetry is dying because "poetry illusions" are dying. The author held that certain beliefs are inherently "poetic," and that, since we can no longer believe these "poetic" beliefs (as the belief that the world is the center of the universe), the very basis of poetic dignity is destroyed. In contrast with this attitude, he now says, in his introduction to his newest volume: "Whatever man is capable of believing is potential material for literature." And his volume is built around the ramifications deducible from this shift in position. He relates art to life by showing that art utilizes for its effects the same "premises" as people live by, that the artist moves his readers by exploiting the convictions and preferences which influence their conduct in actual life. Hence, the rise of different schools which stress different aspects of "consciousness" can determine "to a far greater extent than is generally realized both how people are going to act and what . . . it is going to feel like to live." And by this schema, it is generally the work of the literary critic to study the processes of literary appeal and to orientate these with reference to other biological or social processes.

Mr. Kutch tends to situate the appeal of a work in its arousing and satisfying of desires: "In Hamlet—as in any great work of art—emotional anticipations are always satisfied and each hunger we are led to feel is immediately fed." Or again: "Each individual work undertakes to satisfy the emotional anticipation which the spectator is encouraged to entertain." Naturally, in keeping with this, he stresses the fact that the artist works in a kind of "syllogistic" medium, for the artist can only lead people to "emotional anticipations" by working on the basis of the things they already believe and the attitudes they already hold. When you count up to nine, ten is "in the air," but you can put it there for your "audience" only because they concur in

*147*

your way of counting. Similarly, if people strongly believe that a certain act is despicable, the artist can arouse them to indignation by the picture of a "villain" who commits this act. For such reasons, Mr. Krutch decides that drama and poetry achieve importance and power "when they are genuinely believed—when the structures that they erect receive the support of religion, of patriotism, and of philosophy."

Such a position naturally requires a different statement of the "poet's problem" from that which Mr. Krutch made in *The Modern Temper*. Now, instead of saying that poetry is dying because "poetic illusions" are dying, he seems to feel that the possibilities of powerful and comprehensive literature are limited mainly by the fact that society now happens to lack a powerful and comprehensive ideology, or body of convictions, for the poet to work with. We cannot ask literature "to assume unaided a task which the literatures of other times could perform only with the help of philosophy and religion." Magic, religion, and metaphysics, all helped in the past to substantiate structures of convictions which the artist could tap or manipulate to arouse his audience. But such systems have given way to science—and science so far has done more to obliterate the older structures of beliefs than to establish sound new ones.

Yet, as Mr. Krutch wisely says, there is evidence of emergent new beliefs which may be "humanized" by poets of the future (the critic thus tending to adopt what we might call the "attitude of Wordsworth"). "Crowds carry transatlantic fliers in triumph from the field just as crowds are said to have carried Cimabue's Virgin in triumph through the streets of Florence"— which would certainly indicate that the poet of today who wanted to warm his audience's heart by the symbolization of a hero, yet did not like to feel that he was merely relying for his effect upon a "poetic illusion" out of the past, might find available for exploitation a new belief as to the nature of the heroic (mechanical prowess) just as Homer symbolized heroism for the Greeks by his picture of physical strength (Hercules). The example is particularly apt, and suggests, indeed, the genuine emergence of a new belief, when we recall that in Graeco-Roman mythology the god of mechanical ingenuity was lame, and even in Teuton mythology skill of such sort was in the hands of dwarfs.

Mr. Krutch, rightly, I think, questions those schools of literary criticism which would relegate the enjoyment of poetry to a mere "make-believe" corner of the mind. He holds that art bears upon the coordinates of living in general, giving us those emphases in the imaginative sphere which are relevant to "other human interests," to man's "other activities" outside of art. He upholds the notion of our aesthetic interests as integral to our entire lives, ruling out the once fashionable doctrine of the special "aesthetic sense."

The fact that poets can write poems on riding to the moon or that Dante can, though building upon beliefs now discredited, impress many readers of today, has led many critics to diagnose wrongly the "make-believe" aspect of art. If Dante's poetry is still effective, it is effective only because the beliefs upon which it is erected are still effective, some being preserved as "echoes" or survivals (as in our vocabulary of "sins"), and some preserved as contrivances acutely adjusted to constants of human thought (as when Dante, looking up, sees above him Beatrice, also looking up—a symbolism permanently effective because people will forever "look up," and this ingenious symbolization of the process of looking-up by the use of two stages instead of one brilliantly brings the process before us). Similarly, if the poet delights us with a poem "On Riding to the Moon," he appeals only insofar as he exploits very real and active "convictions" as to the nature of the fearsome, the awesome, the ecstatic, the invigorating, and so forth. A poet is like the man who cried "fire" in a theater: the man's "genius" resided in the fact that the word was so well adjusted to the emotional dispositions, the apprehensions, the "beliefs" of people in that particular situation.

I can indicate here only the "midrib" of Mr. Krutch's argument, which seems to be in many ways sound, though complicated with some survivals more in keeping with his earlier position. I would take issue mainly with his statement, which seems to me unnecessarily modest, that "it grew simply and informally out of my own experiences with various works of art." Mr. Krutch is a very well-read critic, and I believe his book profits by his discriminating acquaintance with current tendencies in thinking, particularly as regards the problems of literary criticism when viewed from the standpoint of communication, or meaning, the tendency to study art as a reader-writer relationship rather than from the standpoint of mere reader or writer alone.

# Gastronomy of Letters

*ABC of Reading* by Ezra Pound. Yale UP
*The Nation*, October 1934, 458–459

Pound repeatedly assures us that all previous books on the appreciation of literature have been swindles, and he begins with a bow to science—a word which usually does the same work among the sophisticated that Old Glory performs among the naïve. It is "scientific" to look at specimens of poetry like the man in the laboratory examining smears on a slide; and in the name of science Pound proposes to do just this. Yet having begun so promisingly, he slips into a subterfuge. He completely passes over the fact that if one looks at the smear on a slide without the assistance of a vast critical vocabulary, one will see mighty little. Pound seems to feel that the naked exposure to the specimens is in itself "scientific." He aggressively and repeatedly asserts that people who ask to be told the rules of good workmanship are trying to get something for nothing. The craft of literature in its important aspects cannot be taught, he says: you either see that something is good or you don't, and that's the end of it.

This position may have something to be said in its favor—but I do not understand how it could be called "scientific." Science is numerology. It is concerned with qualities, such as literary excellence, only insofar as qualities can be given quantitative equivalents. The scientist would like nothing better than to define an emotion or a color perception by measuring its corresponding manifestations in the blood and nerve texture. The nearest practicable approach to this ideal in the realm of aesthetic appreciation—at the present time at least—would seem to be a system of critical concepts or definitions. For a critic's definitions are a kind of incipient measurement, just as the act of measurement is applied definition. (When we measure something with a foot rule, for instance, we are pragmatically defining it with reference to a concept of the inch.) Our nearest possible approach to scientific numerology in the field of values, therefore, would seem to reside in the attempt to express in conceptual symbols (or abstract analogies) the effects which the poet attains by imaginative symbols.

To illustrate: The poet makes a joke. At this point Pound would remind you that you either see the joke or you don't. One can't "prove" to you that the thing is really a joke. But if you concede that it is a joke, one *can* offer you a conceptual translation of the joke, giving you an abstract mechanistic account of the psychic explosion it touches off and its ways of doing so. One *can* find a conceptual parallel to the non-conceptual event, just as psychoanalysis provides an abstract account of associative processes which the symbolists originally exemplified without any thought of such doctrines. It would seem that a truly "scientific" criticism would attempt to trace such emotional-conceptual correlations; yet Pound in the name of science makes a virtue of refusing to do this. The "science" he has in mind could hardly be of the typical Occidental sort, which may explain why he talks about Chinese ideograms, rather than Galileo or Bacon, in introducing his subject.

In another way Pound unconsciously tricks us. He continually reminds us that the ways of good writing cannot be learned from manuals which conceptually oversimplify the poet's procedures; and thereby he seems to forget that his book is by program a treatise not on writing but on reading. We may accept it that "you cannot hand out a receipt for making a Mozartian melody." But the fact remains that, even if you have no intention of making a Mozartian melody, you may receive from a melodic expert, apt at conceptual analysis, some revealing clues as to what a Mozartian melody is, and these clues can give you a sounder and sharper equipment for discerning kindred miracles in melody even totally non-Mozartian.

Pound is valuable for the stress he lays upon the *sound* of literature. He offers good suggestions as to why poetry should not venture far from song. But his position leads him to underestimate the role of ideas here, so that he cannot do full justice to such a man as Pope. Ideas likewise can have their tonalities; and one might show that even the simplest *carpe diem* lyric depends largely for its appeal upon an ideological background which is gently set a-tremble as one reads. One could not possibly construct a tragedy—which is a kind of crime, trial, and sentence in one—without containing in one's head an ideological structure much more complex than that of the Code Napoleon.

This book is a treatise on the gastronomy of letters. It tells you where to find exquisite cuisines. It is not much of a contribution to dietetics (the art-as-propaganda school is dietetic). It is written with a pleasant insolence, in Pound's usual haphazard manner. If one is oppressed by the rigors of the day, and minded to seek relief by reading of people that walk beneath palms, one may even like it for its medicinal contentment, though it is too fragmentary to satisfy as a Baedeker to masterpieces. The author writes like a man who feels that his investments are sound—be they of the Wall Street or Grub Street variety. The clearest echo of our present difficulties is to be noted in an occasional admission that writers may be the victims of bad economics, but the lesson so far seems to be that if they just got more money everything would be all right. The most disappointing feature of the book is its paucity of technical criticism. As an admirer of method, and a man whose attainments undeniably equip him to discern examples of good method, Pound should have prodded himself to say much more about ways and means, noted for their own sake. A gastronomer of poetry is hardly in the best tactical position to revile a gastronomy of criticism. Such an attitude would seem to fit better into the program of the propagandist, or dietetic, school.

# Coleridge Rephrased

*On Imagination: Coleridge's Critical Theory* by I. A. Richards. Harcourt, Brace & Co.
*Poetry*, October 1935, 52–54

A theory of poetry is likewise a theory of reality, a psychology, and an ethics—and its perspective may even be transferred to an account of historical or economic trends, if the times are such that we ask for the transference. In his new book, Richards specifically discusses the fact that the apologist of poetry is in a much better position strategically at present than was the case a few years ago—for now that science has become sufficiently critical of itself to discern the "mythopoeic" function in all thought, including the speculations of scientists, the poet's myths can no longer be dismissed as mere "illusion." The issue seems to take a new form; and instead of seeing a blunt contrast between "scientific truth" and "poetic fabulation," we begin to understand exactly why materialistic scientists have a very limited view of reality, and why some other kind of insight is required if we are to employ the "whole man."

Richards shows that Coleridge had explicitly recognized this situation. Expertly translating passages from Coleridge into terms that more easily reveal their relevance to the present, he enables us to glimpse the ways in which a poet's myths may be of the utmost importance to mankind in the most pragmatic sense conceivable: by providing the frame-work through which our minds may be organized and ordered. To think of such helpful structures as merely "illusory" is materialism of a suicidal sort. For if the mind is such, by its very nature, that it cannot be a mind in the full sense without a rich and highly sensitized store of symbolism, we may justly think of our "mythopoeia" as grounded in something as genuinely real as universal necessity. The choice is not between myth and reality, but between full myths and scant ones. As the old master Goethe wrote in the album of young Schopenhauer (and that is where he should have written it) we can only get out of the world what we put into it. Richards shows us Coleridge keenly at work putting in a great deal.

Coleridge saw that true judgment, or Common Sense (not average opinion), is poetic. It is poetic, a new creation, an "illumination," to gauge one's situation and one's needs so accurately that one can produce the symbolism he requires to cope with them. The result is a synthesis such as each man must find for himself, whether he make the poem by actually arranging the symbols as he must have them, or by reading into the symbols which another has arranged for him. The result is not knowledge, but wisdom—as in our outlines giving us an undigested clutter of facts, we have not wisdom, but knowledge. Until fused by imagination, such material is psychologically a mere burden.

Richards makes out a good case for this great introspectionist, who had "a mind which gave him, in its incessant activity, more remarkable material to inquire into than is ordinarily combined with such capacity to inquire," and who knew that "to ask about the meanings of words is to ask about everything." And Richards' great linguistic sophistication enables him to show us the bearing of many a statement which we might otherwise tend to reject as too inspirational for critical usage. Furthermore he remembers, to our profit, the admonitions he acquired from his earlier study of the old Chinese moralistic psychologist, Mencius.

*On Imagination* is a very important book, fertile in suggestions. Yet we may ask whether Richards has given sufficient attention to the *non-literary* aspects of the poet's problems. He frequently talks about the ordering of the mind as though it were a wholly private act, politically vacant. All that he says seems extremely valuable—but while "projecting" Coleridge's formulas into the contemporary scene, should he not also discuss their bearing upon our economic quandaries? When a society's practical purposes and methods are in order, individuals can order their minds with reference to the patterns of the State. But if these patterns are in disarray, how can the mind be wholly ordered, except by reference to some new scheme of purposes and methods, still to be attained? Such thoughts would suggest the possibility that, to be completely serviceable for our needs, his book should not so cursorily dismiss the "propagandist" element in poetry today.

# Cautious Enlightenment

*The Double Agent: Essays in Craft and Elucidation* by R. P. Blackmur. Arrow Editions
*Poetry*, October 1936, 52–54

Those who take pleasure in technical criticism are certain to find Blackmur's recent collection of literary essays unusually gratifying. A man of taste, he has a patience that is more often found among critics deficient in taste. And he is too tactful to worship consistency with the over-zealousness of our contemporary doctrinaires who would leave us little choice between the "logical conclusions" of their thesis and its "reduction to absurdity." His appeal as a critic probably resides in the fact that his attitude towards his subject comes first, and his rationalization of this attitude comes afterwards. And he consistently avoids the dangerous reversal of this process, as when a critic takes his rationalization as his starting-point, and works back to his subject.

Thus, to employ in a good sense a word that is usually employed in a bad sense, I should say that Blackmur's method of criticism is highly "opportunistic." He does not break, because he can so readily bend. He is the opposite of a critic like Granville Hicks, who might be quite willing to assert that some local proletarian tract poor in imagination is superior to a great "non-proletarian" work of the past, if his rationalization as already formulated led him "logically" to this conclusion. Were Blackmur to find himself confronting such a difficulty, he would quite naturally decide to remake his rationalization. "Opportunistically," he would start over, laying out new coordinates, whereas Hicks would remain stubbornly loyal. Significantly, the pages on Hicks mark the one occasion in this book when Blackmur loses his composure. Hicks' counter-Blackmur treatment of Blackmur himself was presumably too great a trial, and jolted him out of his method.

But though the method produces a book full of concepts, it is not easy to characterize in summary. What is Blackmur "for"? It even seems at times that, through being so deficient in pigheadedness, he must derive his power from the pig-headedness of others. Others must be excessive, that he may admonish us how to discount their excesses (thus to an extent, they die that he may live). He does not work by simple antithesis, as were he to adopt the diametrically opposite position. Rather, he *appreciates* the other statement, but warns of its limitations. When we have finished, we carry away a general attitude of qualification (and a valuable attitude that is)—but when we come to summarize for review purposes, there is nothing we can quickly seize upon and "play up" as thesis.

It is a great privilege for a contemporary poet to have Blackmur as interpreter. He begins by a careful attempt to set down the salient traits of his subject, not in the billboard sloganizing manner that prevails in our "outline of literature" tradition, but with subtlety and penetration. In workman-like fashion, he proceeds to the analysis of method, at which he is exceptionally accomplished—and gradually he expands the implications of method until the intellectual and moral aspects of the technical have also been considered. Cummings, Pound, Stevens, Lawrence, Crane, Eliot, and Marianne Moore are characterized and studied in definitive fashion. The thorough essay on the prefaces of Henry James is also here. His criticism of critics, however, seems to me less scholarly. He is sharper at *discovering* the gist of poets than at *restating* the gist of critics. For the poet's imagination, he finds the apt critical concepts to match (the point of his term "double agent"?), but when dealing with critics he tends rather to select than to assimilate.

These "essays in craft and elucidation" are implicitly an answer to those who seem to be saying, in effect: "We must write hastily, superficially, and crudely, for the good of the proletariat." No cause can provide the blanket of morality that would cover the immorality of slovenly workmanship. People who write abominably should vociferously love God, mankind, or class, that their critic be put in an unstrategic position, as it is hard to attack their individual badness without appearing to attack their collective cause. Much of this sound trickery has gone on. But in proportion as the rawness abates, and we come to realize that the morality of one's craft is close to the source of all morality, Blackmur's patience will be rewarded. His book should be welcomed as one of our finest pieces of contemporary criticism.

# Exceptional Improvisation

*Some Versions of Pastoral* by William Empson. Chatto & Windus
*Poetry*, March 1937, 347–350. Also in *The Philosophy of Literary Form*

This is unquestionably one of the keenest, most independent, and most imaginative books of criticism that have come out of contemporary England. Since Eliot has been encumbered with so much troublesome extra baggage in recent years, his value for us is lessened. And the three most fertile works on literature since *The Sacred Wood* are I. A. Richards' *Principles of Literary Criticism*, Caroline Spurgeon's *Shakespeare's Imagery*, and this new book by the author of *Seven Types of Ambiguity*.

The step from *Seven Types of Ambiguity* to *Some Versions of Pastoral* is considerable. Empson is still, unfortunately, inclined to self-indulgence, as he permits himself wide vagaries. But presumably that is his method—so the reader, eager to get good things where he can, will not stickle at it. He will permit Empson his latitude, particularly since it seems to be a necessary condition for the writing. He will take what he gets, and will proceed to *delve* there. He will enjoy the author's suggestions, looking elsewhere for four-square schematizations.

By the "pastoral" Empson appears to designate that subtle reversal of values whereby the last become first. They do this, not by assuming the qualities of the first, but by suggesting the firstness implicit in their lastness. Hence, we get the long literature of transvaluation whereby humble rustics, criminals, children, and fools are shown to contain the true ingredients of greatness. They are uplifted, not by renouncing their humbleness, but by affirming it, until out of it there arises the prophetic truth.

We can discern the workings of this process in thought as superficially divergent as primitive Christian evangelism and Marx's "proletarian" morality. We may note it in the reshaping of the Parsifal legends, where the knightly half-wit becomes transformed into the saint of the Holy Grail, his earlier Quixotic *credulousness* being metamorphosed into insight. Empson chooses, for his examples, *The Vision of Piers Plowman*, Spenser's *Faery Queen*, Gray's *Elegy in a Country Churchyard*, Marvell's *Garden*, *The Beggar's Opera*, Swift, and *Alice in Wonderland*. Apparently stimulated by sources so different as the propounders of "dialectical materialism" and Fraser's *The Golden Bough*, he makes explicit many of the complex psychological ingredients implicit in "pastoral" revolutions.

"If you choose an important member the result is heroic; if you choose an unimportant one it is pastoral." But also: "In my account the ideas about the Sacrificial Hero as Dying God are mixed up in the brew," the "unimportant member" becoming, by pastoral transformation, the really "important member," and hence the heroic redeemer. There is much here that is necessarily tenuous, and that a rigorously schematizing mind might not have thought of.

The book is also made valuable by many incidental passages opening up new resources of literary "appreciation." We should mention, for instance, the author's acute way of appraising the appeal in a poem on the ways of fish, by Rupert Brooke. And as a sample of his improvising powers, we might close by citing his exegetic comments on the passage from Gray, about the flower that "is born to blush unseen":

> Full many a gem of purest ray serene
> The dark, unfathomed caves of ocean bear;
> Full many a flower is born to blush unseen
> And waste its sweetness on the desert air.

What this means, as the context makes clear, is that eighteenth-century England had no scholarship system or *carriere ouverte aux talents*. This is stated as pathetic, but the reader is put into a mood in which he would not try to alter it. . . . By comparing the social arrangement to Nature he makes it seem inevitable, which it was not, and gives it a dignity which was undeserved. Furthermore, a gem does not mind being in a cave and a flower prefers not to be picked; we feel that the man is like the flower, as short-lived, natural, and valuable, and this tricks us into feeling that he is better off without opportunities. The sexual suggestion of *blush* brings in the Christian idea that virginity is good in itself, and so that any renunciation is good; this may trick us into feeling it is lucky for the poor man that society keeps him unspotted from the world. The tone of melancholy claims that the poet understands the considerations opposed to aristocracy, though he judges against them; the truism of the reflections in the churchyard, the universality and impersonality this gives to the style, claim as if by comparison that we ought to accept the injustice of society as we do the inevitability of death.

One will look long among the writings of most self-professed "Marxist" critics before he finds such profoundly Marxist analysis of literature as this.

# Responses to Pressure

*Wordsworth and Milton, Poets and Prophets. A Study of Their Reactions to Political Events* by Sir Herbert J. C. Grierson. Macmillan Co.
*Poetry*, October 1937, 37–42

Grierson's new study of Wordsworth and Milton is organized on the basis of a distinction between prophetic and didactic poetry, the prophetic poet "putting into the language and pattern of his poetry his deepest intuitions as these have been evoked by a great political and religious experience." The author contends that didactic verse "may at times rise, as in Dryden and Pope, to the level of effective poetic oratory, poetic declamation," but "it never becomes poetry, pure and simple, till the didactic becomes merged in the prophetic, till you feel that the poet is not expounding or defending a thesis but pouring forth in imaginative language and moving rhythms the intuitive images which rise from the unanalyzable blend of sense, emotion, and thought."

Though he objects to those who would accuse Milton of a breach in "unified sensibility," he concludes that, in *Paradise Lost,* "the poet and the prophet, or to put it otherwise, the poet as creator and the poet as critic, meet but fail to coalesce, come even into conflict with one another, leave on the reader's mind and imagination conflicting impressions." Didactically, the poem "aims at one effect, the justification of God's ways to man." But "if any moral springs straight out of the story itself it is . . . that man must be the ruler in his own house." In other poems of Milton, notably *Lycidas* and *Samson Agonistes,* he finds closer integration.

Of Wordsworth: "*The Prelude* abounds in passages of dull or awkward narrative and reflection. The poet emerges when a skating experience, the vision of a mountain raising its head suddenly seen from a stolen boat, a girl's dress tormented by the wind, becomes a mystical, imaginative, spiritual experience." Whereas Milton "throws himself as passionately as Wordsworth" into the telling of his story, he does it "not in the same way, not intuitively recording the voice, as it were, of some inner revelation, but argumentatively." Milton's method was "that of a lawyer, accumulating texts to establish each position." But in Wordsworth we get "more in the nature of the prophetic, intuitive feeling . . . for in that feeling Wordsworth found, after his period of *Sturm und Drang,* a message for himself and the world."

If you make a distinction, things are going best for your readers when you deal with antipodal cases. One has no trouble, for instance, in distinguishing roughly between a crop-report and a poem on the seasons, between a market-forecast and a prophecy of future redemption. Even here there is sometimes a margin of overlap, but the general tenor of your dichotomy is clear. If, however, you seek to maintain your distinction precisely in that area where the margin of overlap confronts you at every point, things don't go so well. And since both these poets were well acquainted with philosophical or conceptual vocabularies of motives (involving a reasoned criticism of social relationships), and since they necessarily wove such coördinates into their interpretations of human burdens and enjoyments, it seems to me that you are, by the very nature of the case, dealing primarily with the margin of overlap, precisely where the joys of the dichotomous are not. Thus, a reader trying to manage Grierson's distinction for himself, and noting in Wordsworth those flashes of recognition that Milton, with his lumbering and impersonal baggage, rarely attained, might place Wordsworth in the class of "what oft was thought but ne'er so well expressed"—yet this formula names the "didactic," of which Wordsworth is offered as the opposite.

But though one may still be left feeling vague about the author's basic distinction, the book has incidental values that are considerable. Reading it somewhat as Grierson would read *Paradise Lost,* dividing the "message" from the "story," we find much material that provides suggestive perspectives for our contemporary exigencies. We see two earnest men each in his way building a structure that no one could take from him. Both had placed much hope in the regeneration of mankind through political expedients. For both, the ideals of liberation had strong connotations of evil. Milton's movement "toward the left" began in earnest with his heterodox views on divorce, thereby inaugurating his long guilt-laden list of refutations, defenses, apologies, and justifications. For Wordsworth, a similar movement was associated with his illicit love for Annette Vallon; hence "France of the Revolution his mistress was; England and her morals, customs, prejudices, became his wife."

Each had seen a revolutionary cause go sour; and each in his way worked out a poetic economy designed to take his disappointments into account. Milton ended by turning a project for the glorification of his cause into an indictment of mankind. Trained in the prayer and invective of the sermon, forever playing the organ of his sonorous Latinity (for if he wrote "as a lawyer," his legalism was theological, as far as possible from the secular style of Bentham), he enjoyed incantatory resources that could always enable him to keep a stake in the heavenly thunder. Hence, by identifying himself with the figure of Samson, he could profit by the increment of such association, transforming something like vindictiveness (even sheer spite) into a partnership with Jehovah, God of wrath and justice. And if Milton, by equating his political issues with theological ones, had the theological resonance left when the politics was balked, Wordsworth seems in contrast to have found his solution in the role of prodigal son. He became the master of the "revisit." After a short period of over-generous spending, he returned home, to confess and repent and be reconciled. He became a child again, his strategy thereafter being to transform his politics in terms of pre-political imagery. He returned to mature his childhood, to take up where he had left off, his appreciation sharpened by the intervening excursion.

"Wordsworth," says Grierson, "in the years from about 1797 to about 1803, was like one who has been converted, or who has recovered his faith, and the poems he wrote are read with most understanding and enjoyment if one reads them as the outpourings of such a convert, a convalescent, the joy of a recovered faith in God which for Wordsworth is in Nature." "Man" and "Society" became merely adjuncts of "Nature"—and Nature was his parent hills, sometimes kindly, sometimes, as Grierson suggestively notes, threatening (as when, remembering his theft of a boat, he recalls how the "grim shape" of a peak "strode after" him). His love of simplicity (particularly where it approaches the state of "glee") suggests something like an adult cult of "baby talk." His recurrent sense of coming from another world was probably sharpened by his own ambiguous situation (in that he was now "back home," yet he was home as a "convert," so that the home was at once new and vestigial). His somewhat trancelike sensuousness suggests such well-being as an infant might express if it could do precisely what an infant by definition can't do: speak. And he was probably kept in this track by the fears and remorse connected with the "traumatic" interim in France.

So, in sum, we find assembled in this book the documents of two different strategies: How Milton persevered by annexing the very heavens, and their relevant sermonizing style, to sustain him in his unregenerate role as fighter. How Wordsworth "retrenched" by "symbolic regression," becoming, in Grierson's words, "a poet of joy, of recovered joy, of joy drawn from the purest sources" (plus, we might add, a series of financial breaks that enabled him to forget the social thunder beyond the hills).

This, I submit, is the "story" underlying Grierson's "message." Though it is not thus pointed by the author, it is there in his documents. It is important, I think, since we can find, all about us, variants of these two prototypes, with different degrees of thoroughness. The revolutionary situations under which Milton and Wordsworth wrote are in many notable respects different from the situation today. Hence, we may expect a correspondingly different formula for their encompassment. And critics on the look-out for the contemporary formula may find, in Grierson's book, "leads" that add precision to the search.

# On Poetry and Poetics

*The World's Body: Foundations for Literary Criticism* by John Crowe Ransom.
  Scribner's
*Poetry*, October 1939, 51–54

John Crowe Ransom can treat knotty material with great suavity. He is a master of discriminations—and writes with a natural independence that spares him the painful choice of styles we so often see now, the shift between the fighter intimidating and the fighter intimidated. He stands among the foremost of those critics who "have learned to talk more closely about poems than their predecessors ever did" (a school with an exceptionally large percentage of Americans, either Americans who stayed or Americans who left).

When doing criticism of this sort, he is as entertaining as Eddington writing on an almost equally subtle field, the universe. And he writes with the lecturer's dialectical aptitude at pointing up a theme by the use of a countertheme, a happy choice of comparisons that suggest a notable contrast, as when introducing *Samson Agonistes* to sharpen our perception of *Murder in the Cathedral:*

> The best thing that Milton had, looked at from this distance, was copia, God's plenty, unlimited wealth in poetic stock; it did not give out, not need reinforcement, nor require dilution. Thus in the Samson play, a chorus of wise old men but not for decoration. Their lines not only lyrical but religious, and not only religious but hammering incessantly on Samson's own religious agony, discussing and emphasizing the truth which is the truth of the play. So has the Becket play a chorus, but of silly old women, who are picturesque and lyrical, but very aimless and repetitive, garrulous old women, going on about life and presently going on about death; above all, knowing nothing in the world about poor Becket's inner tragedy.

In his study of Edna St. Vincent Millay, he similarly clarifies, here by comparing and contrasting with Donne—the chapter being a very neat deployment, as it is written around Elizabeth Atkins' appreciation of Miss Millay, and the exposition weaves among four subjects: the poet, the poetess, the work on the poetess, and Ransom's observations on all three. Donne serves even more rewardingly in the long and engrossing piece, "Shakespeare at Sonnets," a "close" examination of poetic technique, wherein Ransom contrasts the Metaphysical's way of "presenting a figure systematically" with the dramatist's preference for "a procession or flight of figures." The opening essay, on *Lycidas,* ("I venture to think . . . that [it] was written smooth and rewritten rough; which was treason") takes off from Spenser.

But though there are bits of "close" examination scattered throughout the book's fifteen chapters, the major portion of the material is more in line with Ransom's statement that "the good critic cannot stop with studying poetry, he must also study poetics." In this wider area, the critic is equally penetrating. The two essays written around Aristotle's *Poetics*—"The Cathartic Principle" and "The Mimetic Principle"—would alone justify the use of "foundations" in the subtitle. And when discussing Richards, he does some pulling this way and that, with bright results:

> The theory of poetry as agitation gives us a muscular or gymnastic view of poetry: the poem resembles a gymnasium with plenty of dumb-bells and parallel bars for all the member interests; and what the member interests obtain from it is pure or abstract exercise, which does not pretend to have any relation to affairs. Now emphasize the gratifications and the pleasures they receive from it, and we obtain a hedonistic view. But think how imaginary and unreal are the objects that engage them, and we come to a view of poetry as a form of self-abuse. Then talk about the inalienable right of the little interests to "function" just as freely as the big public ones, and it becomes a doctrine of expressionism.

The gradual widening of speculation from "poetry" to "poetics," however, has given rise, in the case of the present reviewer, to uncertainties as to just how Ransom ultimately conceives of the status of art. When he is focusing his attention upon technical criticism, the autonomy of poetry is implied in the very nature of the investigation. But the widening introduces a more social, even sociological, perspective, which necessarily forces a concern with the overlapping, of realms, impinging upon politics, economics, anthropology, psychology, etc. And he seems to prefer too sparse a set of coordinates for a description of such inter-relationships.

Thus, the, "aesthetic" is presented, dialectically, as the opposite of the "scientific"—while the "scientific" is in turn equated with the "utilitarian" and the "predatory." But it is hard to see why pure science would be any more "predatory" than pure poetry would be, or that applied art is any less "utilitarian" than is applied science. Again: the attachments of sentiment are placed in the "aesthetic" bin—and if one had to make a flat choice, in labeling the sentiment of patriotism either "aesthetic" or "scientific," I cannot imagine anyone's putting it in the "scientific" bin—yet there have been many occasions when we could call it "predatory."

In such speculations, it seems to me, Ransom is encroaching upon the field of sociology, without availing himself of the "closer approximations" that the terminology in this field would make possible.

The title of the book well conveys Ransom's desire and determination to establish poetic truth as "objective," as against the many subjectivist and impressionist doctrines of recent decades. This is a battle well worth fighting, and Ransom fights it valiantly. Sometimes, however, I feel that he wins by an unconscious stylistic subterfuge, by merely speaking of a poem's "object" where we should ordinarily have spoken of the poem's "subject." What is the "object" of Hamlet, and where, that a dramatist might hope to "know the object as it might of its own accord reveal itself"?

But too blunt an attempt at seeing the fifteen chapters as systematized parts of one piece would be irrelevant—for they were not so written. Each chapter, taken by and for itself, is perfectly clear in design, extraordinarily so. And all the chapters, taken together, are perfectly clear in their point of view. It is the point of view of a critic who is among the keenest in the appreciation of poetry's attainments, and among the ablest in bringing this keenness to poetry's defense.

# Towards Objective Criticism

*The Rime of the Ancient Mariner* by Samuel Taylor Coleridge. Illustrated by Alexander Calder. With an essay by Robert Penn Warren. Reynal & Hitchcock
*Poetry*, April 1947, 42–47

Surely it is a rare writer, here or anywhere, now or at any time, who could have a critical work of exceptional merit appearing when an exceptional work of fiction by him was also new before the public. Yet here it is, in Warren's essay on *The Ancient Mariner*, published in book form, with notes, while we are still mulling over his recent novel.

Though it is not a very long study, it is a packed one, with many excellencies of detail which the reader should savor for himself. I shall here confine myself to only its more salient aspects, which are also its more problematic aspects.

Warren is among those who would treat of Coleridge's poem from the standpoint of Coleridge own favorite word: Imagination. A poem may be viewed in many perspectives (that is, in many critical terminologies); and high among them, always, in criticism, is the insight got by viewing the poem in the perspective set by the poet's own favorite title for poetic method.

With "fancy," the junior partner of Coleridge's dialectical pair, Warren is not concerned. He focuses the attention on the other, and follows a line of reasoning designed to prove that the killing of the Albatross symbolizes a crime against the imagination. To do this, he distinguishes between a "primary" and "secondary" theme in the poem. Of the primary theme, which "may be defined as the issue of the fable," he writes:

> In *The Ancient Mariner* it receives only a kind of coy and dramatically naïve understatement which serves merely as a clue—"He prayeth best, etc." But the theme thus hinted at is the outcome of the fable taken at its face value as a story of crime and punishment and reconciliation. I shall label the

primary theme in this poem as the theme of sacramental vision, or the theme of the "One Life."

This "One Life" theme, as distinct from the "story of crime and punishment and reconciliation," is probably most joyously expressed in "The Aeolian Harp," where an aesthetic of impulsive unity is expanded to universal scope in the somewhat pantheistic lines:

> And what if all of animated nature
> Be but organic Harps diversely fram'd,
> That tremble into thought, as o'er them sweeps
> Plastic and vast, one intellectual breeze,
> At once the Soul of each, and God of all?

However, Warren is centering his attention upon *The Ancient Mariner*, where the oneness is most explicitly stated in the "moral" that arises out of the Mariner's sin and suffering. Hence, he distinguishes the "One Life" theme from the "secondary theme," which he calls "the theme of the imagination." Having thus taken the two themes apart, he later asks us to rejoice in their rejoining; though, once so unitary and unifying a principle as Coleridge's "imagination" is introduced, it is hard for one to avoid seeing the fusion everywhere.

Warren next takes several important critical steps hinging about a contrast between "personal" and "objective" motives. He wants to deal only with the "objective" ones. But if he were to be *wholly* "objective," I think that much of the material he introduces would be excluded by the rules of evidence. For a truly "objective" analysis of a poem (as Warren uses the term, in contrast with the "personal") would seem to require that one discuss that poem *without any reference whatsoever to its author*. Insofar as one treats the poem in terms of other writings by that author, one is relying upon facts involved in its *authorship*. Hence, these facts would be "personal" insofar as the knowledge of the author's identity figures in the interpretation of a symbol or image in the poem. A criticism that wholly avoided "personal" reference could say only such things about the poem as could be said even if its author, or personal source, were wholly unknown.

Warren's interpretation, in hinging about the proposition that the killing of the Albatross symbolizes a crime against the imagination, secondarily involves an interpretation of the sun image, which is

> the light of practical convenience, it is the light in which pride preens itself, it is, to adopt Coleridge's later terminology, the light of the "understanding," it is the light of

that "mere reflective faculty" that "partook of Death." And within a few lines, its acceptance by the mariners has taken them to the sea of death, wherein the sun itself, which had risen so promisingly "like God's own head," is suddenly the "bloody sun," the sun of death.

If we on our own account turn to Coleridge's writings, however, we find such highly relevant passages as these:

> (From *The Friend;* Shedd edition, p. 100): The light of religion is not that of the moon, light without heat. . . . Religion is the sun, the warmth of which indeed swells, and stirs, and actuates the life of nature, but who at the same time beholds all the growth of life with a master-eye, makes all objects glorious on which he looks, and by that glory visible to all others.

> (On the next page, we find vice discussed in terms of moonlight, thus): This is indeed the dread punishment attached by nature to habitual vice, that its impulses wax as its motives wane. . . . Its own restlessness dogs it from behind as with the iron goad of destiny.

> (*Aids to Reflection,* 131): the sun of love, the perfect law of liberty (P. 167) : the dawning of this inward sun, the perfect law of liberty.

Though there are very many passages in Coleridge where he speaks ill of the imagination, I know of no reference in Coleridge's conceptual writings where the sun has the content which Warren has attributed to it, and which is more like the content he "personally" gives to the "day self" (in contrast with the "night self") in his own excellent novel, *Night Rider.*

There is a crime indeed. And this crime involves the imagination. But it is not a crime against the imagination, as Warren would contend. It is a crime of *imagination against reason* (which in Coleridge's language is equated with religion). There was a morally suspect ingredient in the nature of Coleridge's aesthetic itself (his aesthetic of pure spontaneous "impulse" as contrasted with the ethics of a straining, striving will). Carried to its ultimate metaphysical or theological limits, his aesthetic was a pantheistic offense against God. And the sun became severe after the commission of the crime because its severity represented the conscience (*Friend,* 140: "The conscience bears the same relation to God as an accurate time-piece bears to the sun").

Warren finally introduces the subject of the *poète maudit* purely in terms of "ambivalence." But "ambivalence" is not an explanation, it is a gerundive, a to-be-explained. And he does not use the new interpretation to revise the whole. If one interprets the crime as a crime against religion, one can relevantly note that Coleridge's aesthetic of pantheistic coadunation is similarly but furtively described even in "The Aeolian Harp," as I indicated in my *Philosophy of Literary Form*.

Of course, when one examines the letters and theological writings with this interpretation in mind, the symmetry of the pattern is complete. We know exactly wherein the "crime" of imagination consists "personally," with Coleridge, in the interweaving of his impulsive aesthetic with the euphoric stages of his drug. And there are also plenty of references that link his drug addiction with an offense against his marital duties (not the least of the "personal" things that were symbolically slain when the Albatross was shot was his "pensive Sara"), while these duties themselves are equated with both religion and the sun. But I am willing to go along with Warren in his feeling that Coleridge's drug problem and marital problem may, in their particulars, be exceptionally "personal," and so should fall outside even his modified rules for an objective criticism. I cite them merely because they help clinch the case. But it seems clear enough without them, once you make the one central correction that follows when one sees the sun as religion, bringing "the Terrors . . . that precede God's love." And as for the cure by moonlight: precisely because it is a cure by moonlight it is not completed. But the moralistic ending was prophetic indeed. Coleridge was henceforth to rely more and more upon such language, using religion to undue the damage which his imagination, as tainted by his weakness, had done to him.

Unfortunately, my engrossment in Warren's engrossing essay has prevented me from discussing the book as a whole. I should add that it contains a beautifully printed copy of the poem, along with several unforgettable line drawings by Alexander Calder, whose deft gestures of simplicity in many ways parallel the archaizing simplicity of the verse in what is perhaps the world's greatest *sophisticated ballad*.*

---

\* The proportions of this review are not quite satisfactory. There is no mention of the many incidental observations, which I liked greatly. The gloss on the "objective" significance of the "silly buckets" seemed to me exceptionally good. [K.B.]

# Untitled Review of *La Poesie et le Principe de transcendance* by Maurice Duval

*La Poesie et le Principe de transcendance: essai sur la creation poetique* by Maurice Duval. Librairie Felix Alcan
*The American Journal of Sociology*, July 1938, 167–168

The "principle of transcendence" is approached from various angles: "The principle, the biological function, of transcendence. . . . that the artist should succeed in detaching himself from his experience to reveal within him the intimate sense of universal life." "One transcends society, not in neglecting it, in disdaining it, in denying it, but on the contrary in affirming it, to surpass it." Transcendence in both artist and society is "a continual demand for creation." "Humanity is an exile on earth," exiled from universal life, at once recalling its origins and suffering from its separation—and by the principle of transcendence the artist is stimulated either to regain contact with his source or to suffer insofar as he fails to do so. Transcendence is "the necessity, felt and willed by nature, to surpass itself, to recreate that which exists, to invent that which is not yet realized or discovered, and even to make plausible the impossible." Though "time functions to prevent everything from being given at one stroke," by the principle of transcendence we seek to get the total truth, not "step by step, moment by moment," but simultaneously, non-temporally (*en une fois, intemporellement*). The principle is at once life, the source of life, the drive of life, the method of life, and the improvement of life. Life itself is a transcendence of matter; but it becomes trammeled in the practical, of which the ideal poem is a transcendence in turn (to be itself eventually transcended by other poetry, insofar as no poem ever gets quite to the center of universal life, being held back by the very materials in which it would embody the transcending act).

The author is strongly indebted to Bergson—but too often, instead of soberly rephrasing Bergson, as Karin Stephen does so ably in *The Misuse of Mind,* he tends rather to accentuate the master's rhapsodic, inspirational tonalities, thereby being led into an overreliance upon *spiritualization* as a way of treating social and aesthetic processes. Ample and eloquent tribute is here paid to the creative "explosion," and the author's appreciation of poetic masterpieces plays much the role that the glorifying of the Creation would play in a sermon not thus secularized. Being against utilitarian, positivistic science, and the kind of education that goes with it, perhaps the best feature of his book is in making clear what kinds of stylistic action are stunted by a pragmatic emphasis. Also, there are many penetrating observations on the nature of narcissism, hermetism, and "pure" poetry, bearing upon the relationship between preparatory rot and assertive fulfillment. Unfortunately, despite professions to the contrary, the writer's concern is much more with the mystical aspects of art than with its realistic aspects, so that "transcendence" is treated too much within itself, without sufficient reference to the specific social situations which a poet's symbols are designed to integrate.

# The Sources of "Christabel"

*The Road to Tryermaine: A Study of the History, Background, and Purposes of Coleridge's "Christabel"* by Arthur X. Nethercot. U of Chicago P
*The New Republic*, May 1940, 617

This book would apply the same treatment to "Christabel" as Lowes's "The Road to Xanadu" applies to "The Rime of the Ancient Mariner" and "Kubla Khan." Primarily, it seeks to establish the identity of the lovely but ominously disfigured Geraldine ("demon, witch, snake, vampire," yet withal fascinating sympathetically)—and to this end it retraces Coleridge's readings in demonology and kindred gloomy lore. The method contributes to the description of the strange rites in "Christabel" mainly by bringing into unmistakable relief important traits that might be discerned on inspection of the poem alone, but often appear there too fleetingly for one to feel quite confident in building theories upon them. Also, by his patience and enterprise in assembling in one place so many important observations about "Christabel" by himself and others, the author has helped much to clarify the strange mixture of piety and satanism in the Mystery Poems of Coleridge, a great dialectician, with an equally great sense of guilt, materialized in bondage to a drug. Anyone with a special interest in Coleridge will certainly want to examine this study, though it will not have the broader appeal of its brilliant prototype.

# Toward the Perfectly Poisonous

*The Artist as Critic: Critical Writings of Oscar Wilde* edited with an introduction by Richard Ellmann. Random House.
*The New Republic,* May 1969, 28–30

In his expert introduction to this book, Richard Ellmann remarks on Wilde's cult of the "dangerous":

> What muddies this point of view in Wilde is his looking back to conventional meanings of words like sin, ignoble, and shameful. He is not so ready as Nietzsche to transvaluate these, though he does reshuffle them. His private equation is that sin is the perception of new and dangerous possibilities in action as self-consciousness is in thought and criticism is in art. He espouses individualism, and he encourages society to make individualism more complete than it can be now, and for this reason he sponsors socialism as a communal egotism, like the society made up of separate but equal works of art.

Wilde's preference for such old-time words as "sin" has its counterpart in what would otherwise be a surprisingly frequent use of "perfect" and "perfection." The following passages indicate the range:

> In Mr. Pater, as in Cardinal Newman, we find the union of personality with perfection." . . . "Art has no other aim but her own perfection." . . ."The condition of perfection is idleness: the aim of perfection is youth." . . . "Life and literature, life and the perfect expression of life." . . . "To be premature is to be perfect." . . . "Made perfect by the critical spirit alone." . . . We might make ourselves spiritual by detaching ourselves from action, and become perfect by the rejection of energy.

Wilde sums up in that most uneasy of all literary species, an outraged author's Letter to the Editor, when attempting to defend *The Picture of Dorian Gray*. "It is poisonous if you like, but you cannot deny that it is also perfect, and perfection is what we artists aim at." In a review of poems by Henley, he says that rhyme "gives that delightful sense of limitation which in all the arts is so pleasurable, and is, indeed, one of the secrets of perfection." However, he can as readily go in the other direction. When noting that through poetry Mrs. Browning "realizes her fullest perfection," he further observes, "'She would rhyme moon to table,' used to be said of her in jest; and certainly no more monstrous rhymes are to be found in all literature than some of those we come across" in her poems, with results that give "a splendid richness to her verse."

And with regard to Whitman's remarks on "the possibility of a form which, while retaining the spirit of poetry would still be free of the trammels of rhyme and of a definite metrical system," he uses exactly the same formula he applies to Mrs. Browning: "In her very rejection of art she is an artist. She intended to produce a certain effect by certain means, and she succeeded."

In "The Soul of Man Under Socialism" ("soul" is another of his now quaint words, and Wilde's ways of advocating socialism are about as far from the cult of the working man as are the "perfect" writings of his Walter Pater), he writes, "A healthy work of art is one that has both perfection and personality," another word for "personality" being "individuality." And though he foretells an era when painting will no longer be "an artificial reaction against the ugliness of life," but "the natural expression of life's beauty," he is persistent in his dictum that "the sphere of Art and the sphere of Ethics are absolutely distinct and separate."

There is a wide difference, he contends, between saying that "only a painter is a judge of painting" and his thesis that "only an artist is a judge of art." For "in art there is no specialism." All arts "are in their essence the same, and he who knows one, knows all," whereat he adds a twist, "But the poet is the supreme artist."

Presumably in saying, "There are not many arts, but one art merely," he was motivated by the feeling that the same aesthetic *attitude* was involved in one's approach to all art. And insofar as his sense of secret "sin" was at odds with his popular repute, this attitude went beyond advocating that artistic innovation was merely in a different channel from the ethical, and culminated in his challenge, "All art is immoral."

One feels like a plodder, in trying to put together Wilde's critical theories. For instance, we read in "The Decay of Lying" that "As a method, realism is a complete failure"; art "is not to be judged by any external standard of resemblance." In "The Truth of Masks," an essay on the dramatic value of costumes, we are told that "Perfect accuracy of detail is necessary for us." The point is developed at great length; but the shift is concealed by his saying that such "archaeological" strictness is necessary "for the sake of perfect illusion." "The archaeologist is to supply us with the facts which the artist is to convert into effects." Though he writes that "neither in costume nor in dialogue is beauty the dramatist's primary aim at all. The true dramatist aims first at what is characteristic," the statement must be understood as modified, three pages later, by a reference to "that joy in beauty for beauty's sake without which the great masterpieces of art can never be understood."

Mr. Ellmann's introduction sums up things admirably, as regards both Wilde's aestheticism and its relation to his "sinful" man-love. Even so, it is worth noting that, in his essay on the gentlemanly poisoner Wainwright, Wilde hits upon a stricter definition: "Sin should be solitary, and have no accomplices." How closely should we read that text? Would it mean that, after his "fall" into homosexual entanglements (presumably in 1886) he could not wholly embody the ideal of individualism which he hoped for in Utopian socialism? Insofar as sexual analogues for socio-political situations are concerned, the "perfect" *individualist* could have erotic commerce only with himself.

As regards the book proper, there are two ideal places to begin. The first is "A Chinese Sage," the review of a translation of Confucius, which begins, "An eminent Oxford theologian once remarked that his only objection to modern progress was that it progressed forward instead of backward." Throughout, the stress is in keeping with paradoxical thoughts on "the uselessness of all useful things." Wilde suggests that the English publication, two thousand years after Confucius' death, "is obviously premature." The quality of Wilde's sympathy with this book well indicates the quality of his own conceits, when they now and then come nearest to "perfection."

The other recommended starting point is "Poetry and Prison," a review of poems that Wilfrid Scawen Blunt wrote in connection with his imprisonment. "Literature is not indebted to Mr. Balfour for his sophistical *Defence of Philosophic Doubt,* which is one of the dullest books we know, but it must be admitted that by sending Mr. Blunt to gaol he has converted a clever rhymer into an earnest and deep-thinking poet." In the light of what happened to Wilde later, these pages are particularly touching (I almost said "arresting"). But the causes of the two men's imprisonment varied greatly. Blunt's had the dignity of a political offense, whereas Wilde, though poetically identifying himself with Christ, had to suffer the burdens of mere scandal. As Mr. Ellmann aptly puts it, "So long as he had been a scapegrace the door to comedy was still open; once having accepted the role of scapegoat the door was closed" After his release from prison, Wilde tried to write another play in his former manner, but the kind of continuity best suited to his gifts was broken. "There was nothing to do but die, which accordingly he did."

His reviews are a charming combination of perception and patter. They are much better than his more pretentious pieces, which are not so well defined by the requirements of the business at hand, and which seem more deeply affected by the complications of the "Dorian Gray complex" (a guilty sense of too great a hiatus between secrecy and publicity).

A quite differently slanted review might have resulted from a selection of his witticisms. Also, along with much social shrewdness, engagingly expressed, there are many serious passages of great sympathy and beauty, for instance his pages on *The Divine Comedy*. But of the kind of passage we most spontaneously think of as Oscarian, here's the "perfect" one: "Mr. Whistler always spelt art, and we believe he still does, with a capital 'I.'" Wilde did too.

But let's consider one more exhibit, a review of only seven lines (which, incidentally, may throw light on Wilde's resistances to what he calls realism):

> "The Chronicle of Mites" is a mock-heroic poem about the inhabitants of a decaying cheese, who speculate about the origin of their species, and hold learned discussions upon the meanings of Evolution, and the Gospel according to Darwin. This cheese epic is a rather unsavoury production, and the style is, at times, so monstrous and so realistic that the author should be called the Gorgon-Zola of literature.

# Father and Son

*Father and Son: A Map of Misreading* by Harold Bloom. Oxford UP
*The New Republic*, April 1975, 23–24

This is an exceptionally subtle and complex work which, it seems to me, is doing several things at once. Whatever I pick as a quotation to start from seems to give a wrong impression of the book's tenor. But on the author's own authority, I'll try this:

> Let me reduce my argument to the hopelessly simplistic; poems, I am saying, are neither about "subjects" nor about "themselves." They are necessarily about *other poems;* a poem is a response to a poem, as a poet is a response to a poet, or a person to his parent. Trying to write a poem takes the poet back to the origins of what a poem *first was for him,* and so takes the poet back beyond the pleasure principle to the decisive initial encounter and response that began him. . . . *Only a poet challenges a poet as poet,* and so only a poet makes a poet. To the poet-in-a-poet a poem is always *the other man,* the precursor, and so a poem is always a person, always the father of one's Second Birth. To live, the poet must *misinterpret* the father, by the crucial act of misprision, which is the re-writing of the father.

Primarily, it seems to me, the stress is upon the relation between the poet's poetic "precursor" and the poet as an "ephebe" who resents being "belated" with reference to his origins. But just as the dead precursor lives on in him, so his poems in turn are "refusals of mortality. Every poem therefore has two makers: the precursor, and the ephebe's rejected mortality."

Bloom plays down a concern with the kinds of "anxiety" deriving from the fact that, in many cases, the poet's choice of vocation involves a quite painful and conscious break with his actual parents who, at the very least, were grieved by his alternative lineage. However, this turn is considered near the end of the book in the case of Whitman's "Sea Drift," which amounts to a reconciliation with his deceased father (in a poem that reflected anxiety over the threatened loss of the "inspiration" characteristic of the poetic posturing in, say, the "Song of Myself"). And the problems to do with poetic breakaway trends in general are not given the constant attention that, it seems to me, any radical rejection of one's parental judgments requires.

Just how such problems of "ancestry" relate to the forbears of critics is not an issue in this book. It seems to me that such things are left dangling by this kind of summarizing sentence: "As literary history lengthens, all poetry necessarily becomes verse-criticism, just as all criticism becomes prose-poetry"—whereat we dare assume that, on many occasions, Bloom would like his criticism to be viewed thus, and rightly so.

Another line enters from the pedagogic angle:

> All literary tradition has been necessarily elitist, in every period, if only because the Scene of Instruction always depends upon a primal choosing and a being chosen, which is what "elite" means. . . . No teacher, however impartial he or she attempts to be, can avoid choosing among students, or being chosen by them, for this is the very nature of teaching. Literary teaching is precisely like literature itself; no strong writer can choose his precursors until first he is chosen by them, and no strong student can fail to be chosen by his teachers. . . . What is the particular inescapability of literary tradition for the teacher who must go out to find himself as a voice in the wilderness? Is he to teach *Paradise Lost* in preference to the Imamu Amiri Baraka?

Bloom turns up with an ingenious bit of diplomacy here when he proposes to feature Milton's Satan as "representative of the entire canon when he challenges us to challenge Heaven with him." But how about the precursors of teachers? When, for instance, we think of Matthew Arnold's deference to his own distinguished academic father, what of its relation to *Sohrab and Rustum,* where father and son engage in combat unaware ("unconscious"?) of their identity, and the father slays the son? In brief I'd like to read more about the ways in which the *poetic* genealogy of "influence" relates to the motives of actual biological genealogy. For the most part, it seems to me, Bloom keeps the two lines too distinct.

In particular I am puzzled about his comments on Browning's grotesque fantasy, "Childe Roland to the Dark Tower Came." Let me quote a few brilliantly impressionistic descriptions (there are many more of the same sort): "his perverse and negative stance . . . a turning against the self . . . a quest for failure is a synecdoche for suicide . . . its 'realism' a pure self-imposition . . . an inward impulse [suicidal self-punishment] . . . yielding to instinctual demands that his ego-ideal finds objectionable . . . we feel, as readers, that death must be at hand. . . . to accept his place in the company of the ruined . . . sacrificed, not to the energies of art, but to the near-solipsist's tragic victory over himself . . . Childe Roland dies, if he dies" (a reference particularly worth considering in the light of the traditional association between death and sexual orgasm).

Add now such considerations as these: Bloom has already quoted Freud's notion that writing, "which consists in allowing a fluid to flow out upon a piece of white paper," has "acquired the symbolic meaning of coitus," hence "is as though forbidden sexual behavior were thereby being indulged in." But we should recall that usually in our tradition the conscience-stricken poetic "ephebe" (an adolescent just before manhood) such as Browning was, chooses his calling as a writer prior to the conveniences of coitus, though an independent form of indulgence was available. Add also the thought that, going Freud one better (or one worse) there is the proverbial expression, "As I take pen in hand." And recall Bloom's own assurance that "The poet-in-a-poet *cannot marry,* whatever the person-in-a-poet chooses to have done." In the light of all that, go back and read the previous paragraph—and surely Bloom was providing all we needed for the suggestion that this wayward poem by a mature monologue-artist is a fantasy of onanism (for Bloom also stresses the fact that poets are forever going back to their origins, and most such vocations originate during the lonesome passionate severities of adolescence).

Of course I could quote many similar lines from the poem itself, including above all the stanza in which the poet even signs his name, as the "Childe" nears the squat "brown" turret where he "came," as announced in what Bloom calls "Roland's final act of blowing his slughorn." But I would not agree to interpret the Childe's ruined "Band" as "precursors" in Bloom's sense. They, along with the "ominous tract" (that will stand for what Bloom brilliantly calls the Child's "ordeal, his trial by landscape") and the many incidental gnarled figures, are all tautologies, embodying the rhetorical principle of amplification, various repetitions of the same sinister theme that is, in sum, a highly dramatized exaggeration (or "hyperbole," to use a term that Bloom does exceptionally well by) for this temporary fanciful "return" to the exacting conditions under which his "poetic ancestry" took form. Here is another notable respect in which the motivations of the poetic breakaway are not dealt with throughout; yet one can't deny that they are there.

Two other major fields should still be considered. Having glancingly noted that Vico and I stress the four "major tropes" (metaphor, metonymy, synecdoche and irony), Bloom adds hyperbole and metalepsis (or transumption). And he does wonders by them all. I started this review on that theme. But I abandoned that start because it involves issues too specifically literary for a general approach to the book. As I understand Bloom's added emphasis, atop the stylistic exaggeration (hyper-bole) of the "Childe's" temporary imaginary return to guilt-laden origins (essentially experienced as a relationship to his actual parents as vs. his new poetic unnaturalization), I'd take it that metalepsis, or transumption, would involve considerations of this sort.

The *Phaedrus* takes us from seed in the sense of sheer sperm to the heights of the Socratic erotic, as transcendently embodied in the idea of doctrinal insemination. And similarly, via hyperbole and metalepsis, we'd advance from an ephebe's sheer *physical* release to a *poetically* ejaculatory analogue, implicit in the imagery of Childe Roland's horn-blow.

There is at least one more major strand that should be mentioned in a review (the "news") of this exceptionally and admirably subtle and complex work. Whereas, in my *Rhetoric of Religion,* for the start of things I had been content to borrow secular "logological" analogies from the opening chapters of Genesis, Bloom prefers a "logocentric" version by Isaac Luria, "a sixteenth-century master of theosophical speculation," who "formulated a regressive theory . . . in a revision of the earlier Kabbalistic emanation theory." In any case we coincide to the extent that his "Lurianic story" contains "a vision of creation-as-catastrophe," and mine builds around the orthodox biblical account that integrally connects the "Creation" with the "Fall." Maybe we could settle for this quotation from Coleridge's *Table Talk:* "A Fall of some sort or other—the creation, as it were, of the non-absolute—is the fundamental postulate of the moral history of man."

Bloom announces that he intends to do more with Luria's visionary ways. I am sure that the job of following him will be well worth the effort of any reader who, along with both poetry and poetics, also loves criticism in general for its own sake.

# Untitled Review of *Wallace Stevens* by Harold Bloom

*Wallace Stevens: The Poems of Our Climate* by Harold Bloom. Cornell UP
*The New Republic*, June 1977, 24–27

Harold Bloom is so ingenious in his speculations, and so urgently responsive to his texts, it seemed fitting to start things by an epigraph adapted from Gilbert and Sullivan's opera, *The Pirates of Penzance:*

> When vocabulary duty's to be done—
> To be done,
> The reviewer's lot is not a happy one.

For Bloom does indeed keep us watching every word, what with his highly organized lore concerning the "post-Wordsworthian crisis-poem" and the developments of the Emerson-Whitman "American Sublime," along with his statements of indebtedness to Kabbalism, Nietzsche, and Freud.

The present volume, in bringing this equipment to bear upon the poetry of Wallace Stevens, opens and closes with helpful summarizations of Bloom's theories. The twelve intervening chapters comment on particular poems by Stevens in a detailed way that may not make this the ideal text for a reader more interested in an overall characterization of Stevens's work than in close step-by-step exegesis. But Bloom's procedure does produce many expert interweavings which pay off handsomely when his discussion of Stevens (who complained of poems when "They do not make the visible a little hard / To see") culminates in Bloom's formula, "No more involuntary Transcendentalist ever existed than the Stevens of the final phase, but the text under consideration is wildly indubitably Transcendentalist." The more closely we have followed Bloom's analyses in the preceding chapters, the better equipped we are to appreciate the poignancy of the last poems where the poet, nearing his end, undergoes a turn that might be called the craftsman's equivalent of a death-bed confession.

This overall situation which Bloom is dealing with is in its barest simplicity reducible to this:

In one sense a poet, like each of us, could be called a kind of "Solipsist." Whatever his relations to other people may be, his pleasures and pains, his immediate sensations, are his and no one else's. They are grounded in his nature as a sheerly physiological organism, his "animality" that separates him as an individual from all other animals, human or nonhuman.

His poetry, on the other hand, is grounded in a public, or social medium, involving the vast structure of "Identifications" that he acquires through language. This universe includes not just his personal relations (beginning with members of his family as he emerges from infancy, and gradually widening), but also extending to his increasing knowledge in all its aspects (history, government, geology, geography, astronomy, etc.—a fantastically complex network of information available only to our kind of creature ("human"), so much of whose experience of "reality" is shaped by the communicative medium, language, which the poet shares with his fellows generally and which he adapts to his particular purposes as a poet.

Such localized vocation, or "Election," involves his personality as a composite of these two quite different realms, the realm of speechless physiological motion and the realm of linguistic (or more generally symbolic) action. "Symbolic" is a better word than "linguistic" or "verbal" for contrasting these two realms in the most general sense, since there are also the "languages" of other traditional symbol-systems such as painting, music, sculpture. But J. L. Austin's word "speech acts" would serve for present purposes.

Whereas the poet's medium does not have the immediacy of bodily sensation, he tries (by such resources as imagery) to give the illusion that it does. His ways of drawing upon the language of the tribe will involve him in various cooperative and competitive relationships to other poets. His hopes that his poems may survive him impinge upon the ironic fact that they can't "die" because they never "lived" in the first place, as tested by the sensations of the body. But *he* as a body will die—and on the occasion of such destiny—conscious stock-taking as a "crisis-poem," thoughts along that line will turn up, along with less radical kinds of death such as loss of love, or of professional competence.

To these three moments (the realm of immediate sensation, or physiological motion; the realm of symbolic action; the poetic personality that is a composite of the two) add the fact that by the "form" of any good poem is really meant a "transformation"—and Bloom is in there, in a big way, ever on the alert for "Crossings of Election," "Crossings of Solipsism," and "Crossings of Identification." The only trouble is that Bloom works into these three moments through actual examples, which never have the schematic simplicity of our disembodied outline.

True, it does seem to me that Stevens's persistent "reductive" concern with what he called a "First Idea" was a valiant self-defeating attempt to recover, or discover and convey (by an act of "re-imagining") the sense of an object as it would be if approached through a vision *prior* to speech and thus "beyond" speech, in the prime realm of physiological speechlessness. But in any case, Bloom's necessarily complicated study of the three "crossings" is further complicated by an adroit theory of rhetorical "tropes," the application of which leads in turn to tropes atop tropes. In Hegelian style we could class the three "moments" of our over-simplified outline thus: nonsymbolic motion would be the thesis, symbolic action the antithesis, and the poet in his "poethood" would be the synthesis. But the issue in its particularities gets us into considerations of this sort:

A poem begins because there is an absence. An image must be given, for a beginning, and so that absence ironically is called a presence." Freud figures here because, according to Lionel Trilling, "it was left to Freud to discover how, in a scientific age, we still feel and think in figurative formulations, and to create, what psychoanalysis is, a science of tropes, of metaphor and its variants, synecdoche and metonymy." And we can add to such insight now "by tracing the derivation of Freud's formulations, from ancient rhetoric through the transitional discipline of associationist psychology. But I wish that Freud had used the ancient names, as well as the old notions, so that we could call a reaction formation what rhetorically it is, an illusion or simple irony, irony as a figure of speech." Where Stevens says of colors that they "Repeated themselves," the expression "requires to be read as its opposite, 'failed to repeat themselves.' . . . To get started, his lyric had to say the exact opposite of what it meant." Bloom is discussing here a poem in which "the striding night tropes upon a trope, in a metaleptic reversal, raising the poem's final lines to an almost apocalyptic pitch of rhetoricity, of excessive word-consciousness (a 'text's equivalent of human self-consciousness')." Where de Man says "to put into question," his formula equals "to undergo the process of rhetorical substitution by, as he says, 'the word,' *logos* in the sense of meaning. . . . Rhetoric, considered as a system of tropes, yields such ore readily to analysis than does rhetoric considered as persuasion, for persuasion, in poetry, takes us into a realm that also includes the lie." And we read one poet rather than another because "We believe the lies we want to believe because they help us to survive.

I could go on citing many many more passages that variously illustrate the dexterity of the truly daedalian range in which Bloom develops his intricate application of rhetorical devices for his analysis of the "post-Wordsworthian crisis-poem." And I should note that, with regard to his step-by-step analysis of particular poems, one exceptionally gratifying reward of his method is the insight derived from the tracing of key words through the whole body of Stevens's work.

# Untitled Review of *The Sovereign Ghost* by Denis Donoghue

*The Sovereign Ghost: Studies in Imagination* by Denis Donoghue. U of California P
*The New Republic*, September 1977

Any text that deserves some measure of appreciation can consider itself lucky if Denis Donoghue chooses to write about it. To his intuitive ability as a lover of the word, he brings a wide range of learning (he is Professor of English and American Literature at University College, Dublin, and has published several volumes of criticism in which he has proved himself particularly skillful at suggesting the "personality" of literary works, along with his great alertness to matters of craftsmanship). He has here put together much highly interesting and relevant material, even though he says intrepidly of his subject:

> Imagination is not one of our key terms. . . . Our nature is no longer an object of sustained reflection. . . . If the situation has changed in the past fifty years, it has resulted in a further suppression of the word in favour of such words as style, genre, and structure; it does not figure prominently in current linguistics. The best that can be reported is that imagination has survived as a critical term, without flourishing. . . . Only a wilful or nostalgic critic would now use Blake's term "genius" or "vision." We are patient with problems, but not with mysteries.

The underlying design of the issue with which Donoghue is concerned is probably best indicated by reference to Coleridge's post-Kantian distinction between "primary" and "secondary" imagination. Whatever may be the ultimate nature of "reality in itself," we experience it through such physical sensations as light, sound, scent, taste, touch, heat, cold, pleasure, pain, in an overall matrix of time and space. Here would be the realm of the "primary" imagination, "immediately" common to all human organisms insofar as they do not suffer privations such as blindness or deafness. By "secondary" imagination would be meant such skill as the poet has, at adapting the terms for sensory experiences in ways whereby his medium gives us somewhat the feel of such primary "immediacy."

I am paraphrasing the summary that Coleridge gives, at the end of Chapter XIII, in his *Biographia Literaria*. Or am I? I hear cries of indignation. For here is how Coleridge says it:

> The primary IMAGINATION I hold to be the living Power and prime Agent of all human Perception, and as a repetition in the finite mind of the eternal act of creating in the infinite I AM. The secondary Imagination I consider as an echo of the former, co-existing with the conscious will, yet still as identical with the primary in the kind of its agency, and differing only in degree, and in the mode of its operation.

There, grandly contrasting with my pedestrian version, Coleridge's statement is in much the same spirit as the lines from Wordsworth's *The Prelude* which Donoghue quotes as an epigraph for his book:

> The love more intellectual cannot be
> Without Imagination, which in truth
> Is but another name for absolute strength
> And clearest insight, amplitude of mind,
> And reason in her most exalted mood.

Putting together some lines from Donoghue's first chapter and his last, we offer these quotes as perhaps most succinctly summing up his own view:

> Imagination, as distinct from mind, is that mental power which finds unnecessary the strict separation of conscious and unconscious life . . . which deals with contradictions not by subordinating one to another but by accommodating all within a larger perspective; and which entertains feelings and motives before they have been assigned to categories or organized into thoughts, attitudes, statements, values, or commitments . . . Imagination and mind are not two things, they are one intellectual power, separable only if we choose to call upon a limited effort of that power or upon the complete power. . . . Imagination is the name we give to

> the intellectual power which we call upon when we propose
> to deal with the chaos of our experience merely by putting
> its constituents in separate compartments.

And he explicitly avows: "I cannot believe that the imagination is other than divine in its origin." Thus he is so strongly personalistic in his attitude towards all texts, behind his various comments there are his uneasy differences with the "structuralists," who "maintain that in speaking we are more the slaves than the master of our language," and "are used by language at the very moment in which we think ourselves most independent in the use of it." The structuralists would "insist that the tokens of creative freedom are illusory, that instead of free acts we are witnessing formal operations of language." And Mallarme's later style "is congenial to structuralists because it presents itself as a network of simultaneous relations and does not imply a source more mysterious than language itself."

Donoghue's succinctly documented purview of his subject encounters many related considerations en route: for instance, the important place of *feeling* as a function of the imagination, the shifting line between the "immediate" and the "mediate" with regard to the role of poetry as a medium, the elusively suggestive ways in which the terms "attention" and "intention" keep turning up *passim*—and I'd love to haggle, not with Donoghue, but with Coleridge, about Coleridge's failure to do well enough by his treatment of "fancy," whereby I'd enlist on my side Donoghue's six-word flash, "Satire, the strongest form of survey," if one can class satire as "fancy" (including, say, a work like *Ulysses* with relation to *The Odyssey,* as vs. the solemnly imaginative relation of *The Aeneid* to Homer).

But when proposing a "definition of man" that would be based upon "imagination as his essential quality," Donoghue might at least have referred to the long tradition according to which the imagination, because of its tie-in with image and sensation, was rated low, in being classed as a faculty we share with speechless brutes. Or there's Pico's *De Imaginatione,* at the beginning of the 16th century, with such typical chapters as "On the numerous Evils which come from the Imagination" and "How we can relieve the Voluntary Evils of the Imagination by the use of Reason." Or one could quote from a letter of Coleridge, written at the height of his productivity as a poet (1797): "Frequently have I (half-awake and half-asleep, my body diseased and fevered by my imagination) seen armies of ugly things bursting in upon me." And when Donoghue writes about "fictions," why not a word about Bentham's "theory of fictions," shows how, though such "products of the imagination" are necessary, they must, as we'd say now, be methodically "discounted"?

Be that as it may, Donoghue's appealing championship of his chosen term presents us with the ups and downs of another tripartite design, thus: There is a kind of imagination that, taking pleasure in the *images* of sensation, uses them to give you corresponding *feelings*. Or there is a second kind that transforms images into *metaphors* not equatable with sensory things. And there is a closely related paradoxical kind that centers in the *negative,* as though "nonbeing" were a profounder kind of "being." The second and third almost turn the first around. In this regard there is the essay that takes us from "The Eye as Benevolent Despot," through "The Purer Eye," to "The Mind's Eye."

For his wind-up Donoghue ends on a rousing set-piece built around *Henry VIII* (surely much of which at least is Shakespeare's). Though he says "It is not the purpose of imagination to act as cheerleader for the spirit of the age," he does a handsome job by a play that *could be* interpreted as coming to a climax in a grandiosely imaginative act of cheerleading for the departed "Virgin" Tudor Queen and her Stuart successor (Elizabeth being equated with the Christ Child, the Phoenix, the Virgin Mary, and "royal sempiternity" in general). And be it "imagination" or just good showmanship, there is nothing more effective in drama than the account of a "historical" incident in which an appropriate character "prophesies" in terms of appropriate topics of a state of things represented as having now come about. One could not reasonably ask of Donoghue a more eloquent plea for his cause.

Incidentally, on going back over Coleridge's *Biographia Literaria,* I ran across a footnote in which, with regard to the "desynonymizing" of the terms "imagination" and "fancy," he says: insofar as any such distinctions become accepted, "language itself does as it were think for us." It is a chance remark which the structuralists would make much more of than would either Coleridge or Donoghue. But regardless of whether texts are to be viewed as portraits of personalities or as but the exercising of language, obviously this book's title represents "imagination" (it is culled from a poem by Wallace Stevens). And the subtitle stands for an alertly sympathetic "mind's" (Donoghue's) efforts "to deal with the chaos" of his exhibits concerning this subject "by putting its constituents in separate compartments."

# Prelude to Poetry: Scales and Fugue

*Knowledge and Experience in the Philosophy of F. H. Bradley* by T. S. Eliot. Farrar, Straus & Giroux
*Notes on Some Figures Behind T. S. Elliot* by Herbert Howarth. Houghton Mifflin
*Bookweek*, January 1965, 4, 8

Mr. Howarth writes that, a year or so after completing his doctoral thesis on Bradley in April, 1916, Eliot "was rescued from the Bastille of philosophy and recalled to his natural life as a poet. But he has always valued the training he received among the philosophers." He adds, "Various critics provoke his comment that he would admire them more if their work had been strengthened by a philosophical technique." The change is attributed mainly to the influence of Ezra Pound and to the attractions of London: "The physical City helped to gain Eliot for England and the Anglican Church; possibly it helped to regain him for poetry."

In any case, his plans to become a teacher of philosophy at Harvard were dropped. He did not even complete the requirement for the doctor's degree. And the manuscript of his thesis, "Knowledge and Experience in the Philosophy of F. H. Bradley," has remained until now unpublished.

Despite Pound's imagistic indoctrination, however, "Eliot's habit of thought favored the use of abstractions, and by 1939 he developed a method of employing them," whereupon seven lines of the poetry are quoted, containing the words: "accident," "design," "deprivation," "destitution," "desiccation," "evacuation," and "inoperancy." To get the point, think of typical lines in such of our poets as William Carlos Williams and Theodore Roethke.

In discussing Eliot's thesis, the reviewer's life is not a happy one. Despite the work's obvious relevance to the question of "figures behind T. S. Eliot," Howarth barely mentions its existence, though he does help out by pointing to an ingenious passage in Conrad Aiken's *Ushant,* and to a connection with a book by May Sinclair. One problem for the reviewer is in trying to give an adequate report of Eliot's thesis without getting too involved in an attempt to sum up somehow the idealistic theories of Bradley on which it is based. Matters are still further complicated by the fact that, whereas Bradley's whole overarching system has as its keystone (its term of terms) the "Absolute," the lines of inquiry in Eliot's thesis are so set up that "the ultimate nature of the Absolute does not come within the scope of the present paper. It is with some of the intermediate steps that the following chapters are concerned."

Bradley's terministic tactics, I think, operate somewhat as follows: As regards "immediate experience," each of us is necessarily subject to the relativity that marks his own particular "point of view." How, then, might the philosopher be able to assert that he can in some way experience the totality of the infinite and Absolute, when his experience, in its immediacy, is necessarily finite and fragmentary? After many subtle distinctions that are in one sense asserted and in another sense denied, the answer boils down to this: Even in our typical, fragmentary experiences, such "mere feeling, or immediate-presentation" gives us "the experience of a whole." Thus, insofar as the Absolute is defined in Bradley's system as a whole, we can in principle experience something that is true of the Absolute's wholeness, even though we cannot know the Absolute in any way near its actual range.

Further dialectical deployments are found necessary. For instance, since we have the immediate experience of pain, the philosopher must prove to his satisfaction that the sum-total of the Absolute is not pained, but happy. And ways must be found to answer an opponent's suspicion that, if the Absolute is approached from the individual's point of view, the Absolute may be nothing but one's own private self writ large (as with the technical charge of "solipsism" that is usually leveled against such philosophies). Further, there arises an orderly incentive to treat the many "points of view" not as all on the same footing, but as sensitive to varying "degrees of reality."

Bradley delineates the complexities of this terministic realm with as much patience and subtlety as though he were deliberately trying to work out a metaphysical analogue of the British Empire itself (even to the extent of putting God in a relation to the Absolute somewhat like the secondary role that we associate with the British monarchy). And Eliot is every bit as patient and subtle in his defining, analysis, and criticism of Bradley's terms, though his thesis does not at all suggest to this reviewer, at least, the structural nature of Bradley's system. For this reason, I think that the best place for the reader to begin this book is with the two articles (one on Leibniz, the other on Leibniz and Bradley) printed in an appendix.

What one does see, I think, is the compelling emergence (in *metaphysical, epistemological,* and *psychological* terms) of the very emphasis which, though it is strongly present in Bradley, points towards such a cult of "immediate experience" as got its *aesthetic* analogue in Pound's imagism. Eliot, though, was to become imagistic with a decided difference. So, let's try again. After saying, "I find myself unable to think in the terminology of this essay. Indeed, I do not pretend to understand it," Eliot adds that the book shows "how closely my own prose style was formed on that of Bradley and how little it has changed in all these years." As I see it, the two statements fit together thus:

> (1) When Eliot quotes Bradley as saying, "the union in all perception of thought with sense, the co-presence everywhere in all appearance of fact with ideality—this is the one foundation of truth," or "there is an immediate feeling, a knowing and being in one, with which knowledge begins," we can see the kind of speculation that Eliot develops in his characteristic concern with the "dissociation of sensibility . . ." Concrete historical man, in community with his fellows, in faith open to Transcendence encountered when everything has gone shipwreck: this is the "image of man" to be found on every page of Jaspers' writings over half a century.

This is the "image of man" that will be found in these three essays, though in very different ways. The essay on Leonardo is really a feat of the imagination since what we know of him is so limited and so cryptic that any number of diverse interpretations are possible. Jaspers' interpretation is revealing and impressive—impressive as an imaginative construction, revealing of Jaspers' own understanding of life. The essay on Descartes is a very different matter. It is a brilliant and erudite piece of philosophical analysis, sympathetic yet merciless. Jaspers penetrates to the heart of the Cartesian achievement and failure. Every inner striving of Descartes' philosophy was directed toward reaching being in its undiminished reality; but his systematic misapplication of his method led to a dualism in which both man and the world were lost in one-sided abstraction.

The final essay on Max Weber, first published in 1932 and then amended and supplemented in 1958 and 1964, is a veritable *tour de force:* it is a work of love, of gratitude, of interpretation and criticism. American readers who know Max Weber largely as a sociologist will gain a new understanding of even that phase of Weber's thought; they will certainly be impressed by the picture of Max Weber as political thinker and man. But again the essay tells almost as much about Jaspers as it does about Weber. And, in the last analysis, that may prove the enduring value of these essays.

# Criticism of Literature

*Given my way of cutting the Gordian knot, I believe I can successfully review this ingeniously tangled book of literary criticism within the thousand-word length commissioned.*

—Kenneth Burke to Malcolm Cowley on reviewing Harold Bloom, *Selected Correspondence* (394)

# On Re and Dis

*The Newer Spirit, A Sociological Criticism of Literature* by V. F. Calverton.
   With an introduction by Ernest Boyd. Boni and Liveright
*The Dial*, August 1925, 165–169

Mr. Calverton is a sociological critic. He believes that aesthetic values are the result of certain environmental situations, and that our tastes in the style and substance of art change in accordance with vicissitudes of social evolution. "Literature which fascinated one age," he says, "suffices but to dull and stupefy another." And for such reasons he believes that we must approach past art from an understanding of its conditions of origin. In proof of his theory of causation, he cites three stages of social evolution in European and American history, and shows their counterpart in literature. The feudal system was accompanied by a system of values which held that artistic dignity was confined to the depiction of the aristocracy, an attitude which Mr. Calverton finds notably exemplified in the tenets of tragedy. But with the rise of the *bourgeoisie,* middle-class figures laid claim to the tragic prerogative—a process which is carried still further as the growing strength of the proletariate manifests itself in a corresponding growth of a proletarian aesthetic, so that we now have even the "tragedy of the drab." Thus, aesthetic standards are impermanent, and one age approaches the art of another age with a different frame of mind, a different set of judgment s, the difference being caused by the difference in sociological conditions between the two ages. In some way not specifically explained, the sociological approach to art helps us to "understand" the art of any given age. In order to exemplify the functions of the sociological critic, Mr. Calverton contributes an essay on Sherwood Anderson, wherein the author's work is consistently understood in terms of its setting. Some instances of the proletarian environment out of which the works arose are established by quotation from the works themselves; and one feels that to this extent at least the environmental approach would not be necessary to any reader at any future age, since the work itself would provide it. (It is as though one were to read some helpful sociologist on the conditions at Rouen in the time of Flaubert as a preparation for the understanding of *Madame Bovary*.) However, Mr. Calverton also contributes facts of his own, giving us a kind of sociological impressionism, telling in his way what Mr. Anderson has told in another—a method of illumination (so far as it is illumination) which arises not from the placing of a work in its setting, but from the addition of a new point of view ("*The Man's Story* is a haunting study in schizophrenia"). Yet he does not by this same testimony prove him either a good writer or a poor one, nor does he show why we must know that the aesthetic has a "proletarian" origin in order to enjoy its results. In fact, Mr. Calverton's causal theories are arrived at without much laboratory testing. After showing that a change in social conditions accompanies a change in aesthetic attitudes, he concludes that the conditions caused the attitudes. If mere concurrence proves causation, why could not an opponent assume from the same evidence that the attitudes caused the conditions? We know, for example, that the feminist "aesthetic" was a necessary preparation for the enfranchisement of women: here is an obvious example of an attitude's causing a change in social structure.

The standard genetic argument is well known; but for the sake of clearness we may quote it in its purest form from Mr. Calverton's own text:

> The plain fact is that we appreciate the [Greek] tragedies in an historical sense, just as we approach them in an historical manner. To one acquainted with the brilliance and profundity of Hellenic culture these tragedies have a meaning that is almost entirely lost to the contemporary layman. It should be clear in this alone, if no other evidence were offered, that appreciation or criticism of Greek tragedy or Roman tragedy, or any ancient or non-contemporary piece of art, cannot be legitimate if it disregard the significance of the social element.

Thus, the work of art must be interpreted in terms of its genesis—but genesis sometimes means environment and at others causation. If Swift, for instance, makes a sly gibe in *Gulliver's Travels* at some current political intrigue now forgotten, the modern reader must have the relevant environmental facts of this intrigue restored for him by editorial annotation if he is to appreciate the "value" of the gibe. An element of Swift's social context was involved in his meaning, the words themselves not being an adequate statement of the situation. Here is genesis as environment. But were I to explain why some "complex" in Swift caused him to write of giants and pigmies, or what sociological conditions induced him to write Gulliver as an adventure story rather than as a pamphlet, here genesis would be synonymous with cause. In this second kind of genesis we have the discovery of a principle, in the former we have the recovery of a fact. Whatever the arguments in favour of discovery may be, let us be sure that the superb one cited by Mr. Calverton in support of recovery is not allowed surreptitiously to help out. It in no way justifies his thesis that we must understand the causal relation between proletarian society and proletarian aesthetic in order to appreciate a proletarian writer.

The ambiguity in Mr. Calverton's use of such words as "understand" and "appreciate" is troublesome. For although he talks much of "understanding" the work of art, he never pauses to understand the word itself. If a man says, "I am going down the street," I understand him insofar as I know what he is referring to. But if he says, "I am Napoleon," I understand him by adding some causal interpretation to his words, as "he is a lunatic," or "he is a liar," or "he is joking." The aesthete usually understands in the former sense, the genetist in the latter. While if all artists were jokers, liars, and lunatics, such genetic understanding by the discovery of a *cause* would be the only reasonable sort.

Thus, recovery provides us with understanding in the sense of *knowing what the artist is saying*, while discovery, or causal theories, provides us with understanding in the sense of *knowing why the artist is saying it*. Some works need more recovery than others. A knowledge of Plato's archetypes may be useful in reading of Wordsworth's clouds of glory. *The Divine Comedy* utilizes aspects of scholastic thinking which are no longer current and the recovery of which is essential. When we read, "Speak to it, Horatio, you are a scholar," we must know, or be able to infer, that erudition was once supposed to enable its possessor to talk with ghosts. In some cases the matter to be recovered is so remote (involves a channel of thinking so different from our own) that an editorial gloss explaining the former condition is not adequate. This is always true in some degree—but the relativists make too much of it; for after all, any reader surrounds each word and each gesture in the art work with a *unique* set of his own previous experiences (and therefore a unique set of imponderable emotional reactions, or "values") and communication exists in the "margin of overlap" between the writer's experiences and the reader's. Awareness of this fact goes far towards clarifying fluctuations in preferences; it need not be made the basis for the claim that each of us is "imprisoned within the walls of his personality" (as the subjectivists would interpret it) nor imprisoned within the walls of his times, as the historians would interpret it. And while it is dialectically true that two people of totally different experiences must totally fail to communicate, it is also true that there are no such two people, the "margin of overlap" always being extensive. Absolute communication between ages is impossible in the same way that absolute communication between contemporaries is impossible. Environmental recoveries help us to understand what the author is saying, and generally—though not always, as explained above—to "feel" it. Causal discoveries lead to something else.

Just what they do lead to is a strange form of "hitting below the belt." If a man formulates, for instance, twenty reasons for the superiority of the *bourgeoisie,* the non-genetic approach to a judgment of these reasons would involve an examination of their logic and cogency. The genetic approach would be to discover that the author was himself a *bourgeois,* and that his twenty reasons were a "rationalization" of his class prejudices. Obviously, the same technique could be applied with equal profit to "explaining" twenty good reasons or twenty poor ones: the fact that there were reasons is the point of discussion. Spengler, the most thorough-going adept of this method, realizes just what this process is: it is to "understand" all creation as *symbol,* which is a more friendly word for *symptom.* The criterion thus becomes not excellence, but typicality, or intensity of characteristics. What will come of this method (the farthest reach of inductive thinking) remains to be seen; just now it is pretty much in its Dark Ages, with almost any conjecture capable of statistical proof, and with few corrective razors. Its principal danger of impoverishment lies in the fact that it has the whole world to choose from. While in the meanwhile the "pseudo-aesthete" may feel contented that there is a way of "understanding," say, the words "cold pastoral" without the discovery that they were written on a warm day sublimated by the poet into its mental negation.

# A New Poetics

*Principles of Literary Criticism* by I. A. Richards. Harcourt, Brace & Co.
*The Saturday Review of Literature*, September 1925, 154–155

It is frequently objected, as the author of *Principles of Literary Criticism* points out, that to concern oneself with problems of artistic excellence in an age of practical, economic ills is like being a "passenger on a short-handed ship." Art is looked upon, aside from valedictory addresses, as a distinctly minor influence in the life of a community; and there are many literary historians who would derive artistic standards directly from the sociological conditions along with which they arose, so that art by such a scheme becomes less a propelling force than an indicator of the direction of other forces. As pain is for us empirical evidence that our hand is on a pin or in the fire, so art is considered the empirical evidence of an age's discomfiture or well-being. Or otherwise stated, art is taken as the cheek, whose complexion, sallow or blooming, is to be directly attributed to more "internal" conditions.

Mr. Richards's book goes a long way toward interfering with this patient and humiliating code, and restoring to art its position as the predominant moral factor which it is—a thesis he can motivate easily enough by calling attention to the effect of bad art in blunting reactions and debasing standards of value. He treats artistic experience as being in no qualitative way different from actual experience, asserting that neither one nor the other leaves us quite sane, our possibilities after either having altered in some degree. While at least one advantage which the artistic experience may have over the experience in life is that in life certain imperative needs of action and composure demand us to limit the impulses which we receive, whereas in art we are free to admit a much greater number and variety of impulses. The principal value of art, therefore, he situates in the production of attitudes, or states of incipient action:

> Every perception probably includes a response in the form of incipient action. We constantly overlook the extent to

which all the while we are making preliminary adjustments, getting ready to act in one way or another. Reading Captain Slocum's account of the centipede which bit him on the head when alone in the middle of the Atlantic, the writer has been caused to leap right out of his chair by a leaf which fell upon his face from a tree. Only occasionally does some such accident show how extensive are the motor adjustments made in what appear to be the most unmuscular occupations.

Now, an unconscious system of moral values is precisely such a system of attitudes, or "unconscious preliminary adjustments"—and art, by its subtle insinuations of what aspects of life are to be desired and what to be avoided, contributes moral standards in that manner which seems most penetrative: by unaware absorption.

Such an interpretation involves an attack on some contemporary codes. For the emphasis on attitudes involves minimizing the importance of the immediate sensations in art, art deriving its values not from the "intensity of the conscious experience, its thrill, its pleasure or its poignancy [such factors being merely the means to a further end] but the organization of its impulses for freedom and fulness of life."

Thus, Mr. Richards's attack is directed first of all against the doctrines that there is some special artistic experience which is Beauty. And while taking into account very fully the technical aspects of art, his book is a constant attempt to avoid such words as Beauty, Form, Construction, Design, Rhythm, Expression in accounting for artistic efficacy. It would be impossible to summarize adequately his methods for doing this, methods which involve a keen and extensive study of the nature of communication. He distinguishes between the scientific and "emotive" use of words. Beauty being classed as "emotive," since it is a word without any direct reference, being the *evidence* that something has happened in the mind and not the *cause* of its happening. His application of this distinction is gratifyingly fertile.

In his discussion of "Poetry and Beliefs," the author very ably disposes of the Revelation theories which are threatening to become a movement at the present time. Advancing from Aristotle's dictum of tragedy's catharsis through pity and terror, he indicates in what way the work of art may exhilarate us and make life suddenly "simple" for us by fusing logical opposites into a single emotional unity, (terror being the movement away from an object, and pity the movement towards it). Thus, we are left with all the buoyancy of belief—and it is this "pure" Belief, these rewards of Belief without specific reference or *thing believed,* which he contends may give us that feeling of certainty so badly needed in an age of doubt. Up to this point he sees such exhilaration as a social asset, ministering, as Conrad Aiken might say, to our "psychotic needs." He then goes on to explain how this "pure" Belief may be mistaken for belief in some particular thing—the sheer "affirmation" of some phrase in music, for instance, being interpreted as metaphysical or "noumenal" insight. His careful distinction between scientific knowledge and this emotional knowledge might be very profitably read by the Arrow Collar Mystics who are arising in our midst, and who are constantly mistaking the *comfort* of Belief for actual insight into some specific *object* of belief.

# The Technique of Listening

*Mencius on the Mind: Experiments in Multiple Definition* by I. A. Richards.
   Harcourt, Brace and Co.
*The Nation*, April 1933, 416

Mr. I. A. Richards, the author of *Principles of Literary Criticism,* and coauthor, with Mr. C. K. Ogden, of *The Meaning of Meaning,* here undertakes what he calls *Experiments in Multiple Definition.* For this purpose he selects an ancient Chinese treatise on psychology, a work arising out of a social context greatly different from our own, yet probably as influential in Chinese thinking as Plato has been to the thought of the Occident. But instead of proceeding by the customary rough-and-ready method of translators, seeking the words in one language which seem to afford the most "natural" parallel to the words of the other, he has made the process-of-translating itself the subject of his book. The practical translator exerts himself particularly to "suppress" the divergencies between the two mediums of expression—but it is precisely these divergencies which Mr. Richards here asks his readers to dwell upon. Accordingly, we do not have merely a finished product, an Englished Mencius. Instead, he makes use of the bad "matching" between the two languages to point his observations on the subject of "meaning." The author thereby brings forward a cluster of scruples and questions which serve to suggest that "we are, as regards our systematic sorting and dividing in the field of meanings, much as primitive man was before the early mathematicians or systematic measurers came to help him divide his grain lands."

The results of this shifted approach—whereby we get, not a translation-made, but a translation-being-made, a distinction which should gratify the Andre Gides and the Gertrude Steins—are remarkably fertile. Besides covering the schematizations of *The Meaning of Meaning à l'inverse*—by proceeding this time from specific issues to their relevant generalizations—he pauses here and there to open up psychological vistas. He even affords us ground for believing that a conception of how the mind works may actually make the mind work that way, that an investigator, by introspection, merely finds mental processes which are already implicit in the terms of his vocabulary—an aspect of "creative ideology" which our Marxians might find suggestive for the development of Marx beyond Marx. He indicates reasons for believing that certain places where Mencius makes important omissions or unjustified leaps—as judged by our Western ways of logic—are not to be explained merely as "weaknesses," but as integral to a different approach—a point which Professor Dewey has emphasized in the study of savage tribes, whose mental processes are often described by the Occidental investigator in terms of Occidental "lapses" instead of as positive accessories of their particular aims and interests.

Most valuable of all the material in this book, I think, are Mr. Richards's reflections on "the survival in philosophic practice of the combative habit of mind." Taking a typical paragraph written in the vocabulary of "Oxford idealism," he first shows how the "Cambridge-trained realist" could pick it apart with promptitude and glee. Thereupon, he proceeds to "translate" this paragraph into "Cambridge"—and the actual burden of the paragraph is found to be wholly acceptable to the Cambridge point of view. He says:

> The first effect of a general practice of multiple definition would be a strange peace in philosophy. A philosopher engaged in refuting another—not of his own party—would become a laughable spectacle. Actually at the moment he is a more sinister figure. Nationalism in thought! The defense of the West! Of historic China! Poor little wretches that we are. For with the increasing pressure of world contacts we do pitiably need to understand on a scale we have never envisaged before. Warfare in the intellectual world as in the physical is a wasteful survival.

If criticism were discussion, intellectual cooperation in a search for understanding, based upon the morality of *listening* instead of the morality of *combat,* how different our scene might become! When recalling the valiant "litry" hosts that have gone forth to give battle in the last year or two, who have slain one another's Phoenix selves with broad, wholesome *reductiones ad absurdum* and *argumenta ad hominem,* and have surely felt very proud of themselves each night as they switched off the light and tumbled into bed after a bold day's work, when recalling all these Jungle boys slaying tigers with their own typewriters and with the emotional dispositions of their readers, one knows that it will be some time before this book by Mr. Richards can really be accepted, deep within us. Yet I do not hesitate to say that a man who sets himself up today as a literary critic, and has not exposed himself to the hesitancies and insights brought to the subject of literary communication in the works of Mr. Richards and his colleague Mr. Ogden, is simply in the position of a quack in medicine or a shyster at law.

# The Encyclopaedic, Two Kinds of

*Literary Criticism: A Short History* by William K. Wimsatt, Jr. & Cleanth Brooks. Alfred A. Knopf
*Anatomy of Criticism: Four Essays* by Northrop Frye. Princeton UP
*Poetry*, February 1958, 320–328

In his *Anatomy of Criticism,* referring to "the clerical poet who, like Gower or the author of the *Cursor Mundi,* tries to get everything he knows into one vast poem or poetic testament," Mr. Frye says: "The encyclopaedic knowledge in such poems is regarded sacramentally, as a human analogy of divine knowledge." Accordingly, we might say that both the prose works here under consideration are in this technical sense "divine." For each in its way is a survey vast in scope, involving a ton or more of knowledge—and each has its own rare excellence, though as kinds of survey they differ greatly.

The Frye volume starts from a unitary principle, which becomes modified and supplemented in the course of adaptation to the various problems that arise en route. The Wimsatt-Brooks volume (a "short" history, they say, of their 755 large, packed pages) begins with a great diversity of material which must be presented primarily in its own terms—and then the attempt is made gradually to sift things down until something like an over-all picture emerges. But the rules of procedure underlying these two books are so different that, though the Frye *Anatomy* has a much wider sweep than the Wimsatt-Brooks *History,* paradoxically the *Anatomy* gets but two pages in the *History*—yet Mr. Frye can consider himself lucky; for by the nature of the case, many good critics rate even much less space, in the discussion allotted to their theories. Sometimes an over-simplified statement that represents a doctrine to excess gets better coverage than more fully developed and better rounded views that lend themselves less readily to quick summarization and placement. To an extent, the sheer "dramatics" of such a survey invite to a featuring of overly partial positions. But often, where a theory is not treated in the body of a chapter, the authors seek to make amends by quoting in a supplement good samples of the critic's views. Another notable contrast between the two books: In the Frye volume, there are almost no quotations except for fragmentary references in a few pages of notes at the back of the book. Everything is made stylistically of one piece by being viewed solely through the eyes of the author. But the Wimsatt-Brooks volume quotes copiously.

To begin with the "short history": The summarizations are done with exceptional scrupulosity; the authors cover an astounding amount of ground without becoming superficial. Part of their skill at characterization comes from the fact that, while reporting on *ideas,* they seem always on the look-out for whatever succinct *images* may have been used (by either friend or foe) to suggest the tenor of a given position. Nor do they aim at a false symmetry by Procrustean methods. Besides saying in effect, "He says this, *therefore* that," they often go on to say in effect, "He says this, *however also* that." And while keeping uppermost the stress upon literary criticism as a specialty, the authors seek to make clear the points at which literary criticism impinges upon other fields (philosophy, psychology, anthropology, and the like).

Part One deals with Greek and Roman classics of criticism (primarily Plato, Aristotle, Horace, Longinus, Plotinus). Part Two goes from the mediaeval period through the Renaissance, and on through eighteenth-century neoclassicism. Part Three reviews developments from Wordsworth and Coleridge (also with relation to "poetic diction" and "German Ideas"), Shelley, Arnold, art for art's sake generally, with special honors at the end to Croce's expressionism (and culminating in a chapter where the history surveys the historical method itself). Part Four deals with the issues uppermost in the critical practices of writers now living: Symbolism, "The Semantic Principle," Richards, Pound, Eliot, "myth and archetype." And in an Epilogue the authors mull over all that has gone before, explicitly discussing their own eclectic preferences (comprising the mimetic emphasis of Aristotle, the stress on the "affective" in Richards, and Crocean expressionism—with, of course, special stress upon the values of metaphor and irony; and finally the notion of poetry as a "tensional union of making with seeing and saying"). But surely the most succinct presentation of their particular slant occurs on pp. 517–519, where the authors draw up a "balance sheet" of the things to be said for and against the "Crocean system."

The book forcefully reminds one of the many other voices (besides those of his own choosing) that have been asseverating throughout the centuries; and it takes advantage of much fine criticism that might otherwise be neglected. It helps one, in methodological asceticism, to suffer oneself to be blown every which way by the shifting winds of doctrine. And it makes Saintsbury's history seem somewhat "quaint," as viewed from the standpoint of the issues that most exercise us at present. (Perhaps every age should write its particular history of literary criticism, just as every age requires its particular retranslations of the classics.)

The authors have done a great service in lending their authority to the notion that the *Rhetoric* as well as the *Poetics* should be considered when one is thinking of Aristotle as literary critic. Critics have been almost psychotic in their determination to overlook the fact that in the *Poetics* itself the reader is explicitly referred to the *Rhetoric* when considering the element of drama which Aristotle places after Plot and Character; namely: Thought (*dianoia*, a term that Mr. Frye makes much of). However, their definition of *Rhetoric*, "a study of how words work," does not point up the full resources of Aristotle's *Rhetoric*. (Aristotle's *Rhetoric* is particularly rich in observations and methods that would automatically guard critics against making the "close" inspection of texts synonymous with narrowness of outlook.) Again, their definition somewhat dissociates from rhetoric the principle of "affectivity" that runs through all rhetorical theory, the concern with ways of "bending" an audience (if we may shift to Cicero's word, which Augustine adapts to his treatise on Christian rhetoric). Thus, note that the lines quoted from Edmund Burke (on p. 299) five times use the word "effect" in one form or another, as would befit the rhetorical slant natural to him as an orator; but the authors here stress rather the equally relevant point about the relation between Burke's position and the theory of "association."

Incidentally, among the best sections in the book are the pages that deal with the "association of ideas," in its position midway between the Augustan stress upon "wit" and the Romantic stress upon "imagination." But it has recently been called to my attention that next year is the hundredth anniversary of the birth of the French critic, Remy de Gourmont, who proposed the term, "dissociation of ideas," in an essay with that title. The authors cite Pound's dictum that "De Gourmont prepared our era;" and they refer to De Gourmont with relation to Eliot and the "dissociation of sensibility." But I submit that they should also have included an account of De Gourmont's graciously nihilistic essay, in which De Gourmont thus rounds out the subject of associationism by an experimentally negative approach. For this essay goes far toward analyzing the kind of "harmonious discords" for which these authors express a clear preference.

This preference I share with them, as per my section on the "gargoyle-thinking" of "perspective by incongruity" in an early book of mine, *Permanence and Change*, recently re-issued. The section is concerned with the ways whereby (in poetry, philosophy, and science) a kind of vision or vista is got, through the abrupt juxtaposing of categories that were otherwise felt to be disrelated or even mutually exclusive. Besides being a fit for the French Symbolism of its day, the De Gourmont approach can also point back to the seventeenth-century Metaphysicals and forward to contemporary Surrealist trends. In my discussion of such "planned incongruity," I temporarily forgot the role of De Gourmont, despite my earlier salutes to this essay in *Counter-Statement*. I was busy watching instead Spengler's use of the method in ways adapted from the "perspectivism" of Nietzsche (to whom, incidentally, De Gourmont himself acknowledges indebtedness, though not on this particular matter). But I have since tried to make amends, as I am now doing, and as with a section on De Gourmont in my *Rhetoric of Motives*. All these points, I feel, bear directly upon what the *History* calls "the formal principle of anachronism in poetry." Also, they help restore the prestige of "fancy," which suffered when Coleridge, having so explicitly "desynonymized" fancy and imagination, proceeded to praise imagination so highly that, by the sheer dialectics of the case, fancy rated low.

As a rule, the authors are not interested in a possible dimension of symbolism whereby the objects of pure poetry or pure theory may be in effect a pageantry reflecting the social order out of which such expressions arise. Yet when considering Pope and Dryden, they make some exceptionally apt observations along such lines. And when, discussing the turn from the Augustan to the Romantic, they speak of a flight "from authority to the outdoors," here they offer a good lead into possible further speculations as to just how the cult of "nature in the raw" might implicitly contain its own analogue of the social order, however irrelevant such a cult might seem on its face. Though the authors show little patience with Marxist criticism, such observations as theirs on Pope and Dryden could be called Marxist criticism in the best sense of the term (as could Empson's book on pastoral).

Obviously, every critic could haggle over details, in a book of such range. The main thing, however, is to salute it.

In the "short history" ("short," they say!) Northrop Frye is discussed in connection with his stress upon the importance of "archetypes" in literature. The *History* notes that the term, "borrowed from Jung, means a primordial image, a part of the collective unconscious, the psychic residue of numberless experiences of the same kind, and thus part of the inherited response-pattern of the race." Mr. Frye's own definition in his book (a considerable development beyond the early *Kenyon Review* article which serves as the basis of the historians' report), is: "A symbol, usually an image, which recurs often enough in literature to be recognized as an element of one's literary experience as a whole." And elsewhere in the book he says that though Jung accounts for the communicability of the archetypes by a theory of the collective unconscious, "this is an unnecessary hypothesis in literary criticism, so far as I can judge." But in any case, the archetype does seem to be the generative principle of his four essays. And apparently his belief in it is what provides the ground for his other perceptions, which come thick and fast, and are often quite unusual in themselves, and are brilliantly put.

I would do Mr. Frye a disservice if I attempted here, in a brief space, to give a summary of his four essays. His analysis of modes, symbols, myths, and genres is complicated by subdivision into themes, phases, imagery, *mythoi,* rhythms, forms (with even spring, summer, autumn, and winter brought in to throw a suggestive semi-Spenglerian light on comedy, romance, tragedy, and irony or satire, respectively), all these being in turn further subdivided and crossed with other terms. I cannot lay claim to having yet made myself at home in his nomenclature. Matters are still more complicated by the fact that, being what he himself calls a "terminological buccaneer," he frequently uses traditional words in a sense peculiarly his own. However, though such special usages may add somewhat to your discomfiture when you are first trying to find your way around in Mr. Frye's rich reticulation of variously interrelated terms, they also help to give the *Anatomy* the liveliness of an exceptional personality. With this author, new slants on things come easy, urgently, with a rush—and the best policy for the reader is to relax and enjoy them.

But one should mention at least the five "modes" which the author develops from Aristotle's distinction between the two genres of tragedy and comedy. These are: "myth" (having gods as heroes), "romance" (the hero being human, though capable of marvelous acts in a marvelous environment), "high mimetic," (most epic and tragedy, having "the kind of hero that Aristotle had in mind"), "low mimetic" (most comedy and realistic fiction, having a kind of hero who "is one of us"), and "ironic" ("where the hero is inferior in power and intelligence to ourselves, so that we have the sense of looking down on a scene of bondage, frustration, or absurdity"). In his first essay, he "encyclopaedically" surveys the many species of works he would class under each of these heads, incidentally dealing with such related matters as tragic flaw, pity, fear, romanticism, pathos, *Angst,* the *miles glorious, eiron* and *alazon,* the *pharakos* or scapegoat, melodrama ("advance propaganda for the police state"), play, ghosts, tonality, plausibility, and what he considers the "two poles of literature" (one, the "mimetic tendency . . . to verisimilitude and accuracy of description"; the other, "a tendency to tell a story which is in origin a story about characters who can do anything"). The chapter ends on a distinction between Aristotelian "catharsis" and Longinian "ecstasies," which are rated as better suited to plays and lyrics respectively.

The second essay is on the "theory of symbols," the author meaning by symbol "any unit of any literary structure that can be isolated for critical attention." As might be expected, "image" plays a big role here—but the best way to understand this chapter is to think of it merely as on the road towards the next chapter, on the theory of "archetypes," here defined as "associative clusters" which "differ from signs in being complex variables." His distinction is suggested neatly in this illustration: "As an archetype, green may symbolize hope or vegetable nature or a go sign in traffic or Irish patriotism as easily as jealousy, but the word green as a verbal sign always refers to a certain color." Or at another point, after defining an archetype as "a typical or recurring image," he proceeds:

> I mean by an archetype a symbol which connects one poem with another and thereby helps to unify and integrate our literary experience. And as the archetype is the communicable symbol, archetypal criticism is primarily concerned with literature as a social fact and as a mode of communication.

The quotation should serve also to indicate how his theory of archetypes leads finally into a theory of genres, considered as different "rhythms" (recurrence, continuity, decorum, association) and "forms" (drama, lyric, epos, prose fiction, the "encyclopaedic") that are designed to produce effects upon an audience. The genres and modes in turn shade into "narrative pregeneric elements" ("*mythoi* or generic plots") in the sense that by "tragedy" or "comedy" we may have in mind not "names for two species of drama," but merely "a certain kind of structure or mood."

All told, though he would reintroduce a variant of the classical concern with literary genres, his classifications are so manifold, and so like a sliding scale rather than a fixed system of differentiations, they suggest somewhat the sort of thing that happened with Schoenberg in music when he expanded the principle of modulation, making it so ubiquitous and constant that it could become hardly distinguishable from no modulation at all. Here is a good example of his shadings:

> Romance, therefore, is characterized by the acceptance of pity and fear, which in ordinary life relate to pain, as forms of pleasure. It turns fear at a distance, or terror, into the adventurous; fear at contact, or horror, into the marvellous, and fear without an object, or dread (*Angst*) into a pensive melancholy. It turns pity at a distance, or concern, into the theme of chivalrous rescue; pity at contact, or tenderness, into a languid and relaxed charm, and pity without an object (which has no name but is a kind of animism, or treating everything in nature as though it had human feelings) into creative fantasy.

Everywhere we turn, from whatever point of view the author happens to be dividing up the literary realm, we encounter things thus shading into one another. Hence, "the center of the literary universe is whatever poem we happen to be reading." Such a flower-in-the-crannied-wall position culminates in what he calls, somewhat redundantly, "apocalyptic revelation." Or, as he puts it elsewhere:

> Anagogically, then, poetry unites total ritual, or social action, with total dream, or unlimited individual thought. Its universe is infinite and boundless hypothesis: it cannot be contained within any actual civilization or set of moral values, for the same reason that no structure of imagery can be restricted to one allegorical interpretation. Here the *dianoia* of art is the Logos, the shaping word which is both reason and, as Goethe's Faust speculated, *praxis* or creative act. The *ethos* of art is no longer a group of characters within a natural setting, but a universal man who is also a divine being, or a divine being conceived in anthropomorphic terms.

Presumably Mr. Frye's notion of the anagogic, as a poetic analogue of the all-enfolding Logos, would amount to a kind of lyric transcendence, an idealistically mythic (or "archetypal") view of everything as contained within an over-arching or all-encompassing Monas Monadum, in a scheme that would be a post-Leibnitzian, post-Hegelian reclamation of Neo-Platonism. It culminates in his notion of the "quest-myth" as the archetype of archetypes. And thus, like the "monomyth" school generally, he stops his generalizing at the point where he might, by just one more step, end with a dialectic of purely abstract design (if, for instance, he went from "quest" to some notion such as "transformation" or "development" in general.)

Messrs. Wimsatt and Brooks raise against Mr. Frye's position an objection that, in one form or another, they raise against many: "The inert and valueless 'document' will submit to the kind of classification that Frye specifies just as well as a valuable poem." And, as he indicates in his "Polemic Introduction," Mr. Frye would agree with them, though without feeling at all down-hearted:

> Value-judgments are subjective in the sense that they can be indirectly but not directly communicated. When they are fashionable or generally accepted, they look objective, but that is all. . . . We begin to suspect that the literary value-judgments are projections of social ones. . . . Every deliberately constructed hierarchy of values in literature known

to me is based on a concealed social, moral, or intellectual analogy. . . . . The substitution of subordination and value-judgment for coordination and description, the substitution of "all poets should" for "some poets do," is only a sign that all the relevant facts have not yet been considered. . . . The positive value-judgment is founded on a direct experience which is central to criticism yet forever excluded from it. Criticism can account for it only in critical terminology, and the terminology can never recapture or include the original experience.

Value-judgments, says Mr. Frye, are necessarily circular, ultimately reducible to ways of saying: "'all plays that have unity of action must have unity of action,' or, more simply and more commonly, 'all good plays must be good plays.'" So there! And meanwhile, Mr. Frye will persist in his frenzy, or orgy, of rheostatic classifying.

# Henry Miller and Harry Levin on James Joyce, New Directions

Remarks on H. Miller, *The Window of the Heart,* and on George Orwell on H. Miller in *New Directions* (1940), and on Harry Levin, *James Joyce Direction*, February-March 1942, 18

There is a very good essay on Miller, "Inside the Whale," by George Orwell, in *New Directions: 1940,* in which the author treats brilliantly and at length of Miller as an inverted Whitman. And if you cannot get hold of his *Tropic of Cancer* yet would enjoy something of his narrative style, I would suggest the story "Mademoiselle Claude" in the volume *The Window of the Heart,* recently published by *New Directions.* It is not wholly representative of his style in the novel, in that the elects are not piled up and piled on as they are there (in accordance with the author's admiration for the "over-elaborated," which he considers as the sign of struggle, "struggle itself with all the fibres clinging to it, the very aura and ambiance of the discordant spirit"). But for this very reason there is more deftness—and there is literature in the peculiar quality of virtuousness and almost mystic exaltation which the hero derives from the contemplation of himself in the role of pimp.

Another book published by *New Directions,* a really splendid little Baedeker on "the great blind Milton of our times," is Harry Levin's *James Joyce.* I have not yet read it all; but the parts that I have read strike me as being of a very high quality in the genus guide-book. There is some tendency to write Joyce over again; but, since a labyrinth is all paths, Joyce's peculiar kind of invention invites this. The author of this study is the best kind of scholar, making up for his lack of originality by his assiduousness and by his very good judgment in borrowing the conceptual frames of others and knowing how to apply them.

"All of Joyce's books, like Thomas Mann's," he writes by way of introduction, "fit into the broadening dialectical pattern of *Künstler versus Burger.*" And by way of conclusion: "For Joyce, there will always be a hiatus between the naturalistic texture and the symbolistic structure of his work—a formal reflection of the emotional ambiguity and intellectual equivocation that made him a Janus-faced figure in the history of literature."

This is the first of a series of "critical baedekers" which James Laughlin of *New Directions* has planned for publication "at the rate of several volumes each year." If the numbers still to appear are as good as this one (and the list of critics he has engaged indicates that they will be), I think Laughlin will have here a shelf of extremely valuable and engrossing studies.

# Untitled Review of *On Native Grounds* by Alfred Kazin

*On Native Grounds* by Alfred Kazin. Reynal & Hitchcock
*Chimera*, Autumn 1943, 45–48

Mr. Kazin's book, *On Native Grounds,* having by now been generally introduced, I shall here restrict myself to consideration of its bearing upon the development of critical method.

Whether we agree or disagree with Mr. Kazin's observations and evaluations in the case of a given author, we should generally agree that his kind of comment, like the field of literature on which he has chosen to comment, is well suited to reading at top speed. The appeal of his studies seems to reside in the fact that whereas his characterizations are average in their insight, they are offered with a conviction much above the average. One is continually invited to read his book in a state of total relaxation. Indeed, there is even a sense in which one can be tempted to read his comments on fiction with far less attention than readers usually give to the fiction itself; for in Mr. Kazin's book there is no thread of development to lose track of. Turn to any paragraph at random; to get its full significance, it is hardly even necessary to read the paragraph preceding. Nothing need be carried in the mind except the title of the book or author under discussion. His terms undergo no development that requires preparation. And in keeping with this method, Mr. Kazin, never discusses the developmental aspects of the books on which he comments. That is, he never sets himself and his readers any problems in the exegesis of structure, as were he to be concerned with the attempt to decide what principles underlie the transformations of scene and action in a given story.

Similarly, though as his title indicates, he places his authors and their books against the background of the contemporary world, the correlations he observes between work and ground are of the most obvious sort, as when noting that a book is written about a financial depression because there was a financial depression, or a given author's work is "sick" because the whole modern world is "sick," and so on. His environmentalist considerations rely exclusively on the most readily recognized counters: general references to the factory, the farm, business, possibilities of revolution, political and moral confusion, signs of hope, etc. These counters are used for purposes of quick characterization; and of course he simply ignores the many vexing problems to do with environmentalist criticism (problems the patient contemplation of which can be very illuminating even where definitive answers are impossible).

I am not even sure that much is gained by knowing the books Mr. Kazin discusses. At least, the sort of thing he says about them is the sort of thing one can readily follow without having read them. Which should remind us that the primary value of *On Native Grounds* is its value as a report, or survey. The author undertakes to read and characterize a great many books for us. He is at pains to give us an impression of their salient traits: what they are about, the point of view they embody, their kind of style, the writer's status. And by the very nature of this essentially impressionistic enterprise, Mr. Kazin automatically skirts the embarrassment of analytic criticism (in both its formalist and environmentalist aspects), which must either assume in the audience a state of knowledge similar to the critic's (usually a false assumption), or assume that the audience will consult the text while reading the analysis (usually an equally false assumption), or expend a preponderant amount of time and effort on the sheer preparatory retailing of the work to be analyzed.

Impressionism too often presents you with an unitemized bill, in that it assigns qualities to a work without offering citations that verify the claims (as per the great delight one can take in Coleridge's way of criticism, while there is also a delight in the *precision* of qualifications that the Coleridge method makes for, a precision that is of course completely lacking in Mr. Kazin's procedure). Still, one must grant that Mr. Kazin's method has obvious advantages in a survey. Any great reliance upon sharp conceptualization with citation would have made an already long book much longer, since epithets are naturally summational, hence are the handiest way of "sizing up" a subject briefly. And besides, prose fiction does not readily lend itself to representative citation as does poetry (with which the Coleridge procedure works best), or as with purely conceptual literature (which one can review by quoting the basic propositions *verbatim*). A novelist usually does, of course, have passages that sum up his "philosophy," but these don't go far towards indicating the most important matter, his ways of developing a narrative. Dreiser's "chemism," for instance, is important mainly by reason of the fact that he violates it by giving us the portraits, not of chemicals, but of people.

The central thing about it would not be something that could be represented by quoting a statement of the philosophy itself.

Mr. Kazin so consistently avoids the embarrassments of formalistic and environmentalist speculation by the devices of the reporter, that for his wind-up he writes of the W. P. A. guidebooks, thus giving us, not a summing-up of his own book, but a report on other books which are of such a nature that his report of them can be summarizing in quality. I cite this purely as a character trait. However, my statement was not quite accurate. For at the very end, following his survey of the state guides, he reports on the Van Wyck Brooks effusion against "coterie" writers; and confronting Mr. Brooks' unreasonableness, Mr. Kazin is gratifyingly reasonable. He says that Mr. Brooks' animosity led him to miss "the laborious integrity of modern writers, their will to understand, to live, to create insofar as the world will allow them to." In such a chastened spirit Mr. Kazin might well have gone back and revised his treatment of his critical colleagues. Many of them he slew, but he didn't always leave them without first picking their pockets, both the environmentalists' and the formalists,' as even his index will testify.

Stylistically, Mr. Kazin has one great fault. It is not so much the fault of any one sentence, but resides rather in the accumulation of such sentences. It also derives from his impressionism, hence from his reporting. And it takes the form of a sentence got by the tacking-on of impressions, one after the other. If the first impression does not quite cover the subject, the temptation is, instead of starting over again, to leave it, and revise simply by the addition of others, each of which in turn is revised not by omission but by further additions. Thus: "Yet something always remained: the shadow of the past on the land the Okies had left behind . . ." plus: "the land itself that lay everywhere ready to be discovered and reclaimed . . ." plus: "the framework of a whole American civilization . . ." plus: "richer and more curious than any in the depression generation knew . . ." plus: "greater than any crisis . . ." plus: "waiting and begging to be known." No one of these observations would be much to dwell upon, but if one races across them in a kind of blur, all told they establish a kind of tone, or attitude. They function not as analysis, but as a survey's variant of the Whitmanite catalogue.

At one point in his discussion of criticism, Mr. Kazin writes:

> The poet lived only for the perfection of his poem, as criticism lived only for the elucidation of that perfection. Hence Ransom's unforgettable remark on Wallace Stevens's *Sea Surface Full of Clouds:* "The poem has a calculated complexity, and its technical competence is so high that to study it, if you do that sort of thing, is to be happy." Hence his

> notation on the Macbeth soliloquy: "I do not know why *dusty death;* it is an odd but winning detail." Criticism had become expert at last; it had finally turned its full attention upon the poem itself; it missed nothing; it was stainless in motive, happy only to study the calculated complexity of those few poems whose technical competence was "high." It had become "a sort of thing," a game of devotions by knightly grammarians, and it made one happy.

The citation well illustrates what I would consider the great wastefulness of his literary policies, at least so far as the serious development of criticism is concerned. Rather than trying simply to give us an impression of Mr. Ransom's criticism, would it not be better to see that Mr. Ransom's perception does not go unused? Might one not, for instance, try to build upon it by the search for another step in the same direction? One might begin by noting, for instance, that death could be "dusty" for the same reason that ashes are consigned to ashes and dust to dust. Or one might depart from the fact that the two words are both so much alike in sound despite their differences. "Dusty death" is but a slight modification of the sound we'd get if we could speak of "duthy death," so that the adjective and the noun are almost identical in consonant structure but with different vowels. A great dramatist having put the words into a great soliloquy, and a perceptive critic having singled them out as a specially demarcated episode, the next step is not to strike a posture about it, but to see whether one can advance the matter a step farther by inquiring into the imagistic and tonal logic that may account for some of the appeal in the words.

One should want greatly to be happy at noting felicities wherever they may come, be they in rock formations, in the progress of a disease, in mathematics, or in rare poetry. And the most serious job of criticism is not, as with the reporter's survey, to look for suggestions that might in effect help to write the books over again, but to develop the resources of a *systematic conceptual analysis*. There is a place for Mr. Kazin's book: indeed, a quite reputable place, but only so long as he does not attempt to enforce upon criticism a method that would avoid the extremes of formalist and environmentalist criticism mainly by being too superficial and haphazard to go very far into either.

And rather than dismiss work of such obvious penetration as the formalists and environmentalists have produced, one should seek to develop a perspective that makes it more available by bringing its many aspects into closer relationship with one another; and one should work for the invention of critical concepts that will serve both to make the critical enterprise more methodical and to clarify its bearing upon the subject of human action in general.

# Criticism for the Next Phase

*Elizabethan and Metaphysical Imagery* by Rosemond Tuve. U of Chicago P
*Accent*, Winter 1948, 125–127

Let's begin this review with a Word to the Wise, a market tip. Namely: if you think you are seriously interested in literary criticism, *get this book*. And if you don't find it both engrossing and rewarding, here's another tip: give up the idea that you are seriously interested in literary criticism. Probably you are but a poetaster, or a frustrated novelist, who would conceal the truth from himself by improvising impressionistic translations of original works.

Rosemond Tuve's *Elizabethan and Metaphysical Imagery* is particularly important, in our opinion, because it can mark a stage in literary criticism. Here, clearly observable, is *a major position* among the several which any critic must incorporate into his thinking, if he would develop a well-rounded terminology for the analysis of literature now. It is not an original book (ironically, much of its value resides in the fact that it is not original); it is good because it shows such maturity and independence of judgment in the recovery of an earlier tradition. But we venture the blunt flat assertion that no really well-rounded criticism can be written today unless the critic can make himself at home in such thinking as this book embodies.

The immediate purpose of the book is to correct a present-day misreading of Elizabethan and Jacobean poetry by applying to this poetry the critical methods and criteria flourishing at the time when the poetry was written. The result, had the author been so minded, could have been almost rousingly bellicose. For underlying the work, quietly and often imperceptibly, there is a thesis which, with but a little "pointing up" for the purposes of rhetorical saliency, could make some of our *best* contemporary critics look almost comically nude, when they pontificate on the poetry of the Metaphysicals. By a patient and scholarly reconsideration of the earlier criticism, she shows convincingly that it is well qualified to analyze the forms and purposes of the best poetry then being written; and in the course of this task she shows, just as convincingly, that some of our best modern critics did a monstrously incongruous thing, in applying unsuitable contemporary Symbolist and post-Symbolist criteria to this earlier work.

The book is divided into two parts. The first deals with "Sensuousness and Significancy as Functions of Imagery." Here we have a very perceptive inquiry into such matters as

> "embellished Nature" as poetic subject; "delight" or pleasure as part (or all) of the poet's aim; the demand for "significancy"; the acceptance, for poetry, of certain aims (the didactic) and certain methods (abstract "statement") of reasonable discourse; the demand for rhetorical efficacy; and, most pervasively influential of all critical concepts, "Decorum" as a regulative principle.

The second section deals with "The Logical Functions of Imagery." Here, it seems to me, is the place at which the book begins to transcend its immediate purpose, suggesting ways of thought that must be systematically adapted to the study of imagery in general. But the author's concern is still with the immediate application, to the study of the image as used in Elizabethan and Jacobean poetry. She is advocating no mechanical application of pre-Symbolist criteria to post-Symbolist writing—since such a procedure would be but the reverse of the fallacy she is exposing.

But the important consideration, for criticism generally, is this: Far too often, today, the study of imagery has reduced a piece of literature to a mass of jelly. A writer's work is described as though it were no more defined than a smell of gas. And repeatedly, we find books of criticism saluted though they contain not one single analysis of formal development nor any method which could be applied to such ends.

Over and above its worth in correcting a current misevaluation of certain past literary movements, this book on *Elizabethan and Metaphysical Imagery* is particularly valuable, it seems to me, for its contribution in restoring logical and formal criteria to the study of imagery. There may be respects in which the "logical" and the "imaginative" are antithetical to each other. There may be cases where imagery is little more than a smell of gas, or even an imperceptible gas which nonetheless acts to put the reader into a semi-comatose state. But these thorough pages on the Logical Function of Imagery should go far, with an intelligent reader, towards breaking down the spontaneous assumption, so generally rife in modern esthetic theory, that the "logical" and the "imaginative" are always necessarily antithetical to each other.

Closely connected with this is her sharp reintroduction of rhetoric into the analysis of imagery. We thus get a clear picture of the ways in which logic, rhetoric, and poetic are interwoven (in contrast with the doctrines of those who would confine logic to science, rhetoric to propaganda or advertising, and thus leave for poetic a few spontaneous sensations not much higher in the intellectual scale than the twitchings of a decerebrated frog).

To be sure, when all the returns are in, some further adjustments will be found necessary. The author's very stress upon imagery, for instance, reflects a modern era in which the term, "Imagination," has taken on a complexity of meaning which it did not characteristically have in pre-Romantic terminologies. "Imagination" is now a club-offer, or Miscellany, with meanings ranging all the way from the visible, tangible, here-and-now to the mystically transcendent, from the purely sensory and empirical, even the scientifically factual, to the dramatistically emphatic and sympathetic, from the literal to the fantastic, including all the shades of sentiment, emotion, and judgment, plus the "unconscious" (or the various varieties of "unconscious," for this catch-all term is capable of division, *demands* division, and many of the slovenly critical tributes to the power of the "unconscious" in "Imagination" reflect little more than the critic's "unconscious" realization that his very term, "Imagination," is much like the dusty clutter in an old attic). And only insofar as "Imagination" is cleared up, (as Richards did *not* clear it up) can we expect to see the subject of "imagery" cleared up (and v. v.). But, in the meantime, we might well ponder this: Insofar as a poet's images are organically related, there is a *formal principle* behind them. They could be said to *body forth* this principle. The principle itself could, by a properly discerning critic, be named in terms of *ideas*. And thus, the imagery could be said to convey an invisible intangible idea in terms of visible, tangible things. (Is this Platonism? Or isn't it just a technical statement about organic poetic language?)

Meanwhile, bring together all three—logic, rhetoric, and poetic—in the analysis of imagery, with the proper rationale for doing so, and you are ready for the Next Phase. Because Rosemond Tuve's book on *Elizabethan and Metaphysical Imagery,* "imaginatively" following old texts, does this so well, I consider it a very important book for literary criticism.

# On Covery, Re- and Dis-

*A Reading of George Herbert* by Rosemond Tuve. U of Chicago P
*Accent*, Autumn 1953, 218–226

Some time back, in these pages, the present reviewer was happy to salute an earlier book by Miss Tuve, *Elizabethan and Metaphysical Imagery*. And he'd like to spread glad tidings about her recent work, *A Reading of George Herbert*. To be sure, he saluted her earlier book because of its stress upon rhetoric, whereas on this occasion the word is hardly mentioned, the major concern this time being a plea for scholarship.

But the kind of scholarship she would advocate is quite in the spirit of rhetoric, for it concerns the problem of establishing the proper relationship between writer and audience. Miss Tuve holds: We cannot be adequate readers of a poem such as George Herbert's "The Sacrifice" unless we consciously *recover* (or "uncover") certain important facts about a cultural tradition that was still vigorous at the time when Herbert wrote, but is much weaker now, and in many notable respects has even been lost.

By the dialectics of the case, her position is somewhat opposed to contemporary critical trends that aim rather at *discovery*. Thus, she quarrels with a modern critic who, when writing on "The Sacrifice," exclaims, "What fun, all the Freudian stuff." And instead of trying to discover new things about the workings of Herbert's mind by applying modern terms quite alien to his thinking, she wants us to make ourselves as good readers as possible by getting to understand him in his own terms.

On the other hand, she contends that close textual analysis of a work may not be enough, no matter how scrupulously and perceptively such analysis is contrived. For certain important meanings that may be "in" the language of a given poem at the time it was written, may later be "outside" the poem, insofar as the tradition implicit in that language drops away. And with regard to a religious poet like Herbert, she says, "It is perilous to be too sure of 'the meaning' of his poems without some attempt to be the reader he wrote for." Or again:

I would call attention to the fact that often what we require is plain ordinary information, for that is what time and history have done us out of. In the approach to poems, as in the approach to reality in any other form, we have right to only a limited amount of ignorance, or we shall quite simply not understand what we see. It is perfectly possible to claim that Herbert's poems are not worth the labour of understanding them, and I have been at pains to meet that objection. This is very different from the claim that understanding is not valuably or reliably advanced by information directly bearing on consciously intended meaning. Not until modern times has such a position been considered tenable by any serious criticism; it is now widely held.

The issue reminds us of a place in Chapter XVI of Croce's *Aesthetic*. Here, writing on "Taste and the Reproduction of Art," and considering the problem of historical restoration, Croce says:

> *Historical interpretation* labours for its part to reintegrate in us the psychological conditions which have changed in the course of history. It revives the dead, completes the fragmentary, and enables us to see a work of art (a physical object) as its author saw it in the moment of production.
>
> A condition of this historical labour is tradition, with the help of which it is possible to collect the scattered rays and concentrate them in one focus . . .
>
> Where the tradition is broken, interpretation is arrested; in this case, the products of the past remain silent for us.

He then proceeds to consider what he calls "palimpsests." These are due to "erroneous historical interpretation," and are "new expressions imposed upon the ancient, artistic fancies instead of historical reproductions. . . . 'The fascination of the past' depends in part upon these expressions of ours, which we weave upon the historical."

> Thus "the terror of the year 1000" has recently been discerned on the faces of the Byzantine saints, a terror which is a misunderstanding, or an artificial legend invented later by men of learning. But *historical criticism* tends precisely to circumscribe fancies and to establish exactly the point of view from which we must look.

Though Miss Tuve is far indeed from being a Crocean, her book does concern itself with one kind of "palimpsest," a kind resulting from the neglect of historical facts needed to make us the right kind of readers. And to this end, discussing "The Sacrifice" in accordance with "the idea that a poem is most beautiful and most meaningful to us when it is read in terms of the tradition which gave it birth," she points out that

> Herbert's poem belongs with two interlinked groups, both well known, of medieval lyrics; both groups belong as does his poem to a larger group, the Complaints of Christ to His People. All possibly had their spring in the liturgical offices of Holy Week, most obviously (for one group) in the *Improperia* or Reproaches of Good Friday.

Such placement of the poem provides her with leads that make her reading of it most appealingly sympathetic. And in the course of detailing the liturgical and iconographical traditions which lie behind the poem and which she thinks have not been given the consideration they require (she says that "Neither Canon Hutchinson's notes nor any critics of Herbert notice these liturgical connections"), she arrives at a new view of the stylistic devices we associate with the "Metaphysical" poets. "The secret of Metaphysical wit," she says, "lies in a reading of life . . . inherited through at least the ten or twelve preceding centuries." Thus, she would give a "demonstration of likenesses between the 'Metaphysical' manner and the great religious and secular allegorical tradition, regnant for centuries, upon which it was nourished." Or again, when discussing "a late-Romantic association between the witty and the audaciously unconventional," she says:

> I think that nothing but good, for the poems, comes of disrupting this association and of foregoing these praises, founded as both are on rather superficial notions of individuality and originality. Poems meant to be quietly moving will be differently read from poems meant to startle. They may gain in depth of meaning. My final instances of witty conventional images belong together in a definable group—from the poems on the church as a building with its parts, its adjuncts, its ornaments, and its priest. They have brought on Herbert more than one charge (sometimes even thought of as praise) of novel quaintness and engagingly childish naïveté: of late they have rather been seen as "Metaphysically" clever, chiefly pleasurable for their capac-

ity to surprise through dissonant and unexpected combinations.

Few of us are quite as heathenishly ignorant of the traditional lore as Miss Tuve, in the heights of her advocacy, sometimes seems to suggest. And even some of the heathens may have chanced upon works like Remy De Gourmont's *Le Latin Mystique,* where many oddities of mediaeval piety are assembled by a godless literary epicure who nostalgically savored as style what he could not even dream of accepting as doctrine.

But in any case, criticism generally seems to have considered the Metaphysicals' "wit" and "conceits" rather in terms of their cavalier origins than as a selecting of salient expressions traditional to religious commentary. And in the course of her study, she gives a very good survey of the stylistic or terministic resources traditionally available to sacred poetry. Thus anyone interested in studying, or even passively reading, the Metaphysical poets in general and Herbert in particular should find this book engrossing.

In effect, Miss Tuve's consideration of "The Sacrifice" with regard to the traditional "Complaints of Christ to His People" helps define it as a literary species. And in effect her attributing of the Metaphysical style to liturgical and iconographical sources redefines this style as a literary species. We mean that, just as the emphasis upon "scholarship" somewhat concealed the underlying concern with a problem of rhetoric, so it also somewhat conceals an underlying concern with a problem of poetics. In statements like the following, she would seem to be discussing, in the name of "scholarship," terministic deployments that involve the resources of dialectic in general:

> All these poems belong to a mode of writing wherein there is nothing strange whatsoever in a body which is both fruit and vine, in an earthly rood-tree grown out of an apple of Paradise, in an apple which is a sword held in the hand of him who ate it. Symbolical writing (including Herbert's) is confusing only when we read symbol as picture. . . . Christ is the fruit, He is the oil of compassion from the tree of life, He is the babe, He is the king reigning from the tree, He is the life which makes it burgeon, He is Sapientia itself, and the tree is the knowledge of good and evil, and when they ate of it they should be as gods—all these are ways of saying the unsayable connexion between the doing of the sin and the undoing of it, and there is paradox and mystery at the heart of the whole conception Herbert knew and his predecessors knew.

As regards the genesis of the Metaphysical "wit," one might agree with Miss Tuve's contribution, but use it differently. One might see such wit not just in terms of a theological tradition, but as the fusing of it with a courtly tradition. For instance, in his introduction to *The Works of George Herbert*, F. E. Hutchinson writes of Herbert's mother:

> Donne describes her high intelligence and "sharpness of wit," as well as her devotion to the Scriptures and the services of the Church: "the wit of our time is profaneness; *nevertheless,* she that loved that hated this"; "her house was a court in the conversation of the best."

And surely, if we are to make ourselves into readers such as prevailed at those times, we could hardly go wrong in taking Donne's comments on wit as quite relevant to our views of its implications. Furthermore, where matters of "reverence" are concerned, should we not consider such possibilities of fusing social eminence with divine eminence as would be indicated by the similarity between "My Lord" and "milord"? In trying to make ourselves fit readers for works written in such a time, why should we not consider also such relationships between the language of worldly hierarchy and the language of the supernatural hierarchy, each with its great stress upon the exercising of one's desire freely to praise? In the case of Herbert, certainly, we have a man who, despite his early vows to write only sacred poetry, made many attempts to launch himself in a career at court; and only after the death of all those (including King James) who were his best hopes for preferment, did he finally decide to take orders in the Church of England.

We do not offer these remarks "debunkingly." For both by reliable historical data and by the internal evidence of Herbert's own writings, we are led to believe that, as a priest, he was exceptionally scrupulous in his ministry of the religious services and in his relations to his parishioners. But such considerations bring up another matter:

If we read but "The Sacrifice," the scholarly aids *from without,* as provided by Miss Tuve, are very necessary indeed. And if only that one poem survived from that era, her admonitions would be invaluable. Actually, as it so happens, since we have quite a body of poems by the same author, if we read the lot, carefully "indexing" them, and letting them throw light upon one another, we shall find, within, nearly all the interpretations that Miss Tuve assembles from *external* sources. (We say *"nearly* all.") But Miss Tuve seems to us essentially right in her contention that, insofar as a tradition weakens, many important elements once "in" the poem must be supplied "from outside" it. Only if scholarship had already produced a perfect dictionary, acquainting us with all the important public associations that clustered about a given word at the time of the usage in question, could "criticism" thereafter dispense with "scholarship." And Miss Tuve's work is, in effect, an attempt to suggest that certain meanings were more clearly "in" the poem at that time because at that time they were "in" the words which the poem used, whereas later some of these meanings faded from the poem because they faded from the poem's terminology. But often she would seem to suggest that more is lost than really has been.

Miss Tuve does make very helpful comments on about a dozen other poems by Herbert, thereby beginning an internal analysis. But once we mention the possibility of reading and "indexing" *all* the other poems of Herbert as an "internal" step towards making ourselves the kind of reader he himself was, we confront further possibilities. For instance, what of those twelve hundred or so "Outlandish Proverbs" he collected? They are a charming part of the man, and many of them throw another kind of light upon the themes in the lyrics. Or what of his engaging prose work, *A Priest to the Temple*, where he draws up rules of conduct for an ideal Country Parson ("that I may have a mark to shoot at")? Much of it is even shrewd, in a quite humane sort of way. And though a majority of Herbert's lyrics was written before it, it surely reveals the kind of context in which such sacred verse was in those times received.

We have no right to ask that Miss Tuve write a book different from the good one she did write. That's not the point we are trying to make. Let's try it this way:

Miss Tuve aims to *intensify* for us the mood of the poem she is analyzing. To this end, she asks us to consider other works, not by this author, but in the same tradition. Her purpose is to make us into the kind of audience for which Herbert wrote. At this point, the reviewer proposed to get "inside Herbert" by reading all of Herbert, and letting his various works serve as comments upon one another. But as soon as you do that, you come upon some works that, while they are as moralistically directed as "The Sacrifice," would serve as *latitudinarian modifiers* of the mood in that poem rather than as *strict intensifiers* of it.

Thus, when Miss Tuve writes, "Nothing we can do to this poem can prevent it from being a poem about man seen as guilty of wrong-doing, and faced with the choice of redemption," one may recall (in *A Priest to the Temple*) the brief Chapter XXVII, on "The Parson in Mirth":

> The Countrey Parson is generally sad, because hee knows nothing but the Crosse of Christ, his minde being defixed on it with those nailes wherewith his Master was: or if he have any leisure to look off from thence, he meets continually with two most sad spectacles, Sin, and Misery; God

dishonoured every day, and man afflicted. Neverthelesse, he somtimes refresheth himselfe, as knowing that nature will not bear everlasting droopings, and that pleasantnesse of disposition is a great key to do good; not onely because all men shun the company of perpetuall severity, but also for that when they are in company, instructions seasoned with pleasantnesse, both enter sooner, and roote deeper. Wherefore he condescends to humane frailties both in himselfe and others; and intermingles some mirth in his discourses occasionally, according to the pulse of the hearer.

Or when she refers to "the awfulness of evil incarnate," one may think of these lines, on "The Parson in his house":

> He keeps his servants between love, and fear, according as hee findes them; but generally he distributes it thus, To his Children he showes more love then terrour, to his servants more terrour then love; but an old good servant boards a child. [*Boards* in the sense of *borders* on.]

The Absolute Charity and cult of Praise in the great liturgical moments may thus be seen as a pious completing, or rounding-out, of social scruples, such as find their expression in rules of thumb like this:

> The Countrey Parson owing a debt of Charity to the poor, and of Courtesie to his other parishioners, he so distinguisheth, that he keeps his money for the poor, and his table for those that are above Alms. Not but that the poor are welcome also to his table, whom he sometimes purposely takes home with him, setting them close by him, and carving for them, both for his own humility and their comfort, who are much cheered with such friendliness. But since both is to be done, the better sort invited, and meaner relieved, he chooseth rather to give the poor money, which they can better employ to their own advantage, and sutably to their needs, then so much given in meat at dinner.

The title of this review is adapted from a review (in *The Dial*, August 1925) of the late V. F. Calverton's book, *The Newer Spirit, a Sociological Criticism of Literature*.* The reviewer there accused Calverton of failing to distinguish between "the discovery of a principle" and "the recovery of a fact." To appreciate *Gulliver's Travels*, we said, one would not need to know what

---
* See "On Re and Dis" in this collection.

psychological "complex" made Swift write of giants and pygmies, or what economic considerations led him to write his satire as an adventure story rather than as an essay. But "If Swift . . . makes a sly gibe . . . at some current political intrigue now forgotten, the modern reader must have the relevant environmental facts of this intrigue restored for him by editorial annotation if he is to appreciate the 'value' of the gibe." Or, elsewhere the issue was stated as a distinction between genesis as "cause" and genesis as "environment" ("environment" here being quite close to the sort of considerations Miss Tuve offers in the name of "tradition").

Obviously criticism should be for both Dis-a and Data. Suppose one could make oneself the perfect fall guy for an earlier writer. Miss Tuve seems to feel that therein would lie knowledge. But would it? Or if it is "knowledge" we ask of art, rather than of science, then at least, once we had equipped ourselves to be the wholly sympathetic enjoyer of another's text, might there not still be room for a further kind of knowledge, the kind that comes of meditating upon our memories of such enjoyed experiences?

And what sort of rationale would that further kind require? We believe that, as regards the aesthetic of Re, it would look like Dis. Recall, for instance, Herbert's magnificent poem, "The Collar," with its rebelliously spirited movement that suddenly veers in the closing lines, as the poet, who had slipped his collar, then at the last puts it on again, meekly answering, "My Lord" to a voice he heard addressing him as "Child."

What goes on here? First, we may note that, the relation between "My Lord" and "milord" being what it is, a poem addressed to a supernatural eminence could be interpreted as also ambiguously addressed to a worldly eminence. In fact, parody of this sort might be so readily available, that a scrupulous poet writing in the religious mode might even be troubled now and then lest his reverence secretly contain a modicum of such parody despite himself (being too narrowly conceived after the secular mode). Such a temptation is all the more likely inasmuch as human speech can have no positive terms for the supernatural order, all expressions for this order necessarily being borrowed from our terms for the other three orders: the natural, the social, and the linguistic.

Crashaw can make his readers go another way by using, for his accounts of supernatural love, a terminology so obviously sexual that readers are made ashamed of their own suspicions. In his literary devotions he can come so dangerously near to parody that his readers blush, not for him, but for themselves in thinking of such things.

But though one might parody the Herbert poem by ending it not "My Lord!" but "milord!" there is another important consideration here. We refer to the possibility that the role of his mother, too, figures in his ideas of "lordship," and that such motives overlapped momentously upon his poetic art. For instance, bear in mind the *mater-metra* pun in one of his Latin poems to the memory of his mother, or his references to sucking at the words of Scripture like a nursling. Recall also that he attributed flowing female breasts to his God. For though Miss Tuve justly reminds us that this usage, too, is traditional, it is possible that this fact may be Dis-regarded. (Since the idea of divinity has been traditionally equated with just about everything in the way of imagery, the important consideration may be not so much the traditionality of a choice as the significance of that particular choice.)

Herbert's mother might with all the more reason figure in Herbert's sense of Supernatural Lordship, since his father died when he was scarcely past infancy. And there are, of course, the famous lines in "Longing":

> From thee all pitie flows.
> Mothers are kinde, because thou art,
> And dost dispose
> To them a part:
> Their infants, them; and they suck thee
> More free.

Here would seem to be dialectical (or "linguistic!") considerations worth pondering. If one uses a familial image, such as "mother" or "father" for the idea of godhead, and then moves "towards a higher level of generalization or abstraction" (as with the Platonist view of the dialectical progression from "the senses" towards "divinity") one comes next upon a term like "parent" that combines the nature of the two. If, then, one reduced the idea of "parent" to a corresponding image, androgynous attributes would seem inevitable.

Further grotesquenesses are possible here; for if the godhead, in his sacrificial capacity, is expected to take on (or *stand for*) all human sins, then insofar as the ambiguities of devout imagery can stand roundabout for perverse practices deemed evil by the doer, the devout sinner may preferably conceive the godhead in such terms of unintended parody as come closest to the imaging of his transgressions. (Think, for instance, what the imagery of Saint Sebastian would most readily lend itself to, for purposes of parody. The thought is not just "Freudian," but concerns relations between idea and image generally.)

In sum: There are quandaries that concern both "psychological" and "sociological" motives, if we must accept Miss Tuve's alignment of terms as final. But we, rather, would think of these quandaries as problems of "knowledge" that works of art do not resolve for us, though they give us invaluable material for use in our search, a search over and above the delight that we can have if we read and ponder texts with the help of such able investigators as Miss Tuve.

# The Criticism of Criticism

*The Lion and the Honeycomb; Essays in Solicitude and Critique* by R. P.
  Blackmur. Harcourt, Brace
*Accent,* Autumn 1955, 279–292

Mr. Blackmur is first of all a technical critic, an analyst of texts, (a "New Critic"), one of the best we have. Second, he makes social observations that impart an air of distinction to the life of books (an accomplishment especially welcome to any of us who may hope that books of our own may somehow some day make us, if not distinguished, then at least distinguishable). Third, he sometimes puts forth statements of policy, quasi-diplomatic releases designed to serve some turn in the rhetoric, or politics, of the republic of letters.

Not that these emphases are always confined to separate essays. Sometimes they are relatively pure, sometimes interwoven. And even in discussion of one particular author, his concerns are regularly on the side of criticism in general (as with his "radical allegiance to language," if we may apply to him a formula that he applies to T. S. Eliot). Hence, the title, "the criticism of criticism," for this review of his new book.

From the standpoint of readers especially interested in the resources and embarrassments of words, I think that one of the most fertile things this critic, or any critic, ever did in technical criticism was his analysis of the word "flower" as used in e. e. cummings. In this essay (the first in his first collection of critical essays, *The Double Agent*) Mr. Blackmur was working at rock bottom—and one might adopt or adapt his observations without necessarily sharing his attitude or putting his remarks to the same use.

The present collection does not reprint this. (However, it was reprinted in his third volume of criticism, *Language as Gesture.*) But another early essay, a masterly piece of characterization, "The Critical Prefaces of Henry James," does reappear. Perhaps the two best pieces of characterization in the present collection are another essay on Henry James, and an attempt to give the gist of Eliot's criticism, "In the Hope of Straightening Things Out."

The new James essay gravitates about problems of form along lines in keeping with Aristotle's *Poetics*. However, despite the Jamesian slogan, "Dramatise it!" (a slogan that led James dramatistically to view his problems primarily in terms of "act," "agent," and "scene") there are notable differences between the application of this formula to drama proper and its extension to problems of the novel. Mr. Blackmur does not attempt as thoroughly or systematically as critics like Ronald Crane or Elder Olson might, to differentiate between the principles of drama and those of the novel. Possibly he is deterred somewhat by his pudency as regards what he calls "methodology." But in any case, his close looks at the texts he is discussing make everything he says worth watching here, and do expertly follow the leads of Aristotle's method, in considering the Jamesian novel primarily from the standpoint of its nature as a literary species.

Shopping about among the seventeen pieces here assembled, and trying to survey as fairly as possible in a brief space the mere contents of the book, let us first give tidings of the pieces not already mentioned or not to be discussed later:

"The Politics of Human Power" is a review of Lionel Trilling's *The Liberal Imagination*. Here Mr. Blackmur subscribes to "the tory anarchy which is just the other side of liberalism." He holds that "The true business of literature, as of all intellect, critical or creative, is to remind the powers that be, simple and corrupt as they are, of the turbulence they have to control. There is a disorder vital to the individual which is fatal to society."

"The Artist as Hero" considers such "expressionistic" heroes as those in Dostoevsky, Joyce, Gide, Mann's *Dr. Faustus*—for "the place where morals hit hardest on the arts is in the center, where the hero is."

"The Economy of the American Writer" is built about the thought that "the theory of a cultural market does not work."

"The American Literary Expatriate" is an exceptionally good survey of variations in the type, including the species that "stayed at home and practiced ingrown expatriation." The essay includes many astute references to the social and economic elements that figured in the phenomenon. It is indebted to Henry James at one end and to Mr. Malcolm Cowley at the other, though only James gets quoted.

"The Expense of Greatness" is an efficient digest giving us the gist of Henry Adams. "I want to regard him as he often chose to regard himself, as a representative example of education: but education pushed to the point of failure as contrasted with ordinary education which stops at the formula of success." For: "Success is not the propitious term for education unless the lesson wanted is futile. Education has no term and if arrested at all is only arrested by impassable failure." This is an early essay (1936), and perhaps Mr.

Blackmur himself would be willing to grant that it could profit by greater stress upon Adams' use of the dialectic pair, "multiplicity" and "unity," with the colonies of terms that come to duster about these poles.

"The Everlasting Effort" treats of T. E. Lawrence and his "problem of the obsessed sensibility." ("We say that Dante was a master of disgust; lacking St. Thomas and Aristotle, Lawrence is a master of disgorgement.")

"The Craft of Herman Melville" discusses Melville's "radical inability to master a technique—that of the novel—radically foreign to his sensibility."

"Humanism and Symbolic Imagination" builds up Mr. Blackmur's notion of the "symbolic imagination" by contrast with the doctrines of Irving Babbitt, who "was a praiser of gone times because he had none of his own." This look back at Babbitt's legislating brings the author close to vehemence, as when he says of Babbitt: "In almost the exact measure that he secures assent to his main position he rouses antipathy by the blows—blind, brutal, and arrogant—which he strikes from it." However, I just happen to have been reading a paper, "Irving Babbitt and Benedetto Croce," by Folke Leander; and I was here reminded that, for all the shortcomings of Babbitt when on the relation between poetry and ethics, his stress upon the "inner check" does serve to bring out the essentially *negative* aspect of "conscience." But there's no denying that, by the rhetorical and/or dialectical device of defining the idea of the "symbolic imagination" by antithesis to Babbitt, Mr. Blackmur at least makes us feel very forcefully what such imagination is *not*.

In "Notes on Four Categories in Criticism," these four divisions are proposed: (1) "superficial techniques," such as meter, plot, stanza, rhyme, alliteration; (2) "linguistic technique," such as images, tropes, and idiom, which is "speech breathing with perception"; (3) "the ulterior technique of the imagination," by which is apparently meant the elements of cultural background that may be necessary to an understanding of a work, elements that can be lost and that can be restored somewhat by historical criticism, conventions that served as authority even when rejected (what Malinowski might have called the "context of situation," or Carl Becker the "climate of opinion" that may be lost insofar as it is merely implied in a given work); (4) the "symbolic imagination," by which an "image" becomes a "symbol." The previously-mentioned negative approach to the "symbolic imagination" is here matched by a very good positive example, thus:

> In *Madame Bovary* the widowed doctor reaches the desire to marry Emma when he sees her tip her head back and insert her tongue into a cordial glass: she is given as nubile, ripe, romantic, and ready. In this image—this touch of the actual—are present, by authority, the institutions, conven-

tions, and fictional formulas that have to do with marriage. Flaubert knows how little he has to put in—the tongue in the glass—and how much he can leave out—all the human needs that are conveyed in marriage . . .

And later, with a just stress upon the element of anticipation in form, he says:

> In *Madame Bovary* is it not Flaubert's *anticipation* of Emma's collapse exactly what leads to it and makes it inevitable? There was nothing in the situation that might not have been changed by a single different step; but then the satisfaction of the anticipation would have been lost and the book would have fallen apart. Is it not perhaps the actuality of that anticipation that craves reality? . . . As she collapses she becomes a symbol satisfying Flaubert's anticipation and much more, articulating in her figure and in the configuration of the novel both the anticipation of the author and the actuality of her experience.

The reference to *Flaubert's* anticipation is perhaps a bit misleading, as here quoted. It refers to the ways in which Flaubert, by his ways of anticipation, produced a book that shapes our anticipations as readers.

"Between the Numen and the Moha" is an ingenious refurbishment of two old dialectical favorites, variously called mind-body, spirit-matter, spirit-letter. It contains a brief anecdotal interlude (the page-long section III) that is picturesquely morbid (suggesting somewhat the sort of effect Mann sometimes gets in hospital scenes). The tenor of the chapter is indicated in the reference to "the sickness of our times, which have invented the term 'ideology' and have puerilized the term 'dialectic'"; accordingly, "If there is a destructive criticism of Mann's novels, it is that his conceptual structure is sometimes so schematic that it invades and destroys his substance." All told: "This is one of the ways the struggle between the *Numen* and the *Moha* actually takes place." Though Mr. Blackmur thought highly enough of this essay to end on it, I cannot give it the attention it thus would seem to deserve. In particular, his working of the refrain, "T'have seen what I have seen, see what I see!" seems a bit rhetorically forced. But the closing words do provide a most appealing resonant note to end on:

> Was it not the old peasant, in *War and Peace,* who cured Pierre by his nightly proverbial prayer in the garden of their prison: Let me lie down, oh God, like a stone, and wake like fresh bread? That is, between the *Numen* and the *Moha.*

"Dante's Ten Terms for the Treatment of the Treatise" is perhaps Mr. Blackmur's most forthright sally into dialectic, here on the subject of poetics, and in line with Dante's definition of poetry as a "rhetorical fiction." It is built around Dante's description of the *Divine Comedy*, as "poetic, fictive, descriptive, digressive, transumptive; and likewise proceeding by definition, division, proof, refutation, and setting forth of examples." Mr. Blackmur tentatively makes pairs of terms by variously matching the terms and speculating on the results. He uses this dialectic maneuvering heuristically to suggest perspectives on various literary works, as when he says: "Miranda is poetic definition; *The Alchemist* is fictive division; Proust is descriptive proof; *Joseph in Egypt* is digressive refutation; *Lear* or *Hamlet* is transumptive example." He goes on to list the remaining possible pairs, though he does not give any applications that these other sets may have suggested to him, and he does not apply the scheme elsewhere in the book.

The essay that gives the book its title is decidedly in the third of the classes I mentioned at the beginning of this review. It is a statement of policy . . . designed to serve some turn in the rhetoric, or politics, of the republic of letters. In keeping with the genius of his subtitle for the book, I assume that he would class it among his "solicitudes."

Dated 1950, it calls for a new start, beyond the "New Criticism." Asserting that the New Critics, including himself, had been too exclusively concerned with problems of rhetoric, he calls upon them to repent somewhat, not by dropping rhetoric, but by adding two other dimensions: dialectic and poetic.

I would gladly have joined in his clarion call. I'd have come shouting "Me too!" But alas, without referring to any specific treatment of dialectic in my writings, or to items of mine that I would place in the field of poetics, Mr. Blackmur says that "In Mr. Burke rhetoric always does all the work."

This severe sentence is offered also as prophecy for my subsequent work, with regard to which Mr. Blackmur says: "If we remember that one of Mr. Burke's favorite key devices is contained in the remark that language is either *symbolic* action or symbolic *action,* I think we may hazard it that rhetoric will be doing the work in the symbolic."

Part of the trouble may be due to the fact that different people draw the line between poetic and rhetoric at different places. For instance, we saw Mr. Blackmur himself quoting Dante's definition of poetry as *fictio rhetorica*. Similarly, the line of demarcation between rhetoric and dialectic wavers (as one might expect in the light of Aristotle's observation that rhetoric is the "counterpart" of dialectic). In this same essay, Mr. Blackmur states abruptly, "Dialectic has nothing to do with Hegel"—and if that's the end of Hegel, what right have others to complain? But as regards the possibility of accenting the expression "symbolic action" on either the adjective or the noun: I would consider it a dialectical fact that an expression compounded of two elements can be slanted two ways, though such a *dialectical* potentiality can be exploited for *rhetorical* purposes. For instance, if you define poetry as "an imitation of life," you have an expression that slopes two ways, since some observers can stress the nature of the imitation, while others can stress the ways in which the imitation derives vitality from its origins in real life. And if you wanted to sum up this distinction by a shift of accent (a resource natural to language as tonal gesture) you could say that one school hears the expression as "*imitation* of life," while the other hears it as "imitation of *life*." And whereas *rhetorical* battles of the books could arise from these choices, we could look upon them as grounded in a *dialectical* condition, a duality of possibilities implicit in the compound expression itself.

Somewhere in the Shawcross edition of Coleridge's *Biographia Literaria* there is a similar observation, with regard to the distinction between "imagination" and "fancy." It is suggested that you might think of imagination as "*unity* in diversity" and of fancy as "unity in *diversity*." And if Mr. Blackmur, in a dialectical exercise, would permit himself to consider many possible "permutations and combinations" among ten terms of Dante's, surely this analyst of "language as *gesture*" (or "*language* as gesture"?) should allow for the possible heuristic shift of an accent as a way of revealing the elements of dialectical instability that may be concealed in a term.

Surprisingly, though the "Lion" essay calls for "the mutually related and interinanimated modes of poetic, dialectic, and rhetoric," it itself is essentially an exercise in rhetoric, built around the rhetorical use of Yeats's poem on the "Second Coming." (That is, the poem is introduced not as a theme for study as poetics, but in order that its imagery may be exploited by the essayist for rhetorical purposes, to dissuade an audience.) Yeats having vatically prophesied along Spenglerian lines that the world is in decay and that a repugnant Caesarish Rough Beast will arise, Mr. Blackmur suggests that the New (= Rhetorical) Criticism fits the sinister recipe. This Criticism he next identifies with a somewhat ungainly term, "methodology." All told, he builds up this persuasive set of equations: New Criticism = exclusive stress upon Rhetoric = "Mere anarchy . . . loosed upon the world" = "methodology."

"Methodology" *could* mean simply the systematic criticism of method. In this regard, it could be related to professional scruples on the part of a critic who paused in his criticism of others' poetry to criticize his own criticism. As so viewed, one might grant its proneness to excess, without feeling that it was to be identified with Yeats's horrendous Rough Beast, as in this essay.

However, Mr. Blackmur's treatment of it is not *exclusively* rhetorical. "Method becomes methodology," he says, "when a means becomes an end."

Though this formula is often used rhetorically, it does have a grounding in dialectic. But ironically enough, any really thorough analysis of the ways in which means tend to usurp the role of ends will be good in proportion as it itself thinks along methodological lines. There is a sense, for instance, in which even the best of art could be called a transforming of means into ends (as when an artistic medium is used for its own sake rather than for some utilitarian purpose, or when a poet uses sheerly as poetic forms the rhetorical devices which an orator uses to make an audience change its mind in some controversial issue).

As part of his program, Mr. Blackmur also pleads for a greater concern with Aristotle's Poetics. To this end, he selects, for intelligent relish, certain of Aristotle's key terms, which he places succinctly and aptly. However, since he is stressing essentials, I wish he had taken the further space needed to bring out the importance of Aristotle's concern with literary works in terms of their nature as *species*. For this is the very essence of Aristotle's approach to his subject, and it is a matter often neglected in post-Crocean criticism.

The omission has strategic bearing upon one of the definitions. I refer to Mr. Blackmur's definition of tragic catharsis as "the purging, cleansing, purifying of the *mythos* subject to *mimesis*." That is, he here treats catharsis as a process sheerly internal to the work, quite as though, through "incidents arousing pity and fear," the poetic action of the work so "accomplished its catharsis of such emotions" that the story itself could be considered as undergoing the purge. And the loss of Aristotle's writings on poetic catharsis, along with the fact that he treated of this subject in the Poetics rather than in the Rhetoric, helps us all the more to assume that Aristotle was here discussing the symbolic purging not of the *audience,* but of the *plot* (which he variously calls the end, purpose, principle, life, and soul of tragedy).

But though I incline to share what I take to be Mr. Blackmur's feeling, that poetics should ideally treat of a work in its internality, and though I think we should aim as fully as possible at a purely internal account of "catharsis," there seems good reason to doubt that Aristotle had such purely internal reference in mind when thinking of "catharsis." For he is very much concerned with the nature of tragic pleasure. And whereas one might, for methodological reasons, legitimately object to introducing here his references to catharsis in the Politics (where the term deals with the purging of tendencies toward political unrest), surely we can make up for the loss of the section on purgation in the Poetics by citing related lines from his treatise on Music, which he classes as another kind of *mimesis* (that is, imitation, or, in my proposed heuristic translation, "symbolic action"). Here he writes:

> Music should be studied, not for the sake of one, but of many benefits, that is to say, with a view to education and purgation (the word "purgation" we use at present without explanation, but when hereafter we speak of poetry, we will treat the subject with more precision). . . . In education the most ethical modes are to be preferred, but in listening to the performances of others we may admit the modes of action and passion also. For feelings such as pity and fear, or, again, enthusiasm, exist very strongly in some souls, and have more or less influence over all. Some persons fall into a religious frenzy, whom we see as a result of the sacred melodies—when they have used the melodies that excite the soul to mystic frenzy—restored as though they had found healing and purgation. Those who are influenced by pity or fear, and every emotional nature, must have a like experience, and others insofar as each is susceptible to such emotions, and all are in a manner purged and their souls lightened and delighted. The purgative melodies likewise give an innocent pleasure to mankind. Such are the modes and melodies in which those who perform music at the theatre should be invited to compete. But since the spectators are of two kinds—the one free and educated, and the other a vulgar crowd composed of mechanics, laborers, and the like—there ought to be contests and exhibitions instituted for the relaxation of the second class also. And the music will correspond to their mind; for as their minds are perverted from the natural state, so there are perverted modes and highly strung and unnaturally colored melodies.

Here, obviously, Aristotle is discussing catharsis, not as a "purifying" or unfolding of the melodic line, but as a response that music aroused *in an audience*. And precisely at this point he refers to his use of the term in the Poetics. A lesser reason for thinking that the formula can deal with a rhetorical consideration (the "purifying" effect that the work has *upon an audience*) is that questions of audience appeal are considered elsewhere in the Poetics (hence, are not categorically excluded). And modern works, such as George Thomson's *Aeschylus and Athens*, studying the derivation of secular tragedy from a religious ceremony, can justify us in looking for its corresponding function as a kind of *secular* "medicine," however modified, and however amply analyzable in its own right.

One other point should be mentioned as regards this titular essay. When setting up Coleridge's *Biographia Literaria* as another norm to be followed, Mr. Blackmur focuses on three terms: esemplastic, coadunative, and synergical. He gives a brief definition of each, in accordance with his own interpretation of them.

Since I don't know where "synergical" appears in Coleridge's works, and since Mr. Blackmur gives us no quotations from Coleridge, though he does well by it we cannot wholly share his relish in it. But it looks like a term that might be profitably scrutinized for a possible relation to the doctrine of "synergism." (There seems a chance that, whereas the theological term designates a heresy, its analogue in Coleridge might reveal interesting transformations when thus transplanted).

As regards the other terms, "esemplastic" and "coadunative," there is the opportunity for a closer look; and I think that Mr. Blackmur's definitions require a closer look; for otherwise the reader may puzzle himself in an attempt to discern a distinction where none may really exist.

"Esemplastic" he defines as: "forming, shaping, at a rhetorical level if you take rhetoric as a creative agent." And "coadunative" he defines as "having to do with the union of similar substances, at a dialectical level if you take dialectic as an aesthetic agent." He nowhere quotes from Coleridge to establish this distinction. And I greatly doubt whether he could find any quotations to back him. I think he is improvising here (perhaps in accordance with his own wisecrack elsewhere, that there is a taint of "original genius" in our critics). So far as I can make out, the terms are wholly synonymous, except that one of them is an artificial construct of Coleridge's from Greek elements, the other being the nearest equivalent from the Latin (*coadunatio* is in the big Harpers' Latin Dictionary).

Let us consider a passage from the collection of Coleridge fragments, *Anima Poetae*. Here the words seem to be used interchangeably, though one of them appears in a slightly modified form. (As has been noted in the Shawcross edition of the *Biographia Literaria,* Coleridge seems to have read something into the German that is not etymologically there, but no matter.)

> How excellently the German *Einbildungskraft* expresses this prime and loftiest faculty, the power of co-adunation, the faculty that forms the many into one—*in-eins-bildung!* Eisenoplasy, or esenoplastic power, is contradistinguished from fantasy, or the mirrorment, either catoptric or metoptric—repeating simply, or by transposition—and, again, involuntary as in dreams, or by an act of the will.

Here, you will note, he specifically uses "co-adunation" to name imagination, or "the faculty that forms the many into one." But in his *Biographia Literaria*, his subtitle for chapter XIII is "On the imagination, or esemplastic power." And there is the much-quoted passage at the beginning of chapter X, where he made up the Greek form of his term "from the Greek words, *eis hen plattein,* to shape into one."

It seems to me that Mr. Blackmur is here asking his readers to use the terms in accordance with a distinction that Coleridge himself did not make. And the distinction is explained by another distinction that in itself needs to be explained. I refer to his distinction between: "esemplastic" as rhetorical "if you take rhetoric as a creative agent"; and "co-adunative" as dialectical "if you take dialectic as an aesthetic agent."*

In another essay that we would class among the statements of policy, "A Burden for Critics," Mr. Blackmur builds his position around three Latin formulae: *Omnis intellectus omniformis est; fides quaerens intellectus; corruptio optima pessima.* The second and third are slightly wrong, with corresponding errors in translation. In the case of the third, the difference is negligible. And elsewhere in the book it appears correctly. But the slight difference in the second makes for a notable difference in translation that is worth dwelling on. For it is not a mere error; rather, in the form he gave it, it reveals

---

* So far as I can see, the line "Plastic and vast, one intellectual breeze" (in the "Eolian Harp" poem) is dealing with the same unifying effect of the imagination as this note in *Anima Poetae:*

> As when the taper's white cone of flame is seen double, till the eye moving brings them into one space and then they become one—so did the idea in my imagination coadunate with your present form soon after I first gazed upon you.

In another note Coleridge speaks of feelings being "more confused, and thereby, coadunated"—then continues: "Just as white is the very emblem of one in being the confusion of all." Coleridge attributes this unifying power of imagination to Wordsworth as a poet; and such *poetic* faculty (which, at the end of chapter XIII he calls the "secondary Imagination") is either "esemplastic" or "co-adunative," as you prefer.

The only possible distinction I can see concerns not public dictionary meanings but private poetic overtones. When Coleridge writes that *plattein* means "to shape into one," we catch a glimpse of the way in which his critical word *esemplastic* and his poetic word *plastic* (used with reference to his vision of ideal unity, in his "Eolian Harp" poem) both contain, at one remove, a word that was greatly resonant for him: the word "shape." To pick but three spots along its fatally ambiguous range: "These shapings of the unregenerate mind"; "A speck, a mist, a shape, I wist!"; "My shaping spirit of Imagination." The word "coadunative" would lack the traces of "shape" that lurk in "esemplastic." [K.B.]

something essential about the dialectic pattern that seems to lie at the basis of his thinking.

Mr. Blackmur writes:

> The temptation of the Middle Ages was to identify God with either one's own knowledge of him or with one's particular form of faith. *Fides quaerens intellectus* is a motto meant to redeem that temptation; for it is faith alone that may question the intellect, as it is only the intellect that can curb faith. The very principle of balance, together with the radical precariousness of its nature, lies in the reversibility of this motto.

The traditional formula accredited to St. Anselm has not *intellectus* but *intellectum*, (an accusative where Mr. Blackmur puts a nominative). *Grammatically*, there is no "reversibility" in this version of the formula. It can be translated in but one direction: "faith seeking understanding." And as regards the *doctrinal* nature of the formula, St. Anselm himself happens to have explicitly discussed its singleness of direction. "Right order requires," he says, "that we believe the profundities of Christian faith, before we presume to discuss them rationally." (*Rectus ordo exigit, ut profunda Christianae fidei credamus, priusquam ea praesumamus ratione discutere.* See on Anselm in the Ninth Edition of the *Encyclopaedia Britannica*.)

Emile Brehier's history, *La Philosophie du Moyen Age*, makes it clear that the singleness of direction was re-enforced by a third stage, *intellectus* being but an intermediate step between faith and vision (or *contemplatio*), which transcends the ergotizing ways of the understanding. And in Chapter II of his *L'Esprit de la Philosophie Medifvale*, Etienne Gilson brings out the same irreversibility thus:

> *La hiérarchie traditionnelle des modes de connaissance, chez les penseurs chrétiens, est toujours la foi, l'intelligence, la vue de Dieu face à face:* "Inter fidem et speciem," *ecrit saint Anselme,* "intellectum quem in hac vita capimus esse medium intelligo."

True, there is a sense in which the third member of a three-term dialectic may look like a state of "reversibility" between both members of a two-term dialectic. As regards the dialectical design of Hegel (*absit nomen!*), the "synthesis" has certain elements in common with the "thesis" and others in common with the "antithesis." And if you were compelled to state this three-term relationship in a two-term system, about the nearest you could come to it would presumably be by treating the two terms as mutually checking each other, except insofar as you might, with another accent, treat them as mutually reinforcing each other.

We should further note that, despite the triadic nature of the thinking *behind* St. Anselm's formula, it is dyadic on its face, and has in history repeatedly gravitated towards a two-term pattern, with *fides* and *intellectus* as the two slopes, and *quaerens* as the ambiguously intermediate sloper. But our main point is that Mr. Blackmur's notion of two terms, with a relation of "reversibility" between the terms, seems typical of his own thinking. Also it seems to be the dialectical pattern underlying the first essay in his book, an essay which we turn to next.*

With his first essay, "Towards a Modus Vivendi," we face the full complexity of our problem. In the titular essay, "The Lion and the Honeycomb" (dated 1950), Mr. Blackmur had called for the subordination of rhetoric to poetic and dialectic. But in the much later essay with which his book begins, he deals exclusively with a rhetorical problem, the relation between writers and audiences. It is an observant article, excellent in its way, a highly reputable contribution to that realm midway between literature and sociology that has been called the sociology of literature.

Though imaginatively written, the essay contains no elements of Poetic. Its stress is overwhelmingly upon a consideration of Rhetoric. And insofar as it is implicitly dialectical, its dialectic is that of a sociologist (dealing, as it does, with problems of "the intellectual proletariat and the technical elite"). Matters are still further complicated for this reviewer by the fact that, despite the strong rhetorical stress in the essay, I find myself obliged to maintain that in one notable respect it is not rhetorical enough!

The essay deals with the problem of the "New Illiteracy," a kind of *corruptio optimi* that "has followed the course of universal education." We here have a report (with facts and figures) of Mr. Blackmur's "reactions to peoples and politics in thirteen months of brief visits to England, France, Germany, Austria, Switzerland, Italy, Egypt, the Lebanon, and Turkey." Its "bias" is

---

* As regards the sheer grammar of the Latin formula, I assume that, in interpreting it as reversible, Mr. Blackmur had something of this sort in mind: The two nouns *fides* and *intellectus* were to be considered as nominatives, in apposition. The participle *quaerens* midway between them was to be thought of as capable of shifting its attachment to either one or the other of the nouns. An inspection of such dialectical resources would suggest either *fides quaerens (est) intellectus* or *fides (est) quaerens intellectus*. Or, translating generously, we might get, respectively: "a questing and/or questioning faith is intellect" and "faith is a questing and/or questioning intellect" (or, for the second: "a questing and/or questioning intellect is faith"). [K.B.]

"toward retreating or even creating *de novo* at the cultural and intellectual level the sense of a modus vivendi."

A "new intellectual proletariat" has arisen, we are told, and the corresponding new illiteracy "represents those who have been given the tool of reading . . . without being given either the means or skill to read well or the material that ought to be read." The result is a state of affairs where "the inflammable opinion of the new illiterate is mistaken for the will of the people, so that arson becomes a chief political instrument." All countries need "a larger truly literate class; educated to the needs and purposes of the society." Such an "elite" would be an alternative to "the new intellectual proletariat," the "class of intellectually trained men and women the world over who cannot make a living in terms of their training and who cannot, because of their training, make a living otherwise with any satisfaction." (Mr. Blackmur here offers a superb variation, by the way, on the sociologist Veblen's concept of "trained incapacity.")

"The dilution of literacy, and the intrusion of the new illiteracy into higher education" lead us to "opine that we must *distrust the ability of the audience*," whereupon "we end up inferior to the potential response of the audience." Our "distrust of the audience," resulting from "our distrust of our own reason and our own imagination," leads us to put our faith in such rhetorical resources as "psychological warfare" ("sometimes we call it advertising or aiming at the target").

Next come eight factual pages on the general state of the reading public, the sparse circulation of good magazines, etc., as he found in the course of his travels. (He says some gruesome things about the quality of the "culture" being exported from the United States. But perhaps his most startling remark came earlier: "We find the USIS in Tel Aviv competing against Russia with the Tarzan books as indicator of the American way of life and all its superiority to the Russians who came bringing Tolstoy.") Then follow eight pages built about the "maxim" that "the new illiteracy prevents a modus vivendi." Instead of an influential cultured elite, we have "an intellectual proletariat."

In the last five pages, noting that "the paying audience has, under present conditions . . . nowhere grown in relation either to population or to performance," and avowing that "the problem of audience belongs to education, both within and outside the educational systems," Mr. Blackmur ends earnestly but somewhat vaguely as regards his recommendations.

He is clear enough in his attack upon "professionalism and trades-unionism (of which it is another form)," contending that "professionalism is a form of illiteracy." But on the positive side, we are told only that "the populace must be educated to the level required for the honest and informed discovery of their will" and we should welcome anything that can "persuade" to the "multiplication and heightening of individual intelligence."

Thus, finally:

> Some people call the mode of this intelligence in action criticism. It had better be called the charity of compassionate understanding. Its aim is no less than a modus vivendi for those who must live together.

In sum, confronting "the explosions of universal education," Mr. Blackmur seems to be in line with the frequent current plea for major stress upon a general education in the humanities, as against merely vocational education or, what is worse, mere indoctrination for the efficient stimulating of desired responses. Insofar as education can help solve the problem, I imagine that most readers of this magazine and of Mr. Blackmur would agree with such a slant. I certainly do.

But here is where my embarrassment enters. For at this point I find myself required to hold that, on the basis of Mr. Blackmur's own evidence, what we need is not less attention to rhetoric, but more, though not precisely to the kind of "rhetoric" that would be most characteristic of the "New Critics." I would hold that, in the kind of education Mr. Blackmur seems to call for, the *systematic study of rhetoric* be given the high place it had in classical Athens, Rome, during the Middle Ages, the Renaissance, and after. (It lost its relative importance in the curriculum, I believe, only after the gradual rise of aesthetics during the nineteenth century. Then, being exiled, rhetoric found a partial home in the new "professional" disciplines, such as anthropology, sociology, social psychology, "semantics," and in such techniques as the analysis of public opinion.)

I was mildly scandalized once when one of our outstanding critics, writing on Aristotle as literary critic, never so much as mentioned his Rhetoric. Yet Aristotle was, first of all, a teacher of rhetoric. And until contemporary teachers of English overcome a resistance that they inherited from nineteenth-century aesthetics, their views about a general education in the humanities must continue to be quite warped. Mr. Blackmur's view that "Education is a lever, not an evangelist" has much to recommend it, but only if we make sure that education tells us a lot about the levers of evangelism. When Mr. Blackmur warns against the "arson" of a demagogue, does he not automatically pledge us to a jealous study of such arsonists' devices?

Thus when, in his titular article, he called upon contemporary critics in general and upon Ransom, Brooks, Empson, and Burke in particular, to subordinate their overwhelmingly "rhetorical" concerns, he was making a plea that was more complicated than it may have seemed. And not until now have we established the coordinates for our answer, which is:

By all means, let us *lessen* the emphasis upon "rhetoric," insofar as we mean by rhetoric the concerns inherited simply from nineteenth-century aesthetics. But let us *increase* the emphasis upon rhetoric, insofar as we can replace aesthetics with the classic trio (rhetoric, poetic, dialectic) that Mr. Blackmur commended in his titular essay. If we really give poetics and dialectics their due, as Mr. Blackmur rightly exhorts, then we can safely restore to their rightful place in the study of language such major texts as Aristotle's *Art of Rhetoric* and Cicero's *Orator* and *De Oratore* (to which I would add at least the fourth part of Augustine's *De Doctrina Christiana,* concerning the rhetoric of Christian persuasion).

Thus, as regards the problems of "arson" ("demagogy and hysteria") we should train ourselves in the art of catching such doings *flagrante delicto,* as the systematic study of rhetoric helps us to do, whereas aesthetics could but coax us to turn our eyes elsewhere, in blushingly superior pudency. It is in this sense that one could call simultaneously for less rhetoric and more. Less, if you equate rhetoric with a mere excess of aesthetics (or "methodology," in Mr. Blackmur's special definition of that term). More, if, having discounted aesthetics, you can systematically allow for the full development of rhetoric, dialectic, and poetic, all three.

We have said there is no concern with Poetics in the article (inasmuch as the concern with audiences and with the business of writing is divided between the two provinces of rhetoric and the sociology of literature). As for Dialectic, if you mean the systematic analysis of dialectical resources and embarrassments, you would have to say that it, too, is missing. But a universe of discourse being what it is, every writer necessarily employs a dialectic *implicitly.* And we have tried to suggest that Mr. Blackmur here seems to follow the dialectical pattern indicated in his comments on the *fides quaerens intellectum* formula.

I have in mind particularly the question he asks at the start: "How do we go about converting energy and momentum into intellect?" Here, presumably, "energy and momentum" would be analogous to *fides,* in its role as a kind of initiating intuitive power like faith. Then the cultural task would be to find for this raw drive a truly intellectual counterpart that might properly "curb" it. And if we may postulate the principle of "reversibility" that Mr. Blackmur has advocated as a guide for critics generally, we may assume also that the underlying power would in turn "question" the intellectual frame arising out of it.

The design is complicated, however, by the fact that the underlying power (which he apparently respects, though his essay gives no indication that he did more than sense it beyond the barriers of nationality and language) is not attaining its true cultural counterpart. Instead, it is being corrupted by the "new illiteracy" (the "*kitsch* culture," with its "lip-service, eyewash, and pi-jaw," its "professionalism," and its "packaged goods").

There thus seem to be *two* kinds of "reversibility" here. First, there is a drastically actual kind, whereby the "new illiteracy" that arises in response to the underlying "energy and momentum" provides but a grim caricature of *intellectus* (in a form that not only does not mitigate the original potentialities of rawness but intensifies them). And second, there is a hoped-for ideal kind that would truly represent the underlying possibilities, and thus in its refinement would be expected to act as a "curb" on them.

If I am right in this summary of the dialectical pattern that is at the roots of the essay, I would say that it has one great shortcoming: its failure to show us evidence of a *wholesome* "energy and momentum" that would be even remotely a match for his evidences of cultural corruption. In brief, the materials for a *fides* are very scant in this article, while the materials for a false *intellectus* are profuse. That is, there is no detailing of a *fides* (as regards whatever evangelical possibilities there may be in the seething local situations which he studied). There is very little of an *intellectus,* in the good sense. So, for the most part, there is little to strike our imagination and thus to feed our contemplation (or "vision") but a very persuasive picture of *intellectus* in the bad sense. We cannot know whether this was all there was to see, or all that Mr. Blackmur was able to see first-hand, beyond the difficulties raised by nationality, language, and tourism.

In any case, it seems to me an exceptionally interesting report, vigorously written, the record of an alert observer. Secondarily, it is an act of self-portraiture: the situations it describes are seen through the eyes of an expert bookman who writes of cultural atrocities and cultural possibilities very entertainingly.

Perhaps to some extent one bit of Hegelian dialectic, as modified by post-Marxist thinking, does figure here after all. I refer to the fact that, though Mr. Blackmur's bias is strongly idealistic (as is perhaps the case with all educators, whether they know it or not and whether they want it or not), he does quite often fall into passages where something much like a variant of the Marxist genealogy is followed. (I refer to a dialectic whereby, beginning with conditions in the economic substructure, one derives from them the state of the ideological superstructure.) Thus, he talks about his alienated intellectuals as an economic class whose consciousness is formed in response to their economic conditions. And again and again, his concern with problems of *literature* centers not in questions of poetics but in matters of *livelihood*.

"Culture is the mind's money," he says, "and everybody not forbidden wants a little of it in his pocket, if only to rattle. Culture is the cash and carry of human action: the one form of currency we ought not to debase, or inflate, but must enrich." That is to perfection a shift of accent, a bright dialectical maneuver whereby, though starting on the material slope, before the sentence is finished, all is spirit.

## Addendum

I still don't feel that I did wholly right by either Mr. Blackmur or myself as regards the scholastic formula, *fides quaerens intellectum*. The difficulty is that an element of controversy kept interfering with the main thing, which was merely a matter of discussion.

It is to me a notable fact about an author's dialectic when a three-termed system is transformed into a two-termed system, with corresponding subsidiary adjustments. But there is the further consideration that the "faith-reason" alignment was repeatedly debated as a two-term system (quite as St. Inseam's formula, when considered in itself, gives no indication of its place in a three-term system).

In an earlier draft I also considered how the "faith-reason" pair, while retaining its dyadic form, later becomes critically transformed in its *attitude*. For instance, in Schopenhauer's pessimism, "faith" becomes merely a blind universal craving (a *Wille* that might more accurately be translated as "sheer restless meaningless drive"), while "reason" becomes the conversion of this subhuman metaphysical greed into *Vorstellungen* ("ideas" that are on the slope leading to the psychoanalyst's concept of "rationalization" or the political theorist's concept of "ideology").

For a critical variant of the three-term system, see Spinoza's *Ethics*, Book II, "On the Nature and Origin of the Mind," Proposition XL, Scholium 2. There the three stages are: (1) *opinio*, or *imaginatio;* (2) *ratio;* (3) *scientia intuitiva*.

An analogous problem figures in purely aesthetic theory. There can be the stress upon art as self-expression, or the stress upon art as communication (evocation, medium for affecting an audience). Most writers of my generation began in a period when self-expression was a slogan; but the stress upon communication gradually gained prominence, until now "communication" is almost a password in certain circles.

Accordingly, critics might choose to debate the issue in those terms. One group might stress self-expression as the essence of art, others might stress communication, others might compromise by proposing a judicious mixing of the two (such mixtures being conceived in accordance with either the notion that self-expression and communication reinforce each other or the notion that they act as a check upon each other, or that they do a bit of both). Or we might proceed by the addition of a third term, thus:

(1) Art begins in *self-expression,* spontaneous utterance, as with outcries, oaths, interjections.

(2) Such motives are matured by translation into the great complexities of language that owe their development to the use of language as a medium of *communication* (itself rooted in forms of practical cooperation).

(3) But the work of art moves *towards the transcending of both self-expression and communication.*

This third stage would come about in the following way:

The artist would choose themes that engrossed him personally ("self-expression"). He would develop them by the use of a public medium ("communication"). But in the course of perfecting his work, he encounters possibilities purely internal to the medium; and he may exploit these possibilities "to the end of the line," regardless of either self-expression or communication.

Joyce's later work is an example of this development. Few writers have paid greater attention than he to the public lore (the materials of communication). Yet he did not develop this material purely from the standpoint of its communicability, but rather from the standpoint of its ultimate possibilities (possibilities that might be more efficiently exploited if he deliberately rejected the standards we usually associate with communication). In following out such possibilities, he would presumably be answering a call (he would be "expressing himself" in a very full sense). Yet the resulting product would be *consummatory* in a way that could not be adequately confined to either of the first two stages, but would have something of both in being beyond both.

Thus the three theological stages involved in St. Anselm's formula would have as their secular, aesthetic analogues:

(1) *Fides:* self-expression.

(2) *Intellects:* communication.

(3) *Contemplatio:* consummation.

# The Dialectics of Imagery

*Symbolism and American Literature* by Charles Feidelson, Jr. U of Chicago P
*The Kenyon Review*, Autumn 1953, 625–632

Since symbolism means many things to many people, perhaps in seeking to place Mr. Feidelson's interesting book on *Symbolism and American Literature* we might properly begin by a general survey of the term's main meanings.

In one sense, all linguistic or artistic expression is symbolic. Whereas a stone is a thing in nature, the *word* for stone is symbolic. In this sense, not just poetry, but rhetoric, dialectic, and even any scientific or "factual" statement would be symbolic. The same would be true not just of modern "symbolic logic" (or "logistics") but of *all* logic.

"Symbol" is sometimes best defined by contrast with "sign," with "sign" generally referring to the more "intellectualistic" kind of meanings, "symbol" to the more emotional kind. Or "sign" is on the sharply particularizing, or denotative side, while "symbol" is applied to terms with multiple connotations, or blurred edges.

"Symbolic" can also be used in contrast with the "practical," in describing actions. "Symbolic actions," in this sense, would include not only the use of language (as in art, theory, and reporting or description) but also neurotically motivated conduct. To build a bridge would be a practical act; to write a poem about building a bridge would be a symbolic act in the artistic sense; and it would be a symbolic act in the neurotic sense if one tried to make or design some kind of connecting device between spot A and spot B, not just for the practical reason of getting more conveniently from one to the other, but because one was trying to resolve some emotional conflict, and the bridging device somehow stood for the resolution.

Obviously, not only poetic acts, but even practical acts can possess a measure of such neurotic symbolism. And, in general, we might ask ourselves to what extent even the most apparently practical of acts contained some symbolic ingredient, in either the poetic or the neurotic senses.

In accordance with this consideration, even the material things of nature might be said to possess a symbolic ingredient for man, who approaches them through his own nature as a typically symbol-using animal. And to seek for such a symbolic ingredient in things would be in effect to see "beyond" the things in their sheer materiality (to look for their *ideality*). The most thorough-going enterprise of this sort is with the theologian's "anagogic" interpretation of the visible and tangible (the view of all things in nature as somehow standing for hierarchal relationships in the realm of the supernatural). Symbolism in the psychoanalytic sense would be a secular variant of such "beyonding," and so likewise with the attempt to explain mankind in terms of certain basic "myths." Another variant (to which this reviewer has given the name of "socio-anagogic") would be concerned with the ways in which man's view of nature can be furtively symbolic of the prevailing social order, as it shapes the nature of language and is in turn shaped by man's linguistic (or generally symbol-using) genius. And when a work of art is said, by materialists, to reflect the material conditions out of which it arose, for "reflect" we might substitute "symbolize."

The French literary movement specifically labelled Symbolist contained many strands, but its explicit reference back to Baudelaire's *Correspondances* sonnet proclaimed its programmatic concern with a variant of "beyonding." The Symbolist poets attempted to glimpse and suggest the ideal or symbolic ingredient in natural objects and situations. There was vagueness as to the exact nature of this realm. Sometimes, it was even viewed in a quite individualistic way: "What things mean for *me*." At other times, the vatically visionary seemed to have eschatological pretensions (at least an anagogic peering into hell, if not into heaven). Sometimes, the efforts faded into a mere literary counterpart of pictorial or musical impressionism, an attempt to build up "atmosphere" by the use of associations that had some notable suggestion in common.

These meanings seem to cover the field in general, but perhaps a secondary consideration belongs here, too. We have in mind the fact that a symbol-system, by reason of its internality, allows for a second order of the symbolic, since symbols can be to varying degrees symbolic of one another. The most obvious cases, of course, are those of direct substitution, as when we describe three different classes, and then announce that here-after we shall refer to them as Classes A, B, and C. Things are a bit farther afield in philosophers' "equations," such as Spinoza's "God or Nature," and Berkeley's "*Esse* is *percipi*." And finally, we can extend this study of internality to the point where we could say that all contexts having a certain expression in common are to that extent classifiable together. (Such study of terministic clusters might be said to apply the "principle of the concordance.")

Though some modern philosophers refer to a "dialectic of nature," dialectics in the classical sense referred to purely internal resources of terms. If we began with a term like "condition," for instance, we might spin from it such related terms as "conditioning," "reconditioning," the "unconditioned," "preconditions," "condition of conditions," "first-order conditions," "second-order conditions," etc., by the sheer resources of language, and without the need to have specific things in mind. Often this kind of internality is present, but concealed, in a terminology. It could be concealed, for instance, if we used a varied set of synonyms, as were we to say, "determining" for "conditioning," "reconstituting" for "reconditioning," "transcendent" for the "unconditioned," "implicit" for "preconditions," etc.

Such internality has another notable resource, however. The purely internal spinning of terms can be done largely with the help of images, or other similarly localized expressions. For instance, instead of "unification" we might say "Eden"; instead of "division" we might say "Babel," or "the Fall"; instead of "development" or "transformation," we might use some such particularizing terms as "dying" and "being reborn." And once you have translated the formal principles of dialectic into terms of any such particular "images" or "myths," your internal spinning not only seems much more outwardly directed, but also you have resources of symbolism so complicated that an accurate account of the verbal forms implicit in only a few pages of a text would be as full of lines and angles as the analysis of motion in a Cubist painting such as Duchamps' *Nude Descending a Staircase*. Allow further for the ease with which words slide between generalization and specification (as "Adam" can be one man, the first man, or every man), and you have resources for grouping and regrouping by analogy, a great extension over classification by identity.

We might say that Mr. Feidelson means by "symbolism" this last kind of going-on. But while he stresses the internal nature of language, noting how it culminates in a self-involved symbolizing of symbolism, he also keeps working tentatively with the notion that the "symbolistic imagination" does really see into a realm beyond the natural order. "The theory of symbolism," he says, "is really a theory of knowledge." The symbolist tries "to view the subjective and objective worlds as functions of each other by regarding both as functions of the forms of speech in which they are rendered."

Generally, he works with a series of three terms, "logic," "dialectic," and "symbolism." In this line-up, when he speaks of "the capacity for symbolic thinking," he would not include logical thought here. In his terminology, logic is *antithetical* to symbolism, and dialectic stands midway between these opposites. Also, in this line-up, logic is equated with the principle of division or exclusion, while symbolism is equated with the principle of unification, as when he writes of the symbolist: "It is the divisiveness of logic that occasions his effort to live in the unitive world of language." In sum:

> The dialectician closely approaches the symbolistic point of view. The language in which he works is an autonomous realm of meaning; place the focus of attention in objects outside the medium, and his function simply disappears. Confronted with the divisiveness of logic, the fact that we can define a word only as meaning *this, not that*, he assumes that "opposition can occur only between the parts of a whole." Dialectic can only partially counteract the inherent disputatiousness of logical method. . . . In the very act of resolving an opposition, it must always respect the law of opposition, the "either-or" of logic. In symbolism no "either-or" can arise. "Beatrice is not *either* a real girl *or* a symbol of Love, but a real girl *and* a symbol of Love *and* of the Holy Spirit *and* of the Divine Sun." Having the structure of logic and the status and purposes of symbolism, dialectic is a kind of transitional stage between the two.

With this pattern to guide him, Mr. Feidelson undertakes many engrossing analyses of representative American writers.

In Chapter I, on "Four American Symbolists," he writes of Hawthorne, Whitman, Melville, Poe. The stress here is upon the kind of "image-making faculty" or "symbolic imagination" that sees in things a problematical principle of reality *beyond* their material nature. In particular, the analysis of Whitman's "When Lilacs Last in the Dooryard Bloom'd" brings out what the author calls "the anti-rational conception of a poem as the realization of language."

Chapter II is entitled "The Symbolistic Imagination." "To consider the literary work as a piece of language is to regard it as a symbol, autonomous in the sense that it is quite distinct both from the personality of its author and from any world of pure objects, and creative in the sense that it brings into existence its own meaning." This chapter contains the long passage previously quoted. The author here stresses the "antilogical" or "counter-rational" aspect of poetic ambiguity, with its wealth of meanings beyond even the resources of multiple explanation.

Chapter III, "An American Tradition," discusses the theological tradition, with regard to the interpreting of worldly objects in terms of a transcendental meaning. It notes how the Puritans preserved Biblical "typology" (the devices for interpreting figures and incidents of the Old Testament as "types" of figures and incidents in the New Testament), even while gravitating towards strictly scientific ideals of terminology.

Chapter IV concerns Emerson as dialectician, his work being like "a continuous monologue in which the genesis of symbolism is enacted over and over." Here, Emerson's strongly image-tinted dialectic for avowing the emblematic nature of material things is treated as a systematic turning away from logic towards symbolism.

In Chapter V, "The Fool of Truth," Melville is considered at some length, as our most thorough-going exemplar of the symbolistic imagination. Here the circle is rounded. We come to "the symbol of symbolism," the verbal creator's involvement with verbal devices that have "created the creative." As Melville "got deeper into himself, what he discovered was not so much hidden traits of his own personality, the secret motives of a self-expressive art, but rather the nature of his calling."

While considering all of Melville's major works, Mr. Feidelson centers upon *Pierre;* for, "Defective as it is, *Pierre,* not *Moby Dick,* is the best vantage point for a general view of Melville's work." And this book, with its "ambiguities" as proclaimed in its subtitle, he in turn illuminates by comparison with Gide's *Counterfeiters,* though without reference to the sexual ambiguities usually associated with that work. Rather, the books are linked, with reference to the reflexive principle, the within-the-within design that Mr. Feidelson describes as "an infinite regress." He trails down this principle of internality to the point where it culminates in Pierre's "radical nihilism."

Thus, the ultimate picture is of a movement that gravitates towards a kind of writing which becomes its own subject-matter, and where the affirming of the poetic word as absolute and intrinsic source of insight culminates in Pierre's in-turning discovery of Nothing:

> I am a nothing . . . We dream that we dreamed we dream
> . . . A nothing is the substance, it casts one shadow one
> way, and another the other way; and these two shadows cast
> from one nothing; these, seems to me, are Virtue and Vice.

The author describes his own position as being "experimental" and "problematical" like the literature he chronicles. His book is exceptionally humane and intelligent; and it should make good reading either for those who approach problems of language schematically or for those who prefer to see the discussion of such problems emerging from specific analyses of poetic and novelistic texts. There are many subsidiary notes that guide the reader to other sources—and this review has by no means adequately covered a list of the writers considered in it.

In a final brief section (with reference to Hulme's attack upon "humanism," and his affirming of Original Sin as the prime ethical fact; and to Eliot's stress upon the fact that new work fits itself into a traditional order, even while altering that order), the author speaks of a tragic discrepancy "between the world as given to reason and the world as given to aesthetic apprehension." He says, "This it is the mission of the symbolist to render." He calls such symbolism "a critical humanism." And he places the symbolistic discipline under the aegis of a methodic morality of guilt, taking as his device the words of Conrad's Lord Jim: "To the destructive element submit yourself." Literature is "autotelic," he says. But "in serving itself alone" it furthers the cause of art, even while "it acknowledges the defeat that is always implicit in the victory."

These are good sentiments, and especially good ones to end on. Surely we can't be too far off if, when confronting man's symbol-using genies, we methodically vacilate between appreciation and fear. And, on the appreciation side, we should decidedly salute Mr. Feidelson's great spiritedness, skill, and learning as a guide through the specific works which he analyzes in the course of his study.

Mr. Feidelson may put more stress than necessary upon the "illogicality" of poetic form. True, had he been considering great classical dramas, with their rigorous concern for the "fatal inevitability" of formal development, this objection would be a stronger one. When the stress is placed upon imagery, rather than upon the principles of consistency, of placement, of expectation and retrospection that are involved in the persuasiveness of great drama, the ambiguous and latitudinarian may seem more important than the logically controlled. Yet even here, one could make out a case for "logical" norms as necessary to the guidance of literary form. Using Mr. Feidelson's own suggestion, we might ask that symbolism be analyzed less as a step *beyond* logic and dialectic, and more as the use of imagery in ways that necessarily involve both logical and dialectical principles.

True, for the analyzing of such an art, we might need a logic that was less like theories of statics and mechanics than like modern theories of gases. When the astral physicist uses such a calculus to describe the motions and conditions of distant galaxies, he could hardly be said to abandon logic; and in this sense we might look for a "logic" in the "atmospherics" of poetic imagery.

There is also a problem as regards the kind of "knowledge" to be got from such purely verbal manipulations as Mr. Feidelson ascribes to the poetic products of the peculiarly "symbolistic imagination." His own book would be evidence that, in at least one notable sense, there may be a purely "logical" kind of understanding that transcends poetic symbolism. For inasmuch as the nature of such linguistic resources in general is methodically analyzed, another way of "symbolizing symbolism" is being taken. He says that the symbolistic imagination, in its stress upon the "autotelic" nature of language, leads finally to the discovery of its own forms; but would it not follow that, when linguistically meditating upon such withinness-of-withinness, the critic has added a further step in this business of talking about talk-about?

Accordingly, if art truly is symbolic of some realm beyond itself (as the symbolist sometimes suggests, whether in genuine scientific conviction or as a good showman who knows how to endow his work with the appealing accents of the vatic) then it would seem to follow that some sort of "logic" is needed, to *complete* the poetic "vision." Such a logic would seek to place the resources and limitations of poetic symbolism, not just for the purposes of "appreciation," but in the attempt to discover fully what is involved in the use of poetic language as a means to "discovery."

Mr. Feidelson's book by its very nature points in this direction "beyond poetic beyonding," even while it meditates on the nature of such literature. Specifically, when his book rounds the circle by the discovery that symbolism, as he defines it, culminates in Melville's "radical nihilism," has he not brought language to the point where, in confronting its own forms, it confronts the *negative?* This situation can be explained in many ways, but there is first of all a purely technical consideration: Since sensory images are "positive," a symbolist who uses them to signalize a realm beyond the sensorially positive must endow them with a *negative* significance (quite analogous to the terms of "negative theology" whereby words for a supernatural being are constructed by the negating of words for positive, natural being, as when God is called "unbounded," "undying," "invisible," "intangible," etc.).

A symbolist like Melville, who claims to be symbolically peering into another realm, and whose peerings encounter the forms of symbolism itself, might properly be expected to find things coming to a focus in the discovery of "nothing." But beyond that, there would be room for the analysis of linguistic negativity as such. (Melville gives us the cue here, too, when his talk of "Nothing" becomes interwoven with talk of Virtue and Vice—in brief, when his talk of "Nothing" breaks through to the realm of *No,* of the Negative Command, such as we find in the Decalogue. *And here is the genuinely and exclusively symbolic, or linguistic, realm.* For whereas one might try to think of "Nothing" as a "scenic" term, like a big black hole, or *a-byssos,* one never would try to look anywhere for the location of "Don't." One knows that "No" is an *idea,* an artifact of language.)

We do not mean that Melville, as symbolist, should have specifically brought his book to a focus in talk of "the negative" rather than in talk of

"Nothing." As the modern Existentialists amply show us, talk of "Nothing" is much more poetically resonant. We are only saying that there is another way of rounding the circle which Mr. Feidelson deals with. Quite as the *poetic* symbolizing of symbolism culminates in the visionary discovery of "Nothing," a *theoretical* discussion of symbolizing would correspondingly culminate in the discovery of the all-importance of the Negative. Then would begin a search for a logic of the Negative. And, whatever else this search led to, it would at least point not just towards the forms of language, though it would greatly stress these forms. For, however purely linguistic may be our ability to understand the negative *qua* negative, the negative as used in every language becomes vitally interwoven with the world's systems of property, government, law, virtue, beauty. No wonder Spinoza said that "all determination is negation."

# A Sour Note on Literary Criticism

*A Note on Literary Criticism* by James T. Farrell. The Vanguard Press
*The New Republic*, June 1936, 211

Farrell has written in defense of what he calls "pluralism" in literature. The substance of his position is in his expression, the "carry-over value of literature," referring to the fact that, although a work of art be built to emphasize *one* point of view, its appeal may so "carry over" that it can be enjoyed by people with *another* point of view. Different periods of history, or different classes in a given period, or different individuals in a given class, bring out particular emphases in the selection of their artistic materials. But these emphases are not mutually exclusive. There is a margin of overlap among them. The skeptic de Gourmont, for instance, found much in the literature of the Church that impinged upon his own interests.

The basis of Farrell's book, if I have stated it correctly, is highly agreeable to me. And I beg to be enrolled as a fellow pluralist on the subject of literary appeal, offering in support of my candidacy my discussions of "recurrent patterns of experience" and the "margin of persuasion" or overlap, as formulated in *Counter-Statement*. As one who has reluctantly made the "dialectical" admission that the same work of art may have a progressive effect at one time and a reactionary effect at other times, I am conquered in advance. So surprising are the destinies of literary effectiveness, that I have wondered, in perverse moments, whether our commercial advertising might not be one of the most powerful forces making for revolution in America, since advertising stimulates with scientific efficiency expensive appetites that the "inner contradictions" of capitalist economy must frequently leave ungratified.

If one were a Communist in Russia, and invented a weapon for the defense of the Communist state, there is no guarantee that his invention could not be "taken over" by Fascists, and used against this same state. Hegel forged philosophic weapons that Marx "took over" for revolutionary purposes. A contraption's possible uses in new contexts are unpredictable—and European thought is the history of schools who proved themselves "ready to take over" the implements of opposing or divergent schools. On this point, Farrell has so much evidence in his favor, that I am surprised how niggardly he was in making use of it.

Instead, he devotes his time to attacking Left critics who have been attempting to discover how effectively the literary weapons may be "taken over" for the emphases of *here and now*. These men think (1) that radical social change is necessary, (2) that political awareness is a valuable weapon in shaping "consciousness" in behalf of change, and (3) that imaginative art and critical comment, taken together, shape this consciousness by both emotional and conceptual proddings. Surely they are not blunt enough to overlook the fact that art and politics are not a perfect fit. As one just observer remarked to me, Farrell might have clinched the issue by citing the authority of the Oxford dictionary, where the mere definitions of "art" and "politics" disclose the discrepancies between the two. But for purposes of social change, to be brought about with the aid of political thinking, these leftward-looking critics attempt to discover how close the correspondence between art and politics can be. Aware that the bourgeoisie of the eighteenth century put forth an enormous amount of propaganda art in preparation for the French Revolution, they ask themselves how much of this same procedure can be "taken over" for the enforcing of new social emphases. Tactically, the issue resolves itself in irony: the critics speculate as to how close the fit between art and politics can be, and Farrell pops up brightly with the "refutation" that art and politics are not a perfect fit.

If you feel vengeful toward some of the men discussed, you may rejoice that young Lonigan sometimes catches them when their gang is not around and gives them a trimming. If you feel that their efforts are desirable, you may regret that Farrell makes no positive contribution to the issue. The book's deficiencies, as a new contribution to literary criticism, might arise from the indirectness of the approach. The philosophic vocabulary employed is too unwieldy, too roundabout. The direct coordinates proper to literary criticism are those of rhetoric. Rhetoric deals with literary processes, with the response to literary processes and, by extension, with the non-literary factors (economic, biological, psychological) that underlie our response to symbols. Above all, it requires one to discuss the destiny of the artist's medium, as it lives in artist and audience. Though Farrell's instruments are keen enough, their keenness is for other purposes; he is dealing with the problems of rhetoric without choosing instruments precisely adjusted to the needs of his subject.

The failure to consider explicitly the destiny of the artistic medium, for instance, leads him to damn as "subjective" a statement that the poet "gives names and values"' to life. The charge is unfortunate on two grounds. First, it is confusing: Farrell had already defined the esthetic as "subjective," in contrast with the "objective" or "use-value" that we get in simple propaganda—and though he had consistently spoken in behalf of this subjective element, we now find subjectivity interpreted as a fault. He is presumably using a word in two senses, a weakness that he never forgives in his opponents. Second, an explicit consideration of language would have made him more precise. For language *does* give names and values to life; yet it is not "subjective" because, as a public or collective product shaped by people working with practical necessities, it must take objective realities into account. Its "myths" are thus grounded in objective references, and the poet's work assumes similar objectivity in that it is shaped by this public *communicative* equipment. Language "gives" names and values in the sense that, if we were not taught to speak, we could not develop the full complexities of "consciousness." The concept of class struggle, for instance, gives not only new names but also new values to life in that its perspective shapes our understanding of historic processes. If someone asks, "How about the 'myth' of the Nazis?" I answer: "It too gives values, but wrong ones—and the objective, communicative, cooperative tests will prove their wrongness."

Farrell rightly attacks naïve Marxists who would rail against "abstraction" as the devilish invention of the bourgeoisie. *Das Kapital* is nothing if not a masterpiece of abstract thought. But one may wish that Farrell's abstractions had been framed with closer reference to his own concrete procedures as a writer. One often senses behind his book a defense of his own methods (as in his able comments on "decay" books and "success" books), but it is a loss to criticism when so able a technician fails to give us the explicit technical discussion of literary appeal he was equipped to provide. In the end you are left merely with the feeling that some critics, in their necessary work of simplification, have sometimes oversimplified—and you are a dumbbell if you needed a special book to tell you that.

# A Trail Trails Off

*From These Roots: The Ideas That Have Made Modern Literature* by Mary M. Colum. Charles Scribner's Sons
*The New Republic*, December 1937, 205–206

After the first few pages of *From These Roots,* I wrote down tentatively, for the title of my review: "A Nice Pale Book," A few pages further, and I had become ashamed of myself. I decided that I had wronged both author and reviewer atrociously, in even thinking of such a title tentatively as the organizing basis of my review. So I wrote down a possible title having totally different leads: "Information About Critics, Gracefully."

The radical change was a wise one. In her characterizations of the pivotal literary critics in Western history, from the time of Lessing until the recent past, Mrs. Colum has done a remarkably discerning piece of work. Her task was to bring out the salient traits of each such writer, to give the summarizations and apt citations that name the writer's number. Such naming must satisfy at least three major tests: (1) It must locate the man in the general continuity of Western thought; (2) it must give the essence of the man, as a total personality, regardless of his indebtedness to others; (3) it must give the essence of his special contribution or emphasis, his addition as innovator.

On the first point Mrs. Colum is weakest, as treatment of the general philosophic trend that lies behind literary critics is skimped. It is also this skimping, perhaps, that accounts for her superficial treatment of the relation between the esthetic and the practical, and her blunt analysis of moral rhetoric. But I believe that she will repeatedly delight her readers by her taste and discernment in the featuring of the salient, as per points two and three. She is not an impressionistic critic; yet her characterizations are highly evocative. By a deft mixture of conceptual formulas and revealing metaphors (usually selected from the authors themselves) she "places" her subjects with a minimum of detail. A mode of presentation that she admires in modern poetry, she has herself effectively employed in its critical counterparts.

As the book proceeds, a subtle change of emphasis takes place. While still looking for key formulas and crucial metaphors, Mrs. Colum becomes increasingly concerned with the specific works of art that embody critical theories, rather than with the theories themselves. As I noted this gradual change from a book *about* literary criticism to a book *of* literary criticism, I wanted to revise my title once more, seeking this time something that would "sloganize" a change of emphasis perhaps unintentionally made by the writer in the course of following out her program.

The shift is responsible for some of the best pages in the book. Her discussion of Flaubert and Baudelaire, and of subsequent offshoots from their writings, ranks high in the field of appreciation. But this gradual shift from critics to poets also has an unfortunate consequence, as we note drastically when we arrive at her concluding chapter, "Where We Are." We are presumably nowhere—so the author ends on a devout and exalted prayer, calling in vatic terms for someone to come and redeem us. And as parting recipe for solace, we are told that "the despair of modern philosophies would be intolerable if one did not know with Proust that Time touches everything, that Time changes everything, that spring succeeds winter . . ." etc. The chapter also says some cutting things abort "trade-writing," a category that includes not only the output of the commercialists, but also the output of those who would imaginatively exhort against commercialism. Thus does Mrs. Colum get us coming and going, with no specific solution, but only a blanket solution, "Time." At this point, I hope, the reader will become quite irreverent. I do plead with him to interject: "To hell with 'Time'—what about 'the times'?"

It would seem that Mrs. Colum, in her gradual change of stress, narrowed down her interests from *criticism in general to one specific poetic movement embodying past criticism* (the movement that culminates in such writers as Valéry). The result is that she doesn't even consider recent innovations in critical technique. She has trailed down a trail to the point where it trailed off. Hence, without so much as mentioning recent trends in literary analysis, she makes her moving appeal to a kind of seasonality that would operate without men and measures.

Mrs. Colum frequently pays tribute to innovators. Even too much tribute, I should think, since innovation *per se* has no value. The important test is: *innovation for what?* But present changes in our social situation require corresponding changes in the technique of analysis; we are getting this change in technique; and ironically, Mrs. Colum, who has praised many dead innovators, does not so much as refer glancingly to the new trends. Even so well known a work as I. A. Richards' *Principles of Literary Criticism* is totally neglected. Similarly with Empson and Spurgeon, or with Wilson's *Axel's Castle* and Blackmur's *Double Agent* in America. There is no consideration of the part that has been and can be played by Gestalt psychology, studies in the development of meaning by investigators like Piaget, or the many sociological speculations stemming largely from Bentham's analysis of language. There are under development new instruments for the description of poetic organization, of linguistic action, of appeals and commands to audience and self. Maybe it will come to nothing—but the thought of this rich field, with its fertile leads already scattered through a hundred or so intelligent books, is enough to make one ask himself whether Mrs. Colum, for all her appreciation of past glories, isn't even something of a vandal when she trails off into a prayer, precisely at a time when such fresh critical departures are gaining vigor and clarity of formulation. Presumably she had invested so strongly in a movement of the recent past that she could not see values in anything else. Such absorption is to her credit as an individual. But however much respect we pay it as a moral attribute, we must recognize the limitations it places upon her perceptions as a critic.

# Exceptional Book

*English Pastoral Poetry* by William Empson. W. W. Norton and Company
*The New Republic,* May 1938, 81

*The Colyumist's Dream* is of a book that lays down its thesis in the opening sentence, expands it through the entire introduction, repeats it with variations through several hundred pages, and winds up by summarizing it in an epilogue. By such a test, the superb literary analysis of William Empson would be the colyumist's nightmare. I have read this book three times, and each time I find more in it to reward the attention. In fact, I should like, if I am able, to make this review simply a plea, a "come and buy," recommending *English Pastoral Poetry* to those readers who are also frugal purchasers, and who would thus prefer a work of literary criticism that they can live with to one that they can hurry through.

Empson, who is an offshoot of I. A. Richards, is an honor both to his *magister* and to himself. He has made Richards' teachings his own, and thereby has been able to give them new developments, particularly in laying more stress upon the historical-transitional aspect of literary psychology, which Richards tends more to consider in its arrested, or "flat" aspects. His feeling for literature as a social manifestation is acute, fertile and well documented. There are few psychological novels that have the appreciation of nuance, the ironic pliancy, in which Empson is a specialist. You may legitimately complain that often his perceptions are too refined, leading him into a welter of observations that suffer from lack of selectivity and drive. He is far better at marginalia than at sustained exposition. Obviously, this critic could write an intelligent gloss upon every single line of a long work—and often he seems to have proceeded in precisely this way.

The underlying concern of *English Pastoral Poetry* reflects Empson's response to the salubrious effects that the "proletarian school" has exerted upon the course of literary criticism. To turn from Empson's earlier volume, *Seven Types of Ambiguity,* to his present book, is to realize the importance of the new dimension that the Marxist emphasis has given to his work. Here the balloons of his earlier pure estheticism are effectively tied to a social basis of reference; the later work has a kind of "gravitational pull" in which the former is lacking. Yet he has by no means abandoned the liquidity of his previous volume—the happy result being that there is here no sociological simplism.

The opening chapter, on "Proletarian Literature," considers some representative statements of the proletarian school, and offers reasons why, for the author's purposes, the esthetic of proletarian literature should be considered as part of a wider literary strategy, named by him the "pastoral process." Some quotations from this chapter may serve to characterize the general tenor of his approach:

> The essential trick of the old pastoral, which was felt to imply a beautiful relation between rich and poor, was to make simple people express strong feelings (felt as the most universal subject, something fundamentally true about everybody) in learned and fashionable language.
>
> The usual process for putting further meanings into the pastoral situation was to insist that the shepherds were rulers of sheep, and so compare them to politicians or bishops or what not; this piled the heroic convention onto the pastoral one, since the hero was another symbol of his whole class.
>
> The praise of simplicity usually went with extreme flattery of a patron (dignified as a symbol of the whole society, through the connection of pastoral with heroic). . . . It allowed the flattery to be more extreme because it helped both author and patron to keep their self-respect. So it was much parodied, especially to make the poor man worthy but ridiculous, as often in Shakespeare; nor is this merely snobbish when in its full form. The simple man becomes a clumsy fool who yet has better "sense" than his betters and can say things more fundamentally true.
>
> The realistic sort of pastoral . . . also gives a natural expression for a sense of social injustice. So far as the person described is outside society because too poor for its benefits he is independent, as the artist claims to be, and can be a critic of society; so far as he is forced by this into crime he is the judge of the society that judges him.
>
> My own difficulty about proletarian literature is that when it comes off I find I am taking it as pastoral literature;

> I read into it, or find that the author has secretly put into it, these more subtle, far-reaching, and I think more permanent, ideas.

The author then proceeds, first to the analysis of double plot, with the ironic complexities arising from the juxtaposing of the central heroic thread with its burlesqued counterpart, and thence to many variants of his paradox, in the figures of poets, fools, children, madmen, rogues, who are in subtle and devious ways the bearers of sharp social criticism. Thus, we have the "Twist of Heroic-Pastoral Ideas into an Ironical Acceptance of Aristocracy" (elucidated by reference to Shakespeare's Sonnets); "The Ideal Simplicity Approached by Resolving Contradictions" (Marvell's *Garden*); "The Pastoral of the Innocence of Man and Nature" (Milton); "Mock-Pastoral as the Cult of Independence" (*Beggar's Opera*); "The Child as Swain" (*Alice in Wonderland*).

One may, if he chooses, insist upon the important element of *difference* between this general "pastoral" category and its manifestations in books of specifically proletarian cast. For my own part, I much prefer Empson's way of considering the matter, by seeking the permanent forms that underlie changing historical emphases. Indeed, I should contend that one could not properly define the qualities of specifically proletarian works until he had first placed them in some such *genus* as Empson here proposes. Let us first see the whole line, in its long historical continuity, before attempting to differentiate the particular characterizations at any one stage along this line. Trying this approach, in this book by a man who has a most delightful sensitiveness to the fluctuant ways in which the tactics of compliment and insult (coupled with bids for immunity) are managed in works of imaginative scope, you will, I submit, get here an analysis highly provocative.

# The Serious Business of Comedy

*The Theory of Comedy* by Elder Olson. Indiana UP
*The New Republic*, March 1969, 23–27

This is an unusually able and superior work. Though one might consult a theory of comedy with the quite reputable intention of finding out why a joke is funny, and though Elder Olson touches upon the subject with considerably suggestive methodic skill, the best portions of this study are the chapters that deal with various specific comedies, analyzed in the light of his definition. As Olson puts his case:

> I am old-fashioned enough to mean comedy when I say comedy, and tragedy when I say tragedy; by which I mean the dramatic forms designated by such terms, and not forms which are narrative. And I do not want to talk about the tragic sense of life or the comic sense of life. It may be narrow to me, especially since it is so fashionable now to do so, but I simply do not want to.

That's admirably plain talking, and Olson does well by it. Yet he also says: "We may take a grave or light-hearted view of human life and actions; tragedy develops out of the grave view as comedy does out of the lighthearted. . . . When we say, thus, that tragedy imitates a serious action, we mean that it imitates an action *which it makes serious;* and comparably, comedy imitates an action *which makes a matter for levity.*" So I take it that Olson's decision not to discuss a tragic or comic "sense of life" in this book is a matter of method, not of an assumption that such extra-literary attitudes have no proper place in speculations on the appeal and role of literary forms.

There is also, however, a more immediate problem. For "if we are to discuss comedy, we must of course discuss the comic"—and the comic is by no means confined to the realm of specific "dramatic forms." In fact, an example Olson deals with in his preparatory chapter on "The Problem of the Comic," is a case chosen by Jean Paul Richter from Cervantes: "Sancho clings all night long to the edge of a shallow ditch which he supposes a bottomless pit." However one might account for the comic element here, surely all readers would agree that it is a perfect example of the quality.

Olson strikes telling blows at theories which, while they really do apply to the comic, also fit "many things other than the laughable." Thus, of terms "expressing purely *logical* relations—such as 'incongruity,' " he says, "The universe is full of incongruities, and if this theory were true, we should never stop laughing." To guard against over-simplification, he contends that an explanation of the comic, to be sufficient, must consider three factors: "(1) a certain *kind of object,* (2) a certain *frame of mind* in us, (3) the *grounds* on which we feel." Here we must regrettably cut many corners, for Olson is subtle, succinct, and thorough in developing these notions. But things sum up thus:

> Properly speaking . . . the comic includes only the ridiculous, the ludicrous, the things which are taken as such by analogy, the witty, and the humorous. All of these, differ as they may, have a common characteristic: their minimization of the claim of some particular thing to be taken seriously.

Also, the comic object "must not arouse desire or aversion or emotion" too strongly, otherwise we could not minimize its claim to be taken seriously. I am not sure just how this recipe fits with the conditions of Galgenhumor, for instance, this joke from the thirties about the terrifying dust storms in the Middle West. "Uncle Ebenezer ought to be coming along soon. I just saw his farm go by." In such a case, a kind of spirited "minimization" seems to coexist with a recognition of the disaster in its full scope. Similarly, though the porter scene in *Macbeth* is comic, it seems to derive much of its poignancy from the audience's still intense memory of the murder. The appeal of the comic here is not in the porter's speech alone, but seems to draw upon the audience's continued response to the play as a *tragedy*, with the grounds of its seriousness not minimized.

Olson's definition of comedy proper (as distinct from his concern with "the comic" in general) runs thus: "Comedy is the imitation of a worthless action, complete and of a certain magnitude, in language with pleasing accessories differing from part to part, enacted, not narrated, effecting a *katastasis* [that is, relaxation] of concern through the absurd." While specifically proclaiming the Aristotelian aspects of his theory, and modeling his definition of comedy after the definition of tragedy in the sixth book of the *Poetics*, Olson makes one notable shift. Instead of looking for a mode of comic *katharsis* (or cleansing) to match the purgative power that Aristotle ascribes to tragedy, Olson turns to the *Rhetoric,* where the appeal of comedy is situated not in a kind of purgation but in a kind of relaxation.

Thus as regards the examples just given, he would doubtless consider "relaxation" a sufficient explanation, though he does say at one point that "The human body tends to cathart any excessive emotion by certain physical outlets, such as laughter and weeping." But in any case, whether you call comedy "catastic" or "cathartic," there needs to be a distinction between the kind of relaxation that is due to *relaxed* conditions and the kind that runs counter to *tense* conditions. There is the relaxed humorousness of an easygoing man in easygoing circumstances, and there is an antithetical kind of relaxation, as with a friend who said: "By far the funniest movie I ever saw was a Benchley short making sport of an insomniac. I roared so convulsively, my wife threatened to leave the theatre if I didn't control myself. It was at a time when I was suffering extremely from bouts of insomnia." Despite my great admiration of Olson's book, I do wish that he hadn't disposed of catharsis so quickly.

I have mentioned his warnings against attempts to situate the comic in perverse examples of the logical (as with theories overstressing "incongruity"). In the following, this admonition, combined with his equally just comments on "minimization," seems to blunt his point:

"The proposition 'Smoke talks and makes noises' is not funny; it is simply a false proposition. But anyone who happens to believe it, or to believe that anyone else could believe it, is a fool. In Aristophanes' Wasps there is a scene in which the old man—whom his son had shut up in the house to keep him from indulging his mania for serving on juries—tries to escape by the chimney. He makes a noise and is heard and challenged; to put his guards off, he says, 'I'm smoke coming out.' What is funny here? Not simply his self-betrayal, the frustration of his own intent, but the stupidity of supposing that a patent impossibility would deceive anyone. Precisely the same form of a stupidly self-defeating act is the basis of many jokes. Chickens do not talk, any more than smoke does; but you remember the chicken-thief surprised in the hen-house. 'Who's there?' 'Nobody but us chickens, mister.' Or Ole Olesson hiding from the sheriff in a bag marked CHAINS; when the sheriff kicks the bag, Ole, remembering his disguise, says 'Yingle, yingle.' In all of these cases the act is contrary to the right thing to do, and it produces a result contrary to the one intended."

But surely the joke about Ole Olesson comes to its comic completion in the fact that Ole says "Yingle" for "Jingle"; an example of what Olson elsewhere calls diction that "is appropriate if it is *inappropriate* in the right way." The hen-house joke, as I remember it, is based on a white man's stereotype about blacks as chicken thieves. And in cleaning up its racial bias, Olson deprived it of its particular quasi-logical "confirmation" of the butt as "naturally" stupid. As for the one about smoke, at first I was stumped; for I thought that Aristophanes, of all experts in the comic, should be able to do better than that. But on looking up the original, I find that Olson stopped too soon. The sequence proceeds thus:

> Bdelycleon: By Zeus! what is that noise in the chimney? Hullo! who are you?
> Philocleon: I am smoke coming up.
> Bdelycleon: Smoke? smoke of what wood?
> Philocleon: Of fig-wood.

The notes tell us that smoke from fig-wood is particularly "acrid." Thus the extra twist (an absurd kind of logical "confirmation") resides in the fact that Bdelycleon has called himself a "stinker."

Because of the need to build a general theory concerning "The Problem of the Comic" and "The Poetics of Comedy," (all of it a delight to read, as superb examples of critical formulation) Olson necessarily skimps on the analysis of particular cases. But the second half of the book (the chapters on "Aristophanes, Plautus, Terence"; "Shakespeare and Moliere"; and "Moderns") abounds in gratifyingly acute comments on particular texts.

True, by strictly adhering to his own definition of comedy, Olson concludes that only five of Shakespeare's plays properly fall under this head. In fact, though he says that every true comedy could be called "Much Ado About Nothing," he rules out Shakespeare's own play so entitled, contending that one of the two plots is too serious—and we must "consider not parts but the action as a whole." The question "is not whether our definition fits everything called comedy, but whether a given play fits our definition and so is or is not comedy in our sense of the term." It's more rewarding to go along with him, in this regard, than to haggle about his list. For in any case, his discussion of particular plays is a long succession of apt comments, involving both generalizations about their nature and analyses of notably relevant spots in the texts. There are many ingenuities here, for instance his masterful pages on that most felicitous of comedies, *A Midsummer Night's Dream*. And one finds many sharp observations involving the movement from the Old Comedy in Greece, through Menander, thence to Plautus and Terence, into the comedy of manners, and so eventually to such miracles of humane invention as a comic character like Falstaff.

There is also an interesting discussion of the role of the "base" in comedy. According to Olson's theory at its simplest, "comedy must avoid the base—the really base—as it must avoid the noble." For it must be "lighthearted," and the base is too serious. In Ben Jonson's comedies, the characters "approach base action very nearly, almost to the point where the action itself becomes serious." But Moliere "was able to handle the wicked, the mean, the base in comedy as Shakespeare apparently was not." Though Tartuffe gives his name to Moliere's play about a base religious hypocrite, Olson would save the day by placing the emphasis upon "his dupe, Orgon, who in his infatuation with Tartuffe commits one extravagance after another." In sum, "It is not baseness which Moliere makes comic, but folly." And he quotes a passage in which Tartuffe's baseness itself is made an object of ridicule. Whether or not you go along with such qualifyings, they are good things to watch and to try figuring out.

Toward the end, Olson's concern with the element of the absurd in comedy results in some excellent comments on the difference between true comic absurdity and the Theatre of the Absurd (a discussion led into by his shrewd remarks on what he calls "suspense of form" in Shaw's plays).

I could cite many other places I found enjoyable as criticism. And though I personally still hanker after a theory of comic catharsis, in addition to, or as against mere "catastasis," I must say I greatly admire this book and hope it gets the attention it deserves.

# Kermode Revisited

*The Sense of an Ending: Studies in the Theory of Fiction* by Frank Kermode.
   Oxford UP
*Novel: A Forum on Fiction,* Autumn 1969

The publisher calls this book "a pioneering attempt to relate the theory of literary fiction to a more general theory of fiction, using fictions of apocalypse as a model." Allen Tate says that it "gives us further proof of the depth of [Kermode's] learning and of his philosophical range. [It] will be a landmark in twentieth century critical thought." The Virginia Kirkus' Service says, "This is the most important book on aesthetics and culture to appear since Rosenberg's *The Tradition of the New* and Sypher's *Loss of the Self.* . . ." I like it, too. It is an exceptionally intelligent book on an undyingly interesting subject.

There are ends in the sense of aims, in the sense of cessations, and in the sense of terms or boundaries. Also there's the fertile fact that one can't meditate for long on endings without the discovery that one is also involved in thoughts about beginnings and middles, with corresponding insights derived from those two different but integrally related standpoints.

So maybe the handiest way to *begin* a review of this book's well-documented observations about endings would be by recalling the passage in Aristotle, just after he has said that a tragedy must be a "whole," and that a whole has a "beginning, middle, and end." A beginning, he tells us, is that which doesn't need to follow anything, though something else grows out of it. An end is what necessarily or as a general rule grows out of something else, but nothing comes after it. A middle is both preceded and followed.

When I first read that statement (which occurs in Chapter VII of the *Poetics*) it seemed to me like a boringly obvious piece of sheet pedagogic busywork. Yet the more I have pondered on it, the more problems and possibilities and paradoxes it has seemed to reveal, discoveries to which the present book makes an admirable contribution.

For instance, though we may haggle with one another as to just how any particular drama or novel does develop out of its beginnings through its middle to its end, surely we can all agree at a glance that, insofar as the structure has some unity, in some way or other these three crucial moments must be interwoven, whereby the essence of any one such stage is somehow implicit in the other two. (Francis Fergusson would probably state the case by saying that in a classically formed work they are 'analogously present' in one another.) And other paradoxes readily arise because, even though history itself has no beginning, middle, or end, every *book* on history does.

To see how readily the author's topic lends itself to radiation from its center, we need but quote this early paragraph (emphasis mine):

> I *begin* by discussing fictions of the *End*—about ways in which, under varying existential pressures, we have imagined the *ends* of the world. This, I take it, will provide clues to the ways in which fictions, *whose ends are consonant with origins, and in concord, however unexpected, with their precedents,* satisfy our needs. So we *begin* with *Apocalypse,* which *ends, transforms,* and is *concordant.*

In brief, the author will begin by choosing for heuristic purposes a theological model that comes to a focus in the last book of the New Testament. He will next proceed to ask what modifications are needed if one applies this theological model to the ends of wholly secular analysis. For instance, as the books makes clear, a quite different world-view is implicit in the step from the kind of absolute ending we confront in Biblical Apocalypse (or, as it is usually called, Revelation) to the more limited individualistic kind of ending in a tragedy such as *King Lear.*

Though the author is succinct, it would take too much space for me to give an adequate summary of his ingenious and sensitive and learned observations. Suffice it to say that, though not in a simple one-two-three order, the reader is given a categorizing of the various literary forms (and corresponding attitudes towards life) as viewed in the light of the Apocalyptic model and its secular forms. In this respect Kermode's book is to be classed with much contemporary work (both literary and psychological) which uses ancient "myths" as models for analysis, the assumption being that they disclose basic morphological truths even though we do not take them literally.

Though never loose in the way of a McLuhan or a Norman Brown, the book is in its own way tentative. Thus, whereas it explicitly *begins* with the design of the Apocalypse as a model, in the final chapter it features a literally autobiographical report, *Solitary Confinement,* by Christopher Burner, because this work can serve "as a model of a more general solitary confinement, of the fictions and interpretations of human beings 'doing time,' imagining ends and concords." The kind of end conceived of here is not that of universal Apocalyptic holocaust, but of a hopefully imagined time when the victory of the imprisoned writer's compatriots will terminate his individual solitude.

Thus, as Kermode adopts the Apocalyptic model to the discussion of secular forms (such as the ingenious pages on Sartre's *La Nausée*) his argument undergoes subtle transformations. The original model, which served as a point of departure, becomes enough transformed to call for and call forth a different model as windup. This in turn leads to a further development, a culminating concern with modes of transfiguration in poems of Wordsworth (whose poems move "out of fear into a moment of love," and who also anticipated modern tendencies to write poems about writing poems).

To indicate some of the other matters that get considered *en route:* the Church was moved by a principle of "clerkly skepticism" whereby it "frowned on precise predications of the End." However, "when we refuse to be dejected by disconfirmed predictions we are only asserting a permanent need to live by the pattern rather than by the fact, as indeed we must." The pattern of Apocalypse involves a "potent imperial myth" by which people constantly have "a sense of living at a turning point in time" (middles here coming to take the place of ends). And in some contemporary novels the stress upon the middle is so great that "this departure from a basic paradigm . . . seems to begin with the first sentence." "Already in St. Paul and St. John there is a tendency to conceive of the End as happening at every moment; this is the moment when the modern concept of *crisis* was born." "Apocalypse, which included and superceded tragedy, was itself to be included in tragedy; and tragedy lost its height and stateliness when the single unritualized death became the sole point of departure." (That is an interesting instance of a statement in which ending becomes beginning.) As regards the "myth of crisis": "we should make more sense of it if we could reduce it from the status of myth to the status of fiction." Yet "the age of perpetual transition in technological and artistic matters is understandably an age of perpetual crisis in morals and politics." "The main object is the critical business of making sense of some of the radical ways of making sense of the world." "The apocalyptic types—empire, decadence and renovation, progress and catastrophe—are fed by history and underlie our ways of making sense of the world from where we stand, in the middest." "Naïvely predictive apocalypses implied a strict concordance between beginning, middle, and end . . . Such a concordance remains a deeply desire object, but it is hard to achieve when the beginning is lost in the dark backward and abysm of time, and the end is known to be unpredictable." Yet the "instrument of change" that is ever driving toward this end is "the human imagination."

I confess I can't keep "myth" and "fiction" as clearly differentiated as the author seems to consider feasible, though the distinction is clear enough as a statement of policy, according to which a myth would be somebody else's fiction improperly discounted by "clerkly skepticism." Part of my trouble may be due to the fact that Bentham's theory of fictions got only a part of one sentence, though some readers may feel that this lack is compensated for by the pages on Vaihinger's adaptation of Kant's "as if." It is all clear enough when we are told that "*Lear* is fiction," of that "anti-Semitism is a degenerate fiction, a myth." But I get into trouble when I try to decide whether the distinction between a myth and a fiction is a fiction, or whether we need a third term. And though Dante's *Inferno* is obviously a fiction, one cannot respond to it adequately unless one believes *beyond question* that such sufferings really would be hellish. In any case, when the author writes "nobody, so far as I know, has ever tried to relate the theory of literary fictions to the theory of fictions in general," I see no reason to dispute him this priority, if only he will grant that many other writers have been exercised by the same sort of problems, though not exactly in those same terms.

The exhibits having covered such a range of gradations from ultimately theologic scruples to culminative devices thought up by some contemporary anti-novelistic novelists, it would be almost an act of superrogation to ask for more. Yet the book's very comprehensiveness within so brief a compass requires at least passing reference to aspects of the subject that were not developed. In particular a book on endings should also formally consider the *terminal* nature of sheer *terms,* as when we note that the subject is first treated *in terms* of one model, and later develops into the description of another. Also, an interesting fact about terms is that, even when they are not featuring the temporal kind of development stressed in this book, terms also have the property of bringing beginnings and endings together. For without terms, we could not even begin a discussion, and the terms we use determine both the quality of our attention and the direction of our conclusions (which is another word for "endings"). Furthermore, insofar as terms constitute a medium, they are in effect a kind of *middle;* and thus in their purely technical way, a discussion turns about them, analogous to the kind of "perpetual crisis" which Professor Kermode's overly temporal approach to the subject of endings deflects attention from this non-temporal aspect of terms. (For note that, by their nature as "boundaries," terms are innately "eschatological," since boundaries also bear upon "first and last things," though not in the sheerly temporal sense embodied in the Apocalyptic model.)

Professor Kermode rightly reminds us that "The Bible is a familiar model of history . . . The first book is Genesis, the last Apocalypse." And I have myself done considerable work on terms, using the opening chapters of Genesis as my point of departure. But there is also the opening sentence in the Gospel of John, "In the beginning was the Word"—and, just as the word for "Word" is *Logos,* the secular analogue of this principle (which Professor Kermode never mentions) involves us in kinds of purely *logical* priority that turns our attention to terms rather than to sheerly *temporal* firsts.

Accordingly, when Professor Kermode says, "*The Waste Land* is intended to be outside time, though of course it has a temporal aspect; this is progressive form, as Kenneth Burke talks about it, a 'temporizing of essence,'" I do not feel that this statement quite conveys my meaning. By the "temporizing of essence," I have in mind specifically "mythic" or narrative devices whereby the non-temporal can be stated in temporal terms (as when, instead of saying that someone is *essentially* loathsome, one might either impugn his ancestry or prophesy that he will end on the gallows, thereby defining him "eschatologically," in terms of either "firsts" or "lasts"). Thus in my *Rhetoric of Religion* I try to show how the opening chapters of Genesis in effect define man as "in principle" a sinner (but do so "mythically" or narratively, by a story about the *first* man who disobeyed the *first* command addressed to him by the *foremost* authority). True, such temporal or narrative ways of defining essence do involve "progressive form." But another notable consideration enters here:

It involves the sort of thing I take Joseph Frank to be concerned with, in his talk of "spatial" form (to which Professor Kermode objects). I take it that media such as literature and music are "progressive" in that they unfold step by step; and media like painting or sculpture are "static," insofar as the object is there before us simultaneously, in all its parts. However, just as we "read time" into the static forms by observing piecemeal how they develop from one point to another or how their parts embody certain relationships to one another, so we gradually piece together a set of *fixed* relationships within a progressive form such as a story or an opera.

There are places where Professor Kermode seems almost to be saying this same thing. Yet in objecting to the idea of "spatialization," he sums up his position thus: "Forms in time have an almost negligible spatial aspect (the size of the book). Their interrelations had much better be studied by reference to our usual ways of relating past, present, and future." But why? The relationships among the scenes of a play or among the *dramatis personae* just *are,* though these relationships are progressively *revealed* (and let's not forget that "apocalypse" means purely and simply "revelation").

Something similar figures in Professor Kermode's reference to cases where "all ends in fiction" are represented, "as they are for example by Kenneth Burke, as cathartic discharges." This statement, too, needs modification. True, I would take it that profuse weeping at the end of, say, *Oedipus Rex,* can be a curative release, even to the extent that such an ending can provide in a different setting a surrogate for the original Dionysiac rites whereby the equivalent of an audience's weeping in unison could be attained more directly by a communal sexual orgy. But there are other kinds of endings (the fictive equivalent of Platonic transcendence, for instance, as I have tried to show in my analysis of James Joyce's story, "The Dead").

However, the main point is this: even if one did care to interpret all such other resolutions as variations on the one theme of cathartic discharge, here again the overly narrative view of ends restricts our view on the whole subject. Thus, of the five basic terms I use in my *Grammar of Motives* (act, scene, agent, agency, and purpose), the last most decidedly involves "the sense of an ending," though in ways other than those brought to the fore by Professor Kermode's model. And once we lay stress upon the sheerly terminal nature of terms, Sartre's elaborate shadow-boxing with problems of action, freedom, and imagination collapses into a nontemporal cluster of this sort: whether or not men are free, implicit in the idea of an act there are ideas of purpose and freedom. The exercising of our symbolic resources (often called "imagination") is a species of action ("symbolic action"). Thus, we necessarily relate to one another as persons who *act* (hence posses elements of purpose and freedom), in contrast with things that can but *move* or be *moved*. Maybe yes, maybe no. My point is that Professor Kermode's model does not allow us even to consider "the sense of an ending" along such lines.

Unquestionably one of the most ingenious sections in the book is concerned with the theoretic problems that led Thomas Aquinas to develop the concept of "a third duration, between that of time and eternity," a kind of "duration" for which the author also finds secular analogies. Since Aquinas classed angels as a kind of being which is essentially different from both God and man, just as God is in eternity and man is in time so angels were thought to need some kind of temporal background peculiar to themselves. For all his stress on endings, Professor Kermode here helpfully notes that this issue "is ultimately as argument about origins." And surely it is the most thoroughgoing instance of *essence translated into a temporal equivalent* since Plato invented his "archetypes" (whereby a merely logical name for a *class* of objects, such as "house," could be translated quasi-temporally into terms of house as a pure "form" or "idea" experienced by us in an existence prior to our life on earth). Professor Kermode here gives me a splendid addition for my exhibits on this subject (which I have dealt with mostly in my *Grammar of Motives* and *Rhetoric of Religion*), even though his use of it is turned in another direction.

In sum, a wholly narrative model of "fictions" gives us too temporal a view of the subject, unless the model is itself discounted by a measure of "clerkly skepticism." Our sense of endings needs rounding out by thoughts on terministic interrelationships that are "nontemporal" in the sense of the distinction between the temporally prior and logically prior. However, such reservations would not in any way detract from my great admiration for this book, which has already engrossed me through nearly three readings, and to which I shall surely keep returning.

# Swift Now? Swift Then

*Jonathan Swift: A Critical Introduction* by Denis Donoghue. Cambridge UP
*The New Republic*, May 1970

Denis Donoghue (Professor of Modern English and American Literature, at University College, Dublin) patiently makes it clear that "Swift Our Contemporary is merely a fraction of Jonathan Swift 1667–1745." The "sense of life" that "is operative in his work" is hard to locate "in contemporary attitudes." In Swift's perspective, at the top there was "the God enunciated by the Anglican religion and sustained by Tory politics," the equivalent of which was "an appeal to the landed class, rather than to the moneyed men, the City." When reading Swift with the vatically terrifying close of Pope's *Dunciad* in mind, one continually glimpses the pressure of the coming turn in literary fashion. The constraint that Swift was forever trying to impose upon himself was but a microcosm of the constraint that (in his hatred of "Enthusiasm" and all its squirming brood) he would if possible have imposed upon the rebellious course of history (the literary analogue of which could perhaps be summed up in the turn from "wit" to "imagination" as key term). In keeping with his inhibitory attitude, which in his poetry came to a focus in the strict formalism of rhymed (tetrameter or pentameter) couplets, "Swift made up for constraint by training himself to live with it; as he would deal with misery by reducing his desires." He was in principle under the wholly un-Amurrican sign of one who would try to cut down his expenses rather than increase his income.

    The delightful aspect of the present book, as literary criticism, resides in Donoghue's constant return, by various routes, to a discussion of what blows are struck, or blocked, or dodged, or followed up, and how, in Swift's endless stratagems to make the world "poor but honest." The result is an expert presentation of the profuse inventiveness that enlivens Swift's stylistic tactics. For instance, in contrast with much contemporary writing which tries to get "power" by the wearisome overdoing of a few four-letter words, think of the passage where, satirically adumbrating the key analogies of Carlyle's *Sartor*

*Resartus,* Swift calls "Religion a Cloak, Honesty a Pair of Shoes, worn out in the Dirt, Self-Love a Surtout, Vanity a Shirt, and Conscience a Pair of Breeches, which, tho' a Cover for Lewdness as well as Nastiness, is easily slipt down for the Service of both."

"To begin with," Donoghue "would propose Swift as a master of the Negative."

> If Swift were God, he would declare himself through the Decalogue, the series of Thou-Shalt-Nots; and persist thereafter in silence. As it is, he builds his great work from the resources of negation, featuring as his characteristic gestures the imagery of veto, voiding, riddance, cleansing, deletion, and the like.

In keeping with his somewhat metonymic trick of translating "spiritual conditions" into terms of physical analogues, he "gets rid of sin and evil by treating them as excrement," a stylistic resource that could become a kind of psychologic subterfuge, permitting by negation "an acceptance of what is repressed" (Donoghue is here quoting Freud). But the aptitude for such ingenuities also has its risks:

> Unofficially, then, Swift could admit into his consciousness anything and everything that insisted on coming his way; while officially he would rid himself of it, or some of it, as the Yahoos employed their excrement, by discharging it on their enemies. As long as this magic worked, he could live, if not happily at least productively. The horror of his last years is that his mind was unable totally to rid itself of excremental experience.

Perhaps, despite himself, and despite his hatred of all human pride, part of his trouble had its roots in a devious course whereby Pride had crept up on him unnoticed. For Donoghue goes on to say, "In those years, he thought of himself, 'my blood soured, my spirits sunk, fighting with Beasts like St. Paul, not at Ephesus, but in Ireland.'" Perhaps Swift was yielding here to what Donoghue, in another connection, calls "threat by imagery."

Be that as it may, these are the trying days when one must leave it for the salesmen of business and run-down religion to "accentuate the positive." The welter of our technologic powers, coupled with their burdensome "side-effects," calls for a corresponding profusion of *negativity,* at least as regards the criminally or stupidly wasteful ways of living that are *absolutely necessary,* if our current modes of production and distribution are to be kept going.

Donoghue gives us telling glimpses of respects in which Swift's battles against the world-without are dangerously paralleled by battles-within ("deep in the dreadful unconscious"). But he seems almost as reluctant as Swift himself would have been, to venture upon speculations as to just what, or what all, such a fate-laden ambiguity might eventually involve, so far as personal motives are concerned.

Thus, on the subject of "perspective," he considers at some length the effect of microscope and telescope "upon the English literary imagination." With regard to what Gulliver refers to as a "pocket-perspective," Donoghue says: "Looking through one end, Gulliver saw the Brobdingnagians; through the other, the Lilliputians." But though he proves his point (and all the more so when he quotes ungentlemanly verses on "Celia's magnifying Glass" and its gross reflections when she is squeezing blackheads, specifically called "Worms"), I doubt whether we should stop at this point. For there were fabulous tales of giants and pygmies long before the telescope was invented. To me they suggest an origin in such disproportions as a child must feel in contrast with "Brobdingnagian" adults, or on the other hand with "Lilliputian" insects and small animals. Neither microscope nor telescope quite shows us a Yahoo at one end and a Houyhnhnm at the other, though I could understand such a virtuous horse as an idealized mother-symbol. Incidentally, Donoghue himself remarks that "the Brobdingnagians are to Gulliver in their country as Gulliver is to a weasel in England." And elsewhere he says, "The King of Brobdingnag makes fun of 'human grandeur,' which 'could be mimicked by such diminutive Insects' as Gulliver." Such observations would also fit well with Freud's notions about dream-surrogates for children.

Donoghue might justly say that the attempt to track down such possibilities would, at best, belong in another book. What interests Donoghue is the expressed, not the hidden Swift, and particularly his literary tactics. The first chapter, "One Lash the More," is concerned among other things with the distinction between such a figure as Gulliver and the kind of character we expect of such works as the Jamesian novel. In the second, on "Perspective," while stressing the stylistic resourcefulness of perspective, pressure, irony, discontinuity, parody, comparison, contrast, and burlesque, Donoghue also makes it clear how such devices tie in with Swift's beliefs and limitations. The third chapter, on "Body, Soul, Spirit," discusses his tricks of reduction, as when taking literally what is offered metaphorically. Thus, if the Aeolists say that "the Original Cause of all things" is Wind, Swift proceeds accordingly, by equating eloquence, belching, religious enthusiasm, breaking wind, and inspiration. Similarly, there are endless possibilities of parody, "given that 'spirit' can be construed as ghost, vapour, soul, breath, air, wind, distilled liquor, and many fugitive things." And again, where the ostensible aim of Inspirational artifices in religion is "to scale the height of spirit," Swift proceeds to imply, that their real aim is "to achieve an orgasm." Donoghue also notes how, in order to score, the possibility of Swift's "vexing the world often led him beyond the strict boundary of belief or disbelief."

Then comes a long chapter on "Words" that demonstrates how exacting the tie-up can be between a sense of stylistic propriety and the sense of commitment to a certain position in religion and politics. One could never find a more puzzling tangle of pride and revulsion against pride. There is something both grand and fearsome in Donoghue's remarks on Swift's attitude: "A man is known by the company he keeps and, with equal justice, by the propriety of his style. Swift once told Lord Orrery that he refused to sign a Report until 'the words *Mobb* and *behave* were alter'd to *Rabble* and *behaved themselves.*'" But when one critic objected to Swift's style as "somewhat hard and dry," Donoghue re-minds us that "to Swift 'hard' and 'dry' are terms of praise."

The next chapter, "The Lame Beggar," gives us what we had been waiting for all this time: a discussion of *Gulliver's Travels,* plus relevant references to other works and authors. It's a marvelous field to work in and Donoghue does delightfully by it, though perhaps no one will ever get to the bottom of this book (by an author who, as Donoghue points out, was almost brutal in the perhaps fear-ridden attempt to keep from going below the surface).

The last chapter, "The Sin of Wit," treats of Swift's poetry. Precisely here, where love should enter, it does. Yet how perversely, as Swift's belief in the body gets entangled with imagery of the body's ills and secretions. Reading Donoghue on Swift in love I am reminded: I knew a woman who knew another woman; and this second woman told me what the first woman had told her about a certain man; namely : "I loved him unbearably. I idealized him. And the only way I could keep from him was by always making myself think of him as in the act of defecation." Her strenuous imaginings worked. Thereby, having successfully repressed her adulterous love, she remained a loyal wife, up to the time when her husband divorced her, and married his private secretary.

Similarly, several of Swift's poems are eager to plague themselves by visions of a lovely woman sitting on the can, or otherwise burdened with body-bathos. It may have some devious bearing upon the gnarled satirist's enigmatic relations to his Stella.

# Irony Sans Rust

*A Rhetoric of Irony* by Wayne C. Booth. U of Chicago P
*The New Republic*, July 1974, 25–26

It is gratifying to read so calm and academically mellow a book in days like these when so much is hurried and harried and always going awry. But *A Rhetoric of Irony* is hard to review. For besides its saying so much so well, the appeal of the subject matter makes the reviewer, like Jimmy Durante's everybody, want to get into the act.

Take an unforgettable passage on the subject of "why explaining an irony is usually even less successful than explaining an ordinary joke, and why to mistake literal talk for irony is an unforgivable sin":

> I once had a student who wrote a paper about the joys of deer hunting, including a vivid description of the thrill that "coursed through" his veins as he cut the deer's throat and watched the life dying in those "large, beautiful, childlike eyes." It was evident to me that he was satirizing blood sport. But I found, in what seems now to have been one of the most ineffectual conferences I have ever had with a student, that my ironic reading was to him plain crazy. I made the mistake of lingering over his bloodthirsty phrases, trying to explain to him why I had thought them ironic. But he was simply baffled, as well he might be; to read irony into any one of his statements was to misunderstand his entire perception of what his life and the deer's were all about. Wrestling with irony, he and I were not talking only about "verbal" matters; we were driven into debate about how a man should live.

Things get still worse if we indeterminately wonder: Suppose Booth had been correct in assuming that the passage was intended to be read ironically; might it not, even so, be worth examining for possible suspect traces of the student's attitude? But speculations of that sort are not Booth's concern. By "rhetoric" he has in mind the ways whereby the use of irony establishes a bond of "communion" between writer and reader. When a sentence would be interpreted one way if taken straight, quite as it says on its surface, and a wholly different way if read with the proper ironic discount, then ironic writer and ironic reader are in league. They share a realm for which the literal-minded are self-excluded. This is what Booth seems to be saying.

Building his method of analytic "reconstruction" by beginning with cases of rudimentary "stable" irony (and at the start they can be as rudimentary as saying "what a beautiful day it is" when the weather is awful), Booth gradually takes us into more and more exacting areas, through "Essays, Satires, Parody," "Ironic Portraits," "Local Instabilities," and for the grand finale, "Infinite Instabilities." Along the way he deals with such related concerns as "Clues to the Ironic," "Learning Where to Stop," "Is There a Standard of Taste in Irony?" and "Reconstructing the Unreconstructable."

Having led us eventually to such advanced ironics as the novels and plays of Samuel Beckett, Booth uncorks a prize irony of his own, when concluding (persuasively, I think) that Beckett "aspires to the condition not of non-being but of perfect being"—and if Beckett were to "unmask himself" by translating the "covert affirmation" of the values implicit in his writings into "some 'straight' medium, he would sound like Norman Vincent Peale."

Discussing Beckett as a traditional ironist whose "constant running allusiveness to the whole history of culture" makes him vulnerable to "the traditional charge of elitism," Booth further refers to acquaintances who have "identified not with the elitist author but with his vermiform characters," at the price of "hypersolemnity and self-pity and thus of failed comic effects." Even Beckett himself "seems more and more to risk taking himself seriously in this same self-destructive vein," whereas his "major works convey a positively bouncy verve, a joyfully rich inventiveness." But whether it is God or Godot one is waiting for, a writer might come to feel less and less bouncy at the thought that his admirers are loyally waiting for him to be more and more bouncy.

The book has so many interesting considerations of method and so many bits of specific analysis, many quotes would be needed to do it justice. Along with Booth's own highly independent contributions, there is responsive testimony to the works of others. A few passages may serve to indicate the range of the material.

With reference to Kierkegaard's definition of irony as "absolute infinite negativity," Booth says:

> pursued to the end, an ironic temper can dissolve everything in an infinite chain of solvents. It is not irony but the desire to understand irony that brings such a chain to a stop. And that is why a rhetoric of irony is required if we are not to be caught . . . in an infinite regress of negations.

Discussing "the famous scene when Huck, rejecting the voice of his 'conscience,' decides not to turn Nigger Jim back into slavery: 'All right, then, I'll *go* to hell,'" Booth formulates the development thus:

> It is upon the convictions shared by Samuel L. Clemens, Mark Twain, and every successful reader that the wonderfully warm moral comedy of Huck's "mistake" is built; it is thus Huck, with his verbal misjudgments and his essential moral integrity, that we read for.

Or he quotes the summing-up of Hegel on the "absolute cunning" of Providence as Supreme Ironist thus:

> God lets men do as they please with their particular passions and interests; but the result is the accomplishment of—not their plans but his, and these differ decidedly from the ends primarily sought by those whom he employs.

One tentative "however" keeps nagging at me: Booth's specifically ruling out of his territory the "ironies wrought by the author's unconscious," though he concedes that "a complete rhetoric of irony" would probably include such "deeper communings." One cannot object if, for methodological reasons, Booth explicitly decides that his book will be "about the meeting of conscious minds through irony, not the meeting of the critic's conscious mind with the artist's unconscious." The only objection would be if, under the head of the "unconscious" there are exclusions which do not properly fall under that head. I feel that something of this sort is going on when Booth neglects the sly *sexual* connotations (or "significances") in E. M. Forster's concern with *social* ratings. We have plenty of evidence in Forster's fiction to assume that he was quite aware of such ambiguities in "the snobbery and glitter in which our souls and bodies have been tangled," while "in some other category" there is to be "forged the instrument of the new dawn." Or, turning the whole thing around, what of the fact that we are "unconscious" even of how we contrive to be "conscious"?

# General Criticism

*All living things are critics.*

*—Permanence and Change* (1)

# Engineering With Words

*Geography and Plays* by Gertrude Stein. Introduction by Sherwood Anderson.
  The Four Seas Company
*The Dial*, April 1923. 408–412

Perhaps, by way of a show-down, I should begin an approach to Miss Stein's new volume, *Geography and Plays,* by admitting that I find in parts of Milton pretty much the flowering of certain modern aesthetic worries. Milton writes, for instance,

> Where He now sits at the right hand of God

and the beauty of the line lies precisely in its "significant form." I say this in spite of the fact that Mr. Clive Bell finds significant form a quite negligible factor in determining literary excellence. The significant form in this instance (the structural framework which appeals to us over and above the "message" of the line) is to be found in the fact that the two words "now" and "right" are unaccented in scansion, but accented in sense, so that a complexity of movement and counter-movement results. Incidentally, both of these normally unaccented words are further brought into perverse relief by the violent prominence of the "ow" and "i" sounds. But this is no doubt in the versification books, so I pass hastily on to a quotation from Miss Stein:

> Point, face, canvas, toy, struck off, sense or, weigh coach,
> soon beak on, so suck in, and an iron.

Here, too, we have the appeal of significant form. The sentence is structurally contenting; it begins with a group of four isolated words, follows with three groups of two words, then two groups of three words, and finally a curt swing to a close. I quote one more instance, where the appeal is just as spontaneous, although more complex and difficult to analyze:

> Lie on this, show sup the boon that nick the basting thread
> thinly and night night gown and pit wet kit. Loom down the
> thorough narrow.

Surely one does not have to be persuaded into liking the happy chunks of verbalism Miss Stein has given us here, the sharp ticking off of the words, with a plunge at the end like a boat grounding on thick mud. In all three of these instances we have those purely formal elements which go to make up the appeal of nursery rhymes. Here, after all the varnish, is the return to the primitive. But Milton's line has something more than Miss Stein's. The significant form is backed by subject matter, and this backing produces a heightened emotion. For, as Mr. Raymond Mortimer once said in these pages, if form is sufficient to produce an emotion, subject matter is required to heighten it. Art, that is, is a process of individualization; form is general, subject matter is specific. To illustrate, if I speak of a crescendo, the reader *knows* what I am driving at, but the *crescendo* does not live for him until I play one specific assemblage of notes which forms a *crescendo*. Similarly, I get *climax* by one specific set of circumstances which fall into a climax. Which is to say, by the individualizing process of subject matter.

Now, in Milton's case, the subject matter actually contributes to the formal element, and gives it a satisfaction beyond the mere arrangement of the vowels and the fluxes. In Miss Stein's case the satisfaction stops with the form itself. Even the nursery rhyme, by its semblance of a "message," goes farther in this particular than the quotations from Miss Stein.

We find, then, that Miss Stein's method is one of subtraction. She has deliberately limited her equipment so that she has *less* than Milton to begin with. In this matter I should say that she had ignored the inherent property of words: that quality in the literary man's medium which makes him start out with a definiteness that the other arts do not possess. That is, if the musician plays G-sharp he has prescribed no definitions; but if the literary man writes "boy" he has already laid down certain demarcations. Now, obviously, any literary artist who sets out to begin his work in a primary search for music or rhythm, and attempts to get this at the expense of this "inherent property of words" . . . obviously this artist is not going to exploit the full potentialities of his medium. He is getting an art by subtraction; he is violating his *genre*. One might, in a pious moment, name this the "fallacy of subtraction." The formula would apply to a great deal of modern art.

Miss Stein continually utilizes this violation of the *genre*. Theoretically at least, the result has its studio value. If the academies were at all alive, they would teach the arts in precisely this manner. By approaching the art-work from these exorbitant angles one is suddenly able to rediscover organically those eternal principles of art which are, painful as it may be to admit it, preserved in all the standard textbooks. Similarly, as Severini has shown us recently, cubism is (or can be) simply the first glue-eyed nosing around for the teat of classicism. The musician has always run his scales, has had his counterpoint; the student of writing, on the other hand, begins with stories or poems *about* something. It is exclusively outside the accepted channels of education that all technical research has been done in letters since God knows when. What a pity that Mallarmé was so supersensitive; for he was the man to found a really vital literary Academy.

Perhaps it has been noted with resentment that up to this point I have avoided discussing Miss Stein's use of associated ideas. I have done so because associated ideas *per se* are of no more value than are the Ozark mountains *per se*. Their encroachment into art is justified only when some sound aesthetic value is acquired thereby. And their value, it seems to me, lies precisely in the opportunity they offer for throwing into relief the *functions* of the art-work (as in the above quotations from Miss Stein's new book). A logical sequence (the perfectly lubricated novel, for instance) moves with a minimum of relief; the purpose is to conceal the form beneath the matter; the form is used to "sell" the matter. But if I wanted to emphasize, say, a transition; not try to sneak across a transition, but to throw it into relief so that the reader knew that at this moment he was going through a transition; I could get this by a chain of associated ideas, used like steps going in one direction. I should move from point to point by a *psychological* sequence rather than a *logical* sequence. To illustrate rather bluntly; let us suppose a series of nouns, running from ideas of complete stability, into ideas of inceptive motion, then gentle motion, then accelerated motion, speed, precipitancy, and finally ending in some violent cataclysm or explosion.

But this, obviously, would bring in the need of the taboo. To produce this art-form, I should have to rule out ideas of precipitancy at the beginning, and ideas of stability towards the end. The work of art, then, implies the erection of a temporary set of values, true at least for the particular problem at hand. But in the first flush of our "freedom," certain artists like Miss Stein refuse to recognize even these temporary taboos. Here is the absurdity of romanticism, or individualism; here we see carried to the extreme the tendency to take the personality of the individual as a virtue in itself; for the only unity of these associations is the unity of their having been written by one person—which is the absurdity of Dadaism. Such material may be excellent data for the psychologists; but its aesthetic value is nil, unless some further use is made of it. This further use, I maintain, is to emphasize the functional values in a work of art; and we are at least entitled to this view until someone cares to suggest another use.

At any rate, Miss Stein does get this aesthetic value at times into her sentences. And at such times they have a *raison d'être* not merely as fever charts, but also as bits of art. But here again the choppiness of her subject matter limits her achievements enormously. I think of Lycidas, and of the "program" in the stanza sequence: the change in flux, for instance, which is acquired by the slight deviation from the stanza of

> Weep no more, woeful shepherds, weep no more

to the stanza of

> And now the sun had stretched out all the hills,
> And now had dropped into the western bay.

Miss Stein, by her short sparrow-pecks, can get a certain analytic form, the form of her sentences. But the synthetic form of paragraph or stanza, or beyond, of the art-work *in toto,* is denied her. While even her analytic form is seldom brilliant, and shows beyond a doubt that the focus of her attention is elsewhere. This, of course, results in her being diffuse. And her method leaves us with too little to feed on. One might almost say that it argues for the insignificance of significant form. Further, her book is a continual rebeginning. No sentence advances us beyond the sentence preceding. For such advances involve this synthetic form, and this synthetic form can be brought out only by a greater stability of subject matter.

(Mr. Eliot, in *The Waste Land,* goes as far as the poet can go without falling into this "fallacy of subtraction." The sudden elevation from "Ta ta Goonight, goonight" into "Good night, ladies, good night, sweet ladies" is psychological rather than logical, makes a step forward, that is, by means of an association of ideas; and it is one of the finest examples of the functioning art-work in modern poetry.)

It is, perhaps, egregious to have pursued Miss Stein with Milton throughout this review. But, at least, it is not *mal á propos.* For I have wished to bring out exactly what is sacrificed by an under-emphasis on the *selection* of subject matter, and how little is gained. For if there *is* significant form in letters, this form can only be brought out to its fullest beauty by the most cautious deviations from the norm, the logical. Which probably explains why Mallarmé, seeing one of his young admirers produce a piece of excessive violation, remarked grimly that the man had gone farther than he himself had dared after twenty years of concentration on this very problem.

# Key Words for Critics

*The Intent of the Critic* by Donald Stauffer, ed. Princeton UP
*The New Criticism* by John Crowe Ransom. Greenwood Press
*Reason in Madness* by Allen Tate. G. P. Putnam
*The Kenyon Review*, Winter 1941–1942, 126–132

An ideal procedure for a critic, in putting forward a policy of criticism, would be for the critic to say: "I shall here propose a set of key terms for the consideration of the work of art. Other sets of terms also yield results, but not the results I am after. I shall show what resources of illumination and evaluation I have discovered in my terms. I shall show the kind of problems they solve. I shall try to show why these problems, rather than other problems (for which other terms would be better suited) are the ones that it is of most importance for the critic to solve. And, since every terminology has the defects of its qualities, I shall try to make apparent the kinds of problems for which the terms are not suited." Thus, ideally.

Actually, the critic is so closely identified with his terminology that he does not recognize it as such. He becomes intent simply upon telling you *how things are*. And, particularly in the present state of reviewing, he will grow quite wary at the thought of specifying what areas his terminology cannot handle. If you want to know about his limitations, you must hire detectives (i.e., reviewers representing rival schools of thought), since he has probably done all he can to conceal such untoward facts from them. For if he did not, they might well seize upon his own admissions, and feature them as the theme of their reviews. Hence, when considering problems which he knows, at the bottom of his heart, his terminology cannot solve, he usually adds zestfully: "And I am wholly in favor of having those problems solved too," though he says this in such round-about ways that you are invited to think those problems are included among the solved. He may, it is true, warn you that he is limited and fallible—but such warnings serve merely to disarm your criticism so long as he states them in a general way rather than by specific consideration of terministic resources.

The books I am about to consider were written by some of the best men writing literary criticism in America today. There is not a single one of these seven writers who does not offer you very sound and very usable observations. Naturally, all of them fall somewhat short of the terministic ideal I proposed at the start. But if you think of this while reading them, you will get ample benefits from their pages.

In *The Intent of the Critic*, there are discussions of critical policy by Edmund Wilson, Norman Foerster, John Crowe Ransom, and W. H. Auden, with a supple introduction by Donald A. Stauffer in which important comparisons and contrasts among the four are made with great competence.

Mr. Auden's paper is constructed about a distinction between two idealized types of society, the "closed" and the "open," an opposition that he develops with a good mixture of learning and imagination. The closed type is that of the homogeneous primitive tribal community; the open is the perfection of modern diversification and internationalism (the completion of the liberal pattern, except that the slogan of "progress" would be replaced by the recognition of guilt as normal). Applying these terms to literary criticism, Mr. Auden derives a strategic change in the concept of tradition. Whereas a single tradition is all that is available to the closed society, in the open type there is a whole clutter of traditions, and the artist must make a conscious choice of the tradition in which he would enroll. Hence the critic should acquire as wide a familiarity as possible with the various traditions (or in our view, artistic "idioms"), that he be able to grasp the full significance of the art. The notion seems to be an ingenious variant of Gauguinism, perhaps with the trips to Tahiti replaceable by trips to the gallery, museum, or library. Since a tradition is a group product, in deliberately adopting a tradition (like a son adopting a father, by the way—an old theme of Auden and his group in England) the artist would convert his individualistic identity into a collectivistic identification. And thus the great heterogeneity of trends that has often been decried in Spenglerian tonalities as the cultural mongrelism of the decadent megalopolis is here presented again in Spencerian accents of promise (indeed, *progress*). This resource is indigenous to Mr. Auden's terminology by reason of the fact that, in his dialectic, "open" traits prevail in inverse ratio to "closed" traits. A different calculus would have been possible, however, as he could have employed a dialectic whereby the two traits required each other, so that each got accentuation *pari passu* with the other. Thus, the vast amount of industrial routine, commercial and political bureaucratization, fixities of transport schedules, and the like could be called "closed" phenomena that arose *concomitantly* and necessarily with the "freedoms" of cosmopolitan liberalism ("open" phenomena). But in this calculus there would be a different "fate," a kind of "Neo-Stoic" destiny wherein great cultural "openness" would require an absolutistic "closedness" as its corrective.

Mr. Foerster, using a typical Neo-Humanist idiom, would guide us between a Charybdis of the "heresy of the aesthetic" and a Scylla of the "heresy of the didactic." The former heresy resides in the search for "pure" literature, Mr. Foerster tells us, whereas the most important characteristic of literature is not its "purity" but its "articulateness." "Articulateness" exposes literature to the opposite heresy, the didactic. "From the Greeks till the late 19th Century, the greater peril was didacticism; since the Décadents it has been aestheticism." While Mr. Foerster warns that the critic must consider the work both ethically and aesthetically, you will note that his terminology necessarily gives all the weight to the ethical member of this pair; for in choosing "articulateness" as his key word for literature, and discarding "purity," he thereby automatically immunizes himself to the heresy of the aesthetic (which is lurking in "purity") and makes himself liable to the heresy of the didactic (which is lurking in "articulateness"). Hence when Mr. Foerster pays tribute to the importance of the aesthetic, it may be just a little like a Secretary of State's generous ways of welcoming a foreign diplomat. Every critical terminology has some typically unsolved problem—and when Mr. Foerster writes, "A poem like 'Tintern Abbey' is great aesthetically; as we have come increasingly to see, it is ethically vital but unsound; in sum, this poem is a superb expression of unwisdom," I think that he should have presented this, not merely as the bright observation that it is, but as the typical dilemma of the Neo-Humanist terminology. For, since Neo-Humanism considers the aesthetic and the ethical as "interdependent" and "indissoluble," to call a work aesthetically good and ethically bad would be a contradiction in terms. Also, his calculus leads to the conclusion that "the only completely scrupulous critic is, therefore, the silent critic." Since criticism is by its nature discursive, I think that any critic's calculus must be wrong insofar as it leads to this conclusion.

Mr. Wilson's article, after some opening remarks on the non-historical type of critic (like T. S. Eliot, who tries to see books "as God might," bringing them "to a Day of Judgment," or like the late George Saintsbury, who tasted books as a "connoisseur of wines"), turns to "the discussion of literature in its social, economic, and political aspects." This is done mainly by retailing the sequence of high spots in the development of the geneticist vocabularies, including the Marxist and psychoanalytic, though necessarily in the broadest terms. In the course of this succinct historical survey, he devotes several very valuable pages to the relation between literature and censorship in Russia. Thus:

> In Russia there have been very good reasons why the political implications of literature should particularly occupy the critics. The art of Pushkin itself, with its marvellous power of implication, had certainly been partly created by the censorship of Nicholas I, and Pushkin set the tradition for most of the great Russian writers that followed him. Every play, every poem, every story, must be a parable of which the moral is implied. If it were stated, the censor would suppress the book ... Right down through the writings of Chekhov and up almost to the Revolution, the imaginative literature of Russia presents the peculiar paradox of an art which is technically objective and yet charged with dynamic social messages.

Mr. Wilson seems to feel that, since we do not in America write under a political censorship, the critical tradition of sensitivity to "implications" is irrelevant to our situation. We can't be sure how Mr. Auden would apply his calculus here, but I should think that it would entitle the American critic to adopt the Russian critical tradition, with its sensitivity to a work's "implication," if he preferred. The presence or absence of formal political censorship would not be the test here. The test would be whether or not one could disclose that a book can be implicitly something different from the book it pretends to be explicitly. Such is, I think, the case. Every book embodies a set of values—and implicit in every set of values there is a social attitude, or program of conduct. One might think that Neo-Humanism, at least, could sharpen its critical instruments if, instead of choosing to deal with our modern complexities "in the light of a few simple ideas firmly established" (Mr. Foerster's policy), it looked with at least political sympathy upon attempts to methodize the study of the relation between art and conduct by the specific analysis of value-structures as concretely exemplified in individual works.

As for the remaining essay, by Mr. Ransom, since it gives a curtailed version of his thesis in *The New Criticism,* we shall consider it in its roomier treatment. Mr. Ransom is continuing his doughty battle in behalf of poetic realism, as contrasted with such restricted characterizations of the world as we get in the terminology of positivism. Unlike I. A. Richards, he claims an important cognitive ingredient for poetry; but at the same time, like most teachers, he thinks of poetic assertion as the opposite of educative, or didactic assertion; and like most aestheticians in our present economy, he treats the aesthetic and the practical as opposites.

In addition to its function as a statement of attitude towards poetry, *The New Criticism* lays out a project for the technical analysis of poetry (an exposition that is developed through analysis of key terms in the criticism of T. S. Eliot, I. A. Richards, William Empson, Yvor Winters, and the "semasiologist," Charles W. Morris). These local contests are fascinating to watch, but we must here confine ourselves to the general thesis that grows out of this dialectical interchange. I am sorry thus to hurry on, as it would be especially interesting to observe the ways in which Mr. Ransom squares the terms of these other critics with his own.

His key terms are "structure" and "texture." If structure is the warp, then texture is the woof. Since the terms are used not positively, but dialectically, they do not name two "different "things," but a *relationship*. Hence, what is "structure" in one linguistic situation may be "texture" in another, and vice versa. Usually, a dialectic of this sort treats the details of a work as consistent with some unitary generating principle or "idea." The novel twist in Mr. Ransom's terminology derives from the fact that he stresses the *divergent* nature of the details. Using a kind of Separationist aesthetic, he calls the unitary interpretation of a poem "Hegelian," and "mystical"; and he likens the poem instead to a "democratic" organization that gives a distinctive measure of local autonomy to the details, or "texture" of the work. In a poem, he says, this textural material is enjoyed for itself, independently of its function in the whole; but prose is "totalitarian," in that it subordinates "texture" to the requirements of the central plan, the logical "structure." Texture comprises "a great deal of irrelevant foreign matter which is clearly not structural but even obstructive" (which suggests that at this point he could even have selected as his pair, not structure and texture, but structure and "obstruction"). He calls his position "the doctrine of logical irrelevance in poetry," contending that heterogeneity, rather than homogeneity, is "the specific, the characteristic mode of poetry." Were I to suggest a slogan for his version of the poetic state, it would be not *e pluribus unum* but *ex uno plura*.

The great virtue of this terminology is in its ability to keep us fully aware of the fact that a good poem is not just one steady over-all concentration, but a constant succession of minor concentrations, each with some stylistic virtue of its own. Each incidental metaphor, for instance, is then perceived as a kind of poem in miniature, capable of being savored for itself, like the individual sonnets of a sonnet sequence. But I do not feel that his terms are as well suited as he would have them for differentiating poetry from prose. When he says, for instance, "We might sum it up by saying that the poem is a loose logical structure with an irrelevant local texture," is that really the formula for a poem? Or wouldn't it serve better as the formula for bad prose?

Besides the logical structure and the incidental departures or texture, I think that Mr. Ransom could profitably round out his terminology by some such third term as the "structure of texture." Studies like Caroline Spurgeon's

*Shakespeare's Imagery,* for instance, or Lane Cooper's treatment of the fascination theme in Coleridge's Mystery poems, remind us that the poem does have some principle of organization other than the mere logical structure (or situation or plot or development, or whatever may be the element in a poem capable of prose paraphrase). There is a general tenor discernible among the heterogeneities, something that limits the range of variations, or that points them thematically in the same direction. And if the term "structure" is reserved for the logical element which the poem's "texture" uses as its point of departure, then "structure of texture" could designate the element of consistency limiting the range or quality of these departures. We spoke, in passing, of the father-son design in Mr. Auden's concept of a deliberately adopted tradition, with the son adopting the father rather than the father begetting the son. Were we to tinker with Mr. Ransom's terms in this spirit, but making them into a trinity, logical "structure" would be the father, rebellious "texture" would be the aesthetic (slightly Promethean) son, and we'd have "structure of texture" as holy-ghost term, or maternal synthesis.

Mr. Tate's *Reason in Madness* is a collection of reprinted essays, some of them specific analyses of literary texts, the others general articles, usually of polemic cast, on contemporary cultural trends. "Historicism, scientism, psychologism, biologism . . . the confident use of the scientific vocabularies in the spiritual realm"; the middle-class "intellectual movement variously known as positivism, pragmatism, instrumentalism"; the "professional 'educationists' and the sociologists"; the "vulgarity of the utilitarian attitude" which is responsible for the "cloistered historical scholarship of the graduate school"; behaviorist and operationalist theories that leave no place for cognition, in that they treat interpretation not as "an act of knowing by a knower" but as "an interaction among certain elements of a 'situation'"; "teachers-college racketeers"; tendencies "to extinguish our moral natures in a group mind"; "collectivism—the archetype of the un-traditional life"; finance capitalism that is "hostile to the development of the moral nature" because it has "removed men from the responsible control of the means of a livelihood." . . . these are the themes that Mr. Tate selects as his enemies, and that he attacks with both imaginative and philosophic resources of considerable scope.

I think, however, that his best work here is done on the specific analysis of texts. In particular, I think that his essay commenting on the tactics of his "Ode to the Confederate Dead" is engrossing, and is quite the kind of criticism upon which other criticism can be built. In textural analysis, Mr. Tate is always rigorously pursuing his subject; but in his general articles he is more given to pursuing the enemy, thus tending not to let the enemy's thoughts develop, and rather visiting upon them such scorn as would quickly cause them to pine and wither. He is strong for the treatment of poetry from the intrinsic point of view. Or, as he puts it programmatically: "Religion ought always to transcend any of its particular uses; and likewise the true art for art's sake view can be held only by persons who are always looking for things that they can respect apart from use (though they may be useful), like poems, fly-rods, and formal gardens."

# Action, Passion, and Analogy

*The Idea of a Theater* by Francis Fergusson. Princeton UP
*The Kenyon Review*, Summer 1950, 532–537

Wholly alert to the ritualistic, developmental, and consistent or repetitive aspects of dramatic form, Mr. Fergusson has written an unusually suggestive book, in fact an excellent book. For the most part, by centering on the close analysis of particular texts, he can keep his observations well focussed; yet at the same time, since the theory of drama is so directly relevant to the theory of human motivation in general, the reader is continually getting glimpses down long corridors, vistas that reach far beyond whatever work happens at the moment to be under close scrutiny.

The first part contains four major essays: on Sophocles' *Oedipus Rex*, Racine's *Berenice*, Wagner's *Tristan und Isolde*, and Shakespeare's *Hamlet*. Each is capable of being read quite independently of the others. Yet when considered as a group, and in this order, they take on an added dimension; for in notable respects they complement one another. Though we cannot here do justice to the many incidental precisions with which Mr. Fergusson dots his pages, we would attempt at least to give the main lines of his argument.

Beginning with *Oedipus Rex,* which serves as "landmark" for the entire study, the author first notes how, at the "literal level," the play is "intelligible as a murder mystery" in which "Oedipus takes the role of District Attorney." And "when he at last convicts himself, we have a twist, a *coup de theatre*, of unparalleled excitement." But there are other "levels" of interpretation. And, in contrast with various "reductions" of the play that aim to bring out a single emphasis, Mr. Fergusson asserts:

> Other interpretations of the play, theological, philosophical, historical, are available, none of them wrong, but all partial, all reductions of Sophocles' masterpiece to an alien set of categories. For the peculiar virtue of Sophocles' presentation of the myth is that it preserves the ultimate mystery by focus-

ing upon the tragic human at a level beneath, or prior to any rationalization whatever. The plot is so arranged that we see the action, as it were, illumined from many sides at once.

You may want to object to the somewhat anti-rational implications you may see in this statement. For the element of rationality in a Greek tragedy is central; indeed, the hero's sufferings could with much justice be explained as an "imitation" of the ills man necessarily undergoes because of his peculiar nature as a rational being (involved in a social order that arises from the fruits of his rationality). But you are silenced when Sophocles' treatment of myth is contrasted with the "rationalist" use that Euripides usually made of myth— and the point is still clearer when the author considers the rationalism of the "Baroque" theatre at the time of Louis XIV. Similarly Mr. Fergusson shows how Sophocles' use of the chorus in tragedy, by widening the scope of the scene, thereby enriches the terms of motivation proportionately, pointing beyond the extremes of both the Corneille-Racine rationalism and the Wagnerian overstress upon passion:

> When the Neoclassic and rationalistic critics of the 17th Century read *Oedipus,* they saw only the order of reason; they did not know what to make of the chorus. Hence Racine's drama of "Action as Rational," a drama of static situations, of clear concepts and merely illustrative images. Nietzsche, on the other hand, saw only the passion of the chorus; for his insight was based on *Tristan,* which is composed essentially in sensuous images, and moves . . . according to the logic of feeling: the drama which takes "action as passion." Neither point of view enables one to see how the scene, as a whole, hangs together.

We could explain the appealing combination of precision and resonance one encounters throughout this study, by noting that it derives from Mr. Fergusson's concern with what we might call a *thesaurus of action,* as illustrated by representative works written for four different "theatres." "Action" and "passion" are so central to human affairs, that discussion in such terms naturally makes you think of motivation in general even while you are directly occupied with the inspection of some detail in some particular play. Similarly, the analysis of ritual has profound anthropological and sociological implications; a concern with the relation of act to underlying situation leads towards the areas of philosophy, ideology, and myth; and considerations of development and consistency in dramatic form lead to kinds of observation that can deal sharply with the minutest technicalities of play-writing while at the same time revealing perspectives of much wider encompassment.

The account of Racine's devices for "demonstrating an essence," and of the ways for constructing a play to this end, is engrossing. And the counterpiece, on Wagner as spell-binder, is even more so. The analysis of the means whereby Wagner overwhelmed his audience is convincingly reinforced by a brilliant review of the Nazi film, *Der Triumph des Willens,* considered as a politicalized application of the Wagnerian aesthetic.

Throughout these three chapters, we have encountered references to "unity by analogy." The expression now comes into its own in the study of *Hamlet.* Here Shakespeare's theater is treated as "the direct heir of the realist tradition of Sophocles and Dante, appealing to the histrionic sensibility, and representing the familiar mystery of the human animal in diverse, shifting, and analogous images." And whereas some critics complain of their inability to find "unity" or "intellectual consistency" in *Hamlet,* while others would "reduce" the play to an overly unitary motivation, Mr. Fergusson makes out a wholly convincing case for his interpretation of the play's unity in terms of analogy.

Thus, instead of looking for something reductive, like an "Oedipus complex," to account for the play's nature, a critic following Mr. Fergusson's leads might feel quite at home in a more varied kind of unity. Consider, for instance, the variants of the father-son relationships: young Fortinbras' zeal to avenge his father, the comedy of Laertes as a young replica of Polonius, and Hamlet's dual relation to the Ghost and Claudius. Add next the mother-son and father-daughter relationships. Such repetitions of a pattern, with the several kinds of "reflectors" (or different points of view) it allows for, would in Mr. Fergusson's terms be called "analogues." Or again: if the "supreme analogue" (also called "underlying theme" or "main action") of the play is characterized as "the attempt to find and destroy the hidden 'imposthume' which is poisoning the life of Claudius' Denmark," then the many diverse ways in which the characters interpret this situation (with their many kinds of uncertainty and distrust) could be treated as an assortment of "analogies." In sum:

> The anagoge, or ultimate meaning of the play, can only be sought through a study of the analogical relationships within the play and between the world of Denmark and the traditional cosmos. There are the analogous actions of all the characters, pointing to the action which is the underlying substance of the play. There are the analogous father-son relationships, and the analogous man-woman relation-

ships. There are the analogous stories, or chains of events, the fated results of the characters' actions. And stretching beyond the play in all directions are the analogies between Denmark and England; Denmark and Rome under "the mightiest Julius"; Hamlet's stage and Shakespeare's state; the theater and life. Because Shakespeare takes all these elements as "real," he can respect the essential mystery, not replacing them with abstractions, nor merely exploiting their qualities as mood-makers, nor confining us in an artificial world with no exit. He asks us to sense the unity of his play through the direct perception of these analogies; he does not ask us to replace our sense of a real and mysterious world with a consistent artifact, "the world of the play."

Mr. Fergusson occasionally extends his term, "analogy," to the point where its great serviceability threatens to become an embarrassment. Thus, he can even speak of "Aristotle's notion of analogous actions," an expresion that would doubtless cause acute anguish to those who *contrast* Aristotle's methods with the "analogizing" of Plato.

But so much is certain: the approach is extremely handy when applied to certain kinds of dramatic structure such as *Hamlet*—and after Mr. Fergusson has applied it, we understand what he means by speaking of modern plays as "artifacts" and "fragmentary," in comparison with works that fully utilize the resources of "unity by analogy" (a term ambivalent enough to comprise "similarities and differences" both). His method gives fresh insight into the artistic principles whereby unity can be diversified.

When we come to the second section, on "the partial perspectives of the modern theater," we realize how well the four major essays have prepared the way. Of the works he has selected here (by Cocteau, Obey, Eliot, Pirandello, among others), Mr. Fergusson writes:

> Each play has ... some form of limitation which ... is essential for art; but none of them aspires to the absoluteness and finality of the ideal theaters of Racine or Wagner, each of which is implicitly *the* theater. And with reference to the theater of Shakespeare, the perspectives upon which they are based (however beautiful, or brilliant, or true, or touching) are partial—highly developed fragments of his great mirror, which can only be considered together by keeping it in mind.

Mr. Fergusson does admirably by his view of contemporary experimental art as the fragmentation of an earlier unity. But couldn't he with some justice have been a bit more lenient here? Might we not also note certain *positive* elements in the modern "experimental" forms? Besides their nature as fragmentations of an earlier unity, they may have a new integrity to this extent: there is a certain wholesome semantic training discernible in the growing ability of audiences to accept whatever rules of the game the playwright adopts for his particular play. Such methodic setting-up of arbitrary conventions *pro tem* involves more than the mere collapse of past conventions. And in such a situation, the artist is not "imposing" a form: he is *utilizing resources natural to our culture.* In this respect, couldn't we adopt a broader "analogue" for the modern art, looking upon the "experimental" as thoroughly grounded in our pragmatic ways generally, hence seeing our culture as an institutional frame that allows for the *tour de force* as a norm, and putting forward the idea (or "analogue") of a *single* contemporary, experimental theater that finds its "analogical" existence in plays on their face as different as those of Cocteau, Obey, Eliot, and Pirandello?

(We recall no mention of the "experimental theater" as such. And we can understand why the author would prefer to shun the hackneyed unction of the term. Yet, surprisingly, as his discussion proceeds, we begin to feel that some such term is needed here. The growing willingness to let the artist set the terms of the contract between himself and his audience is a form of thinking that is active in its own right, and not merely the fragmentary survival of a past integrity.)

Maybe yes, maybe no. In any case, whether you would hold to this less down-hearted view of modern artistic conditions or would vote for Mr. Fergusson's point about fragmentation, these "partial" plays are studied with the same patience and discernment as in the four major essays. The analysis of *Murder in the Cathedral* is especially penetrating.

All told, in this book many "analogues" of action are surveyed with scrupulous care. Maybe "action" is even given too much weight, as "action," "passion," "analogy," and the "histrionic sensibility" seem to carry burdens some of which might better have been assigned to "catharsis" (an important aspect of Aristotle's definition which Mr. Fergusson necessarily slights, in selecting "the imitation of an action" as his formula for the "tragic rhythm"). But around the edges of his book there have been references to Dante's *Purgatorio* as the ideal instance of the "tragic rhythm." And perhaps "purgation" is slighted here because, in the author's psychic economy, it falls better under his work on Dante, which we hope is now in progress. Meanwhile, our salute to the many pages of really superb criticism that this book contains.*

*Addendum:* Looking over this review, I fear that the demon of envy must have been working in me. For I intended to do a zestful salute to this unusually valuable book, the mature product of much thought and practice. And somehow or other, the "howevers" managed to creep in. So let me, in ending, state my unqualified belief that this is a work of major importance in contemporary literary criticism.

---

\* "Histrionic sensibility" in Mr. Fergusson's terms is to drama what an eye for color is to a painter, or what an ear for music is to the intuitive perceptions that are the grounding of that medium. But here is a puzzle we chanced upon, and we offer it, without knowing exactly what to make of it. Mr. Fergusson approves of methods for training the "histrionic sensibility" by asking the actor to decide what "the 'main action' and the smaller actions of his character" are, and to indicate them "by an infinitive phrase," as a way of knowing "what he has to reproduce in his stage-life." It struck us that the clarity needed to sum up one's part in an infinitive phrase was anything but "analogical." In fact, it seemed about as "rationalistic" as one could be, in finding a label for a role. And it seemed exactly like the dramaturgic directions that Corneille gives for his "rationalistic" drama in his *Second Discours,* thus:

> Le hut des acteurs est divers, selon les divers desseins que la variété des sujets leur donne. Un amant a celui de posséder sa maltresse; un ambitieux, de s'emparer d'une couronne; un homme offensé, de se venger et ainsi des autres. [K.B.]

# Likings of an Observationist

*Predilections* by Marianne Moore. Viking
*Poetry*, January 1956, 239–247

This book is splendid. My enthusiasm is due not just to the great satisfaction I find in reading it, but also to the fact that it can be used. I can think of no book better able to make clear the kind of scruples that can be involved in the writing of a sentence. If *Predilections* doesn't quickly become required reading for students of college English throughout the country, then the fault lies with our English departments.

Miss Moore is so inveterately apt at quotation, one is tempted to review her book similarly, even to the extent of quoting her quoting someone quoting. Her critical "predilections" are the perfect analogue of her poetic "observations." She shifts so naturally between the *liber scriptus* of art and the *liber vivus* of nature, one is never quite sure whether her subject is personal conscience or poetic imagination. She can make us realize the innate rottenness of a person who squanders commas just because they are readily available. Or more specifically, she makes us so alert to the conscientiousness of the comma, in keeping with her view of punctuation as a form of punctuality, that we begin to fear for our own souls, asking ourselves uneasily whether we have erred, too, in these subtly significant matters. And when she quotes in her special way of quoting, we see her carving a text out of a text, much like carving a personal life out of life in general.

Though her book is essentially a record of appreciations, my delight in its usefulness induces me to praise it primarily as an ever wary sequence of admonitions, a study in stylistic scruples. Sometimes perhaps she is too severe, and she might send a man through sheer despair on the downward path of loose writing, when a bit more leniency might have kept him still striving for improvement. But in general her book should have a wholesome effect as regards the problems of Advanced Remedial Writing, thereby helping us readers, too, with our inborn problems of Advanced Remedial Reading. (I had started to say "a very wholesome effect," but Miss Moore warns us against the use of intensifiers that don't intensify.)

Her criticism is done with the kind of generosity that is sure to reward readers, since she is always eager to note, for our delectation, those moments when a writer is at his best. Reading her criticism is like borrowing a book from the personal library of a skilled reader who underlined all the good spots. Even in the case of a bad book, we couldn't be robbed by reading a selection of the brief flashes in which the book may have been good. And we are further protected by the fact that *Predilections* treats of no bad books, the selections dealing with the best in the best of our contemporaries.

Miss Moore's penchant for quotation leads naturally into a love of the succinct (or derives from it). Fittingly, she refers to the aphorism as "one of the kindlier phases of poetic autocracy." And the reprinting of some early remarks on Sir Francis Bacon helps us to see how the cult of the succinct (in either image or idea) can lead, through the love of aphorism, to a particular concern with the maxims of morality, and so to an interest in strategies and tactics generally, as with her citations showing how Bacon's "insight into human idiosyncrasy has a flavor of Machiavelli."

But her very love of precision, in leading her to dot her pages with "porcupine quills," also raises the problem with which she is constantly wrestling. For precision snips things off; its particular good pickiness and choosiness tends to break the continuity. Though she says that the poet writes under the sign of "therefore" (as when she finds in William Carlos Williams "the *ergo* of the medieval dialectician, the 'therefore' which is the distinguishing mark of the artist"), we dare remember that she entitled one of her own volumes *Nevertheless,* while her ways with the quotation mark make for a maximum number of cullings connected by "and" (though with the word itself usually omitted, or supplanted by some transitional remark designed to usher us from one exhibit to the next).

The principle of "nevertheless" doubtless sums up her unchallenging kind of independence. It seems to say, in effect, "Everybody is going that way; nevertheless I will go this way, even to the extent of sometimes going that way." As for the "therefore" (which she can discern beneath Dr. Williams' "chains of incontrovertibly logical apparent non-sequiturs"), in her criticism it rarely if ever has such a sheerly Aristotelian form as we might get were we to say: "The poem has such-and-such a beginning; therefore it has such-and-such a middle; and given its developments up to this point, it therefore has such-and-such an end." Her therefores suggest rather a cogent relationship between the artist as personal center and his art as impersonal circumference, as were one to say: "The center being such-and-such, therefore such-and-such notable radiations are to be found at various points along the circumference."

Or, "The poet has such-and-such scruples, therefore he makes such-and-such observations."

Her very aptitude at quotation and her love of condensation incline her to leave unanalyzed whatever aspects of a work do not naturally lend themselves to treatment in terms of aphorism or imaginal miniatures. Perhaps her early essay on Henry James is the weakest in this regard. Though the novel is a form in which the shell is every bit as important as the kernels, here too she expends her main efforts on extracting such kernels as might be the major virtue of a La Roche-foucauld or of her favorite lyric poets. But we miss a concerted concern with the problems of over-all development, of situational involvements, of thematic alignments, of ways in which the dramatis personae (or "novellae personae"?) mesh with one another.

The opening sentences of her piece written in connection with the granting of The Dial Award to William Carlos Williams indicate how well she can infuse an almost pedantic literalness with the moodiness of impressionistic criticism:

> William Carlos Williams is a physician, a resident of New Jersey, the author of prose and verse. He has written of "fences and outhouses built of barrel-staves and parts of boxes," of the "sparkling lady" who "passes quickly to the seclusion of her carriage," of Weehawken, of "The Passaic, that filthy river," of "hawsers that drop and groan," of "a young horse with a green bed-quilt on his withers." His "venomous accuracy," if we may use the words used by him in speaking of the author of *The Raven,* is opposed to makeshifts, self-deceptions and grotesque excuses." Among his meditations are chicory and daisies, Queen Anne's lace, trees—hairy, bent, erect—orchids and magnolias. We need not, as Wallace Stevens has said, "try to . . . evolve a mainland from his leaves, scents and floating bottles and boxes." "What Columbus discovered is nothing to what Williams is looking for." He writes of lions with Ashurbanipal's "shafts bristling in their necks," of "the bare backyard of the old Negro with white hair," of "branches that have lain in a fog which now a wind is blowing away."

Her pages thus become a kind of critic's Mardi Gras, a pageantry of sharply diversified characters momentarily and partially glimpsed as they hurry by. Since the quotation marks escape notice when such writing is read aloud, the page becomes wholly an act of collaboration, a good thing that seems to transcend any one person's ownership, though only someone as expert at this art as she could bring such effects into being.

Similar fine acts of identification mark her chapters on Wallace Stevens ("in each clime the author visits, and under each guise, the dilemma of tested hope confronts him"), T. S. Eliot ("words of special meaning recur with the force of a theme: 'hidden,' 'the pattern,' and 'form'"), e. e. cummings (his book "a thing of furious nuclear integrities"), Louise Bogan ("Women are not noted for terseness, but Louise Bogan's art is compactness compacted"), W. H. Auden ("stature in diversity"), and the past master of the adapted quotation, Ezra Pound (in whose Cantos "The ghost of Homer sings," and whose literary patchwork, making for a special focus upon each individual bit, readily lends itself to her methods).

Jean Cocteau's play, *The Infernal Machine*, is reviewed under the title, "Ichor of Imagination," thereby alluding to a motive suggested by another Cocteau title, *Le Sang d'un Poète*. Perhaps it is typical of her ways that, despite the great critical to-do about the nature of "dramatic irony," she prefers to discuss the subject without mention of the term and as though starting from scratch, thus: "A potent device in fiction or drama is that in which one character describes another to that other, unaware that he addresses the person to whom he speaks."

When she reviews a work by that monumental reader, George Saintsbury, we realize that they have the love of books in common; they compare and contrast most directly at that point where, when she is being minutely painstaking, he must cast darts while hurrying on. But each has a way of trying for a quick succession of characterizations. Other brief items are a review of Georg Brandes' volumes on Goethe (under the suggestively dialectical title, *Besitz und Gemeingut*, combining thoughts of individuality and commonalty), and a three-page review of Sir George Sitwell's book *On the Making of Gardens*, a review that makes us quickly realize how "poetic implacability" can figure in this vocation.

The longer retrospective essay on the 1920–1929 period of "The Dial" might best be characterized by a remark she applies to a book by e. e. cummings: It is "primarily a compliment to friendship" (though, come to think of it, I guess this formula could fit well with every chapter in this list of "predilections"). It is neatly stepped off, proceeding paragraph by paragraph from topic to topic like the rungs of a ladder: outside, as seen from inside; inside, as seen from outside; notable contributions; personalities; incidents; relations between editors and authors, and so on, through many stages. There is also, at one point, a twitting note, regarding certain "Dial" policies of the earlier years:

> Such titles as *Sense and Insensibility, Engineering With Words, The American Shyness;* and the advertising—especially some lines "Against the Faux Bon" and "technique" in lieu of "genius"—seemed to say, "We like to do this and can do it better than anyone else could"; and I was self-warned to remain remote from so much rightness . . .

She refers to a "constant atmosphere of excited triumph"—and after a paragraph built about a bit of strongly ideational imagery in a remark of Lawrence, she cites a brief imagery-tinged idea of Yeats. Even the sheerly business details are listed (for instance, the scrupulous equality as regards payment to contributors)—and there is the brief wind-up, ending " . . . I think happily of the days when I was part of it." As one who himself vividly remembers the more obvious of the things here observed (but was always woefully lagging as regards her subtler observations), I find her account so nostalgically appealing that perhaps I am not qualified to be a judge of it. "Those were days when, as Robert Herring has said, things were opening out, not closing in." Yes indeed, except insofar as an opening out might itself be but the incipient stage of a closing in.\*

Looking over the list of her personal predilections, we find that several of them clearly reflect her own salient traits. She is Stevens fastidious, Eliot conscience-probing, Williams aid-bringing, Pound citational, Saintebury bookloving, Bacon aphoristic, Louise Began womanly, Cummings inventive, and a stay-at-home Henry James. And what of that long essay on which she ends, her tribute to Anna Pavlova, a high priestess of the dance?

---

\* "A good sign if not always a good thing." Surely that is perfect precision. For the record, I might offer this addendum: Miss Moore's generous inclusion of me in the list of managing editors could be misleading. At various times, and ranging from weeks to months, I worked as a substitute for members of the regular staff when on vacation. These jobs went up and down the scale, in no particular order. And I was paid at the regular rates for all my reviews, articles, and translations whereas, as Miss Moore rightly says, "Any writing or translating by the editors was done without payment."

I might also point out alas, that included in her paragraph of the twitted is a title of mine, *Engineering With Words.* It concerned what I would now call the "rhetoric" of Gertrude Stein. If I thereby contrived to terrify Miss Moore's somewhat, then I can have the satisfaction of knowing that at least once I repaid her for the ways in which she, by the gentle mastery of her ways of writing, has terrified me over and over again. Also, I whisper to myself, she has shown that the title was at least material for a good sentence, as when she says in connection with the book on gardens: "Engineering zeal in any case is seen to have its verbal prototype." [K.B.]

Pavlova seems to have fascinated her as one who represents her ideals to perfection, though as translated into the terms of a quite different medium. "To enter the School of the Imperial Ballet," we are told, "is to enter a convent whence frivolity is banned, and where merciless discipline reigns."

Pavlova's eyes, she says, were "sombered by solicitude." There is almost a manifesto-like quality in the statement: "in her dancing with persons, remoteness marked her every attitude." And those who like the trappings of a flimsy mystery might well ponder this fundamental formula: "She was compelling because of spiritual force that did not need to be mystery, she so affectionately informed her technique with poetry." Poetry written under that rule is bound to be downright. And you can take your choice whether to call this descriptive vignette a perfect instance of critical predilection or of poetic observation:

> It seems to have been an idiosyncrasy of Pavlova's that one hand should copy rather than match the other, as in the Aime Stevens portrait, in which the hands, holding a string of jade and lifted as though to feel the rain, tend both in the same direction, from left to right (Pavlova's right), instead of diverging equilaterally with the oppositeness of horns. In *Spring Flowers,* the right foot turning left is imitated by the left foot's half-moon curve to the left. Giselle—hands reaching forward, feet (tiptoe) in lyrelike verticals—is all of a piece. Everything moves together, like a fish leaping a weir.

So far, we have been considering the pieces that go from the particular to the general. The two opening essays, "Feeling and Precision" and "Humility, Concentration, and Gusto," proceed rather from the general to the particular. However, the difference between the two kinds is narrowed by the fact that Miss Moore never allows herself the characteristic shortcut of the philosopher or scientist, who may follow along a chain of abstractions. On the contrary, at each step she generalizes only to the extent allowed by the specimen she holds in front of her.

Another word for "feeling" in the first of these two essays ("Feeling and Precision") is the "inarticulate," while "precision" is correspondingly equated with the "articulate." "Needs" and "emotion" are other synonyms for the "feeling" side; other equivalents for "precision" are "expression," "diction," "exactitude," "accuracy," and "explicitness." Thus, when she says that art "is but an expression of our needs," the two sides of the duality are clear. But when she goes on to say that art "is feeling, modified by the writer's moral and technical insights," the two-term alignment seems to be splitting into a three-term one. For whereas "technical insights" would presumably be on the "precision" side, the "moral" element would seem to be on this side only insofar as it is *insight,* while in other respects I should think that it belonged on the side of "feeling" ("emotion," "needs," the "inarticulate").

Thus, we could say either that the term "moral" in her scheme ambiguously belongs on both sides of the feeling-precision alignment, or that it reveals a tendency of the dyadic system to become triadic. Elsewhere in the book (p. 46) she says: "there is in Wallace Stevens a certain demureness of statement, as when—setting down what he has to say with the neatest kind of precision . . ." etc. In effect this remark equates "precision" with "demureness of statement," whereat we note that the word "demureness," when applied to "statement," also combines the "moral" and the "technical," as in her previously cited expression, "the writer's moral and technical insights."

At first glance, this slight terministic perturbation might look like imprecision, and at the very moment when the talk is of precision. But in a subtler sense it is the fifth essence of precision. For the motivational center of Miss Moore's work, both as poetic observation and as critical predilection, is in the fusion whereby one can never be quite sure whether her judgments are ethical or esthetic.

In any case, whether you think of this two-termed essay as having a further term which partakes ambiguously of both, or as incipiently three-termed, the essay that follows it in the book, and was written four years after the first, is explicity three-termed. "Three foremost aids which occur to me," she says, "are humility, concentration, and gusto." And near the end of the essay she gives her three terms a pedagogic slant when she sums up: "Humility is an indispensable teacher, enabling concentration to heighten gusto."

It would make for confusion rather than clarification, if we tried to trace exactly how the cuts made by these three terms overlap upon the cuts made by the previous two. It should be enough for our present purposes to note that whereas people generally tend to think of "humility" as a moral virtue, Miss Moore often thinks of it as an intellectual or technical one—or, rather, as the point at which personal character and poetic aptitude meet. It shades into "judicious modesty," which is apparently motivated more by diplomatic considerations than sheer humility would be, yet which she also seems to look upon as genuine in its way.

Perhaps we should mention another three-part set, in one of the essays already mentioned, some pages on Ezra Pound entitled: "Teach, Stir the Mind, Afford Enjoyment." As she points out, the formula, to which she subscribes, is after the analogy of Cicero's three offices of the orator (an alignment also borrowed by St. Augustine in Part IV of his *De Doctrina Christiana,* on Christian rhetoric). But whereas both Cicero and Augustine look upon both teaching and pleasing as but preparatory offices leading to the changing ("moving" or "bending") of people's minds, it is notable that in the version to which Miss Moore subscribes, the second and third offices change places. The rearrangement is presumably in response to the fact that she is adapting to the *ends of poetic appeal* a terminology originally concerned with *rhetorical persuasion.*

Looking at the book from another angle, let us review some of the problems with which Miss Moore is characteristically exercised.

First, there is the problem stemming from the fact that "precision," frankness, uncompromising honesty of statement must coexist with "reserve," "restraint," the effort to keep within the bounds of "our natural reticence."

Closely allied with this search for a mean there is her great predilection for the "art of understatement." Thus she links Wallace Stevens and T. S. Eliot on the basis of their "reticent candor and emphasis by understatement." Elsewhere, she speaks of a "fascination" in "mere understatement." We might say that she writes Under the Sign of the Figure of Litotes. (A possible minority report here could plead that the classic ideal of to *prepon* should distrust understatement, too, except as an occasional rhetorical device that is most effective when sandwiched in among statements that amplify and statements that are neither over nor under. Miss Moore herself would be the first to recognize that understatement can be supercilious. For she notes that the attempt to be concise, by making one say too little rather than too much, can make writing "seem over-condensed, so that the author is resisted as being enigmatic or disobliging or arrogant.")

Her main concern is with the dignity and responsibility of her calling—a calling in which, by her rules, one avoids the risk of arrogance by imposing upon oneself whatever stylistic commandments one would impose upon others.

Since she is ever on the alert for new ways of saying old things, if we habitually think of A as acting upon B, she will be sure to like the mild stylistic perversity whereby B is presented as acting upon A. Thus, as an example of "precision" in Hopkins she quotes "his saying about some lambs he had seen frolicking in a field, 'It was as though it was the ground that tossed them.'"

She inclines to cull Beatitude-like paradoxes of failure: "He's due to fail if he succeeds" . . . "hope that in being frustrated becomes fortitude" . . . "The right to fail that is worth dying for" . . . "How wrong we are in always being right" . . . "Weakness is power . . . handicap is proficiency . . . the scar is a credential" . . . "an inescapable lesson that discipline results in freedom." Nor should we forget the variant in one of her own poems: "hindered to succeed."* However, at one point the idea takes on the appearance of a slightly less Swoboda-like method, when she says: "A critic that would have us 'establish axes of reference by knowing the *best of each kind of written thing*' has persisted to success." And her view of humility as "armor" falls somewhat within this realm.

Her kind of thinking shows up tonally in inclination towards punlike expressions: art vs. "artificial art"; "reverent, and almost reverend, feeling"; "imagination and the imaginer" as distinct from "images and imagers"; "by heresay—or heresy"; "humility, alas can border on humiliation"; "reverie which was reverence"; "will power has its less noble concomitant, willfulness."

She is for the writer who "goes right on doing what idiosyncrasy tells him to do." She would "ensure naturalness." Typically, she picks from Henry James the maxim: "Don't try to be anyone else." If one but knows how to be overwhelmingly honest, then he can safely and emphatically subscribe to her dictum that "any writer overwhelmingly honest about pleasing himself is almost sure to please others." And it is almost a forgone conclusion that, given such a point of view, she would quote with approval Wallace Stevens' line, "As the man the state, not as the state the man."

There are lots of things still to be noted. But we have covered the ground generally. However, we find one especially superb distinction still left over. What to do with it?

Let's put it last: "William Carlos Williams objects to urbanity—to sleek and natty effects—and this is a good sign if not always a good thing."

---

\* In my copy of Corneille's *Cinna* there is this note (from Louis Racine's memoirs) concerning the words of Emperor Augustus, "*Et monté sur le faîte, il aspire à descendre*":

> "Remarquez bien cette expression, disait mon pére arec enthousiasme à mon frère. On dit: aspirer à monter; mais il faut connaître le coeur humain aussi bein que Corneille l'a connu pour avoir su dire de l'anbitieux, quil aspire à descendre." [K.B.]

# The 'Independent Radical'

*The Tradition of the New* by Harold Rosenberg. Horizon Press
*The Hudson Review*, Fall 1959, 465–472

This is an exceptionally lively book, on painting, literature, and the realm of the socio-political. It is a good brisk breeze. And it should be greeted with acclaim. Since it is a collection of essays written over many years, with notable shifts, from time to time, in the "objective situation," perhaps to do full justice we should take up all twenty chapters, one by one.

Or a good place from which to spin everything would be Chapter 11, "Character Change and the Drama," the slightly revised version of an essay originally published in the July 1932 issue of a critical quarterly then edited by James Burnham and Philip Wheelwright, *The Symposium*. This essay centers in a distinction between "personality" and "identity." The personality is one's individual character—and "whatever unity" it "maintains at the base of its transformations is something mysterious." "Identity," on the other hand, is treated primarily as a social or legal concept:

> The law is not a recognizer of persons; its judgments are applied at the end of a series of acts. With regard to individuals the law creates a fiction, that of a person who is identified by the coherence of his acts with a fact in which they have terminated (the crime or the contract) and by nothing else. The judgment is the resolution of these acts. The law visualizes the individual as a kind of actor with a role whom the court has located in the situational system of the legal code.
>
> In contrast with the person recognized by the continuity of his being, we may designate the character defined by the coherence of his acts as an "identity."

*311*

Law, drama, and religious thought are thus said to be concerned not with "personality" but with "identity" and "changes in identity" ("a 're-identification,' wherein the individual is placed in a new status, is 'reborn,' so to say, and given a new character and perhaps a new name"). Hamlet, for instance, is cited as the example of a "personality" who "is transformed into a dramatic identity . . . in response to his role—which he performs as required of him by the plot." In the beginning, "It is not a weakness of personality that impedes his action but the fact that he is a personality"; and "this character must be changed if the play is to become a tragedy."

Ideally, I'd like to trace how the pattern of thought at the basis of this basic essay (which I saluted as far back as 1937, in my *Attitudes Toward History*) remains always at the roots of Rosenberg's thinking. But there is a readier approach than by dealing with the problem sheerly in its terministic abstractness. That is, we might ask how the distinction between "personal" continuity and "changes in identity" is exemplified in these essays themselves, considered as the signature of a highly independent, expressive, and volatile critic who has responded with especial vigor to contemporary controversies in the realms of literature, painting, and politics.

In a bit of "personal testimony," Rosenberg testifies to having begun "under the touch of a spirit which the thirties banished—a spirit whose native habitat was international Paris (where none of us need have been)." However, when he "first encountered" the "'Marxist' generation in the mid 'thirties,'" with its opposition to "personal radicalism and Bohemian life," he was "too young to be solidly anchored 'in the twenties,'" and though, "like everyone else," he "became involved in Marxism," from the start his "Marxism was out of date." He was interested in Marx because he found in Marx's writings "a new image of the drama of the individual and of the mass"; and in Lenin he saw "a new kind of hero, a sort of political M. Teste." To him Marx "seemed more interested in the deities I had brought with me than in my contemporaries' Marxism," a discrepancy which "did not help me to understand them nor their vision of themselves." Later:

> As the literary leaders of the former Left flopped over, they found it increasingly easy to come to terms with older members of 'our' generation, especially the more conservative ones. But not with the few who, like myself, were chronologically, as well as temperamentally, on the edge between two generations and actually strangers to both.

Many chapters of the book testify vigorously to the ways in which, as a "person," Rosenberg remained a "non-conformist," not without awareness that even non-conformism is threatened with its own peculiar kinds of conformity. He would seem happiest if he could think of himself as in a minority of a minority of a minority. And the opening chapters of the book indicate how this trait of his personality has now culminated in his identification with the "American Action Painters," for whom he is a zestful spokesman. (Characteristically, while analyzing, sloganizing, and defending such a position, he has also explicitly voiced his distrust of "positionism.")

Here are three details which, when put together, provide a good example of the author's "personality" or underlying continuity (as distinct from what might be any changes in his "identity"): (1) In an excellent dramatistic analysis of Marx's *The Eighteenth Brumaire of Louis Bonaparte,* he sympathetically presents the notion that "with the elimination of myth and heroes the basic structure of the historical epic would be transformed." (2) He also has a brilliant satire on "the Communist" as a type ("made in Lenin's image," that is, in the image of a Communist leader whom he had at one time admired as a "hero," whereas we are now admonished against "the sign of the hero," in the Communist's "total identification" with the "total act" of Lenin's revolutionary struggle "24 hours a day"). (3) The book also contains a forceful, well-reasoned statement in protest against an article by Leslie Fiedler sanctioning the execution of the Rosenbergs. This bristling item is included in an analysis of the confession-literature ("Couch Liberalism") that blossomed during the McCarthy era. It is almost hilarious in spots, and it might well make Fiedler feel like a fool.

There is the not inconceivable possibility that, if someone wrote a book voicing one of Rosenberg's views, in reviewing it he would shift to a different view, not through sheer perversity but because, even if he himself had written the book, by the mere fact of finishing it he would have moved into another phase. Thus, in his final chapter, on such sociological laments as Whyte's *The Organization Man,* his negativism becomes transformed into a modified brand of "positive thinking" thus:

> Having accepted self-alienation in trade for social place, the post-radical intellectual can see nothing ahead but other-direction and a corporately styled personality. . . . Within these limits the deploring of "conformity" is simply an expression of self-pity . . . With his own success achieved the only issue the intellectual can see as remaining for society is "personality." Somehow, this seems unattainable in "the dehumanized collective" in the building of which he is taking a leading part. The result is depression—and it is by the power of the depression it generates, in contrast to the smugness of the old-time boosting, that the present sociol-

ogy is a force against a more radical and realistic understanding of American life.

The book thus ends on a recondite species of flag-waving, as it began by affirming that "Action Painting is the abstraction of the *moral* element in art" (in contrast with his satiric attack on "the Communist" as "first and foremost of the abstract substance of heroes").

Of all things to be said about Realism, he characteristically digs up this odd angle: "As the Hindus say, Realism is one of the fifty-seven varieties of decoration." I particularly like the sentence for reasons still to be considered. In the meantime, viewed as an intelligent, ebullient critic's realistic self-portraiture, *The Tradition of the New* is seen to be giving us, in sum, one of the several possible developments from an early estheticism, through deviant Marxism, to neo-estheticism with strong socio-political remembrances (in contrast with artists and writers to whom the new estheticism is a farewell to socio-political concerns in any form except "Farewell").

Whether history is an unfolding of the *Zeitgeist* or merely a reflection of the headlines, I think Rosenberg would have done better to retain the actual progression in which these articles were written. Then, as regards the wavering battle between "personality" and "identification" (for his case, we might better propose "counter-identification") we could have followed the steps consecutively, along with interesting shifts as regards the relation between artist and community. (These shifts culminate, I believe, in the notion that the community of the artist as a *person*—in contrast with the local communities with which people become *identified* from time to time—is mankind in general, as marked by some direct relation to a principle of creativity.)

I personally wish that, what with the nature of the modern weapons (or even of modern Technology in general) Rosenberg had been less uncharitable towards persons whose modes of "identification" lead them to favor better relations between U.S.A. and U.S.S.R. But in any case, it remains a simple literary fact that his antinomianism allows him a maximum number of positions from which to level his picturesque attacks. Where others may on occasion feel inclined to pull their punches, Rosenberg's catch-as-catch-can approach can catch a lot of people in awkward postures—and the resultant observations make for good comedy, than which no one likes more than I than which.

Here is a passage, in the introduction, that makes clear why I'd have liked to see the articles placed in their first order of appearance (or at least, I'd like to have some indication just what that order was):

> Whoever undertakes to create soon finds himself engaged in creating himself. Self-transformation and the transfor-

mation of others have constituted the radical interest of our century, whether in painting, psychiatry, or political action. Quite ordinary people have been tempted to assume the risk of deciding whether to continue to be what they have been or to exchange themselves to fit a more intriguing role; others have had self-substitution forced upon them.

Metamorphosis involves the mechanisms of comedy and tragedy. Never before has there been such wholesale participation in the secrets of the ridiculous, the morbid and the idyllic. It is through these, however, that the physiognomy of an epoch must be recognized.

This would seem to be a "post-Marxist" restatement of the possibly "pre-Marxist" pattern I have already mentioned with regard to the early essay on character-change. Isolate "transformation" and its verbs, then spread out, to include such synonyms and related concepts as: formation, self-substitution, metamorphosis, change, turn, conversion, self-creation, self-recognition, self-identification, self-definition, self-transcendence, self-displacement, resurrection, self-disguise, disinheritance, alienation, estrangement, revelation, revolution (the "constant revolutionizing" of poetry's "tradition"; evolution is mentioned but seldom), personal revolt, tension, inner contradictions (when poetry encounters "an inner contradiction as well as a practical one," it becomes "loaded with generative power"), "a new moment in which the painter will realize his total personality," Action Painting as a succession of moral choices in which the painting has "talked back" to the painter and so contributed to his unfolding—such is the central cluster of terms around which Rosenberg's version of The Development through the spirits of time and tide seems to be constructed. Add also the many statements that present the dialectic of the new art as a kind of scientific experiment, a position Rosenberg upholds even as regards torn minds like Baudelaire's, Poe's, and Rimbaud's, whose pronouncements are quoted as perfect examples of his views. The estheticizing of the political revolution is completed in the formula: "Modern poems are often notes on a secret experimental activity conducted by the poet in order, in the phrase of Rilke, to 'transform the earth,'" a statement that should probably be read in the light of another remark: "Today, everyone is aware that revolution in art and revolution in politics are not the same thing and may even be in opposition to each other."

The book begins with some of his latest writings, on the subject of "Action Painting." Rosenberg is credited with having coined the term, "which is now being used from London to Tokyo, with as many different meanings as there are writers to misunderstand it." For a critic with so barbed a tongue, he is surprisingly generous in his tributes to such "Coonskinism" (which he opposes to traditionalist "Redcoatism," in an amusing transformation of his earlier concern with Reds). Not without uneasiness, I would approach this aspect of his theorizing thus:

Painters, I take it, have three choices: They can illustrate, decorate, or doodle—and traditionally their canvases have been, in varying proportions, mixtures of all three (along with sophistications whereby: the "illustrations" could imitate attitudes as well as things; the "decorations" could extend into the realm of the ugly; and the sort of enactment thought to be implicit in the sheer lines, forms, and colors of a picture, its nature as a dignified kind of "doodle," would vary with the critic's notions about "kinaesthesia," "empathy," and the like.)* One might conceive of "Action Painting" as "abstract" in the sense that it makes for the efficient stressing of a limited field, generally gravitating towards the dignified kind of doodle, though there are often appealing elements of decoration and its sophistications (the result being an "unStyle or anti-Style" that can also use "the mistake, the accident, the spontaneous, the incomplete, the absent," and that often has forms fragmentarily suggestive of illustration whether or not the artist so intended them). Rosenberg, if I understand him, sees such art as a kind of symbolic action expressive of creativity in general rather than simply being the Rorschach-like portraits of individual psychoses. For although the permanent "revolution" of such painting has "re-entered America in the form of personal revolts," and though in this collection he adapts a statement by Stevens to the effect that poetry "is a process of the personality of the poet," Rosenberg does not consider the results "personal" in the sense of sheer "self-expression."

I take it that he particularly likes such art because it promises to involve the painter's "total personality" rather than sheer changes in "identity," though unfortunately, on p. 31, he seems to use "identity" and "personality" as synonyms, in contrast with the essay (earlier in time but later in the book) where the terms are clearly and schematically distinguished. If I have got him wrong here, I have not done so in any attempt to catch him in an inconsistency. The distinction between the pure "personality" in a "revolutionary" Action Painting and "identification" in terms of some socio-political role (be

---

* Once you extend the concept of "illustration" to the point where it includes the imitation of a state of mind, I can see how such art as the "geometric style" in Greek vase-painting might be classed under all three heads. And one may doubt whether an "illustration" could possibly be good, even as illustration, unless a "doodle" were implicit in it. "Calligraphy," I take it, is often used in ways that could cover all three aspects, as a more or less clearly indicated something is represented *in terms of* doodly-decorative gesture which, in various modifications, is maintained at least for the duration of the one "action." [K.B.]

it Left, Right, or Center) seems to me technically at the bottom of his preference (though someone writing of it in terms of what he calls "depth politics" would probably accuse him simply of shifting to much less risky kinds of "revolution"). In any case, he says that the "mark" of such painting is "moral tension in detachment from moral or esthetic certainties"—and he sees its constant succession of moral choices being taken under the guidance of the hortatory negative (the painter "must exercise in himself a constant No" . . . "Art is not, not not not" . . . surely the esthetic counterpart of a Mosaic decalogue, heralding a movement which at its center "was away from, rather than toward").

Though Rosenberg describes such esthetic "conversion" as "religious," at the same time he is militantly insistent that it is "secular." Disputing Maritain, he proclaims the "revision of the profession of poetry through the scientific conversion of divine Being into definable states of consciousness." (We have already noted that he classed outright religious conversion under the head of "identity" rather than "personality." It is a terministic alignment which some might object to, but at this point I am merely trying to characterize his calculus.)

An objection that I might raise would enter from a slightly different angle. I think that Rosenberg's insistence upon the sheer secularity of his position conceals somewhat the nature of that position. For, technically, the relation between the "material" and the "spiritual" (or to use his word, "psychic") remains much the same (so far as symbolic action on a canvas is concerned) regardless of whether one views the Ultimate ground of the esthetic act in terms of the natural or the supernatural. Technically, the basic distinction is between the *taste* of an orange (which would be "material," existential) and the *words*, "taste of an orange" (which would correspond to the spiritual, and would name an essence). Rosenberg puts the issue thus:

> If the ultimate subject matter of all art is the artist's psychic state or tension . . . , that state may be represented either through the image of a thing or through an abstract sign. The innovation of Action Painting was to dispense with the *representation* of the state in favor of *enacting* it in physical movement. The action on the canvas became its own representation. This was possible because action, being made of both the psychic and the material, is by its nature a sign.

And a bit later he quotes from Rilke, "Dance the orange."

Now, once you grant that one must dance the orange *in terms of signs,* you are technically in the realm of "spirit," quite as with the *words*, "taste of an orange," in contrast with the tasting in its actual physical immediacy. The stress upon esthetic *secularity,* as contrasted with a possible ultimate *religious* dimension, can make the artistic "experiment" look as though it could attain fuller physical gratifications than is really the case. Insofar as it is a system of "signs," "Action Painting" is no more physical than any other kind of painting (except to the extent that it may eliminate some *traditional aspects* of what we have come to expect as signs). "Dance the orange" be damned. Physically, the test is: *Pick* the orange and *eat* it. Or dance a dance and paint a painting. On the other hand, as regards the clement of sheer physicality involved in any motion, if the stroke of a pen or a brush is bold, is it any less bold through being used to represent an object?

The main point is: Once you're in the realm of sheer signs, their "spirituality" is of a sort whereby "secular" and "religious" terminologies overlap—and any militant stress upon the secular as though in this regard it were quite different from the religious merely obscures the situation, thereby encouraging one to hope for kinds of fulfillment or gratification which simply cannot be got from art, or from any symbol-system as such. In brief, along the lines of my own special interests, I feel that Rosenberg's arguments for *Action Painting,* good as they are, need rounding out by further reference to the resources and embarrassments of *symbolic action in general.*

In conclusion, I should add: One great virtue of this book which I have completely failed to indicate is its high percentage of incidental hits. I have always liked that old Western "Coonskinism": "It's good to be shifty in a new country." Rosenberg keeps his thinking new by keeping on the move—so that things keep getting said with a flick that makes them interesting. His paradoxical title is a good instance of his mentality, as are expressions like "the herd of independent minds," or his asking whether "a consistently revolutionary attitude" can itself be called "revolutionary." "Art kills only the dead," he says, on the grounds that "Revolution in art lies not in the will to destroy but in the revelation of what already is destroyed." He is aware of the tangle that comes of "choosing choice itself" rather than making specific choices. As soon as he begins talking of "kitsch," you can feel sure that he'll round things out by getting to "kitsch criticism of kitsch." And, typically he writes: *"An End to Innocence* adds perhaps the final dimension to penitence. Fiedler's line is: We have been guilty of being innocent."

I could cite many more such. But let's end on this suggestive proportion: American life in general is to "individual life in the U.S." as a billboard is to "something nameless that takes place in the weeds behind it." The billboard, I take it, would call upon us to "identify" ourselves with something or other; but what goes on back there in the weeds would be "personal."

# Sociology

*An art may be of value purely through preventing a society from becoming too assertively, too hopelessly, itself.*

*—Counter-Statement* (105)

# Realism and Idealism

*The Reform of Education* by Giovanni Gentile. Translated by Dino Bigongiari.
    Introduction by Benedetto Croce. Harcourt, Brace and Company
*The Dial*, January 1923, 97–99

For some centuries the Western world has been on a rampage of volitionalism. This produced a religion of action, of expansion, to the inevitable accompaniment of imperialism. Volitionalism reached its economic *reductio ad absurdum* in the cataclysm of the late war. It has reached its artistic *reductio ad absurdum* in the countless individualistic universes of the modern artist, each artist carefully cherishing his own bias like a precious gem, each *willing* his own world. And idealism, the schematization of volitionalism, is the philosophic parallel of those economic, artistic, and political movements which have led us to the impasse of modern civilzation. It was no mere accident that Hegel was the official philosopher of a rising Prussianism, or that idealism has been flourishing during this last century which marks the highest concentration point of the nationalist spirit. For idealism, with its strong emphasis on the creative will, brings about an abnormal, almost superstitious, emphasis on the value of the individual, the national entity, man triumphant. Now, the idealistic philosophers themselves have hardly been a militaristic lot. Indeed, as in the case of Signor Gentile, one's objections to them are weakened by their almost pietistic attitudes. But one can hardly stress the sacredness of the individual to such lengths without giving formal sanction not merely to such harmless pursuits as the study of folklore and national spirits, but also to the more ominous demands for "a place under the sun," and all that, as experience has taught us, lies behind that phrase.

But in *The Reform of Education,* Signor Gentile finds that if we are to save the world we must stamp out the lean wolf of *realism,* luring the lamb of idealism to its place. It is only, he says, by stressing the unity of knowledge and culture, information and discipline, that we can save the world from the present absurdity and suicide of specialization. He concludes:

> The dislike for the *purus mathematicus* is traditional. But whether he be a mathematician, or a priest, or an economist, or a dentist, or a poet, or a street cleaner, man as a fragment of humanity is a nuisance.

We are coming to see that this is quite true, while the world is gradually turned into monsters. One monster has an hypertrophied index finger, the rest of his body remaining undeveloped; another has excellent eyes, and is unable to walk; and so on. And that specialization passes completely to one side of culture is shown by the fact that in the recent war practically all the scientists and the artists went stupid. There is, further, very little difference between the man who devotes his life to writing symphonies and the man who devotes his life to inventing a wireless outfit. Both are morons. At least, that is inherent in their activity; they may, in addition, be refined and balanced individuals, but such balance would be an accident foreign to the actual discipline of their pursuits.

But just how can this difficulty be remedied by stressing the unity of knowledge and culture? Rather, the whole complacency with our modern dilemmas results precisely from the fact that we have unconsciously accepted the idealist's confusion of knowledge and culture, so that we have not realized that the technician had acquired nothing but knowledge; that the professional cutting up of bodies, for instance, is not conducive to a sense of tenderness. But if the realist in education points out this breach, our technically-minded civilization may realize that it is making simply for barbarity, or at least for enormity. Signor Gentile, however, considers realism as an arrant and vulgar superstition. Perhaps this is because he has not lived in America, where technical skill is constantly being confused with culture, and where education is conceived almost exclusively in quantitative terms.

Signor Gentile, on the other hand, insists that by proclaiming the unity of knowledge and culture, of science and morality, we can in some way restore humanism to education. But on the exact details of this point he is distressingly vague. Indeed, pedagogues will find this work highly dissatisfactory, for while the philosophy of teaching is gone into at great length, the methodology is almost completely neglected. Just how, for instance, is one to get humanism into the binomial theorem. The teacher may have a persuasive voice, and an excellent personality—but it is hard to imagine just how this theorem *per se* has any cultural value. While by falling back powerfully on realism, and stressing the difference between knowledge and culture, one can advise the mathematician to seek his humanism elsewhere.

Of idealisms we now have two kinds: optimistic idealism and pessimistic idealism. Optimistic idealism may be defined as idealism which has not thought itself out sufficiently to become pessimistic idealism. Signor Gentile is of the former variety; and in the light of Spengler, he seems like a man who has walked on the edge of a precipice all his life without ever suspecting that the precipice was there. The vaunted glory of his idealism was that it preserved the dignity of man by showing him as a free creative spirit, a creature of triumphant free will who was continually mis-seeing the world in his own image. In the first place, one may legitimately question whether this is, after all, the highest imaginable type of freedom. It would be like envying a lunatic who thought he was king of the universe, and strutted about grandly with a feather duster tied to his coat. For here surely is the acme of idealistic freedom. While furthermore, pursuing the question into a study of the timespirit (the logical corollary of idealism) one is simply forced into the historical determinism of Oswald Spengler. For if our mis-seeing moves in a gradual march of rhythm, then we are simply the acts of this mis-seeing, and mis-see (or "stylize") in accordance with our own civilization and our own period.

True, Signor Gentile can object to my word "mis-see." For the idealist identifies object and subject; and the subject cannot mis-see itself, it can only *become* itself. But now we have a philosopher who has followed through this process of becoming, and who finds that the philosophy of history is nothing other than a physiognomy of history, and that the idealist's conception of becoming admits a *chart* of this becoming . . . and when we have the chart we have nothing short of determinism. The philosophy of history (the basis of idealism) has thus completed the rounds, and led to the bleakest philosophy of determinism on record. And this is precisely what Signor Gentile's program was designed to avoid.

# Idols of the Future

*Notes on the American Doctrine of Equality* by T. V. Smith. U of Chicago Bookstore
*The Dial*, July 1926, 42–46

That external act which seems best to symbolize for our minds the quality of European thought during the last four hundred years is Galileo's assertion that the earth moves. The loss of the belief in geocentricity was the first blow to the vocabulary of human dignity then in force. It was thereafter but a matter of time and further meditation until the intuitions which led to this formula should, as they were trained successively and with accumulating power on one subject and another, finally leave man's entire lexicology in distress. For the opposition to Galileo was not a kind of prejudice *de luxe,* not merely an arbitrary objection made by persons who were in no way materially affected by the issue. It is probable that the detractors of Galileo were much more sensitive to the importance of his doctrine than many of the sympathetic liberals: the equipoise of only the most discerning among these liberals being due to genuine adventurousness, while the greater number were helped to accept the teaching without discomfiture through their inability to imagine the scope of its consequences. As an instance of how passionate the opposition was, Mr. Smith, in his *Notes on the American Doctrine of Equality,* cites the following "burning prophetic words of Father Inchofer, a contemporary of Galileo":

> The opinion of the earth's motion is of all heresies the most abominable, the most pernicious, the most scandalous; the immovability of the earth is thrice sacred; argument against the immortality of the soul, the existence of God, and the incarnation should be tolerated sooner than an argument to prove that the earth moves.

Man's entire code had been geocentric. Since then he has lost (lost, that is, the machinery of logical proof for) his intimate and consoling relationship with an anthropomorphic God, his transcendental connexions with a metaphysical absolute—and now, of late years, since behaviourism, he is threatened even with the loss of his own individuality. The doctrine of external motion finds its internal counterpart: man loses all basis of external authority (a destitution which has its rewards in another sphere, however, since the loss of *metaphysical* authority led, by the logic of the emotions, to the rebellion against *temporal* authority, and this rebellion netted much material betterment).

The place which was once occupied in human thought by metaphysics is now divided among such methods of research as anthropology, sociology, ethnology, psychology, history. In the place of absolutes, we have the *homo mensura omnium*—and thus serious-minded men came to rediscover in their own way the "frivolous" doctrine of the Sophists. For a time, in such a market-place of relativism, it seemed as though we could never again permit ourselves to talk of standards. The vocabulary of transcendental dignity was ruined, man being a kind of incidental by-product from a vast mechanism whose processes, so far as human ambitions and terrors are concerned, are totally depersonalized and without purpose.

Yet once relativism was complete, it became evident that this change could not be designated as merely destructive of an organism, but rather as a metabolistic activity within that organism: the inductive method which had broken down the older system was found amenable to the erection of new systems within its own terms; and principles of conduct which could no longer be derived deductively from the absolute could now draw their defense by induction from considerations of the future. A few focused facts to indicate what man "may" become by acting in such and such a way, and we have our justification for counselling such action. Perhaps the most vigorous thinker to attempt a thorough-going "psychological," or "non-metaphysical," ethics is Nietzsche. His definition of man's duties is based wholly upon a concept of man's highest potentialities, the one axiom or rock-bottom assumption being that the race wants to improve its station. And although, since Nietzsche, there have been many philosophers who disagree with his concept of what man's highest potentialities are, they must, to develop ethics out of relativism, inevitably parallel his method.

To turn now from Nietzsche to Mr. T. V. Smith, and to assert that Mr. Smith's *Notes on the American Doctrine of Equality* are methodologically Nietzschean is, I admit, to find the *Notes* a bit more disappointing than they might be without such orientation. Still, though they are totally devoid of poetry (being martyred, we might say, to their subject) they are very expertly handled, and are rich in suggestiveness. In his historical sense, his relativism, his deference to behaviourism and the fundamentals of psychoanalysis (rationalization, compensation, sublimation) Mr. Smith's *Notes* are thoroughly "modern." They are modern, too, in their arbitrary optimism derived from the tenets of evolutionistic thinking (arbitrary because he seems to find nothing but encouragement in the thought that changes can be deliberately produced in plastic organisms: whereas the same arguments which would prove it possible to change man for the better, thus justifying the optimism, would also prove it possible to change him for the worse). In a way, Mr. Smith's lexicology is a rearrangement, within the terms of contemporary pragmatism, of conclusions which Karl Marx arrived at through the vocabulary of Hegelian absolutism.

*The Notes* are composed of three essays: *The Transcendental Derivation of Equality in America, The American Doctrine of Equality in the Light of Evolutionism,* and *Co-operation as an Equalitarian Sanction.* The first two are predominantly historical, the third is hortatory. The two historical essays deal with the specific details in American history which represent the gradual loss of any absolutist sanction for equality. Heretofore, specific equalities (such as the assertions that all men should be equal before the law, that all men should have equality of suffrage, and that all men should have equal opportunity) had been justified by deduction from some doctrine of transcendental equality. The three important doctrines of this sort were, according to Mr. Smith, Christian theology, the Kantian ethic, and utilitarian philosophy. Christian theology sponsored the deduction: "Men ought to be equal civilly and politically, ought to have equal opportunities, *because they are equal—before God.*" By the Kantian ethic, "Men are equal and should be treated only as ends precisely, because as *moral beings* they tower above the phenomenal world of measurement and are consequently infinite." Utilitarianism led in the same channel more by implication than explication, as it assumed a static soul, a uniformity of purpose among souls, a "given self"; and "a simple substantial soul furnished to all alike from an unchanging matrix is . . . admirably adapted to serve as a basis for equality."

After analyzing the decline of deductive equalitarian arguments under the spread of evolutionism, Mr. Smith next sketches "the rise in American thought of a more empirical conception of the human individual." By this conception, the rigid metaphysical or theological mold which was once thought to turn out souls is now replaced by the flexible matrix of environmental influences. The "soul," in other words, is seen as the result of social processes. Whereupon, by controlling the social processes, we may hope to alter the resultant individuals.

> The old contention insisted upon an inexpugnably given somewhat, so fixed as to inhibit any thought of fundamen-

tally changing it and as to discourage any thorough-going effort at re-making the social and natural order . . . The newer conception has also its biological given, but its given is plastic enough to raise hope that something may be done progressively to eliminate the undesirable elements of man's inheritance.

The author is now ready for his imperative. Whatever cultural good man has attained, has been attained by cooperation. "Some measure of co-operation is prerequisite to any human life at all," and "a maximum of co-operation is the *sine qua non* of that good life to which the social prophets and spiritual seers of mankind have long pointed the way." But co-operation is the external manifestation of a feeling of equality: since as an incentive to co-operation there must exist among the co-operators, if not equality, then at least that state of mind wherein their sense of equality is more pronounced than their sense of difference. Thus, we find the sanction for equality in the fruits of equality: co-operation. "If men are not actually equal, they nevertheless ought to be treated more equally than they now are, as regards access to education, distribution of economic opportunities and goods, and participation in other privileges"—for in this way the feeling of equality necessary to co-operation is best fostered.

Throughout these *Notes,* Mr. Smith treats his subject, which had seemed heretofore to make automatically for either the waving or trampling of flags, with close reasoning and calm: the caution of a gardener. And it seems to me that he succeeds in doing what he had set out to do: in finding a secular principle of ethics in keeping with the canons of philosophical thought now current. Assuredly, even did we feel ourselves adequate to the task, this is not the occasion to attempt evaluating those canons in themselves.

# Hypergelasticism Exposed

*The Secret of Laughter* by A.M. Ludovici. New York. The Viking Press
*Hound and Horn*, July-September 1933, 732–736. Also in *The Philosophy of Literary Form*

Mr. Ludovici having creatively noted the fact that we laugh or smile under a wide range of circumstances, looks for a *lex continui* that might apply to all of them. He reviews past literature on the subject, but finds it wanting, except in the case of Hobbes, who held that laughter had its genesis in self glory, thus: "The passion of laughter is nothing else but sudden glory arising from some sudden conception of some eminency in ourselves, by comparison with the infirmity of others, or with our own formerly." And again: "Sudden glory is the passion which maketh those grimaces called laughter; and is caused either by some sudden act of their own [the laugher's] that pleaseth them or by the apprehension of some deformed thing in another by comparison whereof they suddenly applaud themselves. And it is incident most to them that are conscious of the fewest abilities in themselves; who are forced to keep themselves in their own favour by observing the imperfections of other men."

The author shows that this formula of Hobbes can be startlingly developed if we supplement it with a behaviouristic description of laughter. For when you have listed the significant aspects of the *act* of laughing (elevation of the head, baring of the teeth, emission of harsh guttural sounds) you have given us the symptoms, not of laughter, but of an animal enraged. Such would suggest that laughter has a jungle origin, in the "showing of teeth" as an indication of challenge or threat. However "civilized" the situations at which we laugh, there will be observable in them a pronounced superior-inferior relationship (are there many other relationships?) such as would characterize the encounter of two jungle beasts, displaying their weapons and conveying their ominous attitudes.

If the reader applies for himself this Hobbes-Darwin-Behaviourism device of Mr. Ludovici, he will find that the most disparate kinds of laughter-situations and smile-events can, with a little squeezing, be made to fit. We may expect pleased laughter when some discrepancy, discordancy, or defect exalts us by a feeling of "superior adaptation"; conversely, we may expect a man to laugh or smile "dishonestly" when he is on the under side of such a disproportion and would suggest "superior adaptation" by "bluff." The author tries his formula on fifty or sixty different laughs, with helpful results. Thus: a child laughs when, running from a mock-pursuer, it reaches the haven of its mother's skirts. Or the condescending gods of Olympus laughed at the sight of lame Hephaestos. Or the villain laughs a mirthless, you-are-in-my-power laugh. Or we laugh if a portly and pompous squire, such as might foreclose our mortgage, has his dignity punctured. We laugh when tickled, for the most neurologically direct reason of all: because we must bare our teeth as the attacks upon our body produce inevitably in us the stimulation of our defense reflexes. We laugh at our own pun, buoyed up by that proud conquest of the syllables we have mangled; and we are generally quite greedy to laugh at another's pun if we perceive it through the fog of a foreign language with which we should like to appear at home. Mr. Ludovici saw a young woman slip on a wet pavement; her clothes were soiled, and she laughed and laughed, though it is hard to imagine that she thought the episode really funny, and much easier to suppose that she was covering her embarrassment by a nervous mechanism ("showing of teeth"—"display of weapons") which gave her a compensatory "superior adaptation" for a situation otherwise humiliating. And Mr. Ludovici's formula would explain our delight in stage characters whose stupidity is total, as though nothing less than *sheer nonsense* could now serve to provide us with that wholesome feeling of *superiority* which we so greatly need.

The formula is also very useful as a conversion mechanism. For the combat patterns, as spiritualized or "sublimated" into corresponding social modes, will naturally lack jungle "purity," and may yield their secret only through the exegesis of Evolutionism. In the Jungles of Society we may more likely discover, not alignments involving life and death, but the subtler calls upon our machinery of competition which are to be found in the Battle of Wits. Though one woman, it is true, may break into irrepressible giggles at the sight of her husband tumbling down stairs, we usually have to track our jungle far: to the good Professor, perhaps, with his faintly ironic guying of a student's faulty answer (the cultivated and widely documented perception of the delicately comic). This Professor might "show teeth" when his student slipped on a question—yet he would not deign to show teeth, like a mere savage child, had this same student slipped on a banana peel. The concept of "superior adaptation" would explain the laughter of a girl well-dressed and courted (she would seem to live among great wits); and "bluff superior adaptation" would explain the strained frozen twitching smiles of nervous people who really ought never to see one another, but who happen to be compelled by the usages of society to sit down at table together, and so proceed dutifully in a circle to show teeth on the slightest provocation.

It does seem to me, however, that in the interest of his thesis the author is more thoroughgoing than he need be. One might hold completely to the jungle origin of laughter, without attempting so strenuously to interpret each laugh or smile by carrying them back to their jungle equivalent. The socialized snarl of laughter may often be due to what we might call "secondary" or "derived" meanings. That is: if we grant that verbal speech probably originated in the mimetic, in bodily posture, we might conversely find occasions in which the mimetic is still used exactly as verbal speech is used. Some laughter might then have to be explained "lexically." To illustrate: Suppose that A had laughed just because he "felt good." Such a phenomenon would be strictly accountable within Mr. Ludovici's formula—since to "feel good" is to "feel superior adaptation" in a general way, and one in an expansive mood might properly show teeth at the entire universe. But if A, in his burst of smiling, had smiled upon B, note how a new kind of "meaning" for this smile might arise. For B might whisper to himself, "This is obviously the time to ask a favour of A. A's mere sense of physical wellbeing will be superiority enough for him today. He will do me no damage with teeth, or with their social counterparts." In other words, A's laughter of good health may suggest to B nothing other than a *promise of sufferance or service*. And as bearded savants, studying the preferences of babies, have discovered that bottle-fed babies bestow upon the bottle the love that would, with breast-feeding, have been bestowed upon the mama, we may experimentally establish it that from a *promise of service* arises a *judgment of value*—the *lovable*. And once we have established a recurrent type of situation in which laughter, by being a promise of service, takes on connotations of the *lovable*, we may expect subsequently to find occasions wherein a man, employing this derived or "conditional" meaning, will show teeth purely as a sign that he would like to be deemed lovable. To explain the use of the smile-sign on such an occasion wholly by its snarl-origin would be exactly as though one were to discover a "socialized snarl" lurking in some actual verbal equivalent, such as "I want you to like me." This charitable reservation will be seen for the pacifistic thing it is when we attempt to exegetize the smile of a defeated opponent. We should be cruel in calling his smile simply a "bluff superior adaptation" to conceal chagrin. Rather, we might take it as gesture-speech for saying, more economically and fleetingly than words, "This is to indicate that our contest will not be carried by me beyond the limits of the game."

With such a minor reservation as a way of guarding against that "fallacy of origins" to which nineteenth-century science erected all its altars, I think the author's thesis can be followed with much profit. And his closing suggestions that the sense of humor is especially prized today (hypergelasticism) because it offers us a ready "disguised inferior adaptation" to the many perplexities and indignities besetting us, may not tell the whole story, but they certainly tell much of it. Here would be trench humor, to maintain trench morale (which might incidentally suggest that we state the laughter-disproportions the other way round, calling the purpose of laughter not so much a glorifying of the self as a minimizing of the distresses menacing the self).

Somewhat tangentially to Mr. Ludovici's thesis, I was led to speculate on the fact that precisely *Hobbes* was the first thinker who attributed laughter to "self glory." For it was precisely Hobbes who, alone of English philosophers (and perhaps alone of important philosophers, except Schopenhauer) was "distinguished" by an extraordinary willingness to display vanity, self-importance, self-esteem, etc. Some might say, "His vanity so marked him that it even led him to find vanity and selfishness in the abnegatory and companionable activity of laughing." For my own part, in view of the man's great insight on many matters, I should credit him with a much more complicated process. Practically all culivated Englishmen were schooled against the obvious show of self-glory in its conventionally recognized forms (as in boasting), so it would not be asking a great deal of Hobbes to expect that he should be equally sensitive to this convention, and to the kinds of censure and handicap that might come of violating it. My explanation accordingly would run somewhat as follows:

Hobbes appreciated, as well as the next man, the social proscriptions with relation to overt self-glory. He saw that his countrymen had a rigid code concerning such matters, and were obedient to it. On the other hand, since they did not detect the covert self-glory of laughter, their prizing of the sense of humor would enable them to gratify the impulses of boasting, vaunting, etc., while apparently complying with the most rigorous code of modesty and polite self-effacement. With his theory of laughter as self-glory, he naturally saw them as forever glorifying themselves in varying degrees of supercilious smilings while thinking of themselves as the very soul of retirement. Hence, he lived in a world where everyone was a monster of incessant boastfulness. What more natural than that he also should be contaminated finally, by this general orgy, and begin boasting himself? And what more natural than that, being a good metaphysician and recognizing the *deviousness* of smile-boasts, he would prefer to take his boasting straight, with that consistency, that thoroughness, that quality-of-seeing-a-thing-through-to-the-end, which is the most distinctive feature of the metaphysician's calling?

# The Age of Enterprise

*The Age of Enterprise* by Thomas C. Cochran and William Miller. Macmillan Publishing Company
*Direction,* Spring 1943, 3–5

*The Age of Enterprise,* by Thomas C. Cochran and William Miller, is designed "to chart the course of our history from a business point of view." Perhaps the best way to present their perspective is to let them resent it in their own words:

> Men's lives are determined chiefly by habits formed in daily activities. In the United States each year after 1800 more and more men spent their days in factories and mines, on canals and railroads, tending machines, locomotives, and steamboats, keeping accounts, selling commodities, digging coal, copper, lead, and iron, drilling oil and natural gas. As time passed they spent their profits, wages, and commissions on goods announced for sale in newspapers supported by business advertisements and friendly to business objectives. Their literature was issued by publishers engaged in business enterprises. Their amusements were not spontaneous street dances but spectacles staged for profit. Their colleges, founded in many cases to prepare young men for the ministry of God, became devoted to science, and their scientists became servants of business. Their public architecture concerned itself with banks, insurance offices, grand hotels for commercial travelers. Their mature philosophy discarded metaphysics—or so its practitioners claimed, describing their speculations felicitously for our pecuniary culture as the quest for the "cash value" of ideas. To get attention in industrial America, a school, a mechanical invention, a cure or a game had to be presented, as Veblen said, as a "business

proposition." No one explained industrial America better than Richard Croker of Tammany Hall when he cried to Lincoln Steffens:

> *Ever heard that business is business? Well, so is politics business, and reporting—journalism, doctoring—all professions, arts, sports—everything is business.*

The interpretation is "based upon the existing monographic materials in American history, economics, and related social subjects." And though the authors speak of themselves as "entering an unexplored field in American history," we may also expect them, in the course of their explorations to come upon many well-worn paths. The distinction of their approach lies in the fact that, rather than presenting an economic history in general, with business being treated as one economic factor, they treat of the political, economic, and cultural structure in general, but always from the standpoint of the business motive as the key factor. The business motive, we might say, is their motif.

At the same time, it would be misleading to characterize their book as distinctly a "history of business." For though the "enterprise" they study culminates in the practices and rationales of business, it required at every turn the use of materials that are not intrinsically or necessarily "business" materials at all. For instance, even the wheat that the farmer raises as a "cash crop" is not intrinsically or necessarily a material of business. Wheat "transcends" business, as is evident in the fact that wheat was raised in eras prior to the business culture. This could be stated the other way round too: business "transcends" wheat; for when wheat is raised as a money crop, we might say that the monetary motive pervades it as a "spirit," causing it in turn to transcend its nature purely as a "food" and to become instead a "commodity."

I think it was this "spirit" in goods produced under capitalism that Marx sought to isolate in his concern with "the fetishism of commodities." When a thing is considered, not for what it is itself, but for what profit it may bring as an investment, men thereby manifest a more "idealistic" attitude towards it than when it is considered materialistically, or realistically. To conceive of it exclusively in terms of its possible monetary return (as with the speculator in wheat "futures") is in effect to "transcend" its brute nature as material, and to approach it rather in the more "spiritual" ways of monetary symbolism.

A history of this sort, then, must deal primarily with two sources of motives. There is the over-all, pervasive motive of business, the "art of making money." But there is also the great heterogeneity of motives arising out of our great occupational diversity. That is, there were the motives peculiar to each specialized activity or situation, the motives derived from the exigencies and opportunities implicit in its materials. Whereas money was a kind of public and universal motive mediating among a great complexity of private and local motives, the state of the materials in any given form of specialized economic activity provided a set of motives peculiar to this activity. For instance, a farmer, a construction engineer, and a lawyer might all share in the use of monetary symbolism as a rationale common to all three of their economic ways, but each of them would have a set of motives peculiar to his own economic situation and deriving from the nature of the materials in which he specialized.

In the long passage we quoted above, the authors refer to the typically American philosophy of pragmatism. One can see how both levels of motives (the motives peculiar to the many kinds of occupation and the over-all motive of money that mediated among the lot) gave rise to the pragmatist emphasis. For pragmatism is a philosophy that features agencies, means, instruments, stressing their important role in the formation of our conduct. And all the great heterogeneity of occupations, as affected by the increase of inventions, made men very conscious of the strategic part that instruments were playing in the motivating of their lives. A man's preparation to *use* these instruments also meant his preparation to *serve* them—hence, his concept of *ends* was shaped by the nature of the technological *means* (or we could state it, *purpose* was derived from *agency*). So in both levels of motives we see the incentive to the pragmatist philosophies: on the material level, the claims which the different specialties made upon men's attention in the need to use, develop, and coordinate them: and on the "spiritual" level, in the nature of monetary symbolism, as the medium into the terms of which all the many diversities of our culture could be translated, the *means of means*.

Thus, in both money and technology we had this great stress (the pragmatist stress) upon the means as the source of motivation, the ancestral cause of ends. And the aesthetic of capitalism showed a similar underlying logic. For it either stressed the purely utilitarian motive, as in our applied arts, advertising, and the like. Or, in its apparent dialectical opposition to the utilitarian emphasis, its doctrine of "pure" art (a totally impractical art, to *contrast* with the world of the practical) it discovered its own version of the pragmatist emphasis. An art for art's sake is a means for means' sake, a derivation of the artist's purpose purely from the nature of his medium.

Money, in such a structure, was in the truest sense the "god-term." For it was the ultimate rational and public ground that mediated among the many diversities of occupation and preoccupation. And perhaps we can also glimpse a deeper motive behind the adaptation of temple architecture for banks—and may add psychological overtones to our reading of a statement about bankers on page 192: "Gradually . . . they came to make a veritable fetish of monopoly, sincerely believing in the end that it represented the only source of order in mature capitalist society."

Indeed, the tendency of means and ends to change places (a tendency implicit in the fact that, under capitalism, money, the *means* of exchange, becomes the *end* of exchange) makes always for an important *reversal* that will manifest itself in a great variety of ways. "Urban congestion feeds upon itself," the authors write, in discussing the ways in which the monetary rationale (a thoroughly social rationale) interfered with social planning. Or we may note how the general tendency to use legislation as a secular substitute for prayer led (largely under pressure from the Progressives) to a great proliferation of laws, which in turn became the condition out of which arose our cunning reversal in the meaning of the word, "protection." The same reversal is neatly signalized in a passage which the authors quote from Adams' *Epic of America* to the effect that, by the fifties, business had "ceased to be a mere occupation which must be carried out in accordance with the moral code. It had itself become part of that code. Money-making having become a virtue, it was no longer controlled by the virtues, but ranked *with* them, and could be weighed against them when any conflict occurred."

But I have been taking over, somewhat. That is the trouble with these gentlemen's book. It tempts the reviewer to put in an oar of his own. This should be accounted a virtue, however, as regards readers who will doubtless be similarly moved.

The book does well in isolating strands that must otherwise, in their interwovenness seem to us wholly a confusion. And primarily what we observe is an irony (i.e., as per our references to "reversal"): the growth of *monopoly* under a rationale of *laissez-faire*, of *combines* under a rationale of *private enterprise*. We watch a long succession of steps designed "to make private capital out of the public domain" (a movement that still continues, as with the use of government credit for the suport of private investments, or with radio's private development of public resources of the air, though the authors' remark refers specifically to a much earlier stage in our history). Discussing the power exercised by business associations and business leaders in the twenties, the authors write:

> Business had, as Babson said, "the press, the pulpit and the schools." It had, besides, the movies and the radio. Even more important, business leadership seemed "to deliver the goods"; as Frederick Lewis Allen said, the systems "worked." The twenties were vexatious for large portions of our population. But nowhere, at any time in the world's history, had there been so much wealth so widely distributed. No won-

> der, then, that business pressures were most successful. No wonder that, while many groups in America won some laws in the twenties, very little legislation was passed that business opposed and very little legislation failed that business wanted.

This last sentence is, I think, momentous in its implications. The business and financial interests were getting, in a form as near to their liking as is possible in this imperfect world, the kind of legislation they asked for. Similarly the Courts had, for over half a century, been interpreting the Constitution in a sense favorable to business. Yet precisely here came the greatest financial smash in all our history. It is a development we should always keep firmly in mind.

One may decide that, in our industrial state, some form of business must, will, and should continue. But if history can teach us any thing, the lesson of the twenties teaches us that the assertions of business must be amply modified by a free dialectic interchange with other assertions. For if not, as with the hubris of a character in Greek tragedy, this assertion drives towards destruction in the very act of getting its will.

If I might end on a paradox, I should say that the authors, in treating of our history "from the standpoint of business," have not wholly supplied the need for a *placement* of the business motive. For a vocabulary designed to place business should have its locus farther outside the business orbit.

My personal preferences, for instance, would be for a vocabulary that treated business primarily in terms of "communion," "justification," "purification," and the like (in brief, a vocabulary considering business as a secular expression shaped by such motives as were once formulated in theological terms). This would be particularly desirable in view of the fact that we should thereby be better enabled to contemplate alternative modes of justification, should it be shown that, with the greatly increasing "union of business and government," the age of enterprise is near its close.

But though I think a more extrinsic terminology would be needed for over-all purposes, such preferences by no means blind me to the value of the authors' work, quite as it is. Here is a convincing document, written out of the documents.

# Renaming Old Directions

*Redirecting Education: Vol. I, The United States,* edited by Rexford G. Tugwell and Leon H. Keyserling. Columbia UP
*The Nation*, August 1935, 166

If all the world were crooks, and the ideal of crookedness were enshrined in all its institutions, would you prepare a youth for citizenship by condemning thievery or by teaching him to steal? Would you ask him to work for a better world, or to get ahead by the standards of this one? There are many scrupulous people who might choose the more Machiavellian course as regards the individual. But the cooperative virtues form an important aspect of our equipment for survival as a race. And since "goodness" is fundamentally so close to social utility, when considering youth as a group (as educational theory must) even the toughest *Realpolitik* can lead to the conclusion that the young must be taught to reject the status quo. For in the end, a considerable percentage of "civic virtue" must be embodied in a society's methods of production and distribution if that society is to be workable—and there are times when people must endanger themselves as individuals to benefit themselves as members of a group.

Hence the predicament in which the proponents of the "new" education have always found themselves. They begin by noting that the economic system under which we live comes pretty close to organized crookedness—i.e., the systematic effort of individuals to draw more from the communal pile than they put into it. Yet educators are by trade a peaceful lot—and here enters Anomaly One: That even in a world highly militant, the educator may most easily set himself at peace with his fellows by subscribing to the rapacious values in authority and training his students to accept things as they are. To be sure, he need not deny the evidences of trouble all about him. He may parade some modicum of discontent with the present. It is even advisable that he call for a better future, if only his pleas do not imply a basic attack upon current institutions which, if preserved, would make this better future impossible. "Futurism" of this sort may be in exceptionally good repute, if the several complimentary tributes to the forward-looking uttered by the authors of *Redirecting Education* are evidence.

Unfortunately, it is quite reasonable that an educator's attempts to alter the social framework in any serious respect should be resisted. A society which believes in itself and its values will insist that its schools be used to perpetuate these values. A society of crooks which firmly believed in crookedness as a "way of life" would probably insist that its children be taught how to steal. And similarly a society built around the expropriative devices of capitalism will insist that the fundamentals of expropriation be taught and hallowed. In the natural order of events, *education is a function of society*. If we imagine an ideal world, for instance, we think of a just and stable economic structure, with a system of education designed for teaching youth how to maintain this justice and stability.

But insofar as a society is in disorder, and a group arises which questions the set of values in authority, we may expect a tendency to reverse the relationship between education and society. The dissident group wants to make education an instrument of social change. Or, in Dewey's terminology as cited by Tugwell, *it wants to make society a function of education*. It would make education evangelical or reformative, rather than conservative. To educate for socialism in a capitalist country, for instance, would be a schismatic, evolutionary, or revolutionary act, designed to make society a function of education. But to educate for socialism in a socialist country would be a conformist and conservative act, designed to make education a function of society.

The five authors represented in *Redirecting Education* have, on the surface at least, aligned themselves with the society-as-a-function-of-education view. In principle, they would equip people for The Scramble, not by teaching youth to be Perfect Scramblers, but by casting doubt upon the Scrambled system of values. Tugwell is particularly vocal on this score.

As symptomatology, the book is commendable. Tugwell offers much to substantiate his formula for America as "an individualism in people's heads finding various characteristic embodiments but always being forced to compromise with a developing collectivism" (in short, the doctrine of the "cultural lag"). In his chapters on Social Objectives in the American College Leon H. Keyserling indicates the essential difference between a truly integrated social structure and the smatterings of survey and outline which are now mistaken for it. Charles Woolsey Cole discusses some major problems of the historic method—and those who feel that we have solved everything by learning to think in terms of historical development would do well to consider his chapters. Ex-comptroller Joseph McGoldrick contributes a subdued jeremiad concerning our political disorders and their effect upon the teaching of Political Science in the College.

Perhaps the most important trait of this book is best revealed in the article by Thomas C. Blaisdell, Jr., on Economics and the College. For it is precisely here, in the most radical paper of the lot, that we see how intellectuals of this stamp can get themselves shunted off from criticism of the ailing economic structure into championship of the elaborate Hoover-Roosevelt projects for preserving private business at public expense. Blaisdell decides to lay foremost emphasis upon the fact of business cycles. In the same way, Tugwell had laid foremost emphasis upon the phenomena of individualism. By these slight shifts, one can discreetly evade the central problems of private ownership. One can get to talking encouragingly of such things as collectivism or social planning, and ease past the fact that he is proposing to leave the fundamentals of the business structure intact.

In recent years, we have seen many fantastic ways of proving that Mr. A is incipiently fascist for all his obvious love of human betterment. As the simplest rule of thumb I vote for the following test: A fascist is one who would integrate politics and production through the medium of business. And conversely, an anti-fascist is one who would integrate politics and production by the abolition of business. If this test is acceptable, I hold that all commercial abolitionists are entitled to distrust this book somewhat, and to suspect that the more vital means of propaganda will originate elsewhere.

# Without Benefit of Politics

*Truth and Reality, A Life History of the Human Will* by Otto Rank. Authorized translation from the German, with a preface, by Dr. Jessie Taft. Alfred A. Knopf
*Will Therapy, An Analysis of the Therapeutic Process in Terms of Relationship* by Otto Rank. Authorized translation from the German, with a preface and introduction, by Dr. Jessie Taft. Alfred A. Knopf
*The Nation*, July 1936, 78

One can with much "truth" view life as a race, a fight, a ship setting sail, a business enterprise, a search for solace (man as valetudinarian), a nightmare ("fitful fever"), a recruiting of one's band, a building of a house, the paying of debts, and so on. One may consider it, with the churchmen, as a "preparation." Or one may prefer Goethe's secularized equivalent of preparation—with man having the vocation of eternal student, passing from apprenticeship to journeymanship, and incorporating the ideal end in the name chosen for his artistic identity, "Will Master."

Thus, one must also admit into the pantheon of metaphors Dr. Otto Rank's apparent preference for looking upon life as an endless dying and being born. Particularly in an era like ours, beset by conditions of crisis, we may note the relevance of a perspective shaped by an emphasis upon the "trauma of birth." On every side one picks up books wherein one finds authors symbolically slaying some portion of the self. Some men would even revise their family trees, treating their actual forbears as bar sinister and putting an ideal ancestry in their stead. After Byron, there have been many forms of symbolic regicide, as old authorities are deposed for new. Gide seems to identifiy his deepest sympathies with the role of bastard. Even those who talk of "evolution" are stressing the state of emergence, the process of "struggling to be born," though they mitigate the emphasis of those who talk of "revolution," a more dramatic and traumatic form of birth (the "r" being added to indicate the growl of the class struggle).

But though one must salute the relevance of Dr. Rank's key metaphor, one may not be so happy with the use he has made of it. Unless the reader is willing, as he reads, to supply supplementary material of his own, the contents may seem to him as remote as some primitive creation myth or as the weirdly fanciful structures of a Plotinus. Redemption, guilt, death, God, separation—the overtones of the vocabulary are almost those of the funeral oration. And one cannot help feeling that much of the anguish with which the author deals derives from that luxurious form of unemployment we call leisure.

It is my impression that the word "politics" does not occur once in these many hundred pages. In fact, there is not even an oblique handling of mass phenomena in any form, be it only a crowd at a football game. Dr. Rank completes the individualistic emphasis. His "analysis of the therapeutic process in terms of relationship" is focused within the limits of a private interchange between patient and doctor. The curative power of collective manifestations is given honorable mention, but no technique is offered whereby the private therapeutic situation shades into relationships outside the study. The infant seems to profit by a kind of "tapering off" whereby the change from a completely gratifying existence to an existence with resistances, is gradual. But Dr. Rank offers no "bridge" from the study to life except the upbuilding of the patient's "will." Is it possible that he should be analyzed for the presence of unconscious cruelty in the way he dwells upon the thought of shoving the patient from the therapeutic nest, as though he resented the function of therapy-motherhood the patient-child had forced upon him? Freud, sturdy patriarch, wanted to retain his authority over his patients, in the form of the ideology he gave them. This may explain the fact that his disciples so often think of themselves as "splitting off" from him, rather than as carrying on the torch. But in any case, I think that Dr. Rank underrates the Freudian emphasis in this respect. To give a man a philosophy is to make him obedient and independent both, since he can respond to its authority even while manipulating it in ways peculiar to himself.

Dr. Rank devotes many pages to an explanation of the differences between his approach and that of Freud. In the course of doing so, he unintentionally discloses at least that Freud is the superior as a dramatist, and dramatics is by no means an unimportant aspect of cure. But whatever the reader may think of Rank's additions and revisions, there is a point of view that can make them look very much alike. Thus, after condemning Freud for his great stress upon the "infantile," Dr. Rank finally settles down to handling everything in terms of "birth trauma." For a time he proposes to avoid this by centering his attention upon the artist, which is certainly a more adult emphasis. But even when approaching human relationships with the metaphor of the artist in the foreground, he typically stresses the individualistically "creative" aspect of the artist to the neglect of the collectivistically "communicative" aspect. And eventually the artist is found to have dropped away, and the "birth trauma" becomes the focus of attention.

Freud's and Rank's emphasis seem equally "infantile" in the sense that they consider human relationships in terms of non-political or pre-political coordinates (quite as the child himself does). Both lack the Aristotelian emphasis upon the *forensic* that must figure largely in our dealings with contemporary reality (and that Dr. Rank himself might have come upon, had he persisted in his approach through art). Both lack even the Church's emphasis upon *institutions* (in incipiently political form) that identify us as members of corporate units. Both deal with psychological forms at too great remove from the economic and vocational realities.

It seems that, where Dr. Rank's system of therapy succeeds, it succeeds because it is simply one more way of doing what successful therapies have always done—i.e., it gives the patient an attitude, filled out with documentary substance, that enables him to be humble and self-reliant simultaneously. The question is whether the substance, as presented exclusively in infantile, pre-political, non-forensic, non-economic material, is sufficient to enable us to encompass our full contemporary situation with accuracy. Somewhat inclining toward Freudian patriarchalism, I like to think that a philosophy ("ideology") equips a man by giving him both a father-authority and an instrument for him to use with independence. But psychoanalysis must face another birth trauma, so modifying its identity as integrally to encompass economic and forensic thought. The Marxist challenge suggests that it does not encompass enough—hence the man who takes this philosophy as his father-principle may be like the man of whom it was said that he had a dumb pap.

# The Constants of Social Relativity

*Ideology and Utopia* by Karl Mannheim. With a Preface by Louis Wirth. Translated by Louis Wirth and Edward Shils. Harcourt, Brace and Company
*The Nation*, January 1937, 131. Also in *The Philosophy of Literary Form*

Discouraged by the ways in which the perspectives of different people, classes, eras, cancel one another, you may decide that all philosophies are nonsense. Or you may establish order by fiat, as you bluntly adhere to one faction among the many, determined to abide by its assertions regardless of other people's assertions. Or you may become a kind of referee for other men's contests, content to observe that every view has some measure of truth and some measure of falsity. If they had asserted nothing, you could assert nothing. But insofar as they assert and counter-assert, you can draw an assertion from the comparison of their assertions.

Professor Karl Mannheim's "sociology of knowledge" is a variant of the third of these attitudes. He would begin with the *fact of difference* rather than with a *choice among the differences.* But in erecting a new perspective atop the rivalries of the old perspectives, he would subtly change the rules of the game. For the new perspective he offered would not be simply a *rival perspective;* it would be a *theory of perspectives.* Insofar as it was accurate, in other words, its contribution would reside in its ability to make the *perspective-process* itself more accessible to consciousness.

Faction A opposes Faction B. To do so as effectively as possible, it "unmasks" Faction B's "ideology." Faction B may talk nobly about "humanity" or "freedom," for instance. And Faction A discloses the "real meaning" of these high-sounding phrases in terms of interests, privileges, social habits, and the like. Faction B retaliates by unmasking Faction A's ideology.

Each faction exposes, as far as possible, the conscious and unconscious deception practiced by the ideologists of rival camps. But in the course of exposing the enemy, a faction comes upon principles that could be turned upon itself as well. Hence, it can spare its own members from the general

*343*

censure only by "pulling its punch." And precisely at this point there enter the opportunities for a "sociology of knowledge," if only the sociologist can so change the rules of the game that he finds no embarrassment in completing and maturing this "unmasking" process.

This he does in the easiest way imaginable. Whereas the ideologists of the opposing factions "point with alarm" to the fact that there is a difference between the face value of an opponent's idea and its real value in social commerce, the sociologist starts out by taking such discrepancies for granted. He begins with the assumption that an idea must be "discounted" by the disclosure of the interests behind it. Hence, he can treat the difference between the face value of an ideology and its behavior in a social context not as an "unmasking" but as an "explanation" or "definition" of the ideology. Thus, instead of being startled to find that an idea must be discounted, and taking this fact as the be-all and end-all of his disclosures, he assumes at the start the necessity of discounting, and so can advance to the point where he seeks to establish the *principles of discounting*.

Such, at least, is the reviewer's way of understanding Professor Mannheim's point in tracing a development from the "unmasking of ideologies" to the "sociology of knowledge." And his book presents a great wealth of material to guide the sociologist who would define ideologies in terms of their social behavior. Incidentally, in his gauging of the case, he suggests reasons why members of the intelligentsia are not a perfect fit for strict political alignment. Their working capital is their education—and insofar as they accumulate this capital to its fullest, they venture far beyond the confines of some immediate political perspective. He does not use this thought, however, to disprove the value of political affiliation. On the contrary, he suggests that there are ways in which this somewhat "classless" ingredient in the "capital" of intelligentsia may serve to broaden and mature the outlook of the stricter partisans, and enable them to take wider ranges of reality and resistance into account.

As for the key terms, ideology and utopia, their "discounting" in social textures makes it impossible for the reader to follow them as absolute logical opposites. In general, the term ideology is used to connote "false consciousness" of a conservative or reactionary sort—while utopia stresses the same phenomenon in the revolutionary category. If conditions have so changed, for instance, that the landed proprietor has become a capitalist yet "still attempts to explain his relations to his laborers and his own function in the undertaking by means of categories reminiscent of the patriarchal order," he is thinking by "ideological distortion." And the "spiritualization of politics" in the thinking of the Chiliasts is treated as a typical utopia, surviving even in the thought of anarchists like Bakunin. However, although the conservative is not naturally given to utopian imaginings, being content to accept the status quo, the competitive pressure of revolutionary utopias spurs him to the construction of counterutopias. Hegel's romantic historicism, erected in opposition to the liberal idea, is given as a prime example. Perhaps the following quotation illustrates the difference most succinctly:

> As long as the clerically and feudally organized medieval order was able to locate its paradise outside of society, in some other-worldly sphere which transcended history and dulled its revolutionary edge, the idea of paradise was still an integral part of medieval society. Not until certain social groups embodied these wish-images into their actual conduct, and tried to realize them, did these ideologies become utopian.

The book is concerned with the ramifications and subtilizations of this distinction, and with a theory of knowledge to be drawn from the plot of history as charted in accordance with these terms. The discussion being conducted largely in abstractions, the book will probably not endear itself to the general reader—but anyone interested in the relation between politics and knowledge should find it absorbing. Perhaps we could venture to summarize the case this way: whereas the needs of the forum tend to make sociology a subdivision of politics, Professor Mannheim is contributing as much as he can toward making politics a subdivision of sociology.

# Untitled Review of *The Ethics of Competition* by Frank H. Knight

*The Ethics of Competition and Other Essays* by Frank Hyneman Knight. Harper & Bros.
*The American Journal of Sociology*, July 1938, 242–244

In this collection of essays there is a constant procession of sharp observations, definitions, and distinctions that make its admonitory value high for the student or practitioner of criticism. Unfortunately, we can here but make a general salute to these incidental "hits," attempting rather to abstract, for review purposes, some basic principles of organization that characterize the tenor of the work.

Thus, locating the book by the rules of reviewing, we should describe it as the conversion of a "pure" economist into a sociologist (or, otherwise put, the "expanding" of one field into another). The author's conception of economics is of the "perfect world" sort. That is: He is concerned with the statement of ideal market relationships. And while he is as much aware as anyone that the world of actuality (which in the technical sense we might call an "imperfect world") does not follow this ideal pattern, he says that it "tends" to. His use of "tendency" thus serves as the bridge between the ideal and the actual (or between the "pure" market and the market as a going concern). It is a strategic concept, even containing its opposite (as the statement that a planet "tends" to fly off into space is a way of making allowance for the fact that it doesn't).

The gradual turn toward a sociological emphasis (from "ideal" to "material" subject matter, from "positivistic" to "participative" method) is motivated by the author's statement that "the 'economic' man is not a social man, and the ideal market dealings of theory are not social relations." Explicitly aware of the way in which thinkers rely upon the concept of *caeteris paribus* (they locate area A by lumping area non-A under the head of *caeteris paribus,* or conversely locate area non-A by treating area A under this head), he gradually shifts his emphasis from "pure" economics to sociology (based on "humane naïve realism") by analytically dissolving precisely what he had begun by lumping as "datum" of the other-things-being-equal sort. Or, otherwise stated: He centers his attention upon the contrary aspect of his word "tendency," coming more and more to deal with the factors in the charting of human relationships that lie outside the "pure" market.

> By the nature of its fundamental conceptions, theoretical economics is an *individualistic* science . . . The science takes its economic individual as a datum, in his three aspects of wants, resources, and technical knowledge . . . and it abstracts from all his relations with other human beings, except those of the perfect market, which are really relations to commodities as such. A social science is concerned with "economic" data in the aspects excluded from economics as an analytical science, the historical and genetic explanation of the individual himself, the phases of market dealings which do not fit the pure theory of exchange, and especially the moral and legal framework in which economic life is lived, the field in which practical social problems take their rise.

But in this "imperfect world" the author is not happy. And in particular his final provocative essay, "Economic Theory and Nationalism," bears testimony to his misgivings. Here, after considering the ways in which current political exigencies threaten the pursuit of truth, he advocates the setting-up of a secular priesthood among the "intellectual, critical, and constructive 'learned' class," that will, we might say, "tend "to function as "auxiliaries to political leadership" while being "kept completely out of politics, and as free as possible from the spirit of competitive individual advancement in any form." He bases this exhortation on the "paradox," motivated in the essay, "that a non-practical, 'pure science' of society . . . is a practical necessity."

Increasingly, we find the author's concerns shifting into the field covered by writers like Mannheim and Lasswell. We also note, as with so many contemporary theorists of science, the formulation of science in such a way, with such ideals of formalistic rigor, that tributes to "art" are required to complete the picture of actuality. The "perfect world" of any abstract pattern, thoroughly pursued, must require a corrective deference to the "perturbations" of actuality, and this corrective is usually supplied under some such heading as "art." Is it not possible, however, that one should hesitate to introduce tributes to "art" without completing the circle by focusing explicit attention upon the processes of art? The encroachment seems under way (via the sociological implications of "applied" art, the rhetoric of propaganda, advertising, and news control, though the depths of conviction are seldom touched in such rhetoric). "The ultimate motives or interests," we are told by the present author, "must be referred to by such terms as exploration, problem-solving, fellowship, power, beauty, rightness, etc., which are not descriptive in an objective sense." One may or may not believe that such terms are best given content by reference to specific works of art, as the concentration points of human strategies. But even if one does not so believe, we may contend that generous references to "art" are not complete until the field of art has been integrally introduced into the discussion, and its value in supplying "leads" either systematically utilized or denied.

# Homo Faber, Homo Magus

*The Myth of the State* by Ernst Cassirer. Yale UP
*The Nation*, December 1946, 666–668

In his *Myth of the State* the late Ernst Cassirer has provided an illuminating survey of some major texts in the history of theory, such as Plato's *Republic,* Machiavelli's *Prince,* the doctrine of the "social contract," Carlyle on hero-worship, Hegel's metaphysics of the state, and so on. The exposition is keen and clear, well reflecting the author's thorough grounding in philosophy. A reader shown over the field by such a guide can consider himself well guided indeed.

The political "myth"—there is no talk of "ideology"—is here placed in terms of a dualistic distinction between the "magical" and the "semantic." The "magical" use of language, we are told, "tries to produce effects and to change the course of nature," while the "semantic" serves to "describe things or relations of things."

> The historians of human civilization have told us that mankind in its development had to pass through two different phases. Man began as *homo magus;* but from the age of magic he passed to the age of technics. The *homo magus* of former times and of primitive civilization became a *homo faber,* a craftsman and artisan. If we admit such an historical distinction our modern political myths appear indeed as a very strange and paradoxical thing. For what we find in them is the blending of two activities that seem to exclude each other. The modern politician has had to combine in himself two entirely different and even incompatible functions. He has to act, at the same time, as both *homo magus* and *homo faber.*

Much valuable insight is got through this approach. Yet it may cause contemporary doctrines of political motivation to seem somewhat more "strange and paradoxical" than need be. For although there are aspects of language

*349*

that cannot be comfortably reduced to either the "magical" or the "semantic," when we have but these two bins whatever cannot be classed as "semantic" must be classed as "magical." As a result, with so much disturbing evidence of reversion to savagery in the modern world, we are invited to conclude that there is even more.

What seems to be missing in this study of political "myth" is a systematic concern with the functions of speech that fall under the traditional heading of "rhetoric." When one human agent sets other human agents in motion, for instance, by calling for help, such a persuasive use of words is not sheer magic spell, as with the attempt to coerce physical nature by incantatory means. Nor is it quite the semantic use of language to "describe things or relations to things." It is the motive that goes into rhetoric.

True, it may be greatly misused, as with race doctrines designed to promote social cooperation for sinister ends. But in itself it is a normal and proper function of words. Being hortatory rather than descriptive, it would fall outside the "semantic" bin; yet its essentially realistic nature, when properly used, would make it a bad fit for the "magical" bin. If we give it a bin of its own—the category of the "rhetorical," with a systematically generated set of terms to round out the analysis—we can study its ways shrewdly enough, but without so many extremely discouraging incentives to believe that presumably civilized populations are running around with rings in their noses.

Technically, the dualistic approach here seems to get an important aspect of language turned backward. For if there is any sort of real experience motivating primitive magic, it must be rooted in the fact that one person's expressions, commands, and requests, when interpreted by other persons, really can produce desired effects. Error arose when men transferred the use of the verbal instrument to areas where it does not belong, as when trying by incantation to influence natural things that do not understand language. But if, as with the Cassirer dualism, you begin with natural magic, the hortatory use of language to influence *human* conduct seems derivative from this derived magical use, rather than existing in its own right. Hence verbal inducement, even in the sphere of human communication, is treated roundabout, as a "social magic" that descends from natural magic. The point is worth stressing because it is characteristic of much modern theory, with its tendency to define human motives by matching science against some antithetical term.

But whether or not the modern political "myth" might be approached more directly, and with less distressing implications, than in *The Myth of the State,* there is much of great moment to be observed about it when viewed in the Cassirer perspective, which considers it primarily as a mixture of bad poetry and bad science. For large areas of it are just exactly that. And much of the book is an apt summary of works in their own terms.

# More Dithyrambic than Athletic

*Love's Body* by Norman O. Brown. Random House
*The Nation*, March 1967, 405–407

According to Norman O. Brown, the suggestive nature of aphoristic, fragmentary expression makes for continual resurrection, in allowing us to be reborn with each fragment, whereas systematic thought condemns us to death. However, I assume that a reviewer should be as systematic as possible, even if it kills him; for any attempt to sum up a book's contents will necessarily require him to ask how one fragment fits with another. And there's always the paradoxical possibility that even the errors of an unsystematic book can be shown to have a systematic origin, from which they are forever born anew, thereby at least proving to that extent the author's claim for an intimate tie-up between resurrection and the fragmentary.

For instance, when we are told that "there is no literal truth," we are in the presence of a statement that on its face is in dire trouble. There would be no point in making the statement unless it is to be taken literally, as univocally "true." Yet it could be true only by being false.

Similarly, we are told that "the conflict between science and religion in the modern world stems . . . from modern literalism: Protestant literalism and Catholic scholasticism; both exterminators of symbolism." And whether or not we agree, what is the author's purpose in making the statement unless he *literally means* what he says? Here certainly is a kind of tangle from which many others could spring.

The book's title is accurate, so we might well proceed from there. As regards the term "body," I'd propose one premonitory observation. The more one speculates upon the paradoxes of the term "substance," the more difficult becomes the task of isolating the "individual." We all merge into our environment, the circumference or scope of which can be extended to the farthest limits of "nature" (and beyond, to the "supernatural," if you are theologically minded). Even when considered close up, the identity of the "self" or "person" becomes part of a collective texture involving language, property, family, reputation, social roles, and so on—elements not reducible to the individual. The same is true of our physical nature, but with one notable exception. Physiologically, the centrality of the nervous system is such that, although I as a *person* may sympathetically identify myself with other people's pleasures and pains, in my nature as a sheer *body* the pleasures of *my* food and the pains of *my* toothache are experienced immediately by me alone. Thus, although even as a body I merge into my environment, there is this physiological condition (in the realm of sheer "matter" or motion) that serves as a rudimentary "principle of individuation," the grounds for a purely empirical distinction whereby, however social our nature in other respects, we are born and die one by one, with certain pleasures and pains experienced *immediately,* bodily, or if you will, "carnally," and not identically experienceable by others.

So far, I have made two quite different moves. First, working from within the book itself, I singled out a basic statement of terministic policy that manifestly undoes itself. Next, when turning to the key word, "body," I introduced a preparatory consideration of my own. Brown says nothing about the "centrality of the nervous system." In fact, the main emphasis throughout his book is upon the respects in which the individual is rather like a drop in the ocean, though somehow divided from its fellows by a kind of primal "fall" from the ultimate oceanic oneness.

But when he says: "Love and death are altogether carnal, hence their great magic and their great terror," I would suggest that before we ever get to the "magic" and the "terror," we should try to be as explicit as we can about that word "carnal." I have explicitly proposed the need for this notion of an individual human body's susceptibility to certain sensations not thus immediately experienced by other human bodies (in the sense that, though other bodies may have physical pleasures and pains *like* mine, they don't have *mine*). And I have suggested that, although Brown does not mention such a concept, he greatly needs it: and a concept of that sort is at least *implicit* in his statement about the immediately carnal nature of love and death. (True, I would want to haggle considerably about his reduction of love to nothing but carnal terms, since the norms of love and friendship are strongly modified by social factors. But in any case, there must be an ultimate bodily reference of some sort, even if it takes the form of strictly ascetic dissociation.)

Even if neither the author nor the reader would consent to my proposal as regards a sheerly "material" or *bodily* principle of individuation, surely all can agree on this minimum basis: once a writer chooses to build a nomenclature that features the word "body," there are certain resources readily available to that term. Thus, whatever might be your definition of a "carnal" *human* body, it must differ considerably from the meanings implicit or explicit in references to the state as a *political* body, or to the Church as an *ecclesiastical* body. Surely, no political or ecclesiastical body can experience the carnality of sex or food as the particular members of such collective bodies can.

Further possibilities are available. There can be words for another kind of body, individually resurrected after death, though somehow not divisively. Such *terms* are possible, whether or not there can actually be such a state. This requires further bookkeeping operations, as per the statement that "incarnation is not to be understood carnally."

A related but different set of transformations is possible. Bodies don't only sex, they also eat. In fact, without a lot of preparatory eating, there'd be no sexing. Hence, along with his pansexualism, Brown includes many terms connected with food. And well he might, if one can believe reports to the effect that when war prisoners are deprived of both food and sex, their dreams are not of beds but of banquets. In any case, food as well as sex provides a basic bodily terminology of appetition, plus corresponding connotations of substance, and hence of *con*substantiality, in keeping with the "carnal" notion that we can all become alike by partaking of the same substance (individuals thus being made one by participation in a common body, as per the popular aphorism, "tell me what you eat and I'll tell you what you are"). This line of development allows for notions of transubstantiated body, when bread and wine are *ritually* transformed into the blood and body of a Divine Word shared by all believers. And although, as I tried to show in my *Rhetoric of Religion,* a sacrificial principle is intrinsic to the nature of the social order as such, you might (like Brown) center attention upon the purely "carnal" aspects of eating whereby one thing lives by the "sacrifice" of another.

I have suggested that you might begin with some overall term such as "appetition," under which you might include terms for food and terms for sex as subdivisions. "Desire" would be a handy synonym if we recall Spinoza's formula, "It is of the essence of man to desire," along with the etymological admonition (too often overlooked by current myth men) that desire in general is the basic meaning of the Greek word eros. Proceeding thus, you will have no difficulty in seeing how Brown's book might have chapters on both food and sex. But if you begin with the particulars of such imagery and the corresponding problems of terministic accountancy (as the book encourages you to do), you are almost sure to get lost; and you will doubtless be left vaguely wondering how you got from body to sex to person to food to sacrifice to resurrection and on finally to the culminative celebration of "Nothing."

As for the other word, the possessive, in the title: I submit that Plato's *Phaedrus* can serve us best, to indicate what kind of potentialities (corresponding to those implicit in Brown's word, "body") are implicit in the word "lose." I have in mind the "literal" fact that the *Phaedrus* begins on a quite low concept of sexual dalliance, then graduates through a solemnly ecstatic view of "noble" love, to such kinds of courtship as come to fulfillment in the Socratic erotic (the whole constituting a dialectic ladder that leads from sexual seed to doctrinal insemination). In brief, the idea of communion embraces a range of meanings as wide as the differences between sheerly lustful coupling, unity in love, and such modes of persuasion, or communication or correspondence in principle, as flower in ardent rhetorical appeal to love of wisdom. (Brown's book features the sex side of such a continuum. Working at the other end of the spectrum, Marshall McLuhan's *Understanding Media* features some considerations to do with the sheer technology of communication.)

Brown tells us that "symbolism is mind making connections (correspondences) rather than distinctions (separations)." Here we confront the same kind of self-canceling statement with which we began. For if Brown's statement makes any sense at all, it is making a distinction. He might answer that he never intended this particular kind of sentence to be thought of as "symbolism." I would call it "symbolism" in the sense that it uses a symbol system, and thus is a kind of "symbolic action." I thought of solving the problem by reference to these remarks by Socrates, also in the *Phaedrus:*

> I am a great lover of these processes of division and generalization: they help me to speak and think. If I find any man who is able to see unity and plurality in nature, I follow him, walking in his steps as if he were a god. And those who have this art, I usually call dialecticians.

But this possible distinction between "symbolism" and "dialectics" won't help us. For Brown also says: "Every sentence is dialectics, an act of love"; and "all intercourse is sexual intercourse"; and sex itself is "symbolic." Brown further tries to equate "union or unification" with eros, and "separation, or division" with "the death instinct," though bodies grow and reproduce by the division of cells, and metabolism involves both anabolic and catabolic processes.

Brown seems to leave no room for the sheerly technical aspects of the communication spectrum. To be sure, one may say that love (or sex) is "dialectical," in the sense that it involves both disparateness and unification. But dialectics, as the use of words for unity and words for plurality, cannot be intelligibly reduced to an utterly "carnal" concept of love. Such an equation would amount to saying that the distinction between a word like "books" and a word like "library" can be adequately discussed as an "act of love." Or, if you must call it "love," then please at least admit that it's not in exactly the same "carnal" category as sedentary eating or recumbent sexing, though we might gain a certain perspective by incongruity if we transferred a term from one such realm to the other (as were we to call some beauty queen an "inviting morsel").

If you would equate "symbolism" solely with the unity side of the unity-diversity pair, no one need haggle with you, in case your scheme somewhere explicitly allows for both. But, so far as I can make out, Brown can admit such considerations only roundabout and unintentionally, as when making a distinction in the very act of outlawing distinctions, or when saying that *all* language is a kind of "fall" (as it unquestionably is, in the sense that it necessarily makes Brown's statement of his own unitary ideal undo itself, since even his word "unification" implies the unifying of a diversity).

The trick is: Where do you start, and where do you go from there? If you start with particulars, well and good. But if you try to make them do the work of generalities, the prognostications are bad. I mean: there's nothing wrong with *sex* as a "way in." But when, like Brown, you first reduce "love" to penis and vagina, and then imperialistically expand until you find "a penis in every convex object and a vagina in every concave one," you're necessarily out of bounds. For geometric forms must also be treated in their own right, fall or no fall. Even if you began with a purely psychoanalytic interpretation of the egg-and-dart motif, you'd have to grant that its use in Greek friezes "transcends" this "origin."

Too often Brown merely re-enacts the terministic devices we have been discussing, rather than helping to make us more conscious of their operation: in this respect his book becomes obfuscating, rather than the "apocalyptic" enterprise he apparently wants it to be. And now, after a reference to some surprising omissions, we shall, have finished:

One might have expected that a stress upon the body would also entail a cult of bodily motion for its own sake. But the satisfactions of the kinetic in general are treated in keeping with the genius of the possessive in the book's title, thus: "All movement is phallic," a doctrine temperamentally more dithyrambic than athletic. A greater surprise lurks in the fact that despite urgent praise of poetry, there is no concern with such kinds of sensory response to nature as John Crowe Ransom deals with in his thoughts on the relation between poetry and the "world's body." The stress upon unity makes the book in effect even more severe than orthodox churchmen in frowning on the principle of divorce. And perhaps the dithyrambic element is also responsible for slighting the major role of body-thinking in connection with disease and the imagery of the ethically problematical: bodies sick or soiled.

# The Second Study of Middletown—
# Albert Rhys Williams on the
# U.S.S.R. and Ortega in Spain

*Middletown in Transition: A Study in Cultural Conflicts* by Robert S. Lynd
and Helen Merrell Lynd. Harcourt, Brace, and Co.
*The New Masses*, June 1937, 22, 24. Also in *The Philosophy of Literary Form*

If one had to find a quick slogan for summarizing the way in which science is effective, I should propose the formula: stooping to conquer. Such is the experimental method at its best. Insofar as is humanly possible, it begins by *listening* rather than by *asserting*. It is postponed assertion, somewhat as investment is said to be postponed consumption.

The Lynds are expert listeners. Their method makes of us all their laboratory. They use the representative town of Muncie, Indiana., as their specific field of study, and as control, their study of the same town ten years ago. One man figures out, let us say, that "everything will turn out well in the end." And so does the next man, and the next. But an important qualitative change takes place when you have added up all these quantities, thereby getting a kind of statistical view of this homely little invention.

The Lynds have done, without the note of guying, what Mencken and Nathan used to do in their collection of Americana. And the omission of this note makes considerable difference. What Mencken and Nathan did polemically, and Sinclair Lewis did inspirationally, they complete by the strategy of stooping to conquer.

As a result, they have given us two books (and earlier and present studies of "Middletown") contributing greatly to the charting of American mores. We already had the topographical maps surveying the hills and valleys of America. Here we get a survey of the country's mental contours.

The findings could hardly be saluted as new. Anyone who has surveyed America either from the standpoint of the earlier aesthetic criticism (culminating in expatriation, actual or symbolic) of from the standpoint of current political emphasis will probably feel, in reading *Middletown in Transition*, that he is more often being reminded than informed. The general outlines of the map are already known. The service of these authors is (a) in giving it greater precision and (b) in the working attitude which their study embodies. The second is particularly of value as a hint to our formal and informal propagandists. For the criticism, radical as it seems in its implications, is voiced by investigators who are eager to make sure that the bonds of participation between investigators and investigated are not broken. The emphasis, in other words is not upon exposure, but upon analysis, with the result that, although the analysis is in effect a drastic exposure, the stylistic change in emphasis prevents the breaking of contact. I can imagine Middletown being troubled by the work; but I cannot imagine it being furious.

The book being over five hundred pages in length, and being largely an assemblage of graphs and statistics written out, I shall not make a pretense of giving it in summary. What one sees, on the whole, is the spectacle of a people attempting to handle new situations by symbols developed under past and different situation, people who still tend to look upon the dislocations of capitalism as an "act of God," who have worked out a bewildering hash of religious and secular coordinates, who strive hard to be friendly under an economy that too often makes for anger (and thereby become all the angrier when their friendliness is frustrated), whose weakness for scapegoats is resisted mainly by lack of some rationalization speciously complete (a lack of making it awkward for them to deflect all of their resentment upon one fixed symbolic victim.) One sees in the main the struggle to form the mind by the acceptance of ailing institutions. This is a disastrous struggle, since the tendency of the individual to locate himself with relation to an institutional frame is in itself *natural* and *wholesome* enough—you can safely think of changing institutions only when you have some *alternative* institutional basis upon which to erect your purposes, as for instance the basis you may derive from the body of anti-capitalist criticism, a criticism rooted in organization and method, but the ailing institutions, as the Lynds make obvious, themselves serve to perpetuate lines of thinking that obscure the issues.

There is one fundamental problem in a book of this sort. The investigators are, by the very nature of their investigation, looking for the typical. And when you have finished, you begin to ask yourself whether there might be some important difference between the typical and history. Middletown, for instance, went 59 percent for Roosevelt in the last election. Yet this shift from Republicanism is not adequately foreshadowed in the Lynd's survey. Insofar as *Middletown* is typical of America, and this survey is typical of Middletown, the material would have led you to expect a national sweep for Landon.

We are left with two possibilities. Perhaps the choice of Roosevelt over Landon was more spectacular than significant. The individual voter, for instance, may have been almost undecided whether or not to vote one way or the other, and *just barely did* finally decide for Roosevelt (this tenuousness adding up, in the deceptiveness of statistical aggregates, to a landslide, quite as the small difference in percentage of votes adds up to a blunt all-but-Maine-and-Vermont in the electoral college). Or else: there may be something about the typical that is itself misleading, as a way of historical gauging and forecasting.

I propose that the second of these possibilities should be considered, in approaching surveys of this sort. The typical is, in a sense, the relatively *inert*. It is *what people answer when present with a questionnaire*. It is a *quantitative* rather than a *qualitative* test, since it assigns to everyone the same rating, regardless of his activity. And though history is moved by quantities, is not this movement accomplished by those people, rare rather than typical, most awake to new qualities, which the changing quantities have brought forth? In other words, might not the *single song of one poet,* under certain conditions, put us on the track of something that the *typical platitudes of a group* could give us no inkling of?

In any case, one thing is certain: those hired to sing for the Landon perspective had a painful job of it—and those hired to sing for the Roosevelt perspective had a much easier time of it. The unhired songs further to the left went practically unheard—but one may believe that they will gradually make themselves heard, and that they will act precisely *because they are not typical,* containing rather the *emergent factors,* such all-important trends of history as the inertly typical conceals from us.

Another problem is suggested by the subtitle, "a study in cultural conflicts." Following leads provided by Bergson, we may note that every state of moral or social "balance" can, by the very nature of language, be analyzed as a conflict between opposing tendencies. Thus even Newton moralistically plotted the curve of planetary motion in terms of opposing centrifugal and centripetal tendencies. And Aristotle, by dint of patient thinking, made the phenomenal discovery that when something is just right in its proportions, it is neither too big nor too small. All moral journeys go between Scylla and Charybdis.

Are not conflicts, in this technical sense, inevitable and everywhere? Can you possibly analyze any social manifestation except in terms of conflict? Many of the conflicts noted by the Lynds seem to me of this linguistically engineered sort. Every state or local portion of a state, for instance, must face in some form a conflict between the attempt to keep down the tax rate and the attempt to promote public enterprises by taxation. Or every state must face a conflict between the ideals of work and the ideals of leisure, between individual preferences and group necessities, etc. Many of such conflicts noted by the Lynds do not seem to me quite on the same plane with the inner contradictions engendered by capitalism's dilemma in trying to develop mass production without reordering its property relationships to facilitate mass consumption.

An explicit acceptance of the Marxist analysis would, it seems to me, form a sounder basis upon which one might proceed to make distinctions between these two kinds of conflicts, the conflicts caused by a system working against itself and the conflicts arising linguistically from the fact that *any* adjustment must be expressed, in analystic terms, as the juggling of opposites. Once we have carried out such a weeding, it is true, we may very well find that the essential contradictions of capitalism serve greatly to aggravate conflicts all along the line, causing dislocations that turn all consciousness into dilemmas (a theme that Norbert Guterman, in collaboration with Lefebvre, has exploited strikingly in *La Conscience Mystifiee*.) But we may be warned that not even socialism can alter the nature of analytic speech in accordance with mystical ideals of non-conflicting unity. The balance of the tight rope walker, as translated into analytic terms, is attained by adjusting the opposing weight of the right and left sides of the body. And so, in any mature society, there will be balancings of individual and group, manual workers and brain workers, industry and agriculture, or among regional divisions. A "good" state is not one that can eliminate them (the notion of eliminating them is meaningless, unless you are proposing to eliminate language itself as an instrument for the analysis of interrelationships.) A "good" state is one that can eliminate some of the obviously man-made contradictions as contained in the capitalist distribution of profits. The others, arising from our position as mere parts of a universal totality, will remain, to form the stimulus for the "symbolic bridges" erected by thinkers and poets. The Lynds show us a people who instinctively grasp this necessity, who know that man's proper enterprise must be expended in developing modes of thought that enable him to *accept* the world, but who are tragically engaged in trying to extend such modes of acceptance to institutions that can and should be *rejected*. The descriptive and admonitory value of such a study cannot be praised too highly.

# In Quest of the Way

*A New Model of the Universe* by P. D. Ouspensky. Translated by R. R. Merton under the supervision of the author. Alfred J. Knopf
*The New Republic*, September 1931, 104–106

The many absurdities in which pure science has found itself, coupled with the many grave problems of social readjustment which applied science has brought upon us, have provided both intellectual and emotional grounds for a turn to other attitudes. Thus, there are signs that the positivistic West would gladly renounce its positivism in favor of a mystical guidance, though men of intelligence and emotional decency have, for the most part, been denied much opportunity in this direction unless they were content to piece together little religions of their own. The dogmatists of the contemporary Church could obviously offer them nothing, as these men were generally of a very unenterprising nature—and whatever talents they had were enlisted more in the cause of institutionalism than of insight. Accordingly, when Mr. Ouspensky came forward some years ago with his "Tertium Organum: A Key to the Enigmas of the World," the situation was considerably improved. In him mysticism found an apologist of distinction.

It is no wonder that a very reputable group of readers rallied behind him. For here is a man of broad learning and even broader sympathies, an ingenious and independent thinker, and above all a mystically inclined person who realized that the organized forces of virtue are much farther from a sense of religious values than a thief or a child-slayer could ever be. To Californian Christianity, the doctrine that customers go streaming into the Kingdom of Heaven by the millions, if they have but earned good salaries and advocated more laws, he is wholly impervious. Whereas our cults have generally been recruited among the slow witted, this man's critical weapons are sharp enough to make any contented statistics-gatherer-in-the-name-of-science uneasy. He knows that insufficient facts can often be more misleading than no facts at all; and since we must admit that on "ultimate" questions our facts are always insufficient, he has here a good entering wedge for what he calls the "psychological method," the "revaluation of all values from the point of view of their own psychological meaning and independently of the outer or accompanying facts on the basis of which they are generally judged." That is, if one under gas dreamed a metaphysical "revelation," we could not dispose of the "revelation" by saying that the man was under gas; it would remain a revelation regardless of the "facts." The universe can look entirely different, if we but make this one slight change in our rules of thumb for thinking.

There are, says Mr. Ouspensky, four ways that lead to the Unknown, "four forms of conception of the world—religion, philosophy, science and art." These ways have diverged until they contradict themselves and one another. But "the more they have broken up and separated from one another, the farther they depart from truth. Truth is at the center, where the four ways converge. Consequently the nearer they are to one another, the nearer they are to truth, the farther from one another, the farther from truth." In Egypt, Greece and India, "there were periods when the four ways constituted one whole." The knowledge of these times was "esoteric" knowledge—and the author lays great weight upon this knowledge in the attempt to construct his new model of the universe which, in contrast with the specializing works of the contemporary West, would tend to make religion, philosophy, science and art again converge. The convergence, as one might expect, cannot be readily followed within the exclusive field of any one of the four. He considers knowledge "based upon senses which surpass our five senses and upon a capacity for thinking which surpasses ordinary thinking." He holds that "ordinary logical language" is but an approximation to the "truth." For there is also the insight of mysticism, which is "entirely emotional, entirely made up of subtle, incommunicable sensations, which are even more incapable of verbal expression and logical definition than are such things as sound and color and line."

The author has examined holy texts, in particular the religious lore of the East. His chapter on "Experimental Mysticism" would lead us to suppose that he had made many tests with hasheesh, deriving from it that sense of impersonality, of the subjective merging into the objective, of "unity," which this drug seems to have induced even in people much less mystically inclined than he. He studied the symbolism of the Tarot. He stood beneath the Sphinx, or listened to the remarkable set of echoes which went hurtling about the mausoleum of the Taj Mahal when one of the gatekeepers had called out the name of Allah—and at such times he felt himself in the presence of a profound secret which was all but revealed to him. He looked into the matter of the five Yogas, which teach "the way to find the hidden truth concealed in things, in the actions of men, in the writings of great sages of all times and peoples." He holds that our development must be toward a "higher consciousness." There is an inner circle of humanity, those in possession of esoteric knowledge, who have had a great influence upon the course of mankind, though such effects are generally disguised, particularly as the masses pervert the doctrines by bringing them to lower levels in the very process of accepting them. Nature is purposive: there is the great laboratory of nature which produced all the inferior forms of life as "preliminary experiments" in the attempt to create a "self-evolving being," which is man. Man has the power, by the selection and disciplining of certain faculties, to become "superman," and thereupon to pass into that higher plane of being which transcends the cycles of such life as we, of the outer circle, live.

This constitutes in brief summary the part of the present volume preceding the chapter on "A New Model of the Universe" proper. This chapter, whatever else one may think of it, is certainly among the world's most ingenious pieces of thinking. It considers the underlying factors of "old physics," shows how certain discoveries of "old physics" led to a breaking of the frame—then concludes that certain considerations of "new physics" must break the frame in turn and lead to the supposition of some such universe as he describes. Old physics broke down, the author says, primarily because it did not consider time as a "fourth dimension." But the new physics is inadequate because there are in reality three dimensions of time, whereas the new physics considers but the "line of time." Thus:

> Motion by itself is a very complex phenomenon. At the very first approach to motion we meet with an interesting fact. Motion has in itself three clearly expressed dimensions: duration, velocity and "direction." But this direction does not lie in Euclidean space, as it was taken by old physics; it is a direction from before to after, which for us never changes and never disappears.
>
> Time is the measure of motion. If we represent time by a line, then the only line which will satisfy all the demands of time will be a spiral. A spiral is a "three-dimensional line," so to speak, a line which requires three coordinates for its construction and designation.

Six-dimensional space is reality, "the world as it is." We see this reality only "through the slit of the senses," thus translating it into a world of three space dimensions and one time dimension. The author now proceeds to examine these added dimensions more closely. Direction, velocity and duration are not, of course, their "real" description, but merely their translation into the terms of our limited vision. They have properties which take them beyond the realm of physics. Thus:

Let us, he says, consider a three-dimensional body in space as a point in time. Now let us draw a line, with "Before" at the left end and "After" at the right end. Anywhere along this line let us choose a point to call "Now." And we can choose other points along the same line to call "Now." Let us next imagine perpendiculars drawn from these Now's. Each one of these perpendiculars will be the "Perpetual Now" for that particular moment. This is the fifth dimension. Each Now will, by the nature of this dimension, exist forever, though we, on the line of the fourth dimension, or "historical time," will move on from one Now to the next as we progress from moment to moment. Each moment, that is, has its Perpetual Now going off "perpendicular" to it.

> But each moment of "now" on the line of time . . . contains not one, but a certain number, of possibilities . . . I may actualize one of the existing possibilities, that is, I may do something. I may do nothing. But whatever I do, that is, whichever of the possibilities contained in the given moment is actualized, the actualization of this possibility will determine the following moment of time, the following now . . . Thus, the line of the direction of time can be defined as the line of the actualization of one possibility out of the number of possibilities which were contained in the preceding point. The line of this actualization will be the line of the fourth dimension, the line of time. We visualize it as a straight line, but it would be more correct to think of it as a zigzag line. The perpetual existence of this actualization, the line perpendicular to the line of time, will be the line of the fifth dimension, or the line of eternity.

And the sixth dimension will be the "line of the actualization of other possibilities which were contained in the preceding moment but were not actualized 'in time.' . . . The line of time, repeated infinitely in eternity, leaves at every point unactualized possibilities. But these possibilities, which have not been actualized in one time, are actualized in the sixth dimension, which is an aggregate of 'all times.'"

I had some difficulty in thinking of these "possibilities" until I imagined them as bottles on a shelf. At a given moment on the line of "historical time" there are a number of bottles, variously labeled, sitting on the shelf, and we choose one of them. This choice presumably affects the number and assortment of bottles that will be on the shelf at the next moment of time. But the bottle we chose at the preceding moment will have an infinite extension in the fifth dimension; it will be the eternal bottle for that moment. The bottles we did not choose, however, will not be destroyed; they are still on the shelf, the shelf of the sixth dimension.

This hypostatizing of "possibilities" seems less arbitrary when we see what the author does with it. We understand the nature of these two dimensions better when we understand the conclusions and exhortations which he draws from them. They are, in brief, coupled with a doctrine of recurrence. A man lives over and over again, "in the same town, in the same street." He will have the same relatives, "will make the same mistakes, laugh and cry in the same way," etc. This explains the feeling we sometimes have that this has *happened before.* It also explains the unerringness with which some men play their roles: their certainty as to the outcome of some act indicates a previous acquaintanceship with the situation. Thus, if we are to improve ourselves, and are implicated in the events of our previous cycles, we must remove the evil by *remedying the past.* We now see the function of the bottles of "unactualized possibilities" which were left standing on the shelf of the sixth dimension. We can make a different selection, putting back the bottle which we had taken down before and choosing another in its stead.

"There would be no possibility of thinking of the *evolution of humanity,* if the possibility did not exist for individually evolving men to go into the past and struggle against the causes of the present evil which lie there. This explains *where those people disappear who have remembered their past lives.*" That is, they have reincarnated into the past, have gone to influence the choice of possibilities. Reincarnation, however, is possible "only into places which become free, into 'vacancies.'" These vacancies are made either "when a soul, after many lives of conscious struggle, obtains freedom, leaves the circle of lives in the particular 'place in time' and goes in the direction of its source, that is, into the past." And there are also undesirable vacancies left when a soul has so degenerated that, as it were, it drops out the bottom, "ceases to be born." The closing chapter, on "Sex and Evolution," suggests that as sex is ordinarily employed in birth, it may, as is evidenced by the pronounced attitude toward sex usually taken in religious disciplines, be "transmuted" into a mechanism for spiritual rebirth. Sex alone contains, for ordinary man, something of the ecstasy which marks the normal mystic state; and the melancholy which often accompanies strong sexual feeling is perhaps an admonition, a dim foreboding, of the "departure" into higher realms of being that might occur if this sex were more accurately transmuted.

Such are the outlines of this work. They should serve, I think, to indicate that the work is practically beyond "argument." There is nothing to "disprove." In the sixth dimension, the author says, "every point of time touches every point of space and everything is anywhere and always." To offer such a conception in opposition to the paradoxes of relativism may seem to some like "reconciling" the logical absurdities of a four-dimensional system by postulating a fifth dimension in which all logical absurdities are reconciled. If someone cares to say that there is such a dimension, there is certainly no mechanism for saying him nay. One can, if he is out of sympathy with the author, simply test the message by aspects with which he is in sympathy. It takes no "believer," for instance, to find much that is admirable and overwhelming and even "revealing" in the vast mythology of Blake. Similarly, in the present work one will find many observations which indicate great sensitiveness to human values, though in this case the perceptions are critical rather than poetic. On the whole, those of us who, however grudgingly, are still weighted down with positivism will prefer our "new models of the universe" as a Blake or a Milton conceives them. The great cry for synthesis is more popular than compelling. No one would ask for a synthesis between bridge building and botany. Two different fields of investigation are "synthesized," not by the merging of their concepts, but by a similarity of method; there is "synthesis" when we develop a "form" of procedure which can be applied *mutandis mutatis* to varying subject matters; botany and bridge building are "brought together" when our ways of studying the one have their equivalent in our ways of studying the other—and this essential aspect of synthesis is already with us. And whatever the values of a synthesis may be, they are hardly great enough to justify an approach which mingles the dialectic of philosophy, the metaphors of art, the measurements of science and the "higher knowledge" of religion. The result is an indeterminate shifting of vocabulary which, far from avoiding the deceptions of speech which Yoga equips us to reveal, makes it possible for deceptions of speech to flourish at their greatest.

# Protective Coloration

*Redder Than the Rose* by Robert Forsythe. Covici, Friede
*The New Republic*, July 1935, 255–256

The most notable quality about Robert Forsythe's tracts on the blotches, itches and agues of the day is that they can make you feel good. Have you flushed or grown dizzy in helpless fury when contemplating the antics of Dr. Frederick B. Robinson, president of the College of the City of New York? If so, Forsythe's hilarious article on "The All-American" will give you the first relief you have had in months. Have there been occasions when you felt that the blunt police were positively monumental in their obstruction of economic decency? In "Cops Are Funny People—if at all" you will find catharsis. Have you winced somewhat at the grotesque avidity of our typical murder trials, gladiatorial combats for decadent eras wherein purely imaginative tragedy will no longer suffice, and there must be real live victims thrown to the lions? Then you will be glad to participate in the vindictive descriptions (in "Five Star Final") of the major commercial enterprise constructed about the fate of the lone wretch Hauptmann. Similarly, for many other of our contemporary ills, Forsythe provides the effective verbal specific.

At one point in this collection of satiric essays (many of which originally appeared in *The New Masses*) the author says that "hypocrisy appears to be a perverted form of satire," since "in satire you appear to be writing about one thing when you are actually writing about the reverse." Forsythe is far too much a Savonarola of late capitalism to maintain the simple pattern of "hypocrisy in reverse" throughout the book. Frequently his zeal in assembling objects for the Pyre of Vanities, or in describing the directives of Soviet Russia, induces him to drop the strangely complex smile by which satire is contrived, and to speak without stylistic subterfuge. He stops guying, and becomes the earnest swearing preacher. Occasionally this shift of pattern bothered me on esthetic grounds, as a slightly broken frame. Some readers find it hard to make the adjustment necessary for the appreciation of satire in any case, and Forsythe's tendency to shuttle between the serious and the mock-serious may trouble persons not completely at home in his point of view. But if readers can shift each time the writer shifts, if their judgments are sufficiently like his for them to meet him halfway, they will be happy thus to "prepare" themselves mimetically for better days with the aid of Forsythe's symbolic revolution against contemporary evils.

There is a notable distinction between the satiric propagandist (such as Forsythe) and the universal satirist (best exemplified for us in Swift). The universal satirist attacks all mankind; and his occupation may in the end assume almost diabolic attributes. The satiric propagandist, on the other hand, has no quarrel with mankind. He is against some class or group of men. In contrast with the austerity of the universal satirist, there are definite areas of humanity that he is obliged by his program to spare. Of course, no one's condemnation is absolute: even Swift tended to forgive people insofar as they possessed the gentility of horses—but such a spiritual test could not make for clear practical alliances of the sort that marks the satiric propagandist. There is some fundamental difference between the gnarled anguish of a Swift, who, beset with a rare, exacting sense of degradation, attempted in myth to drag all mankind down with him, and the selectiveness of Forsythe, who distributes praise and blame in accordance with the demands of a particular social platform. Though he might never in all his life run for office, Forsythe is engaged in *political* excoriation; his work is typically editorial-writing in a party organ.

The job of the satiric propagandist is also notably different from the job of the catch-as-catch-can funmaker (so prevalent in America today), who can engage us by scrambling our values in purely haphazard fashion. "What one must have, to be a success with *The New Yorker*," Forsythe writes, "is an ability to make even the most transcendental event trivial." It is not hard to understand why satirists who change the scale of things, turning major terrors into minor annoyances, are much sought after—for with the help of such magic, the Vague Shapes of Historic Calamity are whisked away to be replaced by odd discomforts, reassuring in their tininess.

The difference between these comic exorcists and the satiric propagandist is that the former, like Swift, can train their stylistic guns in all directions, whereas the propagandist has a clear alignment of friends and foes. (Incidentally, as it works out in practice, the catch-as-catch-can school will be found on closer examination to be partisan also, if not consistently, at least in the predominant quality of their work, for though they are theoretically at liberty to spoof anything, they learn in time that certain butts sell better than others, and in thus accommodating themselves to their market, they are imperceptibly inspired by the genius of partisanship implicit in that market.)

When a satirist is competent, our heel of Achilles is the most prominent part of our anatomy. Anybody, without exception, can be pictured as fool, coward, compromiser, hypocrite, snob, liar, opportunist, coxcomb, vulgarian, etc., given the proper "angle of approach." The important consideration thus becomes: What angle of approach is implicit in the work of the particular satirist? Forsythe, exemplifying a pro-communist perspective, stimulates us to confront the ills of the contemporary world, not by a magical device for converting them downwards into the little and remote—as though seen through the wrong end of a telescope—but by implying throughout his work that these ills can in large measure be remedied. He would doubtless admit that vices will always be with us, in any social or economic texture; but the important thing for him is to point out the ways in which late capitalism has *organized* the anti-social, giving it efficiency, voice and authority, and consolidating it with the help of the educative, legislative and constabulary forces. Thus he may etch, where those of *The New Yorker* school must smudge: he may present evils in magnitude (since he also has a theory of cure) where the others, the conscious or unconscious apologists, must dwarf. By the pleasant embellishments of his wit, coupled with the encouragement of his doctrine, he better enables us to look a bungled situation in the face.

Of course, satire of this sort is closely interwoven with the texture of the news. Forsythe, like Dos Passos, writes from the headlines (is more publicist than poet). A story breaks, flooding the public consciousness for a few hours, days or weeks—and Forsythe appears with some cutting comments that neatly polish it off. Thus, your interest in his book will be largely dependent upon the extent of your familiarity with the outstanding gossip of telegraph and radio, that convincing brand of "reality" constructed for us through channels of organized news-gathering (and one can only conjecture what a warped picture the news may provide, so thoroughly identified with "reality" has this brand of selection, interpretation and focus become for us).

One may argue how vital the news is, and how long a given fragment of it remains vital. Insofar as a story withers from the public memory, losing its immediacy, I suspect that the satiric comments erected upon it tend to wither proportionately. But insofar as the events and personalities about which Forsythe constructs his articles retain vitality as news (which is now the case), *Redder Than the Rose* should gratify with its deftness, sophistication and clearly demarcated point of view. The author is not merely out to gorge you with giggles. He is infused with the belief that "gangsterism is only a lesser phase of the gangsterism of Big Business"—and perhaps we might call this the pivotal judgment about which all his philosophy revolves.

# Storm Omens

*Pittsburgh Memoranda* by Haniel Long. Santa Fé: Writers' Editions
*The New Republic*, August 1935, 83

Haniel Long's *Pittsburgh Memoranda* make a volume that is grave and disquieting. The author is concerned with the "new pioneering," the search for purpose and solace among those "who fight not Indians but insanity." To watch at night, from the Pittsburgh hills, the "goblin forges" by the water's edge is to wonder at the rage that tore out the natural beauty, putting in its place a smoke-laden clutter as

> Some men, driven by a haste cosmic and not human, built furiously, like titans or like idiots, a new world.

In verse and fragmentary prose, Long assembles significant details of his town with scholarship that is vital, but drooping. His choice of outstanding figures and events connected with the Pittsburgh scene provides an expressive array of symbols: the Homestead Strike (with "non-proletarian" glimpses at the human material involved that make you wince); Stephen Foster, seeking in melody that resting place which the earlier men had sought in migration; John Brashear, maker of lenses, pious in a secular vocation, fascinated by the stars in a city where they were hardest to see; Andrew Carnegie, who gave half a million sterling in five-percent bonds, as he said, "to bring into the monotonous lives of the toiling masses of Dumfermline more of sweetness and light," author of *The Gospel of Wealth,* wherein is outlined an intricate system of celestial accounting for balancing exploitation and philanthropy; the warden's wife, Mrs. Soffel, who read the Bible aloud to the Biddle boys while they sawed the bars of their cell; George Westinghouse, whose mechanical ingenuity built up a great plant for others, with financial ingenuity, to take from him; *My New Born Son* and *My Fellow Stockholders;* Frank Hogan and Fred Demmler, two local men of promise killed in the War; Duse, who died in Pittsburgh; and many others whose destinies impinge upon this city at some notable point. The book lacks tension, through being pinned together rather than formed. But as a songful survey, combining the statistical and the impressionistic, it unquestionably suggests the magnitude and the quality of the psychological issues arising from the confused ways in which late capitalism both stimulates and frustrates ambition.

# A Radical, But—

*The Neurotic Nightingale* by Vardis Fisher. The Casanova Press
*The New Republic*, October 1935, 221

To those in search of a sour song the four essays of *The Neurotic Nightingale* may be commended. The author writes intently, even brilliantly—and he is rich in things to complain about, for he is very hard to please. "When I discovered," he says, "that sexual frustration and a sense of guilt had made a Socialist of me I repudiated socialism"—which could be all right if only corresponding discoveries and repudiations had been made by our radical business men. But the absence of matching somewhat fortifies the enemy, while Mr. Fisher proceeds to carve up his natural allies. He is in the "I am a radical, but-" school of pamphleteering, wherein the line of battle wavers until one becomes dizzy; he is as likely as not to throw comradely arms around Mr. Wiggin for a few paragraphs, or to find as his spiritual colleagues under certain circumstances "such men as voted for Mr. Hoover three years ago."

He seems quite eager to assert that much vanity, greed, idiocy, hypocrisy, arrested development, superstition, vindictiveness, pruriency and cowardice mark mankind—yet he is more likely to be hurt when noting these traits in radicals, while tending to condone them as normal and human in reactionaries. The book is provocative; and if one knows how to discount an author, it can even be profitable. But at present Mr. Fisher threatens to be too good for this world.

# Anatomy of the Mask

*Propaganda: Its Psychology and Technique* by Leonard W. Doob. Henry Holt.
*The New Republic*, February 1936, 371–372

In this book the author "makes clear what propaganda really is, upon what principles it is based, and how one may recognize it in its false-face." Readers of such a magazine as *The New Republic* will find little that is new in its general tenor. Its value for them will be less in its message *per se* than in its systematization of this message. Mr. Doob has patiently worked out some "principles of propaganda"; he has assembled representative case histories that illustrate these principles; and he has detailed the many communicative channels open to organizations that specialize in the manipulation of our minds. In particular his volume corroborates by precise evidence the radicals' assertion that partisanship inevitably lurks behind much of the avowedly "impartial." And we are helped to see how, even in the humble task of getting people to buy a brand of coffee, the copy-writer may serve to reshape or reaffirm important social and political attitudes.

One cannot talk about propaganda without first talking about something else. At the time of Aristotle, propaganda would obviously have been treated under the heading of "rhetoric," the art of persuading people by the use of symbols. But though the formal devices of rhetoric can be discussed in themselves, the problem quickly shades off into the field of politics—and politics, as handled today, quickly shades off into such fields as economics, psychology and sociology. For this reason, the study of rhetoric seems to me as quick an entrance to the modern scene as one can get. Hence the importance of a twentieth-century rhetoric, which centers in propaganda and advertising, that is, in the selling of goods and attitudes (the connecting link between propaganda and advertising usually being called "good-will advertising").

The relation between rhetoric and environment can be illustrated quickly enough: People necessarily develop patterns of production and distribution. Out of these patterns, "values" arise. Insofar as people would maintain the productive pattern, for instance, traits that are felt to assist in the maintenance of the pattern are considered virtues, and traits that are felt to disrupt the pattern are considered vices. Thus, the great amount of sales enterprise necessary to keep the factories running in America tended to reinforce the ideal of the breezy, get-ahead live wire—and the shut-in, pessimistic, knock-don't-boost type was resented as uncooperative.

Once such values are established, the artist "exploits" them. He can make a character that appeals to people, for instance, by endowing him with the live-wire characteristics, and by so shaping his plot that such characteristics triumph. Conversely, he can picture a knock-don't-boost type as villain—or perhaps he may appeal by having this type see the light in the end, and reform like Scrooge into a boost-don't-knock type. There is thus a tendency to establish a vicious circle: the productive pattern gives rise to values which the artist exploits—and in exploiting them, he helps to reinforce their authority.

Propaganda, as an "applied art," works by this same process. The propagandist wants to recommend Item A (be Item A a brand of soap, a war, a political philosophy, what you will). And he does so by identifying it with some value, or attitude, that already enjoys prestige in the productive pattern. Thus, since science now enjoys prestige, because technology is so important to our productive pattern, we find advocates as different as Dr. Dewey and a toothpaste firm recommending their products under the aegis of science. When God enjoyed prestige, you might have best sold soap by suggesting that cleanliness is next to godliness. When necking enjoys prestige, you might better sell your soap by suggesting that body odors are an obstacle to necking. The author notes the workings of "suggestion" in the technique of our neo-sophists, the propagandists. But I think that the process of suggestion itself could have been analyzed in turn. The power of suggestion could be considered as a kind of implied syllogism, that gains its strength through being implicit rather than explicit. When a toothpaste advertiser attempts to recommend his product by printing a picture of the package along with the picture of a scientist in a laboratory holding up a test-tube, we might reduce the appeal to a bastardized form of argument, such as: "You trust science; this article is scientific; therefore you should trust this article." But inasmuch as the syllogism is merely implied, the reader approaches it "creatively." He is involved as an ally, made a participant in the formation of the message. He is invited to tell himself something, precisely because the writer of the advertisement has not completed the statement. It is as though the advertisement were to count up to *six,* and the reader, getting the cue, "creatively" proceeds to supply *seven.*

The simplest act of propaganda, an argument performed purely by mimesis, is perhaps the baby-kissing of the politician. The implicit argument here, which you are invited to grasp intuitively (with the explicitly syllogistic left out), might run somewhat like this: "You are uncertain about my future conduct in office; but you feel that the love of babies indicates a love of mankind;

my baby-kissing makes it obvious that I love babies; therefore I love mankind; we try to do right by those we love; since I am a lover of mankind, and you are members of mankind, I mean to do right by you." Such arguments are more effective when approached "creatively" rather than "critically."

Bentham, enraged at the use of "question-begging terms" (with their implicit assumptions) that formed the basis of rhetoric, wanted to invent a technique for eliminating them completely. And he did manage to provide devices whereby we could counteract many of their ravages. But he himself, at the same time, was a skilled rhetorician—and in the end, his impartial method is found to have been merely a more subtilized form of partiality. Thus, I think there is greater justice in Mr. Doob's position, where he recognizes that, without propaganda, action is impossible—the issue then becoming "Which Propaganda?"

I do wish, however, that Mr. Doob had paid more attention to the specifically linguistic and formal aspects of his subject. He says: "The aim of the writer is to enable the reader to grasp propaganda in such a way that he will be able to understand the phenomenon in all its various manifestations. The weapon selected to achieve this goal has been social psychology." But a complete discussion would also require the consideration of our modern rhetorics (propaganda, advertising, tendential news) in line with writings by men like Ogden, Richards, Sapir, Malinowsky. It is surprising that even Veblen does not figure here, despite the high comedy in his analysis of "creative psychiatry" and the bands of "economic mercenaries" hired to fight the trade battles of rival commercialists. Too often the author turns to pedestrian sources, so that his book is diffuse, exhaustive rather than sharp.

Yet the reader should be grateful for having so much assembled in one place. Out of it all, one gets a very disturbing picture. How can we ever be wise, when wisdom is a very difficult matter at best, and in addition we are systematically beset by so many apostles of untruth and half-truth as he describes? Only if the "road to excess leads to the palace of wisdom" dare we hope that the people will become sophisticated enough to see through the maze of trickery to which they are subjected. Not merely that, by surfeit, the appetite may sicken and so die—but rather as the man who applied for a job as proof-reader, giving as his main qualification the fact that, since he has made all possible errors in proofreading, he knew what to look out for. Can we learn by being fooled often enough? Or is it permanently as impossible to anticipate fraud in propaganda as it is impossible to anticipate fraud in law (where a new fraud takes its shape precisely from the laws written to stop an old fraud)? An earlier age used to smile at the confusions of Mrs. Malaprop. Reading this volume, we are invited rather to tremble at the confusions of Mr. Malapropaganda.

# Property as an Absolute

*Who Owns America? A New Declaration of Independence,* edited by Herbert
   Azar and Allen Tate, Boston Houghton Mifflin
*The New Republic,* July 1936, 245–246

You tend your livestock, you grow your crops, you cut your timber with husbandry, you raise your family, you erect appropriate structures for living and working. In all that, there is health, correctness, morality. Unfortunately, your circle of rights and obligations was not confined to these limits. There is a medium of exchange, for instance, a system of currency and credit, and a group arises to specialize in this medium. This financial group may be no wiser in its way than you were in yours. But its specialty gives it a grip upon the market. It may be closer to the "spirituality" of the courts and legislators. It may thereby work its will. And if there are many of you, acting somewhat independently of one another, the things you bring to market, for getting the money that pays your taxes and any goods you import, may impair your bargaining power. The financial group, working in connection with industrialists, may put through tariffs that raise the price on industrial goods, so that your unprotected market suffers in comparison. For a while you make up the differential by a mortgage. But as the disproportion persists, you are eventually unable to meet the mortgage, and lose your property. Irony: All your life you have managed conscientiously and well, you have produced in abundance—and as a reward, you are destitute.

   The twenty-one writers in the new regionalist anthology of the Southern agrarians have given us this picture with poignancy, brilliance and persuasive bitterness. Their attacks upon the financial manipulators who "own America" converge from many angles, in a collective enterprise that speaks well for writers averse to collective enterprise. But in noting that big business is developed by the growth of corporations, the agrarians would lump fascism and communism together as merely the extension of the corporate idea. Hence, they would draw upon our resistance to big business as a way of exhorting us against all collectives.

There is this to be said in their favor. Although Marxists like to foresee the "withering away of the state" (revealing here the effect of their "united front" with anarchists in the revolutionary struggles of the nineteenth century), it is hard to imagine how this withering away can take place. A complex social order, such as is required by industrial-agrarian collectivism, would necessarily require planning on a large scale. If we mean by the state the "bourgeois state," we can picture its atrophy. But if we mean by the state the legislative, educational and constabulary organization that assists the forces helping a given economic order and discourages the forces obstructing this order, we realize that a collective state is far from the anarchistic ideal. In fact, as others have pointed out, the anarchistic ideal is but the logical conclusion of the laissez-faire ideal. It is a heretical affirmation of the commercial orthodoxy.

Our agrarians may also be a heretical sect reaffirming orthodox commercial values. For they, like the commercialists, would extol properly as an absolute, whereas the collectivists treat property as a relationship. The system of private ownership glorified by the agrarians was developed gradually with the rise of the commercial ethic. The merchant-landlords, aided by judicial interpretations, fought long and hard for the "right" to make property "alienable" (that is, to withdraw this means of production from communal use and reserve it exclusively for private exploitation). After 1688, in the English Acts of Enclosure, judicial complicity in the development of these "rights" was reinforced by explicit legislation. Eventually the serf was "freed" and "mobile." The two-way relationship, whereby he was bound to his land and his use of the land was bound to him, had been dissolved. Many of the people thus "freed" died in abject poverty. Many migrated to the cities, where the new industries absorbed them. Many came to America, to dispossess the Indians and set up the same system of private ownership that had victimized them abroad.

It is unfortunate that the earlier feudal-collective usage of the word "property" has been obscured by later bourgeois usage. One used to speak, not of "having property," but of "having a property in" something. The earlier relativistic usage might have a modernized application by suggesting that the citizen of a collective state has a "property in" his citizenship, in the regularity of communicative or distributive resources, in any security afforded by the productive order, the political devices or the courts, in the marriage customs of his society, in the opportunities of study and enjoyment, etc. If he has a job and is performing that job with ability, he has a *property* in it insofar as the usages of his society help to keep him in possession of it and to guarantee him its rewards. Such thinking would suggest that property is as present in a communist state as in a commercial state. The question then becomes, not "Is there property?" but "What kind of property is there?" Every state is a property state.

But by treating property as an absolute rather than as a relationship, the agrarians enjoy a one-way conception of property rights. When things are going well, their ideal private farmer, proud and free in the untrammeled possession of his acres, dismisses the government with dignity. He does as he pleases, without "interference": if the market is favorable, he sells; if unfavorable, he retains for his own use. No necessities can dispossess him, since his land is inalienable. The land is "bound to" him, though he presumably is not "bound to" it (which would entail immobilization, hence a feudal impairment of freedom). Perhaps the land is even untaxed, as the logic of the agrarians' position would require, since the farmer must be wholly independent of the market's financial compulsion, otherwise the deterministic genius of the "money crop" may get him. On the other hand if there are adversities, the government must be called in. Such matters as flood control, drought relief, education, road building and medication are to be handled with governmental assistance. The project suggests a "spoiled child" theory of politics, where the papa-government is dismissed by the proud bearers of "freedom" as intolerable interference, until it must be called on for help. Once we introduce a two-way conception of rights, noting an *ambivalent* situation wherein "rights" are interwoven with *obligations,* and vice-versa, the proposal appears less realistic.

But though the agrarians neglect the ambivalent feature when advocating their own cause, they remember it when warning against collectivism (since they note that collectivist security requires central planning, and central planning necessarily restricts private arbitrary choice). We may note a strong sense of reciprocity in our earlier revolutionary slogan, "Taxation without representation is tyranny." The slogan implicit in the agrarians' one-way revolutionary theory would seem to be, "Representation without taxation is liberty." One can question whether freedom, as so conceived, meets the needs of the modern economic order. But one must admit that it would be fun.

Those who consider social welfare as a *human* problem, rather than a *class* problem, may be disturbed that there is not so much as a single paragraph devoted to the Negro question. Particularly when one author suggests that some are endowed by natural quality to rule, and others are endowed to be hired. A property state such as they propose would fix a disproportion between owners and dispossessed. These writers emphatically reject the slovenly way in which finance capitalism has divided the class of those fit to rule from the class of those fit to be ruled, yet they offer no explicit Binet test as an alternative for disclosing the radical difference in quality. Nor do they tell us whether the estates will be held intact by primogeniture, or whether some sons and daughters of the owners must also in time shift to the class of dispossessed, with attendant disadvantages in bargaining power.

As one writer observes, the regionalists refer often to the past, while the "proletarian" school of social criticism has its eyes upon the future. Yet it is the *proletarians* who talk always with reference to the great laboratory of history. The agrarians are almost vandalistic in their destruction of historic lore by omission. There may be good reason for this. History shows us, again and again, how private ownership of one productive plant operates to turn possession into dispossession. Such training in ambivalence were best dismissed by these advocates as "determinism." The "distributist" state could be maintained only by periodic redistribution. No wonder the master of the agrarians, Jefferson, who pleaded for the private ownership of productive plant, also suggested as a corollary that we should need a revolution every twenty years.

# Methodology of the Scramble

*Politics: Who Gets What, When, How?* by Harold D. Lasswell. Whittlesey House
*The New Republic*, December 1936, 250

Imagine a country where men rose to preeminence in accordance with their skill in a peanut race. That is, the men who could push a peanut with the nose over an official course in the shortest length of time became the country's heroes and leaders. Obviously, such a revolution in values and practices would make for a wholly new kind of selectivity. There must be at present, scattered throughout the nation, potential peanut-pushers who are condemned to rot as mute, inglorious Miltons because the present rules of eminence are not *their* rules. But given the appropriate ideology, they would rise to form a new "élite."

Some, it is true, might gain their national prominence by sheer fraud. They might bribe the judges, or contrive other manipulations, whereby they *passed* as great peanut-pushers and enjoyed the honors and privileges accorded such talent, when they were not *bona fide* goober athletes at all. Or they might contrive to keep new candidates from entering the race, shunting them into lowly occupations (science, industry, art and the like) that did not permit them to perfect and express their peanut capacities to the fullest. But in the main, the tests of selection would make for a reshuffle whereby a class superior at peanut-pushing came to the fore and molded the policies of the state to their liking. And this class would so guide the educative, legislative and constabulary functions as to perpetuate their privileges.

Lasswell is a specialist in the study of selectivity. His thinking, which would fall roughly in the Pareto category, is concerned with the historical shifts in popular allegiance whereby a peanut race takes the place of a potato race, or some such, and the group best fitted in one way or another to profit by the new rules rises to authority. His book is a "study of influence and the influential." It pleads for no particular kind of race (or, to decode our trope, he does not propose to justify a preference for one economic system rather than another). "This book, restricted to political analysis, declares no preferences. It states conditions."

"Conditions" are purely and simply the Scramble, the reshuffling process whereby, as people shift their allegiance from one symbol of authority to another, a new group arises to profit by the change. The profits are not necessarily material ones—they may even be largely confined to the categories of honor and prestige. But whatever the legal tender of the given social norms may be, a new set of bankers arises to manipulate this subtle medium of exchange. They are the "influential"—and

> The influential are those who get the most of what there is to get. Available values may be classified as deference, income, safety. Those who get the most are élite; the rest are mass.

His first chapter amplifies this definition. He next proceeds to a discussion of "methods." We are shown how "any élite defends and asserts itself in the name of symbols of the common destiny"; how such defense involves the use of force; how the use of goods in élite attack takes the form of destroying, withholding, apportioning—and, finally, we are permitted to examine the procedures by which élites are recruited and trained by tactics in policymaking and administration.

In another section he examines matters of "skill," "class," "personality" and "attitude" as they figure in deciding "who gets what, when, how." We are shown, for instance, how the rules of selectivity may sometimes be such that even highly pathological types can be the best candidates for the élite. And though his book is very easy to follow, he clinches matters with a final chapter of recapitulation.

The admonitory value of his book is considerable, particularly for those who would employ it as an intellectual weapon against fascism. Its swift manner, with its wealth of concrete examples, should earn it an important place in our better popular literature of the debunking sort. One may question, however, whether his approach to the subject is as "impartially scientific" as the author apparently assumes. One may even doubt whether his terminology is as broad as required by the situation it would chart. His analysis of human relations seems too strongly motivated by the typically commercialist view of human psychology, with its overemphasis upon the get-ahead, foot-on-the-neck notions of "success" in living. There are important aspects of communion and appeal that are perhaps not given their accurate location when handled in a vocabulary so exclusively of the debunking sort. The "genius" of his subtitle tends to obliterate vitally important qualifications; a Lenin becomes practically the same as a Mussolini or a Hitler.

Like all works of the purely debunking sort, the book should be serviceable for the purposes of negativistic, disintegrative criticism. In fact, its essentially disintegrative character is manifest in its very form, as it is pieced together from many disparate sources, and suggests a shell without a core. If science is to serve its complete social purpose (analyzing human conduct in an *integrative* vocabulary, whereby people may actively cooperate, instead of becoming merely shrewd spies upon one another), Lasswell's science might be called backward and incomplete. It would be excellent for disclosing the misuse of symbols like "liberty" or "solidarity," but its very efficiency would interfere with our allegiance to such symbols when they are properly used. It might lead us to say "thumbs down" even when we should say "thumbs up."

# Synthetic Freedom

*The Restoration of Property: An Essay on the Modern Crisis* by Hilaire Belloc.
   Sheed and Ward
*The New Republic*, January 1937, 365

A fairly superficial statement of Belloc's plans for giving political and economic direction to the "spirit of reaction" against "capitalism and its socialist fruit." A source-book for those who might be interested in tracing the full genealogy of the Jeffersonianism now advocated by our Southern agrarian school. Belloc is a kind of protectionist Adam Smith, with a patchwork scheme for putting security and laissez-faire together. Apparently, all that is needed is to pick the best features from two systems, and forget the worst. He believes that the historic process is taking capitalism toward fascism or communism (which, for him, are almost the same thing); he grants that "you cannot reverse the process without acting *against* natural economic tendencies"—hence he advocates a "reversal" or "reaction" by the deliberate governmental subsidizing of an independent middle class, a project for economic "re-afforestation" by the federal planting of petty-bourgeois "seedlings." "Either we restore property or we restore slavery"—hence his speculations upon legal measures that would recreate a sufficient body of small landowners and independent craftsmen "to give their tone to the state." The rest of the populace could presumably enjoy the freedom of this class by proxy, as it got the spiritual advantage of sharing their "tone."

All that is necessary, to implement this "healthy" reactionary process, is to introduce the kind of laws that give small enterprise the advantage over large enterprise, in accordance with "the principle that everything should be done by the artifice of law to make it easy for the smaller man to buy land from the richer man and difficult for the larger man to buy land from the smaller man," a cute notion that would sound better if expressed in some of Belloc's delightful nonsense jingles and may indeed have derived originally from this topsy-turvy aspect of his genius. The scheme he offers is hung upon the pegs of peasantry, craft guild, universal church and a (beneficent) monarch. For each of these he substitutes an attenuated modern equivalent. The attenuations finally attain such ambiguity that this Catholic can frame his apologetics in the name of "liberty"—the basic slogan of the sinful when Catholicism was in its heyday. Perhaps the book should be of most interest to the students of logomachy, who would watch the ways in which the symbols of appeal are stolen back and forth by rival camps. And it must be conceded that recent laws against chain stores are somewhat in the spirit of Belloc's proposals, as are also the scattered "resettlement" projects instituted under Roosevelt. Everything depends upon how much importance you attach to this drop in the bucket.

# Spender's Left Hand

*Forward from Liberalism* by Stephen Spender. Random House
*The New Republic*, August 1937

If a man has organized his values about the slogan "liberal," and he is addressing people who have similarly organized their values, it seems as good a starting point as any other. Everything then depends upon the qualifications introduced *en route.*

The qualifications usually present much trouble. Liberalism as a *practice* (as Spender points out, along with many other writers) is connected with private ownership of the productive plant. But its needs and opportunities generated an *ideal* that, in the minds of some, is felt to require the abolition of such ownership.

One might conceivably frame the issue in another way. Beginning with the Creation as given, and employing the customary strategy of science in using it as the material basis of reference, one might note that the body lives by locomotion, or freedom of movement. One might hold that the value arising "superstructurally" above this biologoeconomic "substructure" is a love of freedom. And one might then deduce that the drive for the alienation of property (that began in earnest with the rise of the bourgeoisie) was the translation of this value into the idiom of a specific economic texture. One could then proceed to show that the resources of this idiom have been exhausted (that it never did offer the highest communicative possibilities, and is now further impaired by having come close to the limits of its "inner contradictions").

If you go back to a "biological" foundation for the value of liberty, however, you frighten your colleagues, to whom the mere mention of biology automatically suggests the genetic theories of Nazism. And if, on the other hand, you leave the matter wholly on the historical plane, you must always be at once asserting and retracting. For liberalism as a historic movement is bound up with bourgeois modes of ownership. And as a historical ideal, it cannot be severed from its historical economic context. Hence, if one would shun a biological basis of reference for liberalism (with bourgeois modes of ownership being located as a restricted and eventually self-destructive way of expressing this biologically grounded value) one must be continually floundering in an ambiguity, admiring as pure "ideal" what one must condemn in its historical practice.

Spender traces this ambiguity throughout liberal thought. Yet he does not himself manage to "transcend" it. In the end, you are left wondering where his value is grounded. Is it grounded in business, or isn't it? If it is, how can it survive business—or what new shapes must it take?

As things stand, his equating of communism with liberalism (viewing communism as the logical conclusion of liberalism, and all departures as merely regrettable but temporary) is not illuminating. He would sever the ideal from the practice—and is so confined by his efforts to solve this basic dilemma that he cannot advance the discussion beyond its customary stage. His position is not essentially different from that of Wilde in his "Soul of Man under Socialism."

Collectivism, in other words, is not considered as a new perspective that alters individualism. Instead, collectivism is merely the extension of individualism in the same direction. I submit that such an approach will, and should, prepare one for disillusionment.

The book rarely calls forth the flashes we have come to expect of Spender as a poet. In fuming from poetry to prose, he says in effect that he does not place a very high value upon prose. Only occasionally, in a short passage that seems like notes for a poem, do we feel that the writer has recommended his cause (as a writer should) by packing it with invention to the extent of his abilities. (He comes nearest to this in the short chapter "Questions and Answers: Statement," which, along with some pages on Aldous Huxley, we should rate as by far the best portions of the book.)

# More Probes in the Same Spot

*Counterblast* by Marshall McLuhan, designed by Harley Baker. Harcourt, Brace & World
*The New Republic*, February 1970, 30–35

"To say that any technology or extension of man creates a new environment is a much better way of saying that the medium is the message." To this recent revision of the over-simplified slogan in McLuhan's *Understanding Media,* one can decisively say "amen." Indeed, not only is it an improvement, it is saying something quite different. And had McLuhan built his message thus rather than as he did, many of the half-truths with which he (so profitably!) cluttered his pages could have been avoided.

But precisely while at work on a review of his present offering, I also read his earlier book, *The Mechanical Bride: The Folklore of Industrialism* (originally published in 1951). The contrast between that work and *Counterblast* points up a development that struck me as interesting in itself, without regard to the intrinsic merits or demerits of either. I'd call it a kind of "methodological conversion," and I'll try to trace briefly the sort of transformations I have in mind.

*The Mechanical Bride* reproduces many typical examples of advertising, along with a zealously adverse critique of such "poisonous bilge." We are given countless variations on the theme of the adman's demoralizing appeal to our stupidities and vices as a way of unloading a maximum of manufactured commodities in a mass market. The book strikes many effective and ingenious blows, though the ad tricks are usually so dismal that in the end the reader tires of even seeing them exposed and castigated. But the twist is this:

The earlier book is devoted to a relentless analysis of the various exhibits' *contents,* including their appeal to our "unconscious" motives. (McLuhan had not yet latched onto "subliminal," though he was on the way, when observing that popular images of the sleuth, businessman, and scientist were "subterranean.") However, at almost the mathematical center of the book, turning of a sudden from advertisements to a quite different kind of example, he says:

"Mallarme and Joyce refused to be distracted by the fashion-conscious sirens of content and subject matter and proceeded straight to the utilization of the universal forms of the artistic process itself." (Previously there had been a passing, punning reference to authors who, influenced by the technique of sales promotion, were "eager to sell their souls for a pot of message"—and thus was the slogan of *Understanding Media* a-borning. Also, we should recall that, whatever may have been Joyce's and Mallarme's interest in the sheerly formal aspects of literature as a medium, their work was as notable for its contents as was that of an earlier master who doted on the thought of pure form, Flaubert. Nor should we confuse *artistic "form"* with McLuhan's *engineering* stress upon "medium.")

*The Bride* had been concerned exclusively with the products of the machine. McLuhan's later distinction between mechanical technology and electronic technology simply did not exist. In fact, the nearest adumbration of it that I could find is a glancing reference to "Professor Wiener's type of prospect that the electronic brain will certainly eliminate the ordinary man from the human scene."

But note what a radical shift of alignment can take place, once McLuhan postulates a critical cultural distinction between the kinds of business that are associated with mechanical technology and the kinds that are associated with *electronic* technology. The stress now was not upon the *contents* of the new electronic media (such as TV), but upon their nature and effects simply as *media*. Hence, whereas one might readily conceive of a tract that pursued TV commercials as relentlessly as McLuhan had pursued the "techniques of persuasion" typical of printed advertisements, now all was changed. Come the new dispensation, he summarily dismissed all criticism of TV's *contents*, whatever might be its "pot of message." Instead, the bare medium, the sheer TV electronic instrument itself, became the "message." Thanks to this shift, his own later message could become the darling of precisely such pitchmen as he had started out by despising. For instead of discussing the dismal contents of TV's typical "wasteland" wares, he could stress the medium itself as "subliminal" harbinger of the future. Add a touch of the "mythic," "apocalyptic" unction now going the rounds—and whereas he once wrote "headlines mean street sales," the converted version is "headlines are icons."

I must leave it for you to decide how such notable fields as chemistry and biology fit into a flat distinction between an earlier mechanical era and the emergent electronic one. Also, you must decide for yourself just what kind of bookkeeping we're in for when, after his mediumistic way of dismissing a concern with "content," he ended up by discovering that, in the New Age of electronics, we are all to become, above all, something so content-ridden as "information-gatherers."

In any case, *Counterblast* gives the mediumistic angle a different twist. In an intermediate contrivance, *The Medium as Massage: An Inventory of Effects,* McLuhan had teamed up with a collaborator who helped him restate his message by sandwiching it in among a batch of photographs (many of them quite interesting). This time for his repeat performance he has a collaborator who resorts to quite a range of typographical devices (including some upside down, some wrongly syllabified, some set backwards for reading in a mirror, some gnawed at, some spiralling, some Lilliputian, some Brobdingnagian, and others variously at odds). While many of these devices are interesting in themselves, when the message gets administered in this encapsulated manner there develops an unpleasant side-effect, a jumpiness that makes even a minimum of concentration difficult. Perhaps this is why after about 100 pages of such fare, the procedure is abandoned for a spell, and the exposition, in at least ocular continuity, weaves hyper-symptomatically among the media and their imputed effects. (The designer's jaggy manner would serve best, it seems to me, if a batch of aphorisms, each in a universe by itself, were to be assembled on a single page. Under such conditions, the greater the sense of discontinuity the better, as you went from one bit to another, in no fixed order.)

Yet in some respects this book is an improvement. For instance, it has eased up on the worthless (but catchy!) distinction between "hot" and "cool" media. Apparently, however, the distinction itself has become a fixity in the lingo of the sales priesthood, who seem to use it as synonymous with the distinction between "hard sell" and "soft sell." (As so applied, the terms would be misused, since they would involve differences of *content* rather than *medium*. For instance, since TV was labeled a "cool" medium, a "hot" commercial on TV would be impossible, quite as one could not play a thunderous fortissimo on a harpsichord.)

A second improvement may derive from the fact that, if McLuhan is to go on getting out books, it was only a question of time until printing would turn out not to be so obsolescent after all, since it better lends itself to certain kinds of analysis than do many other media.

But the more he tries to get his message "hotted up" with the aid of guileful collaborators skilled in other manners, the more his product gives the effect of cosmetics on a skin grown sallow. Yet about the edges of "blast" there flickers the sound of "blessed": beside the cruel cry to "Blast The Sports Page pantheon of pickled gods and archetypes & The Comic Strip upholder of HOMERIC CULTURE," there is the compensatory avowal (which I must quote without benefit of the designer's typographic prowess): "Bless Madison Avenue for Restoring the Magical Art of the Cavemen to SUBURBIA."

The improvements in *Counterblast* suggest that McLuhan may eventually temper his message in keeping with many of the excellent quotations which he assembled in *The Gutenberg Galaxy* and which he drove to excess when setting up shop on his own. He still transcends the distinction however, between "prove" and "probe," both from the Latin *pro-bare*. "Proof" requires a considerable sense of continuity; "probing" can be done at random, with hit-and-run slogans or titles taking the place of sustained exposition. And in the medium of books, McLuhan with his "probing" has "perfected" a manner in which the non sequitur never had it so good.

# Quantity and Quality

*Modern Man in the Making* by Otto Neurath. Alfred A. Knopf
*The New Republic*, November 1939, 22–23. Also in *The Philosophy of Literary Form*.

Standard procedure: You find a sentence, expand the sentence into a paragraph, the paragraph into a chapter, and the chapter into a book. You start by stating what you're going to prove, you proceed, "now I'm proving it," and for a grand finale you summarize.

To turn from such mighty projects in deforestation to Otto Neurath's *Modern Man in the Making* is to realize how much filibustering takes place, where we were never taught to look for filibustering. As against a species of historiography that resembles the worst kind of naturalistic novel (wherein two hundred thousand details are twice as great as one hundred thousand) you have here an essay in *reduction,* and a splendid one.

The contemporary cult of "the facts" must gain strength in part because, by this cult, systematic plagiarism has been made the norm. "The facts" are a species of quotation which one can appropriate without the quotation marks. They are collections by Bartlett, signed as though Bartlett had made them up himself. "The facts" are, to be sure, the basis of Neurath's book—but he establishes his right to them by a fresh act.

It is his intention to locate the modern world for us by comparing and contrasting quantitative aspects of today with quantitative aspects of the past, sometimes with intermediate points showing the rate at which these quantitative changes occurred. And he has sought to translate his exposition into the idiom of visualization, his so-called "isotypes," a picturizing method that is hardly new with him, but is employed so deftly and methodically as to give one always the feeling of newness, both in the isotypes themselves and in the succinct kind of text that, in being designed to accompany them, became imbued with the same reductive genius.

The reduction to quantities necessarily eliminates important qualitative ingredients. Neurath has an isotype, for instance, visualizing the changed proportions of work, leisure and sleep in a day "formerly" and "now." The sleep quantity remains the same; the leisure quantity has greatly increased and the work quantity greatly decreased. But we are left with the important possibility that many ingredients in the quality of work in the past have been shifted to the quality of leisure now. And though the quantity of sleep is the same for both periods, anyone who has slept (a) by a traffic-laden street after a day at the office and (b) in a mountain cabin after a day of physical exercise, knows that there may be important differences in the quality of sleep.

The author, fully aware of this problem, attempts by a method of "silhouettes" so to combine quantities as to give us an inkling of quality. We are shown, for instance, the silhouette of a town in the middle ages and in modern times. In each we see a church surrounded by secular buildings. In the middle ages, the church overtops a little cluster of dwellings, in about the proportion of a hen to her chicks. In his visualization of modern times, we see the same church, now surrounded by skyscrapers, in about the proportion of the hen to a batch of electric refrigerators. And the same qualitative question is approached from another quantitative answer by indicating loss of religious influence thus: By coupling a rise in the suicide rate with the fact that religious authority is generally against suicide, Neurath interprets this change as a quantitative indicator of a change in the quality of religious authority.

But though the beginnings of a statistical approach to quality are made here, with great ingenuity, I question whether the problem has been completely solved. Look at one of the isotypes, for instance, with its neat rows of little standardized men, all alike, and each "representing" some tens, or hundreds, or thousands of his fellows. Is there not an important omission in the very concept of representation that is embodied here? We may recall an alternative kind of representation, a culminative sort, such as we might get in the culminative quality of a great portrait painter. Or otherwise put: we might distinguish between the kind of representation that sums up an era and the kind that strikes the average of an era. As for the average-man sort, statistically disclosable by little regimented figures, often left uncompleted to indicate that they represent the portion of a quantity, I am always uneasy when noting that this "average man" marries the fraction of an average woman, together they get some fraction of a job, in time they produce the fraction of a child, and they all go riding in two wheels and the bumper of an automobile.

# The 'Science' of Race Thinking

*Race: A Study in Modern Superstition* by Jacques Barzun. Harcourt, Brace
*The New Masses*, February 1938

Jacques Barzun's study of "race thinking" is a tremendously valuable survey, that assembles in one place a most astounding record of flimsy theorizing. One will certainly do well to avoid it if he would make his own baleful contributions to the "science" of racial discrimination. Here is a house of horrors if there ever was one—and I think that its evidence should be included in the exhibit of lynch ropes, Klan robes, and kindred devices assembled at Commonwealth College. The ropes themselves are "neutral." They might have been used for tethering cattle, and the robes would probably do quite well as night shirts. Here, however, is the record of the "ideas" that guide their use for malign purposes.

The book, for me at least, contained surprises. It was surprising to be reminded that "race-thinking" was not always reactionary. Tacitus, for instance, played an important part in "starting the powerful race dogma of Nordic superiority, yet he was actuated by the exact opposite of chauvinistic purposes. His "essay on the Germans, which contains so many of the facts and so much of the feeling that animates modern racialism" was motivated by emancipatory intentions:

> Tacitus wrote as traveler, historian, and moralist, but especially as an embittered foe of the imperial tyranny. Hence his eulogy of the Germanic race is systematic and politically painted. According to him the Germans are an indigenous race; they are virtuous, individualistic, freedom-loving, and jealous of their racial purity; physically they are tall and blond, brave and tough, they live frugally and are adventurous rather than toilsome.

In other words, he was building up the picture of an "ideal" race as a political weapon against tyrannical trends at home. It was apparently a roundabout way of saying, "Let *us* be virtuous, brave, tough, frugal, adventurous, individualistic, and freedom-loving." Later we see the uses of such thinking begin to shift.

> Leaning on the *Germania* for a description of the special gifts and institutions of the Frankish or Germanic race, the Count Henri de Boulainvilliers (1658–1722) evolved the still lively notion that all freedom and independence come from the Germanic strain. Hence Louis XIV's absolute monarchy, based on the Roman idea of the imperium, was a government fit only for slaves. Boulainvilliers wanted the nobles of his day to revolt against slavish institutions and restore the aristocratic freedom of the German forest.

We also find that race-thinking serves, a little later, to enunciate a muddled doctrine of class-consciousness in an emancipatory direction:

> Just before the French revolution the Abbe Sieyes, the author of *What Is the Third Estate?*, had tried to settle the race issue for all time. The nobility, said Sieyes, claims that its political rights are based on the inheritance by blood of the privileges won in the Frankish conquest. "Very well. We, the Gallo-Roman plebs, will now conquer the nobility by expelling and abolishing them. Our rights will supersede theirs, on exactly the principle they invoke."

Hence, after the revolution, when "the bourgeoisie had overthrown both the monarchy and the aristocracy and had lumped the two," we find that "'Freedom' had thereby changed camps, from the Franks to the Gallo-Romans. This is the initial alteration of the Nordic myth of freedom found in Tacitus."

The general pattern was now secure, though its variants would be endless, with all sorts of new strains introduced each time some new scientist found another way of classifying differences. Those who tend to feel that race-thinking is "peculiarly German" (an attitude that is itself an example of race-thinking) will discover ample evidence that it is ubiquitous, with far more important systematic contributions coming from writers in France than from writers in Germany prior to the rise of Hitlerism (the "Franks" enjoyed a special tactical advantage as vessels of liberty, because of the pun lurking behind the name).

Much of such thinking, as Barzun points out, was not cast in the "superiority-inferiority" mold at all. It was liberal, neutral. Particularly in aesthetic theories as to different "racial" or regional characteristics, the distinctions were frequently made along "parliamentary" lines, with the notion that each "race" had its own special contribution to make toward the common cultural pool of mankind. Herder's romantic historicism was of this sort. However, such theories incidentally reinforced the belief in racial distinctions by *taking it for granted that they existed.* Hence, such a mode of thought indirectly served reactionary ends since it maintained the belief in distinct "racial" traits (with a trait like "humor," or "musicality," for instance, being allocated to some particular "blood"). Political rivalries arising from economic pressure could always provide the groundwork for resentments that converted such *neutral appreciation* of differences back into an *invidious comparison* of differences.

And always, as the author shows, in the heat of such impassioned controversies the crassest inconsistencies could be charitably overlooked. For you worked the system two ways: first you discovered "Aryan," or "Semitic," of "Celtic" traits—and whenever you found an "Aryan" that didn't fit the "Aryan" pattern, you thereby "discovered" that he was *really* "Semitic," etc. Or you extolled a certain "blood stream" as all-powerful, capable of winning out over any other (along the "nobility will out" line of thought), and coupled this heroic disclosure with admonitions lest this all-powerful "blood" be contaminated by other "bloods."

Each advance in physiology, geography, philology, anthropology, history, laboratory technique, psychology, and medicology was in turn drawn upon for service in the cause of racial quackery. Any innovation in scientific measurement provided a fresh opportunity for "us vs. them" racial patterns of one sort or another, with each suppositious faction slightly revising the terms for the opposing traits. "We" had "boldness" on "our" side, for instance—but a thinker on "their" side would name this same trait "brutality." "Merimée was right when he said that racial historiography was the democratic form of dynastic history."

The book concludes with a summarized critique of such thought, and with suggestions as to the great number of ways in which it must be modified if it is to be anything but damned nonsense (nonsense serviceable for the uncritical scapegoat devices of political demagogues). The book should also be read by Marxists because it indicates how both "class" and "regional" divisions can, in naïve hands, lead to a schematization of psychological traits that is hardly other than a concealed variant of the same oversimplified pattern as prevail in "race-thinking." On Marx's own testimony, a theory of purely economic classifications must be subtilized when one is analyzing the expressions of any specific individual.

# Corrosive Without Corrective

*The Folklore of Capitalism* by Thurman Arnold. Yale UP
*The New Masses*, February 1938. Also in *The Philosophy of Literary Form*

Arnold's *The Folklore of Capitalism* is a continuation and amplification of his *The Symbols of Government*. Perhaps it is more profitably to be approached as a lexicon than as an argument. For it is attempting to chart some hitherto uncharted areas of speculation, particularly as to the relations between business and politics; and such attempts are necessarily more concerned with the rounding out of a point of view, suggesting a perspective by giving examples of its major aspects, than with rigorous advance from premise to conclusion. Arnold himself names this perspective "Political Dynamics," which is probably as good a trade name as any. But for purposes of general location, I think we could class it with Mannheim's *Ideology and Utopia,* as a contribution to the *sociology of politics.*

Arnold's analysis of capitalism's dilemmas and antics seems at once *on* the track and *off* the track. And it is not easy to differentiate one phrase from the other, without relying merely on appeal to prejudice. Above all, a reviewer should not allow his representations to obscure his obligations as a mere reporter of the book's contents. For to my mind, everyone interested should read *The Folklore of Capitalism,* quite as he should read Jeremy Bentham and Thorstein Veblen.

Attempting to simplify a complex volume, I should reduce *The Folklore of Capitalism* to two main strands: the one that, by my notion, puts it *on* the track, and the one that puts it *off.* Both exemplify the use of planned incongruity for interpretive purposes.

By planned incongruity I mean a rational prodding or coaching of language so as to see around the corner of everyday usage. Impressed by the great development of machinery, for instance, many thinkers have sought to explain the workings of human beings after the analogy of the machine. Or others, impressed by the documents of biological evolution, have sought to explain the workings of human beings after the analogy of apes. Such modes of interpretation would be examples of planned incongruity, whereby the thinker coached the migration of a perspective from its special area into wider area. This would be a kind of metaphorical projection.

One can very easily coach words in this way, by subjecting them to a *functional* test. For instance, not many years ago, when men spoke of morals or ethics, they meant only good morals, good ethics. But suppose you apply a purely functional approach to some term like moral code. You say, "morality *is* as morality *does*," whereupon you may with propriety speak of criminal ethics, the moral code of gamblers, etc. By simply passing over the barriers of the word, as built up in the pieties of everyday usage, and rationally using it instead to name a function or process, you may coach it to migrate beyond its customary barriers, often with valuable interpretive results.

Arnold's books seems to gravitate about two such metaphorical projections. One is the mode of interpretation obtained by projecting (and then toning down) the perspective of the psychiatric institution until it covers all human relations. This leads to a picture of society as a farce, hilarious on the surface but somewhat grim in its ultimate implications. I should call this the dubious aspect of Arnold's book, though it contributes much to its value as entertainment. The dramatic and ritualistic elements he notes in the historic process are, I think, given a radically false interpretation, by reason of the quality of indictment inherent in this psychiatric perspective itself.

The *useful* projection, for interpretive purposes, is in the amply documented transformation he performs upon the word "government." In the pieties of popular usage, business and government are usually treated as *opposites:* Arnold, by subjecting the words to a functional treatment, sees beyond this piety. As you read, in particular his ironic chapters on "The Benevolence of Taxation by Government Organization," and "The Malevolence of Taxation by Government," you find accumulated a mass of clearly pointed material that is perfectly designed to dissolve the quackery of such writers as Walter Lippmann, Mark Sullivan, and Dorothy Thompson. Arnold makes it apparent that his business is purely and simply a government, and a nondemocratic form of government at that, even having its own regularized modes of taxation. In fact, he clearly shows how this business government has repeatedly resorted to the *capital* levy, despite the fact that such a notion strikes horror into the hearts of our conservatives when presented in political forms.

I should also salute a chapter like "The Ritual of Corporate Reorganization," in which Arnold amasses from many contemporary sources the evidence disclosing the unreal and filmy nature of the concept of property under finance capitalism, and the ways in which this breach between legalistic ideals and practical actualities is manipulated to the advantage of insiders.

Again and again, however, the author's showmanship leads him to overstress the part played by ritual in the judicial pronouncements of our legal and economic priesthood. The picturesqueness of his farce, for instance, is greatly heightened, at the expense of interpretive accuracy, by playing down the factor of *interests* behind the continual shifting of principles and ideals. Suppose, for example, you were to give a general picture summarizing, through the course of American history, the continual shifting back and forth between state's rights and federalism. You would find the same group on one side of the issue one day and on the other side the next. Then suppose that, for purposes of farce, you simply made a composite picture of all such shifting. By simply playing up the verbal and logical contradictions, and playing down the consistent pressure of the interests behind them, you might put on a good show that entertained by making people look extremely irrational. But your result at this point would be more valuable as entertainment than as diagnosis.

When reading Arnold's composite picture of such endless shifting, and hearing him explain it by stressing it as a purely ritualistic act, you make a paradoxical discovery.

You find that a man who continually refers such antics to the pressure of interests, no matter how mean these interests may be, would actually enable you to receive a much less desolating picture of human motives than the one Arnold paints. For you at least have a process essentially rational, however complicated it may become as the result of other factors. But Arnold's version of human motivation, by attributing mainly to ritual the cause of men's "inconsistent, irrational, and illogical" shifts in thinking, makes even downright hypocrisy on the part of our reactionaries seem an almost wholesome motive, by comparison.

Arnold justifies his farce on ritual in an appealing way, I must admit. He contends that history, being it dramatic process, must be approached as drama. And since ritual is an aspect of drama, we seem to get from such a view a justifiable ground for playing up the ritualistic and playing down the factor of interests in his picture of the human drama. The deception here arises, I think, from the fact that Arnold does not base his dramatic metaphor upon a preparatory analysis of drama itself. A couple of passing references to hero and villain in melodrama, with passing references to the dramatic nature of trial by combat in the law court, are the nearest he comes to explicit dramatic criticism, as a basis for the remarks about drama and ritual that flicker about the edge of his book throughout. As it is, you get here a glancing reference to art without an explicit study and philosophy of art.

The dramatist is not only a ritualist. Or rather, ritual itself is not merely a lot of passes in the air. The dramatic ritual *materializes,* and does so by reference to an audience's interests. Arnold is apparently a rationalist who has simply kicked over the traces, getting a flat irrationalist antithesis. His version of drama is simply legal principle in reverse. In going from the *ideals* of law to drama, he got farce (*i.e.,* legal ideals turned upside down). Had he begun with drama, I think that both the uses and misuses of law could have fallen into place, with more definite relation to the rational pressure of interests.

Toward the end of the book there is a noticeable chastening, as Arnold begins to feel the necessity for a more positive statement. So, what in his earlier work he had made ludicrous, as principles, and in the earlier portion of this one is taken for a ride as abstract ideals, is subsequently restored to good favor, by an apparently unconscious subterfuge, in the name of propositions and a philosophy. Thus, to keep his universal corrosive from corroding everything, he must cheat a bit. So he resorts to a little contraband, as he begins to discern the fact that not only do organizations play their part in twisting ideals, but also that ideals play their part in guiding the rise of new organizations. But they are brought back, not as ideals, since that would spoil the symmetry of his book (he had already made perfect hash of ideals). So he brings them back in the name of propositions, thereby saving face.

All told, there are several counter-movements going on at once in this book, as is probably inevitable in an investigation of this sort at this time. And Arnold's great respect for administrative tribunals in contrast with courts very well might, if carried out, tend to perfect and regularize an N.R.A. economic structure that perpetuated the present privileged status of business leaders rather than deposing them. On this point, however, the book is vague, since there is also a general tendency favoring the increase of political government's activity, which would probably entail a corresponding atrophy of private, business government. Such elements in the book are as uncertain as they are in the contemporary scene itself. In short, the vacillations in the book reflect the present economic conflicts, so that *The Folklore of Capitalism* is more valuable in picturing for disintegrative purposes the breach between capitalism's slogans and capitalism's realities than in developing a positive program. But the main reason why I think it should be read is for its shrewd comments on the practices of both our business leaders and their ideological priesthood. The book is certainly not to be considered an alternative to Marxism, as many reviewers have proposed; but if read by readers who discount it from the angle of a Marxist critique, it is very serviceable indeed.

# The Work of Regeneration

*Angel in the Forest: A Fairy Tale of Two Utopias* by Marguerite Young. Reynal and Hitchcock
*The Kenyon Review*, Autumn 1945, 696–700

If you happen to be at all interested in those ambiguities of motive whereby religious calling is implicit in the secular, you might well find *Angel in the Forest* an engrossing book. Here is a somewhat destiny-laden record of two American Utopias: the first avowedly supernatural in its ideas of human purpose, aiming at a kind of "Scriptural communism," and organized about a profound belief in the unworthiness of sexual union; the second programmatically renouncing religion for a man-made heaven on earth, denying above all else the doctrine of original sin, proclaiming the pursuit of earthly happiness to be the "primary and necessary object of all existence," holding that such happiness "cannot be individually obtained" but is essentially communal, and promising that by an organized cult of equality there will be formed "a terrestrial paradise . . . in which harmony will pervade all that will exist upon the earth, and there will be none to hurt or destroy throughout the whole extent of its boundaries."

You will have here a good opportunity to contemplate the exquisite scruples of the turn from sacrificial motives (under the sign of Redemption) to the "scientific" promises of Progress. In an age that is being taught to value most the "streamlined," I am obstinately becoming more and more convinced that the books best worth our attention are not the "sweeping" and the "powerful," but those over which we may ponder. And I salute *Angel in the Forest* for being a work of this meditative sort.

The material itself is so intrinsically engrossing, Miss Young's stylistic prettification of it often seems obtrusive. But one's resistance is likely to be strongest at the outset; in time one surrenders to the moodiness of her treatment, allowing it, for better or worse, to become the norm within the conditions of the chronicle. There are many motivational possibilities one yearns to see considered more systematically. And this desire is frustrated by Miss

Young's poetizings, which lend themselves to the evasiveness of the Whitmanesque catalogue, the apparent summarizing quality of lists alphabetically scrambled ("taverns, banks, gallows, ancient dynasties, undertakers, numerous patriarchs, fortresses, churches, bride-wells, preachers who read the Bible upside down, slave ships from Guinea, meaningless rebellions, whores of Babylon, vultures, manias for land speculation," and so on, for a surprisingly much longer stretch).

Though many stages before and after are considered, the book centers about the comparing and contrasting of the Rappite community (found in Harmony, Indiana, at the beginning of the 19th Century) with its Owenite successor, New Harmony. George Rapp had brought to America his band of pious German peasants, inspirited with the theory that "Adam, before he fell, was possessed of both sexual elements, the male and female conjoined. He was, in that pristine state, himself a horn of plenty, himself a receptacle, who might have reproduced without the adjunct of woman." Such rationalizations as these lay behind Father Rapp's distrust of woman so that, in his zeal, he had exacted a vow of chastity from all his band, even those already married, considering it far preferable that the human race perish from this world. And when his own son thereafter got his wife with child, the inexorable leader caused the boy's death by castration.

The irony which Miss Young convincingly builds up for us involves the great worldly plenty which the devout, in their austere abnegation, amassed for the colony ("the product of a marvelously fecund nature, operated by celibates, who believed all things fleeting but themselves, the instrument of God"). Their communistic renunciation of private property had, as its counterpart, the complete personal ownership of the enterprise by George Rapp. And when his adopted son, Frederick, helped frame the first Constitution of the State of Indiana, "a communist, a celibate, a slave of God, and a millenniast, he voted in favor of capitalistic banking laws, property laws, family arrangements, schooling, freedom from slavery black or white, the future world of imperfections, yea, of delusive hopes, of fountains yielding both salt water and sweet."

Yet there is no evidence that the colony itself, despite its trade in capitalistic markets, was capitalistically motivated, unless perhaps in reverse, as Rapp, having made Harmony highly prosperous, of a sudden decided to abandon it. He moved elsewhere with his entire flock, to undertake the solemn upbuilding all over again. "The idea of power required expression," Miss Young suggests, "continual conquest over the enemy, continual moving on. For this community's perpetuation, there had to be a wilderness proportionate to their objective and a feeling of nameless fears." One glimpses another possibility here, that might modify or reinforce Miss Young's tentative suggestion: that the removal took place because Rapp had reached a stage in his own spiritual development where such a change was necessary; that the entire colony was held together as a function of his personality. They were vowed to chastity as a reflex of his imposing the vow of chastity upon himself; and might they similarly have been required to undergo the rigors of a second transplanting ("the destruction within and the construction without") when Rapp himself was ready for this change in the symbolism of his own motives? Such are the ready possibilities with those who look upon the world "as a field of stubble burning."

Whatever the motives may have been, Rapp returned with his followers to Pennsylvania, where he founded the new community of Economy, having sold the site and equipment of Harmony to Robert Owen for $150,000. In his theories of social motivation, Miss Young reminds us, Owen, the philanthropic mill-owner of New Lanark, Scotland, stood midway between the French Revolution and the dialectical materialism of Marxist revolutionary socialism. Believing in the innate goodness, or at least the innate non-badness, of man, dissatisfied with the "division of the human race into nationalities, classes, sects, families," looking upon religion as a survival from savagery and as a modern method of enslavement (most notably in doctrines holding that class distinctions and the special privileges of private property represent the will of God), modifying his Utopian idealism by the materialist tenet that "to change human character, it is necessary only to change the circumstances," Owen set about to replace the servitude of Harmony with the freedom of New Harmony (a humanitarian freedom that was, in, one sense, corrective to capitalism, and in another sense typically capitalist).

Miss Young relates for us, with sympathetic irony, the embarrassments of this freedom. Indeed, besides treating the internal difficulties, she gives us an account of the resistance that the Owenite doctrine encountered from without, resistances that took forms relevant to conditions with us at present. "Physicians on the payrolls of cotton lords swore before Parliament that if children perished in the cotton mills, it was because their bodies were constitutionally weak to begin with." Similarly the supervision of the cotton mills was left to officials on the payrolls of the manufacturers. The Malthusians were vigorously proclaiming that such "natural means" as war and poverty, were necessary to keep the population down. Irish priests decried reforms on the grounds that "the greater the suffering, the greater the vision of good." And Mme. Tussaud was persuaded by her Jesuit confessor not to make a wax likeness of Owen for her Museum. "She might have as many murderers as she liked, but no infidels."

We witness the many idealistic oddities of personality that gravitated about the Owenite venture in America. Thus there was a Mr. Bakeweli, who followed it closely because he intended to found "a community of glass blowers, all blowing glass, all equal." (I even dare wonder whether his project may have been an ideal way of materializing his own name.) Another, who attributed the word's downfall to the "flowers of rhetoric," proposed "to drown the self in an ocean of sociality." Another had a rational project for the proper naming of cities, so that the sheer structure of the name would indicate the location. A committee was appointed to consider the matter:

> New Harmony, 38.11 N, 87.33 W, received, accordingly, its rational name—Ipba Veinul. New York emerged as Otfu Native, Pittsburgh as Otfu Vietoup, Washington as Feili Neivul, London as Lafa Vovotu.

The project was clearly far ahead of its day; yet it did come into use in the life of New Harmony itself; for when one group of schismatics separated from the mother colony, "they called their community Feiba Peveli, a name denoting latitude and longitude, whereby they could be located between the last of the hop fields and the old Rappite bull pasture."

"Alas! how many islands this world contains!" the author exclaims—after she has shown us so many of them, eagerly seeking to be a single continent. Fittingly, we find Robert Owen himself, in his later years, finally coming upon a world of supernatural motives, as communicated to hint through spiritualist mediums, until he became convinced that "Were it not for these new and most extraordinary manifestations, there would arise a conflict between the evil spirits of democracy and aristocracy, which would deluge the world with blood, and would create universal violence and slaughter among all nations." Yet his spiritualism was "only a restatement of his socialist teachings—to unite all hearts."

Rounding out her friendly irony, Miss Young inserts two semi-symbolic figures into her chronicle: an undertaker, who is for life; and a sewer cleaner (Glaucas, 1940) who is in New Harmony but not of it, "the only man who ever goes down and comes up again" (except, let us hope, those of us who, with our authoress as guide, follow this deathy narrative of the better life). And finally there is a miller, who holds that no two millers can make the same flour: "The flour from one miller will seem like the flour from another, but a chemical test will always show that there is a great chasm, caused by something so slight that nobody can name it, nobody can catch hold of it."

Miss Young, you may have observed, does not quite commit herself (except perhaps in an assumption, and a dubious one, that nationalism and humanitarianism are opposite Motives). She has not given us a book in which the motivational strands are quite clear. But she has given us a book in the motives of which one can become quite resonantly lost. She has thus done amply for one book, having written what is both a somewhat playful and a profoundly serious piece of work.

# The Carrot and the Stick, or

*How Much by Promise, How Much by Threat? or*
*What's Loose in the World? or*
*Does Man Demand a Goat? or*
*What of Bunyan's Compulsive Slogan, "Sell him, sell him!"? or*
*See How, Like a Hurricane, It Goes Forward While Going Round and Round*

*Battle for the Mind* by William Sargant. Doubleday
*The Hidden Persuaders* by Vance Packard. David McKay
*The Organization Man* by William H. Whyte, Jr. Simon and Schuster
*The Hudson Review*, Winter 1957–1958, 627–633

First, of *Battle for the Mind, A Physiology of Conversion and Brain-Washing*—, or, as per the jacket: "How Evangelists, Psychiatrists, Politicians and Medicine Men can change your beliefs and behavior." The author, William Sargant, a "physician in psychological medicine," is not concerned "with the truth or falsity of any particular religious or political belief." His purpose is "to examine the physiological mechanisms involved in the fixing or destroying of such beliefs in the human brain."

His theory concerns ways of influencing the "mind" by physically affecting the "brain." Or, Dramatistically stated: Starting from Pavlov's experiments with the conditioning of dogs, he asks how symbolic action can be controlled through the medium of physical motion. For instance, there are purely physical means by which one can increase human suggestibility, most notably drugs and exhaustion.

From the standpoint of Aristotelian Rhetoric, a "physiology" of indoctrination would involve the use of "inartificial proofs," a variant of such "persuasion" as is got by torture, even when outright physical pressures such as flogging, burning, or the rack are avoided.

Though it contains nothing essentially new, the book is full of morbid marvels. And though the reader, before beginning it, thought of himself as fairly obstinate in his beliefs, after reading it he will be considerably chastened. At least, I had the feeling that, within a "reasonably" short time, anyone who used these methods of "persuasion" on me could have me eating obediently out of his hand, or salivating as ecstatically at a painful electric shock as I might now do at the savor of a good steak.

Among the marvels was an incidental story of a non-believer who attended the meetings of a religious snake-handling cult, and before he was discovered, managed to engineer several easy seductions. There is a photograph of a young woman, in a frenzy of surrender, placing her hands upon a poisonous snake. True, she has no relation to the story of the non-believer; but when viewing her rapt expression caught in the photograph, we can understand how profound are the resistances which have been broken down, once one has brought oneself to yield in an act so antithetical to one's "normal" responses. And conceivably, immediately after such radical relaxation, more ordinary resistances would also be weakened, between the time of such "cleansing" and the time when the leader of the cult had doctrinally re-established them.

But whereas the author convincingly describes many purely physical devices and operations for the forming and reforming of attitudes, with corresponding effect upon ideas, I still doubt whether his book is as exclusively physiological in its emphasis as he would have us and himself believe. For instance, his chapter on Wesley's methods of conversion deals with the power of the word as such, to build up, by sheer eloquence, first the dread of hell's fire and then the promise of redemption, with the resources of social organization next being employed to prevent back-sliding. Such procedures, it seems to me, concern the "symbol-using animal" as such, and are not reducible to sheer physiological conditioning. Similarly, in the discussion of "brain-washing," it is noted how the sense of guilt is built up in a person not by accusing him of anything, but by using various kinds of quietus (such as forbidding him to tell anyone about the interviews to which he is being subjected) which finally induce him to work up accusations against himself.

One can grasp the difference between symbolic and purely physical persuasion by quoting against the author a statement of Jonathan Edwards which he quotes as though it were on his side. Edwards regularly brought about conversion by seeking to make as intense as possible the sinner's sense of guilt, before finally offering him solace in the name of Christ. On this point, Edwards writes:

> Another thing that some ministers have been greatly blamed for, and I think unjustly, is speaking terror to those who are already under great terrors, instead of comforting them . . .
> To blame a minister for thus declaring the truth to those

> who are under awakening, and not immediately administering comfort to them, is like blaming a surgeon, because, when he has begun to thrust in his lance, whereby he has already put his patient to great pain, and he shrinks and cries out with anguish, he is so cruel that he will not stay his hand, but goes on to thrust it in further, till he comes to the core of the wound.

Actually, the similitude here should be interpreted in the light of the *difference* between such surgery, which is purely physiological, and Edwards' metaphorical probing along the lines of dramatic catharsis.

To speak of "probing" is to hit upon a perfect transition into *The Hidden Persuaders,* by Vance Packard, "An Introduction to the New World of Symbol Manipulation and Motivational Research," an inquiry into "What Makes Us Buy, Believe—and Even Vote—The Way We Do." In the course of his comically gruesome study, Mr. Packard has read so many advertising slogans, his style has a kind of billboard epigrammatic briskness, as indicated in his chapter headings, for instance: "The Depth Approach," "Self-Images for Everybody," "The Built-In Sexual Overtone," "Back to the Breast, and Beyond," "The Psycho-Seduction of Children," "The Engineered Yes," "Care and Feeding of Positive Thinkers," and "The Packaged Soul?"

Whereas in *Battle for the Mind,* persuasion was approached in terms of Pavlovian conditioning, here it is approached in terms of Madisonian *salesmanship.* More specifically, the book is concerned with the use of "depth psychology" in the marketing of goods and ideas. Readers who love to contemplate mild variants of diabolism should certainly take a look at it, though most of the scheming here studied has to do with the respectable, everyday Madison Avenue job of keeping the citizenry madly at work producing and consuming the largely unnecessary things with which the combination of business, industry, politics, miseducation, and our fast dwindling natural resources is now able, and even compelled, to flood us. By miseducation, in that line-up, I could very often mean simply advertising, as the author's particular collection of cultural horrors makes amply evident.

The work adds up to a proposition of this sort: How to sell everything for some reason other than the use for which it is pragmatically designed? For instance, don't sell a car simply for the purpose of efficient, reasonably priced transportation. Sell it to patch up some poor devil's inferiority complex (though at the same time, of course, you must keep his inferiority complex squirming vigorously, so that you may soon sell him another car for psychological reasons and before he pragmatically needs a replacement).

In fact, to read this book is to wonder where in the devil our national pragmatism (whether vaunted or maligned) has gone. You see the "Depth" people transforming every material commodity into some kind of *symbol*, and selling it, not for its material usefulness, but for some real or supposed *symbolic* value with which, by their schemings, they can manage to identify it. For instance, inasmuch as there are dozens of soaps on the market capable of keeping you clean, obviously one soap manufacturer can't compete against another simply on the grounds that his soap is a cleanser. Hence, "depth" probing, to discover some sales angle that, whereas it might apply to all brands of soap, could by astute advertising slogans be associated with a particular brand.

To get the cream of the book, look at the index and follow all the references to one Ernest Dichter, who must be consulted on a high hill, whither his devotees repair for sales advice, reportedly at $500 per diem. Presumably, said "earnest poet" has it all figured out this way: When confronting this mighty pile of junk (called "the higher standard of living") which is offered us daily in untold acts of persuasion, we find ourselves acquisitively goaded. But even while greedily wanting all we can get, we have vestiges of Puritanic guilt which require that our greed be moralized.

Thus, for instance, if you would induce a man to buy a car by identifying the horsepower of the car with a thereby symbolically aggrandized power within himself, you should also find some slogan that would justify the purchase on a "moral" basis, as were you to say that the extra horse-power would give "that added margin of safety." Or, when the depth-prober has found that people associate candy with the idea of reward (as a result of childhood experiences, when they were given candy for "being good") then you might buck the low-calorie slogans by presenting candy as something one can allow oneself after a hard day's work.

Primarily, this book is dealing with the manipulation of symbols (and usually to such an extent, you tend to forget that very many of the commodities you here see being sold by tricks could also be recommended on purely rational grounds). As symbol-manipulation, it is in the field of rhetorical artifice, generally outside the physiological emphasis of the Sargant volume. Yet, ironically, the most gruesomely winsome story of all leans towards the Sargant side:

> *The London Sunday Times* front-paged a report in mid-1956 that certain United States advertisers were experimenting with "subthreshold effects" in seeking to insinuate sales messages to people past their conscious guard. It cited the case of a cinema in New Jersey that it said was flashing

ice-cream ads onto the screen during regular showings of film. These flashes of message were split-second, too short for people in the audience to recognize them consciously but still long enough to be absorbed unconsciously.

A result, it reported, was a clear and otherwise unaccountable boost in ice-cream sales. "Subthreshold effects, both in vision and sound, have been known for some years to experimental psychologists," the paper explained. It speculated that political indoctrination might be possible without the subject being conscious of any influence being brought to bear on him.

Though the author says that this story is not yet authenticated, it stands as the ultimate "scientific" ideal of the principle of hidden persuasion. It is, to perfection, the sort of thing "depth" advertisers are looking for. I love to contemplate the idea, and to think that probably I'm getting my daily dose of subthreshold indoctrination along with my daily dose of invisible fall-out.*

Mr. Packard shows us how anthropologists, sociologists, psychologists and the like are willing to contribute their best, or their worst, towards the prodding of the citizenry into unintelligent voting and improvident purchases, thereby enlisting science in a cause in which the arts had already long been active. *The Organization Man,* by William H. Whyte, Jr., also touches considerably on this same point. This book is concerned with "the clash between the individualistic beliefs" which the Organization Man is "supposed

---

\* Since the time when this review was written, many reports have been published confirming the authenticity of the *London Times* story. In *The Wall Street Journal* of September 13, 1957, the firm is said to be the Subliminal Projection Company, its founder "a motivational researcher and amateur psychologist who heads his own New York firm specializing in the naming of new products." The company is said to have applied for a patent on the idea, though, if the patent is granted, "it would be a bit like Sigmund Freud getting a patent on his discoveries in the field of psychoanalysis." The article also refers to an experiment where a blank human face was shown on a screen. Also the words "angry" or "happy" were projected, but only in a flash, for a mere fraction of a second, an interval too brief for conscious recording. "The subjects tended to see the face as either angry or happy depending on what word was superimposed on it at the time."

I have also been informed that hearings are being held in Washington to discuss the advisability or possibility of making such enterprises illegal. The thought suggests the somewhat complicated notion that investors in this kind of project should hurry and flood the country with subthreshold suggestions designed to enlist legislators and the public against all Anti-Subliminalism. [K.B.]

to follow" and the "collective life he actually lives." Also, it tentatively evaluates "his search for a faith to bridge the gap." But though such a "damnably inoffensive" Organization Man is typically employed in big corporations that are designed wholly to sell their goods and services to the public, and is apparently a perfect specimen of *homo emptor* (an ideal victim for the wiles of the motivational researcher, down to the last twitch of "impulse buying"), we are assured that the sales department ranks very low in his esteem. Thus, whereas the first book treated of dogs and people in *extremis;* and whereas the second is concerned with efforts at high-powered goading under conditions in which the difference between the buying or non-buying of an unneeded commodity can mean the difference between the success or failure of the seller; the poignancy of this third book is of a different order. For the author seems to fear most that the class he has chosen to study (and in which he classes himself) is in danger of rotting from conformity to the policies of corporations that have the personality of benevolent overlords.

From the standpoint of my own notions about rhetoric, I would say that this third book shifts the emphasis from persuasion to identification. For it is concerned with the ways in which a class of sub-executives both spontaneously identify themselves with the company they work for and are selected by personnel directors who, with the help of personality tests, seek to make such identification the be-all and end-all of the "trainees'" lives.

Since the tendency is for the Organization Man to be given and to demand the kind of education that most directly reinforces his adulation of the status quo, Mr. Whyte would advocate instead a stress upon a counter-principle: he would have education act as a corrective of the trend rather than being merely more of the same thing.

Though we are long accustomed to studies in competitive conformity, Mr. Whyte's analysis is done with all the latest paraphernalia, and makes for entertaining scientific gossip. Here is a novelistic kind of observation, with many illustrative anecdotes well told, and with some broad sociological generalizations serving as the cast of characters.

The book is built around a dialectic posing a contrast between what he calls a "Protestant Ethic" and a "Social Ethic." The Protestant Ethic is equated with the competitive stress involved in the kind of work by which the founders of our big corporations built them. The Social Ethic is equated with the cooperative stress involved in the kind of work done by the "trainees" who now oversee the bureaucratic functions of the corporation. Since there is also the dialectical fact that competition involves cooperation and v.v., by the time you have finished the book the edges of this distinction have necessarily become somewhat blurred. However, predominantly, the author distrusts the attitudes of "acceptance" that go with such "bureaucratization." He calls for more questioning, less automatic tendency to assume that a working force should be one big happy family. And he skilfully backs his observations with enough surveys to floor you in case you needed to be floored.

In an appendix, the author tells you how to cheat on personality tests so that, in case the would-be Organization Man happens to have a spark of originality, independence, or temperamental zing, he can conceal the fact from his scientific inquisitors and can get the job on the basis of a score that makes him look quite non-controversially inane and sheeplike. It's a gallant idea; but the more closely I studied his advice, the more convinced I became that the science of screening out all but the lulus, if that's what the customer wants, is now close to perfection. Most of the spirited people I know would be tricked into self-revelation despite the author's rules of thumb.

All told, the book's comments on ways in which the imaginative aspects of science are being bureaucratized are quite relevant, though he is somewhat caught in his own traps. And just having done some work on Bunyan, I'd say that Mr. Whyte's views on the "Protestant Ethic" are outrageously skimpy.* Similarly, though he identifies "acceptance" with the improvised protocol and etiquette-mongering of his Organization Man, the term can legitimately have ampler meanings, as when applied to writers like Emerson, Whitman, and William James.

In any case, if you're interested in this damned business of motives, which, I must admit, exercises me considerably, these books are all worth looking into. As regards motivational problems in general, I don't feel that any of the books approaches the subject from a sufficiently comprehensive point of view. They all gravitate towards "science" in the specialized sense rather than towards "poetry and philosophy." Yet each does bring out a different basic motivational strand. The first helps remind us how much the body affects our thinking, the second helps remind us that even the most physical of powers can be sought for furtively symbolic purposes, the third shows how imperious an "occupational psychosis" can be, in forming a way of life, and setting up *ad interim* goals that look like final goals.

*Addendum (a few days later):* Now I know a major point I overlooked. Pavlov found that the identical degree of stimulus, when applied to different dogs, elicits different or even opposite responses. This would be a way of saying, in a scientistic parable, that one man's food is another man's poison.

---

* A study of the "hierarchal" motive in Bunyan helps us see how, midway between the two meanings of "noble" (the literal and the figurative) and the two similar meanings of "rich," lay the Puritan paradox whereby the conviction of one's great personal sinfulness testified to one's election. [K.B.]

The thought would suggest the strong possibility that, the more uniform an ideology, the more likely it is to produce resistances on the part of some persons subjected to it. The thought is both heartening and disheartening.

It is heartening insofar as it implies that people will never line up all alike, no matter how skilled the techniques for lining them up and standardizing them. But by the same token it is disheartening insofar as it implies that any pronounced regularity will produce its particular kind of deviation, its special brand of "criminals" (the Ins by one set of rules being the Outs by another). It's like saying that, if a room is stuffy, one person gets drowsy and another throws open a window.

This principle probably applies to education, too. In searching for an ideal system of education, we imply that the same approach would be good for all. Yet what one man gets beaten into him, another gets beaten out of him. And insofar as there are no beatings, one man flourishes from lack of threats where another rots in response to the overly permissive.

All the year round, mankind is an open season. And may the experiments of the physicist, as modified by the military, permit the experiments of the humanist to continue (if fittingly humbled by experience). Spare us the effects of a "progress" from the fall of Adam to the atomic fall-out.

# Democracy of the Sick

*Freud: The Mind of the Moralist* by Philip Rieff. Viking
*The Kenyon Review*, Autumn 1959, 639–643

"In the emergent democracy of the sick," Rieff writes, near the end of his book on Freud as moralist, "everyone can to some extent play doctor to others, and none is allowed the temerity to claim that he can definitively cure or be cured. The hospital is succeeding the church and the parliament as the archetypal institution of Western culture."

Successively in the West, he says, there have been "three character ideals." First there was the ideal of "political man, formed and handed down to us from classical antiquity"; second, the "religious man, formed and handed down to us from Judaism through Christianity"; third, "economic man, the very model of our liberal civilization, formed and handed down to us in the Enlightenment." And now comes a new dominant type, "psychological man," turning from "might" and "right" to "insight," withdrawing "into a world always at war, where the ego is an armed force capable of achieving armistices but not peace." (Rieff lays much stress upon the Stoicism of Freud's attitude, the conviction that at best human discord can be mitigated.)

The Western concern with "self-contemplative manipulation" has come to the fore just at the time "when the Orient, whose westernmost outpost is Russia, has adopted the Occidental ideal of saving activity." And thus, to quote the author's closing words, "Aware at last that he is chronically ill, psychological man may nevertheless end the ancient quest of his predecessors for a healing doctrine. His experience with the latest one, Freud's, may finally teach him that every cure must expose him to a new illness."

This closing sentence is but a special case of the dialectical notion that any "solution" can form basis of a new "problem." And in his "Song of the Open Road," Whitman even found a way of stating the same idea in the accents of a promise: "Now understand me well—it is provided in the essence of things that from any fruition of success, no matter what, shall come forth something to make a greater struggle necessary."

In any event, "psychological man" is "a child not of nature but of technology," a "trained egoist, the private man who turns away from the arenas of public failure to re-examine himself and his emotions." Whereat "Freudian psychology, with its ingenious interpretations of politics, religion, and culture in terms of the individual and his immediate family experiences, exactly filled the bill."

However, for all Rieff's sympathy with "Freud's own unsentimental attitude towards himself, as the first out-patient of the hospital of culture in which we live" (at another point he calls it "medical egoism"), perhaps we could best bring out the virtues of this book by presenting its "thesis" in a slightly different light. Having for some time been much interested in the ways in which problems of "tautology" beset the social sciences, I find *Freud: The Mind of the Moralist* primarily valuable for the light it helps shed upon this problem. Much that passes for "objective observation" in the social sciences is but a systematic way of working out the implications of a given investigator's terminology. Along these lines, for instance, we might say that Rieff's own talk of "psychological man" as a new "character ideal" might be rephrased thus: In previous eras, human relations have been interpreted by reduction successively to terms of politics, religion, and economics; Freud proposes to discuss them in terms of individuals whose origin as infants in a family makes them mentally ill. The "tautological" element enters by reason of the fact that the nature of the seeker's terms determines what he shall find. That is, a "psychopathology of everyday life" would be implicit in the very nature of such a terminology. Terms are like a photographic color filter; the object is real enough, and so is the photograph of the object—nevertheless, the appearance of the object changes, depending upon the particular nature of the color filter in terms of which it is photographed.

I think that Rieff's book is wonderful, in its perceptive and scholarly analysis of the Freudian terminology. And the analysis points always in the direction which seems to me necessary, if we are to understand the limitations—as well as the virtues—of a vocabulary that defines the problems of symbolic action so predominantly in terms of dream, neurosis, the infantile, and the prehistoric (with astounding vagaries of equitability among these four orders). The especially opaque fogs of "prehistory" are sometimes treated as motivationally the most real of all, despite the fact that they are completely outside the field of observation; and anything that one says about them can not be "evidence," but concerns merely inferences implicit in the nature of the terminology that is serving as one's interpretative screen. Such "observations" are sheerly dialectical operations, like a metaphysician's speculations on the nature of God. But Freud's rhetoric is so vigorous, it gives his idealistic fictions (his "scientific myths") the appearance of great materiality. Thus, what might in logic be called a fallacy of *obscurum per obscurius* (proving the obscure by the more obscure), persuades by its constant reference to things so "simple" and "real" as children and human bodies, with their corresponding "psychic energies." Freud is among the world's greatest dialecticians; and the rhetoric with which he backed his dialectic is particularly remarkable in that, while appealing *poetically* to our imagination, it is nominally "scientific."

Rieff approaches Freud's writings with reference to their place in the Western tradition as a whole rather than to psychology in particular. Notably he considers their relation to philosophical romanticism. There is a strategic undertone of reference to Nietzsche, though "From the *Autobiographical Study* we learn that he had deliberately abstained from reading Nietzsche for fear of becoming less original." (Five of the ten chapters in this book are introduced by quotations from Nietzsche.) In all, Rieff characterizes and discusses with considerable astuteness: the emergence of Freud's theories out of a strong physiological emphasis; the strictly humanistic aspect of Freudian "science"; the integral relation between conflict and character (involving a "theory of the prototype" which Rieff handles well, but not so thoroughly as necessary if we are to get a full understanding of Freud's devices for translating essential motivational principles into terms of the temporally prior); the "hidden self" (in which "conscience, not passion, emerges as the last enemy of reason," while all resistance to psychoanalysis is taken as *prima facie* evidence of neurosis); problems of interpretation (involving Freud's "tendency to read a maximum purposiveness into every psychic act," as with the female patient "who dreamed *without* wish fulfillment in order, Freud says, to fulfill the wish that he be shown wrong in his theory that every dream can be explained as a wish-fulfillment"); the ambiguous relations between sexuality and dominance (whereby, since "Authority is Freud's basic problem," psychoanalytic treatment becomes "the therapeutic parody of authority," "a mock warfare of loves, a 'new edition of the old disease'"—the whole resulting in "paradoxes" of the analyst's role as authoritarian in order to break the hold of authority, ascetic in order to cure asceticism, while aiming to make patients attached in order to make them detached); the varying guises of authority, in family, politics, religion, ethics (though "Freud deplored the sense of dependence most people feel in regard to some higher being," Rieff agrees with his "insight" that "the 'love' which the therapist might bestow upon the patient cannot be disentangled from the relation of 'a superior and a subordinate' which analysis presupposes in every erotic relation"); and finally, the emergence of "psychological man."

This book is so meticulous, a review should go from page to page, discussing each remark in turn. But from an overall point of view, we might settle on this issue, where Rieff sums up Freud's grounds for a stress upon the individual: "Both society and the individual psyche depend for their formation on the characteristic actions of individuals engaged first, and thereafter by symbolic repetition, in family life." Whereupon Rieff adds: "Concerning such a fundamental topic of investigation as the powers of reasoning (e.g., of deducing similarity, sequence, number, abstraction) he has no theory at all."

Inasmuch as language, by the nature of the case, emerges out of the "infantile" (that is, the "speechless"), it is hard to see how Freud's speculations regarding the speechless side of this notable human transition could ever come to seem irrelevant, particularly since there is so much of a "collective revelation" incorporated in his lore (as with the material from myth, poetry, and popular usage which said in one way what he has said in another, and which he thus can use as a kind of inductive authority, like quoting a proverb to justify some highly complex and abstruse train of thought).

Freud has characterized so many human foibles, he has made a permanent contribution to the human comedy. And there is the central appeal of his concern with the Erotic, his idea of which is continually expanding and contracting with almost physiological pliancy. But the very scope of his theories must make it increasingly more apparent why an approach to speech in terms of speechlessness is a bit too paradoxical for any but admonitory purposes. There are two problems here: There is a sense in which even the most mature use of language may be a kind of "dreaming," and a kind of "sickness." But there is also a qualitative difference between the articulate and the infantile (or between the "Conscious" and the "Unconscious") whereby terminologies that treat of one field in terms of the other are necessarily parodies. All language can split, multiply, condense, displace, substitute, censor, repress, sublimate, and the like, quite as dream-symbolism does. Also, as Rieff points out, whatever a dream may be in the original experiencing of it, it is exclusively a reduction to verbal terms when it gets to the analyst's couch. And as a matter of fact, there are the equivalents of those various verbal operations in even the non-symbolic realm of sheer motion (or, at least, that's how natural processes seem to man, who must define them in the dual terms of sensation and dialectic). My point is: The areas of overlap do not justify us in taking the reduction to dream, neurosis, the infantile, and the mythically "prehistoric" as the essentially "real" one.

Reading Rieff's book, one will find ample evidence to distrust the Freudian claims to a "science" of psychology. Though Rieff could round out his position by a more systematic concern with terministic problems as such, his book is amply supplied with observations pointing in this direction. However, while holding that psychoanalysis "cannot meet the rigid standards of scientific theory," he would nonetheless celebrate Freud's "wide range and subtlety, his unsurpassed brilliance as an exegete of the universal language of pain and suffering, his willingness to pronounce judgments and draw out the evidence for them from his own life as well as from clinical data." In sum: "For humanists in science, and for scientists of the human, Freud should be the model of a concern with the distinctively human that is truly scientific."

But this review hasn't turned out just right. It has not communicated the fact that I found the book engrossing. Few books are written with greater attentiveness to their subject, attentiveness not merely in the sense of characterization, but also in the sense of exact and exacting critical observation. The trouble is that Rieff's analysis is so alive to the major issues involved in the Freudian terminology, one is tempted to join in, whereupon uncertainty arises as to just when the reviewer is agreeing with the author and when he is tossing in some notions of his own. But the main point is: that the author's attitude toward his subject is both responsive and responsible—and the reader who wants to meditate on these matters will find in Rieff much keen and cautious guidance.

# Religion

*The subject of religion falls under the head of rhetoric in the sense that rhetoric is the art of persuasion, and religious cosmogonies are designed, in the last analysis, as exceptionally thoroughgoing modes of persuasion.*

—*The Rhetoric of Religion: Studies in Logology* (i)

# Fides Quaerens Intellectum

*The Religion of Plato* by Paul Elmer More. Princeton UP
*The Dial*, May 1922, 527–530

In a study of past intellectual currents, there are two elements involved. First, there is simple exegesis. And, second, there is the application of one's exegesis to contemporary conditions. In *The Religion of Plato,* then, Mr. More has sat down to trace for us how some of the most spiritual elements of Plato have added to Christianity. And his applied thesis is that an age which can neglect such spiritual considerations with a few specious sophisms is an inferior age. Plato is an adequate text for such contentions. The tracing of Plato's influences is a matter of study and comparison; while the position of Plato among the Sophists is quite patently that of a master among thumb-twiddlers, a man with enough fire and affirmation to renounce at all costs his clever contemporaries. Further, comparisons between the Sophists and present-day attitudes have become well recognized. Concerning the first contention we shall say nothing, especially since Mr. More's program involves at least three more volumes. It is the application to contemporary conditions which is by far the more exciting.

Mr. More, then, is combatting that specious logic whereby the gods can be looked upon as either non-existent or asleep, and which results in the characteristically Sophistic outlook on man as the measure of all things. One can, for instance, by observing that so many years ago women wore hoop-skirts and today they wear rolled-down stockings, affirm thereby the transitoriness of beauty. Or, by comparing the moral practices of India with those of Europe, one can inside of two minutes reach the logical conclusion that morality is nothing other than custom, and is thus not divine, but human. In some form or other, this is indubitably the contemporary point of view. One will find it held quite generally in colleges by the intellectual leaders of the Freshman class. Sweet young things will tell it to one in more or less lisping form. It is, in short, the first pale blush of thinking. Now, to preserve one's decency, one should certainly hold to other views, even at the expense of an absurdity. And it is precisely to an absurdity that Mr. More has recourse, offering it to us under the aegis of Plato. Pure logic, he says, will always lead to some such denial of standards; for a completely consistent universe involves the loss of the Good and Evil distinction, by tossing it among the cogs of causality.

But Plato refused to take just this step, as Mr. More will convince any one by his muster of quotations. The spiritual urge in him made him prefer an inconsistency in his rational system to the denial of absolute, or intrinsic, Good and Evil. And it is in this ultimate distrust of rationalism that Mr. More places the glory of Plato. While it was, further, precisely this distrust of rationalism which distinguished Plato from the Sophists.

Now, this categorical attack upon rationalism has one particularly unhappy feature. For by it, the intellectual Freshman mentioned above, Nietzsche, and the Sophists must be thrown into one indiscriminate heap with a philosopher like Spinoza. From Mr. More's point of view, all of them would pigeon-hole together: they all err when judged by the Christian ideal of humility. Thus, metaphysics becomes *per se* detestable, for it is the attempt to explain the universe consistently, and thus argues an unpardonable *hauteur* on the part of the human mind. The humble man, with his eye on God, will reach a point where consistency becomes too much for him, because his reason threatens to explain away any ultimate need of spiritual betterment. And he will sacrifice consistency to spirituality.

Now, if Mr. More finds this *hauteur* categorically opprobrious, it is hard to answer him in his own terms. To Spinoza, man's search was not for humility, but for mastery, and in this sense he might be united with Nietzsche as the enemy of *Sklavenmoral*. "*Et humanas actiones atque appetitus considerabo perinde, ac si quaestio de lineis, planes, alit de corporibus esset:* I shall treat of human actions and appetites as if it were a question of lines, planes, and solids." This is almost a triumphant program, and is in an entirely different channel of thought from that of the searcher after subjection. Still, one can point out that Spinoza's doctrine of intellectual domination is nothing other than the furthering of Plato's reasons-emotions-appetites division of the individual. For in such a division, both the appetites and the emotions become eschewed as troublesome, with the reason alone as the seat of a broad and placid outlook. Nietzsche should, of course, be allied with the Sophists, in that he made man the measure of all things, in that his attitude involved the death of God, and in that he could neglect any spiritual (read, "inhibitory") principle. But if the Sophists were smart, Nietzsche was pathetic, while Spinoza is a monument to his own philosophy, the contentment and constancy of his pursuit of it arguing that the intellect had really given him his mastery.

It is, in fact, just this emphasis on the reason which Nietzsche lacked and which places Spinoza, the rationalist, within such close range of Plato.

Mr. More, however, can see no difference between metaphysics and eristic, in spite of Plato's respect for Parmenides the metaphysician and his disrespect for the eristic Sophists. Both are abhorrent to him in that they deny the spiritual affirmation. That the rationalist metaphysician has invariably made some ethical aspiration the very centre of his system, Mr. More escapes rather high-handedly by speaking of the rationalist's "bastard" spiritually. To be consistent, then, is to be a bastard, while the inconsistent are unquestioned sons of deacons. *Fiat.*

Now, when we must approach excellence by such a tortuous method, it is time to question whether there is not some simpler approach. It may be found in examining the process of the philosopher. Scholastic philosophy, for instance, has named itself by the apt formula of *fides quaerens intellectum*, which might be translated as "an emotional predisposition seeking its parallel in logic." In this sense, there is no philosophy but scholastic philosophy, for in the very nature of things a philosophic attitude must precede the means of making this attitude logically cogent. Spinoza, in other words, began with the emotion of his metaphysics, with his *fides*, and then sought logical cogency, *intellectus*, in his method of geometrical demonstration. And in the same way Plato, insofar as he is a philosopher, has an emotional attitude which he will attempt to restate in the parallel terms of logic. Which, I believe, is a correctly pragmatic statement, and therefore in extremely bad taste.

The trouble with the pragmatists, however, lies elsewhere. It is chiefly in the fact that they attribute to their doctrines primarily an ethical content, whereas pragmatism—with its extreme emphasis on the creative—leads directly to aesthetics. If a system of ethic cannot be absolutely true, it can be absolutely beautiful. By the same fact, Dante or the *Summa Theologiae* of Thomas Aquinas may outlast the belief in Christianity. Which is simply saying that without the fear of hell, we can still have an eternal inheritance of beauty in some powerful description of hell. And that, without even remotely experiencing Spinoza's abstractions, we can continue to enjoy their hard logic. Thus, in the great triad of the good, the true, and the beautiful, both the good and the true are treated merely as subdivisions of the beautiful. Reversing Matthew Arnold's formulation of the artistic conscience, we speak of moral taste. (Which is by no means an unusual procedure. In the applied Neo-Platonism of the Renaissance, for instance, the virtuous was deduced from the courtly.) And metaphysics then becomes an examination into a universal structure in this structure's relation to human standards of excellence. This is by no means a reverting to man as the measure of all things. Or at least, it involves a distinction between generic man and man as an individual. The former reading will lead us almost inevitably to God (by which I mean some rigidity of higher standards to which the individual must aspire). The task would be to prove the existence of permanent principles of beauty (a task, by the way, which is being pursued under the modernized discipleship of Plato and Pythagoras by Gino Severini, in his book, *Du Cubisme au Classicisme*) and with this proved, the moral life would demand similar feelings for balance and proportion.

Although Mr. More may protest, I maintain that he is trembling on the verge of just such an attitude of aesthetic priority, as any one must be who chooses to make a study of Plato. In the last analysis, a demand for spiritual affirmation can be justified on no grounds except the one that life is made less beautiful without it. And in any case, the aesthetic standpoint would have made Mr. More's defense of inconsistency less obnoxious. For Plato is so patently the artist that his ideology had best be looked upon as subordinate to his love of beauty. As a creator of beauty who prefers dialectic to narrative, he becomes a philosopher. But his *fides* proves too much for his *intellectus;* his emotion does not attain its complete logical parallel; and where the logic fails, it is a failure and none other. The beauty of the whole may lead us to pardon an imperfection in a part, but let us not, until we are forced at the point of a pistol, find it praiseworthy that the tight rope-walker should fall off his rope. The aesthetic attitude at least has the virtue of being less strained. And further, it does full justice to the particular superiority which Plato manifested over the Sophists: his capacity to touch on permanent standards at a time when his facile contemporaries could see nothing but flux. However, so long as we attempt to systematize Plato's statements from the standpoint of those statements alone, Platonizers and Neo-Platonists and Plato-exegetes can pile up *ad inf.*

# Weighted History

*The Crisis of Civilization* by Hilaire Belloc. Fordham UP
*The New Republic*, February 1938, 375–376

Belloc here gives us a curve of history, succinctly interpreting from a Catholic point of view the development of Western culture through four stages: decay of pagan Rome, with rise of Catholicism; development of the Catholic hierarchy until the flowering of Catholic culture in the thirteenth century; subsequent corruption, leading to the Protestant Reformation; rise of business culture out of Calvinism (with communism as the mere *completion* of capitalistic errors). In a fifth part he discusses Catholicism as the only hope of saving mankind in the "war of religions" between Catholicism and communism. Such redemption would not require a mass conversion to the Church, but merely a sufficiently numerous, active and informed body of Catholics to give their "tone" to society (by upholding values and legislation that made for a maximum restoration of small property owners). Belloc here exhorts mainly in the name of "independence," which would seem to mark him as somewhat Jesuitical (in taking over a *capitalist* value for Catholic propaganda as the Jesuits originally took over Protestant values for Catholic propaganda). Thus, a Catholic reviewer of an earlier and similar volume by Belloc noted that a more genuinely Catholic slogan than "independence" would be "interdependence."

The book, being mainly addressed to believers, would seem to require more good will on the part of general readers than many are apt to muster. On the subject of pre-Reformation decay, for instance, we are told: "It may fairly be said that the main cause of decline was old age." But if it was simply "old age" that was the decisive factor five hundred years ago, impairing "watchfulness and readiness to reform," we must show good will to keep from asking what factor short of second childhood might change the situation half a millennium later. The diagnosis is used when handy, and dropped when it isn't.

*421*

Again, we are given an excellent materialistic explanation of Mohammedan forms, but must be distinctly more spiritual when considering Catholic forms. Or again: we are told that the Church in the fourteenth and fifteenth centuries became corrupt because society as a whole was corrupt—but we must not remember this equation when the author is on the subject of contemporary decay.

Further, it is somewhat of a strain to see the establishment of communism described as "beginning with whole-sale massacres on a scale hitherto unknown among Christian men, comparable only to the Asiatic orgies of the Mongol invaders seven centuries ago," while remembering that the glories of the thirteenth century ("that supreme moment of our blood") were described with a light flick at the Albigensian slaughter in this wise: "The last great effort to destroy Christian society from within, the Albigensian movement, had been crushed."

If you consider the Renaissance and Reformation as natural developments out of medieval thinking and production, you get one result; if you think of them as a kind of "second fall," you get another. The latter is Belloc's.

# Invective Against the Father

*Milton's God* by William Empson. New Directions
*The Nation*, June 1962, 540–541

The underlying structure of Empson's latest book, which has the virtues and vices of a protracted pamphlet, might be reduced to the following strands, though the actual exposition is more complex: (1) He builds up a repugnant picture of Milton's God, especially as depicted in *Paradise Lost;* (2) these notions involve him in more sympathetic treatments of Christ, Satan, Adam, Eve and the angels, whether loyal or fallen (sentiments that Empson also extends to Delilah, as portrayed in *Samson Agonistes*); (3) he holds that Milton's God, "wicked" as he is, is much better than the traditional God of the Christian; (4) these considerations involve the author in attacks upon current "neo-Christianizing literary critics; (5) to round things out, there are some perfervid curses uttered against Christianity in general (a somewhat bloodthirsty diatribe against bloodthirstiness). Here Christianity gets blamed for a lot, and any virtues that persons trained as Christians may possess are likely to be thought of rather as surviving in spite of Christianity.

All told, William Empson, who is best known for his book, *Seven Types of Ambiguity* (later followed by a similarly mercurial book, *The Structure of Complex Words*) and whose book, *Some Versions of Pastoral,* is equally ingenious (it is the book of his that I prefer, along with its imaginatively Marxist twist, though I doubt whether any orthodox Marxist would agree with my description), has chosen this time to exercise in a more "controversial" fashion. And he rises to a pitch of righteous indignation that will either reinforce your own righteous indignation, if you agree with it, or will call forth a contrary kind of righteous indignation, if you righteously disagree with it. Or, in case you simply enjoy watching a good scrap, these pages should entertain you. They should entertain you particularly if, like this reviewer, you are sick of the dismal gossip-novels that are regularly heralded by spokesmen for the trade as great works of literature. In this case, you will be relieved to see how, whatever the problems of Christian doctrine and of a great blind Christian poet who had wrestled so sturdily with them, the orbit of the damned dingy gossip that currently passes for the ideal of fiction or biography or autobiography is necessarily transcended. You can't talk about a brainy and temperamental poet like Milton without finding that you are automatically involved in livelier matters.

True, I'd flatly assert that Empson does not live up to the requirements of his subject. But, at least, he's free of the gossip racket. Milton inevitably did that for him. And in reading his book, you're in a realm where genuine literary exercising really counts. So, regardless of your righteous indignations, be they pro or con, I'd suggest that when confronting this book you relax and enjoy it.

Here is a list of statements (in the order of their appearance), that I have picked verbatim from the book because they seemed to sum up best one or another of the five "strands" I have mentioned:

> A Renaissance Christian Church was itself usually a thorough-going police terror.

> The Wars of Religion so disgusted sensitive and intelligent people with the cruelty of all Christian sects that, after about a century of effort, they managed to prevent the religion from burning people alive any more.

> So long as you gave Mr. Eliot images of someone being tortured his nerves were at peace, but if you gave him an image of two people making each other happy he screamed.

> Milton steadily drives home that the inmost counsel of God was the Fortunate Fall of man [fortunate, that is because it called for Christ as Redeemer]. . . . However wicked Satan's plan may be, it is God's plan too. [Thus Empson quotes lines from *Paradise Lost* to show "that God's actions towards Satan were intended to lead him into greater evil." I believe that secular law would here accuse God of compounding a felony.]

> [When misleading rumors start in Heaven] it is hard to see who could be the ultimate source but God himself, as part of a war of nerves.

> The only good writer who had defended the regicide was ascribing to the devils the sentiment still firmly held by himself and his proscribed party.

It is a tremendous moral cleansing for Milton's God, after the greed for power which can be felt in him everywhere else, to say that he will give his throne to Incarnate Man. [Empson here refers to the notion that Milton tries to patch up God's character by representing him as a despot who wanted to retire, and planned to let his Son take over.]

The picture of God in the poem, including perhaps even the high moments when he speaks of the end, is astonishingly like Uncle Joe Stalin; the same patience under an appearance of roughness, the same flashes of joviality, the same thorough unscrupulousness, the same real bad temper.

One expects the morality of God to be archaic, but this God seems to be wickeder than any recorded society.

What would have happened if Adam and Eve had irritated God by refusing to do what he foresaw is too horrible to imagine.

The conscience of Milton was not quite as corrupt as a neo-Christian's.

[Milton] was himself a man of civilized conscience . . . [and that was] the reason why he was laboring so hard to make his God appear a bit less morally disgusting.

[Neo-Christians] boast of the morally disgusting aspects of the religion which more traditional Christian writers have commonly been anxious to hide or explain away.

Parliament decided to exclude from England the American Horror Comics for children, and a leading Church of England scholar remarked jovially that the kids could get quite enough sadism from Christianity anyway.

[Christianity is the only one of the universal religions] which dragged back the Neolithic craving for human sacrifice into its basic structure.

When the Church had sufficient power, it would regularly happen that a man was promoted to high place in it through a widespread recognition that he was genuinely imitating Jesus Christ; and then he would say to himself "Come now; a man with my responsibilities has a duty not to go on imitating

Jesus Christ; it is time to imitate God the Father; and immediately he would start behaving with monstrous cruelty, apparently without any psychic shock.

The Doctrine of the Trinity is a means of deceiving good men unto accepting evil; it is the double-talk by which Christians hide from themselves the insane wickedness of their God.

Shelley remarked that no man of honor could go to Heaven, because the more he reverenced the Son who endured, the more he must execrate the Father who was satisfied by his pain.

The Christian God the Father, the God of Tertullian, Augustine and Aquinas, is the wickedest thing yet invented by the black heart of man.

The symbol of the Religion of Love is a torture [and] Worship of torture is itself a sexual perversion; [hence] The fires of unsatisfied sex can be relied upon to stoke the fires of Hell.

[In sum:] What Christians are worshiping, with their incessant advertisements for torture, is literally the Devil.

To back such views, Empson builds his interpretations, first of all, by relevant quotations from the text. He also employs paraphrases, often deliberately crude, designed to bring out the nature of the tactics. Thus, "God answers the petition of Adam by saying, in effect: 'What d'you want a woman for, hey? *I* don't want a woman.'" He makes effective polemic use of Milton's references to God's "derision." He plays upon the fact that one-third of the angels revolted (a rebellion that would suggest the presence of tyrannical conditions in Heaven), and plays down Milton's explanation, according to which they got into a state of disobedience to God through hierarchally *obeying* their immediate superior, Satan. (See in Book V such lines as 671–710, and more specifically the passage: "But all obeyed / The wonted signal, the superior voice / of their great Potentate; for great indeed / His name, and high was his degree in Heaven.") He acts more as a debater than as an analyst in failing to bring out the fact that, in *Paradise Regained*, Milton stresses not Christ's "torture" but Christ's resistance to Satan's temptations. And by his stress upon "torture" rather than upon the sacrificial principle in general, he picturesquely deflects attention from the central relationship between religion and the social order. In sum, Empson is being Impson.

But above all, Empson commits what is surely the unpardonable sin as regards his concern with language: for he almost willfully fails to develop a mature, *terministic* or "logological" analysis of Milton's theological and poetic problems. This is no place to argue the matter in detail. But one point is obvious from the start: If only by reason of its borrowings from Judaism, the Greeks, the pagan Mediterranean cultures in general, the successive stages of secular Western thought and many other sources besides the "Neolithic," Christianity could not be so efficiently horrendous as Empson would want us to believe. Thus, though my own approach to the terminology of any and all theologies is secular, I have the uneasy feeling that something of the old Puritan fury shows through Empson's rabid brand of secularism.

# Philosophy

*When a philosopher invents a new approach to reality, he promptly finds that his predecessors saw something as a unit which he can subdivide, or that they accepted distinctions which his system can name as unities. The universe would appear to be something like a cheese; it can be sliced in an infinite number of ways—and when one has chosen his own pattern of slicing he finds that other men's cuts fall at all the wrong places.*

—*Permanence and Change* (103)

# Righting an Ethnologic Wrong

*Primitive Man as Philosopher* by Paul Radin. With a Foreword by John
   Dewey. D. Appleton and Company
*The Dial*, November 1927, 439–440

In his *Primitive Man as Philosopher,* Mr. Radin has given us the useful counter-volume to M. Lévy-Bruhl's *Les Fonctions Mentales Dans les Societes Inferieures.* M. Lévy-Bruhl, whose book appears in English under the title of *Primitive Man,* had distinguished between a primitive and a civilized manner of thinking. The primitive, by this schematization, has a "pre-logical" method of envisaging reality. Every natural event which is of importance to him, a storm or a tree falling across his path, is given a purposive explanation, is felt as having a personal bearing. M. Levy-Bruhl terms this the primitive's "mystic participation" in nature. Whereas civilized man, with an impersonal concept of causality, a "logical" attitude, would explain the storm or the falling tree as being from his standpoint an "accident," and thus as part of a causal sequence in which he did not "mystically" participate.

   M. Levy-Bruhl summons much evidence to show the workings of the "prelogical" system among primitives in contrast to the "logical" system among ourselves. Yet it might be objected that such a logical attitude is with us very often insecure, not imperious to the individual, but allowed by a state of society in which there are few cataclysms and dangers so that, since we are not regularly pitted against natural forces, we have little occasion to feel their "personal" bearing. Still there are those who have cursed into the "teeth" of a bitter wind, or felt the sinister purpose behind a "run of hard luck"—while our gamblers, our thieves, and our Napoleons inhabit a world of destiny and omen. Even yesterday it was my privilege to hear a woman, who wears no ring in her nose, decide that she must have acted properly by her disinherited son since her two hundred new strawberry plants all lived.

   Mr. Radin, however, furnishes us with a much less tenuous answer. He shows that the primitive can attain a stage of intellectual sophistication parallel to our own, possessing all the capacities for abstract thought, and even the skepticism, of the most "modern" man, and manifesting no greater literalness or credulity in his use of mysticism and symbolism. The author points out that our ideas of "civilization" have been based upon the intellectual attainments of a few highly expert thinkers and savants, a class always greatly in the minority, whereas ethnologists have almost invariably derived their conclusions concerning primitive peoples from the sayings and beliefs of the most naïve members of the group. Mr. Radin, on the contrary, hunts for the "intellectual" among the primitives—and finds him to an extent which is sure to ruin negro sculpture with Dôme and Rotonde. He asserts that there are two types of character—the speculative and the practical—in every social group; and he amasses much evidence to show that the concerns and solutions of this speculative type among the primitives parallel those of the similar type of today. "In temperament and in capacity for logical and symbolical thought," he concludes, "there is no difference between civilized and primitive man."

Perhaps the greatest importance of Mr. Radin's contribution lies in the solidity of his proof, while the message itself has appeared in other forms. Even in the last century De Gourmont was talking of man as an "intellectual constant" and doubting whether any modern could surpass in genius the prehistoric inventors of sewing, ploughing, and fire-making. Evolution within the human species is not one of plasm, but of tools, our "advance" being, it seems, merely in the accumulation of documents. Which may be a bleak or a sunshine thought, depending upon the approach: since we can either regret, on reviewing the statistics, that man's shortcomings promise to be eternally recurrent, or we can be relieved to feel that life must inevitably generate out of itself the standard cycle of exhortations.

# William James: Superlative Master of the Comparative

*The Thought and Character of William James, 2 vols,* by Ralph Barton Perry.
 Harvard UP
*Science and Society,* Fall 1936, 122–125

The rich metaphorical genius of William James, in spite of the unsystematic character of his work, has made more stir in the world than that of any of his more rigorous American colleagues. Logical specialists, experts in a vast impersonal system of checking (learning to "think forwards" with an equipment essentially "backwards," as we check addition by subtraction, or multiplication by division), had reason to be annoyed with the laxity of his method, as Professor Perry so well points out in his recent two-volume study of James. He himself admitted that a man must earn his assertions instead of helping himself to them, and that the morality of his craft requires that all assertions should be checked, insofar as the resources for checking are available. Hence, he was apologetic for dealing in a philosophic method which the boisterous mystic, Blood, who had found God in a dentist chair, could salute as "poetry in overalls and blouse." Not until the close of his life was James able to forswear "his *Sturm* und *Drang* propensities forever in order that he might satisfy his intellectual scruples and the 'respectable academic minds' of his colleagues." But having reached this decision, he died. His biographer notes the coincidence without irony, though irony might be justified. Perhaps, having resolved to "be good," he had nothing more to live for. Maybe the prospect was not enticing enough, for a temperament such as his, to keep his bad heart going.

Pierce was James's gadfly, forever making it difficult for James to indulge his weakness for resonance in place of rigorous expression. Thus we find him reproaching James for his generous use of terms, and even being led into this uncomfortable severity:

> It is an indispensable requisite of science that it should have a recognized technical vocabulary, composed of words so unattractive that loose thinkers are not tempted to use them; and a recognized and legitimated way of making up new words freely when a new conception is introduced; and that it is vital for science that he who introduces a new conception should be held to have a *duty* imposed upon him to invent a sufficiently disagreeable series of words to express it. I wish you to reflect seriously upon the moral aspect of terminology.

When James had written that the Kantian "I think" could be reduced to the experience of breathing, the gadfly answered:

> I call your attention to the circumstance that many people, of whom I am one, involuntarily hold their breath while thinking. . . . If I have got to believe that I think with my lungs I will take as my equation: *Ich denke* = I don't breathe.

The theoretical issue between them seems to revolve about a fundamental difference of this sort: James discussed pragmatic effects in such a way that there was always an invitation to distinguish two kinds of effectiveness, an invitation to distinguish between a *good* act and a *shrewd* one. Hence, James had to *engraft* a moral exhortation *in addition,* to make sure that one would vote for the good act and against the merely shrewd one. Pierce seems to have been making goodness implicit in his definition of act or judgment *per se.* "Pragmatism (*my* pragmatism) makes logic a mere special case of ethics." Was not Pierce in this closer to the Greek concept of reason, whereas James's approach made for exposure to the modern stress upon *intellect,* as essentially a non-partisan (non-moral) coefficient of power?

Were we to seek a sentence characterizing James's work we might, borrowing a clue from Fritz Mauthner (who suggests that empiricism is "adjectival"), describe his method by an analogy from grammar; we could call him an expert in the *comparative degree* of adjectives of value. Distrusting absolutism (which is really the *superlative,* identifying the One as the Best), he thought in terms of *more* rather than *all.* Hence his dislike of monism, authority, the rationally finished. To optimism or pessimism, he preferred "meliorism." His assertion of free will, that played so important a part in his moral rehabilitation, owed its shape to similar notions of partiality. Even God was on the make, not a Completed Best but a Candidate for Better, as he wrote to Davidson:

> I can sympathize perfectly with the most rabid hater of him and the idea of him, when I think of the use that has been made of him in history and philosophy as a starting-point, or premise for grounding deductions. But as an ideal to attain and make probable, I find myself less and less able to do without him. He need not be an all-including 'subjective unity of the universe,' as you suppose.

It was this comparative pattern of thought that could lead him to the amusingly ingenious observation on Bradley: "He is, really, an extra humble-minded man, I think, but even more humble-minded about his reader than about himself, which gives him that false air of arrogance." There is something of the same genius in his remark to a friend concerning Royce: "You make some pointed objection to him which needs a definite reply, and his invariable reply is simply to restate his whole system." It promoted a kind of any-port-in-a-storm attitude, annoying perhaps to lovers of the symmetrical when it takes the metaphysical guise of pluralism, but extremely helpful for the moral jugglings we must manage in this imperfect world: "One can meet mortal (or would-be mortal) disease," he writes to his dying friend Davidson, "either by gentlemanly levity, by high-minded stoicism, or by religious enthusiasm. I advise you, old T. D., to follow my example and try a playful *durcheinander* of all three, taking each in turn *pro re nata*." The same distinctions in schematic form seem implicit in his rule-of-thumb trinity: "Rationality, activity, faith." And if, as an adept at the comparative, his world became pluralistic, it followed that as a thoroughly sincere man he would even buy a pluralistic house; his sister Alice reports him as saying: "It's the most delightful house you ever saw; it has fourteen doors, all opening outwards." (We may add, for the sake of the record, that James elsewhere credits it with but eleven.)

Much of James's resistance to the procedures of his "respectable" colleagues seems to have come from his conviction that they were in danger of dealing with too restricted a world. He hated the *"streng wissen schaftlich"* not merely because he was too restless or too physically ill to persist in minute measurement. He also felt that too much of vital importance might, by the nature of the method, necessarily be left out of account. Here we see James spontaneously obeying his father's injunction, striving to maintain the widest notion of vocation, vocation not as a specialist, but as a man. Yet, as we finish the account of his work, we are led to wonder whether, for all his inclusiveness, he could give us a full equipment for today. One is struck, for instance, by an almost total absence of historical and economic considerations. The mention of politics is rare, and naïve:

> Man is essentially an adventurous and warlike animal, and one might as well preach against the intercourse of the sexes as against aggrandizements and piracy.

[It is] a remark which, though one could hardly propose to eliminate human pugnacity by *fiat,* would require a great deal of qualifying before it could be made a serviceable view. And in 1896 he writes to Münsterberg:

> The political campaign goes on admirably—splendid speeches and documents on both sides. It seems difficult to doubt the essential soundness of people where such a serious mass of discussion, pursued on the whole in such a dignified tone, is a regular incident of life. Of course, the silver party must be beaten, but they have much that is ideal on their side.

This would need much "filling out" before it could become an instrument for gauging the nature of events. But James seems invariably to have veered away from such considerations; we must be content when, announcing his zest at the prospects of a philosophic school, he makes an oblique reference to its "drowning the roar of the Russo-Japanese artillery across the Pacific."

In part, I think, the fault lies with James himself. For he did not fill out his message by explicit concern with the economic, commercial, financial categories, despite their tremendous effect upon the culture of his country. We find him, early in life, during his own period of dispersion as a student, sizing up his future in characteristic fashion:

> On one side is *science;* upon the other *business* (the honorable, honored and productive business of printing seems most attractive), with medicine, which partakes of the advantages of both, between them.

In a sense, he *did* choose medicine, medicine of the "mind-cure" sort. But though he thereby united "business" and "science," in making his living as an educator, he did not go on to round out his naming by a critique of economic relations as such. In both these two volumes of his, the only out-and-out passage containing such an emphasis appears in one letter from John Dewey, recommending the work of a "newspaper man," Franklin Ford, who had studied out the following questions:

> (1) The conditions and the effects of the distribution of intelligence, especially with reference to inquiry, or the selling of truth as a business; (2) the present (or past) hindrances to its free play, in the way of class interests; or (3) the pres-

ent conditions, in the railway, telegraph, etc., for effectively securing the freedom of intelligence, that is, its movement in the world of social fact; and (4) the resulting social organization.

Perhaps it is quite natural that, when such themes were not explicitly and exhaustively assigned their place, students could be exposed to Jamesian influence, could be graduated into a flowing, Jamesian world, and still contrive to forget the profoundly Jamesian lesson.

# Untitled Review of *Reason and Emotion* by John MacMurray

*Reason and Emotion* by John MacMurray. Appleton-Century Co.
*The American Journal of Sociology*, September 1936, 283

This is a good book of moral exhortation, based on a concept of reason whereby the author can discover the principle of rationality in art and religion as well as in science. "Rationalism is not reason. It is only the intellect in blinkers." Rationalism is not opposed to reason, but is a restricted manifestation of it, attaining perfection most easily when dealing with less complex materials (as in the physical sciences). The essays should be of value in stimulating readers to extend their thinking beyond the accidental borders of words, as when the author discusses the religious ingredients in collectivistic atheism and the antireligious ingredients in churchly institutions. He gives substance to critics who would resist the attempts to use theological dogmas as a plea for material injustice. The author is to be grouped among those who can note the limitations of science without concluding that we should be wearing rings in our noses. His book is comfortable rather than tragic in its coordinates; hence one may feel its insufficiency in omitting the problems of anguish, sacrifice, militancy, and crime from its discussion of ethical adjustment. One may also ask whether the author's ideals of individual integrity are a perfect fit with his ideals of group cooperation—as the latter may call for kinds of compromise not present in the total frankness he assigns to what he calls personal "chastity."

# Intelligence as a Good

*The Quest for Certainty* by John Dewey. Minton, Balch and Company
*The New Republic*, September 1930, 77–79. Also in *The Philosophy of Literary Form*

Philosophers, after long telling us what the universe is and commiserating with the blunt majority of mankind too brutelike for such refined insight, next began to question their own possibilities of knowledge. The focus shifted from "What is the universe?" to "How can we know what the universe is?" Each new discovery of science put such knowledge farther from us. The world's most thoroughgoing body of information threatened to block out that cosmological vision which seemed sharpest when the data was sparest—until now, in pragmatism, a third stage is reached. The pragmatist says simply: "The universe is." And, the universe being, it does—so the pragmatist will situate his knowledge, not in *what* the universe is, but in *how* it works. He will seek to understand operations, to find in what order things generally precede and follow one another. He will also consider himself as involved in the process, will recognize that one discovers "reality" in accordance with his terminology, that a shift in the vocabulary of approach will entail new classifications for the same events. He will renounce what Professor Dewey aptly calls the "spectator theory of knowledge," the notion that the universe is something like an insect under glass in a museum, and that to know it we must merely go and look at it. Knowledge he will see as arising from an interaction between an organism and its environment. Knowledge is not knowledge of what things are, but a knowledge of when and how they happen.

In the present volume, Professor Dewey has traced this course of thought with great clarity and critical keenness. He has pictured mankind, in its quest for certainty, turning to some rigid metaphysical or theological structure as compensation for the contingencies of actual life. Man fortified himself against the irregularities of life by imagining the perfect regularity of heaven. The consistency, justice, dependability which he could not feel assured of in his intercourse with nature, he relegated to some supernatural realm of "antecedent Being," where it lies intact, an absolute good, truth and beauty. These absolutes are "reality," and they are but obscured by "appearances." The dialectic juggling of these concepts, the vast intellectual legerdemain by which "reality" is first obscured by "appearances" and then traced back through "appearances" to "reality," the strenuous effort required to show how a thing both is and is not, has given rise to the grandiose structure of metaphysics, an imposing monument, but one regrettably rotten at the base and kept standing only by hasty replacements which soon crumbled in turn.

I fear that metaphysics, gentlemen, is a living lie. What does the metaphysician do? He begins, like any artist, with himself and his corresponding set of values. Then he figures out that the world *ought to be* such and such if these values are to be imbued with universal validity. So much has been done under cover. He next comes forward with the assertion that not until now is his process of investigation to begin. Under our very eyes he examines the nature of the universe; he finds the universe to be such and such; and then he says triumphantly, since we have found the universe to be such and such, it follows irrefutably that these values which I am about to sell you have universal validity. Having thought from Z to A, he poses as thinking from A to Z.

Now, Professor Dewey situates the fallacy of the metaphysician's A in the doctrine of "antecedent Being," the notion that there is a fixed reality to be known as it really is, that there is an equation between the thing to be known and the thing as we know it. He holds that we do not perceive in this sense, but translate. An object is perceived as a food is taken into the stomach; it is acted upon in accordance with the capacities and requirements of the equipment receiving it. Further, what would be the gain in knowing what reality *is?* Our whole interest would reside in how to *use* such knowledge—and the progress of science and invention is evidence that we have already gone far in the *use* of reality, while metaphysicians still lag behind, wrangling over their first principles. While they were asking whether or not we could possibly know, the pragmatism of science was steadily increasing its knowledge. And if science, in the newest paradoxes of physics, now reaches what it considers an impasse, so that the old cry of "Can we know?" begins to arise in these new quarters, this is only because science has become metaphysically speculative, and had begun attempting with its instruments to discover what the universe is instead of how it works. But whatever the cosmological difficulties of science, it continues to amass pragmatic certainties. It can, for instance, *use* electrons without even being sure that they exist.

*The Quest for Certainty* is an ideology of science. Professor Dewey, looking over the history of the progress of physical science, discovers that its knowledge has been the knowledge of processes. He sees that, while man tended to retreat from the world of contingencies, compensatorily building a structure of immutable absolutes in the mind, and thus combating the uncertainty of life by getting at least the *feel* of certitude (whistling to keep up his courage), science went ahead with its study of processes and succeeded in greatly increasing the actual certitude of living. One does not depend upon a chance stroke of lightning for his fire, upon the chance dropping of a seed for his crops. Non-metaphysical certainty, pragmatic knowledge, knowledge of the processes by which fires are lighted and seeds grow, has increased the certainty of living. Scientific knowledge is of this sort. The theological or metaphysical system gets certainty by affirming dogmatically how things *are,* how they *must be;* it erects a set of vested interests, which cannot be questioned without imperiling its precious certainty; it cancels by decree the actual fluctuations in human livelihood. So here, in the doctrines of antecedent Being, were certainties which left the world uncertain. Whereas pragmatic knowledge is erected out of doubt, questioning, experimentation. It has no vested interests; to have one of its beliefs undermined is a gain, an aid in the better understanding of processes. It defines as truth *what works.* Possessing no certainties in itself, it has undeniably increased the certainties of living.

Having got so far, Professor Dewey would now argue by analogy. Since the scientific (pragmatic, experimental, instrumental) method has produced such good results despite the many cases of misuse for private ends, he would have us apply this same method to the criticism of values. Values, too, should be grounded, not upon the authority of antecedent Being, but in accordance with their workings. We should not necessarily turn against traditional values because they have been derived from the past. Their survival may in many cases be some proof of their adequacy. But they can be tinkered with, improved like any other process, and these improvements are made by looking to their possibilities. Values, in other words, are to be tested by experiment, experiment either in actuality or in thought (since thought is a kind of deferred, or symbolic, action). The past of a value is used as the past of a laboratory experiment—it is neither glorified nor condemned, but interpreted in accordance with the problem at hand.

Approached in this way, the argument for an analogous application of experiment to the study of values (the ultimate aim of all philosophy) seems quite cogent. But should we situate the success of science in its perfection of measurement, it is harder to see that the application of its method to a criticism of values is analogous. Science owes much to experimentation, to pragmatic knowing, but this method has been reinforced by an instrument equally important—mathematics, the instrument of quantification, of measurement. This instrument enables us to test an operation by means which minimize the opportunities for differences of opinion. When people can look at the scales and agree that they say twenty, or look at the thermometer and agree that it says forty, the experiment is proved. It is not always quite so simple as that; the process of proof itself is often brought into question. But in contrast with an argument about the workings of a value, it is exactly as simple as that.

How do we test the success of a value? Values undeniably work—but they don't necessarily succeed or fail. We have monogamy, bigamy, polyandry, polygyny and a dozen other systems of marriage. They have all *worked*, since people seem to have lived and sung under each of them. Taboo against murder works, since societies flourish where this taboo is prevalent; a systematic killing of aging parents also works. The latter custom is more necessary where food is scarce and existence is hard; perhaps to that extent it is even a pragmatic value. Values are all somewhat pragmatic, since they have arisen to serve human needs, though they undeniably may become a menace when they survive the situation for which they were invented, and the knowledge of the processes by which they arose can do much to break the force of their authority in the minds of those who still hold them. The understanding of processes can clearly contribute greatly to the elimination of such outgrown values.

But the matter is different with the erection of new values by the experimental method. The experimental method would derive its values, not by authority, not by any theory of antecedent absolute good, but by test. It seems, however, that when carried to its logical conclusion, this method of evaluating values presents difficulties of its own. When judging the effectiveness of a value, for instance, we have to utilize some other value to appraise it. Though we may know the processes whereby people are made fat, lean, or middling, we still have to decide whether we *ought* to make them fat, lean, or middling; for there is no judgment inherent in a process. Suppose that we decide to make them lean in order that they may run faster. Then we have founded our value of leanness upon the value of speed in running, which must in turn be founded upon another value, and so on. Where then is our "key value"? By the experimental method there could obviously be no key value, in the sense of its antecedent existence, its acceptance on authority. Even a key value must be dependent upon experiment for its justification, and its worth could be tested only by the adoption of some other value by which to test it. Eddington has already discussed this circular chase in the definitions of physics, each phenomenon being defined in terms of another until you get back to the first. Thus, it should not be surprising if we found the same situation in the evaluating of values when values are treated by an analogous method.

It is interesting to see how Professor Dewey handles this difficult matter. He must necessarily avoid a key value, yet must have evaluations. How does he satisfy both needs? By his writings on the nature of intelligence, in which he praises the function of intelligence, tact, taste in the formation of our judgments. For intelligence is not a value; it is a process, a functioning. Still, it is more than a process; it is a good process. Intelligence, if I correctly interpret Professor Dewey's chapter, both *is* and is *good* (or, more accurately, both *becomes* and *becomes good*). It thus serves as substitute for the key value. For if intelligence is good, it will naturally choose good values. So, being a value in itself, it does the work of a key value in grounding out a criticism, for all other values can issue from it.

I am not competent to judge whether this is a wholly justifiable step, though I do feel that it is the crux, or fulcrum, of Professor Dewey's philosophy. If Intelligence is good by definition, we need not be surprised that a system of good can be drawn from it. In the older systems there was something which, by definition both is and is good, and with so much given all the rest could be deduced, down to the divine authorization of imprisonment for failure to salute the sheriff.

Further, if the arbiter of success is Intelligence, evaluating out of itself, creating the values by which it measures its own success, is this not an intrusion upon the relativistic thinking of pragmatism? Would it not be much like "pure" Intelligence, an absolute? We have done away with the unmoved mover; but do we have in its stead the self-judging judger, the self-measuring measure, a good so good that it perceives its own goodness? Do we face a choice between the circular chase from value to value, and the treatment of Intelligence as an absolute evaluator?

Also, the goodness of the Intelligence, so far as the pragmatic evidence goes, seems much more like goodness in a technical sense, like the goodness of one's liver. Its goodness as an *ethical* good, a good for society in general, is less apparent. For though the functioning of a liver be accounted a good, the functioning of mine enemy's liver is not good for myself. The evidence shows more clearly its goodness from the standpoint of the organism than goodness for all.

The reader may or may not agree with these tentative objections, which seem to me the difficulties arising if we carry experimentalism to its farthest implications and seek to find in it a mechanism for the erection of values without relying upon the existence of a prior good. In any event, my zeal to discover the bare bones of Professor Dewey's logic has led me into a major act of unfairness. For I have failed to convey any notion of the sensitivity, learning and vitality contained in "The Quest for Certainty." Its incidental sidelights on the history of philosophy constitute, to my mind, a constant succession of scores. The total lack of authoritarianism in his thinking is forever leading Professor Dewey into the expansive and adventurous. The book is tolerant and inquisitive. Its extension of strict dialectic by borrowings from psychology, anthropology, history, sociology, economics fits it into a wider scheme than mere matters of dogma and makes it an important contribution to our culture. We see that pragmatism in such hands can disclose its social value without going so far into the subject of the rock that supports the rock that supports the world. And Professor Dewey's good is certainly no tax upon our good will. It is not hard for us to accept that the Intelligence both is and is good, for we act upon this assumption daily, and it brings results. These results are tested by values which just are, regardless of how they came about, or how many no longer fit, or how many should be remedied, or how many would be incapable of empirical proof. Whether or not the scientific attitude could provide the grounding for a world of values, once values are given, it can certainly contribute to their better guidance. And it can always play one value against another, relying upon a kind of relative antecedent Being, since it can take values which are generally accepted as good and use them to argue for values not yet so accepted. If the world prizes justice or happiness, for example, we need not seek the justification for these values; but we can use them to prove that some practice is reprehensible because unjust, or because it leads to misery.

In this respect the pragmatist is strongest when he is more like the artist than like the metaphysician. It is not gratuitous that Professor Dewey has written so brilliantly of art, both in this present volume and in his *Experience and Nature*. The artist says, in substance: "I make this exhortation in the terms of what has already been accepted. Once these terms are accepted, I can go a little beyond them. But I shall argue only for my addition, and assume the rest. If people believe *eight,* I can recommend *nine;* I can do so by the manipulation of their *eightish* assumptions; I need not justify my *nine* by arguing for *one.*"

# The Poet and the Passwords

*Fear and Trembling* by Glenway Wescott. Harper and Brothers
*The New Republic*, August 1932, 310–313

On the nineteenth of his "Attic Nights," Aulus Gellius tells a story of a Stoic philosopher, who was in a shipwreck. Now, this Stoic philosopher, despite his doctrines, had been greatly disturbed during the shipwreck, whereas a certain rich and showy Greek from Asia had been quite calm. After the shipwreck had been successfully weathered and the storm had subsided, the provincial Greek began to twit the Stoic for his uneasiness, saying: "You are a Stoic philosopher, I am not; yet you were pale with terror during that storm, and I was neither pale nor terrified." To which the Stoic answered: "Quite true; I was more frightened than you were. But consider how much more I had to lose."

Like this imperfect Stoic, one may look with boastful uneasiness upon the transitory qualities of the contemporary scene (uneasiness being the emotional counterpart to a deep premonition of change). In change we lose something that we may gain something else—and one becomes uneasy in proportion as he is less concerned with what he might gain than with what he shall surely lose. One may fear the loss of continuity. Precisely through considering what remarkable things have been amassed during the processes of Western culture, one may feel like an owner of them, and may bother himself with the thought that these might be destroyed through some vast international upheaval. He has, before him, an anthology of Europe—and as there is only one copy, he may be gravely worried lest it become misplaced.

The attitude has recently been expressed, with many ramifications, in Glenway Wescott's volume of essays, *Fear and Trembling*. Sometimes with suavity, sometimes with brilliance, sometimes too prettily (the author should either have written less ambitious sentences, or should have taken more time to write them), he states what we might call the "philosophy of privilege"— and with Goethe's dictum that "fear and trembling is the best part of man" to back him, he sets to fearing and trembling at all the factors by which our essential privileges seem to him imperiled.

Wescott's creed, reduced to its simplest terms, would seem to be that other people should enjoy, as much as he, the preserving and swelling of the archives. Life should be a search for simple pleasures. He thus mentions the "miracles of digestion," to indicate that, if we eat at all, we should eat with astonishment. The body is capable of certain sensuous, sentimental and intellectual pleasures. They should be more strongly stressed—our ambitions should be made to stop here, if possible. Turning, then, to the world in general, one should apply the same principle: "Might not the earth simply be enjoyed, as just a larger, fleshier body than the one in which each of us exists by himself, and is almost at liberty to enjoy as he likes?"

Indeed, it might not. Here enters the difficulty. Wescott and three friends, setting out in a car through central Europe, in search of nothing other than such personal gratifications as would be in keeping with this code of amenities, found such humble absorbings wholly inapposite to the season. "Everywhere we kept finding references to affairs of state. Every impression came to us seemingly saturated in advance with unwelcome impersonal feeling." Not what happened to them, but what was in the air, forced them to admit that "no country, nothing in any country, can be regarded from a quite personal point of view these days. Palaces are, above all, examples of either private property or nationalized wealth." When looking at the vegetables in Les Halles, like plucking a daisy and holding it up before one and drawing therefrom a lesson, Wescott is encouraged to find in the murder of these patient things a sweet alternative to the murder of other men; but the harsher kinds of facts, the non-epicurean, non-esthetic facts, the facts of politics, industry, economics, of warped ambitions, of greeds so unnatural that fullness but makes them greedier, compel the author to observe almost archaically: "The problem of pleasure . . . still needs solving."

Hence the underlying machinery of this book. Wescott is really concerned with such milk of human kindness as might come of contented human kine. He holds that if all men had but learned to enjoy their darling personal potentialities, their genius as meditative vegetables, they might never have felt obliged, before they could consider their lives well spent, to drive thousands of their fellows into coal mines at certain seasons, and at certain other seasons drive them out again. He is really concerned with the Voltairean lesson, the culture that comes of tending one's own garden—and this concern, at this time, is malapropos for a peculiar reason: Because people have for so long based their self-respect upon the coercion of other people rather than upon the use of their gifts as human vegetables (superior vegetables, since they really know how they could avoid crowding, as their blunter cousins do not) that they *force* a man into political and economic worries. If one were to plan his life today with no other slogan than the slogan, "Let me alone," even with this non-aggressive slogan he would become a meddler, since he must drive off the meddlers, and since the doctrine of laissez-faire has meant, in practice, not to refrain from interfering, but to refrain from interfering with those who were interfering.

He thus finds the public business upset by the inanity of private lives. He fears "so many men's boredom, and their wish in consequence to have new desires and hopes constantly aroused in themselves, and then, naturally, to have those satisfied." He fears "the resentment of those who are unsuccessful according to these false standards," and foresees them "loosely shifting and settling on an enemy." He fears "the selfishness of investors and industrialists—no, not even their selfishness, but the foolishness of their selfishness at any given moment." Thus, where the book seems inapposite, it seems so through a deeper appositeness: it is really dealing not with the particular expedients that might lead us out of our present troubles, but with the crooked ways of living and thinking that originally got us into them.

For this reason he dares distrust Russia, a country which has shown far too much respect for America, importing too many of our mechanics and plumbers, and whose new social system, so far as the behavioristic symptoms go, would seem to differ from ours primarily in the fact that its economic provisions make possible precisely the materialistic development, the worship of industry and toil, which the profit element in our capitalistic economy is always impairing. Communism, that is, is the perfect scheme for mass production, since it is the perfect scheme for mass consumption, offering a far better distribution of buying power than is possible to orthodox capitalism. Thus we seem faced with the industrialist plague all over again, only this time in a more adequate form: the glorification of a system, not because it provides *leisure*, but because it provides *jobs*. So he fears and trembles at the spectacle of this human beehive, which in its evangelical zeal has glorified workers at work, though man's really vital problem, the "problem of pleasure," is a problem for after-hours.

Wescott's title, however, with its backing in the words of such an "Answerer" as Goethe, can trick him. For by giving him the authority to fear and tremble, it tends to make him go in search of situations whereat he may fear and tremble. In particular, he should find nothing but solace in the Russian experiment, in the thought that it is being carried on, that imaginative and well documented people have had a hand in it, and that the distresses of the capitalist countries have given it more freedom from vital interference than its plotters could reasonably have expected. Here, but for the title of his book, Wescott could have exulted. For as a literary man, he would certainly be pledged in advance to any vast social experiment—and as a citizen, forced to live while it is under way, he may, if he chooses and is luckier than many of us, be comforted at the thought that he is elsewhere while it is going through the stages he does not approve of, and thus can wait, outside the lines, until he sees whether, as the various industrial programs are completed, leisure really does arise there after all (as it has already arisen in ghastly disguise, in capitalist countries, under the name of unemployment). For in time the workers' republic must either become two-car conscious, or become an idlers' republic.

Wescott fears most, however, the next Great War. In its efficiency, and its aimlessness, he fears a great cultural desolation. He does not directly consider how much of our culture was lost already, and precisely during the years of prosperity. He thinks that war will be followed by revolution, that both will entail a great cutting away of amenities—yet he does not evaluate revolution as an alternative of war, as the simplest way of preventing precisely the kind of warped living that makes his dreaded war both a Need and a Tonic, "a very Eleusis of love-making; the thrill of more danger than ever, more picturesque than ever, the chemicals of the killed as well as those that kill making a better aphrodisiac than ever, so that the most moderate of men, physiologically, may have as good a reason to be pleased with themselves as any old eloquent Don Juan." Revolution (change from past practices) we must have—whether it be by direct and bloody confiscation or by the cunning and indirect confiscation that would come of enormously augmented taxes upon private wealth.

Wescott's position is perhaps best typified in his distinction between the nineteenth and twentieth centuries:

> All during the nineteenth century, there was laborious reasoning . . . and tireless scientific experiment: the mind of man busy learning that God was no more divine . . . than the digestion of food, the shattering of light. . . . Now, during the twentieth . . . we must learn . . . the same lesson the other way round. . . . Scientists look at the orchid through a microscope and discover that it is only a little mottled liver and avid sexual organs. Now if we, personally, can look at our liver and sexual organs and see that they are a bouquet of orchids—well and good. . . . Otherwise, haunted by the thought that God is but a vast digestion, the orchid but a little liver, what more natural than that we should go to pieces in the reckless effort to amuse ourselves, seeking distraction from the thought? Piling up fictions in our minds,

and unsound money and unwanted arms all over the world, with sensational shocks to ever touchier vanity and habit-forming salves and facile consolations, treacherous and secretive, in secret disgust—what more natural than that we should all kill each other finally, nation against nation, just as a roundabout way of committing suicide?

Here Wescott fails to pronounce the password, since here he fails to accept a few rudimentary economic principles as the prime movers of historic processes. He is really dealing with *meanings,* with *vocabulary,* as the fulcrum of our behavior in history. In this I think he is closer to accuracy than he may seem. Consider our treatment of the criminal, for instance, if we approach him from the vocabulary of sufficient grace, whereby we look upon his transgressions as a deliberate choice of "evil" where he might as well have chosen "good," so that we make our prison justice "retributive." Contrast this with our treatment of him if we approach him from the vocabulary of determinism, whereby his transgressions become "symptomatic" and justice becomes rather a matter of prophylaxis and reclamation. Here we see the destiny of thousands dependent upon a mere shift in terminology. And similarly: one man, dismissed from a job, but having a Marxian "configuration of meanings," will fit his particular fate into a larger social process, and so feel resentment rather than humiliation, and may perhaps organize an ominous hunger march; another, similarly dismissed, and with only the older pioneer configuration, the doctrine that ability will out, takes his dismissal simply as an evidence that he was insufficiently endowed, and so may slink out of existence with a few pilfered sniffs of the gas company's gas. Such, to my mind, are the matters of terminology that make us act one way rather than another under a specific situation and that, accordingly, deny the situation itself as prime mover. The best argument I can see in favor of getting one's head cracked for Marx would be the denial of Marx's economic determinism—for if our ideas are determined by the situation, then we could quite simply sit back and let the situation determine them, fortified in our knowledge that an inevitable historic process should be a damned sight stronger than the enemy, be the enemy a gang of gangsters or a consortium of bankers.

We have, in recent years, heard much talk of a "new vocabulary." I suggest that Wescott's book gives inklings of what this new vocabulary would be. It would involve the rediscovery of an old vocabulary—and to make myself as unpopular as possible, I shall call it the slave-owners' vocabulary, the leisure-class vocabulary, the vocabulary of the privileged citizens of Athens and the pleasantly corrupted hedonists of late Rome, who pursued their speculations at the expense of countless bended backs—except that in the instance of today, these backs would not be human backs, nor even the backs of beasts, but the insensate forms of engines. Let us but change our words, let us try to put the word "leisure" in the place of the word "unemployment," and let us set about to examine all the implications radiating from this initial shift in terminology (a terminology dating from the days when toil was the prime condition of survival), and the absurdity of plans for "making work" promptly becomes apparent. If Sisyphus were to come among us, complaining, because each time he had borne his rock to the top of the hill it rolled down again, our unemployed would look at him with scorn and envy, since they have been taught to imagine nothing grander than an endless Sisyphean burden, a rock that rolled down a hill each time they got it to the top, and that had to be rolled to the top again, this over and over, plus a living wage (as Sisyphus obviously enjoyed in hell, since he couldn't die there). Yes, the "problem of pleasure" is still unsolved, when the greatest curse upon modern life arises out of the fact that, despite all manner of new needs, our labor-saving devices had begun, inexorably, to save labor—for how could we go on selling cars unless the Guggenheims were willing, with their copper profits, to buy 200,000 Fords annually; and how go on mining copper unless Ford were willing, with his automobile profits, to build himself a copper pyramid to shame Cheops?

This is the economist's day, insofar as the economist must formulate the economic expedients by which the collective wealth is made collectively available, shaping these changes to make them best conform with the past institutions and ways of thought in each individual country. It is the day of the new politicians, and of their pamphleteering and soap-box allies, who must find the strategy for best placing these expedients favorably before the people. It is the day of the poets and the novelists in that they must subtly complement this work by their manipulation of vocabulary, by their almost imperceptible uncrowning of words formerly privileged, and their enshrining of words formerly neglected, so that "dissipation" might even emerge as "relaxation," "idleness" as "opportunity," and "practical ambition" as "grave social risk." The esthetic, the "problem of pleasure," must come to form the fulcrum of our thinking, the basis of our self-respect, the incentive of our new muscularity, lest we become "a finished race, a race that changed in every way but could not sufficiently change its mind."

# Fraught with Freight

*Past Master* by Thomas Mann. Translated by H. T. Lowe-Porter. Alfred A. Knopf
*The New Republic*, January 1934, 257

In this selection of essays by Thomas Mann, who is now among those German writers honored by exile, there is a brooding quality, almost a moroseness. It may be in part explainable by the fact that many of the chapters are written "in commemoration" of one dead titan or another—such as Durer, Lessing, Goethe, Wagner, Tolstoy, Nietzsche—but the sepulchral tone arises also from Mann's general attitude towards life. His patience can seem too great, his sympathies stretched too far beyond the range of biologic service. A cult of suffering, or heroism, or esthetic and scientific "saintliness," lurks about the fringes of his doctrines, to dismay us as to the gravity of living. At times his work suggests to me, not a personality, but a battlefield, an expanse of suffering soil across which the fluctuant and indeterminate conflicts of our day are waged momentously. There is a trampling back and forth, a complexity of veerings and deployings; there is even bewildering vagueness of position whereby men unknowingly fire upon their own comrades; and there are strange lulls which make us almost cry out for the quick resumption of combat and disorder.

The present essays, written during recent years in which conditions have shifted from day to day, are hardly to be judged by the tests of strict ideological consistency. Throughout his career, Mann's work has remained remarkably of one piece, as regards the issues at which he points. But his ways of pointing have been so changeable that one could conceivably play them against one another until they were canceled off to zero. He has even written a defense of this ambiguity: "The intellect should be objective enough to admit that it makes no difference whether a perception is positive or negative in sense, provided it is a perception and a true one." If I understand this remark, Mann does not mean simply that affirmations and negations, or the "constructive" and "destructive," are integrally related. He means rather that were we to say either "I am decidedly a patriot" or "I am decidedly not a patriot" we should be pointing at the same "perception," since in either case we should be making the same issue paramount. Perhaps it is only in this mercurial sense that Mann's critical formulations can be said to possess consistency. He will usually be found at one date advocating as an ideal the very trend or attitude which at another date he will ally with disaster. How eloquently, for instance, he warns the Nazis that they are choosing the way of darkness, of retreat into the primeval womb—and yet how eloquently, on other pages of this same book, he praises the cult of darkness.

One must know Mann well not to be confused by such uncertain tactics, the tendency to use as bogeyman this year the very thing which he had fondly saluted the year before. In a very thorough and discerning essay published in a recent issue of *The Sewanee Review,* Mr. Harry Slochower has discussed other aspects of this same phenomenon, showing how earnestly Mann has sought to cast overboard all parts of his vast intellectual equipment which are not suited for the demands of the hour, yet how, once decision has been programatically taken, he smuggles back part by part all that he had scrapped. One can know for a certainty that when the final choice comes, Mann will always choose on the side of justice, and against the side of bigotry and oppression. But others must force the choice upon him. Left to his own devices, he falls into what Mr. Slochower has called the "bottomless pit of indiscriminate sympathizing."

Mann has written much in the imaginative sphere to make us realize the origins of this duality. He has pictured for us, again and again, the attempt to bid farewell to an older scheme of living and salute a new one, the somewhat prophetic hankering after a "third kingdom" which will restore to us our right to love the world. This typically nineteenth-century pattern of experience leads him to convert nearly everything he touches into a project for the merging of antitheses. This way of seeing is often very suggestive, yet I suspect that in the end Mann has been betrayed by it. Particularly as sharpened by the genius of Nietzsche, it leads to the formulation of false alternatives, and hence false syntheses. Though he himself has come to suspect this, his skill had been developed over too many years. He mentions, for instance, "the widespread, reigning, anti-idealistic and anti-intellectualistic determination to dispute the primacy of mind and reason, to pour scorn upon it as the most unfruitful of illusions, and to set the irrational and intuitive, the powers of darkness and the depths triumphantly in possession of their rights once more."

Does not Mann here deceive both himself and us most egregiously? Have we not, all about us, seen a world move toward confusion through too great an emphasis upon the intellect, the direct, rationalistic, irreligious, "enlightened," "go-getting" type of mind that moves with the sureness of an adding machine? And yet, by Mann's arrangement, were we to repudiate this ideal, we find ourselves hankering after nothing less than some dismal alliance with the darkest of primeval heavings. Having given us a choice between "day" and "night," and having allied the mind with day and the emotions with night, he makes it almost impossible to contemplate some check upon the mind without feeling that we are thereby dedicated to a cult of morbidness. What, indeed, has become of that central region, so swiftly spirited away by this sharp antithesis: the realm of the sentiments, of the gentle and warming affections, kindliness, friendliness, good nature, charity, good will? Is that the "night"—or is it not rather the only sort of "day" that man is entitled to idealize and to materialize? Is not our rising distrust of "mind" based purely upon the fact that power and knowledge have too far outpaced their counterpart in humane gratifications? Surely, the pleasing dispositions by which a social group promotes its cooperative tasks are not exactly "intellectualistic," nor are they by any means a reversion to the "powers of darkness and the depths." They must be known by their own rights, and not by the "merging" of "pure" mind and "pure" passion. They are qualitatively distinct—and if they are not kept so, the well founded distrust of "brain" can easily lead to a cult of dumbly obedient "brawn" that is indeed wholly allied with "darkness and the depths." From a region now given to such alliances, Mann has the distinction of being in exile.

# The Universe Alive

*Nature and Life* by Alfred North Whitehead. U of Chicago P
*The New Republic*, November 1934, 26

These two brief lectures on philosophy give us an entire *Weltanschauung* in miniature, yet at the same time they show a critical penetration that summaries usually lack. Whitehead begins by sketching the "general commonsense notion of the universe" that was in process of formation among the more progressive thinkers of Europe around 1500. He next considers its breakdown, which continues until "the state of modern thought is such that every single item in this general doctrine is denied, but that the general conclusions from the doctrine as a whole are tenaciously retained." And he details the main respects in which Newtonian mechanics and Hume's empiricism seem to him inadequate. He holds that whereas "the status of life in Nature is the standing problem of philosophy and of science," the prevailing positivism is unable to deal with this problem meaningfully. Whitehead traces the difficulty back to Cartesian dualism, in which "the mental substances are external to the material substances." After offering grounds for his assertion that "the characteristics of life are absolute self-enjoyment, creative activity, aim," he shows that the methods of science, based upon sense perception, preclude the discovery of these characteristics. But an awareness of aim, he holds, is as much a fact of our experience as any sensory measurement might be. From this he proceeds to affirm the importance of the qualitative; and in conclusion he states as his key notion: "The energetic activity considered in physics is the emotional activity entertained in life." This would give us a living universe, organically related, rather than grinding wheels conceived after the factory model. The many sharp formulations that occur in the course of the discussion make these lectures as fertile and indicative a treatise on philosophy as one could possibly expect in so short a space.

# Liberalism's Family Tree

*Liberalism and Social Action* by John Dewey. Minton, Balch and Company
*The New Republic*, March 1936, 115–116. Also in *The Philosophy of Literary Form*

Dr. Dewey's new book is divided into three chapters: on the history of liberalism, on the crisis in liberalism, and on "renascent liberalism." About the topic of liberalism, the author groups the cultural values he most admires. His book is written to show with what important and desirable traits liberalism can be identified. He goes through a cycle of virtues, such as peace, liberation, "the development of the inherent capacities of individuals made possible through liberty," tolerance, reintegration, science, rationality, education, charity, courage, and hope—and he pleads that liberalism, as he conceives it, can be included in this cycle.

As a way of beginning his series, he selects an ancestry for liberalism. He sketches its history briefly and suggests a theory of origins:

> The use of the words liberal and liberalism to denote a particular social philosophy does not appear to occur earlier than the first decade of the nineteenth century. But the thing to which the words are applied is older. It might be traced back to Greek thought; some of its ideas, especially as to the importance of the free play of intelligence, may be found notably expressed in the funeral oration attributed to Pericles. But for the present purpose it is not necessary to go back of John Locke, the philosopher of the "glorious revolution" of 1688. The outstanding point of Locke's version of liberalism is that governments are instituted to protect the rights that belong to individuals prior to political organization of social relations.

In this citation, Dr. Dewey seems to bring up the possibility that we have the choice of two different family trees in charting the history of liberal manifestations. If we mean by liberalism a "particular social philosophy," the author finds that "for the present purpose it is not necessary to go back of John Locke." But if we mean simply "the thing to which the words are applied," he finds it possible to begin the family tree with classic Greece. Indeed, since he situates such liberalism in "ideas as to the importance of the free play of intelligence," and since such ideas can obviously be found in periods antedating Greece or in cultures independent of Greece, the attempt to chart all the ancestors in this second family tree might carry us far beyond the "funeral oration attributed to Pericles."

In Dr. Dewey's first chapter he is concerned solely with the briefer, historic ancestry of liberalism. Here he shows the organic connection between liberalism and the rise of business enterprise. He recounts the negativistic, atomistic, "muckraking" elements in liberal thought, demonstrating why the liberal philosophies were much better fitted for sweeping away old resistances than for building up a new positive integration. He traces the ways in which the liberals' doctrines of individual rights were made negotiable in removing the restrictions upon profit and trade. He shows why such theories can be called liberal despite the tremendous cramping of opportunity they necessitate at present. But when admitting that liberalism, as so conceived, is now owned and managed by the reactionaries of the Liberty League, he notes a "split" in liberal philosophy. This split was caused in part, he shows, by the surprising contributions which various brands of Tories made to the maturing of liberal philosophy "in alliance with evangelical piety and with romanticism," and later with the institutionalism, traditionalism, and collectivism in German idealistic thought.

In contrast with the older liberalism, the coöperative aspects of society were now stressed, and the demand for control through social legislation became uppermost. One may question whether this revision of liberal emphasis could properly be called liberalism at all. But it is what the author advocates as liberalism, and the names of historic phenomena are not ordained.

The important consideration from my point of view is that, precisely where this "split" occurs, we covertly shift from the short family tree to the long family tree as the basis on which liberalism (the collective, social-legislation kind) is advocated. For somewhat in line with Veblen's distinction between business and industry, we are told that the really dynamic factor in the development of modern history is not business, or capitalism, with its attendant problem of the "class struggle," but scientific method as objectified in technology. Behind this method lies the functioning of "intelligence" in general. The function of intelligence is, among other things, to integrate old material and new material (to "mediate" the change of status), and this integrative or mediating function is called upon at *every* period of history.

Now, if "liberalism," as "intelligence," is identified with an integrative or mediating function that operates in every period of history, we have obviously gone from the short family tree to the long family tree, plus extensions far beyond or beneath Periclean Athens. The implied origin is not temporal, but universal, as the integrative work of intelligence goes on, *mutandis mutatis,* in all eras.

I think too that the ancestry undergoes still deeper extensions without avowal on the author's part, as his conception of scientific method becomes colored with connotations of love or charity. When one notes that a prize-fighter's skillful left swing to the jaw may be good, intelligent, pragmatic science, one questions just how Dr. Dewey manages to introduce non-violent, non-coercive requirements into his notions of scientific method. He *implies* a difference in kind between the use of a chemical to eliminate vermin and the use of a chemical to eliminate human rivals, but his *explication* is vague at this important juncture. Particularly in view of the fact that Dr. Dewey usually celebrates scientific achievement as a "conquest," we become aware that, when applied to people, his idea of scientific method is not merely that of a *power* but adds hidden connotations of charity or solidarity usually connected with religion, ethics or poetry.

Again, when Dr. Dewey celebrates liberalism as the opportunity for the "development of the inherent capacities of individuals," we realize that there is some such adjective as "good" or "wholesome" implied before the word "capacities." If the adjective were explicitly there and if the attendant steps made necessary by its explicit presence were inserted, or if the author's merging of science as technique with science as a charitable attitude towards people were made the express subject of analysis and rationalization, Dr. Dewey's volume would be more enlightening. As it stands, it seems essentially Ciceronian. It serves primarily as a lawyer's brief, in that it persuades without exposing the crucial steps in its persuasion. Philosophic tracts, if they are of worth, seek to persuade; but the difference between them and Ciceronian exhortation, it seems to me, is that they try at the same time to expose their methods of persuasion. I question whether Dr. Dewey could be said to meet this test fairly so long as the ambiguity as regards "family trees" remains at the keystone of his treatise.

However, as Dr. Dewey warns us in his introduction, a writer cannot say everything at once. And certainly the present book becomes far less "Ciceronian" if one considers it, not in itself, but as a kind of final chapter to such fuller books as *Experience and Nature* and *The Quest for Certainty,* books that, for this reader at least, did a lot of eye-opening. Yet some of the same ambiguity seems to lie at the roots of these also. When one talks of "functions," one necessarily brings in non-historic assumptions of structure. The "function of intelligence" belongs to the long family tree, quite as does the "function of the heart." History may tell us how the heart beat faster on a given day. But behind the effect of that given day, there lies a property of hearts, a "heart function," that is not historical in the same sense at all. The attempt to divorce philosophy from metaphysics will always, I suspect, be merely a protective screen for the setting up of metaphysical assumptions.

# George Herbert Mead

*The Works of George H. Mead. Vol I: Mind, Self and Society,* edited with an Introduction by Charles W. Morris
*Vol. II: Movements of Thought in the Nineteenth Century,* edited with an Introduction by Merritt Hadden Moore
*Vol. III: The Philosophy of the Act,* edited with an Introduction by Charles W. Morris, in collaboration with John M. Brewster, Albert M. Dunham and David L. Miller. The U of Chicago P
*The New Republic,* January 1939, 292–293. Also in *The Philosophy of Literary Form*

The publishers of these posthumous documents print Whitehead's endorsement as follows: "I regard the publication of the volumes containing the late Professor George Herbert Mead's researches as of the highest importance for philosophy. I entirely agree with Professor John Dewey's estimate, 'A seminal mind of the very first order.'" The editors rank Mead, in the pragmatist movement, "as a thinker of the magnitude of Peirce, James and Dewey." And though the reader will probably feel that a philosophy is here mulled over, rather than formed, I cannot see why he should want to disagree with the above testimonials. Anyone who would cherish with gratitude what of great value may have been piled up in this country, must study these books (the journalistic remaining, as always, for those who prefer the like-water-off-a-duck's-back mode of reading, and will not work over the printed page except when doing puzzles, rebuses, and cryptograms).

In search of a text, as a handy way of getting at the gist of these 1,700 or so pages, I should select from the good book, under "Voice—middle":

> Middle voice (Gram.), that form of the verb by which its subject is represented as both the agent, or doer, and the object of the action, that is, as performing some act to or for his advantage.

Mead's philosophy of the act, in other words, takes its start in the idealist's concern with the identity of subject and object. The concept of the Self is pivotal, the very word "Self" suggesting the reflexive form, a subject that is its own object. The strategy of romantic philosophy (which Mead likens to the beginnings of self-consciousness at adolescence) was to identify the individual Self metaphysically with an Absolute Self, thereby making the reflexive act the very essence of the universe, a state of affairs that is open to lewd caricature. But Mead, turning from a metaphysical emphasis to a sociological one, substitutes for the notion of an Absolute Self the notion of mind as a social product, stressing the sociality of action and reflection, and viewing thought as the internalization of objective relationships.

Mead calls his social psychology behavioristic, while distinguishing clearly between his brand of behaviorism and that of Watson. The individual's responses are matured by such processes of complication and revision as arise from cooperative and communicative factors. The communicative, in turn, is formed by language, out of which arises the "universe of discourse," and rational self-consciousness is framed with reference to this universe of discourse.

We have been hearing much of "democracy" and much of "dialectics"—and surely Mead's approach helps us to understand the integral relationship between these concepts. For dialectics deals with the converse, the conversational, while democracy is the ideal of expression in the marketplace, the dramatics of the forum. The truth of the debate arises from the combat of the debaters, which would transform the competitive into the coöperative (somewhat as competitors in a game "cooperate" to make it a good game).

So Mead would envisage the act of reflection as the holding of conversation with oneself—of seeking to contain within oneself, dialectically, the entire drama—of asserting in the form of an incipient act, which is delayed, to be corrected from the standpoint of the "generalized other" ("the attitude of the generalized other is the attitude of the whole community")—and of thus waging this internal dialogue back and forth, in search of truth matured by the checking of an imaginary opponent. It is by this ability (implemented by the character of language) to put oneself in the role of the other, that human consciousness is made identical with self-consciousness, that the subject can see itself as object (an "I" beholding its "me"), and that the subject can mature by encompassing the maximum complexity of roles.

The metaphor of the conversation (uniting "democratic" and "dialectical" by the *forensic* element common to both) is systematically carried throughout Mead's view of human relations. "The parry is an interpretation of the thrust," as one even "converses" with objects, coöperating with them to his benefit only insofar as he allows them to have their say, takes their role by telling himself what their modes of assertion are, and corrects his own assertions on the basis of their claims. To "silence" them by the use of one's dictatorial opportunities is to deny oneself the opportunity to gauge their resistances correctly, an imposing of the quietus that would take its vengeance upon him by restricting his available knowledge of reality. Or again, when discussing two phases of universal societies (the religious, which are treated as extensions of neighborliness, and the economic, which are treated in the spirit of Adam Smith's apologetics, as the exchange of surpluses to the mutual advantage of the exchangers), he writes: "One cannot complete the process of bringing goods into a market except by developing means of communication. The language in which that is expressed is the language of money"—where the philosopher presumably so carries out his conversational metaphor as to say, without irony, that "money talks."

The general tenor of Mead's social psychology is in keeping with the promissory mood that went with the happier days of progressive evolution. Here, man the problem-solver looks with Whitmanesque delight upon that state of affairs wherein each solution is the basis of a new problem. Mead considers the possibility that, in seeking to encompass the total conversation, one might make of oneself an internal wrangle, with more of heckling than discussion (particularly where he would identify himself with a society in which sub-groups are at odds)—but characteristically, he treats this as a complicating factor, as something to look out for and try to guard against, rather than as a basic element of discord in his picture.

The book covers a vast range of material. *Mind, Self and Society* is the volume in which Mead's sociological pattern is developed. *The Philosophy of the Act* deals with his devices for transferring his concepts of sociality and perspective into cosmological interpretations, wherein he uses the physicist's theories of relativity to his purposes. And *Movements of Thought in the Nineteenth Century* is a highly serviceable historical treatment of trends since the Renaissance, mainly centered upon matters of science and revolution. It is a great loss to the quality of discussion in America that the volumes were not publicly available during the period of upheaval and recasting that went with our attempts to refurbish our individualism for collective necessities after 1929. One might conceivably sometimes want to put pluses where Mead put minuses, and *v. v.*, particularly where Mead considers social developments, in promissory fashion, as a straight line towards a kind of ideal League of Nations. Again and again, one misses Veblen. But particularly in his remarks on attitudes as incipient acts, on modes of identification, on personality and abstraction, on the relations between the biological and the social, and on thought as gesture, his writings seem to map out the field of discussion for forthcoming years.

Unfortunately, the piety of Mead's disciples has worked against him somewhat, as they sought to preserve for us his every word rather than to seek condensation and saliency. For there is another sense in which these books hinge about the metaphor of the conversation. They are composed mainly of transcripts from classroom discussion, so that much is repeated, and is said loosely. As a result, there are many paragraphs, but no sentences.

# Monads—on the Make

*Reality* by Paul Weiss. Princeton UP
*The New Republic*, April 1939, 314–315. Also in *The Philosophy of Literary Form*

In a review of John Dewey's *Logic* (New Republic, November 23, 1933), Mr. Weiss writes:

> He grounds the acts of inquiry in the movement of the organism from a state of disequilibrium to one of recovered equilibrium with respect to an environment. But if that pulsational process did not have its roots in the nature of inorganic things as well, his basic "principle of continuity" would be violated and organisms would be made into a special kingdom within a kingdom of nature, forcing a radical break between the sciences of biology and physics.

Mr. Weiss here touches upon a basic problem of philosophic strategy, and from an angle that may help us to characterize his own book. For in *Reality*, his ingenious work on epistemology and ontology, he would confront the issue that he accuses Professor Dewey of slighting. He would move by transformations from the realm of physics to the realm of biology, and would do so without violating the *lex continui* (that is, without the intervention of a miracle, a mutation veiled in an ambiguity).

I can think of but two ways of fulfilling such conditions. You can keep the two realms together by either physicizing your biology or biologizing your physics. Mr. Weiss seems to prefer the latter. And having put a biology implicitly into his physics at the start, he has no trouble in drawing it forth explicitly at the appropriate moment. He contrives this by treating both physical and biological processes in terms of a biological metaphor: the metaphor of eating, of digestion, of assimilation. Individuals, both organic and inorganic, seek to attain self-completion by incorporating external beings.

We might add a third realm: the realm of ethics. And applying our pattern, we should then hold that the philosopher may preserve continuity of realms by ethicizing physics and biology, physicizing biology and ethics, or biologizing physics and ethics. Mr. Weiss seems to remain loyal to his biological metaphor by applying it to this third realm as well.

"To be is to be incomplete." And to be incomplete is to strive to be complete by the assimilation of all others than oneself. "The universe is one where multiple unique beings endeavor to become the Absolute in unique and opposing ways." Every being, either organic or inorganic, "at every instant is at a stage analogous to that ascribed by Leibniz to his monads, but every one endeavors to pass beyond that stage in the effort to achieve the state ascribed by Leibniz to his God."

This monadology differs significantly from Leibniz's in that there is no harmony among the monads, preestablished by God. Perhaps we might even say that Mr. Weiss has replaced this by a kind of "preëstablished disharmony," with each individual enterprise seeking to become a universal monopoly, within a marketplace of mutual checks and balances provided by all the other individuals similarly striving, within the means and limitations peculiar to their natures.

Leibniz characterized his monads as "without windows." Their development was internal, with God accounting for the harmonic interrelationships whereby these internal developments amounted to external interaction. Mr. Weiss, considering this introduction of a common ground as a mere *deus ex machina* to save an otherwise faltering explanation, gives us instead a plurality of individual universes interacting by an overlapping of their "virtual regions." Also, in this way, he avoids the picture of the world as illusory, that arises in such philosophies as Schopenhauer's, positing a single, absolute striving of which each individual will is but a fragment. The individual's striving is real, independent, unique, in accordance with its intrinsic nature. Hence, these are monads with windows, with a view, even a point of view, looking out upon a public world, and seeking to get along in the real opportunities and resistances that the world offers.

Though Mr. Weiss would ground his structure of thinking on the law of contradiction, this does not prevent him, as he approaches ethical problems, from introducing a very cute concept, "privational possession," composed by an incongruity. One can "privationally possess" what one does not have. And, conversely: "It is perfectly possible to eat one's cake and have it too." By knowledge we attain vicarious perfection, as we may, in knowing the structure of the universe, thus vicariously or privationally possess nothing less than this universe entire. But one must *live* his knowledge in action, "until one's mind permeates one's body." Only by thus "infecting ourselves with our knowledge" can we "achieve the only possible perfection open to man."

I regret that, in thus trying to report the main features of Mr. Weiss's picture, I have been unable to exhibit the many subtle and suggestive details encountered *en route*. I refer to such matters as his advance from quest to question; his treatment of the circularity in the relation between epistemology and ontology; his systematic placing of the arts and sciences with relation to his total scheme; and his crucial chapter on "Mellontological Causation." But the book is hard going. Mr. Weiss spins a very fine web of internally adjusted descriptions, and the reader must work very hard if he would be caught in this web—otherwise, he will rip the fabric with inattention and fall through, like a clumsy wasp that blundered into a trap laid for gnats.

# Action as Test

*The Uses of Reason* by Arthur E. Murphy. The Macmillan Company
*The New Republic*, February 1944, 220–222

This book does not attempt to offer "a systematic philosophy in whose terms our present complexities can finally be resolved." The author feels that "we are not likely in this generation to achieve so comprehensive a doctrine"—and "perhaps, on the whole, it is as well no longer to expect it." The reviewer is thereby happily relieved of certain embarrassments. For if the author himself specifically disclaims pretensions to a system, the reviewer cannot be expected to give a wholly systematic report of his book. One should, however, be able to state its "slant."

The two key terms in *The Uses of Reason* would seem to be "reason" and "action." Reason is conceived broadly: one might not be far wrong if he substituted for it the word "reasonableness," in contrast with such extremely narrowed meanings as we get when identifying reason solely with mathematical precision or scientific demonstration. And as for "action": we might substitute some such expression as "cooperation," or "joint effort for a common good."

The author relates these two terms pragmatically, in that reason is placed as the guide of action, and action is placed as the test of reason. Reason guides action in helping us to make a reasonable survey of the situation and to adopt ideals that will serve as the effective aims of action (under the particular conditions that form the "context" of our act). And action will be the test in the sense that reason is as reason does. That is, we won't judge a philosophy simply by adjudicating the claims it makes on paper, but we'll consider its consequences in terms of action. We'll see (or foresee?) what sort of context results when people act out the philosophy—and we'll let that be the judge.

This goes also for "the relation between the theological content of the beliefs recommended and the natural and social conditions under which the beliefs are propagated." Thus:

It is not difficult to maintain, in theological or metaphysical debate, that a belief in a supernatural foundation for the highest values is better nourishment for the democratic virtues than are mere secularism and agnosticism. Since Spain under Franco encourages and insists upon the inculcation of such beliefs, while Republican Spain did not, it might be concluded by the unwary that the Spain of Franco provides a better environment for freedom, enlightenment, and human brotherhood than did the Spain which made the first and bravest stand against fascism in the war we so tardily entered. I shall not, I think, be guilty of overstatement in saying that this conclusion would be a mistake. Men do not gather grapes from thorns, figs from thistles, or spiritual freedom from "values" whose "sanction" is anything less or other than the good that proves itself in their work together, freely, generously, and in the open. When such freedom is not to be found, the authoritarian indoctrination of approved theological principles will not serve to take its place. Where it does exist, democracy has a soil in which to grow, and it is in its growth under natural conditions that the proximate substantiation for our faith in it is to be sought.

Liberal; secular; democratic; proclaiming human dignity in humanistic terms; the author's *via media* is between the overextended claims of scientism on the one hand and the overextended claims of supernaturalist, absolutist philosophies on the other. His treatment of reductionists, over-simplifiers, debunkers and the like should be useful in making clear the invitations to bad thinking that reside in excessively narrowed terminologies of motives. And as regards terminologies not narrow enough, one may enjoy Professor Murphy's efforts to discourage "literary, philosophical and theological loose talk."

Ironically enough, the virtues of the analysis derive preponderantly not from the treatment of the books in terms of action, but by a treatment of them in terms of their nature as books. And this review will be similarly confined (though Professor Murphy's almost complete neglect of esthetic values might lead us to wonder whether his own philosophy, as enacted, could lead to anything richer than a world of well-conducted committee meetings).

The author thinks that the pragmatist "emphasis on the plurality of contexts in which ideas can function significantly" is "the greatest single contribution to critical philosophy of our time." His treatment of the subject, however, is disappointingly skimpy. His book itself should have enacted his admiration for the notion of context by a far more thorough and sustained contemplation of the subject he considers so important. That is, a book should act to "monumentalize" the subject of admiration. But such an attempt at monumentalizing would probably be, in philosophy, the same thing as an attempt at a "system"—and that Professor Murphy distrusts.

Having got through our "however," let's end by recognizing that the book is brightly and vigorously written, and is particularly valuable for its discretion in showing up many ideological works that have recently enjoyed some measure of popular interest. And if the author doesn't monumentalize reason, he does pay it the good compliment of considering, in terms of reason, both the nature of reason itself and the conditions, or "contexts," in which it acts.

# History

*And by 'history' is meant primarily man's life in political communities.*

*—Attitudes Toward History* (i)

# Puritans Defended

*The Influence of Puritanism* by John Stephen Flynn. E.P. Dutton and Co.
*The Literary Review* (*New York Evening Post*), February 12, 1921. 2

On the title page of volume three there is a quotation from Dowden: "If Puritanism did not fashion an Apollo with the bow, or a Venus with the apple, it fashioned virile Englishmen." I suppose one could say the same of cricket, the cat-o'-nine-tails, and teething ring. The author, in glorifying the contribution of Puritanism, has glorified it as something homely but useful. Puritanism, we are made to see, fulfills some sturdy and essentially honest function in the body politic; one might say that Mr. Flynn sees it as a rump which has enabled the Anglo-Saxon tradition to sit its way into greatness.

Certainly, this is one impregnable method of defending the Puritan. Puritanism as a political movement had contributed to the very basis of the English and American governmental systems. The fight of the Commons in England for supremacy over the Lords and the King was carried on mainly by a rising Puritan middle class which stood for thrifty home life and thrifty morality.

Mr. Flynn watches this tendency come down through the centuries. Each new rebellion in the direction of greater freedom, he maintains, was conducted by the Puritan element. It was the Puritan consciences, for instance, which finally abolished slavery in America; and it was the Puritan conscience which forced England to renounce her opium traffic in China.

The author might have added that it was even the Puritan conscience which fought the Puritan conscience. Roger Williams was no less of a Puritan than the Plymouth colony which expelled him. And to read the works of the early Darwinists is to read a record of tremendously Puritan souls whose rugged honesty drove them further than they really wanted to go.

So long as Mr. Flynn sees Puritanism as an ungainly but handy instrument in the conducting of the commonwealth, he has a good many arguments in his favor. It is only when he tries to reconcile Puritanism and art that his theories become highly questionable. For this book does not merely deny that Puritanism is an enemy of art; it asserts that Puritanism is positively friendly to the arts. This claim is backed by quotations showing that some of the earliest Puritans were lovers of music, or had dancing masters for their daughters, and so forth.

Unfortunately, the whole effect is spoiled by a closing paragraph which speaks "of that moderation which tempers our politics, and of that more reasonable spirit in religion which counts art as a handmaid, and not an enemy, of which the spirit of God is the inspirer, and is therefore to be rescued from degradation and consecrated to the highest service man can render."

The author would have been more convincing if he had continued to talk from the standpoint of government. For the religion of Puritanism is the religion of a preeminently "safe" government, with a minimum of dangers and discomforts. And this safe government must be attained at the expense of everything else. Now, while it is safe to have a dead art, it is not safe to have a live art, since live art is disruptive. Puritanism scents out all that which is dangerous to the commonwealth, because it is the religion of good government. And if art is dangerous to the commonwealth, it must be sacrificed. And art, unfortunately, often is dangerous to the commonwealth.

The fact is that the Puritan's sureness of feeling for the wisest policies in government prevents him from being broadminded. The attitude which would be broad enough to encompass an unmoral art, for instance, would be the symptom of its own destruction; a broadminded nation would probably be a dissolute nation within a single decade. A democracy, which is at the mercy of so uncertain a thing as a mob, exists solely by that divine law of human inertia by which whole centuries must be wasted in driving a thing into the people's heads, and whole centuries more wasted in driving it out again. There is no room for toleration here.

To reduce them to their absurdities, art is sick, while Puritanism is obstinate, hard-headed health. That in itself is enough to proclaim them as irreconcilable. And a nation is wise, it seems to me, which crucifies its artists, for it is only stamping out the possibilities of the pandemic. A nation which restrains its artists is a vigorous nation capable of acquiring whole continents, of imprisoning entire peoples, of thriving at the expense of a multitude of other nations.

As to the artists, they will get on somehow. It has been noted before that where there is financial splendor there are also artists, yes, even highly uncommercial artists. And if suppression can stop them from saying what they want to say, then it wasn't worth saying.

The book closes on the theme of the present-day labor agitation in England. Mr. Flynn thinks that everything depends upon the triumph of the Puritan ideals. These people who are in revolt are the inheritors and perpetrators of Puritanism. But he adds with disquietude: "The modern Puritan preachers . . . have, to some extent, failed to keep the flame of Evangelical piety burning on the altar of the nation's heart."

# A 'Logic' of History

*The Decline of the West* by Oswald Spengler. Translation with Notes by
   Charles Francis Atkinson. Alfred A. Knopf
*The Dial*, September 1926, 242–248

Over against the H. G. Wells concept of history as a straight line progressing from savagery to modernity, Spengler opposes the concept of numberless cultural systems, each of which has followed through a cycle of its own, growing, flourishing, and decaying in a fixed order or "periodicity." These cultural cycles, by Spengler's doctrine, evolve in an irreversible sequence through "spring, summer, autumn, and winter" aspects, any "season" of one culture being comparable with the corresponding season of any other culture. These analogous stages of different cultural systems are called "contemporaneous"; and by aligning the stages of our own cultural cycle (that of Europe and European America, which Spengler dates from about 1000 A.D.) with the contemporaneous stages of other cultural cycles, Spengler claims to produce a series of coordinates for determining which of the cultural seasons is now upon us.

Homer, in the Graeco-Roman cycle, would be contemporaneous with the northern sagas in our own, this era always being "rural and intuitive," and marked by the "birth of a myth of the grand style, expressing a new God-feeling." This spring gradually metamorphoses into summer, a period of "ripening consciousness" and of the "earliest urban and critical stirrings"— the pre-Socratics of the sixth and fifth centuries being analogous to Galileo, Bacon, and Descartes. In autumn the city assumes a leading position in the life of the culture. This is the age of "enlightenment" (Socrates and Rousseau) in which the traditional code is now subjected to a rigorous questioning, although it is still powerful as a religious and creative force. The mathematics characteristic of the culture is now definitely formulated, and the "great conclusive" metaphysical systems are constructed (Plato and Aristotle having their contemporaneous parallel in Goethe and Kant).

But each culture, while exemplifying the laws of growth and decay common to all cultures, is a self-contained unit, talking in a language addressed to itself alone. When it has passed, it leaves us its monuments and its scripts, but the experience which these works symbolized has vanished, so that subsequent cultures inherit a body of rigid symbols to which they are psychically alien—much the way one of Jung's typical extraverts would be alien to a typical introvert. In this sense, ancient Greek is as undecipherable a language as Etruscan, since there is no word in the Greek vocabulary which corresponds, in its cultural background, to the word which we select as its equivalent in any one of our modern languages. Consider, for instance, the difference in content between "man" as one of a race who stole the fire from heaven and "man" as a link in the evolutionary chain. It is not hard to imagine how a work of art arising out of the one attitude could be "alien" to a reader in whom the other attitude was ingrained.

Spengler lays great emphasis upon this cultural subjectivism, and even insists upon the subjective element in natural science. For even though science deals with empirically provable facts, a specific kind of mentality is required to meditate upon these facts rather than others. The possible modes of natural investigation are dependent upon the interests of the investigators. Spengler characterizes the science of any given culture as the conversion of its religion into an irreligious field—such concepts as "force" and "energy," for instance, merely being an altered aspect of the omnipotent and omnipresent God conceived at an earlier stage in the same culture.

The growth of science is also the evidence of a radical change in a culture's evolution. At this stage, the intellectualistic, critical, and irreligious elements of the culture gradually rise to the ascendancy. The emotional certainty of the earlier epochs, when religious, metaphysical, and aesthetic systems were built up spontaneously, is now past. The culture becomes a civilization. "In the one period life *reveals* itself, the other has life as its *object*." In place of the city we have the metropolis, and the "ethical-practical tendencies of an irreligious and unmetaphysical cosmopolitanism." Winter, thereby, is upon us. Hellenistic-Roman Stoicism after 200—returning to our concept of the contemporaneous—is paralleled by ethical socialism after 1900. The theatricality of Pergamene art is matched by Liszt, Berlioz, and Wagner—and Hellenistic painting finds its equivalent in impressionism. The American skyscraper, instead of being looked upon as the evidence of a new "dawn," is interpreted by Spengler as the symptom of decay corresponding to the "architectural display in the cities of the Diadochi."

Spengler thus finds that the high point of our culture has been passed, while we go deeper into the closing period, the era of civilization. With intellectualistic elements predominant, we are no longer fitted for the production of great works of art, but for technical exploits, for economic, commercial, political, and imperialistic activities. We are, like Rome, which was the civilization of Greek culture, ordained to be superior as road-builders and inferior as artists. And by his doctrine of cultural subjectivism, even those great works of art which our culture in its more youthful and vigorous stages produced as the symbolization of Western-European experience will become alien as this experience itself recedes before the rise of other cultures having other modes of experience to symbolize. In conclusion, then: (a) Even the greatest works of art are couched, not in the language of "mankind," but in the language of a specific cultural tradition, and the loss of the tradition is like the loss of the dictionary; and (b) since art is inevitably inferior in an era of civilization, we are invited to abandon all hope of further artistic excellence in our cultural cycle.

Let us consider first Spengler's subjectivist argument. In discussing each cultural cycle, he finds some dominant trait which characterizes the entire mode of experience peculiar to the culture. Arabic culture, for instance, is "magian," our own is "Faustian," and the Graeco-Roman is "Apollinian." He then shows how these dominant traits manifest themselves in all the various aspects of a culture's "behaviour." The Apollinian trait can be expanded as a sense of the "pure present," a concrete "thisness and hereness," which is to be found equally in the repose of the Greek temple, the "corporeality" of Greek mathematics, and the Greek indifference to time (the Greeks had no system of chronological reckoning comparable to our method of dating from the birth of Christ). This same attitude naturally resulted in the development of sculpture into a major art. In contrast to this, the Faustian culture has a pronounced historic sense, a mathematics of function and time, an "aspiring" architecture; and it has developed music into a major art. In painting, the "corporeal" mentality of the Greeks led to the exclusion of sky-blue as a color, and the disinterest in perspective; while the Faustian culture, with its feeling for distance, showed a marked preference for this very blue, and developed perspective exhaustively. Spengler considers this as evidence of totally different subjective states; yet could it not, as well, be used to indicate a very fundamental kind of similarity? If blue and perspective are employed by the Faustian for the same reason that they are rejected by the Apollinian, does not this argue a common basis of choice? It is to grant, categorically, that blue and perspective symbolize for both cultures a sense of distance. A genuinely subjective difference between cultures would be undetectable, for it would involve a situation in which the symbols could be employed with directly opposite content. Blue and perspective would then, for the Greek, mean pure present; and we could have formed the Greek temple, rather than the Gothic cathedral, as our symbol of aspiration. The aesthetic symbols of an alien culture could give us no clue as to the mode of experience behind them.

Furthermore, it seems arbitrary that Spengler should stop at cultural subjectivism. Why not epochal subjectivism? If a difference in the traits of a culture involves a difference in the content of its expressionistic symbols, does not his division of a culture into seasons indicate that each season symbolizes a mode of experience peculiar to itself? If a culture speaks a language of its own, then each season has its own dialect of that language.

Why, then, does Spengler not go on to this further stage? What "vested interests" could be endangered for this savant who would so willingly sacrifice an entire culture? The fact is that epochal subjectivism would interfere with his two major conclusions: cultural subjectivism and aesthetic defeatism.

Spengler's division into spring, summer, autumn, and winter is at bottom the formulation of four subjective types, four typical modes of experience which recur in each cultural cycle. Thus, subjectivity is seen to produce its alliances as well as its estrangements. And contemporaneous epochs of different cultural cycles might even be considered to have more in common than different epochs of the same culture—our "irreligious and cosmopolitan" winter, for instance, being nearer to the same mode of experience in the Graeco-Roman cycle than to its own "rural and intuitive" spring. At least, there is more of Apuleius than of Beowulf in the modern *Weltanschauung*. Epochal subjectivity, looked upon in this way, would tend to counteract the estrangements of cultural subjectivity. Cultural subjectivity would not be an *absolute* condition, but an *approximate* one—and the modes of experience in different eras of the world's history would be capable of an approach towards identity. Epochal subjectivity, furthermore, would constitute a sanction of the modern artist. It would force us to recognize that winter, purely by being a different mode of experience from spring, summer, or autumn, is categorically entitled to symbolize this mode of experience in art.

In any case, how can Spengler call modern art inferior? By what subtlety does this absolute judgment manage to creep into a relativistic theory? There is no criterion of excellence inherent in the analysis of a genetic process. His logical machinery provides for no step beyond the observation that in spring we must have the symbolizations of spring and in winter the symbolizations of winter. To emerge with a judgment in such a case would be like concluding, after an explanation of the earth's seasons as being caused by the planet's revolution about the sun, "therefore autumn is better than winter."

The pessimistic connotation which he puts upon the civilization aspect of the culture-civlization dichotomy is purely arbitrary. We might, with as much authority, use a different analogy from that of the seasons, perhaps considering all the earlier stages of a cultural cycle as periods of upbuilding, of pioneering, of grim, hard-working zealotry. Culture, we could say, struggles and wrestles with its environment to amass an inheritance which civilization, coming after it, has the leisure to enjoy. For when a culture is in full swing, it is not only politically and religiously intolerant, but aesthetically intolerant as well. And in any case, the people of Bach's time did not have Beethoven, and those of Beethoven's time did not have Wagner—while in the course of a New York winter we have them all.

Yet, however much one may snipe at Spengler's book, it remains a stupendous piece of work, formidable, lugubrious, and passionate. His historical perspectives are often brilliant and fertile; his methodology\* unquestionably has a future. And European culture does seem to be undergoing some weakening of the pure cultural strain: whatever interpretation we may put upon the fact, we must recognize that our culture is no longer thorough-bred. We now question, where we once asserted—and even art is trammelled by considerations which prey upon it much the way epistemology has preyed upon metaphysics. Such phenomena are given an elaborate orientation in Spengler's system.

But if our own art cannot suffice for us, if appreciation is as powerful an influence with us as creation, we should be renouncing the half of our inheritance by our almost pathological demand for creativeness as the criterion of self-respect. We must not confuse impoverishment with embarrassment of riches. Aesthetic defeatism is made more plausible by our modern tendency to consider the great works of the past as hostile forces rather than as amenities. For my own part, I can imagine but one really drastic kind of aesthetic desolation: if, by some great futurist upheaval, the traditional monuments of

---

\* His treatment of cultural factors differs refreshingly from that of the usual genetic or causalist critic. The sociologist, for instance, will explain aesthetic values as the result of the economic conditions under which they arise. He finds certain aesthetic values paralleled by certain economic conditions; and after observing that any variation in the one entails a concomitant variation in the other, he considers this as evidence that the economic conditions produce the aesthetic values. Spengler, arriving at this point, would merely observe that the two vary concomitantly, and that every other aspect of the same era in history varies concomitantly with them. In place of a causal principle, he would utilize a principle of analogy. He would specify that quality or character of an era which was manifest in any cultural activity of the era (architecture, music, inventions, politics, marriage customs, attitude towards property, and so on) just as we might consider a poet's facial expressions, his method of walking, and his style of writing to be analogous aspects—each in different terms—of his behaviour. This method broadens the horizons of such investigations enormously. [K.B.]

European art were to be eradicated now, so that not one trace of them remained except the *feel* of them in our memory. I imagine us trying to restore, with the bungling of a nightmare, the specific equivalents for these vague qualities which we recalled, trying to find again the actual notes for that suavity which we remember as Mozart, or that severity which we remember as Bach, or that straining Prometheus which we remember as Beethoven. Piecing together, from a line someone half remembers in Australia, and another restored by a traveller in Tibet, the godless rollick of Candide. Consulting *The Dial* of a recent month to recover, with the help of Mr. Rosenfeld's word pictures, the inert leap of an El Greco. And so on. But in the meantime, since all these works are still with us, I insist that it is not our *fate,* but our *privilege,* to receive more than we give. And though holy texts fail to assure us that we are, in so doing, blessed, they do not, on the other hand, acclaim such status as accursed.

# In Vague Praise of Liberty

*History of Europe in the Nineteenth Century* by Benedetto Croce. Translated from the Italian by Henry Furst. Harcourt, Brace and Company
*Hound and Horn*, July-September 1934, 704–707

Croce's *History of Europe in the Nineteenth Century,* which is dedicated to Thomas Mann, has about it something of that retrospective sorrow which we may note in the recent collection of Mann's essays, *Past Masters.* Emphasizing the political and economic movements of the century, as Mann had emphasized the esthetic one, it brings out the same titanic, and even demonic, quality of nineteenth-century effort. Reading it, we ask ourselves if mankind may ever again come to devote itself to more reposeful concepts of the good life. Should a cult of amenities, delights, and kindnesses manage to replace the cult of strain and dominance which prevailed throughout the romantic exaltation in art, politics, and business, no era will look more grotesque and turbulent (or even, to use Santayana's word, more "penitent") than the great "century of progress," with its prodigious exertion, its vast upswing in documentation and equipment, and its bewildering multiplicity of clashing *idées fixes.*

Strange paradox: How, in the name of freedom man drove himself and his fellows as he had rarely driven or been driven the name of servitude— and the world came to seek such rewards as fall to the unsleeping. It may be impossible to select one underlying cause for this complexity of interacting forces, material and spiritual, but Croce's word "liberty" seems adequate as a designation for them in the lump, whether we refer to the great expansionists of nationality and commerce, the iconoclasts of art and thought, or the political rebels who were determined to complete in the patterns of the state the movements already established in the habits of private enterprise. Incidentally, Signor Croce reminds us that our very word "liberal" comes from reactionary Spain, where it was put forward in contrast with the word servil, by men who saw in *servil* mainly the connotations of devotion, of loyalty, and in "liberal" the connotations of licence. Thus, as with many effective movements in history, liberalism would seem to have received its name from its opponents, and to have read into it "new meanings."

Croce's position with regard to this "liberty," which he sees as the genius of nineteenth-century purpose, has about it something of that "muddled" quality which is generally associated with liberalism. Evidently, even a philosopher, with all the conveniences of conceptualization at his command, cannot escape the confusions which underlie the liberal movement. If "liberty" is to have any sound purpose, if it is to serve as something more than a mere slogan for expressing and stimulating perennial unrest, it must be looked upon as a mere transitional device. That is: it will be intelligent only insofar as it performs a directly "pontifical" function, acting as a psychological bridge whereby a society goes from one thing to something else. The notion of liberty is very vague, but the notion of our prison can be very accurate—yet Croce, like the century by which he was formed, tends too naïvely to exalt liberty as a good-in-itself: instead of testing liberty by its ability to procure definite cultural values, he extols it as the ultimate value, the cultural end in behalf of which all else might properly be sacrificed. Our unemployed are "at liberty."

Of all the devices which should be labeled as mere "handmaidens" to social good, the name of liberty seems to head the list. As synonymous with the notion of "infinite progress," as representing the very core of human genius, it seems to me a dismal and even frightening ideal. *Liberty for what?* By the reversibilities of psychology, the very cult of emancipation makes life into a prison, since it is only prisoners who can intensely yearn to be free. In this respect, the cult of liberty must be taken as *per as* the evidence of radical cultural inadequacies. The Croce documents present us with the picture of a century whose most valuable contribution to history might be set down as the somewhat dubious one of having driven the cult of liberty to such excessive lengths that the peoples of the West can even, in their anguish and bewilderment, cry out for strong men to arise and rule them. As capped by the extreme romanticism of business, with its myriads of individual liberties treading drastically upon one another, "liberty" finally led to the drastic confusions of the World War, in which practically every shot was wrongly aimed, though the intellectual equipment behind these errors was a marvel of precision. And the honest philosopher, kindly and mankind-loving, notes this desolation, but consoles himself with the thought that a few pure souls here and there preserve the priceless ideals of liberty hidden away in the catacombs of the mind, a *respublica litteraria* of the elect.

The solution seems detached. Even if one does not subscribe wholly to Strachey's assertion that "liberty" was merely the spiritualized version of the struggle for free markets, for the right to sell one's services (which became in time the need to have one's services sold!) one must recognize that the gradual culmination of this movement in the formation of private or governmental monopolies greatly impairs whatever reinforcement the liberal ideal may have received from the dominant patterns of our economic life. The danger lies in the fact that this impairment of the liberal ideal (as the "economic authority" which once supported it is drained away by monopoly) may become too far advanced before the fruits of the emancipatory movement are attained. When this aborting takes place, and the abolition of "freedom" in business is accomplished without the abolition of commercialism itself, the result is usually called "Fascism." Fascism is particularly dangerous in that it merely *frustrates* the competitive instincts rather than converting them into the channels of a soundly cooperative motivation. It thus tends to foster a state which must seek its unifying principle, not in goodwill, but in racial or national malice. Where there is no strong bond of common good, union must be established by the image of a common evil.

We are so imbued with the "dignity" of liberty that the very thought of relinquishing it (even among the multitude which never had it) suggests some element of retreat or degradation quite as a vigorous old admiral might feel humiliated at being asked to abandon his campaigns and take a seat by the fire. Accordingly, it seems advisable that in attempting to salute the "next phase" we refuse to abide by the nineteenth century's statement of the issue entirely. That is: We must neither reaffirm the cult of liberty nor flatly bid it good-bye—but must simply state the issue in such a way that a choice either *for* or *against* liberty becomes irrelevant. It seems obvious that in any adequate cultural structure the entire notion of a choice between liberty and servitude would fall away, just as it is never paramount when the relations between friends or among the members of a family are compatible. From this point of view, I should suggest that the key word of the past century which we should single out for particular distrust and definite negation is *Werden,* "becoming," with its two antithetical corollaries, "progress" and "decadence." They are closely linked with the entire cult of liberty, but they may serve to present the matter differently. Let us say that we are seeking a condition of stasis, a "new equilibrium," and that our philosophies of "becoming" are justifiable only insofar as we can use them to acquire precisely the status of stolidity in which a philosophy of eternal change would seem irrelevant. Once we have chosen as our ideal the "divine unrest" of a perpetual "becoming," we almost automatically establish a set of premises which pledge us to the dismaying Nietzschean alternatives. The idea of "progress" leads to the discovery that war is the most thoroughgoing symbol of the adventurous, combative, heroic man—and conversely, the slightest evidence of a tendency to renounce this ideal presents itself to us as "decadence," a sinking into deep "Asiatic slumber" (for in the nineteenth century at its worst, nothing served more fitly as a symbol of sloth and death than the placidity of China at her best). Through the philosophy of *Werden*, the cult of "striving" takes on a purely combative quality, until "virtue" is a kind of "justification by conquest," residing not in the qualities and graces of well-ordered social relationships, but in a vain quest of the golden fleece, be this situated in either the accumulation of material commodities or the accumulation of those spiritual commodities which the scientist designates as "facts" or "knowledge." By such a concept of attainment, "goodness" and "success" necessarily became synonymous. It was a century to blow itself up—and it is doing so.

I do not offer these suggestions as a plea for passivity in the face of the current disorders. On the contrary, I believe that these disorders must be radically rectified—for only by such rectification can we establish an economic structure upon which a profound philosophy of *being*, as distinct from our philosophies of *becoming*, could again be erected. The state is an artifact—and it may be at least as imperative for citizens to revise their state as it is for a poet to revise his page.

# Untitled Review of *Stalin: A New World Seen Through One Man* by Henri Barbusse

*Stalin: A New World Seen Through One Man* by Henri Barbusse
*Book Union Bulletin,* November 1935

This is not a formal biography of Stalin. Even its subtitle, "A new world seen through one man," does not quite reveal the nature of its contents. The book begins and ends with Lenin—and it contains many important sections dealing with the purely *collective* aspects of recent Russian history, seen essentially as a group enterprise rather than as background for one man. It is, to be sure, written throughout as a fervent tribute to the figure who is now, in Barbusse's words, "the heart of everything that radiates from Moscow on the surrounding world." But beyond a desire, on Barbusse's part, to make Stalin's perspective his perspective, the book spreads until the subject of the individual is merged into the history of the Communist Party, and the history of the Party is merged into the general history of Soviet Russia.

As we lay down the book, we do not carry away the sense of a personal portrait at all. "Intimate" details are few. It is the phenomena of the 'political' personality that we are here concerned with—those aspects of a human character that one sees when considering him as a concentration point of historical events. The result is not a "family portrait," we might say, but a memorial statue in a park: it depicts the traits that bear most directly upon impersonal or superpersonal relationships. This emphasis upon the political rather than the intimate makes it natural and easy for the author to move, again and again, from the portrait of a man to the epic of a nation.

The word "personality" originally comes from a word referring to the role taken by an actor. In times of increasing passiveness, we have come to think of "personality" as a purely "spiritual" quality, something almost the opposite of one's public relationships. The *political* biography brings back the notion of personality closer to its origin, as it approaches character primarily from the standpoint of the role assumed by the actor in the human drama. And when such an approach is stressed, we find it natural to move, as Barbusse has done, from the man to his theories and his tactics, and thence to the historic context in which they operated.

The first chapter, "A Revolutionary Under the Tsar," depicts the rigors of that "terrible vocation," the calling of professional revolutionary, for which one must be fitted not only by reason of his convictions, but also by "iron health, at the service of indomitable energy, and an almost limitless capacity for work." Without histrionics, Barbusse impresses us with the picture, as he recounts Stalin's acceptance of his difficult role during the pre-Revolutionary days. Barbusse offers no psychological explanation of Stalin's efforts. He smiles at Emil Ludwig who asked Stalin, in an interview, "Perhaps you were ill-treated by your parents in your childhood, to have become such a revolutionary?"—and quotes Stalin's reply, "The reason that I became a revolutionary is simply because I thought the Marxists were right." In any event, Barbusse well shows that the conviction of possessing a *correct* philosophy fortified Stalin constantly, while he was further strengthened by the theory that the triumph of his cause was *historically inevitable.* Contemporary science has questioned the notion of historic inevitably, but it has never questioned the fact that a belief in historic inevitability may be of invaluable assistance in stimulating purpose.

The second chapter, "The Giant," depicts the master-disciple relationship between Stalin and Lenin. The stressing of this relationship is doubtless an important feature of Stalin's appeal to his countrymen. We see, in Barbusse's account, how many ingredients the public figure must unite within himself. He must symbolize not only his Party, and through his Party his people and their historic mission—he must also trace an integral connection with the important features of the *past.* Thus, it is in his role as the Perpetuator of Lenin that Stalin completes his public identity.

The third chapter describes Stalin's activities during the period of counter-revolutionary campaigns which followed the Bolshevik Revolution. This is followed by a very interesting discussion of national pluralism in Russia, the question of "homogeneousness in heterogeneousness," considering the adjustments made between the new unifying Communist framework and the separate national identities.

Barbusse next reviews the incredible difficulties of organizing the coöperative system in a state which had been but slightly industrialized to begin with, whose few industries had been crippled by war, and where the forces of inertia and open resistance were still strong as obstacles to the new modes of production. Then, under the title of "The Parasitic War," he gives an account of the split between Stalin and Trotsky. It is told frankly as a complete partisan of Stalin would tell it.

Next comes a review of Soviet success to date, in the one country in the world blessed with an economic system rational enough for a national surplus to be a national asset. This chapter is followed by an account of the policies adopted with relation to the peasantry. In chapter nine, "What of Tomorrow," Barbusse considers Soviet Russia's equipment, both as regards internal development and as regards protection against external aggression. He next adds a chapter pleading against the belief that there is any possible intermediate position between Reaction and Revolution. And in his brief closing section, "The Man at the Wheel," he returns to the theme of Lenin-Stalin identification.

The book is written with an unmistakable fervor. And as a general picture of the vast unwieldy processes of historic adjustment, as manipulated by key figures who both make history and are made by history, it is an engrossing record.

# Revival of the Fittest

*Darwin for Today: The Essence of His Works* edited and with an Introduction by Stanley Edgar Hyman. Viking
*The New Leader*, December 1963, 22–24

As we are reminded in the introduction to this edition, it was no easy job to select 170,000 out of the three million words that Darwin accumulated, "building, like his corals and earthworms, an enormous change at a pace almost imperceptible." So we can be sure that not all readers will be equally satisfied with whatever set of selections the hard-pressed editor might deem naturally fittest to survive for republication under such exacting conditions.

For instance, "Darwin's *Essay of 1844* is included in its entirety, as a substitute for *The Origin of Species,* which by itself would more than fill the pages of this present volume." And all that here survives of the later and longer work is the six-page "Conclusion." In his "Introduction," Stanley Edgar Hyman gives an expertly succinct review of the gains and losses that follow from his choice. The reader who takes those paragraphs into account should find the solution quite reasonable. And Hyman is a good guide on many other matters.

All told, this set of selections from Darwin does give us an excellent opportunity to consider the "essence of his works." The varied exhibits include: A section on the expression of emotions in monkeys (expressions "closely analogous to those of man"); a section on the most fascinating of plants, the ones that trap and digest insects; the entire *Autobiography* (readers will prize in particular Darwin's anecdotes about his shrewd yet friendly father, and the pages tracing the evolutionist's calm development from religious belief to agnosticism, which make an interesting contrast with Mark Twain's agitated pages on the same subject, published in the recent issue of the *Hudson Review*); from *The Voyage of the Beagle,* excerpts effectively contrasting life in Tierra del Fuego and in the Galapagos Archipelago; two personal letters ("Will you honestly tell me . . . whether you believe that the shape of my nose (eheu!) was ordained and 'guided by an intelligent cause'?"); a respectfully attentive report on the habits of worms, whose "castings" are so beneficial to the soil; and from *The Descent of Man,* a chapter "On the Affinities and Genealogy of Man."

While quietly content to describe himself in his old age as "like a man who has become color-blind" where religious belief is concerned, Darwin did believe in a future interregnum when man "will be a far more perfect creature than he now is," though "he and all other sentient beings are doomed to complete annihilation after such long-continued slow progress." His assumption was, of course, that man's eventual extinction would result from purely natural causes. He was not thinking of the ironically suicidal possibilities with which the recent perfecting of the physical sciences now confronts us.

I think it would be fair to say that the power of Darwin's evolutionism centers in his systematic concern with what he calls "degrees of resemblance." To discern the transitions of an organ (for instance, to observe the various modifications whereby a swimbladder becomes transformed into a lung) is by the same token to observe the notable respects in which unlike things are, *au fond,* like one another.

Thus Darwin's great skill in lining up a set of such modulations through a series of different species naturally prompted him to be on the lookout for respects in which, despite their obvious dissimilarities, the organic functions of various species might be traced back to a common ancestry: "Analogy would lead me one step farther, namely, to the belief that all animals and plants are descended from some one prototype." And man's body "is constructed on the same homological plan as that of other animals." We can see how readily a program of work was indicated by this approach when we read: "In accordance with the principle of evolution it was impossible to account for climbing plants having been developed in so many widely different groups unless all kinds of plants possess some slight power of movement of an analogous kind."

Whereas Western theology proclaimed a qualitative distinction between man and other animals, and whereas many naturalists were similarly inclined (at least partly, perhaps, in response to the same religious tradition), Darwin expressly objected to "placing man in a distinct kingdom." As he himself said, he aimed to show "that the mental faculties of man and the lower animals do not differ in kind, although immensely in degree." Thus he remarks (and I for one wouldn't want to deny it!), "If man had not been his own classifier, he would never have thought of founding a separate order for his own reception." And he quotes with approval Huxley's proposition that there "is no justification for placing man in a distinct order."

Doubtless in keeping with this stress upon considerations of *degree* rather than *kind,* Darwin pays astoundingly little attention to language as a special human aptitude. Typically, for instance, in a passage not here quoted (and I personally wish that Hyman had included Darwin's pages on language, perhaps making room by thinning out some of the stuff on the sheer machinery of mayhem expertly contrived by the botanic insectivores), Darwin speaks of language's resemblance to bird-song on the grounds that both must be learned. But he does not concern himself with the kind of Hegelian evolutionism that stresses "self-consciousness" (or Aristotle's "thought of thought"), a *reflexive* faculty characteristic of human language, with its special aptitude for talk-about-talk.

In sum, *terministically*, there is a paradox (or at least an ambiguity) implicit in Darwin's formula, "origin of species." To get the idea quickly, try substituting purely formal terms for his two quasi-materialistic ones. Then you would have something like: "the common ground (or unitary source) of the specific." Along those lines, and in keeping with the Hegelian proposition that a difference in quantity can make a difference in quality, one might reasonably hold that, regardless of man's biologic origins, his specific aptitude for symbol-systems marks the passing of a critical point (as with the steps that divide water from ice or steam).

In all decency, and lest we dishonor the many non-human species that are trying to eke out an honest living, we should at least categorically distinguish between all those other poor devils and the kind of symbol-wielding animal that can produce Isms, Madison Avenue, Wall Street, yellow journals, a Hitler, a Birchite, an occasional soft-spoken, cross-burning Southerner, and exalted calls to wage thermonuclear, chemical, and bacteriological war in the name of progress and freedom. Mr. Darwin, it was not nice of you to play down the fact that we are something special, endowed with the ability to be the unkindest kind of all.

Incidentally, Hyman reminds us that for all of Darwin's interest in man's sheerly biological pedigree, he took good care of his investments, so that they were worth much more when he handed them on than when he had inherited them. But many persons have already noted the traces of 19th-century British politics in Darwin's philosophy of nature.

Understandably, as regards man's "descent," heraldic shifts show up. So you have stylistic choices, at different stages along the way. You could pick (italics mine): "When I view all beings not as special creations, but as the lineal descendants of some few beings which lived long before the first bed of the Cambrian system was deposited, they seem to me to become *ennobled*." Or you could pick: "Thus we have given to man a pedigree of prodigious length, but *not*, it may be said, of *noble* quality." So much for the problem of human pedigrees implicit in the dialectic of a scientist who, in disclaiming any "philosophic" aptitude, automatically obligated himself, things being as they were then, to overlook the full implications of man's peculiar tricks with "symbolicity."

Many other exciting matters could be discussed in connection with this basic book. In particular, when going back over the pregnant pages in the light of recent controversy—and having in mind the fact that *both* sides of the Iron Curtain, each after its fashion, recently worked up some trick ways of *politicalizing* biology—I was struck by a quandary of this sort: Darwin seems to set up the terministic situation for quite different possibilities. There is the idea of mutations that arise within the mutant and are handed on. (The cunning, totally skeptical free-thinker, Remy de Gourmont, said that the theory of evolution threw out the magic of one big creation—or innovation—by postulating a lot of little ones.)

There are also two differently pointing notions in Darwin. The less "controversial" suggests that, when mutations do arise from within the mutant and get handed on, external conditions decide whether the new form will manage to prevail; that is, the deviation happens from within the given organism, and it survives purely because the new form is a better fit for the situation. Or, though the deviation occurs from within, it may be thought of as having been prodded into being by "external conditions." In this connection Darwin refers to the effects of *food*.

There is another quite different dimension touched on in these expert excerpts. It has to do with Hyman's hunch that Darwin's stomach trouble indicated what we now would call "psychogenic" origins. (That's a different species yet, as regards problems of origin!) We can know for sure only that, whatever was or was not wrong with Darwin's guts, he survived; and this volume is clear evidence that he left a lot of engrossing pages for specific selection.

# Myth

*Experience itself becomes mystical when some accidental event happens to be 'representative of the individual.'"*

—*A Grammar of Motives* (307)

# Untitled review of *An Introduction to Mythology* by Lewis Spence

*An Introduction to Mythology* by Lewis Spence. George G. Harrap
*The Freeman*, January 1922, 478

In the preface to his "Introduction to Mythology," Mr. Spence remarks: "Thirty years ago, if a student of myth had been asked who Janus was, he would probably have replied: 'A Roman god of origins.' Today he might see in him a development of the 'kirn-baby.'" It is thus that relativity is becoming the keyword in the sciences; and in this instance mythology ceases to be the recording of specific myths for their informative or documentary value, and becomes the comparison of myths to determine their common denominators. It is a short step, however, from the grouping of myths by parallelisms or recurrences to the explanation of these parallelisms by the formulation of some underlying principle; for these comparisons show "a regularity of development not to be accounted for by motiveless fancy, but by laws of formation." One finds, for instance, the continual recurrence of the Deluge in the myths of peoples scattered over the entire earth; and if the Hebrew myth is explained as a borrowing from the Babylonian, how is the prevalence of the same subject accounted for in the American Indian? Is this due to some purely physical relationship? Or does it testify to a certain broad similarity in all human brains? On this phase of the subject Mr. Spence is at great pains to maintain no thesis at all; although he does summarize what has been done in the way of establishing monistic principles, while he himself holds to the opinion that such efforts have been more invigorating than true, and that the interrelations of mythology should be formulated on a less wholesale basis. In his chapter dealing with the bearing of myth on folklore, he gives some interesting material relating to the metamorphosis of the former into the latter. The belief in the power of iron, for instance, to ward off evil fairies may be connected with the times of the pre-historic bronze-users, whose weapons were shivered to pieces by the users of iron; iron thus coming to be looked upon as a magic power. If the writer of this note could be permitted to add his mite to knowledge, may not this old iron-spirit be traced in a modest form even to present-day America? In the children's game of "iron-tag," the person who stands on iron cannot be tagged by the person who is "it."

# A Recipe for Worship

*The Hero. A Study in Tradition, Myth, and Drama* by Lord Raglan. Oxford UP.
*The Nation*, August 1937, 201–202. Also in *The Philosophy of Literary Form*

It is not likely that many readers will find the primary thesis of this book its most notable aspect. The author is very eager to prove that the figures and events of myth have no basis in history. Even a character like Robin Hood, for instance, would seem to dissolve under his analysis—particularly when we recall the material on The King of the Wood in Frazer's "Golden Bough," are reminded that there was a Continental story of Robert des Bois, and that "hood" is the word for "wood" in several English dialects. Even the historicity of the Trojan War is brought up for severe and drastic questioning, while the author hurls many amusing darts at the pious savants who would attest their respect for Greek enclitics by believing that there was a real prototype in history for the heroes and events celebrated in "The Iliad," despite the fact that even the stratagem of the horse appears in variation in the myths of other peoples.

When you finish you can still, if you prefer, persist in your belief that there was some actual flood to form the basis of the account in Genesis—and you may still satisfy your hankerings to seek some naturalistic account of Moses's feat in guiding his people across the Red Sea that later closed to swallow up the soldiers of Pharaoh. (You may hang on, regardless of the author's evidence indicating that such magical strewing of obstacles in the path of the enemy was the stock in trade of mythic leaders.) For as the author himself admits, it is impossible to prove absolutely that myths lack a grounding in historicity. Nevertheless he does attain a high degree of inference.

But whether you are convinced of his main thesis or not, I think you will find that, in the course of maintaining it, he turns up an enormous amount of valuable material. It is his contention that the figures and events of myth owe their origin to the ritual dramas of initiation and propitiation (rites for the installation of kings, for rain-making, fertilization, and victory in war).

The origin of myth, therefore, is in drama, and in drama of a purely *ceremonial* sort (such as we saw in the recent coronation). He traces the role played by king-god-hero in these magic rituals for the securing of prosperity. And he holds that tradition was written *backward,* with these dramas providing the perspective for interpretation. In fact, he gives ample reasons to conclude that history in the annalist's sense of the term could not exist prior to literacy. The primitive lives in the "pure present," his rituals linking past, present, and future into one (as they seek scrupulously to reenact a past ceremony in the present, for future efficacy, and their past persists in their present quite as the Catholic will tell you that every day Christ is crucified—the event being not merely "historical," but continuous).

But even though, when you finish, you may still tend to feel that there was an "actual someone" who provided the polarizing principle for the accumulation of mythic details (as Mae West is now the broad basis of Mae West stories), you do feel the important point to be the way in which they were reshaped for ritual purposes. In the course of his argument the author works out a recipe of twenty-two points for the typical hero. Among these might be cited: "At birth an attempt is made to kill him"; "he is spirited away and reared by foster-parents in a far country"; "on reaching manhood he returns or goes to his future kingdom"; "after a victory over the king and/or a giant, dragon, or wild beast, he marries a princess . . . and becomes king"; he "prescribes laws, but later he loses favor . . . and is driven from the throne and city, after which he meets a mysterious death, often at the top of a hill." The author cites as examples Hercules, Perseus, Bellerophon, Dionysus, Joseph, Moses, and Siegfried; and their fidelity to the pattern is quite convincing.

We should make but one major objection to his book. Noting that the details of the hero's life are not realistic, but ritualistic, he seems to underestimate the role of the people in the development of mythic figures. The author seems to assume that, since the details of the dramatic rituals deal with kingly ceremonies rather than with everyday life, the people beheld them merely as onlookers, their participation residing mainly in the fact that they had a share in the successful outcome of the rite.

This emphasis would, I think, imply a false relationship between drama and audience. The spectator, I believe, could not have been attached to these dramas merely because they were spectacular but mistaken ways of doing what is now done by irrigation and reforestation. The dramas could retain their hold only insofar as the spectators were "glued" to them—and one is glued to a work of art only when that work is reliving for him some basic pattern of his own experience, with its appropriate "medicine." The *curriculum vitae* symbolized in the dramas must have paralleled their own, despite the kingly symbols. In their heroic-ritualistic translation, these experiences were, to be sure, "writ large," but the underlying processes of transition charted by the mythic hero's life must have been a replica of their own processes. Thus the author accounts for the fact that so many of the ritual dramas have a doorway or gateway as setting by attributing it to a mere technical convenience of stage presentation; but could we not rather note the relevance of this "Janus" symbol for objectifying rebirth, such changes of identity as investigators have noted in totemic initiation? From this standpoint we might hold that, despite absence of realistic, everyday detail in the rituals, they symbolized the experience of even the most lowly, though expressed "transcendentally," in "stylistic dignification" (as when Shakespeare dignified his own concerns in King Richard II and Prince Hamlet).

The author is strongly antagonistic to Euhemerus and all his modern variants. He does not believe with that genial old debunker of 300 B. C. that the gods and heroes of mythology were merely deified mortals, with their real acts amplified by the imagination. Perhaps my reservation is but another brand of Euhemerism, though with a difference. I am suggesting that, despite the absence of realistic detail in the rituals, it was not the *king's* life but their *own* lives that the onlookers were reliving—and these lives were being made acceptable, or "negotiable," by transmogrification into royal attributes.

# Careers Without Careerism

*A Century of Hero-Worship* by Eric Russell Bentley. J. B. Lippincott
*Kenyon Review*, 1945, 162–166

This book is about a literary and artistic movement which the author has labelled "Heroic Vitalism." Heroic Vitalism is, in brief, the cult of the Superman, the exceptional mortal whom Nicholas Berdyaev would call the man-god, in contrast with the religious cult of a God incarnate, the God-man. Indeed, readers of Mr. Bentley's book might well profit by considering, at the same time, the Berdyaev book on Dostoevsky, in which the dialectic of man-god vs. God-man is traced at some length. Conversely, readers of that overly spiritual study would profit greatly by considering, at the same time, *A Century of Hero-Worship*, with its more materialist, pragmatist, positivist leanings.

The notice on the dust-cover is quite accurate in describing this collection of essays as "a brilliant excursion into the latter-day history of man's attempt to create heroes—as exemplified by Carlyle, Nietzsche, Wagner, Shaw, D. H. Lawrence, Spengler, and Stefan George, in their lives, their work, their influence." The author has aptitude for the characterizing, summarizing, and placement of the persons, works, and trends he reviews (reducing them often to that set of key propositions which, in a given writer's output, are variously interrelated by *therefore*'s, *however*'s, and sometimes sheer *and*'s). He is fairly discreet in his borrowings from the newer vocabularies of motivation, though now and then he makes a journalistic attempt to be exceptionally vivid when the material itself was already clear. There are several intelligent hours of reading in this book.

Mr. Bentley's label is meant "to embrace both a political theory, Aristocratic Radicalism, and a metaphysic which, inverting Carlyle's expression 'Natural Supernaturalism,' we might call Supernatural Naturalism." He contends that Carlyle was "groping" toward this philosophy, which Nietzsche "openly brandished." That is, whereas it is customary to interpret Carlyle's concern with "the good of evil" as aiming at precisely the mixture of immanent and transcendental ingredients which Carlyle did attain by borrowings from the Kantian terminology, Mr. Bentley's placement of him in a *line* of hero-worshippers leads rather to the interpretation of Carlyle's position as it looks when considered from our perspective at the *end* of this line. And the essence of a writer's work can look quite different when we consider the proportions of the ingredients within themselves than when we think rather of their fulfillment as revealed in a writer who, appearing later in the same trend, greatly changes the proportions of these ingredients, explicitly featuring a stress that, in the earlier writer, may have been by comparison but implicit.

Heroic Vitalism is "no creed," but "a faith, a dynamic Weltanschauung" that "adapts itself to the needs of the moment." With the best of intentions, the Heroic Vitalists "used arguments which today come too pat to the lips of demagogues." But although "their attack on democracy was cogent," they "expected too much of the enemies of democracy." Against them the author raises the "Marxist objection" that "no amount of education or eugenic selection is enough unless the hero has control of the commercial and industrial machine which is the modern state." And H-V-ism is indebted to classical education, though the author also observes that Carlyle ignores "the great civilizing principle of the golden mean," and that Nietzsche's, "Hellenic cult of the Whole" was likewise "an un-Greek recognition of the unity of theory and practice."

The book might have profited by two additional chapters, one logical or grammatical, the other psychological. The first would have considered systematically the philosophic points that are continually being introduced *en passant*. Particularly the scattered remarks on pragmatism make one wish that the author had told us just what key propositions, in his opinion, characterize this movement which he evidently considers of signal importance, since his hero-worshippers often grope for motivational statements that pragmatism can now take in its stride.

The second chapter I should wish upon the author might have been centered about the pattern of the sacrificial king (in line with William Troy's article on D. H. Lawrence, a thoroughly relevant contribution to the subject, though it is not even mentioned in the bibliography, and though Mr. Bentley himself says of Nietzsche, in passing, "He would be a Dionysos, torn to pieces that there might be a more abundant life"). The pages on decadence, sadism, surrealism, and the like would have fitted here. And since Mr. Bentley is explicitly concerned with the correlation between the sexual patterns and the intellectual patterns of the figures he is discussing (as when he suggests a probable connection between sexual impotence and the cult of power in Carlyle), much could be added here, I think, on the psychological linkages connecting the ideal of total independence, the cult of the self and its transmogrified replica, the cult of style, with the imagery of incest and self-abuse which can serve as the reflex, in sexual terms, of anarchistic and nihilistic values.

Thus Mr. Bentley cites Nietzsche's deliberate burning of his hand when an adolescent at Pforta school, but he uses the incident purely for purposes of moral portraiture: "He could not bear to hear of the courage of Mucius Scaevola, who did not flinch when his hand was burnt off, without seizing a box of matches and firing them against his own hand." But could not the incident be psychologically related, as well, to Nietzsche's grandiose dictum, "Thou goest to women? Remember thy whip," which would be related in turn to Mr. Bentley's own description of Nietzsche as a "self-flagellator." Mr. Bentley himself is content to characterize here in terms of masculine-feminine ambivalence, in place of a more integral interpretation, that would also, incidentally, fit well with his own notion of Eternal Recurrence as a "marriage-surrogate." On the purely "grammatical" level, such imagery of the independent self could be interpreted as representing, in burlesque, the Spinozistic definition of substance, the *causa sui,* the "hero" becoming a self-sustaining substance, in this sense, insofar as he is his own motive, which he can be by such *Selbsttodtung* as suicidally takes its destiny in its own hands.

Similarly, a formal psychological chapter might have called for other levels of motivation besides the purely rational explanation which Mr. Bentley gives for two grotesque dreams of Zarathustra. He treats these dreams as "cryptic confessions of Nietzsche's two deepest misgivings," the feeling that his work would be misunderstood and that his gospel might be false. Yet are not both these but aspects of a single, deeper misgiving: his appreciation of the dismal disintegrative end toward which his own intellectual development was inexorably leading him? (Mr. Bentley himself mentions Nietzsche's awareness of this trend during the '80's). Should we not thus interpret, psychologically, the distorted reflection of himself he saw in the mirror held by a child—as we recall that his ideal course of development was to go regressively from responsibility-laden camel to proud lion to *child?* And the second dream, with the roaring wind that tears open the gate, to release a whirling chaos of "children, angels, owls, fools, and butterflies," does it not contain a *future,* the future of one who (Mr. Bentley reminds us, though again without psychological application) wrote in 1887: "in me a catastrophe is being prepared"? The quality of Nietzsche's mystic moments, in establishing a complete identity between himself and his scene, adds further grounds for here treating statements about the scene as a portrait of the agent in that scene.

Still offering suggestions for a chapter dealing purely with the *forms* of psychology involved in the nature of his subject, we should want to put there also the thesaurus of powers cited from D. H. Lawrence's Vitalist beatitudes, "Blessed Are the Powerful." Here physical, mental, ethical, spiritual, mechanical, military, and political powers are mentioned. And since all Mr. Bentley's chosen figures are adulators of the power motif, we might have considered formally the resources whereby any one such power can do service for any of the others, by reason of their general kinship in the Power family of terms.

The author has placed Heroic Vitalism as a protest against both the "cash-nexus" of capitalism and the mechanism of applied science. But at the end, turning rather to our liberal word for the cash-nexus, "democracy," he notes a paradox in the democratic faith. For "democratic equality means to respect the individual"; and his respect in turn means "to notice individuality, to welcome variety, to revere superiority—which implies inequality." Anti-democratic philosophies of aristocracy such as Heroic Vitalism, he says, "are part aestheticism, part fascism." And "when the hour strikes, if he cannot swing to democracy, the Heroic Vitalist becomes either pure aesthete or pure fascist." But there is a proper approach to aristocracy, through democracy:

> Democracy, to justify itself, must include aristocracy. It is because democracy alone can produce aristocracy, because democracy alone can offer careers open to talent, that we are democrats.

One who thinks he has a talent has grounds for welcoming whatever situation seems to open a career for that talent. But does not Mr. Bentley end by here offering as his solution the very proposition that most succinctly states the essence of the *problem?* Is it not precisely the inducement to individual ambition that has led to the pushing, elbowing, and scramble characteristic of democracy, even inciting men to strive after improvement of their social status? Our world can be expected to have the defects of its qualities. But the author here ends by discovering as his solution precisely the unsettling aspect of our bourgeois society which induced our Heroic Vitalists to shape their own bourgeois careers by the reversal of bourgeois values. Sublimating the ideals of their class, they liked to imagine a careerist so great that he might abolish careerism, turning a few into leaders and calling upon all the others to rest content in their status as the led.

In brief, the conditions of democracy have made possible and necessary precisely the transvaluation most characteristic of the power philosophies (or power poetries?) Mr. Bentley is studying: the Umwertung aller Werte stemming from the fact that the tragic flaw of *hubris* is transformed into the primary virtue, the defiant courage of Byron's Manfred. Whereupon we are brought back to our belief that Mr. Bentley's book could have profited greatly by those two formal chapters, on the logic and the psychology underlying his inquiry. As things stand, he introduces at many points the central matter of the twice-born, but without a systematic treatment of rebirth. He refers often to the equally central matter of the personalistic revolt against the "machine age," but without tracing the ironies whereby those most personal and human of all things, technology and finance, can serve to depersonalize, or dehumanize, social relations. He deals throughout with the subject of power, but without an examination of the dialectical resources whereby this subject splits into a distinction between moral *action* and natural *motion* (the issue central to Kant's transcendentalism, and lying undetected at the roots of contemporary pragmatism).

However, whatever our reservations, let us end by again affirming our belief that this is quite an intelligent book.

# Folktale and Myth

*Python: A Study of Delphic Myth and it Origins* by Joseph Fontenroe. U of California P
*Journal of American Folklore*, July-September 1960, 270–271

This work gives us between the same covers both a book and the makings of a book. With its codifying of themes and motifs classed and sub-classed (with indications as to where the forty-three themes parallel or differ from the motifs of Thompson's *Motif-Index*), its exhaustive recording of versions and variants, its summaries, appendices, indices, tables, illustrations, footnotes, cross-references, and bibliography, it does indeed impress the reader with the conviction that the author has his subject sewed up for good.

That subject concerns the "combat myth." To this end, it centers in "a study of the combat of Apollo with the dragon Python, the origin myth of Apollo's Delphic shrine." But the search gradually widens, to include "myths, legends, and folktales of many lands, of Greece, Anatolia, Canaan, Mesopotamia, Egypt, India, China, Japan, Germanic Europe, medieval Christendom, even of Central America and the Pacific Coast." Thus the author hopes that his work will appeal to classicists, orientalists, folklorists, anthoropologists, "and all readers who like myths and folktales."

On pages 9 to 11, one will find the "Themes of the Combat Myth" neatly outlined, with regard to the nature of the combatants, the location of the combat, and its form as a story with a beginning, middle, and end. The account so concludes as to make clear the myth's development into "that kind of story which purports to tell of the occasion on which some religious institution, a cult or certain of its rites and festivals, had its beginnings, and of the divine acts which set the *precendent* for the traditional acts performed in the cult." But the search leads to the lineaments of an earlier myth (a contest between dragon and sky-god), which is outlined on pages 262 to 265. This is "a myth of beginnings, a tale of conflict between order and disorder, chaos and cosmos," the dragon side of the equation also being associated with death. (We might here note, incidentally, that in this form the myth comes close to the lore of the alchemists as regards *prima materia* and the dragon of chaos, though in alchemy the ordeal of combat is replaced by the *opus* designed to purge base metals.) On pages 465 to 466, there is a good concluding summary listing sixteen "observations and discoveries" that resulted from comparison of the later myths (particularly Apollo's combat with Python, and Zeus' combat with Typhon) with the "single antecedent myth" of the contest with chaos.

Finally, just as the listing of themes and motifs has broken the vase into tiny potsherds which the three summaries have pieced together again into forms, there is a generalization to include the lot, thus: "So we may look upon the whole combat between life instincts and death instincts that Freud was the first to formulate, albeit tentatively, as the central principle of all living organisms from the beginning; though it was seen dimly or expressed in dramatic or metaphysical terms by poets and philosophers before him. But in life the two kinds of instincts, though opposed, are always mingled. Thus do the fantasies of myth disguise the fundamental truths of the human spirit."

We should also note that in his chapter on myth and ritual, the author holds that, whereas the two "interpenetrate each other," the combat myth "did not grow out of rituals, but had an independent origin and was later imposed upon them" (though he adds, "Certainly some myths had received their whole frame and content from rites").

This work is so thorough, one would be supererogatory in asking that it do anything more than it does. But the very scope of its documentation suggests one possible further development. I refer to speculation that might use the material to seek for the "origins" of such myths not just in some earlier myth, but in something beyond any one myth, the nature of language itself.

I do not have in mind merely such notions as the possibility that "Typhon and Python are variants of a single name," though unquestionably the many modes of etymological transformation are of major importance in such searches. I refer to a further kind of possibility, an attempt to state why, whenever "fundamental truths of the human spirit" are stated in narrative terms (as they are said to be in the case of the "combat myth") certain forms are inevitable, insofar as the expression attains its perfect form.

For instance, we might begin by deducing the very theme of a combat from the principle of contraries and contradictories, of "polar opposites," implicit in the nature of that basic linguistic marvel, the negative. That is, insofar as negatives imply their opposites (as "disorder" implies "order"), such opposition itself is in effect "timeless"; but when it is translated into terms of myth, or narrative, such opposition can become a quasi-temporal "combat" between two terms, with the possibility of one partner prevailing at one time and the other at another, in succession, or alternation, and with intermediate moments of indecision.

Scattered throughout the author's far-reaching and authoratative assemblage of material for the study of the "combat myth's" origins in the purely historical sense, there are many observations that could be drawn upon for such speculative *vativinia post eventa* in this purely linguistic, or "logo-logical" sense.

But either way you take it, it is a tract well worth pondering.

# Myth, Method and Tragedy

*The Agony and the Triumph, Papers on the Use and Abuse of Myth* by Herbert Weisinger. Michigan State UP
*The New Leader*, November 1964, 21–23

The author of *Tragedy and the Paradox of the Fortunate Fall* and editor of *The Centennial Review* here reprints a selection of the expert scholarly and critical papers he has published over the last decade or so in various learned journals. He might well take as his motto his own formula: "There is, in art, no one source of the Nile."

Though quite independent in his judgments, it would seem that, on any given topic, his first impulse is to consult the files, see what others have said on the matter, and prepare a succinct survey of his findings. At times he becomes impatient with this scrupulous but not always rewarding procedure. In one of those impatient moments he writes, "I have come to the most distressing conclusion that the gravest danger to education lies, not outside the academic walls, but directly and deeply within them" (maybe he should here bear in mind that advertising, slanted news, and the "values" implicit in popular art are also forms of "education"); and he also speaks of "my confessedly unsystematic reading in more quarterlies than I know are good for me."

Typically Weisinger writes, "Not even the King Canutes of the new criticism can stem the tides of learning which flood through contemporary literature, and, as to criticism, why, Frazer, Marx, Darwin, Freud, Jung, Lovejoy, Whitehead, Tillich, and Buber are only the starting texts for beginning critics." (Incidentally, he confides that, because of an "irrational reason," he has "an almost pathological antipathy to the Jungian mystique," in contrast with an admiring and admirable chapter on "The Hard Vision of Freud.") In any case his questing, in pursuing the vigorous questions with which he constantly plagues both himself and others, classes him as anything but one of those "academic nullities, the men who believe little and profess less, and know nothing except the date of their retirement."

The sort of reader who wants to get everything settled for good and all will not be happy with this book. And the author himself frankly explains why:

> I suppose it must be transparently obvious to any one who happens to read these papers but it was not until I had brought them together and had read them one after the other that I realized how irritatingly ambivalent they are toward myth, their ostensible unifying theme; they are equally ambiguous with regard to their corollary theme, science. . . . In some of these papers, I find myself still believing in myth as a still viable and fecund form of thought. . . . In other papers, however, I discover that I take altogether the opposite point of view, that myth represents but an early stage in the intellectual development of man. . . . Pandora's box is myth; opening it is science.

On the subject as so put, every civilized man should waver, and Weisinger is highly civilized. Another possibility is to ask whether science as we now have it may itself be building up its own kind of Pandora's box. For instance, I can never bring myself to believe that, despite the material reality and technical accuracy required for a successful moonshot, scientific space travel to the moon is in essence any less looney than a poem about a dream-trip to the moon. And I'm far from impressed when people think themselves superior to an ignorant savage who can thrive in a wilderness; "superior" technology-bred modern imbeciles can thrive only if you give them the money to shop at a supermarket, while the "scientific myth," particularly as vitiated by laxities of business enterprise, is destroying the world's ecological balance at an alarming rate.

In brief, science must unmask not only old myths, but its own; Weisinger's lineup tends to suggest that the world of man-made science would categorically exclude the traditional modes of "symbolic action," whereas it may be only these same modes in a new form. I mean that "myth" would be here, not as a "survival from the past," but as an integral aspect of symbol-systems, even if all the old myths were of a sudden to be miraculously forgotten and we were to begin tomorrow with a brand new set of wholly "scientific" ones.

Weisinger still tends to think of myth too much in keeping with the imagery of "survival," as though it had its "source" in a primitive past. I would contend for a quite different kind of "source," in the real nature of symbolic action here and now. Here's a quick illustration of the difference I am trying to indicate: *The Power of Satire: Magic, Ritual, Art,* by Robert C. Elliott is a study of the likenesses and differences between primitive magic and sophisticated, esthetic satire. The book has many excellent observations on this subject. But its general tendency is to view modern satire as a modified survival of the primitive magical curse. (See above all, his suggestive Appendix on "The Curse.") If you are going to look for originating principles in terms of a historical line, however, you might with as much justice view primitive magic as a confused early striving toward its mature fulfillment in modern satire.

From the standpoint of symbolic action and its resources, one could locate the beginnings of both magical curse and modern satire in a "natural" aptitude of language, in its powers of invective (*vituperatio*). These powers took one form of expression when a magical worldview prevailed, and necessarily take another insofar as the rationale behind the ritual curse is weakened, and modern libel laws alter the nature of the risks that threaten the author of the invective. Elliott's work (and it's a good one) hovers on the edge of this view; but primarily, in borrowing from the lore of anthropology (as he should have), he failed to "de-anthropologize" his approach at this strategic spot. I submit that Weisinger's penetrating work on myth as "source" is similarly off center.

Whether you agree or disagree with this reservation, you will find many ingenious speculations on the overlaps between literature (more specifically tragedy) and the "myth and ritual pattern." Indeed, in keeping with Weisinger's characteristic restlessness, you will find him not only summing up the "pattern" and applying it to his study of Shakespearean tragedy (by his way of figuring, *Othello* comes out on top, and the magic comedy of *The Tempest* does not fare well), but also (in his chapter on "Some Meanings of Myth") he comes to the conclusion that "no myth and ritual pattern as such exists or ever existed in any real sense; it is a modern, scholarly reconstruction of diverse materials drawn from divergent sources, and no two experts agree as to its exact constitution." We'll leave that to be settled between him and Stanley Edgar Hyman, with whom he quarrels somewhat (in his chapter "Between Bennington and Bloomington") and whom he greatly admires.

Here is Weisinger's Roget-like windup, so far as the "pattern" is concerned: "Myth study at present has not so much the purity and integrity of an homogeneous regional cooking as it has the syncretist flavor of international *cuisine*: a dash of Cassirer, a dollop of Freud, a grain of Frazer, a minim of Graves, a pinch of Harrison, a smidgeon of Jung, a taste of Thompson, all intriguing flavors in themselves, excellently cooked, but, "still and all, not really a style." Incidentally, when he referred to my own analysis of *Othello* simply as "the psychoanalytic approach of Kenneth Burke" and hurried on, I wept. But I love him anyhow.

Though the constantly recurring themes of the book are myth and tragedy, the essays cover quite a range of related questions. Among others, one should mention such pieces as his resistance to "The Attack on the Renaissance in Theology Today"; his data on works that view the world in terms of the "extended metaphor" of a theater ("*Theatrum Mundi*: Illusion as Reality"), though I wish he had also considered the "dramatistic" view according to which the nomenclature of "action" can be applied to human relations *literally;* a chapter on Frazer (who, he says, "created the myth of the myth"); some reservations on "euhemerist" tendencies in "Robert Graves as Mythographer"; thoughts on "Dialectics as Tragedy" (he views Marxism as "capable of producing authentic tragedy," except that it lacks the necessary combination of faith and skepticism); a "myth and ritual" approach to the librettos of W. S. Gilbert (here Weisinger comes close to some paragraphs that might, without much forcing, be fitted into *The Pooh Perplex*); and for a finale, an emotional review of the Sacco-Vanzetti case (it is from Vanzetti that he gets the title for his book).

Above all, one should note Weisinger's restless concern with matters of *method,* regarding both scholarship and criticism. He has listened to so many voices, he never forgets the great babble involved in the search for "the sources of the Nile." And though he thinks of himself primarily as scholar, teacher, and critic, perhaps his editorial role is also an important influence upon him—particularly as regards his tendencies to the survey approach.

My main objection to the typical discussion of primitive myth is that it tends to "over-naturalize" the subject. That is, the notion that rituals were developed to the ends of "order" and "control" puts the major stress upon the use of magical devices to influence *nature,* whereas they seem to have been developed and perfected by men who were vitally concerned with the relation that such rites had to the structure of *social authority.* Thus, of all the books Weisinger mentions, there are two quite fertile ones that he seems to have left out of account. They are *The Genesis of Plato's Thought* by A. D. Winspear and *Aeschylus and Athens* by George Thomson. These works indicate superbly how to play down the mythic penchant for such terms as Freud's Eros-Thanatos pair. But Weisinger is so strongly moral and political in his sympathies that there is much in this book which falls wholly outside the charge of mythic "over-naturalizing." All told, these are exceptionally lively pages.

# Language

*Rhetoric is concerned with the state of Babel after the Fall.*

*—A Rhetoric of Motives* (23)

# After-Dinner Philosophy

*The Genius of Style* by W. C. Brownell. Charles Scribner's Sons
*The Dial*, March 1925, 228–231

In his newest book Mr. Brownell has written a series of glosses to Buffon's statement that "Style is nothing other than the order and movement we put into our thoughts." His program, he says, is not that of "defining the indefinable"; he will be content, rather, to "confine it within a compass narrow enough for contemplating comfortably." The result is a work displaying none of the gauntness caused by the lean and hungry pursuit of concatenated thought; and while filled with much sharp detail, the book has a clarity from line to line which it does not possess as a whole, so that it will, I believe, be more easily understood at a first reading than a third.

Mr. Brownell employs puns, not for decoration, but as the backbone of his thoughts. His most vital distinctions are less definitions than jingles, although as jingles they are always charming. He speaks, for instance, with his undaunted mother-wit, of the contemporary tendency to wear less clothes than formerly, and suggests that it is "intrinsically egoistical rather than social . . . originating, perhaps, in a desire to experience a sensation by producing one." Or he complains of modern art:

> Portraying invisible transition, though securing rhythm by falsifying rhyme and reason, destroys the integrity of the dancing lady dislocated for the purpose. She is indeed fatally rhythmic; dance she must since, ceasing, and lacking the wherewithal, she would be unable to sit down.

It is safe to suppose that no more engaging book has ever been written on this "subject of philosophical discussion." Unfortunately, the author takes a positively Puckish glee in digression, not a "that reminds me" type of digression, but the digression of gratuitous distinctions which, while brilliantly lighting up some passing phase of the subject, often remind us that this phase did not, for the purpose at hand, need lighting. We might say that

Mr. Brownell follows the course of his arguments like a terrier out for a walk with its master: he covers five times as much ground as necessary, but is on the highway only long enough to cross it.

*The Genius of Style* is primarily a plea for "aesthetic prose," prose which does not merely possess the more homely and serviceable virtues of clarity and precision, but also makes its appeal to our emotions as well as to our intellects. Mr. Brownell does not mean that pure communication should be candied up with "aesthetic" qualities; what he is really concerned with is a plea for the use of prose in other functions than pure communication. He does not want prose considered as the opposite to poetry, one as a vehicle for the intellect and the other for the emotions. The issue involves merely shifting a centre of gravity. If the purpose of a novel, for instance, is to tell its plot, style becomes dalliance in direct ratio to the acquisition of qualities beyond clarity and precision. But if the tone of the novel is taken as its *primum mobile,* and the plot is considered merely as one of the many potentials for conveying this tone, then clarity and precision are hardly more than a basic framework, and the more "written" aspects of speech come into prominence.

In terms of authority, Mr. Brownell can readily enough establish his issue, by simply recalling the outstanding English authors who have written aesthetic prose. It is in his dialectical justification that he becomes confusing, and I believe this confusion to result from his unconscious use of the word "style" in two senses.

He speaks of "the quality of style, that is, of an *ensemble* of structure and rhythm." Style occurs when the "whole composition is modelled by the details functioning as forces." Style is "the organic factor in art of any kind, the factor in virtue of which every part of any whole becomes at once a means and an end." The genius of style, "which remembers and anticipates in the act of expression." All these statements seem to mean by style that growth and consistency of the art-work which is usually designated as form. Yet we also find "style" used for "pomp," or "ceremony," as when he regrets that the Brooklyn Bridge was not given an architectural finish, "something comparable to the Karlsbrücke towers." Obviously, the Brooklyn Bridge does have style in the sense of consistency, appropriate detail. A piece of engineering, to stand, must have. And if Mr. Brownell wants it to have "more style," he wants it more decorative, more ceremonious. Thus he could praise the style of Newman because it "seems to celebrate the subject rather than expound it, as a song does its words." Mr. Brownell's chapter on style as a chastening influence on our social habits is built entirely on this second meaning of "style," for obviously it is not consistency, but ceremony, which could produce such results.

At other times "style" seems to mean simply "theme" or "message," as when he speaks of "style touched with emotion." And when he quotes as an example of style Arnold's "He is, he is with Shakespeare," he does not seem to mean style as major form, as the relation of detail to some larger unit, as "remembering and anticipation," (otherwise, how could he quote the sentence as an example of style without explaining its exact position and function in its context?); but he is pointing out as style a sentence which has a formal peculiarity of its own. The sentence is a kind of broken repetition, comparable to Yeats's "I will arise and go now, and go to Innisfree"; and its appeal lies in the fact that it is really a rhetorical device not yet abstracted into a formula. The Bible, translated under the close suggestion of the original tongues, frequently has beautiful varieties of non-English in which the stylistic value is, similarly, that of a latent formula. But these other senses of "style" are less confusing, and the major confusion of style as consistency with style as ceremony is all we need consider here.

The basis of Mr. Brownell's plea is that style is a "not-ourselves ideal," and utilizes certain laws of perfection which are outside the individual. ("Not-ourselves" is a misnomer, since if such laws exist, they are not "not-ourselves," but "not exclusively ourselves"; we sense them as individuals, and in common with the rest of mankind.) In opposition to this "not-ourselves" ideal of style (and here surely is meant style as form, as growth) Mr. Brownell speaks of manner, which is the expression of the personality. Although the author gives no specific examples of manner, he does quote Sainte-Beuve to the effect that manner is dictated by the nature of the author's talent. "Manner" seems to signify one specific equipment, readily traceable to the personality, one limiting mold into which the author pours his subject. Waldo Frank's *staccato* treatment of every subject, for instance, would be thus a manner. And perhaps there is also manner in Sherwood Anderson's gesture of the half-articulate prophet.

In this sense "manner" is to be differentiated from form, while ceremony (hitherto masking under "style" as a "not-ourselves ideal") would reveal itself as the expression of the personality, thus being one kind of manner. With such a revision of Mr. Brownell's terms, he could counsel form, the "not-ourselves," as that element which makes for a work's perfection within its kind. It would be a technical, or non-moral attribute, and as readily accessible to the pornographic and the diseased work of art as any other. But he could ask that authors employ a ceremonious, or dignified, or appealing manner, which necessitates the uplift of the personality, and is thus a moral attribute. But Mr. Brownell's avoidance of this dissociation looks like a bit of unconscious Jesuitry, giving as it does the impression that a man must have a noble soul to have a good technique, disguising for a technical age moral values as concerns of craftsmanship, attempting to insinuate ethics into those who have little religion beyond art. I believe that Thomas Mann's discovery of moral values as deeply emotional, and as thus making for the richer art, is a less tortuous and more convincing method of arriving at the same conclusion.

But Mr. Brownell's book, with its hale and balanced prose, is an excellent one, and rides beautifully above what to me seem like inconsistencies in its reasoning. Furthermore, its central purpose is so obviously less the elucidation of its subject than the expression of a sprightly and keen-witted personality (less consistency than ceremony) that it seems almost *mal apropos* to stress its argumentative aspect. *The Genius of Style* is not a discourse on style, but an after-dinner speech on style, tricked out with the most entertaining compliments, anecdotes, and asides. And if, on finishing it, we understand style the less, we may congratulate ourselves upon having seen Mr. Brownell the more, and having enjoyed his jibes at some mythical body of thought which, so far as the mute and inglorious oncoming generations are concerned, might in some vague way be H. L. Mencken, or non-existent, or both.

# Idiom and Uniformity

*The Society's Work S. P. E. Tract No. XXI* by Robert Bridges. Brochure. Oxford UP
*Words and Idioms* by Logan Pearsall Smith. Houghton Mifflin Company
*The Dial,* January 1926, 57–60

*The Society's Work,* by Mr. Robert Bridges, is a modest, and almost melancholy, pamphlet dealing with the motives, the hopes, and the procedure of the Society for Pure English. "Two primary considerations," Mr. Bridges writes, "called our Society into being." First, the English language is spreading all over the world, "a condition over which we have no control." During its evolution it has been "subjected to sudden violent changes of environment, irruptions or interruptions so disconnected that they must rank scientifically as external accidents." And while this has brought much wealth to the language, it has also caused defects, some of which are still corrigible and "have their cure ready to hand in existing dialects." "Again, there are those abundant absurdities common to all receptive languages that can be corrected more efficiently by intelligent criticism than by unguided practice." The second consideration is that the history of languages "shows that there is danger lest our speech grow out of touch" with our inheritance, "the finest living literature in the world," and "losing, as it were, its capital, and living from hand to mouth, fall from its nobility and gradually dissociate itself from apparent continuity with its great legacy, so that to an average Briton our Elizabethan literature would come to be as much an obsolete language . . . as Homer or Aeschylus to a modern Greek." This danger is increased by the fact that the central force of English is so dissipated over all manner of "unrelated environments"; while there is furthermore the "most noxious condition" that "whenever our countrymen are settled abroad there are alongside of them communities of other-speaking races, who, maintaining among themselves their native speech, learn yet enough of ours to mutilate it, and establishing among themselves all kinds of blundering corruptions, through habitual intercourse infect therewith the neighbouring English."

The Society is, therefore, purely centripetal in its ambitions. Its work is essentially catholic, and attempts to arrest midway those very protestant tendencies to which English itself owes its original recognition as a means of dignified expression. The problem thus corresponds to that which, earlier in European history, beset another great imperialistic language. The power of a speech to spread over alien territories becomes, at a certain point, a weakness—just as yeast, flourishing in the fruit mash, multiplies with ebullience and fervor until, by its own processes, it has generated sufficient alcohol to kill it. Latin, like English, spread into "unrelated environments" until the divergent particularities of the various conditions under which it was spoken attained their counterpart in corresponding divergent particularities of speech.

With the example of Latin haunting us, we are constantly tempted to defeatism; yet not totally so, because instruments of standardization are much more in evidence today than they seem to have been during the hegemony of Latin. It is usual to consider, as Mr. Bridges considers, that such things as compulsory education, journalism, and the radio are primary incentives towards standardization. But it seems probable that "all modern improvements" in living conditions, minimizing as they do divergencies of habit, are of much deeper utility. It is they which, for better or worse, promise an eventual sky-scraper hotel in Tibet, a macadamized road through darkest Africa, and steam heat in the igloos. And the fact that English is spoken, with not too hopeless variations, by the two nations best equipped today for carrying on this horse-evangelism, may enable the language to retain a reasonably uniform integrity while widening its geographical frontiers. If this is true, the Society's program should become increasingly successful, since it will be profiting by, rather than militating against, natural forces.

Just how much aesthetic preferences have to do with the settling of such matters it is hard to say. It would seem, however, that uniformity of speech would be best promoted by some such attitude as obtained in the eighteenth century, when the waywardness of idiom, grammatical turns of speech which were logically inconsistent, and "expressive" words fighting their way from popular speech up towards formal recognition, were considered as a nuisance rather than a wealth. Every new candidate, it seems, should be admitted grudgingly; and a circumlocution might even be preferred to the risk of using some new, more direct, more "forceful" method of speech which incurred the danger of remaining regional. Writers would—were individualism suddenly to burn out and conformity become the characteristic aesthetic trend—willingly impose upon themselves a kind of arbitrary restraint, as though a general attempt were made to write in the language of Chaucer. For, if the welter of new popular creations continues, uniformity would thrive best in an aesthetic of *written* words rather than *spoken* words, pomposity rather than conversationalism, "Asiatic" prose rather than "Attic" prose, obscurantism rather than spontaneity. It could be done, and done with sufficient returns, if ever Europe were Chinese enough to do it. And for those who would complain against the "barrenness" of such a procedure, it might be well to point out that one age may find the art of a past age barren not because this past age lacked penetration in its art, but because the penetration was not of the sort which the new age demands. Needing bread, it cries out against those who amassed metals. However, whether it is bread or metal which we demand, the contemporary aesthetic seems directly opposed to the kind of uniformity suggested above—as Mr. Logan Pearsall Smith's new volume, *Words and Idioms,* well indicates.

Mr. Smith's volume is an English equivalent to Remy de Gourmont's *Esthetique de la Langue Francaise.* Both writers admire, not regionalism in speech, but those aspects of speech which by their very nature can originate only in regionalism. And whereas Mr. Bridges, facing the "menace" of dissipation, complains against a statement in The *New York Times* (a blind optimism generated by despair, according to his diagnosis) that "the old lady may be trusted to take care of herself," Mr. Smith writes:

> More and more . . . standard speech, and the respect for its usages, is being extended, and there is not the slightest danger at the present day that its authority or dominance will be questioned or disregarded. The danger lies rather in the other direction that in our scrupulous and almost superstitious respect for correct English, we may forget that other and freer forms of spoken English have also their value, and make useful contributions to our speech.

It is quite possible, of course, that the modern appreciation for the dying folklore has no force as a movement at all, but is rather a kind of last gasp, the sudden jealous clinging to something which becomes most valuable at the moment it is being taken from us. It may be that the ambitions of the S. P. E. will be only too successful; although the sullen prejudice remains that if they are so, "conditions," rather than the efforts of the S.P.E., will be responsible.

In the meantime, we seem in a strange antinomy, wishing with our minds a state of affairs which our palate is continually denying; anxious lest our language develop to a point where Shakespeare and Milton write an English which is obsolete, yet delighting in the continual refreshment and generative power that remains with us; striving for "wealth at all costs"; and with a "poor but mine own" psychology following in our love of newness and invention somewhat the procedure of the Dark Ages, when noble texts were erased from the parchment that contemporary creations, however idle or ill-considered, might be placed in their stead.

# Poets All

*Bentham's Theory of Fictions* by C. K. Ogden. The International Library of Psychology, Philosophy, and Scientific Method. Harcourt, Brace, & Co. *The Nation,* January 1933, 70

Much of Bentham's work on the unmasking of the "ghosts" or "fictions" which men mistake for realities was done in the very year of Waterloo—and as could be expected, this "small still voice of one weighing the meaning of words" went unheeded during stress. "Even less was it heeded when the storm had died down," and men began nibbling at the edges of his doctrines while completely neglecting the core. So here we are, a century after his death, at another time of Waterloo, beset by a whole astral sphere of unexorcised, gibbering ghosts. They are, perhaps, with their vague terrors, their "ingenious perversion of the language of praise or blame, to make it comprehend that which did not properly come within the quality expressed," observable in such terms as "raids on the Treasury," "saving the railroads," "national honor," "sound money," "private initiative," "sanctity of contract," "observance of the law," "good for business," "favorable balance of trade," "wholesomeness of our people under strain," "confidence," "fundamentally sound," "scraped bottom." Bentham dreamed of a vast lexicographical project which would eliminate the vaguenesses of words forever, at least the pivotal words of ethics, politics, and law—and though one can imagine wiseacres saying that the meanings of words are funny things to be fooling with while millions are in danger, they might well recall the past great changes wrought in the social structure by "Encyclopedists," writers of dictionaries—and these same objectors will, if they are "practical agitators," go forth to plead with people, from soapboxes, by the hour, attempting nothing other than the reshaping of the terms in which people consider their situation. A wily old trout lives only because he has learned to distinguish the meaning of bait from the meaning of prey; men dodge automobiles successfully because of the meanings that an onrushing car happens to have for them; and, similarly, our social processes may be as dangerous as unsuspected poisons until we have well defined them. "*Give us our rights,* say the thousands and the millions. *Give us our rights,* they say, and they will do well to say so. Yet of all who say so, not one perhaps can say, not one perhaps ever conceived clearly, what it is he thus calls for—what sort of a thing a *right* is." So it might be an eminently practical matter for us to have a thorough technique of definition. Bentham, to eliminate the tragic human bunglings that come of ideological vagueness, would develop a method for making men fully conscious of the linguistic aspects of our thinking.

Language, to guide us, must be a naming. Yet in all probability language did not originate as a naming at all, but as an instrument for exhorting and conveying attitudes. In its origins and underlying machinery it is probably about as much like "thought" as a dog's perking of his ears and bristling of the hairs along his spine when he scents a cat. Bentham would never overlook this unintellectualistic genesis of speech, and would so codify the rules of definition as to guard as much as possible against it. Thus, in the present book, edited by the coauthor of *The Meaning of Meaning,* we are shown the ambiguities and vaguenesses inherent in speech, "linguistic" structures which man has attempted to read into the very structure of the universe; we see the bewilderments these ambiguities can cause in human conduct; and we find in outline a methodology of definition whereby they may be avoided. Fundamentally, it is a method for forcing one to disclose the picture-thinking and emotional tinges hidden in the necessarily metaphorical language one employs, and for compelling one to carry one's analysis of vague words (such as "obligation," "rights," "justice") to the point where they are made to refer to "something real and observed."

Bentham knows the tricks of the rhetoricians, tricks so deep that even the rhetoricians are seldom aware of using them—for rhetoric as he conceives it is only too constantly at the command of all. By the Bentham teaching, all men are poets, alas! as they judge and act and exhort their fellows by terms which work upon our unsuspected prejudices, or words which are really talking about two things when they seem to be talking about one. And he knows the handy "appellatives" which have ever come to the assistance of "moral" men by furnishing them with the best motives for their acts, as a simple "love of gain" may appear in the "eulogistic covering" of "industriousness" (devices which he calls "fig-leaves" for the "unseemly parts of the mind").

Bentham expected that not merely one century, but many centuries, would pass before we might have hopes of such a quiet and deep-lying change as is at the bottom of his methods. Meanwhile, we shall probably continue to combat old ghosts with new ones, ever fighting wars henceforth in the name of peace, fantastic wars-to-end-war, and adulating such jungle ways of thought as might serve us better if we were trying to rip live meat with our claws than for properly apportioning the national income. Perhaps for a long time yet flags will be torn down only when there are stormers to raise other flags. This, Bentham would call the "license of cheating people for their good." The Benthamite revolution, on the other hand, will never occur in its purity unless criticism and skepticism can enjoy the place of honor in the state, along with a completely non-theological utilitarianism based accurately upon human pains and pleasures, avoiding those strangely gnarled forms of religiosity which are no less religious, and even *magical,* through the fact that the flaming words of their inspirational cult are to be found primarily in the financial columns of our press.

# Concern About English

*Wine and Physic: A Poem and Six Essays on the Fate of our Language* by Alexander Laing. Farrar & Rinehart
*Poetry*, February 1935, 294–296

Though this volume contains both verse and prose covering a considerable range of issues, Mr. Laing writes primarily as an educator. The long opening poem, "The Flowering Thorn," is as instructively allegorical as an old morality play. Indeed, in both symbolism and manner, it harks back to ways of statement that prevailed long ago. And the glosses and archaistic illustrations that line its margins are similarly suggestive of ancient conventions. Thus vulnerably if venerably, the poet tells us of a long lineage, and of the arduous discipline which the bardic apprentice must under-go before he can fit himself to carry on the traditions handed down to us from the days of Chaucer. And allegorically he proclaims his uneasiness at the thought that alien strains have threatened to obscure our pious attachment to this spiritual lineage. In his introduction he writes: "With chaos abroad in our world, it is a basic instinct to defend first that which we most love; and I love this English." The poem is perhaps too loyal. New and alien strains were excluded with over-thoroughness. A little bastardy might have made it sturdier.

However, the author gives us another chance—for in the remainder of his volume he restates his position in straight critical prose that is not antiquarian at all. The dissociation between his right and left-handed manners amounts almost to a complete transformation as we turn from one to the other. Here, with ample material, he pleads that teachers of good English usage should think of their function primarily as conservative, and should not feel their work discredited simply because the relentless process of change exerts itself regardless. His argument is based upon the liberal notion, defended by Eliot, that even a vanquished opposition plays a *cooperative* role in the historic process. There is much to be said for this, as all effectively implemented attempts to produce a "totalitarian" state will in time reveal. Nevertheless, it is hard to get people to think of themselves as losers by profession—and one may doubt whether the author, in proposing that teachers accept as their function a grudging retreat before the forces of innovation, will greatly animate the Guild. The conservatives are not out to lose gracefully, but to win—and from that difference in attitude springs all the difference between humanism and reaction. Mr. Laing's prescription looks best when we divorce it from the surrounding social context. The author would take this into account by pleading that education is a contemplative pursuit rather than an active one—but since contemplation provides us with basic cues as to our modes of action, it is hard to see how his likable distinction can be upheld.

In a sense, it is unfair to single out the "lesson" of Mr. Laing's book for particular discussion. Its main value is in its incidental matter, especially its elucidation of linguistic problems, which are often stated succinctly and picturesquely, as when he says:

> An Eskimo's speech, like his bone weapons, can retain its forms with trivial changes over hundreds of years of the same kind of living; our language, like the tools of our automobile factories, must undergo ready alteration at the dictates of scientific research, social revolution, and mere fashion.

His book can be recommended to those who would like to see important aspects of such issues clearly brought to the fore.

# The Impartial Essence

*Lectures in America* by Gertrude Stein. New York: Random House
*New Republic,* July 1935, 227

The repetitions and blithe blunderings that Gertrude Stein has somehow managed to work into a style make her *Lectures in America* hard for a critic to discuss. Though they have as their subject a theory of writing, they are expressed so girlishly that we are tempted not to ask how the various parts fit together.

The keystone of Gertrude Stein's literary theories seems to be her doctrine of "essence." She would get at the "essence" of the thing she is describing. She thus tends to consider literature primarily as *portraits*. She makes portraits, not only of people, but of landscapes; plays are to her little other than group portraits; and eventually people and landscapes become so interchangeable that a play can describe a landscape by assembling portraits of people. Hence let us, instead of attempting to follow the order of exposition in Miss Stein's book itself, build up her literary schema in our own way with "essence" as the starting point:

The essence of a thing would not be revealed in something that it does. It would be something that a thing is. The search for essence is the attempt "to express this thing each one being that one." A thing's essence is something that makes it distinct from other things; it is, as she says at another point, a thing's "melody." Since it is some-thing that the thing *is,* action would tend to obscure it rather than reveal it. Hence:

> In my portraits I had tried to tell what each one is without telling stories and now in my early plays I tried to tell what happened without telling stories so that the essence of what happened would be like the essence of the portraits, what made what happened be what it was.

Suppose, now, that you held to such a doctrine of essence, and wanted in your writing to get down the absolute essence of each thing you wrote about.

Consider the sort of problems, in both theory and method, that might arise. In the first place, you would have to worry about resemblance. In putting down the essence of Mr. A, you would have to guard against any tendency to think of him in terms of somebody he resembled—Mr. A1. Again, since essence is something that a thing now is, you would have to guard against the tendency to think of your subject is terms of memories (an exaction which might explain in part her tendency to feel that stories or acts obscure the perception of essence). And you would now have brought yourself to the paradoxical position wherein your knowledge of your subject's past or of people like him amounts to "confusion" (a sad state of affairs upon which Miss Stein dwells at some length).

At this point you might rebel; but if you go on, as Miss Stein did at her leisure, you will find attendant considerations arising. You will talk much about getting "inside" things (perhaps thus being led to note as the primary fact about English literature the stimulus it derived from insularity). And since you, as an *outsider,* are busied with the literary task of describing things until you get *inside* them, there will necessarily hover about your theories some hint of mystic communion. In time your doctrine of essence brings you to the metaphysical problem of the One and the Many, for if you start by trying to find wherein each one is that one, you begin to find a general intermingling; and particularly as you make that outside you to be inside you, you come, through the medium of yourself, upon a kind of universal essence:

> And so I say and I saw that a complete description of every kind of human being that ever could or would be living is not such a very extensive thing because after all it can be all contained inside in any one and finally it can be done.

How does this work out in practice? You start to write about something, to describe it, to make its portrait. You have a personal style, a set of mannerisms that suit your particular essence, and as you write you gradually get into the swing of them. When you get going, you are "excited." And since your excitement arises during your description of a thing, you may call this excitement the melody or essence of the thing. You may feel that each subject has its particular essence because you have used a particular combination of words in writing about it. But you feel the "unity" of all subjects because the quality of your excitement is the same in all cases (the way you feel when you get going), and you call this melody of yours the melody of the thing.

If the essence of external things is thus identified with the qualities of your style, you may tend to think of writing (description) primarily as a monologue act, done with little direct concern for an audience. And since this stylistic circulation about an object obliges you to consider the strategy of expression, you may arrive at the thoughts on the nature of naming that Miss Stein verbalizes as a shifty distinction between prose and poetry ("that is poetry really loving the name of anything and that is not prose").

However, you are now on the verge of a change. For the strategy of expression leads into considerations of the audience. From this point, you begin to suspect the suggestive values of narrative, since narrative unquestionably has a significant appeal to audiences. But at this point, if you are Miss Stein, you simply state that you have changed your opinion—and stop. As a kind of compromise between your initial notion of essence as non-dramatic and the fully revised notion that essence might best show itself in action, you may be grateful for her halfway metaphor: the essence is something like the engine in a car—a going without a destination.

It seems to me, however, that Miss Stein should have continued her revisionary process, until all the initial visionary assertions had been similarly modified. She might have considered, for instance, the ways in which remembrance and resemblance are inevitable; the ways in which the primary fact of English literature might be called its transcendence of insularity, etc. And then, and only then, should she have begun her book. As it stands, I maintain that it is (a) the first draft of a critical credo, (b) complicated by the co-presence of its revision, (c) further vitiated by the fact that the revisionary process was not applied to all its parts. Above all, I believe, a complete revision would require her to stress (at least in this "imperfect world" of history) the *dramatic*, the *active*, the *partisan*, in direct contrast with the feature of *passivity* that is now infused through her doctrine of portrait and essence.

# Semantics in Demotic

*The Tyranny of Words* by Stuart Chase. Harcourt, Brace & Co.
*The New Republic*, January 1938, 343–344. Also in *The Philosophy of Literary Form*

In his newest book Stuart Chase has given us a very entertaining and easily read account of a study that is still in the course of mapping out its territory, and may some day have a chair all its own in our colleges, probably called the chair of "semantics." Semantics deals with the subject of communication, meaning, the interpretation of signs.

Sometimes the students of semantics seem to be stressing the genetic, psychological, or historical aspects of the question: they observe and speculate to determine how meanings arise. Anthropologists like Malinowsky throw special insight upon this aspect of the subject, as do experimental psychologists like Pavlov and Watson, Koffka and Koehler. Psychoanalysis also makes a distrusted, but probably necessary, contribution here. Sometimes the emphasis seems to be primarily upon an attempt to perfect an accurate system of signs or pointers, regardless of the ways in which our meanings, or lack of meanings, or muddled meanings, arise and operate in everyday vocabulary. The speculations of the logical positivists, stemming largely from the symbolic logic of the "Principia Mathematica," seem to stress this aspect. Sometimes semantics seems to be mainly a new weapon for the debunker who, revolting at the balderdash meted out daily in the press, pulpit, radio, political exhortation, goodwill advertising, legal and economic theory, etc., wants to find some quick and efficient way of dissolving said balderdash.

In *The Tyranny of Words*, Stuart Chase, like Thurman Arnold in *The Symbols of Government* and *The Folklore of Capitalism*, is interested primarily in this third emphasis. He is looking for a solvent, a corrosive, that will dispatch verbal obstacles with as much speed as possible. To do this, he first picks some salient moments from writers like Korzybsky, Malinowsky, Ogden, Richards and Bridgman that give one an inkling of fields one and two—and then he plunges into a varied assortment of case histories where he debunks with zest the thinking of right, center and left.

By the use of his rough and ready instruments he does good work in making hash of the well-paying verbosities uttered by the priesthood of the right. That is all to the good. But unfortunately, the same instruments also dissolve (as Chase explains on pp. 191–3) a definition like this by Harold Laski:

> I suggest the conclusion that Fascism is nothing but monopoly capitalism imposing its will on the masses which it has deliberately transformed into slaves. The ownership of the instruments of production remains in private hands.

Though conceding that this statement *seems* clear to "a reader of *The New Republic* living in New York," Chase contends that the enlightened student of semantics "is not disposed to argue with Mr. Laski, because the apparent meaning has faded into a series of semantic blanks. Laski is not necessarily wrong; he is saying nothing worth listening to. Knowledge cannot be spread, sensible action cannot be taken, on the basis of such talk."

To arrive at this conclusion, Chase suggests that many necessary ramifications and modifications are omitted from Laski's *definition*. Completely overlooking the fact that a definition is, by the necessities of the case, a *summary,* and that Laski has written a great deal giving explicit body to this summary, he finds the definition itself meaningless. Chase has warned, at many points in his book, against taking words at their face value, without reference to their place in a total context of thought and situation. Yet here he seems to be doing precisely what he warns against. And I do not see how any just theory of meanings could require that a writer give a summarization of his thought without omitting all the ramifications and modifications of that thought.

There must surely be something wrong with instruments of analysis that can debunk so drastically. Chase is dubious about the word "slaves," for instance, recalling that it falls in with "a stock phrase in socialist propaganda." Yet, applying the same enlightened test, we might question the word "tyranny" in Chase's own title, if we simply jumped on this summary of his book without reference to the material with which he gave it body. And he notes that the enlightened student of semantics "never saw an 'ism' imposing its will," thereby debunking Laski's metaphorical shortcut as though it were intended to be taken literally as a completely and explicitly filled-out statement. To show that a summary requires filling out is not *per se* to show that the summary is nonsense. We do not know whether the summary is nonsense until we have examined the ways in which the author himself has given it body.

The difficulties arise, I think, from the overly empirical bias which Chase adopts in his approach to the subject of meaning. Empiricism is, of course, a philosophy—one among several—but Chase begins by adopting it under the "down with philosophy" slogan. *Other* philosophies are philosophies—*his own* is just sound "fact." He proposes to try meanings by the reassuring test of seeing, touching, feeling, weighing, smelling. Hence, since many meanings are *interpretations of relationships* as disclosed from a certain *perspective or point of view,* you are going to find a lot of very necessary meanings dissolved, once you permit a man to impose a naïvely empiricist philosophy in the name of anti-philosophy.

Chase also bolsters up this approach appealingly by borrowings from Bridgman's philosophy of physical science, called "operationalism." According to this, the meaning of a concept is to be tested by some actual operation performed in a laboratory, or recorded on a meter reading. There is no point here in attempting a critique of Bridgman's theory. (The reader is referred to a very stimulating article on the subject by R. B. Lindsay in *Philosophy of Science* for October.) My present point is that, even if we granted its validity for the physical sciences (despite several centuries of fruitful scientific development done largely in violation of it), we could still legitimately demand that Chase offer explicit reasons why one may forcibly induce the migration of this perspective from the realm of physics to the realm of social relationships. The migration may be justified, but the justification is not offered. Chase, by the unconscious ruse of putting forth his philosophy in the name of anti-philosophy, spares himself the trouble; a perspective is simply made to migrate from one realm to another, with no discussion of this migratory process itself, no discussion of the metaphorical function that arises when such migration takes place.

It is my suspicion that, if you would seek an "operation" or a meter reading, or a test of seeing, feeling, tasting, when you come to the interpretation of a relationship as disclosed from a given perspective, you are going to debunk meanings with a vengeance. So thoroughly, in fact, that whenever you want to stop debunking, and would adopt a positive policy of your own, you can do so only by pulling your punch and not applying to yourself the solvent you apply to your opponents. Thus, when in a pure debunking mood, Chase dismisses "the going canons of philosophy, theology and the rest" on the ground that they deal with "ideas and purposes." He distrusts a concern with such matters as "purposes," because you can't see them, touch them, test them "operationally." But when he is in a normative, hortatory mood, he writes, "The controlling issue, the real task for statesmen, is to find the human purpose to be accomplished in a given situation." So far as I can see, you could not do this unless you offered, implicitly, a philosophy of human purpose.

So I question whether it is legitimate for a writer to save himself embarrassment by putting forward a philosophy under the name of no philosophy, a device that enables him simply to avoid the issues at every important point. I question whether a theory of meanings can be put forward simply in the reassuring name of "the facts." Rather, the student of communication must evolve an explicit critique concerned with the processes of making judgments, of putting forth structures of judgments, or rationalizing these structures (by tests of internal consistency), of showing their scope and relevancy to human situations, of verbalizing the role played by metaphorical migrations (transplanted perspectives) in the interpretative process. References to apples, skins, cats, caterpillars and meter readings sound homey, and as such contribute solace by making a complex field look simple. But those who would banish philosophy from the study of meaning must simply make a show of throwing out by the front door what they covertly smuggle in again by the back door.

# Basic and After

*The Loom of Language* by Frederick Bodmer. W. W. Norton, & Co.
*The New Republic*, April 1944, 566, 568

*The Loom of Language* is at least three books in one. In the first 200 or so pages, the author surveys "the natural history of language," tracing the development of the alphabet, analyzing inflection and syntax, and ending with "the classification of languages." The next 200 or so pages comprise a book for anyone who would piece together, with Mr. Bodmer's shrewd assistance, a working knowledge of German, Swedish, Dutch, Danish, Norwegian, French, Spanish, Italian, or Portuguese. There are basic word lists in a copious index—and grammar is studied with an eye for the acquiring of maximum expressiveness with a minimum of resources. This section could also be read purely for the light it throws upon language in general and English in particular, thanks to the author's stress upon linguistic evolution and to his array of comparisons and contrasts between English and other languages, living and dead, primitive and civilized.

A "third book" considers "the world language problem." Here Mr. Bodmer reviews the history of language planning; and on the basis of what he has been saying about the trends and "diseases" of language, he sets down principles which he thinks should be embodied in the ideal international auxiliary language.

All told, it is an engrossing book, a mature and complex approach to the problems of linguistic simplification. Mr. Bodmer is an excellent curator of his "language museum"—and be your interests in language philological, literary, or purely practical, you should find many things here to arrest your attention.

After following the author's many tributes to the virtues of English grammar, along with his unfavorable treatment of Esperanto and similar projects, we were agreeably surprised to find that he does not plump for *Basic English*, or for any of the competing brands of simplified English. As he sums up the matter:

If advocates of constructed languages have been peculiarly blind to the *intrinsic* merits of Anglo-American, those who champion its claims as a world-auxiliary have been equally deaf to its *extrinsic* disabilities. Though Anglo-American is not a rational language, it is not a politically neutral language. If a victorious alliance of the English-speaking people attempts to make it the official medium of a united Europe, its use will make the British nation a *Herrenvolk*. It will perpetuate all the discords which arise when one speech community enjoys a privileged position in the cultural and social life of a larger group. There is only one basis of equality on which nations can cooperate in a peaceful world order without the frictions which arise from linguistic differences. A new European order, or a new world order in which no nation enjoys favored treatment, will be one in which every citizen is bilingual, as Welsh or South African children are brought up to be bilingual. The common language of European or world citizenship must be the birthright of everyone, because the birthright of no one.

This seems like a fair statement of the case. *Basic English* is unquestionably a work of genius—and throughout this book one can discern its salutary influence upon Mr. Bodmer's thinking. There is even a genuine sense of style and poetry in the skill with which *Basic* has stripped itself of all stylistic and poetic vanities. But the mere fact that it has in effect taken a linguistic vow of poverty is no guarantee against imperialist invitations to cash in on it. At the very least, those who believe in the advantages of English structure, as such, should be willing to *rationally distort* it, for the purpose of getting these advantages to the fullest, with total regularity and efficiency. But in the interest of Anglo-American susceptibilities, *Basic* even imposes upon foreigners something so thoroughly unscientific as a large batch of idioms, plus many other kinds of exception and irregularity that are preserved not on their merits but purely as a concession to custom.

Regrettably, the author's own suggestions are confined to the realm of "principles," though we are told in a footnote that his editor, Lancelot Hogben, has attempted to embody them concretely in a language project. Primarily Mr. Bodmer favors a language that would be like a simplified and regularized English in grammatical structure. And its vocabulary would exploit to the fullest the Greek and Latin roots (especially the Greek roots) which the compound words of modern science and technology are making known throughout the world: the roots in such words as microscope, telephone, anthropology, hydrodynamics, chromosome. (A well selected list of these roots is also appended.)

The author states quite saliently his grounds for preferring "analytical" or "isolating" languages (like English and Chinese) as his structural model:

> The complete Sanskrit verb finite, that is the verb without its infinitives, participles and verbal adjectives plus their flexions, has 743 different forms, as against 268 of Greek. From a complete Greek verb we get the enormous number of 507 forms, from a Latin one 143, and from a Gothic verb 94. The English verb usually has four, or at most five forms (e.g., *give. gives, gave, giving, given*). If we add seven forms of *to be*, four of *to have*, together with *shall* or *will* and *should* or *would*, for construction of compound tenses, we can express with twenty words everything for which Sanskrit burdens the memory with nearly forty times as many vocables.

In a completely analytic language, every word would have but one form (as we say "I *must*, you *must*, he *must*," and "*must* list"). As a noun, the word would be the same in singular and plural, like *grouse*—and the possessive form would be periphrastic, as French would say "the hat of John," instead of "John's hat," thereby avoiding the flexional apostrophe-s. Latin synthetically says *amavi*, but English would break this into an analytic equivalent, "I have loved"—and to make the isolating process complete, we should also drop the flexional *d* of *loved*. Grammatical function is analytically revealed by a word's *position* rather than by its *form*.

"With the possible exception of a plural terminal," Mr. Bodmer's ideal interlanguage "would have no flexional modifications of word form." Thus, it would be almost totally of the isolating type. Discussing the fact that earlier planned languages, such as Volapuk and Esperanto, are flexional, he says:

> Nineteenth-century linguists made the same assumptions as nineteenth-century biologists. They took for granted that what exists necessarily has a use. Awareness of the universal drift from flexional luxuriance toward analytical simplicity in the history of Aryan languages was not yet part of their intellectual equipment.

One may question whether a judgment made on the basis of a "universal drift" is in itself any more reliable than a judgment based on "that which exists." One might even accuse Mr. Bodmer of being "linguistically romantic" in his assumption that the ideal world language must try to go the "universal drift" one better.

One can even imagine an irony of this sort: Suppose there were no flexional languages for Zamenhof to have used for a model for his Esperanto. And suppose that some language planner were trying to invent the ideal language. He found himself confronted with the problems of rigid word order which a purely positional language brings to the fore. And he found that an isolating language like English makes for combinations of consonants (like the *t-s-n* of "it's not") that are awful mouthfuls for people of other linguistic habits. Then imagine that he of a sudden hit upon an idea. He could relieve these burdens in a flash, by introducing a few flexions, for instance the use of *-o* as an ending for nouns, of *-e* as an ending for modifiers, of *-i* as an ending for verbs. Wouldn't we hail his simple device as a startling bit of linguistic genius? But as things stand, when he is considered in terms of the "universal drift" away from flexion, he can be dismissed as a has-been.

# Words as Deeds

*How to Do Things With Words: The William James Lectures Delivered at Harvard University in 1955.* 2nd ed. by J. L. Austin. Ed. J. O. Urmson and Marina Sbisà. Harvard UP
*Centrum,* Fall 1975, 147–168

Theories of language involve two kinds of speculation that are quite different yet by no means mutually exclusive. One might be called "scientistic" because it gravitates about language as a mode of *knowledge*; the other "dramatistic" because it approaches language in terms of *action*. The distinction is presented in the opening remarks of David Hume's *An Inquiry Concerning Human Understanding*: "Moral philosophy, or the science of human nature, may be treated after two different manners . . . for the one considers man chiefly as born for action . . . the other species of philosophers consider man in the light of a reasonable rather than an active being, and endeavour to form his understanding." The distinction probably gets its ultimate grounding in the shifts of approach between "ontology" and "epistemology." But I would confine the terms to a *terministic* emphasis.

This summary formulation, on the first page of the last chapter of Austin's *How to Do Things With Words,* is in itself enough to indicate why I would class the book as "dramatistic" in its approach: "The total speech act in the total speech situation is the *only actual* phenomenon which, in the last resort, we are engaged in elucidating." True, his theory of words as deeds is itself a contribution to knowledge, as per his opening sentence: "the only merit I should like to claim for it is that of being true, at least in parts." But the systematic choice of a dramatistic approach to his subject implies that the pursuit of *knowledge* in such matters is best guided roundabout via speculations about language as a mode of *action*.

The book being notes for lectures rather than a definitive text, it is presented in the spirit of a "work in progress," even to the extent that it undergoes en route a "fresh start" (p. 121), with corresponding "sea-change" (p. 150). At the time when Austin began his speculations (which he dates from 1939), I had already been considerably influenced by the dramatistically slanted essay, Bronislaw Malinowski's "The Problem of Meaning in Primitive Languages," published as a supplement in Ogden and Richards' basic volume, *The Meaning of Meaning*. I had got so deeply interested in it, I began building with it in sympathetic ways of my own. Austin begins with two terms, only one of which ("performative") is dramatistic. The other ("constative") is clearly designed to be on the "scientistic" (T-F) slope. He finally abandoned his "belief in the dichotomy of performatives and constatives in favour of more general *families* of related and overlapping speech acts" (p. 150). But my terministic line-up had made it impossible for me, from the start, to find it as clear as he had seemed to do. Yet the very views I had on the subject also get in my way when I try to see the issue as I think he wants us to, in his culminating chapter.

His way of conducting us through the transformations from his initial dramatistic anecdote (presenting "performatives" in terms of such "speech acts" as vows and declarations) to his grand finale surveying "classes of utterance, classified according to their illocutionary force" and "quite enough to play Old Harry with two fetishes which I admit to an inclination to play Old Harry with, viz. (1) the true/false fetish, (2) the value/fact fetish," is itself a performance of appealing virtuosity. It is one long ingeniously self-imposed *aporia*.

When trying to decide on a name for his "performatives," he says:

> One technical term that comes nearest to what we need is perhaps "operative," as it is used strictly by lawyers in referring to that part, i.e. those clauses, of an instrument which serves to effect the transaction (conveyance or what not) which is its main object, whereas the rest of the document merely "recites" the circumstances in which the transaction is to be effected. (p. 7)

I particularly like that kind of anecdote because it lends itself so well to a dramatistic extension. That is to say: If one thinks of such a legal transaction as literally an "act" (in the sense of "speech *act*"), then the recital of the "circumstances" in which the transaction is to be effected defines the "scene" in which it is to be "active," or "enacted." When the pattern is applied to such "enactments" as the U. S. Constitution, the relationship between "scene" and "act" will be found to reveal what Austin might call an "infelicity" of this sort: The Constitution, as a legal "instrument," was "enacted" in a "scene," or situation, quite different from the circumstances in which the Constitution, with its amendments and often innovative judicial interpretations, is operative as an *enactment* now. In this respect can the same utterances, as a speech act, have the same "meaning" they had when first declared? Austin's term, "constative," I take it, would cover the description of the circumstances prevailing at the time of the original enactment or their modified nature now. This is a dramatistic consideration I intend to take up elsewhere, in connection with the terms "meaning" and "significance" ("text" and "context"), when reviewing *The Aims of Interpretation*, by E. D. Hirsch, Jr.

There are some interesting similarities and differences between Malinowski's and Austin's informative (better, "*preformative*"?) anecdotes in conformity with which to form their analytic nomenclatures. Both authors choose cases which clearly involve what Malinowski calls "context of situation"; on page 140, Austin refers to "circumstances of situation," elsewhere to "circumstances," "situation," or "context." Both stress the *conventional* aspects of the verbal behavior they are starting from, and of the human relations implicated in those acts. Malinowski's two anecdotes are much the more rudimentary, being concerned with illiterate tribesmen in group activities:

> Take for instance language spoken by a group of natives engaged in one of their fundamental pursuits in search of subsistence—hunting, fishing, tilling the soil; or else in one of those activities, in which a savage tribe express some essentially human forms of energy—war, play or sport, ceremonial performance or artistic display such as dancing or singing. The actors in any such scene are all following a purposeful activity, are all set on a definite aim; they all have to act in a concerted manner according to certain rules established by custom and tradition. In this, Speech is the necessary means of communion; it is the one indispensable instrument for creating the ties of the moment without which unified social action is impossible.

Having described in some detail the operations of some fishermen, Malinowski sums up thus:

> All the language used during such a pursuit is full of technical terms, short references to surroundings, rapid indications of change—all based on customary types of behaviour, well-known to the participants from personal experience. Each utterance is essentially bound up with the context of situation and with the aim of the pursuit, whether it be the short indications about the movements of the quarry, or the expression of feeling and passion inexorably bound up with behaviour, or words of command, or correlations of

action. The structure of all this linguistic material is inextricably mixed up with, and dependent upon, the course of the activity in which the utterances are embedded. The vocabulary, the meaning of the particular words used in their characteristic technicality is not less subordinate to action. For technical language, in matters of practical pursuit, acquires its meaning only through personal participation in this type of pursuit. It has to be learned, not through reflection but through action. [I take this last sentence to be dealing with what I have treated in terms of my scientistic-dramatistic distinction, though obviously, if there weren't the makings of many T-F distinctions implicit in the tribesmen's "technical terms" and the like, there couldn't have been a living in that way of life.] . . . The consideration of linguistic uses associated with any practical pursuit, leads us to the conclusion that language in its primitive forms ought to be regarded and studied against the background of human activities and as a mode of human behaviour in practical matters. . . . The manner in which I am using it writing these words, the manner in which the author of a book, or a papyrus or a hewn inscription has to use it, is a very far-fetched and derivative function of language.

Malinowski then turns to a different anecdote that brings out a different aspect of language—and his name for this is "phatic communion," not to be confused with what Austin calls a "phatic act." Here "we turn our attention to free narrative or to the use of language in pure social intercourse; when the object of talk is not to achieve some aim, but the exchange of words almost as an end in itself." Verbalizing as so denominated involves "a type of speech in which ties of union are created by a mere exchange of words . . . The whole situation consists in what happens linguistically. Each utterance is an act serving the direct aim of binding hearer to speaker by a tie of some social sentiment or other."

These two anecdotes struck me as almost classic in the simplicity and suggestiveness of their relevance to the subject. And it made good sense to me that the strategic instrument in so major an activity as the gathering of food (a cooperative function that can equally well serve to the ends of competition) should be, we might say, enjoyed for its own sake; for the typically symbol-using animal might be expected to exercise its prowess as the typically symbol-using animal, as fish take to swimming and birds to flying.

And in the offing there were the makings of a third anecdote, suggested by Malinowski's reference to contrasting written texts which would be at least comparatively "self-contained and self-explanatory." When I first read his essay, I had been taking notes on various social and literary "devices," and along those lines I had written a book around the contrast between "yea-saying" and "nay-saying" ("acceptance" and "rejection," with intermediate twists). Accordingly, the first essay in my collection, *The Philosophy of Literary Form* (published in 1941, composed of things done in the Thirties), begins thus:

> Let us suppose that I ask you: "What did the man say?" And that you answer: "He said 'yes.'" You still do not know what the man said. You would not know unless you knew more about the situation, and about the remarks that preceded his answer.
>
> Critical and imaginative works are answers to questions posed by the situation in which they arose. They are not merely answers, they are *strategic* answers, *stylized* answers. For there is a difference in style or strategy, if one says "yes" in tonalities that imply "thank God" or in tonalities that imply "alas!" So I should propose an initial working distinction between "strategies" and "situations," whereby we think of literature . . . as the adopting of various strategies for the encompassing of situations. These strategies size up the situations, name their structure and outstanding ingredients, and name then in a way that contains an attitude towards them.
>
> This point of view does not, by any means, vow us to personal or historical subjectivism. The situations are real; the strategies for handling them have public content; and insofar as situations overlap from individual to individual, or from one historical period to another, the strategies possess universal relevance.
>
> Situations do overlap, if only because men now have the same neural and muscular structure as men who have left their records from past ages. We and they are in much the same biological situation. Furthermore, even the concrete details of social texture have a great measure of overlap. And the nature of the human mind itself, with the function of abstraction rooted in the nature of language, also provides us with "levels of generalization" (to employ Korzybski's

term) by which situations greatly different in their particularities may be felt to belong in the same class (to have a common substance or essence).

Consider a proverb, for instance. Think of the endless variety of situations, distinct in their particularities, which this proverb may "size up," or attitudinally name.

But a *written text* is like the parry to a thrust. The thrust comes from the "context of situation" out of which the text arose. And whereas the thrusts of history keep undergoing changes of position and direction, the written text lacks corresponding immediate pliancy. The written text makes its particular parry statuesquely permanent, whereas the context of situation into which it has survived may have put forth a thrust that calls for a quite different parry. So I waver a bit concerning the extent to which we can recover the original "self-contained" meaning of a text that arose from a "context of situation" greatly different from ours.

But all told, we have (1) words as illiterate instruments in a cooperative act, itself motivated by a "context of situation"; (2) words as the exercise of illiterate human prowess with words in a "context of situation"; (3) words as a literal text that is a context for its own words (with a somewhat problematical relation to "context of situation" in Malinowski's sense). In (3) the exercising of (2) "phatic communion" (in Malinowski's sense) can be developed internally to the extent where the mere social relaxations of gossip can be transformed into such profound exercising of our symbolic prowess as the "tragic pleasure" discussed in Aristotle's *Poetics*. For just as experts in the solving of crossword puzzles will demand the most exacting challenges, so the fullest exercising of our aptitudes in the way of "symbolicity" will have a gratification in and for itself.

But besides the fact that both Malinowski's and Austin's ("*pre*formative") anecdotes concerning words as modes of action involve a great stress upon the role of circumstances in the meaning of an act, we confront important dramatistic considerations to do with the relation between *acts* and the *attitudes* of agents. And as I read Austin, he has offered some remarkable contributions to that aspect of the subject. As I see the issue, he has introduced a wealth of accurate discriminations into an area which is implicitly ambivalent.

To point up the ambivalence in the concept of "attitudes," in my section on "'Incipient' and 'Delayed' Action" (*Grammar of Motives*) I contrasted two excellent works built around the term "attitudes": I.A. Richards' *Principles of Literary Criticism* and George Herbert Mead's *Philosophy of the Act*. Reduced to its bluntest the situation would be thus:

If I felt an attitude of sympathy towards someone in trouble, I may sincerely express my sentiment. Or my attitude of sympathy might lead to an overt act of seeking to modify the conditions that are the cause of the distress. A philanthropic intermediate stage might be, say, as with a coin tossed to a leper, whereby I could give help, but at a distance.

Quite as the acts of agents are grounded in scenes, so those acts are associated with corresponding *attitudes* on the part of the *agents,* attitudes that sometimes *accompany* the acts, sometimes *lead into* the acts, and sometimes *serve as surrogates* for the act (as you might write a poem voicing sympathy for the unjustly treated, and feel that you had done enough—a turn that could also be characterized as "dancing an attitude" of sympathy—and you might do so persuasive a job that, if ushers passed plates, a tidy sum could be collected for the cause).

As a kind of "work in progress" on my part, I want to see what might be done by a view of "illocutionary force" as a synonym for "attitude," and to ask what qualifications might be needed for treating from this point of view the five classes of "illocutionary acts" listed in Austin's last chapter (actually two further "-ives" are mentioned there). But first let's review some of the main steps en route.

A notably "*pre*formative" aspect of Austin's anecdote is its contrast with the collective illiteracy of the speech acts Malinowski chooses as his way-in. And above all, there is the wholly different approach inherent in the ingenious role that is played by an intrinsically related aspect of his analysis: his cautiously qualified use of the "first person singular present active indicative form" as a grammatical test for traces of his "performative" verbs. (There are references on pages 56, 62, 63, 64, 67, 150.)

In particular note the shrewd test of "asymmetry" he discusses on pages 62–63. Here he explains why a sort of *explicit* expansion is needed, to guard against taking a performative utterance "in a non-performative way."

Austin's self-admonitions of this sort were largely responsible for his decision that the constative-performative dichotomy had to be abandoned. For such *explicit* expansion indicated that, by the same token, a performative might be *implicit* in what would otherwise look like a "non-performative." The issue is clearly illustrated in the various references to a "bull in the field" (pp. 33, 59, 62, 74).

In out-and-out "dramatistic" terms, the point might be summed up thus: Implicit in what looks like a constative "description" there may be such a kind of speech act as, if explicitly expanded, would amount to saying: "On the basis of this description you had better do, or not do, such-and-such." That is to say, the mere would-be description, or report, would not just be saying what the situation *is*. The utterance would also imply an *attitude* (such as a warning) towards the situation. Thus, utterances that on their face have the form of a constative locution might also have the illocutionary force of a performative attitude (which might even eventuate in an act having perlocutionary consequences). I am here tentatively anticipating, on the assumption that these pages are being written for readers already quite familiar with Austin's book—and this seemed to be a handy place for indicating my direction. In any case, the ambiguity of "constative" and "performative" is clearly stated on page 33: "'There is a bull in the field' may or may not be a warning, for I *might* just be describing the scenery."

Here, in advance of the relevant passages in Austin's text, are the equations I am tentatively working with: A locution's role as a warning makes it a performative; this performative function is synonymous with its illocutionary force—and with regard to the relation between speech acts and attitudes, I would equate an utterance's illocutionary force with its role in explicitly or implicitly symbolizing an attitude.

In abandoning his two-term start, Austin (p. 95) works with "three rough distinctions between the phonetic act, the phatic act, and rhetic act," which relate thus:

> The phonetic act is merely the act of uttering certain noises. The phatic act is the uttering of certain vocables or words, i.e. noises of certain types, belonging to and as belonging to, a certain vocabulary, conforming to and as conforming to a certain grammar. The rhetic act is the performance of an act of using those vocables with a certain more-or-less definite sense and reference.

Two pages later: The same "pheme, e.g. sentence" (that is, the same "phatic act") "may be used on different occasions of utterance with a different sense or reference, and so be a different rheme" (that is, a different "rhetic" act).

I'd take this triad to be summing up the fact that the mere *sounds* of words, in their nature as mere sounds, are in the realm of *nonverbal motion*. Such sounds are in the realm of a speech act when interpreted as words, i.e. "phatic." Insofar as such words function with reference to contexts (either a context of situation or the text itself as a context) they become "rhetic." And insofar as the same sentence can have different implications in different contexts, its nature as "phatic" takes on different "rhetic" identities. But though Austin does not reject this intermediary line-up of terms, he moves on (p. 98) because "they do not so far throw any light at all on our problem of the constative as opposed to the performative utterance." It's a good basic line-up, though not the best for his purposes. And I particularly want to end by considering more closely the relation between the mere "noises" of words (as "phones") and their nature as "phemes," that is, when their function in the proper symbol-system transforms them into the possibility of speech acts as "rhemes." For the mere noise of words (phones) is related to their role as speech acts (phatic acts, rhetic acts) as the realm of nonsymbolic motion is to the realm of symbolic action. And this reviewer's "work in progress" should end on matters of that sort, in line with concerns that Austin clearly touches upon in Chapters VIII and IX, as per for instance the footnote on page 112: "If we suppose the minimum physical act to be movement of the body . . ." etc. All told, a dramatistic study of Austin's dramatistic book falls into three phases: (1) The relation between speech acts and the circumstances of an act; (2) the role of illocutionary force (equatable with "attitude"?) in the speech act; (3) the grounding of all speech acts ("symbolic *action*") in the realm of wordless "nonsymbolic motion."

By no means do I commit myself to a promise that the issues will be settled. But I do dare hope that the confronting of all our quandaries may contribute towards a better coordination of our future efforts.

There would be good grounds for starting my discussion precisely where we now are. And I tried to do so. But obviously too much would be lost. For though I haven't done justice to the engaging virtuosity of Austin's professional scruples in working out the ingeniously analyzed implications of his "first person singular present active indicative" formula, I trust that I have at least paid tribute to his methodologically grammatical excursions around such prior approaches, as with German metaphysicians who build from an Absolute Ego (as dialectically paired with a Non-Ego)—with perhaps Descartes' *cogito, ergo sum* utterance or pheme or locution as a halfway stage (for I do incline to judge that Descartes' *cogitatio-extensio* polarity was implicitly much closer to a purely empirical distinction between "symbolic action" and "nonsymbolic motion" than his terms' metaphysical trappings permitted to be explicit).

But to proceed. Austin next hits upon the triad that he will settle for: "three kinds of act—the locutionary, the illocutionary, and the perlocutionary" (p. 103). "Our interest in these lectures is essentially to fasten on the second, the illocutionary act and contrast it with the other two." So let's copy out, as our basic text, his summarizing presentation of the three:

>(E.1)
>Act (A) or Locution
>He said to me "Shoot her!" meaning by "shoot" shoot and referring by "her" to *her*.
>
>Act (B) or Illocution

He urged (or advised, ordered, &c.) me to shoot her.

Act (C. *a*) or Perlocution
He persuaded me to shoot her.

Act (C. *b*)
He got me to (or made me, &c.) shoot her.

(E. 2)
Act (A) or Locution
He said to me, "You can't do that."

Act (B) or Illocution
He protested against my doing it.

Act (C. *a*) or Perlocution
He pulled me up, checked me.

Act (C. *b*)
He stopped me, he brought me to my senses, &c. He annoyed me. (pp. 101–102)

The quietly jolting thing about that alignment is in the fact that the verb "persuaded" is not in the same class as the verbs "urged," "advised," and "ordered." This is a radical matter. Traditionally, "persuasion" is the term of terms in texts on rhetoric. (Incidentally, the word "rhetoric" does not appear once in this book. Though we might find a faint etymological trace of it in Austin's term "rhetic," his "rhemes" differ as much from "rhetoric" as his "phatic" act differs from Malinowski's "phatic communion." Perhaps in the light of traditional contests between "rhetoricians" and "grammarians," Austin's basic investment in the "first person singular present active indicative" formula automatically turns his attention away from the traditional formulations of rhetorical theory.)

Except for a brief section on "inartificial" proofs (which would include such "nonconventional" means of persuasion as torture), Aristotle's *Rhetoric* is wholly concerned with the art of persuasion by the resources of diction. In this respect the verb "persuade" would definitely fall under the head of class B (the "illocutionary" act), whereas Austin puts it in a class of "perlocutionary" acts that involve "consequences" outside the realm of speech acts, as the act of murder would obviously be, even if the murder had been a consequence of purely verbal persuasion.

Austin's reasons for his procedure here are clearly stated:

> We must systematically be prepared to distinguish between "the act of doing *x*," i.e. achieving *x*, and "the act of attempting to do *x*."
>
> In the case of illocutions we must be ready to draw the necessary distinction, not noticed by ordinary language except in exceptional cases, between
>
>> (a) the act of attempting or purporting (or affecting or professing or claiming or setting up or setting out) to perform a certain illocutionary act, and
>>
>> (b) the act of successfully achieving or consummating or bringing off such an act. (pp. 105–106)

In the light of Austin's clear distinction, we realize that a wholly accurate title for Aristotle's text would be something like "The Art of *Trying* to be as Persuasive as One can." To this end it surveys various conventional "topics" which the orator can exploit in his efforts to convince an audience by verbal means, though the acts they do as a consequence of expert "deliberative" oratory may involve matters of "ways and means" as clearly in the nonverbal (or more-than-verbal) realm as a colonizing expedition or a military operation.

The traditional position would amount to something like this: "Here are the ways to be persuasive. Sometimes you may use them successfully, sometimes not." And in that spirit, going back to the opening anecdote of Austin's book, we might say that, just as a marriage vow may turn out "happily" or "unhappily," so an attempt to be persuasive may turn out "happily" (if successful), "unhappily" (if not). "And in the course of using speech acts to be persuasive, to the best of my ability I would so design my speech as to form, in the audience, the kind of ATTITUDES that would lead them to adopt the policies or judgments I am advocating."

So now we're ready for the "families" in the last chapter.

We are by no means importing the term ATTITUDE into Austin's text. See, for instance, the definition of "Behabitives" (p. 160): "Behabitives include the notion of reaction to other people's behaviour and fortunes and of attitudes and expressions of attitudes to someone else's past conduct or imminent conduct." On page 152 he says they are "a very miscellaneous group, and have to do with attitudes and *social behaviour*." Page 155: "to blame is a verdictive, but in another sense it is to adopt an attitude towards a person and is thus a behabitive." Page 157: "such exercitives as 'I challenge,' 'I protest,' 'I approve,' are closely connected with behabitives. Challenging, protesting, approving, commending, and recommending, may be the taking up of an attitude or the performing of an act." With regard to Permissives (p. 159):

"Behabitives commit us to *like* conduct. Thus if I blame, I adopt an attitude to someone else's past conduct, but can commit myself only to avoiding like conduct."

> To sum up, we may say that the verdictive is an exercise of judgment, the exercitive is an assertion of influence or exercising of power, the commissive is an assuming of an obligation or declaring of an intention, the behabitive is the adopting of an attitude, and the expositive is the clarifying of reasons, arguments, and communications. (p. 163)

When Austin says, on page 152, "It could well be said that all aspects are present in all my cases," I submit that the essential element they have in common is their common nature as speech acts in general. Insofar as a speech act has "meaning," it involves an *attitude* of some sort—that is why Austin complains that his "Behabitives" are too miscellaneous. The "rhetic" act of *persuasion* is designed to so perform an "illocutionary" act that "a certain effect is achieved" (p. 116). This "effect must be achieved on the audience if the illocutionary act is to be carried out."

I can understand his major triad but in these terms: If I consider the utterance simply as an utterance, it is a "locution." If I consider it in its attitudinal nature (its "force" in expressing or shaping an attitude) it is an "illocution." If I consider it in terms of its *consequences* (that is, if I note how the attitude that it embodies as a purely verbal effect leads to an action in accordance with the attitude it aroused) I am considering it as a "perlocution."

Presumably if it aroused an unintended effect, it would still be a "perloctuion," but maybe for me an "unhappy" one. But if my oration produces three different responses in an audience, does Austin's use of "consequences" as a test of the "perlocutionary" act mean that my *one* rhetorical act *in speech-acting the oration is three perloctutionary acts?*

In any case, I must "dramatistically" take it that all speech acts either as uttered or as responded to, are *intrinsically* attitudinal. Thus Austin's five families (in the chapter he also refers to "permissives" and "descriptives," the latter of which would presumably run the same risks as in the case of "constatives") would be inter-related in ways whereby the attitudinal Behabitives would be the ancestors of the lot, with differentiations emerging slowly. (I'd go along with Austin's notion that language probably developed out of holistic utterances.)

In any case, since the illocutionary act (with its inherent attitudinizing as its "illocutionary force") encounters a boundary beyond which a speech act cannot pass without ceasing to be a mere speech act, Austin's penetrating remarks on the subject of "consequences" bring us to our third consideration.

In Austin we confront to perfection the step from the Metaphysical "I" to the Grammatical "I." But we confront the possible need of a further step, along lines that Austin clearly touches upon. The very nature of the relationship between a speech act and the circumstances (or "context of situation") in which any such act takes place forces us (in *ultimately* dramatistic terms) to ask how all such "conventions" (such verbal or "symbolic" action) must relate to the nonconventional, nonverbal, nonsymbolic ground or context that, by the very "dialectical" nature of the case, must be there somehow. For don't the dialectical conventions of speech itself force us to recognize that our aptitude with *words* emerges from a realm of *wordlessness?*

Such nonverbal, nonconventional, nonsymbolic ground would be a realm of sheer MOTION in the sense that, if all *verbalizingly active* animals were erased from the world (as they in all likelihood some day will be) despite the absence of such speech *acts* there would still be the *motions* of the winds and tides, of the earth's revolutions about the sun, the processes of geology, astronomic unfoldings in general, etc., all going their way without benefit of verbal clergy here on earth. And inasmuch as languages are conventional symbol-systems, by sheer dialectical necessity I'd propose to call such a realm devoid of speech *acts* a realm of nonsymbolic *motion*.

Whatever the uncertainties of the metaphysical or grammatical "I" might be, such an out-and-out dramatistic statement of the case would give us a purely *empirical* principle of individuation to build from; namely: the human body in physiological motion, each with the centrality of its particular nervous system whereby, however its pleasures and pains might resemble the pleasures and pains of other such bodies, it immediately experiences only its own. Hence there would be a drastic qualitative difference between a state wherein it rather than some other physiological organism immediately experienced some particular pleasure or pain. And whatever may be the continuity between such organisms and the environment of which they are a part, the centrality of each one such particular organism's nervous system would be born and would die as that individual. Its "I" in the social sense would be developed insofar as the organism somehow developed the ability and need to learn conventional symbol-systems which, being in their very essence modes of "social behaviour," endowed those particular wordless ("infant") organisms with the ingenious capacity to develop speech acts that could discuss speech acts. And so, in sum, we have the realm of symbolic action that is qualitatively different from the realm of nonsymbolic motion.

Though Malinowski's and Austin's anecdotes have a great deal in common (since both lay great emphasis upon the "conventional" nature of verbal utterance) I had to admit that, since I had approached the subject from the standpoint of Malinowski's analysis and of my building on it (first in *Phi-*

*losophy of Literary Form* and then more definitively in *Grammar of Motives*) I had some trouble with Austin's way-in. For the genius of his own term, "speech act," was guiding his speculations from the start, hence demanding that the difference between "constatives" and "performatives" dissolve into their common identity as speech acts, whereby utterances that explicitly looked like constatives could implicitly have the force of performatives.

Then I have tried to show why, since all speech acts involve attitudes, Austin's analysis of "behabitives" as attitudes could be extended to his other related "families" of "-ives." I argued that the function of the attitudinal weighting or slanting they all performed (though in varying ways) could be equated with what Austin calls their "illocutionary force." I might have borrowed here an expression that Bentham uses with regard to what (in his Table of the Springs of Action) he calls "censorial appellatives," which "have the force but not the form of an argument."

We were here confronting the gradual encroachment of rhetorical concerns ("persuasion") upon an inquiry that was built about a grammatical device (Austin's ingenious heuristic use of the "first person singular present active indicative formula). We must now consider why this stage in our analysis involves a basic methodological concern with the problem of "drawing a line" between the realms of "motion" and "action." The choice of these particular *terms* is not important, but the *distinction* is.

In Austin's text the issue comes up with regard to his distinction between the "illocutionary" and "perlocutionary." The problem comes to a head in Lecture IX, from which I'll quote several representative passages:

> We have then to draw the line between an action we do (here an illocution) and its consequences. Now in general, and if the action is not one of saying something but a non-conventional "physical" action, this is an intricate matter . . . We can, or may like to think we can, class, by stages, more and more of what is initially and ordinarily included or possibly might be included under the name given to "our act" itself as *really* only *consequences,* however little remote and however naturally to be anticipated, of our actual action in the supposed minimum physical sense, which will then transpire to be the making of some movement or movements with parts of our body (e.g. crooking our finger, which produced a movement of the trigger . . . which produced the death of the donkey). (pp. 111–112)
>
> Note that if we suppose the minimum physical act to be movement of the body when we say "I moved my finger,"

the fact that the object moved *is* part of my body does in fact introduce a new sense of "moved." . . . The ordinary use of "move" in such examples as "I moved my finger" is ultimate. We must not seek to go back behind it to "pulling on my muscles" and the like. (Footnote, pp. 112–113)

We do not seem to have any class of names which distinguish physical acts from consequences: whereas with acts of saying something, the vocabulary of names for acts (B) seems expressly designed to mark a break at a certain regular point between the act (our saying something) and its consequences (which are usually not the *saying* of anything). (p. 112)

[For drawing the line] we seem to derive some assistance from the special nature of acts of saying something by contrast with ordinary physical actions: for with these latter even the minimum physical action, which we are seeking to detach from its consequences, is, being a bodily movement, *in pari materia* with at least many of its immediate and natural consequences, whereas, whatever the immediate and natural consequences of an act of saying something may be, they are at least not normally other further acts of saying something [I assume that, as per page 117, he'd call them "responses" or "sequels"?], whether more particularly on the speaker's own part or even on the part of others. So that we have here a sort of natural break in the chain, which is wanting in the case of physical actions, and which is associated with the special class of names for illocutions. [p. 113]

[Footnote, same page:] This *in pari materia* could be misleading to you. I do not mean . . . that my "moving my finger" is, metaphysically, in the least like "the trigger moving" which is its consequence, or like "my finger's moving the trigger. But "a movement of a trigger finger" is *in pari materia* with "a movement of a trigger."

We could quote many other relevant passages. But these should be enough to point up the underlying dramatistic quandaries which speculations along these lines just naturally confront, and which Austin considers with his characteristic acuity. His problem of drawing the line between illocutionary "sequels" or "responses" and perlocutionary "consequences," hence *a fortiori* between speech acts and "minimum physical actions" or bodily "movements," involves us in various considerations that come to a head on pages 114–115, which please consult.

We confront one accidental problem of nomenclature here. The terms "action" and "motion" are not generally differentiated as must be the case for out-and-out dramatistic purposes. We refer to the "actions" of a motor, for instance, whereas in the strict usage required for our purposes one would have to say the "motions" of a motor. Or we refer to the "movements" of a symphony, whereas we'd have to call them different "acts," as we refer to a "drama in five acts."

In this light, consider (p. 114) the "uttering of noises, which is a physical movement," yet can be called a "phonetic act." Confining ourselves to the stricter use of the two terms, we should state the case thus: The utterance, in being called a speech act, would thus be denominated exactly right for our purposes. (Since such a medium is a conventional symbol-system, a synonym would be "symbolic act.") But the term "phonetic act" requires some protective qualification. For the "act" of speaking (and of interpreting an utterance) is made possible only by its grounding in two aspects of *motion;* namely: (a) such *physiological* motions as the neural processes involved in speaking, hearing, interpreting, and the like; (b) such environmental motions as the vibrations in the air which carry the words from speaker to hearer. (As per Austin, footnote page 114, we are "confining ourselves, for simplicity, to *spoken* utterance." Written words would depend on visual rather than auditory kinds of environmental motion, Braille on motions involved in touch.)

When "illocutionary force" (which I would equate with "attitudinal slanting") is viewed thus, a notable principle of duality enters the case. Austin explicitly deals with an aspect of it, when on page 117 he says: "Many illocutionary acts invite by convention a response or sequel. Thus an order invites the response of obedience and a promise that of fulfillment. The response or sequel may be 'one-way' or 'two-way': thus we may distinguish arguing, ordering, promising, suggesting, and asking to, from offering, asking whether you will and asking 'Yes or no?'"

Note the underlying difference he has hit upon here. The "sequel" to an "order" invites a "response" on the part of the *hearer*. But the "sequel" to a "promise" invites "fulfillment" on the part of the *speaker*.

When first presenting his *grammatical I* as test (see page 57), he said: "We need not waste our time on the obvious exception of the first person plural, '*we* promise . . . ' ' 'we consent,' &c." But a *rhetorical* "two-way" consideration has entered. So it's conceivable that the speaker who says on page 117 "I promise" is saying in effect not "I promise that *I* will deliver the goods" (as per Austin's opening anecdotes to illustrate performatives) but "I promise that if we all do what I am advocating we'll all get fulfillment." In either case, the "response of obedience" obviously involves *rhetorical* matters of persuasion. And the "two-way" aspect of the case is central.

Whatever attitude my speech act might utter, note that such utterances can work two ways. I may feel an attitude, say, of resentment. No, let's make it an attitude of friendliness; there's enough meanness let loose these days already. I feel so friendly, my utterance manifests my friendliness. Or, if you will, I'm not friendly at all, but fake an attitude of friendliness. Or suppose that, whether I'm really friendly or not, I would evoke in you an attitude of friendliness. Aristotle's *Rhetoric* gives you many tips on how to go about trying to be persuasive thus, whether or not you happily attain the consequences of the attitude that you aimed to establish in your audience.

The mere fact that I have a pronounced attitude towards something and want you to share it with me is no guaranty at all that my way of expressing the attitude will be the best way of getting you to share the attitude. But whatever the differences between a one-way or a two-way kind of attitudinizing in my speech act, in either case my speech act involves correlative behavior in the realm of motion. Regardless of what attitude any speech act "symbolizes," it can be enacted only insofar as there are corresponding neural motions of the body (whatever they may be). And whatever attitude (response) such a "rhetic" structure of utterances (locutions) may evoke in a hearer, they will necessarily be paralleled somehow in the realm of wordless (nonconventional, non-symbolic) motion.

Behaviorism would be pointing in the right direction here, except for its basic methodological error at the start, its assumption that the distinction between the realms of action and motion is but a matter of *degree,* rather than a difference in *kind.* And having thrown out philosophy (which I'd want to call Logology), Behaviorists can be philosophically (Logologically) obtuse in their projects that by implicit definition, reduce the realm of action to terms of motion. And run-down Technologism being what it is, the more methodologically obtuse they persist in being along those lines, the more grants they'll get. But by a dramatistic reinterpretation, much of their work can be of great use, in helping to suggest the proper admonitions when we are attempting to sum up just what is involved in our being the kind of symbol-using, speech-acting animal we are, as viewed in terms of MOTION, ACTION, and ATTITUDE.

Towards summing up, think of these sample histories:

(1) A drug, introduced into the blood stream, produces physiological effects. The drug functions, let us say, as a kind of irritant. (I go back to a mean example, since my anecdote is clearer thus.) It makes me so irritable that my speech act reflects my attitude of irritation. By the same token, such would be the illocutionary force of my related utter-

ances. Thereby a condition in the realm of physiological motion will have surfaced as a speech act which can have illocutionary force with hearers only insofar as the motions of their bodies and in the conditions of the environment make it possible for those familiar with the conventions of my utterance to receive it and interpret it as the kind of speech act (symbolic action) it is.

(2) Or let's take another route. Mine enemy referred to me in utterances (a rhetic act) the attitude, or illocutionary force, of which I found quite irritating. My response to his attitude had a physiological counterpart in the realm of motion by such "behavior" as increased blood pressure, accelerated pulse beat, secretion of adrenalin, without which body symptoms his attitudinizing couldn't have had such illocutionary force so far as my response to his speech act was concerned.

(3) Or I might address you in a way designed to build up in you an attitude of irritability that would induce you to sympathetically join with me against mine enemy. In any case, whether you went along with me or not (whether or not my illocutionary act attained the consequences that entitled it to be called a perlocutionary act) whatever your response was it necessarily involved physiological and environmental motions of one sort or another.

Basically, the two-way ambiguity ("asymmetry") is this: The speaker's illocutionary uttering of his attitudes is not directly equatable with the hearer's response to such an illocutionary force, the "*pre*formative" aspects of speech, be they explicit or implicit. And in any case, even if there are no "consequences" in the sense that, when A said to B "shoot her," B shot her, there must be the physiological and environmental motions that serve as the "material cause" of the speech act.

Though obviously neither Malinowski nor Austin would have any reason to deny such a grounding of speech in a context of speechlessness (symbolic action grounded in nonsymbolic motion), it is my claim that only an out-and-out, formally dramatistic nomenclature sets the conditions for inquiries into the sheer *bodily* equivalents of the speech acts' attitudes, a realm of *quantification* such as the corresponding *qualitative* nature of the speech act decidedly is *not*.

Given a performer's expertise in speech acts, for instance, his body may be "behaving" in ways that are quite health-giving, or maybe in the ways of psychogenic illness. One dreamer's "brain waves" may be all to the good, another's may be in bad need of repair. A *citizen's* behavior is one thing. His *body's* behavior is something else. In the speech department he may be anticipating or remembering. But with his nonsymbolic body, as with a dancer's symbolizing body, everything is NOW.

As I interpret Richards (and his pal Ogden) along Behaviorist lines, somehow our speech acts are ultimately cathartic insofar as the *symbolic* "resolution" of our conflicts digs down even into its total physiological counterpart. And we are left with this:

In Malinowski's anecdotes there is the featuring of illiterate "they's." In Austin's story, there is featured a highly literate grammatical "I." Now I propose to end on what I want for a starter in sympathy with them all; namely (now brace yourself for this out-and-out dramatistic statement of the case): We start from such things as trees, and draw an *absolute* line between trees and the *word* "trees." And never the twain shall meet, despite Jung's wavering battle to persuade himself that they holistically can.

After all this is over, we confront this summarizing line-up: Speech acts are illocutionary attitudes; all such are grounded in the speechless behavior (motions) of the body; speech acts are not reducible to terms of the body's motions, but we can inquire into their modes of motion, which are *quantifiable* in such terms as brain waves and endocrine secretions, though as *acts* they are wholly *qualitative*. There are ultimate behavioristic ("behabitive"?) correspondences of this sort, to be confronted in our quandaries concerning the relation between *speech acts* (as public, social, "conventional") and their grounding in the individuated *wordless motions* of each communicant's physiological organism (along with the environmental motions needed to carry the "noises," or "phones," from speaker to hearer). The speech act would be in the *collective* realm of "culture." But it would be grounded in each user's *individual* physiological "nature."

# Art

*Art is a translation, and every translation is a compromise.*

—*Counter-Statement* (54)

# Untitled Review of *Greek Vase-Painting* by Ernst Buschor

*Greek Vase-Painting* by Ernst Buschor. Chatto and Windus
*The Freeman*, May 1922, 238

Dr. Ernst Buschor sees the history of Greek vase-painting as "a constant struggle to represent mankind and animal creation." In his opening chapter on the stone and bronze ages, however, he shows that the naturalistic and the highly stylized tendencies have existed side by side; then "life disappears, but fixed decorative formulæ remain, and to them the future belongs." Perhaps at this point the swing of the Greek genius could be said truly to begin. The painter treats man as no different from a design, fills in his space indiscriminately with human or geometric figures, actually painting "birds or fishes between the legs of horses or between the chariot and the bier which rests upon it." Following upon this comes a period of fantasy, evidently of Oriental influence, in which monsters and fabulous creatures are portrayed with rich, carpet-like ornamentation. The borrowing, however, is a fusion rather than an imitation, and it is out of this fusion, which occupies, roughly, the seventh century, that the black-figured style arises. This is the period of legend and narration, with scenes from hunting, fighting, wrestling, dancing, carousing and the like. Names frequently appear; the painter is evidently coming to look upon himself as a conscious, individualized artist. At the peak of the black-figured style comes a reversal of the process, so that instead of the figures being painted, they now are drawn and the background is painted in afterwards, the figures being left in the color of the clay. This permitted a greater accuracy of drawing; and one by one such refinements follow as the portrayal of joints and muscles, of folds in garments, of eyes which see rather than stare. The schematization of the human figure, in short, gradually drops away, although the vases still retain marked decorative features. In this period "the artistic craft had its greatest triumphs and created the most perfect synthesis between ornamental types and delightful naturalism." In his chapter on "The Style of Polygnotos and Pheidias" the author traces a further development of the red-figured style, in which a pronounced element of psychology enters. We have, instead of narrative and action, the warrior being carried off by Sleep and Death, a woman in a softened posture listening to music, or the indecision of Eriphyle, as a necklace is held out to her which will send her husband to death. One further stage is dealt with: the re-conventionalization of forms, a playful and ingenious distortion; at this point the author closes, since the centre of production changes from Greece to Italy. The author continually stresses the fact that the purpose of vase-painting remained essentially decorative; but in this portrayal of indecision, the anguish of Eriphyle is transmitted in a remarkably "ultra-modern" fashion by the hesitant and unpleasantly conflicting lines of her garments. Here certainly the tendency is to place expression beyond beauty.

# Note on *Der Sturm*

*Kunstdammerung in Der Sturm* (13th year, No. 7–8) by Herwarth Walden *Secession*, January 1932, 32–33

On reading Herwarth Walden's *Kunstdammerung in Der Sturm* (13th year, No. 7–8) one asks himself with distress whether two parties of reaction are fighting for dictatorship of the arts. There is the *retour* element, pleading for an art which will have a more fundamental relationship with life; and over against it, there is the struggle to preserve the exclusively esthetic point of view. Says Herr Walden, defending the latter, "The man who requires the representation of water in order to see a blue completely lacks the artistic eye. If, when placed before a color, one must think something before he can experience it, he is without any color sense whatever. A color is not received in the soul, but in the eye. Everything else is simply the association of the subject." Walden's message is strenuous and accurate throughout, but the reader is not compelled to accept it. The choice lies between retaining a method found within the last twenty years, or so, and recovering a method which had sat upon Europe for whole centuries . . . In this same issue, and the one preceding, there is a remarkable article by Jorg Mager on the quarter-tone scale, containing documents on its history, the nature of quarter-tone instruments, music written for the quarter-tone scale, and taking up various points of harmonization. Analysis and synthesis; modern efforts seem to be moving in both directions simultaneously; and to those who object "Why the quarter-tone scale?" the answer is, obviously, "To prepare the way for the eighth-tone scale" . . . In the ninth number Lothar Schreyer begins an article on *The Word*. The drawing of fine lines seems pointless enough up to date; one gets exhaustively what one already knew without exhaustion. "Logokratis" does not appear in the first installment; yet, surely, that is the essential matter, the exact fixing of those regions wherein the word is man's servant and where it is his master. Man's business is primarily that of the slayer; is not the word his best weapon for the slaying of emotions, by transferring them into adequate ideas? Or, conversely, the word cuts through a great complexity of ideas, by creating an emotion. If our prognostics are correct, Herr Schreyer is going to discuss an equally promising aspect, however: the function of the word to staticize a transition; at least, the article ends on that note. In any case, here is a subject which has, up to this time, been in the exclusive possession of philosophical dictionaries; we expect *Der Sturm* to give it a new twist, and await the number 10.

# A Pleasant View of Decay

*Music Ho! A Study of Music in Decline* by Constant Lambert. Charles Scribner's Sons
*The Nation*, February 1935, 200–201

Insofar as a book review is a news item, the only way I know to report on this bright and intelligent volume by Constant Lambert is to quote from it as copiously as possible. To begin with: since it is a survey of music, I might state my belief that a reader could find its pages extremely stimulating though the sounds of music concerned him not at all. Those who are acquainted with the works which the author discusses will of course be better equipped to derive the maximum satisfaction from his lively comments, but the main requirement for the non-musical would be a general interest in the symptomatology of recent cultural movements, in the mental topography of our decades. Pungent, picturesque, aphoristic—the author gives us a succession of succinct characterizations. Himself a composer of great merit, he has a gift for verbalizing his tonal experiences; and though not one single passage of musical notation is quoted in this book, one gets an excellent picture of modern composition.

In fact, Mr. Lambert makes us realize that the "outline" is beginning to take on the dignity of a new literary form. Too often undertaken as a mere business venture, it has affronted serious readers by its superficiality. At its worst, it provides mere identification marks of the "Book of Etiquette" variety. But Mr. Lambert bears witness that it can become quite a civilized medium, with much the same interpretative value as one might derive from a good realistic novel of the panoramic sort. Indeed, such works have certain notable advantages over the realistic novel *per se*. Since they usually deal with some highly barometric aspect of the times—some art or practical activity at its most expressive stage—the writer automatically has at his disposal representative figures. And whereas the realist of the novel must often find that his cult of "reality" pledges him to report the most dismal drivel as the "truth" about people's minds and speech, the realist of the critical survey can be at once accurate and eloquent. He has, as it were, the equivalent of Shakespeare's noblemen. He can give us selective statements, statements made by people who are actually living—yet who show a certain captaincy in their choice of behavior. And in direct contrast with the rules of novelistic realism, the sharper and more brilliant the statement of the critical survey, the greater its "photographic truth."

In any event, Mr. Lambert's book is illuminating. Of Stravinsky's rhythms he says: "They are rhythms suspended in space, arbitrary patterns in time, forming a parallel to Debussy's impressionist use of harmonies detached from melodic reasoning." Of Schonberg's harmonic system: "There are two ways of destroying the significance of the House of Lords—you can either abolish it or you can make everyone a member. We have no sense of modulation in Debussy's music for the simple reason that he doesn't modulate, and we have no sense of modulation in Schonberg's music because the work itself has become one vast modulation." Or to quote another of his ingenious contrasts: he says that Wagner gives us the "appeal of a ship with the hero's sweetheart on board leaving the quay, or the departure of a troop train in time of war," whereas Debussy's appeal "is of the less personal and more subtle order that we get from, the mere sight of an unknown ship in sail." Stravinsky he both praises and condemns as a master of the pastiche, skilled at assembling musical incongruities, and borrowing from earlier styles without any sense of their inner significance but with concern for externals only: "Like a savage standing in delighted awe before those two symbols of an alien civilization, the top hat and the *pot de chambre*, he is apt to confuse their functions."

He disagrees violently with those composers who attempt to build their works upon the traditional folk melodies, which are unsuited to modern harmonic treatment, resist constructive manipulation when used as ingredients of larger symphonic forms, and are too alien to the quality of contemporary life. He likewise shows little sympathy for the "wrong note" school, whose members acquire a doubtful distinction for their compositions by the arbitrary shifting of harmonic intervals.

When discussing the shortcomings of "Exoticism and Low Life," he writes: "There is a definite limit to the length of time a composer can go on writing in one dance rhythm (this limit is obviously reached by Ravel toward the end of 'La Valse' and toward the beginning of 'Bolero')." He makes the quite paradoxical but just observation that realistic music should be used only in connection with the events it describes, concluding: "The place for music of the Honegger type is not the concert hall but the cinema. Those who are bored by 'Pacific 231' in the concert hall would have been surprised at the brilliant effect it made when used in conjunction with the Soviet film

'The Blue Express.'" On the subject of "highbrow jazz," he suggests that the composer must extend the harmonic vocabulary of the popular syncopationists, but "this development must be on the lines of a broader view of what is desirable as consonance rather than on a narrower view of what constitutes dissonance."

Sibelius is this author's giant—and he writes some convincing pages upon Sibelius's virtues. After many sharp chapters devoted to the processes of musical "decline," we appreciate his firm attachment to the lonely Finn. The one great drawback of Lambert's study, from my point of view, is that it shows too little sympathy for the aesthetic behind the new collectivist trends in art. "The artist who is one of a group," he says, "writes for that group alone, whereas the artist who expresses personal experience may in the end reach universal experience." This is not the issue. Art is not merely a problem in production—as in the recent Art for Art's Sake movement. Nor is it merely a problem in consumption—as in the earlier doctrines of "appreciation." It is a problem in the coordination of production and consumption. An occasional great inventor may permit himself a long step in advance; but the trouble with Mr. Lambert's attitude is that it asks all to write as though they were the occasional great.

# Many Moods

*A Treasury of American Song* by Olin Downes and Elie Siegmeister. Music arranged by Elie Siegmeister. Alfred A. Knopf
*The New Republic*, June 1943, 869–870

Here is a plenteous horn of American folksongs, issued in a new edition, "revised and enlarged," on handsome quarto pages, with both words and melodies, and with highly serviceable piano accompaniments by Elie Siegmeister. The book should attract both those who want it for the songs' sake and those whose main interest is in the sociology of music.

The editors subdivide their treasury into sixteen compartments, ranging from devotional music in the medieval church modes to ballads of cocaine-sniffers, from the rollicking barn dance to the dirge of slaves, from the firm and steady tramp of soldiers on the march to the aimlessly shifting rhythms of the wanderers to nowhere.

Nor is this all. Each song, and each section of songs, has its critical comment that points out the distinctive traits of both words and music. This comment is particularly apt at historical and psychological observations that reconstruct for us the kinds of situation out of which the songs arose and the kinds of quest to which they responded. Thus we are reminded that "the singing of chanties with their vigorous and clearly measured rhythms established the regular timing so necessary for the efficient execution of such tasks as weighing anchor, hoisting sail, manning the pumps." Or there is the night-herding song, a lullaby sung by a cowboy to a whole herd of cattle, that they may be kept calm during the night, reassured by the human voice, and so induced to ignore the night sounds that might otherwise cause them to stampede. Whereas each folksong was originally an act appropriate to a particular kind of scene, a scene that is by the nature of the case here missing, Mr. Siegmeister has tried in his arrangements, often with success, to give "a harmonic background in the piano intended to suggest the color originally provided by the physical background."

Like a second-hand-book store, this is a good place in which to browse around. Browsing, one gets a sense of great symmetry, for instance, on noting that the music of "John Brown's Body" came from a hymn popular in Negro churches in the 1850's. There is a jaunty bit of economic criticism developed about the refrain, "Oh the farmer is the man who feeds them all." Indeed, throughout the book, one finds in the words as direct an expression of economic motives as one finds, otherwise couched, in "The Federalist Papers." "When I can read my title clear to mansions in the skies," they sang exaltedly in the old camp-meeting song, "The Saint's Delight"; the promised land was indeterminately a mixture of life-after-death and good Western real estate; and there is the forlorn Negro wandering song, "Ah'm Broke an' Hungry," in a tune that is, as the authors well say, "remarkable for its drifting, shifting quality."

All told, going from page to page in this book, one must be both tone-deaf and intellectually a stone if he is not deeply moved by this spectacle of our country being both vigorously and painfully put together.

# The Esthetic Strain

*Art as Experience* by John Dewey. Minton, Balch and Company
*The New Republic*, April 1934, 315–316

Professor Dewey objects to those theories that hold to a distinct "esthetic sense" operating in a separate realm from the commoner ways of life. At the same time he holds that the esthetic is a distinct strain, that there can be unesthetic acts, and even anesthetic ones. By his definition, a merely downcast frame under grief would be unesthetic, whereas the conversion of this emotion into a work like Tennyson's "In Memoriam" would be a true "act of expression." To quote:

> Irritation may be let go like an arrow directed at a target and produce some change in the outer world. But having an outer effect is something very different from ordered use of objective conditions in order to give objective fulfilment to the emotion. The latter alone is expression and the emotion that attaches itself to, or is interpenetrated by, the resulting-object is esthetic. If the person in question puts his room to rights as a matter of routine he is anesthetic. But if his original emotion of impatient irritation has been ordered and tranquilized by what he has done, the orderly room reflects back to him the change that has taken place in himself. He feels not that he has accomplished a needed chore but has done something emotionally fulfilling. His emotion as thus "objectified" is esthetic.

Here we seem close to the strictly classical concept, the esthetic as the love of order. At other points, however, Professor Dewey brings out different aspects of the esthetic. For it is obvious that order in its purity might be more observable in strictly logical pursuits than in the arts. A man who had converted his unrest into the constructions of mathematics, for instance, would seem further along this same road than a Shakespeare who, for all the grasp of order in his plays, yet retains a great deal of simple disarray. Thus we can understand why the emphasis upon order alone could lead a philosopher like Plato to place the life of pure reason above that of art, with its "sensual" remnants.

Professor Dewey sees the intellectual constructions of science as producing a wholly different kind of insight from those of art. The esthetic strain in science, he says, has provided us with a vast collection of signposts, to assist us in finding our way about the complex avenues of experience; the esthetic strain in art gives us the quality of experience itself. "Such . . . is the newness of scientific statement and its present prestige (due ultimately to its directive efficiency) that scientific statement is often thought to possess more than a signboard function and to disclose or be 'expressive' of the inner nature of things." He offers reasons why this attitude toward science is erroneous, and concludes: "The poetic as distinct from the prosaic, esthetic art as distinct from scientific, expression as distinct from statement, does something different from leading to an experience. It constitutes one." Yet his distinction on other occasions is blurred, as when he discusses "qualitative thought," pointing out that even the most conceptual thinker "feels" his way about among ideas. He writes: "In short, esthetic cannot be sharply marked off from intellectual experience since the latter must bear an esthetic stamp to be itself complete." (The reader might be referred to Richard Rothschild's recent volume, *Illusion and Reality*, as providing a totally different approach to this same issue.)

There are several chapters devoted to the specific arts, the matter being appropriately focused on the discussion of medium. Though one whose interests are trained upon any particular art may find this section written too much "from without," its value as a survey is great. The author's dictum on the present agitation over "proletarian" art may serve as an instance of his accuracy:

> The idea that there is a moral obligation on an artist to deal with "proletarian" material, or with any material on the basis of its bearing on proletarian fortune and destiny, is an effort to return to a position that art has historically outgrown. But as far as proletarian interest marks a new direction of attention and involves observation of materials previously passed over, it will certainly call into activity persons who were not moved to expression by former materials, and will disclose and thus help break down boundaries of which they were not previously aware.

He has also made some acute remarks disclosing how, when we shift our point of view, different aspects of a work are seen as "form" and "matter." And he clearly shows how concepts carried over from philosophy can pervert our understanding of art, though he leaves us suspecting that when a critic's concepts are not explicitly philosophical, they are but implicitly so, and that the non-philosophical critic is not really escaping philosophy, but is merely using an untested philosophy. His comments on the genius of the individual arts are especially stimulating.

Returning to the question of art as experience: Professor Dewey points out that art is not "illusory," since it does actually embody its insight in external objects. Or as he has also stated his thesis: "Art is a quality that permeates an experience; it is not, save by a figure of speech, the experience itself." (Rothschild would handle this same issue by pointing out that *all* interpretation is fictional, be it called metaphysics, science, art or common sense. The two views are possibly much the same, despite their apparent antagonisms of vocabulary. For to say that all judgment is fantasy is also a way of making it impossible to set art aside as a self-deceptive enterprise. Professor Dewey seems close to Rothschild's position when he writes: "If animals are strict realists, it is because they lack the signs that language confers upon humans.")

Professor Dewey subscribes to Wordsworth's dictum that science may eventually provide a new firm body of thought which will affect the poet as religion once did. "But," he adds, "poetry will not on that account be a popularization of science, nor will its characteristic values be those of science." Perhaps the relationship between poetry and science may be established in this wise: The results of science may finally be crystallized in a more stable social structure; out of such a stable structure a code of "proprieties" (customs and aims) may take form; and the poet will then weave these proprieties into the texture of art, both relying upon them and contributing to them.

The chapter on "Criticism and Perception" throws a sharp light upon many faulty weapons in the artillery of modern criticism, particularly as regards the many "genetic" schools which attempt assiduously to relate the artist's esthetic accomplishments to his private difficulties. Every practising critic of the day should look into this chapter for valuable admonitions. But for the general reader I believe that the closing chapter, "Art and Civilization," will prove the most fertile. It seems to me especially significant that whereas Professor Dewey's "instrumentalism" has been avowedly a philosophy of science, as soon as he approaches experience from the standpoint of art he feels called upon to grant the many grave cultural problems to which science has given rise. He seems to feel that these disorders are transitional rather than absolute, especially if the profit motive can be eliminated as the basis of work and tests of humanity can supplant the demands of investment as a guide for practical activities. Though he recognizes that "the mechanical stands at the pole opposite to the esthetic, and production of goods is now mechanical," he suggests that there is nothing in machine production *per se* to destroy a worker's satisfaction in his work, but that the disorder arises largely from psychological factors due to the oligarchy of ownership and its misuse.

One may ask whether the "experimental method" itself is a sound basis upon which to erect a scheme of social solidarity, of group homogeneity, since it is essentially a technique individualistic in genius, providing a definite technique for doubting the beliefs of one's group and hence working fundamentally against the authority of the "proprieties" which art mainly deals in. Perhaps we may eventually be forced to shift our whole notion of "agreement" to a much higher level than now prevails in the usual "for me or agin' me" attitude; perhaps an underlying basis of homogeneity for uniting the vast heterogeneity of scientific disciplines can be obtained by stressing one unified social purpose—but in any event, Professor Dewey's closing chapter offers grounds for believing that the end of private control over the fruits of scientific inventiveness is the paramount opening step required before science can become a genuine instrument of benefit and the present anguish of the arts can abate. Professor Dewey's closing summation makes it clear, I think, that however broad or deep-lying the issue may be, there is no turning back: science is with us, we must accept it and shape it to esthetic ends—and we can never do so until it has been made, in the fullest sense, a group possession.

# The Esthetic Instinct

*Art and Society* by Herbert Read. MacMillan Company
*The New Republic*, August 1937

Mr. Read's new book is a very earnest and provocative volume. It assembles many important observations by the author and by others bearing upon the nature of artistic activity. And its hundred expertly chosen illustrations of various artistic modes would alone make it worth its price.

Yet I feel that it is a profoundly misleading book. Whereas every phenomenon that Mr. Read notes *is* a manifestation of art, the misfortune arises from the fact that his names for the locating of these phenomena are all slightly askew, thereby making a little difference that makes all the difference. A less penetrating discussion would be far less dangerous.

For one thing, his thesis contrives to reaffirm, in however attenuated form, the genesis of art in a "seething cauldron" of the unconscious, a kind of internal bell towards which the artist makes journeys (and from which he returns, like an inverted Swedenborg, to report of his visions, by "compromise," to his duller companions, who could not understand or tolerate them in their chemical purity). "Art, tale murder, will out," says Mr. Read, in pleading for art as an instinctive activity that must be free of moralistic pressure. He reaffirms the Freudian thesis that art has its source in a "pleasure principle," as distinct from a "reality principle." In the course of so doing, he implies that the motives of artist and non-artist are distinct. He assists in bolstering up the Spenglerian emphasis, that equates art with the virginal and childlike. And he gets from the individual to the universal by suggesting that all artists' ultimate intuitions run in the same underground channel. With none of which one could enter head-on objections.

At every point the slight dislocation of his naming does damage. Thus, he complains convincingly against the capitalistically engendered zeal for thinking of art in terms of its marketability, its availability as a commodity—yet his own book is concerned exclusively with the commercially negotiable aspects of art: art *objects*. Such an approach to the subject is an impoverishment, even a slander, since it automatically invites us to pass over without evaluation such unmarketable forms of artistry as we may note in the vital anonymous contributions being made to popular speech, in a statesman's or labor leader's tactics, in comments at an amateur ball game, in the postures and gestures all about us. Art *objects* are but the condensation or crystallization of artistic aptitudes. A commodity such as a dialogue by Plato arose from a texture of Socratic conversation completely lost as a commodity, but "esthetic" none the less.

Such considerations get us to perhaps the most disastrous confusion of all. This seems to stem from a double usage in his concept of the "esthetic" impulse. Sometimes the esthetic refers to a "universal" and "constant" attribute of men—at other times it refers to an "exceptional" attribute, possessed only by a few outstanding individuals in any given age. It is a confusion customary to writers on this subject, who on occasion mean, by the artistic, *all art, any art, pea, bad, indifferent* (such as a "universal" and "constant" instinct Live activity would have to subsume)—and then again they secretly rope off their term to designate only "*good*" art.

The point is not made for mere purposes of heckling. It is made because the issue, as presented by Mr. Read, would throw us radically off the track, in our attempts to discuss the relationship between and art and society. In part, I believe, his misrepresentations of this relationship arise because he has selected plastic and graphic art, rather than drama, as his point of departure. There is probably no fundamental distinction between them. What you found by studying one field should apply in studying the other. But it so happens that, the exception of such concepts as *empathy* (which I do remember Mr. Read's even mentioning here in his discussion of artistic production and appeal), the analysis of plastic and graphic art has approached its subject through the coordinates of elegance and appreciation rather than the coordinates of action and participation. The fault is not with the plastic or graphic works themselves, but with the "commodity" vocabularies critics have traditionally employed in discussing them. If, on the other hand, you start out to detect the "esthetic" from the standpoint of *drama,* you are less tempted by this tradition, and more free to realize that only a small portion of the drama going on in the world arrives at its ultimate commodity stage in formal offerings.

Again, approached from the standpoint of drama, Mr. Read's drastic distinctions between the "intuitive" and the "moral" or "abstract" simply dissolve, thereby emancipating you from his attempts to equate the infantile with a "deeper wisdom." One could tentatively imagine three levels, the abstract, the intimate and the "instinctive." A character (conceived out of an artist's relationships with people) may be shown to embody a point of view (i.e., a philosophy, amorality, related to the "abstract level"). And if the character and his point of view are conceived with thoroughness, the artist may endow him with appropriate mimetic expression (derived from the "instinctive," or "biological," or "visceral," or "unconscious" level—as when the glandular responses of anger give rise to corresponding skeletal postures and muscular expression, while these in turn require verbal or tonal expressions in keeping). And we believe that the organization of action in a painting could be discussed similarly. If the artist feels a given emotion, in response to a given set of moral judgments, he will be moved to round out his expression with appropriate mimetic. And in doing so, he will draw upon the "seething cauldron" of the unconscious, quite as does an inventor, a speaker or an athlete. As for the fact that one man may discern vaster situations than another, or symbolize them with greater depth, complexity, accuracy—you do not "explain" anything by naming the difference "esthetic." You could with as much profit call one man's way of conducting his business more "esthetic" than another's.

In particular, I believe that Mr. Read has employed overly individualistic coordinates in his discussion of artistic processes. He tends to consider communication as essentially a "compromise" between the individual and his audience. And with mystic hankerings, he appears to assume a vision seen by the artist independently of the communicative mediums. Is it not, rather, true that the mind of the individual artist is so thoroughly infused with public matter that his ways of seeing, and his desires for "self-expression," are themselves molded by the communicative medium? Otherwise stated: the content of the "unconscious" is not an object that one can go and look at. Like the universe, it can be charted only in accordance with the vocabularies and meanings already shaped by the public, communicative frame. There is, even in such a view, still room for some mystic kind of "seeing around the corner," an inkling beyond the counters of everyday speech and logical thought. But it is to be attained *atop* the adult world, not *beneath* it. And if you must think of art as "instinctive," let the infantile connotations of your term be tested by examining the highly moralistic elements in Shakespeare (and going from this to their more tenuous expression in forms and colors)— rather than using Mr. Read's deceptive approach, leading to superrealism as his ideal art. A different approach would suggest, rather, that superrealism is the overstressing of one ingredient in art.

# Biography

*Then appears a biographer. He looks at the man, makes a selection of his acts, weights, organizes, interprets, to give us what he considers to have been the gist of this man's life.*

—Kenneth Burke, "A Gist of Gists of Gists"

# Chekhov and Three Others

*Reminiscences of Anton Chekhov* by Maxim Gorky, Alexander Kuprin, and I.A. Bunin. Translated by S. S. Koteliansky and Leonard Woolf. B. W. Huebsch
*Notebook of Anton Chekhov* by Translated by S. S. Koteliansky and Leonard Woolf. B. W. Huebsch
*The New York Times Book Review,* January 1, 1922, 2

Chekhov, we learn in the reminiscences of him by Gorky, Kuprin and Bunin, was a man who received an endless procession of visitors, who came to talk, to beg, to receive advice, to get his signature, to express their admiration. And, as might be expected of an author whose visitors were so varied, Chekhov seems never to have been quite the same man twice. While retaining his own identity almost to the extent of aloofness, he would at least show that side of himself which was most amenable to his interlocutor. So that we now have a Gorky Chekhov, a Kuprin Chekhov and a Bunin Chekhov, each merging into the other, it is true, and yet each with a distinct flavor.

In the "Fragments of Recollections," by Maxim Gorky, we see the Tolstoyan side of the Russian character coming to the fore. Although his works are perhaps as free from the problem of the reform as those of any significant Russian, Chekhov steps forth here as one who is tremendously overburdened with the fate of his people. The juxtaposition of the two names brings out their essential difference, which is that whereas Gorky's heroes bare their teeth and snarl at misery, Chekhov's wither away at the idea. Their common grounds of meeting were the wretchedness and misery themselves. For by the last quarter of a century the outlook had become very discouraging. There could be Gogols while there were still serfs, for the serfdom one could always look forward to the happy days when serfdom would be abolished. But with serfdom abolished, and things perhaps even worse than ever, there seemed to be little chance of further improvement. It was such an environment as this that both Gorky and Chekhov looked out upon. And if Gorky saw frustration at the end of every action, Chekhov saw frustration even before the action. With such a state of affairs confronting him, Chekhov developed a strange mixture of pity and contempt, a hatred against those about him who were so constant in their triviality, their sloth, like the scoundrels of his story, "The Exile," who, when the door blows open on a cold Winter night, leave it open and shiver because no one of them will get up and close it; while this hatred was tempered with a stifled yearning that his people would mend their ways and some day blossom forth like a summer garden.

Kuprin, however, is a more cheerful soul, who, while admitting that things are very much worse than they need be, always finds a little corner of loveliness somewhere. Things are bleak, to be sure, but the situation is by no means without relief. At times, in such a story as "A Slave Soul," the very element of bleakness has its own peculiar sweetness, and even hilarity. In his "To Chekhov's Memory," therefore, we see Chekhov tending his roses and boasting charmingly that all of his orchard was planted by him, in a spot which had once been a wilderness. Here the frustrated yearning for improvement becomes a faith, and Chekhov claims that within three or four hundred years "all the earth will become a flourishing garden. And life will then be exceedingly light and comfortable." In the meantime, that lightness and comfort which he foresaw for his countrymen already existed in his own home, and was exemplified in his own life. Kuprin writes:

> It was difficult not to yield to the fascination of the simple, kind, cordial family. One felt constant solicitude and love, not expressed with a single high-sounding word—an amazing amount of refinement and attention, which never, as if on purpose, got beyond the limits of ordinary, everyday relations. One always noticed a truly Chekhovian fear of everything high-flown, insincere or showy. In that family one felt very much at one's ease, light and warm, and I perfectly understand a certain author who said that he was in love with all the Chekhovs at the same time.

More than either Gorky or Kuprin, Bunin is the pure artist, concerned primarily with problems of artistic excellence. When Bunin cuts into a thing with his descriptions, the incision is made with cold, unyielding steel. The man who wrote "The Gentleman from San Francisco" reveals himself as first of all a connoisseur of effects and of a type of deliberate, calculating cruely which one would associate more with a modern critically-minded Frenchman, such as Villiers, than with the traditional impetuosity of the Russians. It is not surprising, therefore, that in Hunin's reminiscences one should see more of Chekhov as an artist. There is a remarkable passage here dealing with his attitude toward the sea. Chekhov, it will be remembered, loved to deal with the minute and the peopled, so that the vast, lonely sea was an unwieldy thing for such an art as his. Chekhov, then, "dismissed" the sea, for he was too great a lover of companionship to deal with it masterfully. And what the artist cannot deal with masterfully is not likely to figure prominently in his art while he is also discomforted by the mere thought of it, and turns his attention to subjects which he finds more pliable. Then, we see his mind skip, in the conversation Bucin records, from the sea to sitting in a crowd listening to music. Indeed, the reminiscences of Bunin are very beautifully written, starting with opinions of books, critics and the like, and ending with these two artists driving along the sea at night, their conversation drifting imperceptibly from life to art, from the emotions of the artist in nature to the victory over those emotions which the artist scores in his work.

But above and beyond the different phases of Chekhov's character which are brought out by the three authors, there is one common thread which runs through them all, and this thread is a profound respect for one who could be kind, quiet, unassuming and friendly, and yet at the same time reserve something to himself, content to leave unsaid even in intimate speech those processes and cross-currents which lie at the base of the artist. But the book will be found invaluable to those who wish to see as much of Chekhov as Chekhov himself deigned to disclose to his peers and intimates.

During his lifetime, therefore, Chekhov's method of working had always remained a mystery. Indeed, it is not even certain just when he wrote. In such a state of affairs it is no wonder that we find Kuprin looking forward to the revelations which may come out in Chekhov's memoranda, those same memoranda which are now issued in English as his *Notebook*. While these revelations do not quite live up to their promise, they are in any case frequently of great interest. These notes are chance jottings, the description of a woman's face, a plot, a situation, an epigram, some likely odds and ends of material which Chekhov thought of possible value to his stories. As might be expected, such notes are not of the first quality. For if they were Chekhov would have devoted himself not to stories but to notes. And he, no doubt, frequently heard more overtones, felt more connotations, in a simple statement, than we, not being Chekhov, could be expected to see in purely Chekhovian jotting. For instance:

> The wife cried. The husband took her by the shoulders and shook her, and she stopped crying.

It is interesting to know that an author has though in such bafflingly simple terms. The jotting must have had to him a significance, a possibility, far beyond the mere act. And therein, certainly, lie the beginnings of the artist. We are perhaps closer to Chekhov in that pointless note than in his most finished story. The story represents the embellishment, the justification, the apology for such an interest; but the hasty jotting represents the bare interest itself, the artist's subject before the skill of his treatment has given it a significance to other people.

In other places, however, we find notes which are almost complete stories as they stand, and which, therefore, are almost complete mediums of expression as they stand. What more thoroughly Chekhovian world, for instance, than this:

> The club blackballed a respectable man because all the members were out of humor; they ruined his prospects.

While there is the ludicrously pathetic situation of the earnest author who chose only to write of contemporary problems, and who complains like one of Edgar Lee Masters's characters out of the tomb.

> When the locust was a plague I wrote against the locust, and enchanted every one; I was rich and famous, but now, when the locust has long ago disappeared and is forgotten, I am merged in the crowd, forgotten, and not wanted.

The *Notebook* is evidently the work of an appraising eye, which could observe with equal boldness a "hemorrhage; creaking, moisture in the apices of both my lungs; congestion in the apex of the right," and "a Russian's only hope-to win 200,000 rubles in the lottery." Many of these jottings will be found of primary interest through their bearing on the author and his works, while as many more have a value of their own, being the observations of a keen intelligence. While throwing no astoundingly new light on Chekhov as he was already known through his stories, these two books taken together afford us a very well-rounded interpretation of him.

# Art and the Hope Chest

*The Ordeal of Mark Twain* by Van Wyck Brooks. E. P. Dutton
*Vanity Fair*, December 1922, 59, 102

Supposing that A is a lover of flowers, and that I present him with a flower ... and supposing further, that instead of examining my flower, arranging it tentatively against the landscape, and putting it to his nose, A asks me where I got the flower, why I got it, and how much I paid for it. In other words, let us suppose that A talked of all the accidental features of the flower, and quite neglected the central matter, a judgment of the flower itself. In that case A would be a thoroughly representative modern critic of the type I am about to discuss.

Now, some of our most skillful disciples of this extrinsic criticism find Freudian methods very well adapted to their ends. That is, with the help of psychoanalysis, they will take some honest devil who wrote a book, who just sat down and wrote a book, and they will show precisely why the book should have been some other book. Or, failing that, they will show why the book is the book that it is. The book itself comes in for only the most cursory examination. It is not significant as a *fact,* but as a *symptom;* we must learn how much of it came from the heart, the stomach, the groins, and above all, from the author's neighbors. The book is a pimple, which must be diagnosed for acne or measles.

As a very brilliant, but typical, work of this sort, I should mention Van Wyck Brooks's *The Ordeal of Mark Twain.* Mr. Brooks sees Mark Twain exclusively in terms of biography. Yet Mr. Brooks is not a biographer, but a critic of literature; his very evident purpose in this work is, in Waldo Frank's term, to find a "usable past." He holds up Mark Twain as a bogey to coming generations. He shows us how a genius was dissipated. And his plain purpose is to prevent such dissipation of genius in the future. Hear, for instance, the closing message:

Read, writers of America, the driven, disenchanted, anxious faces of your sensitive countrymen; remember the splendid part your confrères have played in the human drama of other times and other peoples, and ask yourselves whether the hour has not come to put away childish things and walk the stage as poets do.

## THE FAULT WITH THE FREUDIAN TECHNIQUE

Thus, Mr. Brooks is not a biographer, but a critic. Yet he sees his subject purely in terms of biography. In his study of Mark Twain's ordeal he has given us a very convincing interpretation of Clemens's spiritual background. He has shown us the author's repressions and compromises, shown us their traces in his works. He has pointed out such things, for instance, as the fact that Mark Twain was waging a continual battle between his real self and his self in society, and that this battle manifested itself in a frequent recurrence of dual personality as a fulcrum for his plots. He has established exactly why Mark Twain was forced into the role of a humorist against his will. He has vividly reconstructed for us the pioneer element and the pioneer attitude which determined the complexion of Twain's production. All told, we have many astute psychological observations here bearing on the internal and external forces which went into the work we now know as Mark Twain.

But there is a prominent leak in this method of attacking the matter of art, and it is just this leak which I wish to talk about. But before going further, I should point out that I am not interested primarily in the truth or falsity of psychoanalysis. What I am interested in is the validity or failure of psychoanalysis when removed from the psychopathic ward to the consideration of art. Thus, I should begin by granting the complete accuracy of psychoanalysis, and then examine some aspects of its one fatal limitation. This limitation exists in its extrinsic handling of art, in the fact that it neglects to smell the rose because it is so busy explaining how the rose came to be there.

In other words, psycho-analysis concerns itself with the *genesis* of the art product rather than with its *status quo*. In this respect it is quite in keeping with the last century's great awe of evolutionism, a form of knowledge which we have not yet learned how to handle. By the evolutionist's exaggerated interest in origins the conception of a spiritual morality is found quite unnecessary, and is thrown over-board. Morality becomes, *au fond,* a higher expediency. Similarly, such a phenomenon as national idealism becomes purely a subject for economics. And the machinery of virtue and vice is allowed to grow rusty, although the less enlightened of us still cling to some vague remnants of it in our admiration for certain actions and our disapproval of others.

## The Iliad as a Social Document

Now, in the same way, aesthetics—art's own peculiar morality—disappears when we devote our time to examining how the work of art came to be, rather than examining the work of art as it is. Evolution, in other words, has nothing to do with a system of judgments. Consider the *Iliad*. I, being a producing scholar, prove that it was written by seven poets who were all blind and who met in a cave to glorify a type of magnificent, sun-lit life which was denied them. I show how the unusually brilliant quality of the Homeric epic results purely from the sublimated yearning for sun-shine. Or let us suppose on the other hand that I am able to establish how a drunken merchant bought thirty thousand Greek alphabets made of ivory, tossed them on the floor out of a jug, and behold! produced thereby the *Iliad*. In neither case has my discussion of origins touched upon the valuation of the *Iliad*. We have the *Iliad* in its status quo, and only when we take it in its *status quo* do we come to the critic's true business of judgment. This is the limitation of the Freudian method.

The Freudians—and, in general, all purely psychological methods of criticism—have supplanted for a system of excellence some vague faith in the "representative." The *Iliad* by this system becomes significant for its meaning in the life of the Greeks. Waldo Frank, in his *Our America*, pursues this method throughout. Contemporaneity becomes looked upon as a force, a more or less blind agent, a universal mold; while the artist is a mouthpiece of this force. Whitman is vaunted as representative of an epoch. We get the formula for the spirit of a city: If Chicago is a hog-butcher city, then someone who writes a representatively hog-butcher poem is glorified for his reproduction of the times. The attempt is not made, for instance, to prove so much that Sherwood Anderson's work is beautiful, but that it is an authentic spiritual re-giving of the Middle West. Excellence becomes lost in the idea of the representation; and there is almost a demand that a broken, unbeautiful age produce broken, unbeautiful books.

Some day we shall receive the apotheosis of this attitude when a critic steps forward to demand that, since his age is boring, all writers must strive to make their works as representatively boring as possible. Thus, so surely do the "genetic" critics avoid a system of excellence in their method that they have actually sought a substitute for beauty. Further, such criticism is really better adapted for other fields. Why take Walt Whitman or Henry James as subjects for diagnosis, when we have Carrie Nation and Billy Sunday? If one is looking for representative symptoms, let him consider whether these two great bar-wreckers are not positive monuments to the American mind. They are certainly points of extreme concentration. Sunday's sermons are documents of a rich representative character; and when studied, not for their excellence, but for such an extrinsic matter as their causes, they should be found of both interest and value.

As to the Freudian "message," it is, quite baldly, that the artist must express himself without bondage, without repressions and compromises. Strangely enough, in Mark Twain's case we have a peculiarly apt disproof that this is the royal road to art. Consider, for instance, the complete lack of distinction of Clemens's early letters, written in all sincerity, before he was forced—in Mr. Brooks's interpretation—by his pioneer public to make the compromise of humor. Or again, consider the documents of truth he has left us posthumously. Here again we see the untrammeled expression, and here again it is without distinction. Such things would not even be worth considering if they had not been written by our supreme humorist. And one might almost offer a vote of thanks to the pioneer civilization which forced Clemens into this role.

## The Autobiographical Novel

A criticism which leaves us with nothing but freedom has left us all dressed up and nowhere to go. The artist is turned loose to lay an abnormal importance on his own personal minutiae. Guided by a system of criticism which entirely ignores discipline, training in the craft, he is gloriously free to tell us the kind of toothpaste he uses and the manner in which he licks a postage stamp. Our prevalent glut of inartistic autobiographical novels is the result; here the matter is not arranged in accordance with principles of beauty, but by the sheer accidents of experience. Each man has but one story to write, as he has but one to live; and there is nothing on the Freudian horizon beyond James Oppenheim and Floyd Dell. But there is, in fact, as much restraint requisite to the artist as freedom. That particular phase in the artist's life which is known as "getting his stride" is nothing other than a laborious set of compromises, a gradual adapting of what he wants to say to what he can say with elegance. Mark Twain may have resented being court-jester to the world; but that was the capacity in which he could excel. He would have been a strange artist if he had not fitted his expression accordingly.

The Freudians make self-expression all of art; they want to clear the way for the artist to give himself freely and without stint; in some vague way a complete self-expression is allied with beauty. But they do not take into account that self-expression is the mere *beginning* of art, the simple desire which the artist shares with every non-artist, the common denominator between *King Lear* and Mrs. O'Grady talking behind Mrs. O'Leary's back. *King Lear* departs from Mrs. O'Grady's conversation in the artistry of the self-expression, which is a matter of technique and aesthetic standards. But it is precisely those qualities marking Shakespeare's departure from Mrs. O'Grady that Freudianism chooses to ignore in its discussions.

There is another phase of the Freudian attitude which brings out how *mal à propos* is the examination of sources. This is the emphasis laid on hungers and vengeances, on art as a vicarious method—like dreams—for settling those disturbances which are found too much for the artist in real life. Art performs here precisely that same function for society as the hope chest of a few decades back performed for the unplucked spinster. Art becomes a substitute for living. It is a sickly wish-fulfillment, a species of daydream. It would be rash to deny that there is a strong element of this in the artist. In Catullus we read of the chaste poet with his vile poetry; Ausonius tells us that "our life is pure, but lascivious our books." We have also the phenomenon of cerebral libertinage in men like Flaubert, Nietzsche, de Gourmont, all of whom had a powerfully Puritanical side to their lives. But this, again, is the mere beginning of their work. Where the Freudian formulas leave off, there the true problem of criticism begins. If a man happens to be suffering under an incest complex, this element might conceivably be discernable in his work. Similarly, if he had lived in Australia, he might have written a novel around his Australian impressions. Such things are facts, but hardly points of critical exegesis. The essential matter is the forms, the proportions, the use of value and counter-value, the technical discipline, with which the artist utilizes this purely accidental background.

### Engulfing Emotions

Further, as to the great emphasis on engulfing emotions, on mad temperaments, on *pure* inspiration which this type of criticism has fostered . . . it should be pointed out that the aesthetic joy is something quite apart from this. The excessive appetite is of itself positively inimical to the production of beauty; in a sense art almost involves the negation of it. If one, for instance, were thirsting in a desert, a discussion of aesthetics would be peculiarly pointless. To the thirsty man a painting of water would be a mere mockery; he would not care for the beauty of water, or for some interesting quality of water or function of water in a picture; he would want *water itself.* Our spiritual hungers are less absolute, but here too the aesthetic emotion tends to disappear behind the actual one. Thus, when we overlook in our criticism this independent artistic activity, this abundant curiosity which is freely and positively excited over the possibility of new beauty, when we substitute for this element an over-emphasis on suppressions and yearnings—which are undeniably there, but are the point which the artist works away from, the point beyond which the true study of art begins . . . when we do this we are pursuing a side-issue.

It must be granted that the followers of this method have made it more worthwhile for us to draw our oxygen. They have, in short, given us some very vigorous contributions to the sum total of culture. But only in a sense that a study of the Greek enclitic is a contribution to culture. That is, they have assembled documents, they have produced focuses, they have approached a subject from another angle. The work of art merits such varied angles of approach. We must be grateful for any new light thrown upon it. But at the same time we must remember that such criticism is not criticism at all in the true sense, that it shifts the centre of gravity from judgment to orientation, that it interprets rather than weighs, that it furthers our knowledge but offers no clear guide to the formation of tastes and standards.

# Heroism and Books

*Romain Rolland, the Man and His Work* by Stefan Zweig. Translated by Eden and Cedar Paul. Thomas Seltzer
*The Dial*, January 1922, 92–93

The predicament of the reformer is this: That if people suddenly take to standing on their heads, he recognizes how egregiously silly it is to stand on one's head, how many needless casualties are caused thereby, and most of all, how much better off the world would be if people stood on their feet. Then he falls to explaining passionately the functions of the feet. Finally certain people are convinced, turn right side up, and for them, at least, the reformer's value has ceased. He becomes purely a historical turmoil, while the world, having passed him by, goes about contentedly on its knees, or its elbows.

In his present volume Stefan Zweig shows plainly that he appreciates this fact even in the case of the reformer he is lionizing. Already we find him defending certain things of Rolland's on the ground that they meant so much more when written, owing to their peculiar adaptability to circumstances which have passed. Rolland and his work are interpreted here almost exclusively in terms of the war. Which signifies a tacit assumption on Zweig's part that Rolland has a greater historical than artistic importance.

Yet looked at from this standpoint we find that Rolland preached against the war, and the war came; that he went on preaching, and the war continued; and that ultimately the war stopped owing to the defeat of Germany. Certainly, this is not participating in history. Rolland, as Zweig shows well, was one of the most passionate champions of common sense during the butchery; but it takes a stupid world indeed to make common sense wise. Or to praise him merely for the elevation of his teachings is like praising Wilson for the formulation of his fourteen points. A great statesman is one who, with all the complications of office, can maintain those principles of decency which are self-evident to any one outside of a madhouse. If Wilson could have upheld the axiomatic simplicity of his peace program, his historical importance would be enormous. But as to the value of the points *per se*, any number of Hillquit's supporters in New York City could have outlined fourteen better ones. . . . In like manner, I do not see how Rolland can be assigned any unusual significance in history. In the light of his inestimable sincerity, I am discomforted by the brutality of such a statement; yet I feel that the fact, as a fact in nature, is true.

Manifestly, to judge Rolland as an artist would have meant to judge the power of his material and the skill of his workmanship, to judge virtues, in other words, which could have been utilized with as much value to glorify war as to denounce it. Zweig, however, turns constantly away from Rolland's methods to rhapsodize on his message. Then taking Tolstoy's creed that genius lies in the power of suffering, he fits Rolland admirably into this definition. I feel a bit abashed at the suggestion, but still I suggest it: That this emphasis on suffering has made more idiots than it has ever made artists. In Rolland's case it seems to have made an admirable man, a man of unmistakably heroic proportions, a man who really experienced agonies over the abstract thought of war, and who was as large in his distress as others have been in their calm. Taking him as a man, Zweig makes him seem authentically a genius; his most convincing pages are written about this phase of his hero.

But so far as art is concerned, to quote one especially delicious artist, Andre Gide, in a sentence which was applied some years back to Octave Mirbeau, it takes a great deal of talent to make genius supportable. And Rolland is seldom talented, unless we except some parts of *Colas Breugnon,* a book which, significantly enough, Zweig rates as his most important work artistically. What he gives, he pours out upon us: earnestness, bitterness, love of man, what not. Yet all such qualities are the mere starting point of art. It is in the resolution of such things that art-values are to be found; and this resolution might happen to be the modelling of an egg.

Zweig, then, has given us here a great deal more of Rolland as a great man than as a great artist, which I think is an excellent testimony to Zweig's judgment even under the stress of an egregious enthusiasm. As to the "world-movements" which Rolland deals with, I think we are too often inclined to place the writer of universal history as categorically above the writer of comic opera; obviously, it all depends on the history and the opera.

# Codifying Milton

*Milton, Man and Thinker* by Denis Saurat. Lincoln MacVeagh. Dial Press
*The Dial*, November 1925, 429–430

Mr. Saurat's book on Milton, despite the total orthodoxy of its treatment, is a very difficult work to approach. On first reading I felt it to be an assembling of *disjecta membra;* yet further examination disclosed that the subject had been parcelled out with perfect logic and clarity. The opening section is devoted to Milton, The Man. It is in turn sub-divided into The Elements of Milton's Character in Youth, and The Man of Action and Passion, the latter sub-division astutely including the polemical pamphlets as a phase of Milton's "action." The other three parts—again sub-divided, while the sub-divisions are sub-divided in turn—deal respectively with Milton's "system," the reflection (and occasionally deflection) of this system in his major poems, and the "sources" of his thought. Having gone so far in the laying out of his book, I suspect Mr. Saurat of simply reversing his process, taking the various notes which he had collected and sorting them into their proper bins. The result is too often a mere sequence of data, a loose mosaic of quotations paralleled by repetitions in Mr. Saurat's own words, or introduced by some such barely serviceable remarks as: "And he concludes in this masterly fashion"; "The praise of books is famous"; "Here is his opinion of contemporary Italy"; "But here is his opinion of England." The work, which originally served as a doctor's thesis, has not wholly lifted itself above its type.

In his introduction Mr. Saurat writes that "Milton's thought is most attractive when studied in connection with its intimate sources in his character and emotional experience." One might begin by challenging this statement in itself. Indeed, Mr. Saurat's own book may be taken as added evidence that Milton's thought is, on the contrary, most attractive when it is left embedded and obscured among Milton's own stylistic specifications. A poet's "thoughts" are not those flat answers to questionnaires which can be extracted, in the form of propositions, from some intricate piece of rhetoric constructed around these "thoughts." Ibsen's "thoughts" on the freedom of women, for instance, are not certain sentences taken from his *Doll's House*.

His thoughts on this subject are the *Doll's House*. The "thoughts" on the subject—as Mr. Saurat understands the word—are, like the thoughts of Milton which Mr. Saurat so carefully outlines, perfectly capable of suggesting themselves to persons of rich or low vitality, and to powerful and niggardly brains alike.

But even allowing Mr. Saurat his assumption, I feel that his book still remains a disappointment. For he possesses only the most antiquated and unwieldy of mechanisms for disclosing to us the "intimate sources" in Milton's "character and emotional experience." In view of the increasing accuracy of psychological nomenclature during recent years, the reader will be nonplussed at a method of investigation which confines itself to talk of "imperious will," "penetrating and systematic intellect," "fullest self-consciousness of a tremendous individuality," "noble humility in his pride." Mr. Saurat tends always to discuss Milton's character in an ethical, rather than a psychological, vocabulary.

A similar objection might be made to Mr. Saurat's treatment of theology in Milton. He does hardly more than cull or rearrange Milton's theological prose, and—by seeing it purely in the terms current in its heyday—restates rather than interprets. (He does, however, draw certain parallels between Milton's system and that of some nineteenth-century philosophy.) As to his appendix on Milton's blindness, and his somewhat loose yet possibly correct reasoning to prove that it derived from hereditary syphilis, this is a fact which—if thoroughly established—might be useful to those savants who keep turning up with the desire to connect genius with disease. In Mr. Saurat's volume it is merely constated, a thesis without an application, left *in vacuo*.

In summary I should say that Mr. Saurat's concerns are decidedly peripheral to those aspects of Milton's poetry which recommend it to modern readers; but in this peripheral territory his work has been extensive, and should prove of most value to students and producing scholars, all those for whom Milton is less a poet than a task.

# The Art of Yielding

*Stephen Foster, America's Troubadour* by John Tasker Howard. Thomas Y. Crowell Company
*They All Sang; From Tony Pastor to Rudy Vallee,* as told to Abbott J. Liebling by Edward B. Marks. Viking Press
*The Nation,* April 1934, 484–486

"I find that I cannot write at all," we read in a letter by Stephen Foster, "unless I write for public applause and get credit for what I write." Foster was addressing E. P. Christy, of Christy's Minstrels. He had sold Christy the right to appear as the author and composer of "Old Folks at Home"; but following the great popular success of this "Ethiopian melody," he had considerably altered his plans for his career as a song-writer. In this same letter he explains:

> As I once intimated to you, I had the intention of omitting my name on my Ethiopian songs, owing to the prejudice against them by some, which might injure my reputation as a writer of another style of music, but I find that by my efforts I have done a great deal to build up a taste for the Ethiopian songs among refined people by making the words suitable to their taste, instead of the trashy and really offensive words which belong to some songs of that order. Therefore I have concluded to reinstate my name on my songs and to pursue the Ethiopian business without fear or shame and lend all my energies to making the business live, at the same time that I will wish to establish my name as the best Ethiopian song-writer.

The art song, no matter how great its pretensions, falls clearly in the category of "business." It was written as a sales commodity in a civilization that was learning more and more to live by a purchase economy. Mr. Howard's thoroughly documented record of Foster's career appropriately has an entire chapter headed Finances, the upshot of which is that Foster averaged something more than $1,300 a year for the period between 1849 and 1860, his productive era as a purveyor of pleasant melancholy to millions.

As a fitting companion piece, the reader is referred to Edward B. Marks's colorful account of Tin Pan Alley from the nineties until today. However, in this second volume we have not a monograph but a panorama, an endless procession of agitated and unstable bohemians who quickly manufactured the raw materials of sentiment into salable objects, generally marketed with some song publisher for ten or fifteen dollars a few hours after their production. The one aim of these individualistic entrepreneurs, each of whom carried about a more or less efficient song factory in his head, was to turn out a commercially useful product. Working in close touch with the stage performers, or the orchestras and singers of the amusement dives, they had the most inexorable test to go by—the delight or jeers of extremely vocal audiences. Originality meant nothing: any work that caught the public fancy was immediately followed by an avalanche of imitators, each of whom attempted to abstract the factor he considered most responsible for the success of the piece, and to put together a commodity which would exemplify this factor still more intensively.

Stephen Foster was their reason for being. "Sober, they acquiesced in the fate society decreed for bohemians. Drunk, they gloried in it. Mostly they were drunk. 'Look at Foster,' they would say. Stephen Foster, their immediate predecessor, whom many of them could remember, had died in a cheap lodging-house in the Bowery, hadn't he? They considered their mode of life a confirmation of their talents, which, truthfully, were sometimes slim." The distinction between Foster and the great run of song-writers seems to have lain in the fact that whereas they were wholly opportunistic, and would write a song for a political campaign, the new electric light, the flying machine, or any other topic of the moment which might dispose the public's interest in their favor, Foster had one underlying principle of stability: his yearning for "home" was deep and permanent. He too seized upon anything that the occasion brought to the fore; but besides, he was possessed by melancholy imaginings of the "good life," a hope for the future which, in keeping with the ways of the times, he symbolized in plaintive contemplation of things far away and long ago. As a consequence, in addition to his host of purely "popular songs," be produced "folk songs."

Though I should be hard put to state just wherein the difference between a popular song and a folk song resides, I am sure there is one, and a momentous one. Perhaps it is only in the fact that the occasions for which the folk song is written are of longer duration, and the pattern of its melodies follows more closely the patterns of experience in our childhood. Yet there is another factor that enters here. For in going through the reminiscences of Mr. Marks, and reading many titles of works which are the essence of triviality, I find that they have strangely appealing overtones, surely not present at the time of their newness. In reading again the songs a nation sang, one must vaguely recall times when he heard them sung—hence their very names possess an evocative power, quite as some odor or natural sound might have if it possessed associational linkages with past events. The magical powers which Proust attributes to Vinteuil's sonata can reside as genuinely in even a dingy piece, since life itself is not dingy, and a work heard when we were emotionally involved is as truly a significant part of the "environment" as sea or hills. It is perhaps for this reason that even a folk song, if written today, might have to incorporate something of the purely popular songs which were heard in the past.

The Foster volume is a piece of research rather than biography in the Strachey manner. It is a valuable contribution to the Foster archives, written by one whose understanding of Foster's gifts and limitations is obvious. The Marks volume is a good-natured and haphazard survey of a turbulent era as revealed in one of its most barometric groups, men who lived by their "weather eye" alone, who speculated as keenly on the daily fluctuations of the market as any in-and-out trader on the curb. But its narrator has been close to his subject for so long, having been in the song-publishing business through many decades, that he often speaks with great shrewdness, as witness this diagnosis of the decay of the minstrel show:

> Mock dignity that grew upon its practitioners until it became real; grotesque exaggeration that mocked a vanishing ideal! When manners flourished in America, their amiable parodists were loved. When the substance departed, the shadow might not linger. It was not that the jokes were old. It was not that the public had seen too many minstrel shows. The public had not tired of them in the previous fifty years. The specialty acts that constituted the olio of the minstrel show continued in the form of vaudeville. The tear-jerking balladists still operate over the radio, and there has been no cessation of trick and soft-shoe dancing. No, the minstrel show passed because the public lost the courtesy which was the underlying motif of the whole institution. The humor of the highfalutin interchange between Mr. Interlocutor and Mr. Bones survives, but its audience has vanished. "What the hell are they batting about?" became the reaction of twentieth-century audiences to these high incongruities. "Get on with the show." And so they

kept the tinsel specialty jewels and threw away the gracious antique setting.

Surely this paragraph is a remarkably acute critical appraisal of the relationship between an art form and a social background. The minstrel show was a comedy of manners, largely precommercial manners; it flourished while the manners were breaking under the impact of new demands but had not yet broken—and then for a time this art form survived vestigially after the manners had passed. Gradually the "irrelevant" features were eliminated entirely until today the minstrel show could appeal only as a "revival," not as the parody of an era, but as its restoration.

# A Gist of Gists of Gists

*One Mighty Torrent: The Drama of Biography* by Edgar Johnson. Stackpole
*The Nation*, May 1937, 622–623

Each man's way of living, as we might say, is his particular way of getting the "gist" of experience. The world is manifold; it has many loose ends, and each man knots a few of them. He knots them in accordance with his own particular vision of necessities and opportunities. Put all his acts together—and they reveal what he has taken to be the "gist" of experience.

Then appears a biographer. He looks at the man, makes a *selection* of his acts, weights, organizes, interprets, to give us what he considers to have been the gist of this man's life. And after many such biographies have been amassed, one may become a kind of "statistician," looking over an entire field. People having lived gists, and writers having given gists of these lives, after a sufficient accumulation one may "transcend" both lives and biographies by taking as his starting-point this "higher level" afforded by the accumulation itself.

Edgar Johnson's *One Mighty Torrent* is an engrossing work conducted on this "higher," "statistical" level. He has epitomized for us the course of English biography from the sixteenth century to the present—including the autobiographies, memoirs, diaries, letters, and biographical fiction that he considers significant. In this large undertaking, I think he has done us a double service.

Like John Chamberlain, in his highly succinct job of reporting the variants of populism (in *Farewell to Reform*), Johnson has put together some important lore, reducing a welter of material to "abstracts," that we may proceed to build upon it in whatever way we please—whereas otherwise we should have first to cover this preparatory ground ourselves. And in the course of thus making a field "handy" for others, who would get at it quickly, he has produced a work packed with "events."

I hope that our young novelists especially will read it. For it might have a healthy effect upon their notions of "realism," which have become disturbingly oversimplified in recent years. Realism has become "naturalism"—and naturalism has come to mean hardly more than an efficiently organized way of running people down. Reading Johnson's book, we are reminded that imaginative enterprise requires much subtler tactics, that realism should not be the mere bureaucratization of debunking and indictment. It should be the attempt to find the acts, thoughts, situations, and speeches in which a character *names his number.* Flaubert thought of it that way. Realism was not to him merely a roundabout way of asking us to pay $2.50 for words that we can get outside of books for nothing. It is the search for *gists,* for those events wherein a character sums up himself and the life beyond himself with accuracy and picturesqueness.

Johnson's book gives us a maximum of such events. He has gone through his material in search of characteristic moments, significant condensations, incidents that reveal the essence of the given biographer and the given biographer's subject. The literary efficiency of wit, of sharp appraisal (the startling kind of short-circuiting we get in the poems of Marianne Moore, where we can leap across gaps suddenly)—that sort of emphasis has become lost as the result of competitive crudeness; and Johnson's connoisseurship might do much to correct such blunt notions of "power."

There is no use here in attempting further to condense his condensations. I might mention, however, the almost frightening effect we get as we move from Chapter VII, Eighteenth Century Apogee (discussing that massive Tory, Samuel Johnson, that intellectual bouncer who perfected epigrammatic ways of kicking out the enemy) to Chapter VIII, Romantic Letter-Writers (dealing with Byron, Shelley, and Keats). I never felt so strongly what was let loose upon the world as the romanticism of business and the counter-romanticism of poetry caught its full stride. Another highly suggestive contrast is got by the matching of Steffens and Lawrence.

If you want not a survey but a final putting together of the material surveyed, perhaps Johnson's book will not be completely satisfactory. The range of the author's appreciation, his pliancy when confronting many different kinds of material, is the virtue here. And that is virtue enough for one book. He has recorded the plenitude of human personality. If you want not only this plenitude but also some underlying logic of unification, you may find the book, comprehensive as it is, still unfinished. Perhaps it were better left unfinished, in this sense. Perhaps men *are* as different as daisies and liverwort—and that's the end of it. And perhaps we should be content merely to contemplate and relish this diversity. In any case, I do not see how a reader could fail to enjoy the documents of diversity as here assembled, a literary springtime wherein the tiny brooks of personality converge to make the sweep onward of a torrential flood.

# Goethe and the Jews

*Goethe and the Jews* by Mark Waldman. G.P. Putnam's Sons
*The New Masses*, March 1935, 25

When one is angry at a man, one strikes him. If angry enough, one strikes him with whatever weapon is at hand. In "law-abiding" situations, the strike is metaphorical, not by a blow but by an epithet; and unless one is exceptionally inventive in speech, here too, one uses the handiest epithet available.

Now, in the competitive struggles that go with capitalism, we practically have chagrin written into the very nature of the State; for each transaction involved in the producing and distributing of goods demands that, in part at least, talent be employed not in helping others but in outwitting them. Under capitalism, the *competitive* use of talent, as distinguished from its *cooperative* use, is Rule One. Hence, there is everywhere the situation that provides incentive for the metaphorical blow, the vituperative epithet.

If gentile outwits gentile in this lofty commercial combat, the outwitted one, seizing the weapon nearest to hand, may call him a "bastard." Though originally implicating his whole family, the word now generally has the quality of damning him simply as an individual. But if, in the peaceful conduct of his trickeries, he is outwitted by a Jew, the enraged gentile reaches for the handiest epithet and calls his commercial antagonist a "Jew bastard," thereby damning him not merely as an individual, but as a member of a race. This linguistic generosity and scope obviously serves his vindictive purposes with maximum thoroughness. Thus does the competitive act, which is at the base of all capitalist interchange, lead in some instances to the imputation of *individual* guilt and in other instances to the imputation of *racial* guilt, depending upon the linguistic weapon that best fits the situation. And this tendency, embodied in capitalist economy, is further perpetuated by Jewish isolation, which is also the embodiment of the capitalist economy.

The present book, *Goethe and the Jews,* shows that even so broad a man as Goethe had moments when he simply took the qualities of his language, as it was, content to get his effects as a writer by using the word "Jew" in the handy connotations which it had derived from competitive vindictiveness. But by far the greatest amount of evidence shows Goethe as a thinker who consciously wove Jewish strains into the texture of his thought, who had learned both Yiddish and Hebrew, and who repaid his debt by vigorously championing the cause of tolerance.

Communistic Jews may find the result somewhat unpalatable, since his borrowings essentially comprise the pious patterns of the Bible and Spinoza, in whom he saw, not the excommunicated atheist, but the mystic, "God-intoxicated Jew." And the book throughout is written in a spirit of nationalism which, while fully justified in light of events, leads constantly to a misplacing of the emphasis as regards the needs of current political criticism. Yet the work does serve unanswerably the purpose advertised on its binder, as "a challenge to Hitlerism," since it shows how thoroughly Jewish thought was imbedded in the works and acts of Germany's greatest Aryan.

# Mainsprings of Character

*The Ironic Temper: Anatole France and His Times* by Haakon M. Chevalier.
 Oxford UP
*The New Republic*, December 1932, 103–104

In seeking a key term for the pattern of thought underlying the works of Anatole France, Mr. Chevalier holds that an insistence upon France's irony as a central fact makes possible "an organic account of the contradictory elements in the man himself." By his interpretation, not only was France ripe for irony, but the times were ripe for irony. That is: France's irony is "explained" as a pattern peculiar to the author as a person, manifesting itself in emergent forms long before he could have accurately gauged the issues of the day; yet the issues of the day were also such as to encourage an ironic stressing. Hence France, like a kind of Leibnitzian monad, could be obeying wide social patterns while obeying his own. This lock-and-key fit between a society naturally making for ironists and a man with many traits of character naturally making for irony resulted in a writer who, subjective, personal, impressionistic, concerning himself with his own particularities of experience, became a popular writer symbolizing trends of thought and feeling which ran through the entire reading public of his day.

Mr. Chevalier's documentation seems to me thoroughly convincing. It is no accident that irony was brought up for deep consideration by the romantics at the beginning of the nineteenth century and became an attribute of many lively writers as the century progressed. His remarks on the nature of irony enable us to understand why the nineteenth century, of all centuries, a century inferior in great drama, should be concerned with a device so integral to drama. As Mr. Chevalier points out, dramatic irony arises from a relationship between the audience and the play. The audience knows that certain tragic events are destined to take place. It also hears some figure on the stage boasting of the good times to come. And in the audience, as *spectator*, arises dramatic irony. The audience is powerless to affect the course of events; at the same time, its sympathy for the characters makes it long to alter the course of events—and this divided attitude, a sense of being *with* the people as regards one's sympathies but *aloof* as regards one's ability to forestall the movements of destiny, this awareness of a breach between one's desires and one's understanding, this is ironic.

Hence it becomes clear why the nineteenth century, of all centuries, reapplied irony by transferring the spectator attitude from the audience to the writer. Hence the irony of men like Renan, France, Henry James. Here was a century in which the men of intellect saw the people headed eagerly towards so many ambitions which these men despised. Feeling that the authority of this movement was irresistible, yet having always a strong desire to change the course of events if they could, they became *spectators,* with the divided, ironic attitude that comes of seeing people headed with confidence towards desolate ends.

The ironic attitude was complicated by the dual position which science played in the life of the century. In the speculations of pure science there was everything which a lover of the "esthetic" could admire: enterprise, independence, spiritedness, imaginativeness, critical keenness. Applied science on the other hand (the adventurous speculations harnessed for business purposes) seemed to make for the very opposite type of mind, with more and more demands upon our acquiescence, our obedient repeating of such parrotlike things as one says to a parrot, our loss of fluid, physical, "earthy" living, our development of cogwheel thoughts to match the cogwheel methods of production. This was cause enough for irony: a sense that the most brilliant aspects of human thought were being steadily converted, by men of a different order, into human impoverishments. The situation was further complicated by the fact that pure science had robbed the social critics of a stable basis upon which they might erect a system of protest, such completely relativistic sciences as psychology and anthropology having destroyed the underpinnings of absolute judgment. Only those who remained staunch Catholics were able to write sturdy invective. They could still base their thunderings upon the old ideology of horrors, thus deriving "strength," but the "new men" had weakened: they could not say, "It is wrong in the eyes of God," nor even, "It is wrong in the eyes of human justice," but simply, "I do not like it." Thus, pure science had not merely put them in a divided attitude as the result of its harsh commercial application; it had also impaired the authoritative, "metaphysical" judgments upon which they could frame an attack against this harsh commercial application. Hence their complaints about the "disillusionment" of science—complaints, be it noted, which never turned them against scientific speculation, for as men of spirit they were necessarily vowed to breadth of inquiry, regardless of where it led.

There was a strong attempt to avoid their dilemmas by making ethics a branch of esthetics. As a matter of fact, the criteria of the beautiful were as fundamentally impaired as the criteria of the good. But ethical crumblings were naturally more noticeable, so a definition of goodness as a subdivision of the beautiful seemed to point in the direction of an area still partially intact. This was, I believe, a move in the right direction, and might eventually have led to such a biologic or psychologic basis of judgment as, "It is wrong because it outrages needs of the mind and body, because it interferes with the felicitous working of the human organism." As a matter of fact, however, all that it did generally lead to was an ultimate realization that beauty also was relative, so at the close of the century this double frustration was in evidence: applied science driving the world towards ways of living and thinking which required the elimination of many past amenities; and pure science having corroded the basis of judgment upon which the disorders of applied science could be attacked.

Mr. Chevalier clearly shows Anatole France at the center of these issues. He shows how certain personal elements, of indolence, of irresponsibility, permitted him to stress this ironic, spectator attitude to the limits, allowing him to remain at home (as regards his page) in these many contradictions, inducing him to live by an "as if" philosophy which could restore the classic amenities once more by permitting oneself on paper to feel "as if" they were still with us, and yet grew apologetic at the awareness of its own subterfuge.

It is customary today to be repelled by the thought of this spectator attitude. There are no spectators. All men, though they have done no more for a living than to exhaust themselves by clipping coupons, are a-tremble. There is no haven, no elevation above the century, from which one can look out calmly upon the hideous Manichean battles that are to be fought between the principle of goodness and the principle of evil during the next decades. So it can be made to seem that there was something cold, something unfeeling, in the ironic temper. Yet whatever else we may hold against it, we must dismiss this charge entirely.

As Mr. Chevalier very pointedly says of France in his closing summation:

> That which he expressed—often with profound sophistication as the naïve, the fresh, the immature approach to experience, the first contacts with life, the budding emotions, the tentative intellectual discoveries that each youth must make anew. Life remains for him always clothed with mystery and enchantment, fraught with danger. It is an ecstatic youth's vision of life, even when his reactions are those of a disabused old man . . . Some of the most appealing human

traits are magically evoked—tenderness, compassion, and childlike wonder, a perpetual fresh surprise before objects of beauty and grandeur.

For all his guise of "complexity," France managed all this by a very simplified kind of poetry. He wrote his books on the top of other books, that his might share the quality of theirs; he found that by "scribbling upon the margins of books," he could restore for us some of the gentler existences out of which these other books had arisen. Like an archeologist, he found a calm Atlantis, which had heaved a huge geologic sigh and sunk slowly to the bottom of the sea, where it now lay, its temples still standing, its marbles posturing, and mournful fishes peering upon these dead splendors. It is not the most "usable" attitude for today—neither is it an attitude which could be dismissed from the mind without great loss.

# One Who Wrestled

*Dostoevsky: A Life* by Avrahm Yarmolinsky. Harcourt, Brace and Company
*The New Republic*, March 1935, 192, 194

Think of some gnarled old magician who had been skillful enough to make a powerful demon take bodily form, where spells and incantations could make this demon do his bidding, but who did not know how to dismiss the monster and lived in dread lest it attack him in his sleep. Foremost among such great demonologists of the nineteenth century is Fyodor Dostoevsky—and who can say whether he is boon or calamity for those who, during the chaos of adolescence, first come upon the turbulent order of his fiction and learn the dangerous trick of interpreting motives in his morbidly agitational vocabulary? Mr. Yarmolinsky's painstaking biography of this unwieldy writer who "regarded his novels as his testament" had the effect of recalling with penetrating intensity the spell his works once exerted over me. The biographer's discreetly emotional pages, his thorough collation of relevant facts, and his many keen critical observations afforded the most persuasive incentive to live again the time of my "Dostoevskian conversion." The first work of his I had ever read was *Notes from Underground,* an accidental choice making for the maximum of impressiveness, for in this early work one finds most succinctly the peculiar kind of psychological grotesque that was Dostoevsky's contribution. I wondered how it would look to me, after nearly twenty years. And rereading, I found:

> A man of the nineteenth century must and morally ought to be a preeminently limited creature . . . Gentlemen, you must excuse me for being overphilosophical; it's the result of forty years underground . . . Why, suffering is the sole origin of consciousness. Though I did lay it down at the beginning that consciousness is the greatest misfortune for man, yet I know man prizes it and would not give it up for any satisfaction . . . I have been for forty years listening to you

> through a crack under the floor . . . Snow is falling today, yellow and dingy . . . I made friends with no one . . . I alternated between despising them and thinking them superior to myself . . . I was always the first to drop my eyes . . . Of the daughters, one was thirteen and another fourteen, they both had snub noses, and I was awfully shy of them because they were always whispering and giggling together. . . . In short, I parted from my schoolfellows as soon as I got out into the world . . . That night I had the most hideous dreams . . . No one paid any attention to me, and I sat crushed and humiliated . . . If I suddenly asked him what he wanted, he would make no answer, but continue staring at me persistently . . . Even in my underground dreams I did not imagine love except as a struggle . . . Even now, so many years later, all this is somehow a very evil memory.

I found the work almost as engrossing as it had been when I first saw it, though I was happy to be able to feel that it was somewhat overdone, that it was not the "whole truth" that I once thought it to be, but simply a bogeyman's truth, an admonition. Dostoevsky's art is not a design for living—it is a "Beware the dog" kind of art. The appeal of the story technically, I think, resides in his great skill at building up vicious circles whereby a character's offenses became self-perpetuating, whereby in trying to extricate himself from one bad situation he creates another. This predicament is always engrossing: we enjoy it in a mildly provocative form when W. C. Fields gets caught in a barbed-wire fence—and here we have its morbid counterpart in the grimly hilarious antics of a wretch whose very yearnings for sociality aggravate his social affronts.

Fear of insanity, strong feeling of both guilt and promise, courting of punishment, humiliation, fascinated concern with crime and gambling, debt, overwork, ill nature, religiosity, sense of duality, foreboding of the "end of the world"; a superstitious belief in dreams (so thorough a cerebralist was bound to realize that dreams had "meaning," but his adumbrations of psychoanalysis would need the revision of other men); violent epileptic seizures which, before plunging him into misery, gave him a sense of complete beatitude and universal oneness; jingoism, reactionary attachment to the Tsar (he identified the Tsar with God and he identified the masses with God, and since things equal to the same thing are equal to each other, he could thereby identify the Tsar with the masses); "and there were a thousand minor vexations." Decidedly, this demonologist was more apt at conjuring forth dark powers than at dismissing them—and Mr. Yarmolinsky gives us the whole drama with great care. Readers who would have the riddle of Dostoevsky definitely solved for them may be disappointed. But if one is interested in seeing all of the novelist's typical acts, emotions, situations and literary symbols assembled before him with scholarship and fluency, he will find in this volume a most stimulating store.

In his chapter of general evaluation, "Life After Death," the biographer says of his subject: "Involuntarily, indirectly, he furthered the cause of revolution. The moral maximalism informing his work is inimical to all reformist and middle-of-the-road policy." The suggestion seems reasonable. For all his attachment to the Little Father, whose government had sent him to Siberia, the antinomian and grotesque patterns of his thought provoked his readers to rebellion. If Mr. Yarmolinsky's estimate of Dostoevsky's effect upon his time is correct, critics must note that there may be a great difference between the face value of an author's exhortations and their social behavior when released into a given environmental texture.

# Why Coleridge?

*Samuel Taylor Coleridge: A Biographical Study* by E. K. Chambers. Oxford UP
*The Life of S. T. Coleridge: The Early Years* by Lawrence Hanson. Oxford UP
*The New Republic*, September 1939, 163–164

Each time I note the signs of the élite boom for Kierkegaard and Kafka, I am disgruntled. It should be Coleridge. Most assuredly, it should be Coleridge. And it is largely, I suspect, because we were all compelled to read his poems in high school, that those lesser figures are focusing attention at his expense. Coleridge would not so obviously be a "discovery." Also, the tangle of these other men was much less complex; they did not even remotely have the scope of Coleridge's mentality. They did well by the stage of masturbatory adolescence—and so their scrupulous quarrels with the father may be interesting and relevant to watch. But their Hamletic labyrinth is a trivial one, in comparison with the twists and turns of Coleridge. They had many fewer cylinders to hit on—they were like a first engine, Coleridge like the engine after long development.

In his life there was a great transitional year, the *annus mirabilis* of 1797–98, wherein his gift for miraculous poetry quickly flowered and went to seed. A few anticipations (most notably, "The Eolian Harp")—and a few after-echoes (most notably "Dejection" and the second part of "Christabel")—but it is in the *annus mirabilis* that the bulk of his significant poetic output is concentrated, with the other few bits as foothills leading up to and away from this peak year.

It was a "watershed" year—a strategic shift from one slope to another. Before it, we had Coleridge the libertarian, the prophet of "Pantisocracy" (the project for a communist colony to be founded on the Susquehanna), Unitarian, the propounder of optimistic determinism. After it, we find him on the other slope, on his way to becoming Coleridge the Tory (I wince at seeming to put him in the same bin with Chamberlain), the apologist of the National Church, the Trinitarian, the exponent of original sin and free will. (It is typical of him that he proclaimed himself a "necessitarian" in the period before his enslavement to opium had become established, whereas he insisted strenuously upon the freedom of the will at a later time, when in his letters he had bemoaned the effects of "this *free-agency-annihilating Poison*," and complained that "by the long long Habit of the accursed Poison my Volition . . . was compleatly deranged.")

In the "watershed" year there was a "watershed" poem: "The Ancient Mariner," with its guilt-laden pilgrimage, no mere *allegory* of sin and redemption, but an organic sequence of internal, personal developments objectified in the imagery of external, natural marvels. The very ship on which the wanderer is driven is an aspect of the wanderer himself; it thirsts and sweats, is fixed or moves, as does the man's own body. It is a "drunken boat"—and when it sinks, something of the Mariner sinks with it. Under the accusing magnetic eye of the Sun at high noon it was—as Coleridge says of his poison—"accursed." But when "the moving Moon went up the sky," it gets release, though a dangerous release, maybe even a *lunatic* release, which would explain why the poor Pilot's boy "now doth crazy go," as the dangerous factors in the cure, effected under the aegis of moonlight, were drained off, with this nameless fellow as the recipient of the ominous charge.

But let us complete the pattern: In this "watershed" poem there was a "watershed" moment—quite where it should be, in the middle, in Part IV of a seven-part lyrical drama. It is here that a radical bit of alchemy takes place—as loathsome creatures, crawling in primeval slime, abruptly change their nature from things ugly and accursed to things blessed and beautiful. It is a kind of second creation, as though the poet had said: "Let dark be light":

> O happy living things; no tongue
> Their beauty might declare:
> A spring of love gushed from my heart,
> And I blessed them unaware.

And immediately following upon this change of identity the Mariner, who had passed through the terrors of ice, drought and rot (in another connection, Coleridge speaks of "the Terrors that precede God's Love")—the Mariner could of a sudden pray, whereat the burdensome Albatross fell from his neck, and "sank like lead into the sea" (later, the ship "went down like lead").

A watershed moment, in a watershed poem, in a watershed year. Enough like the House That Jack Built to engage anyone in search of "critical points." Add, now, the fact that the writer of this expiatory ritual was thoroughly equipped to articulate in conceptual terms the complexity behind it. Add that, owing to the conversational, epistolary and diarist propensities of both himself and his associates, we have an almost embarrassing wealth of documents through which we can observe the personal and social situations digested in his work—and you begin to see: Why Coleridge.

Other sales points could be added. Out of idealism, both Marxism and Nazism are descended—and Coleridge is as thorough an exponent of idealism as Hegel or Schelling, plus the fact that he could write great idealistic verse, as the German metaphysicians could not (unless you take their cumbersome nomenclature to be itself a form of poetry). Nor would we have any difficulty in tracing a strict line of literary tradition from Coleridge, to Byron, Shelley, Keats and Scott, to Poe, to Rimbaud and the French Symbolists, and so to Surrealism (with "Kubla Khan" more fully meeting the requirements of the Surrealist esthetic than anything our contemporaries have done, to my knowledge, since it is the perfect instance of "automatic writing," originating in the "subconscious"—hardly other than *dictated*, with Coleridge as amanuensis, yet it is "beautiful," i.e., publicly negotiable).

I said that Coleridge's poetry went to seed. It did—and the seed germinated, in a mutation, as would be fitting for one who had been through a transformational year. Most notably in "The Friend," in *Biographia Literaria* and in his scattered jottings. Even the religious tracts of his later years repay close reading, if one is interested in the mental deployments of a man with a grievous burden, struggling constantly to keep himself from falling through the bottom, and building up a vast architecture of stabilizing ideas for this incantatory, or self-admonitory end.

And the overall situation in which he wrote is quite "contemporary"—since England then was responding to the French revolution and reaction quite as we today are responding to the Russian revolution and the Fascist reaction (an event beyond the borders that agitated even the less mobile groups within the borders, and thus had an especially strong effect upon the class of greatest mobility, the literary Romantics and political Utopians, all of whom were, to borrow the title of Wordsworth's play, "Borderers").

I could add more sales points—but these should be enough for the moment. Particularly since all this is but designed for leading up to the subject of two new biographies by E. K. Chambers and Lawrence Hanson.

The Chambers one has the merit of covering the entire course of Coleridge's life. But it gives too much the impression of a syllabus filled out with grammaticalisms. It is punctilious in verifying the exact time of day when Coleridge was where with whom and what they talked about—and thus is highly serviceable as a reference book for academic workers who may have need for this minute kind of checking.

The Hanson volume, while equally factual in its method, concentrates upon an ampler kind of fact. Its main short-coming is that it but brings us up to the year 1800, thus leaving us with thirty-four to go, and yearning for the sequel. But it is a good job, quite able to stand by itself—and is done without the impressionistic, monographic emphasis of such works as Charpentier's *Coleridge: The Sublime Somnambulist,* Fausset's *Samuel Taylor Coleridge,* or Potter's *Coleridge and S. T. C.*

A standard biography should probably seek to describe motivations and relationships in the most orthodox of terms: terms like "kind-hearted," "indolent," "conceited," "pretentious," "charitable," "well read," "discerning," "imaginative." This sort of description should be perfected, and amply, as the groundwork prerequisite to any experimental vocabulary of motivation. And it is the kind of description that Hanson has assembled with careful documentation. Thus, when discussing a letter in which Coleridge asseverates an intention of returning to Stowey:

> This statement of his intentions . . . sounded, at first hearing, definite enough. Yet [it] only too probably masked, and was intended partly to bolster up, a sagging purpose. That Coleridge was genuine in his wish, so often expressed, to be at Stowey, need not be doubted. But he had other wishes, at least of equal strength; and these it was he set himself, half-heartedly, to fight; employing a favorite weapon of the weak, the announcement of intentions—but promptly nullifying its effect in the next breath, by attaching to it qualifications providing easy and endless avenues of escape from the implications of his own words.

All told you get, with much relevant quotation, the portrait of the man who characterized himself perfectly when he wrote: "On dipping my foot and leg into very hot water, the first sensation was identical with that of having dipped it into very cold"—the man whose favorite maxim was "Extremes meet," and who knew how to pursue its intricacies to the ends of the universe—the man who justified a journalistic interlude by observing that the subjects of his articles were (a) "important in themselves" and (b) "excellent vehicles for general truths." It is this constant eagerness to consider local situations with reference to universal situations that gives even his most transient concerns their lastingness. And though you may very often disagree with his vote on a given issue, you must repeatedly salute his precision in singling out the issues to vote on.

# Cult of the Breakthrough

*Selected Letters of Theodore Roethke* edited with an Introduction by Ralph J. Mills, Jr. University of Washington
*The New Republic*, September 21, 1968, 25–26

As the editor well says of the turbulent man who wrote these letters (most of them by hand), "All of Roethke's poetry involves search, transformation, the continuous process of becoming, in technique and style obviously, and also in vision, in the depth and intensity of experience he pursued." In an age when scientists speak often of "breakthroughs" in the realm of knowledge, Roethke was interested in a poetic counterpart, though he was not the sort of person who would have presented his search in such terms.

What the scientific searcher might seek to describe or formulate for an observer, the aesthetics of poetry would transform into *experience for a participant*. The possible range would comprise rarity, oddity, magic, the mystical, and breakdown. And Roethke worked his way indeterminately through several of these phases.

His most important breakthrough, it has always seemed to me, took place during the time at Bennington College when he hit upon what I have called his "vegetal radicalism," as embodied in his greenhouse poems. He could thereby say it with flowers, which have always provided a basic poetic terminology for signalling states of mind. These resources had a special potentiality in his case. For among the formative circumstances of his early years was the fact that he had been raised in an environment of greenhouses—and this sudden, exceptionally beautiful breakthrough (with its objectivist sense of the image being drawn from the well of old memories) could also in effect be a species of "regression," vigorously reawaking in him the somewhat magical notions of guilt and authority that we all have at our roots. The psychic riskiness of the poems added to their allurement for the reader (or at least for me, whom they summoned like a gong, from the moment Roethke first showed me some of them). But he was feeling around in a treacherous area—and when some purely personal troubles befell him in his relations with Bennington, he was all ready for the mental tangles that became interwoven with the remarkable longer poems for which the greenhouse pieces were a preparation, and in which they culminated. (I refer to the volume, *The Lost Son and Other Poems,* finally published in 1948. I was astonished in being reminded by the letters that the greenhouse poems had been rejected by both John Crowe Ransom and the editor of *Poetry.*)

Roethke went on to other breakthroughs, sometimes with similar discomforting aftermaths, and many of his loveliest pieces were still to be written. In going through these letters, the reader will get many glimpses of him along his way, snatching somewhat haphazardly at things even while, underneath it all, he kept striving in the direction demanded by his personality. And though we find him repeatedly expressing the hope for a different kind of breakthrough (into drama), his real genius was essentially lyrical, even though his poems were always strikingly "dramatic" in the sense that a good lyric can be dramatic when properly read aloud.

But whereas the reader will find, scattered through these letters, many hints as to Roethke's craft (and even craftiness) as a poet, the main impression that the book makes will probably be of a different sort. His imaginative, idealistic strivings in the poetic dimension find a materialistic counterpart in the most frankly careerist correspondence conceivable. In the Thirties Roethke did some work as a publicity man and he never lost his flair for that aspect of the writer's trade. Yet his self-promotion is so frank and spontaneous, it has a certain winsomeness. He does plenty of boasting but few will accuse him of being pretentious. Since he looks upon many of his important contemporaries as simultaneously his friends and his competitors, he is frank to air his hopes that he has just outdistanced someone towards whom we elsewhere see him taking a most sympathetic attitude. An abrupt sally of this sort is typical: "It saddens me that Mr. Eliot seems to think me a thug. He's right, of course, but I am convinced I can write rings around some of those punks on his list."

The spontaneity of his epistolary scrawls was doubtless increased by both alcohol and the various medicines he took constantly for one or another of his many symptoms, both bodily and mental. (Though quite without authority for saying so, I would attribute his sudden death to the fact that, whenever things went wrong with him, his natural tendency was not to modify his ways, but to keep right on in the same groove, plus pills of one sort or another. Thus, at one point he mentions a great drop in blood-pressure brought about by such means.)

If his letters to me are any test, some of his most entertaining moments (in epithets he applies to one or another of his colleagues) are omitted. I assume that I am similarly spared in some blanks that precede or follow my name.

Whatever kind of favorable or unfavorable treatment a given subject gets at one point, the likelihood is that he'll get the opposite somewhere else, when the circumstances have changed. Here's some advice he gives me for writing to an editor:

> Tell him that some of the zeitgeist, ear-to-the-ground boys in England like John Lehmann think I'm the only bard at present operating in the U.S. of A., that everybody is tired of Tiresome Tom, the Cautious Cardinal, and wants to hear about the new jump-boy, the master of diddle-we-care-couldly. They have to be told, the god-damned sheep. Boom-boom, you gotta believe. (I don't mean Palmer but the public.)

Eliot's stock fluctuated more than any of the others'—and Roethke finally decided: "It's the old love-hate business. He can't stand anyone who will duel with God." Elsewhere he had said that "Eliot is not honest," and had "never acknowledged" his debt to Whitman. "Oh no, he's always chi-chi as hell: only Dante, the French, the Jacobeans, etc." At one stage he grumbled about the agrarians, but later shifted his attitude completely, having been particularly impressed by Allen Tate's reputation in Italy. He complains that one of Dylan Thomas' binges "cost me a pretty penny—even a 30 buck traffic ticket." And his next remarks are beautifully characteristic:

> I'm fond of him, but he does get a bit wearing when dames are around. But as one of the dames pointed out to me, 'Dylan, you have to remember, is a child . . . ' From the lofty heights of adolescence, I make these observations.

Among the omissions, there is a reference to a speech by Edward Teller, "who 'fathered' the hydrogen bomb." The lacunae occur both before and after the name. And from his letters to me there are omissions concerning the role of the now deceased William Yandell Elliott (in connection with a 1950 Harvard Summer School Conference on The Defense of Poetry), and concerning some unsavory problems to do with academic freedom at the University of Washington while Henry Schmitz was president. The editor was more squeamish as regards these matters than I, for one, wish he had been, particularly since such omissions obscure somewhat the unconscious self-portrait that Roethke's letters so appealingly present. For although, every once in a while (when applying for a job or a grant or some such) Roethke settled down with almost Prussian thoroughness to line things up, his interest in self-portraiture as such got its ideal expression in his poems. Indeed, shifting back to the happier subject of his "slobbering egomania and four

I's in one sentence," I would cite this amusing twist after his marriage: "I (we—how hard the plural comes!) were . . ." etc. Yet what of this man who says so disengagingly, "deep in my heart of hearts, where there is nothing but wormy ambition"? I'd like to end by quoting a plug I once wrote for him (and I meant every word of it):

> During the several years when Roethke taught in the English department at Bennington, I got to know him quite well personally and to see him in operation as a teacher. On the basis of this knowledge, I would say most emphatically: He loves his subject, is permeated with it, and can communicate his enthusiasm to his students. His frank, open manner makes him popular with his classes; and he continually hits on felicitously picturesque ways of getting his insights across. Among people concerned with the best in contemporary poetry, he is generally considered a poet of exceptional ability. And as for my own attitude towards his work, I contributed to *The Sewanee Review* (Winter 1950) a forty-page appreciative analysis of his poems published up to that time, poems which, like his work done since then, have a kind of stylistic purity that is profoundly exhilarating. Were he given an opportunity to go farther afield in his studies, I am confident he has the kind of aptitude that would instinctively avoid the mere inclusion of chunks of undigested knowledge. What he took, he would assimilate, in terms of his unusual poetic integrity. And his pedagogy, good as it already is, should be to that extent improved.

# The 'Christ-Dionysus Link'

*Voyager: A Life of Hart Crane* by John Unterecker Farrar. Straus & Giroux
*The New Republic*, August 1969, 24–26

Once I happened to be discussing the "seven offices" that, as I see it, men in their public relations perform for one another. Six of them I could line up readily enough; namely: govern, serve (provide for materially), defend, teach, entertain, and cure. I explained that I had trouble with the seventh. I had thought of calling it "console," having in mind the religious rites that may still be resorted to, even after all hope of cure has failed. But religion also serves the ends of social control, since it was likewise designed to scare the devil out of us. Finally, I hit upon "pontificate," that is, to "build a bridge" between a here and a "beyond," and to talk about the here in terms of that "beyond." I had in mind the fact that whereas the Roman Emperor, in his dual role as secular ruler and divinity, had been called by his pagan subjects *Pontifex Maximus* (or "foremost bridge-builder" between two realms), the expression was later taken over by the Christians to designate the Pope.

Whereat, lo! in the discussion following the talk, from the floor came the inquiry, "In this connection, what would you do with Hart Crane's culminative poem, 'The Bridge'?"

Here was a perfect question. For it helps make clear how the *aesthetics* of Hart's "mythic" interest in his "religious gunman" (including puns on "gun") differs from a directly *religious* view of human motives. Hart's major poem does indeed pontificate. For his treatment of our world (its *hic et nunc*, plus a vaguely visionary future) is *in terms* of an idealized "mythic" past which somehow lives on, so that our history's subsequent developments are somehow infused with the same initial essence. His poem would aim to show "how much of the past is living under only slightly altered form, even in machinery and such-like."

Part of his material for this primal past he got from public, bookish sources, with moments assembled in his sprightly way by consulting The Documents and snatching from them (often with a mixture of alcohol and

Victrola records) whatever details he felt would best fit his need for "a synthesis of America and its structural identity." The rest involved his many ways of transforming personal experiences into quasi-mythic analogues whereby some particular event involving his relations to one particular person at one particular time became, as it were, "timeless" by being divested of its place in his biography and translated rather to some sheerly functional role in his overall poetic scheme. Thus, as John Unterecker puts it: "Though the 'Voyages' set is a consequence of a love for a man, its subject matter is love itself." Or, though Hart was quite explicit as to their relations "privately," the biographer notes that "publicly . . . the poems were meant to link love and sea and death into a dense, affirmative design."

Though this book contains many excellent comments on the poetry as poetry, almost by sheer definition the biographer's job is to go back and locate as many of those utterly personal motives as Hart's way of incorporating them was designed to "mythically" or bridgingly transcend. And Hart's exceptionally frank and circumstantial letters (a great number of which have been preserved), plus letters to him and about him, and the reminiscences of many sympathetic but realistic friends whom the biographer was able to consult, help "demythologize" the poetry (however respectfully) by recovering the personal situations which had figured originally as incentives, or points of departure, for his lines.

First of all, with painstaking and painful thoroughness, we are permitted to follow the ways in which Hart suffered from the quarrels of his parents.

In 1919 (he was born in 1899) he wrote to his mother (whom he explicitly associated with his search for a poetic synthesis): "It's time you realized that for the last eight years my youth has been a rather bloody battleground for your's and father's sex life and troubles." He was "Harold" in his father's house, "Hart" in his mother's. For present purposes suffice it to say that, before the obsessive entanglement was over, Hart's attitudes had undergone a brutally revolutionary change. And whereas for years he had seen his father through his mother's eyes, in time he came to be greatly sympathetic to some of his father's subsequent sorrows; and with the death of his grandmother, "a new crisis developed, Hart finally cutting himself off from his mother completely, hiding his address from her, refusing to answer the pleading letters that found their way to him." Obviously, such an upheaval would do great damage.

However, there was also to be bridged the nagging conflict between his family's ideal of a conventional, well-paying job and his resolve to be a poet (with Hart making repeated poorly paid attempts to abide by the norms of business, even while being as though "put up on a cross and divided," since he was "forced to be ambitious in two directions"). As the biography describes an interview Hart gave in 1919:

> The artist had to cultivate a deliberately split personality. He had to be "two different people," as Crane told his interviewer. One of his lives, if it was to be meaningful, had to be devoted to business; another, to art. And the two lives, "arts and business," had to be kept "entirely separate."

It was, for him, an almost desperate effort—and it obviously involved a situation that had to be bridged (in his case, by a "mythic" celebrating of our country's technologic prowess, though at a later date Spengler was to cause him acute worries for a while).

Another gulf, more and more in need of bridging as time went on, arose between his character when sober and his character when drunk. It was a Jekyll-Hyde situation that was greatly aggravated by his homosexuality, causing problems that even got to the stage of blackmail. Near the end, his alcoholic violence, homosexual promiscuity, and cult of mythic primitivism led him so far afield that he could go farther only by cohabiting with a woman during a Mexican ceremony which Hart loved as another kind of bridging (namely: Aztec survivals in local Christian rites), "while skyrockets splintered the sky and all the bells of Taxco splintered their ears."

"Boys—I did it!" he shouted afterwards. But not long after that he was shouting, "She thinks she can reform me, does she? I'll show her! Why, God damn her, I'd rather sleep with a man any day than with her!" Anyhow, be that as it may, she had moved in with him. And she was with him on the boat when he, who had said, "In the absolute sense, the artist *identifies* himself with life," leapt into the reality of his obsessive symbol, the sea, and was no more.

Given his particular kind of intensity and close family ties, there was also a world of his Middle-Western beginnings that somehow needed to be merged with his later footloose modes of life (themselves sporadically modified by attempts at anchorage).

What I, following the biography, have called the "Christ-Dionysus link" concerns the fact that he identified poetry so closely with alcohol, he worked constantly on that ragged edge between a sudden unforeseen line that could be salvaged and the many lines that (the very next day, he knew in a flash) had to be thrown away. And at no slight risk I will confess: when going back over his poems in connection with this review, I found that they work better if read not in cold reviewer-sobriety, but if one brings to them on one's own part a modicum of alcoholic latitude. Such assistance (mild, mind you!) might better fit the reader for communion with the poet's Dionysiac groove.

All told, the biography is an exceptionally admirable piece of devotion to its subject. And it is especially admirable because the sympathetically documented narrative also includes many telling references to the modes of workmanship that characterize Hart Crane's morality of production. We might start with Malcolm Cowley's description of the "brilliant monologue" that developed during one stage of Hart's frequent transformation from sobriety to desolate excess:

> Everything reminded him of something else: landscapes, of musical compositions; poems, of skyrockets or waterfalls; persons, of birds, animals, or piles of grimy snow; he could abstract the smile from a woman's face and make us see it in the design of the mantelpiece.

In this stage (while it lasted!) Hart came close to his poetic ideal. For instance, when on the subject of "symbolic transformations," Hart wrote to Waldo Frank that his bridge would become in turn "a ship, a world, a woman, a tremendous harp." He expresses worry lest the last section of the poem seem "transcendental," though he felt that other sections would counteract this "tendency." Elsewhere, we hear about "the metamorphosis of Pocahontas (the Indian) into the pioneer woman, and hence her absorption into our 'contemporary veins.'" And the biographer says of "Lachrymae Christi":

> Playing the sort of literary game his readers had come to expect from him, Crane brilliantly assembled a body (that of reborn Christ-Dionysus-earth) from the natural scene— the "smile" of a factory windowsill, "fox's teeth," "flanks of hillsides," "eyes," "tongue," "palm," and the earth's "tendoned loam" compounding into the refreshing experience of spring. . . . (p. 375)

All such devices, to my way of thinking, could be classed as poetic variants of the "transcendental," and particularly since, so often, as the biographer helps us to realize, they embody "the elements of his life that were to serve as a private substratum for the elaborate framework of the 'public' poem." But I must admit: you can take your pick as to which stratum, the public or the private, is "beyond" the other.

All told, then, there were ways of transforming the personal or autobiographical into a transcendent "myth." The realistic situation (the mounting problems of money and technology) could be similarly transcended in terms of a vaguely promissory myth. And the terms of the myth itself could undergo purely internal transformations (thereby getting a reflexive kind of density through the addition of modifications that variously referred back to one another, like words in a dictionary).

As regards this situation, Allen Tate is quoted as saying: "The 'bridge' stands for no well-defined experience; it differs from the Helen and Faustus symbols [of Hart Crane's earlier poem, "For the Marriage of Faustus and Helen"] only in its unliterary origin," which is by no means so wholly "unliterary" as the concept of a "bridge" itself would suggest. The alembications at their extreme probably show up in Hart's letter to Yvor Winters: "It's as plain as day that I'm talking about war and aeroplanes in the passage from F & H (corymbulous formations of mechanics, etc.)."

Though various of Hart Crane's works are dealt with, the book gravitates about his tremendous psychic investment in "The Bridge." The theme becomes so obsessive, one occasionally feels that the pages would have been at their ironic best if but fragmentary bits of the poem itself, with but tantalizing hints of its structure, had survived. There were definitely times when (as during one period on the Isle of Pines) spells of writing allowed him the greatest of gratifications; namely: the quasi-mystic euphoria of living in what Santayana might call the "Realm of Spirit," the delight of total engrossment in the internalities of a symbol-system, the feeling (be it right or wrong, and often it was right) that things were falling into exactly the proper place. But the very delight in such moments (often erroneously assisted by alcohol) can set up the conditions for a frightful letdown. So, when the poem was finished, then what?

Add the tangles he had got himself into, along with the kind of troubled nation to which he was returning in 1932—and the "logic of metaphor" to which he had subscribed gets its analogous fulfillment in a reflexive logic of suicide.

In "Cutty Sark" he says, "I started walking home across the bridge . . ." Boy! you couldn't get home from there. But your biographer has shown how a poignant tale can be told about your search. And what *vitality* you brought to it! And how you punished yourself. It's almost as though nothing but yourself could kill you . . .

All told, the range had been between "Permit me voyage, love, into your hands" and "love/A burnt match skating in a urinal."

# Appendix A
## *New York Herald Tribune Books* Reviews, 1923 to 1929[*]

Ryan P. Weber and Nathaniel A. Rivers

"The Eloquence of Barres"
*The Sacred Hill* by Maurice Barres. Translated by Malcolm Cowley. The Macaulay Company
*The New York Herald Tribune Books,* 6 November 1929, 4

"An Urn of Native Soil"
*Blue Juniata* by Malcolm Cowley. Jonathan Cape and Harrison Smith
*The New York Herald Tribune Books,* 5 August 1929, 2

"Little Men"
*The Paul Street Boys* by Ferenc Molnar. Translated by Louis Rittenberg. Macy-Masius
*The New York Herald Tribune Books,* 4 December 4, 1927, 4

"Love Among the Ruins"
*Maria Capponi* by Rene Schickele. Translated from the German by Hannah Waller. Alfred A. Knopf
*The New York Herald Tribune Books,* 4 March 4, 1928, 7

"Subjective History"
*In the American Grain* by William Carlos Williams. Albert and Charles Boni.

---

[*] Because of the excessively high fees for reprint rights requested by the rights owner (*New York Times Company*), we are not able to reproduce these reviews in this collection. Readers can locate them in digital archives of most academic libraries. We have chosen to present this analysis in lieu of the documents themselves.—The Editors.

*New York Herald Tribune Books,* 1 March 1923."Werthers With a Future"

*The Gateway to Life* by Frank Thiess. Translated from the German by H.T. Lowe-Porter. Alfred A. Knopf
*New York Tribune Books,* 4 February 1928, 7

"Witchcraft in Our Day"
*World's End* by Jacob Wassermann. Translated by Lewis Galantiere. Boni and Liveright
*New York Herald Tribune Books,* 4 January 15, 1928, 2

"Useful Distress"
*The Second American Caravan,* edited by Alfred Kreymborg, Lewis Mumford and Paul Rosenfeld. The Macculay Company
*The New York Herald Tribune Books,* 5 October 1928, 5

"But They Have Settled"
*The American Caravan: A Yearbook of American Literature* edited by Van Wyck Brooks, Alfred Kreymborg, Lewis Mamford and Paul Rosenfeld. The Macaulay Company
*The New York Herald Tribune* Books, 4 September 18, 1927, 2

Burke's literary reviews published in the *New York Herald Tribune Books* from 1923 to 1929 reflect the overarching equipment for living theme that characterizes the entire collection. These nine reviews show Burke grappling with the role of literature in contemporary society, especially the fiction and poetry of his more notable contemporaries. By demonstrating the equipment for living methodology in action, these reviews show the complexity behind Burke's idea that each work of art contributes names and attitudes to recurring experiences. As early as 1923, we see Burke developing and deepening his notion of equipment for living, arguing for literature's need to provide stylized, terminological assistance to recurrent situations. That is, a work must be realistic but also offer more than simple realism; it needs to provide compelling metaphors that make sense of experiences fundamental to readers' lives.

In two reviews, Burke examines the work of two friends and correspondents, William Carlos Williams and Malcolm Cowley. In "Subjective History" (1923) Burke reviews Williams's *In the American Grain,* and while the book is a novelized account of America's founding and development spanning several centuries, Burke is as interested in Williams's metacommentary as he is in the work itself. For instance, in a move that reflects Burke's insistence that all is grist for the mill, he quotes from the book jacket where

Williams describes his artistic program: "In these studies I have sought to rename the things seen, now lost in a chaos of borrowed titles, many of them inappropriate, under which the true character lies hidden." Because naming and terminology are interests characteristic of Burke, he adds his own interpretation of Williams's program as a framework for understanding the text:

> And these new names, if I understand Williams correctly, are intended merely to be the old names with their original charge restored. They are new, not for the love of novelty, but through piety, through husbandry of tradition; new only in the sense that one might change the label on a bottle from "Poison" to "Deadly Poison," employing a modified statement to produce the same effect.

These renamings show us the humanity and perspectives of historical figures like Columbus, Daniel Boone and Eric the Red. And because the purpose of the work is "poetry, not history," Burke focuses on the attitudes inherent in the text, which create complex perspectives on these characters as driven by both heroic and demonic traits. In Burke's view,

> Implicit in Williams's book there is something which fluctuates between these two attitudes, an intermingling of their once divided logics, so that we can no longer distinguish, in these pilgrimages of his heroes, between that which is done in aggression and that which is done in defense, between power and starvation, play and malice.

What Burke finds productive is how Williams's renaming—the form and style of his work—complicates our relationship to historical figures. He finds Williams fluctuating between two attitudes towards the heroic, creating an ambiguity between the noble and desperate motives of American legends.

What Burke finds problematic is that Williams's method results in a history too poeticized, often losing site of the historical context of each figure. Writing that he does not "mean to imply that Williams's method always works," Burke notes that,

> It tends toward a maximum of "interpretation" and a minimum of research; his heroes at times are so busy living that they neglect to do anything else, and their inventions, or discoveries, or battles, or policies, become an unimportant by-product.

The comment is productive in light of Burke's notion of recalcitrance. Though Burke argues as eloquently as anyone for the flexibility of terminology, there are limits to the way things can be renamed (as Burke writes in the "Equipment for Living" essay, an artist "won't sit on the edge of an active volcano and 'see' it as a dormant plain"). Historical work, however poeticized, must bear some relationship to the broader context of the historical figures' lives. Lest we privilege the psychology of form at the expense of the psychology of information, equipment cannot ignore the actuality of lived experienced. Here is one nuance of equipment for living: the balance between form and information.

Burke's review of his childhood friend Cowley's *Blue Juniata* likewise deals with the poeticizing of history, as Cowley's collection of poems describes subjects such as the decay of a Pennsylvania town, the lasting impermanence of New York City, and the upheaval of post-WWI Europe. Burke finds in these works much nostalgia (seen here as a stylized treatment of historical happenings). Nostalgia, as an attitude within the poem, becomes a certain kind of equipment itself. There is a concern for the past lost but also the past that remains in a decayed form.

> For in the midst of its rising, America has known a decay. Elements needed in the nation's building have become useless to its continuance. Modes of thinking, once vital, are no longer necessary. Some forms of energy and courage have outlived their purpose, while certain old men linger, their bodies weakened, their hills and valleys denuded, their very minds fallen into neglect.

This nostalgia functions as a corrective to an obsession with the contemporary, to a myopia which sees the current world as the only possible world. One of the collection's loveliest poems, "Day Coach," offers this corrective by powerfully depicting a return to the long-forgotten landscapes of youth. The poetry also beautifully encapsulates some of our darker attitudes through Cowley's "meditation upon death and upon the stagnation of the mind which may precede death by many years." And unlike Burke's assessment of Williams's explorations of the past, Burke's praise for Cowley is unequivocal. Burke makes a case for Cowley's verse as "by far his most important contribution" when measured against Cowley's fame, "by an ill adjustment," as a critic and translator. Burke also predicts that "perhaps as many as ten" of Cowley's poems may become "permanent acquisitions to our literature."

Many other notable authors of the time, including Cowley and Williams, appeared together in *The American Caravan* anthologies reviewed by Burke in "But They Have Settled" (1927) and "Useful Distress" (1928) respectively. In short works by Ernest Hemingway, Gertrud Stein, Mark Van Doren, Eugene O'Neill, H.D., and others, Burke finds an array of equipment. The authors found within the pages develop attitudes and philosophies through their writing, keeping their concerns close to home and the "problem of the individual and his relationship to life as a whole" (however, Burke points out the irony of lacking wanderlust in a collection intended to serve as a metaphorical "caravan"). Burke's closing lines about the first *Caravan* anthology evoke the equipment metaphor as it will later appear in his 1938 essay.

> These men are not pulling their work out of a hat—their art is a "battleground" on which they are fighting out their "problems." Thus the book is doubly valuable: as a document, as evidence of the temper of the nation; and as a body of work which frequently transcends this purely representative function and recommends itself in terms of excellence.

In his review of *The Second American Caravan,* Burke builds on this line of thinking by arguing that the aggregation of voices provided by the anthology is even more useful equipment than any singular work., The volume, taken holistically, transcends the deficiencies or excesses of any particular author. Burke writes:

> The reader's wisdom may be the sum of the writers' errors; the reader's poise, if he would have poise, may arise from the aggregate of the writers' unbalance. If life is an experiment, art is experimental living, and here we may find many alternatives laid out for our vicarious sampling by poor devils who are, alas, condemned to expertness in their own mentalities.

Seen in this light, the pessimism and neurosis found in the stories themselves add up to what Burke terms a "useful distress" in which the art, like hypochondria, provides protection for readers by symbolically signaling dangers. For instance, Burke praises Waldo Frank's insight on the "fruitlessly prophetic quality of New Year's Eve" as well as the lesson offered by many of the women writers that "sex is something exceptional or remote, and extremely difficult." The idea of useful distress, like Burke's critique of Williams, points towards the sophistication of the equipment analogy: the importance of usefulness balanced with the formal appeal appeals of of literature. as well as the notion that the distresses invoked through art can serve the reader.

An eye for literature as equipment for living is thus present throughout Burke's reviews for the *New York Herald Tribune,* including "Witchcraft in Our Day" (1928) and "Werthers With a Future" (1928). In particular, the reviews "Little Men" (1927) and "The Eloquence of Barres" (1929) demonstrate the poignancy of Burke's famous analogy. Burke criticizes both books from two competing (but not contradictory) demands of the equipment for living analogy: the tension between realism and aestheticism. To be valuable equipment, a book must identify relevant and relatable scenarios. As Burke writes in "Equipment for Living," an artist must, "to develop a full strategy, be *realistic*. One must *size things up* properly. One cannot accurately say how things will be, what is promising and what is menacing, unless he accurately knows how things *are*" (298). But realism is not enough. Burke also writes, "The author may remain realistic, avoiding too easy a form of solace—yet he may get as far off the track in his own way. Forgetting that realism is an aspect for foretelling, he may take it as an end in itself" (299). There are twin dangers here only avoided by a balance of both.

The tension theorized above emerges perfectly in the review "Little Men." Though Burke praises author Ferenc Molnar's *The Paul Street Boys* for its "familiar echoes" that provide one "many occasions to recall his own childhood," his ultimate critique is that the book favors realism at the expense of art. That is, for a literary work to function as equipment, it needs to provide an interpretative, symbolic framework around experiences; without that, for Burke, the work never approaches the level of art.

> [Molnar] seems too often to be copying the details of his novel out of a diary. To the retrospective and the forward-looking, art is handed on a platter; but to one who writes with his experiences of last night uppermost, the use of his impressions as an artist is identical with his reception of them as a voter. The author's characters do not meet the hero; they sit at the author's breakfast table. They are real, that is, but their reality does not forward the purposes at hand.

The last line precisely captures the essence of literature as equipment: it must give purpose to experiences beyond our everyday reception of them. There must be a difference between reading a book and hearing the author talk about what she did yesterday. The difference is the formal, symbolic qualities of a work of art that make meaning, sense, and beauty of narrative. Art must be real, but it cannot be *just* real.

On the other hand, art must not wander too far away from the identifiable, lived experience of the audience. In his review of Maurice Barres's *The Sacred Hill*, Burke seems to suggest that the novel does not ring true enough to the lives of American readers who will read Malcolm Cowley's translation. In contrast to his review of *The Paul Street Boys*, Burke praises the formal and stylistic qualities of Barres's novel. "But Barres, a lover of resonance, begins and ends his book on a note of Ciceronian grandeur, and throughout he rises above the vulgarity of his peasants to ambitious passages of rhetoric." What Burke praises here is the stylization of lived experience. His chief concern, however, is the context in which the work would serve as equipment. Barres's "stylization is grounded upon a very realistic plot," but his book is built "about a situation which did arise in Lorraine," a situation which may not be relevant to its new audience across the Atlantic. The work's focus on a uniquely European approach to the "psychology of heresy" "is not likely to win wide favor with the American public." For Burke, Americans, as "people raised among no religions or many religions," do not bring the same interest in heresy as those from places with a history of the church as a state power. This leaves American readers without the motive to use the novel as equipment for living. As Burke describes it:

> We may be impressed with the author's treatment of his subject, but we do not meet him halfway by prior engrossments in this subject. One is writing under the most advantageous conditions when he is manipulating the fears, desires and prejudices which are already swaying his readers before they open his book.

The statement offers a fascinating counterpoint to the review of *The Paul Street Boys* by privileging experience as an entry point into works of art.

Read side-by-side, these two reviews underscore both the practical and aesthetic aspects of the equipment for living metaphor as well as the contextual value of any such equipment. This attention to the context of a work is another way of underscoring the importance of scene in human motivation and action. Burke concludes his review of the Barres translation by arguing that a universally relatable reader, detached from any particular scene or set of motivations, does not exist. Burke writes, "I have tried to imagine the book which could wheedle the reader starting at zero, an Olympian reader, devoid of aches, itches and hungers. There is no such reader—and Barres was certainly not writing for such a reader when he planned this work for his compatriots." Burke here discounts the work, acknowledging that his own readers require different equipment than do Barres's readers. If literature helps readers to negotiate recurrent situations, then literature must necessarily address the situations of its readers. Without reference to such shared experiences, "a book, to affect a zero public, must appeal by its more strictly 'literary' virtues." In this respect, Burke generously praises Barres, but ultimately finds the artistic merits of the work do not alone recommend it as equipment for the readers he imagines picking-up the *Herald Tribune*.

Unfortunately absent from this collection due to rights issues beyond our control, these early reviews provide a glimpse into a mind at work. In the context of influential contemporaries, we see Burke develop a practical approach to literature. It is not, though, an approach that deflects the formal or the aesthetic. Instead, the approach recognizes the unique and powerful work that aesthetics can accomplish. The equipment for living metaphor finds the utility in beauty without rendering beauty utilitarian. By providing warnings, correctives, new terminology, and even distress, literature prepares readers to face their own lives, provided that literature is both beautiful and relatable. Burke, perhaps America's greatest rhetorician, knew well the intimate connection of form and content, style and substance, and his approach to literature, birthed in a time of social and economic upheaval, is no exception.

# Appendix B: Reviews by Journal

## The American Journal of Sociology

Untitled Review of John McMurray
*American Journal of Sociology 42*. September 1936

Untitled Review of Frank Hyneman
*American Journal of Sociology 43*. September 1937

Untitled Review of Maurice Duval
*American Journal of Sociology 44*. July 1938

## Accent

Criticism for the Next Phase
*Accent 8*. Winter 1948

On Covery, Re- and Dis-
*Accent 13*. Autumn 1953

The Criticism of Criticism
*Accent 15*. Autumn 1955

## The Bookman

A Decade of American Fiction
*Bookman 69*. August 1929

## Book Union Bulletin

Stalin: A New World Seen Through One Man
*Book Union Bulletin*. November 1935

## Bookweek

Prelude to Poetry: Scales and Fugue
*Bookweek 2*. January 1965

## Centrum

Words as Deeds
*Centrum 3.* Fall 1975

## Chimera

Untitled Review of Alfred Kazin
*Chimera 2.* Autumn 1943

## The Dial

Axiomatics
*Dial 68.* April 1920

The Modern English Novel Plus
*Dial 70.* May 1921

The Editing of Oneself
*Dial 71.* August 1921

Modifying the Eighteenth Century
*Dial 71.*, December 1921

Heroism and Books
*The Dial 72.*, January 1922

Heaven's First Law
*The Dial 72.* February 1922

Fides Quaerens Intellectum
*Dial 72.* May 1922

Deposing the Love of the Lord
*The Dial 77.* August 1922

Enlarging the Narrow House
*Dial 73.* September 1922

The Consequences of Idealism
*Dial 73.* October 1922

The Critic of Dostoevsky
*Dial 73.* December 1922

Realism and Idealism
*The Dial 74.* January 1923

Engineering with Words
*Dial 74.* April 1923

Immersion
*Dial 76.* May 1924

Ethics of the Artist
*Dial 77.* November 1924

Delight and Tears
*Dial 77.* December 1924

After-Dinner Philosophy
*The Dial 78.* March 1925

On Re-and Dis-
*The Dial 79.* Aug *1925*

Codifying Milton
*The Dial 79.* November 1925

Idiom and Uniformity
*The Dial 80.* January 1926

Idols of the Future
*The Dial 81.* July 1926

A "Logic" of History
*The Dial 81.* September 1926

Righting an Ethnological Wrong
*Dial 83.* November 1927

Van Wyck Brooks in Transition?
*Dial 84.* January 1928

## Direction

The Age of Enterprise
*Direction 6.* Spring 1934

Henry Miller and Harry Levin on James Joyce
*Direction 5.* Febuary/March 1942

## The Freeman

Short Untitled Review of Emanuel Morgan *Pens for Wings*
*Freeman 3.* June 1921

The Bon Dieu of M. Jammes
*Freeman 3.* May 1921

Short Untitled Review of Lewis Spence *Introduction to Mythology*
*Freeman 4.* January 1922

Short Untitled Review of Ernst Buschor *Greek Vase Painting*
*Freeman 5.* May 1922

## Hound and Horn

Hypergelasticism Exposed
*Hound & Horn.* July/September 1933

In Vague Praise of Liberty
*Hound & Horn.* July/September 1934

## The Hudson Review

The Carrot and the Stick, or . . .
*Hudson 10.* Winter 1957–58

The Independent Radical
*The Hudson Review 12.* Fall 1959

## Journal of American Folklore

Folktale and Myth
*Journal of American Folklore 73.* July/September 1960

## The Literary Review (New York Evening Post)

Alcohol in the Eighties
*The Literary Review 1.* October 1920

Transitional Novel
*The Literary Review 1.* November 1920

Felix Kills His Author
*The Literary Review 1.* December 1920

Puritans Defended
*The Literary Review 1.* February 1921

## Kenyon Review

Key Words for Critics
*Kenyon 4.* Winter 1941–1942

Careers Without Careerism
*Kenyon 7.* Winter 1945–1946

The Work of Regeneration
*Kenyon 7.* Autumn 1945

Action, Passion, and Analogy
*Kenyon 12.* Summer 1950

The Dialectics of Imagery
*Kenyon 15.* Autumn 1935

Democracy of the Sick
*Kenyon 21.* Autumn 1959

## The Nation

Belief and Art
*The Nation 135.* November 1932

The Technique of Listening
*The Nation 136.* April 1933

Poets All
*The Nation 136.* January 1933

The Art of Yielding
*The Nation 138.* April 1934

Gastronomy of Letters
*Nation 139.* October 1934

A Pleasant View of Decay
*The Nation 140.* February 1935

Renaming Old Directions
*The Nation 141.* August 1935

Without Benefit of Politics
*The Nation 143.* July 1936

The Constants of Social Relativity
*The Nation 144.* January 1937

Fieldwork in Bohemia
*The Nation 145.* July 1937

A Recipe for Worship
*The Nation 145.* August 1937

A Gist of Gists of Gists
*The Nation 144.* May 1937

Homo Faber, Homo Magus
*The Nation 163.* December 1946

Invective Against the Father
*The Nation 194.* June 1962

More Dithyrambic than Athletic
*The Nation 204.* March 1967

## The New Leader

Imaginary Lines
*The New Leader 45.* December 1962

Revival of the Fittest
*The New Leader 46.* November 1963

Myth, Method, and Tragedy
*The New Leader 47.* November 1964

## The New Masses

Rugged Portraiture
*The New Masses 11.* April 1934

Goethe and the Jews
*The New Masses 14.* March 1935

Return After Flight
*The New Masses 18.* February 1936

The Second Study of Middletown
*The New Masses 23.* June 1937

The "Science" of Race-Thinking
*The New Masses 25.* October 1937

Corrosive Without Corrective
*The New Masses 26.* February 1938

Fearing's New Poems
*The New Masses 30.* February 1939

## The New Republic

Intelligence as a Good
*The New Republic 64.* September 1930

In Quest of the Way
*The New Republic 68.* September 1931

The Poet and the Passwords
*The New Republic 71.* August 1932

Mainsprings of Character
*The New Republic 73.* December 1932

Fraught with Freight
*The New Republic 77.* January 1934

The Esthetic Strain
*The New Republic 78.* April 1934

Permanence and Change
*The New Republic 79.* June 1934

The Universe Alive
*The New Republic 81.* November 1934

While Waiting
*The New Republic 81.* November 1934

One Who Wrestled
*The New Republic 82.* March 1935

Change of Identity
*The New Republic 83.* June 1935

Two Kinds of Against
*The New Republic 83.* June 1935

The Impartial Essence
*The New Republic 83.* July 1935

Protective Coloration
*The New Republic 83.* July 1935

Storm Omens
*The New Republic 84.* August 1935

A Radical, but
*The New Republic 84.* October 1935

Anatomy of the Mask
*The New Republic 85.* February 1936

Liberalism's Family Tree
*The New Republic 86.* March 1936

By Ice, Fire, or Decay?
*The New Republic 86.* April 1936

A Sour Note on Literary Criticism
*The New Republic 87.* June 1936

Property as an Absolute
*The New Republic 87.* July 1936

Methodology of the Scramble
*The New Republic 89.* December 1936

Synthetic Freedom
*The New Republic 89.* January 1937

The Esthetic Instinct
*The New Republic 90.* April 1937

Spender's Left Hand
*The New Republic 92.* August 1937

Thurber Perfects Mind Cure
*The New Republic 92.* September 1937

A Trail Trails Off
*The New Republic 93.* December 1937

Semantics in Demotic
*The New Republic 93.* January 1938

Weighted History
*The New Republic 93.* February 1938

Exceptional Book
*The New Republic 95.* May 1938

George Herbert Mead
*The New Republic 97.* January 1939

Monads—on the Make
*The New Republic 98.* April 1939

The Book of Proverbs
*The New Republic 99.* June 1939

Why Coleridge?
*The New Republic 100.* September 1939

Quantity and Quality
*The New Republic 101.* November 1939

The Sources of "Christabel"
*The New Republic 102.* May 1940

Many Moods
*The New Republic 108.* June 1943

Action as Test
*The New Republic 110.* February 1944

Basic and After
*The New Republic 110.* April 1944

Cult of the Breakthrough
*The New Republic 159.* September 1968

The Serious Business of Comedy
*The New Republic 160.* March 1969

Towards the Perfectly Poisonous
*The New Republic 160.* May 1969

The Christ-Dionysus Link
*The New Republic 161.* August 1969

More Probes in the Same Spot
*The New Republic 162.* February 7, 1970

Swift Now? Swift Then?
*The New Republic 162.* May 1970

Irony Sans Rust
*The New Republic 171.* July 1974

Father and Son
*The New Republic 172.* April 1975

Untitled Review of Harold Bloom
*The New Republic 176.* June 1977

Untitled Review of Denis Donohgue
*The New Republic 177*. September 1977

## NEW YORK TIMES BOOK REVIEW

Chekhov and Three Others
*The New York Times Book Review*. January 1, 1922

## NOVEL: A FORUM ON FICTION

Kermode Revisited
*Novel: A Forum On Fiction*, Autumn 1969

## POETRY

Concern about English
*Poetry 45*. February 1935

The Hope in Tragedy
*Poetry 46*. July 1935

Coleridge Rephrased
*Poetry 47*. October 1935

Deft Plaintiveness
*Poetry 48*. August 1936

Cautious Enlightenment
*Poetry 49*. October 1936

Exceptional Improvisation
*Poetry 49*. March 1937

Tentative Proposal
*Poetry 50*. May 1937

Leave the Leaf Its Springtime
*Poetry 50*. July 1937

Responses to Pressure
*Poetry 51*. October 1937

On Poetry and Poetics
*Poetry 55*. October 1939

Towards Objective Criticism
*Poetry 70.* April 1947

Likings of an Observationist
*Poetry 87.* January 1956

The Encyclopaedic, Two Kinds of
*Poetry 91.* February 1958

## The Saturday Review of Literature

A New Poetics
*The Saturday Review of Literature 2.* September 1925

## Science and Society

William James: Superlative Master of the Comparative
*Science & Society.* Fall 1936

## Secession

Note on Der Sturm
*Secession 4.* January 1923.

## The Southern Review

Recent Poetry
*The Southern Review.* July 1935

Symbolic War
*The Southern Review.* Summer 1936

## Vanity Fair

Art and the Hope Chest
*Vanity Fair 19.* December 1922

# Appendix C: Reviews in Chronological Order

Axiomatics
*Dial 68*, April 1920
Alcohol in the Eighties
*The Literary Review (New York Evening Post* 1). October 1920
Transitional Novel
*The Literary Review (New York Evening Post* 1). November 1920
Felix Kills His Author
*The Literary Review (New York Evening Post 1).* December 1920
Puritans Defended
*The Literary Review (New York Evening Post 1).* February 1921
The Modern English Novel Plus
*Dial 70*, May 1921
The Bon Dieu of M. Jammes
*The Freeman* 18. May 1921
Short Untitled Review of Emanual Morgan
*The Freeman 3*, June 1921
The Editing of Oneself
*Dial 71*, August 1921
Modifying the Eighteenth Century
*Dial 71*, December 1921
Chekhov and Three Others
*The New York Times Book Review.* January 1, 1922
Short Untitled review of Lewis Spence
*The Freeman 4*, January 1922
Heroism and Books
*The Dial 72*, January 1922
Heaven's First Law
*The Dial 72*, February 1922
Short Untitled Review of Ernst Buschor

*635*

*The Freeman* 5. May 1922
Fides Quaerens Intellectum
*Dial 72*, May 1922
Deposing the Love of the Lord
*The Dial 77*, August 1922
The Consequences of Idealism
*Dial 73*, October 1922
Enlarging the Narrow House
*Dial 73*, September 1922
The Critic of Dostoevsky
*Dial 73*, December 1922
Art and the Hope Chest
*Vanity Fair 19*, December 1922
Realism and Idealism
*The Dial 74*, January 1923
Engineering with Words
*Dial 74*, April 1923
Immersion
*Dial 76*, May 1924
Ethics of the Artist
*Dial 77*, November 1924
Delight and Tears
*Dial 77*, December 1924
After-Dinner Philosophy
*The Dial 78*, March 1925
On Re- and Dis- *The Dial 79*, August 1925
A New Poetics
*The Saturday Review of Literature 2*, September 1925
Codifying Milton
*The Dial 79*, November 1925
Idiom and Uniformity
*The Dial 80*, January 1926
Idols of the Future
*The Dial 81*, July 1926
A "Logic" of History
*The Dial 81*, September 1926
Righting an Ethnological Wrong
*Dial 83*, November 1927
Van Wyck Brooks in Transition?
*Dial 84*, January 1928
A Decade of American Fiction

*Bookman 69*, August 1929
Intelligence as a Good
*The New Republic 64*, September 1930
In Quest of the Way
*The New Republic 68*, September 1931
Note on Der Sturm
*Secession* 4, January 1932
The Poet and the Passwords
*The New Republic 71*, August 1932
Belief and Art
*The Nation 135*, November 1932
Mainsprings of Character
*The New Republic 73*, December 1932
The Technique of Listening
*The Nation 136*, April 1933
Poets All
*The Nation 136*, January 1933
Hypergelasticism Exposed
Hound & Horn, July/September 1933
Fraught with Freight
*The New Republic 77*, January 1934
The Age of Enterprise
*Direction 6*, Spring 1934
Rugged Portraiture
*The New Masses* 11. April 1934
The Art of Yielding
*The Nation 138*, April 1934
The Esthetic Strain
*The New Republic 78*, April 1934
Permanence and Change
*The New Republic 79*, June 1934
In Vague Praise of Liberty
*Hound & Horn*, July/September 1934
Gastronomy of Letters
*Nation 139*, October 1934
While Waiting
*The New Republic 81*, November 1934
The Universe Alive
*The New Republic 81*, November 1934
Concern about English
*Poetry 45*, February 1935

A Pleasant View of Decay
*The Nation 140*, February 1935
Goethe and the Jews
*The New Masses 14*. March 1935
One Who Wrestled
*The New Republic 82*, March 1935
Change of Identity
*The New Republic 83*, June 1935
Two Kinds of Against
*The New Republic*, June 1935
Recent Poetry
*The Southern Review*, July 1935
Protective Coloration
*The New Republic 83*, July 1935
The Hope in Tragedy
*Poetry 46*, July 1935
Storm Omens
*The New Republic 84*, August 1935
Renaming Old Directions
*The Nation 141*, August 1935
The Dialectics of Imagery
*Kenyon 15*, Autumn 1935
The Impartial Essence
*The New Republic 83*, July 1935
Coleridge Rephrased
*Poetry 47*, October 1935
A Radical, but
*The New Republic 84*, October 1935
Stalin: A New World Seen Through One Man
*Book Union Bulletin*, November 1935
Anatomy of the Mask
*The New Republic 85*, February 1936
Return After Flight
*The New Masses 18*. February 1936
Liberalism's Family Tree
*The New Republic 86*, March 1936
By Fire, Ice, and Decay
*The New Republic 86*. April 1936
Symbolic War
*The Southern Review*, Summer 1936
A Sour Note on Literary Criticism

*The New Republic 87,* June 1936
Property as an Absolute
*The New Republic 87,* July 1936
Without Benefit of Politics
*The Nation 143,* July 1936
Deft Plaintiveness
*Poetry 48,* August 1936
William James: Superlative Master of the Comparative
*Science & Society,* Fall 1936
Untitled Review of John McMurray
*American Journal of Sociology 42,* September 1936
Cautious Enlightenment
*Poetry 49,* October 1936
Methodology of the Scramble
*The New Republic 89,* December 1936
Synthetic Freedom
*The New Republic 89,* January 1937
The Constants of Social Relativity
*The Nation 144,* January 1937
Exceptional Improvisation
*Poetry 49,* March 1937
Tentative Proposal
*Poetry 50,* May 1937
A Gist of Gists of Gists
*The Nation 144,* May 1937
The Second Study of Middletown
*The New Masses 23,* June 1937
Fieldwork in Bohemia
*The Nation 145,* July 1937
Leave the Leaf Its Springtime
*Poetry 50,* July 1937
Spender's Left Hand
*The New Republic 92.* August 1937
The Esthetic Instinct
*The New Republic 92.* August 1937
A Recipe for Worship
*The Nation 145,* August 1937
Thurber Perfects Mind Cure
*The New Republic 92,* September 1937
Responses to Pressure
*Poetry 51,* October 1937

The "Science" of Race-Thinking
*The New Masses 25.* October 1937.
A Trail Trails Off
*The New Republic 93,* December 1937
Semantics in Demotic
*The New Republic 93,* January 1938
Corrosive Without Corrective
*The New Masses 26.* February 1938.
Weighted History
*The New Republic 93,* February 1938
Exceptional Book
*The New Republic 95,* May 1938
Untitled Review of Frank Hyneman Knight
*The American Journal of Sociology 44,* July 1938
Untitled Review of Maurice Duval
*American Journal of Sociology 44,* July 1938
George Herbert Mead
*The New Republic 97,* January 1939
Fearing's New Poems
*The New Masses 30,* February 1939
Monads-on the Make
*The New Republic 98,* April 1939
The Book of Proverbs
*The New Republic 99,* June 1939
Why Coleridge?
*The New Republic 100,* September 1939
On Poetry and Poetics
*Poetry 55,* October 1939
Quantity and Quality
*The New Republic 101,* November 1939
The Sources of "Christabel"
*The New Republic 102,* May 1940
Key words for Critics
*Kenyon 4,* Winter 1941–42
Henry Miller and Harry Levin on James Joyce
*Direction 5,* Febuary/March 1942
Many Moods
*The New Republic 108,* June 1943
Untitled Review of Alfed Kazin
*Chimera 2,* Autumn 1943
Action as Test

*The New Republic 110*, February 1944
Basic and After
*The New Republic 110*, April 1944
Careers Without Careerism
*Kenyon Review 3*, Winter 1944–1945
The Work of Regeneration
*Kenyon Review 7*, Autumn 1945
Homo Faber, Homo Magus
*The Nation 163*, December 1946
Towards Objective Criticism
*Poetry 70*, April 1947
Criticism for the Next Phase
*Accent 8*, Winter 1948
Action, Passion, and Analogy
*Kenyon 12*, Summer 1950
On Covery, Re- and Dis-
*Accent 13*, Autumn 1953
The Criticism of Criticism
*Accent 15*, Autumn 1955
Likings of an Observationist
*Poetry 87*, January 1956
The Carrot and the Stick, or . . .
*Hudson 10*, Winter 1957–58
The Encyclopaedic, Two Kinds of
*Poetry 91*, February 1958
Democracy of the Sick
*Kenyon 21*, Autumn 1959
The Independent Radical
*The Hudson Review 12*, Fall 1959
Folktale and Myth
*Journal of American Folklore* 73. July-September 1960
Invective Against the Father
*The Nation 194*, June 1962
Imaginary Lines
*The New Leader 45*, December 1962
Revival of the Fittest
*The New Leader 46*, November 1963
Myth, Method, and Tragedy
*The New Leader 47*, November 1964
Prelude to Poetry: Scales and Fugue
*Bookweek 2*. January 1965

More Dithyrambic than Athletic
*The Nation 204*, March 1967
Cult of the Breakthrough
*The New Republic 159*, September 1968
The Serious Business of Comedy
*The New Republic 160*, March 1969
The Christ-Dionysus Link
*The New Republic 161*, August 1969
Toward the Perfectly Poisonous
*The New Republic 160*, May 1969
Kermode Revisited
*Novel: A Forum On Fiction*, Autumn 1969
More Probes in the Same Spot
*The New Republic 162*, February 7, 1970
Swift Now? Swift Then?
*The New Republic 162.* May 1970
Irony Sans Rust
*The New Republic 171*, July 1974
Father and Son
*The New Republic 172*, April 1975
Words as Deeds
*Centrum 3*, Fall 1975
Untitled Review of Harold Bloom
*The New Republic 176*, June 1977
Untitled Review of Denis Donoghue
*The New Republic 177*, September 1977

# Acknowledgments

The editors would like to thank the Kenneth Burke Literary Trust for their permission to reprint all of the reviews in this collection.

The editors would also like to thank these rights holders for their permissions to reprint the following works:

Reprinted with the permission of *The American Journal of Sociology*

Untitled review of John MacMurray, *Reason and Emotion*. *The American Journal of Sociology* 42 (September 1936): 283.

Untitled review of Frank Hyneman Knight, *The Ethics of Competition and Other Essays*. *The American Journal of Sociology* 43 (September 1937): 242-244.

Untitled review of Maurice Duval, *La Poesie et le Principe de Transcendence: Essaie sur la Creation Poetique*. *The American Journal of Sociology* 44 (July 1938): 167-168.

Reprinted by permission of the publisher, Duke University Press.

"Kermode Revisited." *Novel: A Forum on Fiction* 3 (Fall 1969): 77-82.

Reprinted with the permission of *The Hudson Review*

"The Carrot and the Stick, or . . ." (William Sargant, *Battle for the Mind*; Vance Packard, *The Hidden Persuaders*; and William H. Whyte, *The Organization Man*). *The Hudson Review* 10 (Winter 1957-58): 627-633

"The Independent Radical" (Harold Rosenberg, The Tradition of the New). *The Hudson Review* 12 (Fall 1959): 465-472

Reprinted with the permission of *Journal of American Folklore*:

"Folktale and Myth" (Joseph Fontenrose, Python: A Study of the Delphic Myth and Its Origin). *Journal of American Folklore* 73 (July-September 1960): 270-271.

First Published in the *Kenyon Review* - Old Series. Copyright *The Kenyon Review*.

"Key Words for Critics." *Kenyon 4.* (Winter 1941-1942): 126-132
"Careers Without Careerism." *Kenyon 7.* (Winter 1945–1946): 162-166.
"The Work of Regeneration." *Kenyon 7.* (Autumn 1945): 696-700.
"Action, Passion, and Analogy." *Kenyon 12.* (Summer 1950): 532-537.
"The Dialectics of Imagery." *Kenyon 15.* (Autumn 1935): 625-632.
"Democracy of the Sick." *Kenyon 21.* (Autumn 1959): 639-643.

Reprinted with permission from *The Nation*. For subscription information, call 1-800-333-8536. Portions of each week's *Nation* magazine can be accessed at http://www.thenation.com.

"Belief and Art," from the November 30, 1932 issue of *The Nation*.
"The Technique Listening," from the April 12, 1933 issue of *The Nation*.
"Poets All," from the January 18, 1933 issue of *The Nation*.
"The Art of Yielding," from the April 25th issue of *The Nation*.
"Gastronomy of Letters," from the October 17, 1934 issue of *The Nation*.
"A Pleasant View of Decay," from the February 13, 1935 issue of *The Nation*.
"Renaming Old Directions," from the August 7, 1935 issue of the *The Nation*.
"Without Benefit of Politics," from the July 18, 1936 issue of *The Nation*.
"The Constants of Social Relativity," from the January 30, 1937 issue of *The Nation*.
"A Gist of Gist of Gists," from the May 29, 1937 issue of *The Nation*.
"A Recipe for Worship," from the August 21, 1937 issue of *The Nation*.
"Field Work in Bohemia," from the July 31, 1937 issue of *The Nation*.
"Homo Faber, Homo Magus," from the December 7, 1946 issue of *The Nation*.
"Invective Against the Father," from the June 16, 1962 issue of *The Nation*.
"More Dithyrambic Than Athletic," from the March 27, 1967 issue of *The Nation*.

Reprinted with permission from *The New Leader*. © The American Conference on International Affairs, Inc.

"Imaginary Lines" (Shirley Jackson, *We Have Always Lived in the Castle*). *The New Leader* 45 (December 1962): 20-22.
"Revival of the Fittest" (Stanley E. Hyman, ed., *Darwin for Today*). *The New Leader* 46 (November 1963): 22-24.

"Myth, Method, and Tragedy" (Herbert Weisinger, *The Agony and the Triumph, Papers on the Use and Abuse of Myth*). *The New Leader* 47 (November 1964). 21-23.

Reprinted with the permission of *The New Republic*

"Intelligence as a Good" (John Dewey, *The Quest for Certainty*). *The New Republic* 64 (September 1930): 77-79

"In Quest of the Way" (P. D. Ouspensky, *A New Model of the Universe*). *The New Republic* 68 (September 1931): 104-106

"The Poet and the Passwords." (Essay-review of Glenway Wescott, *Fear and Trembling*). *The New Republic* 71 (August 1932): 310-313.

"Cult of the Breakthrough" (Ralph J. Mills, Jr., ed., *Selected Letters of Theodore Roethke*). *The New Republic* 159 (September 21, 1968): 25-26.

"Mainsprings of Character" (Haakon M. Chevalier, *The Ironic Temper: Anatole France and His Time*). *The New Republic* 73 (December 1932):103-104.

"Fraught with Freight" (Thomas Mann, *Past Masters*). *The New Republic* 77 (January 1934): 257.

"The Esthetic Strain" (John Dewey, *Art as Experience*). *The New Republic* 78 (April 1934): 315-316.

"Permanence and Change" (Thomas Mann, *Joseph and His Brothers*). *The New Republic* 79 (June 1934): 186-187.

"The Universe Alive" (A. N. Whitehead, *Nature and Life*). *The New Republic* 81 (November 1934): 26.

"While Waiting" (Edward Dahlberg, *Those Who Perish*). *The New Republic* 81 (November 1934): 53.

"One Who Wrestled" (Avrahm Yarmolinsky, *Dostoevsky: A Life*). *The New Republic* 82 (March 1935): 192, 194.

"Change of Identity" (James T. Farrell, *Judgment Day*). *The New Republic* 83 (June 1935): 171-172.

"Two Kinds of Against" (e.e. cummings, *No Thanks*, and Kenneth Fearing, *Poems*). *The New Republic* 83 (June 1935): 198-199.

"The Impartial Essence" (Gertrude Stein, *Lectures in America*). *The New Republic* 83 (July 1935): 227.

"Protective Coloration" (Robert Forsythe [Also in Karl S. Crichton], *Redder Than the Rose*). *The New Republic* 83 (July 1935): 255-256.

"Storm Omens" (Haniel Long, *Pittsburgh Memoranda*). *The New Republic* 84 (August 1935): 83.

"A Radical, but -" (Vardis Fischer, *The Neurotic Nightingale*). *The New Republic* 84 (October 1935): 221.

"Anatomy of the Mask" (Leonard W. Doob, *Propaganda: Its Psychology and Technique*). *The New Republic* 85 (February 1936): 371-372.

"Liberalism's Family Tree" (John Dewey, *Liberalism and Social Action*). *The New Republic* 86 (March 1936): 115-116.

"By Ice, Fire or Decay?" (Clifford Odets, *Paradise Lost: A Play in 3 Acts*). *The New Republic* 86 (April 1936): 283-284.

"A Sour Note on Literary Criticism" (James T. Farrell, *A Note on Literary Criticism*). *The New Republic* 87 (June 1936): 211.

"Property as an Absolute" (Herbert Agar and Allen Tate, eds., *Who Owns America*). *The New Republic* 87 (July 1936): 245-246.

"Methodology of the Scramble" (Harold D. Lasswell, *Politics: Who Gets What, When, How?*). *The New Republic* 89 (December 1936): 250.

"Synthetic Freedom" (Hilaire Belloc, *The Restoration of Property*). *The New Republic* 89 (January 1937): 365.

"The Esthetic Instinct" (Herbert Read, *Art and Society*). *The New Republic* 90 (April 1937): 363-364.

"Spender's Left Hand" (Stephen Spender, *Forward from Liberalism*). *The New Republic* 92 (August 1937): 24-25.

"Thurber Perfects Mind Cure" (James Thurber, *Let Your Mind Alone!*). *The New Republic* 92 (September 1937): 220-221.

"A Trail Trails Off" (Mary M. Colum, *From These Roots: The Ideas That Have Made Modern Literature*). *The New Republic* 93 (December 1937): 205-206.

"Semantics in Demotic" (Stuart Chase, *The Tyranny of Words*). *The New Republic* 93 (January 1938): 343-344.

"Weighted History" (Hilaire Belloc, *The Crisis of Civilization*). *The New Republic* 93 (February 1938): 375-376.

"Weighted History" (Hilaire Belloc, *The Crisis of Civilization*). *The New Republic* 93 (February 1938): 375-376.

"Exceptional Book" (William Empson, *English Pastoral Poetry*). *The New Republic* 95 (May 1938): 81.

"George Herbert Mead" (Morris, et al., eds., *The Works of George Herbert Mead*). *The New Republic* 97 (January 1939): 292-293.

"Monads - on the Make" (Paul Weiss, *Reality*). *The New Republic* 98 (April 1939): 314-315.

"The Book of Proverbs" (S. G. Champion, ed., *Racial Proverbs: A Selection of the World's Proverbs Arranged Linguistically*). *The New Republic* 99 (June 1939): 230.

"Why Coleridge?" (E. K. Chambers, *Samuel Taylor Coleridge*, and Lawrence Hanson, *The Life of S. T. Coleridge*). *The New Republic* 100 (September 1939): 163-164.

"Quantity and Quality" (Otto Neurath, *Modern Man in the Making*). *The New Republic* 101 (November 1939): 22-23.

"The Sources of 'Christabel'" (A. H. Nethercot, *Road to Tryermaine*). *The New Republic* 102 (May 1940): 617.

"Many Moods" (Olin Downes and Elie Siegmeister, *A Treasury of American Songs*). *The New Republic* 108 (June 1943): 869-870.

"Action as Test" (Arthur E. Murphy, *The Uses of Reason*). *The New Republic* 110 (February 1944): 220-222.

"Basic and After" (Frederick Bodmer, *The Loom of Language*). *The New Republic* 110 (April 1944): 566, 568.

"Cult of the Breakthrough" (Ralph J. Mills, Jr., ed., *Selected Letters of Theodore Roethke*). *The New Republic* 159 (September 21, 1968): 25-26.

"The Serious Business of Comedy" (Elder Olson, *The Theory of Comedy*). *The New Republic* 160 (March 15, 1969): 23-27.

"Toward the Perfectly Poisonous" (Richard Ellmann, ed., *The Artist as Critic: Critical Writings of Oscar Wilde*). *The New Republic* 160 (May 31, 1969): 28-30.

"The Christ-Dionysus Link" (John Unterecker, *Voyager: A Life of Hart Crane*). *The New Republic* 161 (August 16, 1969): 24-26.

"More Probes in the Same Spot" (Marshall McLuhan, *Counterblast*). *The New Republic* 162 (February 7, 1970): 30-35.

"Swift Now? Swift Then" (Denis Donoghue, *Jonathan Swift: A Critical Introduction*). *The New Republic* 162 (May 9, 1970): 25-26.

"Irony Sans Rust" (Wayne C. Booth, *A Rhetoric of Irony*). *The New Republic* 171 (July 6 and 13, 1974): 25-26.

"Father and Son" (Harold Bloom, *The Map of Misreading*). *The New Republic* 172 (April 12, 1975): 23-24.

Untitled review of Harold Bloom, *Wallace Stevens: Poems of Our Climate*. *The New Republic* 176 (June 11, 1977): 24-27.

Untitled review of Denis Donoghue, *The Sovereign Ghost: Studies in Imagination*. *The New Republic* 177 (September 10, 1977): 29-31.

Reprinted with the permission of *Poetry*.

"Concern about English." *Poetry* 45. (February 1935): 294-296.
"The Hope in Tragedy." *Poetry* 46. (July 1935): 227-230.
"Coleridge Rephrased." *Poetry* 47. (October 1935): 52-54.
"Deft Plaintiveness." *Poetry* 48. (August 1936): 282-285.
"Cautious Enlightenment." *Poetry* 49. (October 1936): 52-54.
"Exceptional Improvisation." *Poetry* 49. (March 1937): 347-350.
"Tentative Proposal." *Poetry* 50. (May 1937): 96-100.
"Leave the Leaf Its Springtime." *Poetry* 50. (July 1937): 226-229.

"Responses to Pressure." *Poetry* 51. (October 1937): 37-42
"On Poetry and Poetics." *Poetry* 55. (October 1939): 51-54.
"Towards Objective Criticism." *Poetry* 70. (April 1947): 42-47
"Likings of an Observationist." *Poetry* 87. (January 1956): 239-247.
"The Encyclopaedic, Two Kinds of." *Poetry* 91. (February 1958): 320-328.

Reprinted with the permission of *Science and Society*.

"William James: Superlative Master of the Comparative" Review of Ralph Barton Perry, *The Thought and Character of William James. Science & Society* 1 (Fall 1936): 122-125.

Reprinted with permission of *The Southern Review*.

"Recent Poetry" (an omnibus review): *The Southern Review* 1 (July 1935): 164-177.
"Symbolic War" (Granville Hicks, Proletarian Literature in the United States). *The Southern Review* 2 (Summer 1936): 134-147.

# Index

action: and philosophy, 466; illocutionary, 535, 540–545, 547–552; incipient, xviii, 197, 460–461; locutionary, 541–542, 545; of expression, 512, 563; perlocutionary, 542–543, 545
ad hominem, 201
advertising, 14, 18, 40, 103, 218, 240, 254, 306, 332, 334, 348, 371–373, 385–386, 404–405, 426, 505, 526; and necking, 372; Madison Avenue, 388, 404, 488
Aeschylus, 116, 235, 508, 515
aesthetics, xvii, xviii, xix, 56, 61, 72, 84–86, 88, 126, 145, 148, 150, 164, 166–168, 170, 173, 174, 190, 193–195, 226, 236, 237, 241–242, 244–245, 251, 268, 285, 287, 291–294, 298, 334, 356, 392, 419–420, 474, 476–477, 500, 512, 516, 517, 560, 579, 581, 606, 610, 621–622
Agee, James, 16, 25
agent, 156, 185, 229, 236, 237, 273, 350, 459, 499, 539, 540, 579
Aiken, Conrad, 93, 97–98, 188, 199
*Alice in Wonderland*, 97, 158, 262
Anderson, Sherwood, 61, 122, 193, 285, 513, 579
anthropology, 163, 203, 241, 325, 393, 444, 507, 531, 596
apocalyptic fiction, 269–272, 355, 386
Aquinas, Thomas, 94, 273, 419, 426
archetypes, 195, 205, 207–208, 273, 387

Aristophanes, 265, 266
Aristotle, 115–116, 163, 198, 203–204, 206, 229–230, 232, 234–235, 241–242, 264, 268, 299–300, 303, 342, 358, 371, 402, 473, 488, 539, 543–544, 550; Rhetoric, 543, 550; and rhetoric, 402; Poetics, 268, 539
Arnold, Matthew, 177, 203, 419, 513
Arnold, Thurman, xx, 394–397, 526
Arrow Collar Mystics, 199
ars poetica, 6, 22, 66
art, 147, 172–175, 194, 195, 197, 198, 220, 242, 245, 286, 317, 318, 319, 553, 560, 563–568, 578, 581, 620; and assumption, 444; and attitude, 145, 147, 193, 316, 474–475, 560, 574; and experience, xix, 149, 564–565; and life, 557; and mysticism, 170; and philosophy, 565; and pleasure, 176, 567; and society, 590; and suffering, 584; and the unconscious, 567, 569; and truth, 361; as a stylized answer, xiii, 538; as communal, xxi, 104; as experience, 102, 205, 207, 620; as medicine, xiii, xxii; as morality, 197; as propaganda, xviii, 117, 151; as reader-writer relationship, 149; for art's sake, 203, 295, 334, 560; modern, 89, 286, 300, 321, 476, 511; organs of, 88; pure, 103, 334, 574
atheism, 53, 108, 438, 594
Atlantis, 30, 598
attitude, xvi, 186–187, 343, 414; aesthetic, 145, 173, 194, 420; and

*649*

action, 461, 539; and art, 145, 147, 193, 316, 474–475, 538, 560; and comedy, 263, 328; and criticism, 144, 155, 186, 228, 244, 579; and Freud, 411, 581; and history, 30; and irony, 596–597; and language, 519; and literature, xiii, 56, 60, 67, 75, 77, 82, 85, 95, 101, 133, 292, 578; and Mann, 85, 451, 452; and morality, 198; and persuasion, 403; and philosophy, xx, 419, 435; and poetry, 12–13, 21, 26, 28, 33, 77, 83, 147, 275, 607–609; and propaganda, 152, 371; and psychoanalysis, 144; and religion, 418; and satire, 113; and science, 360, 392, 444, 457, 564, 596; and sex, 364; and society, 48, 321, 407, 460, 521–522, 566; and sociology, 357, 379; and the reader, 128; and therapy, 342; Communist, 133; contemporary, 275, 417; eighteenth-century, 516; idealistic, 333; logical, 431; nineteenth-century, 85; non-hygienic, 31; of Wordsworth, 148; political, 371; revolutionary, 125, 318; tragic, xix, 31, 263, 596; utilitarian, 294; youthful, 110
Auden, W.H., xv, xxii, 23, 125, 290, 292, 294, 305
Austin, J.L., xxii, 181, 534–537, 539–549, 551–552; speech acts, 181, 535, 540–548, 551–552

Babel, 104, 248, 509
Bach, Johannes Sebastian, 100, 477, 478
Bacon, Francis, 151, 303, 306, 473
Barnes, Djuna, 82
Barres, Maurice, 615, 619, 620, 621
Barzun, Jacques, 113, 391, 392
Baudelaire, Charles, 46, 247, 258, 315
beauty, xviii, 34, 49, 63, 73, 74, 77, 97, 173, 174, 175, 198, 253, 285, 288, 348, 355, 369, 417, 419, 420, 440, 556, 579, 580, 581, 597, 598, 603, 620, 622; and reality, 581

Beckett, Samuel, 162, 280
Beethoven, Ludwig Van, 477, 478
behaviorism, xx, 294, 325, 328, 447, 460, 550, 552; and laughter, 328
Belloc, Hilaire, 381–382, 421–422
belt, hitting below, 111, 196
Bennington College, 507, 606, 609
Bentham, Jeremy, 160, 186, 259, 271, 373, 394, 518–520, 547
Beowulf, 476
Bible, the, 11, 77, 103, 249, 269, 272, 369, 399, 513, 594
biography, xvii, 144, 424, 483, 577, 578, 589, 591, 599, 605, 611, 612, 613
Blackmur, R.P., 155–156, 228–245, 259
Blake, William, 184, 365
Bloom, Harold, xv, xvi, 176–179, 180–183, 191
Book of Job, 33
Booth, Wayne, xvi, 279–281
bourgeoisie, 140, 145, 193, 196, 255, 256, 383, 392
Broadway, 60, 94
Brooks, Cleanth, 202–209
Brooks, Van Wyck, 48, 78, 123, 143–146, 214, 241, 577–582, 616
Browning, Elizabeth Barrett, 173
Browning, Robert, 177–178
Buber, Martin, 505
Buddha, 77
bureaucratization, 290, 407, 592
Burke, Edmund, 204
Buschor, Ernst, 555–556
Butler, Samuel, 56
Byron, Lord, 24, 340, 500, 592, 604

Calverton, V.F., 193–196, 225
Candide, 97, 446, 478
capitalism, xx, 12, 20, 22, 106, 107, 109, 119, 120, 122, 133, 136, 254, 294, 333, 334, 335, 338, 344, 357, 359, 366, 368, 369, 376, 381, 394–397, 399, 400, 421, 447, 448, 456, 500, 526, 527, 567, 593
Carlyle, Thomas, 275, 349, 497–498

Cassirer, Ernst, 349–350, 507
catharsis, 146, 198, 206, 234–235, 264–267, 300, 366, 404
Catholicism, 54, 92, 108, 109, 111, 118, 138, 382, 421, 596
Cervantes, Miguel, 263
Cezanne, Paul, 72
Chaucer, Geoffrey, 97, 516, 521
Chekhov, Anton, 292, 573–576
Childe Harold, 95
Christianity, 54, 57, 92, 157, 158, 204, 238, 242, 308, 326, 410, 417, 418, 419, 422, 423, 424, 425, 426, 427, 610, 612; Californian, 360
Cicero, 125, 204, 242, 308, 457, 620
Clapp, Frederick, 35–36
cocaine, 14, 561
Coleridge, Samuel, xiii, xx, 141, 153–154, 165–168, 171, 179, 184–187, 203, 205, 213, 233, 236, 237, 294, 602–605; Christabel, 171; drug use of, 168, 171, 603; Kubla Khan, 171, 604; motives of, 166, 605; popularity of, 602; *Rhyme of the Ancient Mariner*, 141, 165, 166, 171, 603; The Eolian Harp, 237, 602; theory of imagination, 153, 154, 184; universal situations in, 605
Colum, Mary, 257–259
Columbus, Christopher, 105, 304, 617
comedy: and evolution, 329; and tragedy, 263, 315; theory of, 263–267
Communism, 14, 22, 29, 32, 106–107, 124, 125, 133, 254, 313, 314, 368, 374, 375, 381, 384, 399, 421–422, 447, 483, 484
conceptual parallel, 39, 151
conformity, 17, 101, 312, 313, 407, 516, 536
Confucius, 174
Conrad, Joseph, 93, 97, 188, 199, 251
consubstantiality, 353
corrective, xix, 78, 96, 196, 291, 347, 400, 407, 618, 622
*Counter-Statement*, xiv, xviii, xxiii, 3, 43, 205, 254, 319, 553

Cournos, John, 55–58
Cowley, Malcolm, xxiii, 76, 125, 191, 229, 613, 615, 616, 618, 620
Crane, Hart, xv, xxi, 156, 229, 610–614
Croce, 78, 203, 220, 221, 230, 234, 321, 479, 480
cult, 502; Hellenic, 498; of baby-talk, 161; of darkness, 452, 453; of deity, 117; of equality, 398; of experience, 189; of liberty, 480, 481; of motion, 355; of nationalism, 109; of power, 498; of Praise, 225; of primitivism, 129, 612; of reality, 558; of self, 499; of strain, 479; of striving, 482; of style, 499; of suffering, 451; of the facts, 389; of the succinct, 303; of the superman, 497; of utilitarianism, 520; snake-handling, 403
culture, 8, 9, 26, 35, 40, 48, 94, 96, 125, 126, 240, 243, 244, 268, 280, 300, 321, 322, 332, 333, 334, 410, 411, 421, 436, 444, 445, 446, 448, 473, 474, 475, 476, 477, 552, 582
cummings, e.e., xv, 12–15, 26, 27, 88, 98–100, 106, 156, 228, 305, 306

Dada movement, 54, 287
Dahlberg, Edward, 12, 16, 27, 106–107
Daly, James, xix, xxi, 32–34
Dante Alighieri, 28, 116, 149, 230, 232, 233, 271, 298, 300, 301, 419, 608; *Divine Comedy, The*, 175, 195, 232
Dark Ages, 57, 196, 517
Darwin, Charles, 175, 328, 471, 486–489, 505
Davidson, Israel, 10
De Gourmont, Remy, 45, 55, 57, 204, 205, 222, 254, 432, 489, 517, 581
debunking, 223, 379, 380, 527, 528, 529
Dell, Floyd, 52–54, 580
democracy, 401, 410, 460, 467, 472, 498, 500

Descartes, Rene, 144, 190, 454, 473, 542
*deus ex machina*, 464
Dewey, John, 201, 338, 372, 431, 436, 439–444, 455–458, 459, 463–566
*Dial, The*: The Dial Award, 304
Dickens, Charles, 86
discounting, xvii, xviii, xx, 156, 186, 242, 271, 274, 280, 344, 370, 397
Donne, John, 163, 223
Donoghue, Denis, 184–187, 275–278
Dostoevsky, Fyodor, 55, 71–74, 229, 497, 599–601; as demonologist, 600
drama: as ritual, 140, 396, 495
dramatism, xx, 313, 508, 534, 535, 536, 537, 539, 540, 542, 545, 546, 548, 549, 550, 551, 552
dream-symbolism, 413
Dreiser, Theodore, 55, 213
Dryden, John, 159, 205

economics, xi, xvii, xx, 12, 17, 23, 27, 32, 48, 105, 106, 109, 115, 116, 129, 137, 145, 152, 153, 154, 163, 197, 226, 229, 243, 254, 255, 291, 292, 321, 322, 327, 332–336, 337, 338, 339, 342, 346, 347, 366, 368, 371, 373, 374–378, 381, 383, 393, 396, 397, 410, 411, 435, 436, 444, 446, 447, 449, 450, 461, 475, 477, 479, 481, 482, 485, 526, 562, 578, 587, 593, 622
education, 66, 98, 120, 134, 170, 229, 235, 239, 240, 241, 287, 321, 322, 327, 337, 338, 344, 375, 376, 407, 409, 498, 505, 516, 522
El Greco, 478
Eliot, T.S., xiii, 5, 15, 16, 17, 22, 88, 97, 156, 157, 188–190, 203, 204, 228, 251, 288, 291, 293, 299, 300, 305, 306, 309, 424, 521, 607, 608
Elizabethan, 114, 216–218, 219, 515
Emerson, Ralph Waldo, xv, 143, 144, 180, 250, 408
Empson, William, 157, 205, 241, 258, 260, 262, 293, 423–427

Endymion motif, 52
epistemology, 88, 463, 465, 477, 534
equipment for living, xix, 33, 122, 148
ethics, xvii, 85, 153, 167, 173, 230, 325, 327, 395, 412, 434, 457, 464, 514, 518, 597; ethical, 85, 173, 235, 251, 291, 308, 419, 438, 443, 464, 474, 500, 586, 597
ethos, 208
Euclid, 73, 362
Euhemerism, 496
evolution, 175, 193, 315, 326, 340, 364, 394, 432, 461, 474, 487, 488, 489, 515, 530 578, 329; of humanity, 364, 432

Farrell, James, 108–110, 138, 139, 140, 254–256
fascism, 107, 339, 374, 379, 381, 467, 481, 500, 527
Fearing, Kenneth, 12, 14, 15, 16, 26, 27, 40, 123
Federalist Papers, the, 562
Feidelson, Charles, 246–253
Fergusson, Francis, 269, 296–301
Fisher, Vardis, 370
Flaubert, Gustave, 6, 53, 194, 231, 258, 386, 581, 592; *Madame Bovary*, 194, 230, 231
Flynn, John Stephen, 471–472
form: and style, 513
Forsythe, Robert, 366–368
four major tropes, 178
France, Anatole, 595, 597
Frank, Waldo, xi, xv, 48–51, 75–78, 79, 80, 81, 93, 98, 99, 101, 513, 577, 579, 613, 619
Fraser, Sir James George, 158
French Revolution, 255, 392, 400
Freud:
Freud, Sigmund, 6, 56, 66, 72, 98, 178, 180, 182, 219, 227, 276, 277, 341, 342, 406, 410, 411, 412, 413, 503, 505, 507, 508, 567, 577, 578, 579, 580, 581; and culture, 411; and

expression in art, 580; and politics, 411; and religion, 411; and terminology, 411, 414; life and death instinct, 503
Frye, Northrop, 202–206, 208–209

Gabirol, Ibn, 10–11
Galileo Galilei, 151, 324, 473
Genesis, Book of, 179, 272, 494
Gentile, Giovanni, 321–323
Gide, Andre, 56, 57, 140, 200, 229, 250, 340, 584
Glicksberg, Charles, xvi
God, xii, 7, 10, 11, 41, 53, 64, 75, 85, 90, 92, 99, 100, 108, 117, 118, 156, 158, 159, 161, 162, 166, 167, 168, 189, 224, 227, 231, 238, 247, 252, 273, 275, 276, 280, 281, 285, 287, 291, 324, 325, 326, 332, 341, 357, 372, 399, 400, 411, 418, 420, 423, 424, 425, 426, 433, 434, 448, 464, 472, 473, 474, 497, 538, 594, 596, 600, 603, 608, 612
Goethe, 57, 85, 88, 117, 153, 208, 305, 340, 445, 447, 451, 473, 593, 594
Gospel of John, 272
Grammar of Motives, the, xiv, 273, 491, 539, 547
Gray, Thomas, 157, 158
Greenhood, David, 16, 25, 26
Gregory, Horace, xix, 16, 26, 30–31, 123
Grierson, Sir Herbert, 159–161

Harris, Wendell, xvii
Hawthorne, Nathaniel, 249
Hegel, 75, 182, 208, 232, 238, 243, 254, 281, 293, 321, 326, 345, 349, 488, 604
Hemingway, Ernest, 93, 95–97, 618
Hicks, Granville, 115, 155
history: curve of, 421
Hitler, Adolf, 379, 392, 488
Hobbes, Thomas, 328, 331
Hollywood, 96

Holy Grail, The, 157
Homer, 148, 186, 305, 387, 473, 515, 579
Hopkins, Gerard Manley, 22, 309
Horace, 203
Howarth, Herbert, 188
Hughes, Langston, 123
Hughes, Rupert, 79
Hume, David, 454, 534
humor, 99, 331, 393, 576, 580, 589
Huneker, James, 45–47
Huxley, Aldous, 384, 487
Hyman, Stanley Edgar, 486, 488, 489, 507
hypochondria, biological utility of, 619

Ibsen, Henrik, 129, 585
identification, 21, 123, 181, 182, 290, 305, 312, 313, 314, 315, 316, 407, 461, 485, 558; counter, 314
identity, 75, 80, 99, 104, 140, 166, 171, 177, 248, 290, 311, 312, 313, 316, 317, 340, 342, 351, 460, 476, 484, 496, 499, 547, 573, 603, 611
ideology, 116, 148, 200, 231, 244, 297, 341, 342, 343, 344, 349, 378, 409, 420, 440, 596
*Iliad, The*, 5, 494, 579; random creation of, 5, 579
imagery, 14, 25, 28, 40, 104, 108, 128, 129, 161, 179, 181, 206, 208, 217, 218, 227, 233, 251, 276, 278, 306, 353, 355, 499, 506, 603
immorality, 93, 156
Indiana: Muncie, 356; New Harmony, 399
irony, 27, 32, 104, 105, 109, 120, 121, 128, 178, 181, 182, 203, 206, 216, 234, 255, 258, 260, 262, 277, 279, 280, 281, 329, 335, 395, 399, 400, 401, 405, 433, 461, 487, 501, 533, 595, 596, 597, 614, 619; and science, 596; dramatic, 305, 595

Jackson, Shirley, xxi, 127–130

James, Henry, 46, 156, 228, 229, 277, 304, 306, 310, 437, 579, 596
James, William, xx, 408, 433, 534
jazz, xvii, 560
Jefferson, Thomas, 377, 381
Jesus Christ, 64, 125, 174, 187, 221, 222, 224, 403, 423, 424, 425, 426, 475, 495, 610, 612, 613
Johnson, Samuel, 592
Jonson, Ben, 266
Joyce, James, 57, 72, 80, 88, 89, 104, 144, 210, 229, 245, 273, 386; *Ulysses*, 72, 77, 79, 89, 186
Jung, Carl, 205, 474, 505, 507, 552
Juvenal, 14

Kafka, Franz, 602
Kant, Immanuel, 8, 144, 184, 271, 326, 434, 473, 498, 501
Kazin, Alfred, 212–215
Keats, John, 592, 604
Kermode, Frank, xxi, 268–274
Kierkegaard, Søren, 280, 602
Krutch, Joseph Wood, xix, 140, 147–149

language: and attitude, 519; and myth, 502, 503; and poetry, 35, 180, 181, 183, 256; and values, 256; constative, 535, 536, 540, 541; history of, 515, 530; magic in, 350; negative in, 103, 252, 276; performative, 535, 540, 541; resources and embarrassments of, 228, 242, 318
Laski, Harold, 527
laughter, 265, 328, 329, 330, 331
Lawrence, D.H., 30, 80, 81, 156, 306, 497, 498, 500, 592
Leibniz, Gottfried, 189, 208, 464, 595
Lenin, Vladimir, 123, 312, 313, 379, 483, 484, 485
Leonardo Da Vinci, 190
Lewis, C. Day, 16, 22
liberalism, 229, 290, 345, 383, 384, 392, 410, 455, 456, 457, 479, 480, 481, 500, 521
liberty, 11, 73, 100, 167, 367, 376, 380, 382, 383, 392, 446, 455, 479, 480, 481
Lincoln, Abraham, 64
linguistics, 184, 532
literary criticism: and biography, 577; close analysis, 219; environmentalist, 213, 214, 215; New, xiv, 228, 232, 233, 241, 289, 292; relation to other fields, 203; technical, 39, 152, 155, 163, 228; vocabulary in, 289, 568
literature: and attitude, 56, 60, 67, 75, 77, 82, 85, 95, 101, 133, 292; and essence, 524; and rhetoric, 255; and society, 260, 358; English, 524, 525; French, 92; margin of overlap in, 254; of confession, 63, 313; pluralism in, 254
Locke, John, 455, 456
logomachy, 382
Long, Haniel, 369
Longinus, 203, 206

Machiavelli, Niccolo, 303, 349
MacLeish, Archibald, 16, 19–21, 25
magic, 23, 29, 110, 121, 123, 129, 139, 276, 349–352, 367, 489, 493, 495, 506–507
Mallarme, Stephane, 70, 186, 386
Mann, Thomas, xix, xxi, 33, 37, 57, 70, 84–86, 103–105, 133, 210, 229, 231, 451–453, 479, 514
Mannheim, Karl, 343–345, 347, 394
Marxism, xiv, xx, 106, 125, 136, 140, 158, 205, 243, 260, 291, 312–318, 342, 359, 397, 400, 423, 498, 508, 604
McLuhan, Marshall, 269, 354, 385–388
Mead, George Herbert, 459–462, 539
Melville, Herman, 143–144, 230, 249, 250, 252
Mencius, 154, 200–201
metaphysics, 23, 148, 325, 331, 332, 349, 411, 418–419, 440, 444, 458,

477, 565; as living lie, 440
metonymy, 178, 182
Milton, John, xvii, 24, 159–161, 162, 177, 210, 262, 285, 286, 288, 365, 423–427, 517, 585–586; Lycidas, 159, 163, 287; Paradise Lost, 138, 159–160, 177, 423–424; Samson Agonistes, 159–160, 162, 423
Mimetic, 38, 203, 206, 330, 569
Moliere, 266–267
Molnar, Ferenc, 615, 620
Moore, Marianne, xv, 16–18, 156, 302–310, 459, 592
Moore, Merrill, 16–17
morality, 85, 103, 109, 110, 115, 118, 120, 125, 140, 156, 157, 201, 251, 303, 322, 374, 395, 417, 425, 433, 471, 521, 578, 579, 613; and art, 197; and attitude, 198; and poetry, 115, 208, 579; as equipment for living, 109; morality play, 125, 521; of guilt, 251; of listening vs combat, 201; of production, 85, 613; of toil, 118
Morgan, Emanuel, 5
motion, 181–182, 248, 251, 287, 318, 325, 350, 352, 355, 362, 402, 413, 501, 541–552
motive, 50, 81, 103, 160, 166–167, 177, 185, 215, 227, 245, 250, 277, 305, 333–334, 336, 348, 350, 385, 396, 398, 400, 401, 408, 499, 515, 519, 562, 565, 567, 599, 610–611, 617, 621; religious in the secular, 398
Mozart, Wolfgang, 478
Murry, J. Middleton, 71–74
music, 29, 60, 61, 70, 84, 94, 100, 181, 199, 207, 234–235, 247, 272, 286, 472, 475, 477, 556, 557, 558–560, 561–562, 575, 587, 613; musicality, 26, 31, 393
Mussolini, Benito, 112, 379
mysticism, 14, 20, 54, 94, 105, 108, 118, 124, 159, 170, 210, 235, 293, 359–361, 364, 431–432, 433, 491, 499, 524, 569, 594, 606, 614
myth: American Indian, 493; and drama, 495; and history, 494; and language, 502–503; and literature, 507; and science, 506; as precedent, 104; Babylonian, 493; combat myth, 502–504; Greek, 471, 502–503, 556; Hebrew, 493; Nordic, 392

Napoleon Bonaparte, 64, 151, 195, 431
Nehemiah, 10
Neo-Humanism, 291–292
Nethercot, Arthur, 171
Neurath, Otto, 389–390
*New Masses, The*, xv, 107, 140, 366
*New Republic, The*, xv, xvi, 26, 371, 463, 527
New Testament, The, 250, 269
*New Yorker, The*, 112, 367–368
Newton, Issac, 125, 358
Nietzsche, Friedrich, 32, 84, 86, 172, 180, 205, 297, 325, 412, 418, 451–452, 497–499, 581
nihilism, 204, 250, 252, 499
novel, the: attempts to destroy, 54; autobiographical, 580; by a critic, 46; and characters, 95; and Dostoevsky, 72, 599; and drama, 229 experimentation with, 50; frustrated novelists, 216; future of, 57; gossip, 102, 423; Jamesian, 229, 277, 304; local color, 97; modern English, 59, 61; naturalistic, 389; psychological, 260; and realism, 65, 102, 558, 591; as too rigid a form for the present, 57; society, 61, 94; transitional, 50

Odets, Clifford, 124–125, 138–140
Odysseus, 104
*Odyssey, The*, 186
Ogden, C.K., 200–201, 373, 518, 526, 535, 552
Old Glory, 150
Old Testament, The, 249

656  Index

Olson, Elder, 229, 263–267
Olympian reader, 621
ontology, 463, 465, 534
Oppenheim, James, 63, 65, 580
Orphic, 57, 67, 103
Orwell, George, 210–211

paganism, 92, 118, 421, 427, 610
painting of water to a thirsty man in the desert, 581
palimpsests, 220–221
Parmenides, 419
parody, xvii, 226–227, 261, 277, 280, 412–413, 589–590
pastoral, the, 157–158, 196, 205, 261–262
pathos, 88, 206
patriotism, 41, 140, 145, 148, 164, 207, 452
Pavlov, Ivan, 402, 408, 526
peanut racing, 378
perspective by incongruity xxi, 204–205, 355, 394–395
Petronius, 57
philosophy, xv, xvii, 7, 31, 67, 84, 88, 96, 114, 117, 119, 135, 139, 148, 188, 190, 201, 203, 204, 213–214, 297, 322, 323, 326, 332, 334, 341–342, 349, 361, 365, 368, 372, 396, 397, 408, 418–419, 435, 441, 443, 445, 454, 455–458, 459–460, 466–468, 481–482, 484, 488, 497, 528–529, 534, 550, 565, 569, 586, 597; and empiricism, 528; of history, 14, 323
*Philosophy of Literary Form, The*, xiii, 131, 168, 538, 547
*Piers Plowman*, 118, 157
planetarium, xxi, 127
Plato, 24, 71, 195, 200, 203, 227, 273, 299, 349, 353, 417–420, 473, 508, 564, 568; *Phaedrus, The*, 179, 353, 354
Poe, Edgar Allan, 13, 249, 315, 604
poetry: and action, 182, 234, 246; ars poetica, 6, 22, 66; as matter of welfare, 115; as substitute for living, 581; and attitude, 12, 13, 21, 26, 28, 33, 78, 83, 275, 418, 607, 608, 609; and beliefs, 148, 149; cliché in, 50; and common sense, 154; and complexity, 598; devotional, 10; didactic, 159, 292; and drama, 20, 140; and economics, 27; editorial, 17; Elizabethan, 114, 216; and emotion, 6–7, 19, 25, 235, 585; English, 22; and ethics, xx, 153, 230; and experience, 16, 18, 35, 129, 148, 159, 233, 606; experimentation in, 50; and expression, 33, 38, 163; and form, 234, 251, 288; and Freud, 503; and language, 35, 180, 181, 183, 218, 250, 252, 256, 413; influence of the poet on, 25, 30, 38, 67, 176, 177, 181, 316, 546, 552; Jacobean, 216–217; Metaphysical, 216; and metaphor, 257; and morality, 115, 208, 579; and motive, 160; and myth, 153; and nature, 8, 18, 355; and observation, 307–308; and organization, 6, 259; and persuasion, 182, 309; physicality in, 318; and politics, 14, 17, 22; and propaganda, 24, 117, 122, 152, 154, 405, 508; and punctuation, 302–303; pure, 164, 170, 205; and readjustments, 23; and realism, 292; and religion, 24, 39, 40, 92, 108, 123, 148, 202, 219, 222, 223, 226, 317, 565, 603; and rhetoric, 233–234, 239, 242; and science, 350, 408, 412, 457, 564, 565, 606; and sincerity, 14; and society, 14, 37, 158, 181, 358; status of, 147–148; and structure, 173; and subject matter, subjective, 12; subjective vs. objective, 164; 41, 618; and symbol, 149, 151, 196, 251, 252, 253, 359; and terminology, 7, 32, 76, 150, 165, 185, 450, 519, 538, 606; and values, 209, 365; poetics, 6, 75, 163, 179, 222, 232, 233, 234, 242, 243;

politics, xvii, xviii, 12, 21–23, 31, 48, 89, 109, 119, 123, 125, 135, 140, 145, 159–161, 174, 190, 194, 213, 226, 234, 240, 244, 255, 290–292, 311–318, 321, 333, 339, 342, 344, 347, 349–350, 352, 357, 367, 371–373, 375, 379, 381, 391–393, 395, 397, 402, 406, 410, 436, 447, 455, 469, 471, 475, 479, 483, 497, 500, 508, 526, 588, 594, 604
positivism, 170, 292, 294, 346, 360, 365, 454, 497, 526
Pound, Ezra, xv, 150–152, 156, 188, 190, 203–204, 305–306, 308
pragmatism, xx, 23, 49, 153, 170, 300, 334, 419, 434, 439, 440–444, 457, 459, 467, 497
proletarian, xviii, 115–126, 139–140, 155, 157, 193, 195, 260–262, 369, 377, 564
Prometheus, 478
propaganda, xx, 13, 107, 116–124, 135, 138, 151, 206, 218, 255–256, 339, 348, 357, 371–373, 421, 527; and art, xviii, 117; and satire, 367; principles of, 371
Protestant, 118, 351, 407–408, 421, 516
Proust, Marcel, 232, 258–589
proverb, 114, 178, 224, 231, 413, 539
psychoanalysis, xiv, xvii, 46, 63, 66, 72, 112, 123, 143–144, 151, 182, 244, 247, 291, 325, 342, 355, 406, 412–413, 507, 577–578, 600; and Burke, 507
psychology, 49, 66, 72, 73, 86, 96, 97, 98, 100, 101, 104, 129, 153, 158, 163, 182, 189, 200, 203, 220, 226–227, 240–241, 255, 259, 260, 269, 287–288, 325, 334, 342, 361, 369, 371, 373, 379, 393, 402, 404, 410–414, 444, 460–462, 480, 484, 498–501, 517, 526, 556, 561, 566, 579, 586, 596, 599, 618, 621
Puritanism, xii, 48, 98, 133, 249, 405, 408, 427, 471–472, 581,

Pushkin, George, 292
Pythagoras, 420
Racine, Jean, 296–299, 310
Ransom, John Crowe, 117, 162–164, 214–215, 241, 289–295, 355, 607
rationality, 418, 434, 438, 455, 460, 529; and comedy, 111; and expression, 119; and language, 394, 401, 531; and money, 334; and motive, 396; and propaganda, 405, 499; and religion, 238; and the law, 397; anti-rational, 249, 297; counter-rational, 249; humans as rational beings, 297; in Greek tragedy, 297; irrational, 111, 396, 452, 505; oversimplifications of, 23
realism, 65, 97–98, 114, 127, 136, 138–139, 173, 175, 178, 292, 314, 321–323, 347, 559, 591–592, 616, 620; superrealism 569
Reformation, The, 421–422
relativity, 189, 195, 325, 343–345, 364, 461, 493
religion, xvii, 10–11, 15, 20, 24, 32, 39, 64, 85, 89, 107, 108–110, 114, 115, 121, 135, 137, 139, 145, 148, 159, 162, 167–168, 219–226, 235, 267, 275–278, 312, 317–318, 321, 351, 357, 360–365, 390, 398, 400, 402–403, 410–412, 415, 424–426, 435, 438, 457, 461, 472, 473–478, 486–487, 497, 502, 514, 520, 604, 610
Renaissance, The, xvii, xxiii, 203, 241, 419, 422, 424, 461, 508
rhetoric, xvii, 12, 25, 41, 116, 125, 182–183, 204–205, 216–218, 219–222, 228, 232–242, 246, 255, 257, 279–281, 306, 308–309, 348, 350, 371–373, 401, 402–409, 411–412, 415, 509, 519, 543–552, 585, 621–622; and literary criticism, 255; inartificial proofs, 402; symbolism in, 246
*Rhetoric of Motives, The*, xiv, 205, 509
*Rhetoric of Religion, The*, 141, 179,

272, 274, 353, 415
Richards, I.A., xx, 153–154, 157, 163, 197–199, 200–201, 203, 218, 258, 260, 292–293, 373, 526, 535, 539, 552
Ridge, Lola, 16, 23–24, 26
Roberts, Elizabeth Madox, 93, 97
Roethke, Theodore, 188, 606–609
Rosenberg, Harold, 268, 311–318
Rosenfeld, Paul, 93, 101, 478, 616
Rueckert, William, xi, xiv, xv, xvi, xxiii

Saint Augustine, 111, 204, 242, 308, 426
Santayana, George, 479, 614
Sartre, Jean Paul, 270, 273
satire, xiii, 14, 27, 186, 206, 226, 313–314, 366–368, 507; universal vs. propagandist, 367
scene, 120, 154, 177, 201, 212, 229, 273, 297, 371, 386, 397, 445, 499, 535–536, 561, 613, 621; and act, 535; and music, 561
Schnitzler, Arthur, 46, 67–70
Schoenberg, Arnold, 207
Schopenhauer, Arthur, 153, 244, 331, 464
science, xvii, 7, 37, 40, 63, 72, 105, 148, 150–151, 153, 164, 170, 182, 204, 218, 226, 307, 322, 330, 332, 347, 350, 351, 356, 360–361, 365, 372, 378, 380, 383, 385, 391, 406, 408, 412, 413, 434, 436, 438, 439–441, 454, 455, 457, 461, 474, 482, 484, 488, 500, 506, 528, 531, 534, 564, 565, 566, 596, 597; and art, 564; and attitude, 392, 444, 457, 564, 596; and ideology, 440; and irony, 596; and mysticism, 360; and poetry, 606; terminology in, 150
Scott, Evelyn, 79
Scramble, the, 338, 378–380
semantics, 203, 241, 300, 349–350, 526–529

seven offices, the, 610
Shakespeare, William, 20, 64, 94, 116, 157, 163, 187, 261–262, 266–267, 294, 296, 298, 299, 496, 507, 513, 517, 559, 563, 569, 581; *A Midsummer Night's Dream*, 266; *Hamlet*, 147, 164, 232, 296, 298, 299, 312, 496; *King Lear*, 232, 269, 271, 581; *Macbeth*, 74, 215, 264; *Much Ado About Nothing*, 266; *Othello*, 507; *The Tempest*, 507
sincerity, 10, 11, 34, 95, 123, 580, 584
Sisyphus, 91, 450
Smith, Adam, 381, 461
socialism, 53, 118, 172–174, 338, 359, 370, 400, 474
socialization of loneliness, 32
Socrates, 179, 354, 473, 568
sophists: 417–420, 525; neo-sophists, 372
Sophocles, 296–298
Spengler, Oswald, 59, 196, 205–206, 233, 290, 323, 473–478, 497, 567, 612
Spenser, Edmund, 157, 163
Spinoza, Baruch, 8, 73, 244, 247, 253, 353, 418–419, 594
Spurgeon, Caroline, 157, 258, 293
Stalin, Joseph, 425, 483–485
Stein, Gertrude, xvii, 144, 285–288, 306, 523–525, 618
Stevens, Wallace, xvi, 156, 180–183, 187, 214, 304–310, 316
stream of consciousness, 114, 144
structuralism, 186–187
subjectivism, 12, 48, 70, 114, 140, 144, 208, 248, 255, 361, 435, 474–476, 538, 595
Supreme Court, 104
Swift, Jonathan, 14, 157, 194, 226, 275–278, 367 Brobdingnagian, 277, 387; Lilliputian, 277, 387
syllogisms, 8, 147, 372
symbolic action, xv, 181–182, 232–234, 246, 273, 316–318, 354, 402, 411, 506–507, 542, 546, 549, 551

symbolism, 14, 20–25, 28–29, 59, 65, 85, 108, 100, 110, 114, 129, 138–140, 141, 148–149, 153–154, 165–168, 178, 203–205, 217, 222, 246–253, 333–334, 351, 354–359, 361, 367, 400, 405, 408, 413, 432, 474–476, 484, 489, 495–496, 521, 539, 569, 588, 595; and a dancer's body, 552; of the color green, 207; as stylistic mirror, 35; symbolic communion, 18; symbolic croaking of frogs, 91; symbolic curses, 25; symbolic imagination, 230; symbolic self-immolation, 20–21; symbolic regression, 161; symbolic slaying of self, 340; symbolic transformations, 613; symbolic vengeance, 119
symbol-using animal, xx, 247, 403, 537
Symons, Arthur, 5
synecdoche, 178, 182

Tacitus, 391–392
Tate, Allen, 37–38, 268, 289, 294, 374, 608, 614
tautology, 178, 411
TV, 386–387
Teller, Edward, 608
Tennyson, Alfred Lord, 563
terminology, xvii, xviii, xix, xx, xxi, xxii, 6, 28, 32–33, 48, 50, 88, 92, 98, 108, 115, 129, 136, 144–146, 153, 161, 164, 166–168, 185–190, 193, 194, 200, 202, 206, 208, 209, 212, 216, 218, 219–227, 229–244, 246–252, 258, 263, 264, 268, 271–273, 276, 278, 289–294, 297–301, 304, 307–309, 312, 315–318, 322, 325, 326, 333–336, 338, 341–342, 343–345, 348, 349–350, 352–353, 358–359, 363, 373, 379, 387, 393, 404, 411–413, 418–419, 427, 431, 433–434, 439, 442, 444, 446, 449, 450, 463, 466–468, 477, 488, 498–500, 503, 507, 508, 512, 513, 518–519, 524, 533, 534–536, 540–550, 552, 567, 575, 577, 578, 583, 586, 603, 605, 606, 609, 610, 613, 617, 619, 622; and behavior, 449; and poetry, 7, 32, 76, 150, 165, 185, 450, 519, 538, 606; and reality, 439; buccaneer of, 206; key terms, 184, 234, 293, 344, 466; shifts in, 450; terministic deployments, 222
terrier out for a walk, 512
theology, 145, 160, 167–168, 223, 236, 245, 249, 252, 269, 296, 326, 336, 427, 438, 439, 441, 466–467, 487, 520, 528, 586
Thiess, Frank, 616
Thomas, Dylan, 608
Thurber, James, 111–113
Tolstoy, Leo, 145
Toomer, Jean, 93, 101
tragedy, xix, 19, 30–31, 60, 125, 178, 193, 206, 234, 251, 263, 297, 300, 438, 500, 519, 539, 595
trained incapacity, xxi, 240
tropes, 117, 178, 182, 230, 378
trout, wily old, xxi, 518
Tuve, Rosemund, 216–227
Twain, Mark, 48, 281, 486, 577–582

U.S. Constitution, 336, 399, 535
Untermeyer, Louis, 16, 18
utilitarianism, 40, 164, 170, 234, 294, 326, 334, 520, 622
utopia, 174, 343–345, 398–400, 604

Van Doren, Mark, 16, 24, 618
Veblen, Thorstein, 240, 332, 373, 394, 456
Vico, Giambattista, 178
Virgil, 28; *Aeneid, The*, 186

Wagner, Richard, 45, 64, 296–299, 451, 474, 477, 497, 559
Wall Street, 19, 152, 406, 488
Warren, Robert Penn, 165–168
Wassermann, Jacob, 616
Weber, Max, 190
Weiss, Paul, 463–465

Wescott, Glenway, xix, 87–89, 93, 97, 100–101, 445–449
Whitehead, Albert North, 454, 459, 505
Whitman, Walt, 7, 14, 48, 65, 66, 173, 177, 180, 210, 249, 408, 410, 579, 608
Whitmanites, 60
Wilde, Oscar, 172–175, 384
Wilder, Thornton, 93–95, 125
Williams, William Carlos, xv, xvii, xxiii, 5, 6–9, 54, 71, 188, 303, 304, 306, 310, 356, 471, 615–619; The Great Figure, 9

Wilson, Edmund, 135, 204, 290
Wilson, Woodrow, 583
Wimsatt, William, 202–209
Woolf, Virginia, xiii, 59–61, 144, 573
Wordsworth, William, 148, 159–161, 180, 183, 185, 195, 203, 237, 270, 291, 565, 604

Yeats, William Butler, xv, 143, 233, 306, 513

Zangwill, Israel, 10

www.ingramcontent.com/pod-product-compliance
Lightning Source LLC
Chambersburg PA
CBHW030101010526
44116CB00005B/52